Modern Policing

Modern Policing

Edited by
Michael Tonry and
Norval Morris

Crime and Justice
A Review of Research
Edited by Michael Tonry
with the Support of The National Institute of Justice

VOLUME 15

The University of Chicago Press, Chicago and London

This volume was prepared under Grant Number 89-IJ-CX-0003 awarded to the Castine Research Corporation by the National Institute of Justice, U.S. Department of Justice, under the Omnibus Crime Control and Safe Streets Act of 1968 as amended. Points of view or opinions expressed in this volume are those of the editors or authors and do not necessarily represent the official position or policies of the U.S. Department of Justice.

The University of Chicago Press, Chicago 60637
The University of Chicago Press, Ltd., London

ISSN: 0192-3234

ISBN: 0-226-80813-0 (cloth)
96 95 94 93 92 91   5 4 3 2 1

ISBN: 0-226-80814-9 (paper)
96 95 94 93 92 91   5 4 3 2 1

LCN: 80-642217

Library of Congress Cataloging-in-Publication Data

Modern policing / edited by Michael Tonry and Norval Morris.
    p.   cm.—(Crime and justice, ISSN 0192-3234; v. 15)
    Includes index.
    ISBN 0-226-80813-0. — ISBN 0-226-80814-9 (pbk.)
    1. Police.   2. Public relations—Police.   3. Police—United
States.   I. Tonry, Michael H.   II. Morris, Norval.   III. Series:
Crime and justice (Chicago, Ill.): v. 15.
HV6001.C672 vol. 15
[HV7921]
364 s—dc20
[363.2'0973]   91-43706
                                                      CIP

The paper used in this publication meets the minimum requirements of American National Standard for Information Sciences—Permanence of Paper for Printed Library Materials, ANSI Z39.48-1984. ∞

Contents

Preface

Police practice is in a state of flux. An array of substantial research projects over the past two decades, mostly led and executed by the police themselves, has cast doubt on the efficacy of traditional methods. The police are seen, and now see themselves, as too removed from the communities they serve and protect. Links are therefore being formed with community members and community groups, the better to control crime and to lessen the fear of crime. Diverse patrol and prevention techniques are being tested. Reforms sailing under the flags of "problem-oriented policing" or "community-based policing" are being widely applied. It is a time when the synthesis of knowledge that this volume provides is of particular value.

In *Modern Policing*, the fifth of the *Crime and Justice* thematic volumes, these new initiatives are examined, as is the accumulating body of research that has had an effect on police practice.

This volume's development has followed the standard *Crime and Justice* course. Essays were commissioned from leading scholars, and their drafts were then subjected to the grinding process we have found so useful in the earlier thematic volumes—and in this one, too. A research conference was convened, attended by the authors of the essays and a dozen or so senior police officials and other scholars of the police, the commissioned essays forming the subject of the conference. Written critiques of each essay were solicited from anonymous readers. From the acid test of these processes, essays were rewritten. Further editorial efforts were then devoted to these new drafts. From this ponderous process, a process not always congenial to an author, we believe there have emerged essays that are simultaneously the work of a primary author (or, in one case, authors) and yet reflect critical judgments and insights of many informed professional police and police scholars.

Modern Policing would not exist had it not been for the generous and enthusiastic support of the National Institute of Justice, including particularly that of the former director James K. Stewart, assistant director Paul Cascarano, and Mary Graham, who has worked with *Crime and Justice* and its editors over the course of many volumes.

These volumes reflect the work of many people—long-suffering writers who put up with a protracted and no doubt occasionally frustrating process of critique and review and rewriting, anonymous referees too numerous to mention, and the participants in the midcourse research conference on modern policing. Those participating in the conference, besides the writers, editors, and NIJ staff, were Alfred Blumstein, Anthony Doob, John Eck, Brian Forst, Carl Klockars, Barry Leighton, Stephen Mastrofski, Sheldon Messinger, Lloyd Ohlin, Antony Pate, Peter Reuter, Oliver Revell, David Smith, Jerry Wilson, and Franklin Zimring.

To all those people, and to the readers whose support makes continuation of *Crime and Justice* possible, we express our gratitude.

Roger Lane

Urban Police and Crime in Nineteenth-Century America

ABSTRACT

While much new work has been done over the past decade to add to our
knowledge of nineteenth-century police and crime, the field is still not as
"useful" to policymakers as might be hoped. Two trends observable ten
years ago are even clearer now: the productive use of other "social
sciences" to enrich more traditional approaches to history, and
paradoxically, the failure of "social science" to answer some of the most
important questions in the field. The history of police, first, is subject to
the kinds of controversy, mostly involving class and politics, familiar
throughout academe. With allowance for these, it can still be
reconstructed in ways that most historians and laymen can recognize. The
study of crime, however, is much more difficult. Some of the difficulty
results from ideology and political differences that make even definition
problematic; the nineteenth century and the late twentieth were
concerned, often, with very different kinds of "crime," and in neither
period was or is there a consensus on morality or priorities. The problem
of quantification is even more difficult, as we grow increasingly aware of
holes in the record that make it impossible to answer natural questions
about the comparative extent of various offenses, then and now. What is
offered here, finally, is, at best, a series of educated guesses.

To look again, ten years later, at the current state of the history of
cops and crooks is not quite to experience a sense of déjà vu. A good
deal more has been written; on surveying the same adjoining subfields
for *Crime and Justice* in 1980 I found a "scholarly coming of age." Eric
Monkkonen, referring elsewhere in this volume to the wider history
of police, can now quite properly claim that we have reached full

Roger Lane is Benjamin R. Collins Professor of Social Sciences, Haverford College.

maturity. Even in the survey that follows, largely restricted to nineteenth-century cities—leaving the newer work on state and federal law enforcement and more recent times to Monkkonen—it is no longer necessary, indeed no longer possible, to cite all of the significant studies. But if I have not seen it all before, I do feel that we are still traveling much the same road. And two of the issues, or trends, that appeared most striking a decade ago are more prominent than ever. The first of these is that historians of police and criminality are continually in touch with, often in debt to, scholars from the other and "harder" social sciences as part of the wider effort to tell nonhistorians what we have to tell as usefully and objectively as possible. The second is that this relationship remains problematic, and the ideal elusive, especially as the subjects involved get closer to our own contemporary political agendas, or to our "gut" emotions. And if these generalizations remain abstract, they are not hard to illustrate by considering the quite different states of our "knowledge" of cops and crooks, respectively.

The debt historians have owed social scientists has been evident from almost the beginning as, very simply, they got there first. The serious historical study of police and crime is only about one generation old. But sociologists, political scientists, and even a few anthropologists had long since staked out the turf. Historians of police, during the 1960s alone, found useful material in the work of Michael Banton (1964), Jerome Skolnick (1966), James Q. Wilson (1968), and William Westley (1970). Some of these and others have written directly historical work, or at least work with a historical dimension. And for the history of crime, no scholars have been more important or influential than James Q. Wilson, one of a number who have looked at law enforcement from both sides (Wilson and Herrnstein 1985), or Ted Robert Gurr, who, as both author and editor, has periodically resurveyed our map of scholarly developments both in the United States and abroad (Gurr and Graham 1969; Gurr 1979, 1989).

It is significant that neither Gurr nor Wilson is easily classified; the term "political scientist" seems arbitrary; so, as applied to other scholars, does "sociologist," even, in a few cases, "historian." It is a cliché now that the lines between disciplines have blurred, and even those of us who belong to the oldest and most conservative of disciplines have had to take account of the others. We have had, that is, sometimes to acknowledge what we had always absorbed from long-dead foreigners such as Max Weber and Karl Marx and to search openly for ideas among those more recently deceased, such as Michel Foucault. More broadly, as Monkkonen's survey (as well as much of his original work) makes clear, we have sought to quantify whenever possible, to use social science methods, concepts, and definitions whenever appropriate.

It is clear, then, what historians have gotten from social scientists. It is also clear what, ideally, they ought to get from us. One of the oldest and most valued functions of history is simply to provide perspective, to distinguish deeply rooted phenomena from new ones, or to show that what is was not always so, and thus not always must be so. We all do this at some level of consciousness; a synthetic survey such as James Richardson's *Urban Police in the United States* (1974) does it very directly, reminding interested students of the justice system that problems associated with vice control, for example, or the abuse of force are as old as the cops themselves. History may also serve as a source of factual information that criminologists may use, much as econometricians do, to test their hypotheses retrospectively. Certainly traditional historians take an almost malicious delight in doing this in reverse, when the existing evidence simply will not, in fact, produce the expected results in terms of class, status, power, or whatever.

In general, the history of police may serve these functions. Certainly it is ready to. And in the current search for alternatives to the patrol car as the near-exclusive means of crime control, policymakers as well as academics may find a rich variety in the studies cited in Monkkonen's survey, or even in this one. But it is harder, for many reasons, to find even potentially useful applications for the history of crime.

Part of the problem, it seems to me, lies with the criminologists, a notably incurious lot full of theories drawn from several disciplines with no attempt at quality control. Not merely ignorant of, but too often indifferent to, past experience, they use history only rarely and then as a kind of grab bag of anecdotes or tautologically defined data used not truly to test but to bolster whatever they seek to prove.

But the problem is far deeper than this. Despite continuing efforts to reach what we idealize as scientific objectivity, we all, whether as scholars or citizens, find it hard to think straight about things that touch us deeply.

It is not hard to draw a composite picture of the development of police that most historians can recognize and agree on and others can use. But it gets harder to find such agreement when we deal with their broadly "political" character, often involving controversial definitions of crime. And with respect to crime itself, a subject that arouses truly visceral emotions, there are not only political problems of definition but technical problems with the records. The result is that the historical evidence is so thin in many places that we simply cannot answer many of the most natural and elementary questions that scholars and citizens ask of us.

The survey that follows is divided into four sections. The first two sections summarize, respectively, the origin, development, and characteristics of nineteenth-century urban police and explore writing and theorizing about economic, political, and class influences on policing as well as the evolution of a distinct police culture. Section III examines knowledge about nineteenth-century crimes such as riot, prostitution, vice, and thievery, about which a fair amount is known. Section IV considers the formidable practical impediments that confront efforts to establish whether the major common-law crimes were more prevalent in nineteenth- than twentieth-century America but nonetheless offers tentative answers concerning theft, robbery, assault, rape, and murder.

I. Police History: A Synthesis

Given later scholarly and political developments, it is ironic that the first two scholarly histories of police were written almost wholly without benefit of models in the social sciences. And although once published they benefited from the exploding interest provoked by the "law and order" and riot issues of the later 1960s, they were conceived earlier and quite independently of each other. My own *Policing the City: Boston, 1822–1885* (Lane 1967), and James Richardson's *The New York Police: Colonial Times to 1901* (1970), dealt with a new subject but in traditional ways, as institutional histories drawing on the kinds of evidence, the appropriate bureaucratic reports, newspapers, biographies, and other contemporary accounts, with which our craft was long familiar. It is, then, a kind of tribute to, or confirmation of, the traditional historian's rather haphazardly inductive method that both independently identified substantially the same themes and issues. A partial list would include the origins of full-time salaried police out of a variety of antecedents, the role of riot in precipitating changes, the origins of official responsibility for detective work, the symbiotic relation between police detectives and the underworld, the role of police in local politics, the continuing controversy over enforcement of the vice laws, the appeal of the London and military models for American reformers—and their lack of appeal for American politicians, the class and ethnic origins of policemen, the changing variety of their duties and deployment, and structural reform and bureaucratization.

These subject categories have been expanded since, partly to accommodate wholly new questions raised by scholars in other disciplines, and the original findings have, of course, been disputed at various points. But with respect to the urban police of the nineteenth century, especially those of the Northeast and older Midwest, later work has more often enlarged on or modified these first accounts of Boston and New York than challenged them directly, and so it is still possible to draw a composite sketch of police development, using many studies without doing substantial violence to any.

Well into the nineteenth century, despite much morally and economically ambitious legislation at the state level, American local governments had very limited powers of administration. Enforcement of criminal law, in particular, was largely the responsibility either of the community as a whole or of the individual victim of some offense, rather than something delegated to specialized agents of the state. Towns and cities encouraged individual initiative by offering rewards for the capture of badly wanted felons; groups of citizens might be called to form a posse to chase offenders or break up disorderly crowds; citizens went to court in person to swear out warrants against those who had injured them.

Some officials did deal directly with criminal law enforcement but only as one of a number of duties. Centuries of legal independence and physical distance from the original British prototypes had created much variety among the policing arrangements of early nineteenth-century cities. Still, some combination of watchmen and constables, sheriffs and marshals, elected or appointed, paid by salary or by fee, operated in every major town or city. The watch, in smaller places detailed only under the threat of war (or slave insurrection in the South), patrolled some sections at night, calling the hours, tending the street lamps, watching for fires, and (in theory) breaking up fights, answering disturbance calls, and arresting "suspicious persons." They reported typically to a head constable, one of a body of men who, like sheriffs on the county level, were primarily servants of the courts, doing civil as well as criminal business, the latter largely by aiding aggrieved citizens to make arrests once warrants had been secured. Most of what was considered the "police" function—and the word itself was then very nearly synonymous with "local administration"—was carried on by interested private parties, marshals, and inspectors, who examined health hazards and otherwise enforced compliance with a range of local ordinances.

These arrangements were inefficient—and the watch, in particular, was a standing joke—but they had two related advantages. One was that they were cheap, in that the cost of administration fell largely on those immediately interested, the complainants or victims who paid the fees. The other is shown by Allen Steinberg's very important study of *The Transformation of Criminal Justice* (1989), a book based on findings in Philadelphia that seem also to apply elsewhere. "Crime" control in this era remained a private rather than controversial public issue. In practice, very little was done about prevention, detection, or those moral offenses such as drunkenness that had no individual victims. In practice, aldermen or justices of the peace simply adjudicated cases brought to them by constituents who had been robbed or assaulted, often by their neighbors, and sought restitution and revenge. While criminal in substance, these complaints were essentially civil in form and ensured that the citizens involved—and, in Philadelphia at least, these included many of the very poorest residents, immigrants, and blacks—got precisely the kind of justice they asked for or deserved. Such a directly "democratic" system, too, although obviously open to corruption and abuse, obviated the fears of executive tyranny that had dominated Anglo-American political thought since the English revolutions of the seventeenth century.

The twin fears of governmental expense and power were equally evident on the other side of the Atlantic, in Great Britain itself. But there, after years of agitation, Home Secretary Robert Peel in 1829 was able, for a variety of reasons, to secure the establishment of a Metropolitan Police of London, the first in the English-speaking world. And with this precedent somewhat loosely in mind, the municipal authorities in Boston, New York, Philadelphia, and other major eastern cities in the United States all took parallel steps over the next three decades to strengthen their police. The precipitating issue in most of these places was not ordinary crime so much as riot, one of the areas that new work has illumined greatly since my own relatively glancing treatment a generation ago.

Riot was a novel subject for historians and others in the 1960s, and George Rudé's (1959) analysis of popular uprisings in eighteenth- and early nineteenth-century France and England, now an acknowledged classic, was largely ignored on first appearance. But explosions in the ghetto awakened both American politicians and scholars later in the decade. It is of some interest that both the officially commissioned Kerner report (1968) on these contemporary American riots, which was apparently written in entire ignorance of Rudé's still-obscure work, as well as the several later scholarly studies, which were not, agreed with many of its essential findings: "mobs," whether of mid-eighteenth century Frenchmen or late twentieth-century black Americans, were not wholly mindless, destructive, or made up of the very dregs of society, temporarily released from restraint and giddy with their own power to do violence. They were, instead, made up of relatively settled residents, largely young men, more politically aware and perhaps better educated than most of their peers, who chose their targets with some care and attacked property more often than persons, usually with definite ends in mind. The same profile might apply to early American "mobs" as well.

Following Pauline Maier (1970) for the colonial period, and Gordon Wood for the American Revolution (1974), Paul Gilje, in *The Road to Mobocracy* (1987), has recently summed up the transition into the 1830s, the turbulent Jacksonian era that gave rise to police. Many historians in recent years, loosely inspired by the anthropology of Clifford Geertz, have looked to the symbolic significance of various popular ceremonies, and found that what used to be called "mobs" or "riots" were often outgrowths of ritual parades or demonstrations directed either against small outgroups—Protestants in Catholic countries or vice versa, or against such targets as unpopular politicians, or protocapitalist marketeers who sold food at high prices in times of scarcity. In this country as elsewhere, such activities were often tolerated by governments either weak or wise enough to recognize that, before the advent of democracy, it was foolish to take a stand against what were often deep-rooted community feelings without any legally approved outlets. As Gilje (1987) shows, the elite leaders of the American Revolution—as later the French—often relied on mobs to do their bidding, their illegal violence sanctified in the name of the wisdom of "the sovereign people."

But the political leaders of the new American Republic, although for some time they continued to encourage rioters on "their" side, grew increasingly disenchanted with popular violence, arguing that truly representative government made it no longer necessary. Their disen-

chantment was completed by developments in the long generation between the early 1830s and the Civil War, which several elements combined to make the most riotous in our history.

The painful transition from a local to a national marketing system,
the changes associated with the early Industrial Revolution, squeezed
some workmen out of the urban economy and brought the boom and
bust cycle to all of them. All the eastern cities swelled dramatically
with mutually hostile immigrants from Ireland, Germany, and native
hinterlands, just as national tensions over what would become the Civil
War exacerbated tensions with and among the free black population.
This sort of activity was not directed, as in the glorious days before
the American Revolution, at a few cowed representatives of a distant
crown but at whole classes of private citizens, some of whom had the
power to fight back and did. Rival groups other than the blacks could
often count on support from youth gangs or volunteer firemen, all of
them organized along parallel ethnic, political, and territorial lines, and
all eternally battle-ready in the absence of any form of recreation other
than drinking or fighting (Laurie 1973). The authorities were no better
equipped than in the previous century to deal with mob violence.
Neither elderly watchmen nor elected writ servers offered much help,
once the blood was up. As population grew, it was no longer possible
for a charismatic mayor or alderman to step in and organize a posse
among responsible citizens. The state militia, like the army in Great
Britain, was the weapon of last resort. But militia companies themselves were often organized along the same divisive lines that inflamed
the rioters, and it was both cumbersome and politically embarrassing
for local leadership to call in outside aid. What was needed, the city
fathers were apt to conclude, was a body of men answerable to themselves alone.

Following three major riots in four years, Boston commissioned a
small group of such police in 1838; political jealousies and traditional
fears held up New Yorkers until 1844; Philadelphia, perhaps the most
riot-torn of all, had to restructure its local government entirely in order
to create a single consolidated force in 1854. But in most cases the new
police did serve the purpose intended, generally proving their ability
to obey orders and deal effectively with hostile crowds of pro- or anti-
slavery men and women, Irishmen, and natives, whatever their own
political views or ethnic affiliations. If they were not always
successful—in protecting abolitionist meetings, for example—the failure was traceable not to a lack of means but to a lack of will on the

part of local authorities hesitant to aid politically unpopular groups. But in Boston and, especially, New York, courageous efforts in the great antidraft riots in the Civil War summer of 1863 were proof of policemen's ability to transcend their private beliefs on behalf of those who paid their wages. And with the end of the war and the passage of riot as a normal form of political expression, the fear of conflict between personal inclination and public duty was ended also.

In any case, if riot was often the precipitating cause for the creation of police, it had never been the only one. Whether over the course of fifteen years, as in Boston, or immediately upon their creation, as in Philadelphia, the new men displaced the old night watch and largely confined the constabulary to the service of civil writs. The older system in which most minor criminal business was initiated by citizens directly, using the cops, much like constables, simply to arrest and bring to court those they fingered for injuring them, continued for some years or even decades. But meanwhile, citizens and city fathers alike found that a regular force of patrolmen answering to a central office and on duty round the clock was a conveniently flexible instrument of administration. The men on the beat gave directions, unsnarled traffic, returned lost children, aided victims of sudden accident, and escorted drunks either to the station house or home. The chief often inherited the older functions of watchmen and marshals, remaining responsible in Boston for public health until 1853, and in New York for street cleaning until 1881. Newer functions without obvious place elsewhere in city administration, such as the maintenance of weather records, also gravitated to the police. Homeless drifters, by the late 1850s, were given nightly lodging in the station houses; by the 1870s, in the bigger cities, tens of thousands of homeless were put up in this fashion annually. In hard times, policemen sometimes ran soup kitchens for the hungry. It seemed natural, too, to assign the oversight and sometimes issuance of a variety of municipal licenses—for hackney drivers, pawnbrokers, and, most important, liquor dealers—to the "eyes and ears" of the city.

But from very early on, the 1840s and 1850s, the cops found themselves involved in endless controversy as a result of reformers' insistence that they be used to enforce moral legislation. And the group of issues surrounding liquor sales came to dominate the politics of policing. Indeed, they came close to dominating politics in general, as over the past generation historians have come to recognize the enormous importance of religious and ethnocultural differences in determining the party preferences of nineteenth-century voters. Such divisions often found symbolic expression in battles over enforcement of moral codes. And for politicians the results of these battles had real as well as symbolic consequences. The sale of alcohol was associated with a host of other popular recreations and vices, from roller-skating and prizefighting to prostitution and gambling, and the right to grant or deny such sale was measured in dollars as well as other forms of power. Shifting coalitions of Catholics and Protestants, Irishmen, natives, and Germans, Republicans and Democrats, state legislators, and city councilmen enacted a variety of policies ranging from absolute prohibition to nearly free license. But ultimate responsibility came always to rest on the police, who might enforce these regulations strictly, selectively, or not at all. The inevitable results—shakedown and shake-up, cyclical waves of protest—made this aspect of police work a matter of chronic tension.

Parallel problems marked the emergence of another function, criminal detection. The business of "thief taking" had never been a fully public responsibility in Anglo-American tradition, except for the occasional offer of reward from the treasury. While constables and other peace officers had certain obvious advantages in collecting these rewards, their legal standing was little different from that of any interested amateur or bounty hunter. And in cases involving the return of stolen goods or the finding of an unknown felon, as distinct from the arrest of a suspect named by the victim, it was customary for these experts to hire themselves out to the injured party. Problems arose, however, when such private arrangements were partially transformed into public services.

The first American detective bureau was set up as part of the Boston police department in 1846, a step followed shortly in nearly every other major city. But as most fully shown by Frank Morn (1982), the change from private to public responsibility was never complete. A host of private competitors, like the Pinkertons, flourished through most of the century. And the new public detectives themselves found it hard to walk the line between public duty and private enterprise. In an era before technological aids of any kind, with criminal informants not the main but the sole available resource, an intimate familiarity with, or even background in, the underworld of professional thieves was often the only qualification for success. The need to protect informants and, when substantial sums were involved, the temptation to arrange illegal deals, sometimes at the expense of the victims, were more compelling motives than the duty to prosecute as the law required. Detective work, then, like vice control, involved law enforcers with lawbreakers in a complicated tangle of relationships as much mutually supportive as hostile. Once government and citizens came to expect and then demand that thief catching was public business, and so long as it took a thief to catch another, there was no way out of recurrent scandal and turnover.

Many groups outside of the force never accepted this situation, however. Elite reformers in particular repeatedly called up a somewhat idealized vision of the prototype, the London Metropolitan Police. This was understood as a strictly disciplined, indeed semimilitary body whose major responsibility was to prevent disorder and "enforce the law" almost mechanically and without favor.

Some elements of the London model had been incorporated in American police systems from their origins, and others continued to appeal to politicians in power. It was stressed from the beginning that full-time police on patrol would have a preventive effect. While there were differences as to what they were supposed to prevent and how, it was clear that they were to be more proactive, less purely reactive, than their predecessors. And if this more aggressive activity were to serve useful public or political purposes, from staving off riot to closing (or taking assessments from) saloons, the men would have to be responsive to direction, as in the military.

There was little resistance to some aspects of the progressive militarization of the police. Supervisory officers easily adopted such titles as captain and lieutenant. Given the original importance of mass collective action, as in riot duty, and the prestige attaching to the military during the Civil War, the occasional adoption of such devices as morning roll call and training in parade drill seemed equally natural. Surprisingly little attention or controversy accompanied the official issuance of firearms, although this represented a major break with the British tradition. A host of historical circumstances, symbolized and reinforced by the Second Amendment to the Constitution, had maintained and even extended the colonial gun culture (Kennett and Anderson 1975). Many patrolmen had begun to carry pocket revolvers soon after they became common among sporting men and young toughs in the 1850s, so that the adoption of an official policy ten or fifteen years later only legitimized a long-accepted practice. But the most significant step in the attempt to impose a quasi-military discipline, the adoption of blue uniforms, was bitterly resisted.

The first move to uniform the police, in New York in 1853, was greeted with mass protests, resignations, and a number of civil suits following dismissals for insubordination. The same pattern, in some form, was repeated elsewhere through the decade. Some supporters appealed to traditional democratic objections to the wearing of livery and fancy foreign innovations in general. Underlying these symbolic objections were very real ones for the men themselves; a cop in uniform was easily spotted not only by citizens looking for help but by street toughs looking for trouble and, most important, by "roundsmen" trying to assure that he was walking the beat and not whiling the time away in the comfort of a billiard hall or saloon.

Beyond the instrumental need for a measure of discipline on the force, however, American politicians were generally united in opposition to the deeper implications of adopting the London model in its entirety. The metropolitan police commissioners were answerable not to the London authorities but to the home secretary; their men were deliberately chosen from outside of the city, and to preserve "impartiality" they were encouraged to remain socially and residentially segregated from the citizens they dealt with. Nothing could be more alien to American political culture. Local police in the United States were supposed, like other municipal employees, to be politically active residents and voters. No political faction wanted independent or impartial law enforcement; the real issue was simply which faction, and at which level, would direct the force. Ward leaders, as in New York, attempted to maintain control over precinct captains in their districts; in Philadelphia, the force was routinely named after the mayor currently in power, as for example, "Fox's Police." But the same opportunities for power and profit tempted upstate politicians as well, and the police of Boston and New York as well as those of several other cities in the nineteenth century all fell for a time under state control. If a one-sided partisanship proved intolerable to the minority party, the solution generally adopted, as in many other municipal departments, was not nonpartisan but bipartisan rule in the form of a board of commissioners representing both major political organizations.

At the beat level, however, supervision from outside or above was, in any case, limited by the nature of the job as well as the job holders. While telegraph lines linked district stations to headquarters in the 1850s, call boxes on the beat were not generally introduced until late in the nineteenth century, and radio and motorized communications lay well in the future. Partly as a result of their own success in curbing riot, the police after the Civil War were rarely called out in a body for serious business, although on ceremonial occasions, or parades, it was thought that the sight of the full force in marching array would promote pride in good citizens and second thoughts among "troublemakers." Most of their time by then was spent not in groups, or under specified orders, like soldiers, but walking their beats alone, acting on their own initiative.

Nineteenth-century policemen were well paid but hardly well trained. With yearly if not daily wages comparing favorably with those for skilled labor, men from even the best blue-collar jobs could be tempted into police work. With some exceptions, however, chronic scandal and political vicissitudes created a high turnover. Little experience was accumulated and very little was formally codified. New men were sent out on patrol with no training and few instructions beyond those contained in their cumbersome and largely irrelevant rule books. Left thus to themselves, they had to develop their own strategies for coping with life in the streets.

Relatively little can be learned historically about ordinary patrol work or routine interactions with the public. It is simple, in contrast, to document such highly charged matters as changing enforcement of the vice laws. The nineteenth-century judiciary, often unsympathetic to moral reformers, imbued with common-law notions about the sanctity of property and armed with the Fourth Amendment to the Constitution, made it quite clear how and when vice raids and liquor seizures should be carried out. But the arrest of persons in law depended then as now on matters of difficult definition: "undue force" and "reasonable suspicion." It is hard to tell just how individuals and departments reacted to the variety of characters and situations they encountered on the streets.

Following the Civil War, however, and the period of innovation and experiment led by the major eastern cities, the outlines of formal departmental development are relatively easy to trace. New and smaller cities across the country adopted full-time uniformed police forces, as Eric Monkkonen (1981) has shown, not in reaction to any specific precipitant but almost automatically as a function of rank order in size. And in contrast to the variety of arrangements that had characterized the early nineteenth century, the tendency by its end was toward convergence, a similarity of purpose and function symbolized by the nearly universal adoption of uniform blue. Older departments abandoned such duties as the care of streets, lights, and sewers to more specialized agencies, and new ones never had to deal with them at all. Such charitable activities as the maintenance of soup kitchens and the provision of nightly lodging for the homeless were also surrendered. Since very few policemen ever followed their careers in more than one city, the means of communication between cities remain obscure. But police departments had long exchanged information about wanted criminals, and communication was furthered by the first national police convention, held in 1871, followed in the late 1890s by the establishment of the International Association of Chiefs of Police.

By that time, the formal responsibilities of American police systems had been largely standardized along lines still familiar. While continuing to deal with a variety of citizens' complaints and requests, police were charged chiefly with maintaining patrol, enforcing certain sections of the criminal law, providing detective service, and regulating traffic. The existence of thousands of separate jurisdictions was rarely reflected in innovation but only in differences in size, efficiency, and such politically sensitive matters as job security and vice control.

II. Police Issues and Questions

In 1992 as in 1980, most historians could probably agree that the preceding sketch of police development is still basically accurate as far as it goes. But it is clearer than ever that it does not stretch far enough to encompass all of the relevant new work. Like the original studies it is based on, it is a largely administrative or political account, and as Eric Monkkonen shows elsewhere in this volume, there are a number of other possible approaches—social, statistical, and comparative— that may illumine issues that had been merely outlined earlier or even overlooked entirely. Perhaps even more important, while the narrative above may be mostly beyond criticism, interpretations of what is (merely) administrative and what is (fiercely) political are highly controversial. And studies involving the nature of governance and what may be loosely defined as "social control" in the nineteenth century have been and will continue to be in conflict as long as contemporary politics reflects some of the same issues and viewpoints.

The older studies provided only implicit answers to the question, Who controlled the police? To the extent that the force did not simply grow like Topsy in response to its own developing needs and experience, it was directed by state and local politicians. These nineteenth-century politicians were never a wholly homogeneous group. At the beginning of the period, the city's social and economic elite was often directly involved in government. Continued growth and foreign immigration, however, forced members of that elite to share or surrender power to organized professionals drawn from the lower-middle and even lower classes. Few of these politicians, whatever their backgrounds, had ideological interests of their own, as distinct from personal or organizational concern with power and profit. Their attitudes, as a result, and those of the police they directed, were ultimately shaped by the expectations of the people who elected them. Thus with the notable exception of vice control and certain obviously partisan functions such as poll watching, the police were supposed to operate in a fashion that would not offend any substantial number of constituents. Many functions were a matter of sheer administrative convenience; few denied the need for riot control at the beginning, and it was assumed that most citizens welcomed a visible effort to combat crime and disorder.

Such a consensus view was and is obviously unsatisfactory to those searching for more profound answers about governance. The question of who controlled the police has wide ramifications, after all, if viewed as a subset to the question of who controlled the city or the society or institutional development in general. Among historians and other social scientists, such questions evoke at least some consideration of social class and class conflict—and so they have with the issue of police.

Allen Steinberg's study, *The Transformation of Criminal Justice* (1989), described earlier, suggests what is in many ways the most novel way of reconceiving the relatively straightforward account given above. While not directly challenging its description of the way in which elective politics worked, it goes far beyond it. What he argues implicitly is that the conventional line between "politics" and "administration" is an artificial one, and that although the late nineteenth century was formally a highly democratic era, with tightly organized parties assuring voter turnouts far higher than today's, it already contained seeds of the apathy that plagues the United States in the 1990s. However inefficient and often corrupt, the direct administration of criminal justice, initiated by the injured parties, was more democratic than a system that progressively turned the matter over to organized, uniformed police. And this development was only one symbol of the growth of bureaucracy, which, underneath the democratization of the elective process, progressively surrendered real power to educated experts.

An older, essentially Marxist challenge to the earlier view of police development has been offered most forcefully by Sidney Harring, in *Policing A Class Society* (1982). Harring's view is that urban police were created by a dominant bourgeois elite to serve as "an instrument of ruling class domination" and above all to suppress working class unrest. His evidence is drawn mostly from Buffalo and other Great Lakes industrial cities in the late nineteenth century, and as far as it goes, it is undeniable. Buffalo's force was founded in 1866, just after the Civil War, and there and elsewhere in the succeeding decades, local police were indeed used to put down strikes and harass "undesirables" such as tramps, whom Harring identifies as members of the industrial working class.

This is an argument that will live in some form as long as Marxism itself. And although the great majority of social scientists had discounted Karl Marx's vision of the future long before its collapse in Eastern Europe, virtually all of us are "Marxists" at least in the simple sense that we are trained to consider his categories of analysis and above all to be sensitive to issues of class. But apart from the fact that Harring's approach does not explain the origins of American police in preindustrial American cities, it is inadequate in its own terms. It is, that is, oversimplified, insensitive to the more sophisticated varieties of Marxism itself that stress the complexity of social organization and control, the need to rule through hegemony, defined as a form of implicit consent and earned through at least some measure of impartiality and benefit to all. And although Harring may explain the behavior of some late nineteenth-century jurisdictions, typically mill towns or smallish industrial cities, places with relatively simple and oligarchical social structures, no truly great metropolitan police force was continually and reliably at the service of industrial employers as a class.

There were, however, a variety of other alternatives open to capitalists large and small. Frank Morn (1982) has shown how retail merchants used private watchmen, often officially deputized as "special police," to patrol the central business district; in Chicago, during the 1850s, serious thought was given to the possibility of using these mercenaries alone, eliminating the publicly paid cops with all of their attendant problems and complications. After the Civil War, too, small armies of railroad cops promoted the interests of the great railroads, by then the largest employers in the nation. The Pinkertons were only the biggest and best known of several agencies for hire in times of strike or, more routinely, as guards against vandalism and theft. As the Pinkertons became notorious in some districts, or simply as state politics allowed, state police were organized to serve parallel functions. Only Massachusetts possessed such a force in the nineteenth century, but a number of other states, notably Pennsylvania, followed just before World War I. It is significant that these "cossacks," as they were known to labor leaders, were supposed to live in isolated barracks, free of the local pressures and community sentiment that made urban police seem unreliable to capitalist employers. Following up on a suggestion made by two historians a dozen years ago (Liebman and Polen 1978), others, as Eric Monkkonen shows in this volume, have sensibly viewed the police function as one that might be assumed at different times by private, local, state, and federal agents, as political conditions allowed—or demanded.

But to conclude that local police were not generally reliable servants of capital is not necessarily to conclude its opposite, that they were instead reliable allies of labor. This argument, an ironically dialectical rejoinder to Harring's Marxist one, was made fifteen years ago by sociologist Bruce Johnson (1976). Unlike Harring's, however, it has no long academic antecedents and has not been followed up. The idea that the police formed a useful alliance with the working class seems instead a classic example of reading the present back into the past. For more than a generation now the cop has been a favorite symbol, and "law and order" a favorite issue, among white ethnics who perceive themselves threatened by black neighbors in urban working-class districts. But the symbolism results from the fact that black-white divisions have recently obliterated older ones. In the nineteenth century, the term "white ethnic" would have been incomprehensible for the same reason that a truly united labor movement would have been inconceivable. In a world in which differences in national origin and religion remained too vivid to allow any sense of class unity, the fact that cops were typically recruited from among white working men did not insure that they represented the interests of their "class."

A more sophisticated approach to the issue of class and the police was taken by Wilbur Miller's study of *Cops and Bobbies* (1977), which took its inspiration not from Marx but from Weber. Not only is it the first comparative study, the book is still the best scholarly account of the development of the London police—replacing the turgid, heavily legal, and political account contained in Sir Leon Radzinowicz's massive study of criminal law and administration (1948–68). And as the

British, in the age of Chartism, were far more frank in discussing matters of class than their American counterparts in the age of Jackson, the issue becomes inescapably prominent.

Similar to all the historians who have published in the 1970s and after, Miller is thoroughly conversant with modern sociological studies of police. But his organizing principle is supplied by Max Weber himself: the issue of legitimation, something akin to hegemony, the process by which authority wins acceptance from the governed. It is this, he finds, which explains the often-noted differences between the police in London and those in New York (and, by extension, in America generally).

The central paradox is that the highly undemocratic London Metropolitan Police, founded in 1829 by the last of the prereformed parliaments, was much less tolerant of abusive brutality—largely directed against the "lower orders"—than were their counterparts in democratic New York. The explanation offered is that in England the governing elite was so small and so conscious of its own vulnerability vis-à-vis the "Other Nation" that it was careful to insist that the police were merely impersonal and neutral agents of "the Law." In all encounters with subjects, as a corollary, individual officers were forcefully enjoined to employ patience and politesse. The rule book in New York contained parallel injunctions—but the rules were often honored only in the breach. New York's politicians, in contrast to those in Britain, feared a "dangerous class" composed not of a majority of their fellow citizens but of a minority—albeit a large one—consisting of much of the immigrant population as well as the more disorderly natives. Always recognized as partial agents of the party in power, New York's cops never won the respect eventually accorded Her Majesty's representatives in London. The fiercely partisan nature of American politics in the 1840s precluded any realistic attempt to appeal to neutral law enforcement, and those who founded the police, all of them potential "outs," were careful not to grant unchecked powers of enforcement. But there was a pervasive fear of violent behavior in the streets—New York, Miller (1977) argues, was a rougher town than London, a judgment more recently confirmed by Eric Monkkonen's comparative study of homicide rates (Monkkonen 1989, 1990). And this fear helped prompt politicians, judges, and the middle classes generally to encourage cops, in the absence of such ex officio authority, to use extralegal personal authority, muscle, and hickory in putting down the poor, the criminal, and the riotous.

A great deal of historical attention has been devoted in recent years to those nineteenth-century institutions used, scholars have argued, as instruments of social control, through which an elite hoped to curb dangerous tendencies in the dangerous classes. The relevant literature is too great even to survey here, but much police history, including Miller's, may obviously be considered from this perspective. Two of the most explicit studies are those by John Schneider (1980), and more comprehensively by Eric Monkkonen in two book-length studies written a decade apart (1981, 1991).

Schneider's account of the origins and early development of the department in Detroit is concerned especially with the physical and social geography of the city. He finds that the force was designed especially to deal with the progressively intrusive presence of a "bachelor subculture." The transient young men who populated the fears of the city's more settled residents formed an economically useful labor pool but were also thought to represent a threat to established values, as their habitat, down by the river, was also the scene of much of the city's vice, robbery, and violence generally.

Monkkonen, although less concerned with origins, would agree that the police all over the United States were founded as instruments of social control but never operated simply as agents of oppression. Indeed, they became agents of class control in humane as well as punitive fashion. Even the humblest residents turned to the police for various services best symbolized by help in finding lost children, while transients took shelter in the station houses on cold nights. And it was often the leaders of the cops themselves, seeking a vaguely professional upgrading of their own status, who rebelled against these untidy and unwelcome functions. Late in the century, in a move anticipating the current emphasis, they turned increasingly to the narrower business of law enforcement and crime control.

Those studies that emphasize political battles for control of police usually agree with Schneider and Monkkonen in stressing the cultural rather than the directly economic dimensions of class conflict. The most notable published work in this category is Robert M. Fogelson's *Big-City Police* (1977), a survey of reform efforts which, although largely confined to the twentieth century, begins with a description of the situation at the end of the nineteenth. For Fogelson, the battle for control of the police was simply the symbolic focus of a wider conflict between an entrenched native elite and a largely immigrant majority in the nation's great cities. The points at issue included differences over the nature of public and private morality, the nature of social mobility, and the proper locus of political power. Fogelson, in effect, defines the police in terms of those who were most critical of them, the often-moralistic reformers of the Progressive Era and after. The answer to the question, Who controlled the police? is simply, as in the older studies, local politicians. But in contrast to both Monkkonen and Schneider, Fogelson conceives these politicians as primarily representing the immigrant lower and lower-middle classes—a development Lane (1967) and Richardson (1970) would find typical of the late but not the early nineteenth century. Ward leaders insisted above all on the right to appoint police captains in their districts and used the force to preserve their own decentralized power base, to provide employment and an avenue of upward mobility for their supporters, and to regulate liquor, vice, and gambling interests, protecting them from competition and outside interference.

This view seems flawed in many respects. It overlooks the fact that the police originated in an era when urban politics was still largely dominated by a local elite rather than by representatives of the lower classes and ignores the many and at least partially successful efforts at vice control that antedated the Progressive Era. It tends, further, to confound all ethnic groups, the relaxed and the puritan, the Catholic and the socialist, as well as to identify "ethnicity" too often with "class." But despite these faults it does rather starkly describe many of the political realities of the Gaslight era.

Fogelson's book has the virtue, too, of showing—as do all scholars with the exception, perhaps, of Sidney Harring—that the police were never fully controlled from outside or above. In practice, the generally decentralized governments of the nineteenth-century city were incapable of enforcing real direction along a hierarchical chain of command, as in the London or military models. And whether explicitly or implicitly—through the use of such passive locutions as "the force grew" or "the police developed"—scholars generally agree that in most cases the men themselves were largely responsible for shaping their own development and traditions. Some of the twentieth-century drive toward self-conscious independence was already evident by the late nineteenth century. Samuel Walker, in the first comprehensive study in the field, traced early efforts at civil service, at unionization, and at what later police reformers—although not scholars—would call "professionalization" (Walker 1977). But before such efforts, even before any substantial degree of job security or continuity had been won, some sort of police subculture was developing.

Much of the best work about contemporary cops assumes or describes such a subculture, one that underlies a high degree of internal autonomy. Among historians, David R. Johnson (1979) has been most concerned with its origins. His study, with materials largely but not exclusively drawn from Philadelphia and Chicago, is concerned especially with the response to the crime prevention function. From their beginnings, police on patrol were supposed to help protect citizens from assault and theft as well as to combat vice in the form of drunkenness, gambling, and prostitution. Given only the vaguest of formal instructions from superiors, however, they had to develop their own means of implementing this impossible mission, a task complicated by a variety of legal and social restraints on their behavior. In dealing with real or putative troublemakers, or suspicious persons, patrolmen quickly learned to concentrate on those low-status groups—the young, the idle poor, the intemperate—that excited the least general sympathy and the most distrust. The principal tactic in newly formed departments in particular was to make large numbers of arrests for such minor offenses as drunkenness or disorderly conduct. The tabulation of such arrests, or body count, was also a convenient way of measuring effort in doing a job which, in reality, defied precise evaluation. It was quickly discovered, too, that in making such arrests, or indeed any arrests, a personal or departmental reputation for toughness, even for carrying and using weapons, was a decided asset. Superiors, then, often ignored the rule book in refusing to discipline cops who used their clubs routinely—except when the clubs were used on respectable complainants. The men themselves justified brutality in terms of the dangers of their working environment. Discretion was learned, rather, in dealing with the world of vice—a world close to and thoroughly entangled with their own—whose entrepreneurs bribed, voted for, protested against, and socialized with police and politicians both. The law, taken literally, was no better as a practical guide in dealing with vice than was the rule book in dealing with the street. The result was that the men developed their own code, one that emphasized personal toughness, tolerance of "deviant" behavior, and a spirit of emotional cohesion and mutual support born out of shared experience.

David Johnson's book stands alone in one highly significant respect. Most scholars would assent to its specific findings. In fact, with some stretching, it is still possible to find much common ground, not only with respect to Johnson's work but also among the several differing views or approaches described in this section. Although political differences are real and fundamental, disputes among police historians about the issue of who controlled the cops and to what ends have been relatively subdued, centering around accusations of overgeneralization, oversimplification, neglect, or omission rather than around outright error. Given the many decades involved, and under American federalism literally thousands of different jurisdictions, it may at least be argued that differences of interpretation have simply resulted from the fact that different scholars have concentrated on different times and places. Thus even those farthest from consensus and from each other, such as Sidney Harring and Bruce Johnson, may have something to say about those places—and there were many—that were at least temporarily dominated politically by capital and labor, respectively. Similarly, if Robert Fogelson and John Schneider and I have differed in approach or emphasis, at least some of this is explicable in terms of the fact that New York in the 1890s, Detroit in the 1860s, and Boston in the 1820s were all rather different places. What makes David Johnson's approach unique is simply that he is the only historian on nineteenth-century development who has chosen to focus predominantly on the function that has come to dominate most thought about police work: the control of ordinary common-law or street crime.

III. Crime and Criminals: Prejudices and Problems

The search for a useful consensus, progressively harder to find as historians move from a simple narrative of police history to more politically charged interpretation, breaks down completely as we move (as many, myself included, have done) out of cops and into crime. A number of British and American scholars have treated nineteenth-century crime as a subject in its own right. Moreover, if relatively few have stressed it, all but the most specialized studies of police have devoted at least some attention to crime and ventured some opinions about its nature and extent. The range of relevant scholarship, as a result, is far greater for crime than for the police and much too great for any definitive listing in a survey such as this. Some of it is rather naive, while some, by historians' usual standards, is sophisticated both methodologically and conceptually. The one common point is that most scholars have at least tried to assess the impact of various social institutions or developments, from professional policing to the Industrial Revolution, on the incidence of and concerns about various kinds of activity defined as criminal. But generalization ends right there, as the result of two intractable problems that no degree of socially scientific methodology seems able to conquer.

The first of these problems may be defined as prejudice, the fact that many of the kinds of behavior that we now define as criminal or perhaps immoral were not so defined during the previous century, and vice versa, and that historians as contemporary citizens have powerful feelings about many of them. Some of the latter prejudices are often helpful in opening up new areas for study—the historic attitude toward various drugs, for example, or prostitution—but they may also block the attempt to reach a scholarly consensus. The second problem is that the historic record simply does not allow a definitive answer to many of the most natural questions that we historians are most often asked by the laity. This section deals with the several kinds of crime whose description or interpretation has been most subject to prejudice, as defined above—often involving class, gender, or ethnicity—saving the problems of the historical record and other kinds of crime for Section IV.

When defined at its broadest, the most profitable kind of crime in the nineteenth century, as in the late twentieth, was committed by businessmen wearing white collars, often abetted by politicians. But for present purposes, the history of political bribery and corruption at high levels must be left to traditional political historians, while the history of unlawful business activity is hard to distinguish from the history of business in general. For historians as well as other Americans, crime may be defined, at one level, as the kind of activity we expect local cops to deal with.

By far the most costly of nineteenth-century white-collar crimes in this category—actually one that involved collusion among merchants, artisans, and the criminal underworld—was counterfeiting. While this became a federal responsibility with the adoption of a national currency, the era before the Civil War, when each of hundreds of individual banks put out its own notes, was a kind of golden age of counterfeiting. Engravers hired ordinary criminals and often made deals with small merchants to push blocks of false paper. The profits could be high, and because of the strictly local nature of law enforcement the business relatively safe; it was hard to deal in Boston with phony money made out in the name of a bank in Alabama, and retailers everywhere, more eager to pass it on to the next unwary customer than to blow the whistle, got drawn into the web of illegality. The result, as David Johnson (1991) finds, was that perhaps as much as half of the circulating paper in the United States in that era was illicit, a fact of some economic significance in an immature economy chronically short of liquid capital.

The other, or blue, side of the collar line is beginning to be far more troublesome to historians especially of strike and riot, once thought virtually indistinguishable categories of criminal behavior. Throughout the previous century the inherited common law, often reinforced by state legislatures and almost always by a conservative judiciary, defined most organized labor activity as illegal. In the absence of union recognition, too, with the often-forcible harassment of scabs the only way working people could make a walkout effective, violence, real or potential, was inherent in any labor conflict. This was a problem for employers who often had to find other members of the working class—if not local cops then state or private ones—to do battle for them. It has not, however, been a problem for twentieth-century historians, who have seen strikes as perfectly legal activities and whose accounts of past conflict have overwhelmingly taken the side of underdog labor against dominant capital. But this confident consensus may be shaken by a closer look at the often-artificial line that divides strike from riot.

For modern scholars, much as for early national politicians, attitudes toward riot have been shaped mostly by its apparent ends. Very broadly political or economic riots, especially those directed against an oppressive authority, as in the decade before the American Revolution, have found sympathetic historians, and much work since the 1960s has gone into vindicating mobs from earlier accusations of mindlessly uncontrolled behavior. Modern scholars have, in contrast, universally deplored racial or ethnic riots in which the dominant majority attacks an unpopular minority. But in analyzing the varieties of popular violence in the previous century, when legal authority was often the only protection available to minority groups, and when the work force in a particular factory or trade was often organized along ethnically exclusive lines, it is often impossible to indulge the inevitable tendency to read our contemporary sympathies back into the past. In pursuing the history of black exclusion from the new economic world opened by the urban industrial revolution, for example, I have found that much violent labor activity was directed against blacks, previously kept out by white competitors, who were imported into a given mine or mill by cynical employers only long enough to break a strike (Lane 1986), making it hard for me to choose up sides in any easy way. Parallel issues are beginning to complicate the work of black and labor historians more broadly. For an earlier period, too, Paul Gilje's work (1987) may have a similar effect. Whatever its objects, riotous or group violence has always been carried out by the relatively deprived, by young males with deeply felt grievances. But however real the grievances, the actions themselves were often vain and even ugly, and Gilje has shown how issues involving politics and economics, Protestants and Catholics, blacks and whites, were often deeply entangled, reminding us that, whatever its ends, the resort to violence always has victims, and hurts.

In dealing with issues of class, then, modern historians, having long since inverted the openly elite sympathies of their nineteenth-century predecessors, are just beginning to explore the complications suggested by the introduction of race and ethnicity into what we had once misread as simple contests between haves and have-nots. Similar considerations have also come to complicate our otherwise coherent picture of the nineteenth-century underworld.

A largely descriptive history of the underworld may be and has been constructed simply by abandoning indignation in favor of a more dispassionate attitude, itself a product of historical change. Both the specific foci of concerns about vice and the relative weight given to various arguments—that is, those involving personal health, social order, or a purely abstract morality—have all shifted dramatically. While we are much concerned now, for example, about how or, indeed, whether to draw the criminal line with respect to drugs other than alcohol—about what sanctions should be applied to the smoking of which vegetable products, and where—our ancestors were not. With the partial exception of smoking opium late in the century—which was associated with gamblers, prostitutes, Orientals, and other "undesirables"—the proscribed list of 1990 was mostly legal as of 1900. The largest single class of addicts, as David Courtwright has shown in *Dark Paradise* (1982), was then middle-class white women, "hooked" on morphine by doctors who, before they could do much about disease, struggled at least to make their patients feel good. Heroin was known mostly as a headache powder, and a number of leading medical men were or had been working through naive personal experiments with cocaine. At the same time, from the second quarter of the nineteenth century, American legislators continually debated the wisdom of allowing any consumption of alcohol. Virtually everywhere they adopted the still-existing restrictions as to sales to minors, on Sundays, in residential areas, and so forth, while many states and countless localities passed outright prohibitions, leading to the passage of the Eighteenth Amendment early in our own century. Similarly, although many states in the early nineteenth century, much like the late twentieth, had moved to ease their tax burdens by sponsoring state lotteries, the resultant corruption and excesses contributed to an almost universal outlawing of any form of gambling by the Civil War era. And in an age associated with "Victorian morality," of course prostitution was a crime largely because it was a sin, despite a few attempts at decriminalization inspired by the failure of law and the fear of disease.

Now that drink, gambling, and a variety of sexual activities are more legally available and, among middle-class academics, more socially acceptable than they were once, it is relatively easy to maintain a certain detachment. Modern scholars, whatever their private moral views, are not wholly unsympathetic either to those who sold vice a century ago or to those who bought it and, so, can describe the marketing of many illicit goods and services much as economists have come to do or as they would other and more fully licit activities. The general framework first supplied by Oscar Handlin in *The Uprooted* (1951) has since been elaborated on by a number of others, most notably by David Johnson and Mark Haller in a series of books and articles (Haller and Alviti 1977; Johnson 1979; Haller 1985, 1990, 1991; Johnson 1991). Whether or not boxing, say, or liquor dealing, or gambling are legal at any given time, the worlds of entertainment, drugs and alcohol, sports, gambling, and politics have all been historically intertwined (Lane 1986). Among urban youngsters, physical prowess, street smarts, the ability to command a gang of one's fellows at the polls, on the field, or at the construction site have all been virtually interchangeable assets in the American game of success. Politics, the rackets, and the labor movement were and are traditional avenues upward, just as drink and sport have been traditional recreations all along the social ladder.

The historical sources available to students of illegal marketing, too, pose few problems except that, in common with most others, they become progressively less common as one moves back in time. Penny papers, which first exploited popular fascination with the underworld, date only from the late 1830s and 1840s, followed in a few years by mass circulation magazines. The police and police reports date, not coincidentally, from the same period. Legislative investigation awaited the formation of police, and autobiographies of cops and crooks awaited the necessary public appetite for their stories.

For the origins, the pre–Civil War period seen only darkly, David Johnson's remains the best full account (1979). Johnson is especially good at describing prostitution and gambling as business enterprises. Neither was a simple one. Each operated differently in different areas of the city, with prices and institutions appropriate for each of the classes they catered to. And if prostitution is "the world's oldest profession," essentially timeless in nature, gambling has evolved continually. Johnson gives a richly complex account of changing games and systems, ethnic variations, and the origins of such now-familiar institutions as the numbers racket and parimutuel betting.

The best of the other historical accounts—all of which share the relatively dispassionate viewpoint described above—depend, with the usual irony, on the passionate accounts of contemporary reformers. The journalistic and legislative investigations or exposés of the Progressive Era, beginning shortly before the turn of the century and lasting into World War I, are an especially rich source of materials. One result is that the most sophisticated histories, like those of Mark Haller, concentrate mostly on the twentieth century. But several do reach back at least into the late nineteenth century, including the best full history of prostitution, Ruth Rosen's *The Lost Sisterhood* (1982). Rosen has concentrated on the Progressive Era largely because that is where the materials are richest: the period encompasses, among other things, both the federal Mann Act of 1912 and E. J. Bellocq's famous Storyville photographs. But it also represents the period when the profession was probably at its numerical peak, before either private sexual liberation or the women's vote, when the wages for single females were still too low to support them and the new immigration created a severe sexual imbalance among several ethnic groups.

Perhaps no other area of criminal activity has gotten more significant new attention in recent years than prostitution, and none represents a more complete reversal of attitude between then and now. Among many feminist historians, the reaction against the moralistic passions of a century ago has moved past dispassion into a passionate advocacy on the other side. Prostitutes, if not quite role models, have become cultural heroines of a sort, foot soldiers on the very front line of the battle of the sexes; their profession may be seen, as suggested some years ago by George Bernard Shaw's fictional Mrs. Warren, as based on the same fundamental exchange as matrimony but without the accompanying responsibilities—or hypocrisy. But while contemporary interviews do suggest—much to the dismay of the reformers who conducted them—that many Progressive Era prostitutes were not forced into but did indeed choose their way of life, and made few apologies for it, a modern emphasis on their individual or small-group independence comes dangerously close, it seems here, to romanticization, and ironically downplays the degree to which they were subject to crippling disease, male manipulation, and brutality.

A parallel romanticism, also involving the inversion of Victorian or Edwardian morality, marks the work of a number of those who see the long nineteenth-century effort to combat vice as simply an effort at social control, designed to insure hegemony by imposing middle-class values on a reluctant proletariat. Marxist historians such as Sidney Harring have sometimes adopted this view as part of the argument about the class-control function of police. But perhaps its most notable recent exponent has been Anthony Platt, who has investigated a special subcategory in *The Childsavers* (1977). Platt, in analyzing Progressive Era reforms of the justice system, has illustrated the proposition that yesterday's solution is indeed often today's problem. Modern advocates of children's rights now often deplore the lack of any adversarial role or formal safeguards in juvenile proceedings. This situation, designed early in the twentieth century to free children from lawyers, put their fate instead in the hands of experts. In this new version of an old story, the former heroes, such as Denver's Judge Benjamin Lindsey, have become villains. The experts turned out to be meddlesome reformers, obsessed by class-bound or sexist standards, who simply labeled as "delinquent" or "status offenses," much juvenile behavior, such as adolescent female sexuality, which was acceptable in adult males.

As applied to adults, however, this class perspective—although not wholly wrong—comes close to suggesting that conventional morality was almost wholly the preserve of native middle-class Protestants, and that the working classes, especially racial minorities and immigrants, were partisans of drunkenness, whoring, and gambling. Much recent political history reminds us of the intensity of battles over legalized boxing or liquor licensing, but it is not easy to divide the partisans along simple class lines. While it is true that many Germans, for example, or Chinese did not share the dominant Protestant attitudes toward Sunday drinking or gambling, there is a growing body of scholarship about the rich ethnocultural diversity of the American population, while everyday observation reminds us, too, that individual Baptists, say, or Catholics, have not always followed the dictates of their churches. Mark Haller (1971) has found that Chicago's mayors were often bombarded by letters from immigrant women complaining of nearby saloons and whorehouses. More recently I have found that articulate black Philadelphians, in the late nineteenth century, were bitterly resentful of the fact that the white Protestants who ran the city had apparently zoned their neighborhoods as semi-official vice districts, while, conversely, over half of black children in the city's reformatory were placed there not by reforming busybodies but on request of their own parents or guardians (Lane 1986).

The history of professional thievery, meanwhile, offers an instructive contrast to all of this. The records available to historians of thievery are virtually identical to those of entrepreneurial vice, simply because thieves visited the same places and lived in the same underworld as gamblers, saloonkeepers, prostitutes, and detectives. But perhaps because thievery, as compared to vice, had fewer practitioners then and has fewer partisans now, the relevant scholarship has been much less controversial. The major argument among British historians— echoing worried contemporary observers—was whether the underworld—whose nineteenth-century habits, cons, and institutions could, in many ways, be traced back at least to the Elizabethans—properly constituted a hereditary class, quite distinct from other merely poor or marginal subjects. But this seems to have been settled in the negative, and American historians were never really involved. Our nineteenth-century observers tended, for their own ideological reasons, to deny the importance or even existence of "class," and twentieth-century scholars, for equally ideological but very different reasons, have been concerned only with the working class and its direct oppressors, rather than with those Marx himself classified as "social scum."

Full-time urban thieves, as described in my own police history (1967), seem originally to have grown out of the British underworld. The matter of origins is naturally obscure—David Johnson's account is the fullest—but by the 1840s or 1850s, professional thievery had clearly matured in patterns that were recognizably those of Edwin Sutherland's famous "Chic" Conwell in the 1930s (Sutherland 1937) or indeed of the hard-core professionals described more recently by Charles E. Silberman (1978). Highly skilled specialists in theory—not only con men and fences, pickpockets and forgers but also several varieties of burglar, each distinguished by characteristic methods and targets—they were not quite so choosy in practice. While certain specialties came and went with technological advance and social change, the loose fraternity of American thieves remained marked by common associations, habits, and habitats. The nineteenth century may have been their heyday—a period of relatively primitive protective systems, and widespread if never fully trustworthy police "cooperation." Partly because, like their British cousins, they generally sought to operate through craft and wit rather than violence, the popular press tended to glamorize as much as condemn them. And historians have followed social observers ever since Lincoln Steffens in agreeing that, as with vice, the police in big cities did not so much attempt to suppress as to regulate professional theft, protecting favored sources, confining depredations to acceptable locations and perhaps acceptable victims. But their mutual relations were tense, rarely lasting, and the estimate for the late nineteenth century is identical to that for the late twentieth: professional thieves could expect to spend a third to a half of their lives behind bars (Lane 1967; Silberman 1978).

For historians of crime, then, the most intractable problems lie not with the relatively rational and well-recorded activities of professional thieves nor even with the entrepreneurial underworld whose history, however subject to opposing interpretations, may at least be described in terms that most would recognize. It lies, instead, with the behavior, both more and less routine, of amateur criminals: acts of desperation and violence, disorderly conduct, burglary and petty theft, armed robbery, arson, rape, assault, and murder. There are problems of interpretation here, as with all else. But the bigger problems are technical and, so far, nearly insoluble.

IV. More Crime, Criminals, and Problems

Prejudice, in the sense described in Section III, is sometimes a problem, but it also both inevitable and (often) fruitful, as new concerns generate new scholarship and fresh interpretation. But problems arising from holes in the historical record, while perhaps equally inevitable, have no redeeming features. And for most common-law or street offenses—the ones that ordinary late-twentieth-century Americans think of as "crime"—there are holes ranging in depth from the pitfall to the abyss. While social scientists have helped us to find ways of approaching these holes, they, and we, are ultimately unable to plumb them accurately. We have found out a good deal, despite manifold handicaps, that is relevant to current debate about criminal behavior. But in the end, in addition to the problems of prejudice, those who are concerned with burglary and larceny, arson, assault, rape, and murder are uniquely embarrassed by their inability to give any simple answer to the most common and natural of questions: "How much was there, then, as compared to now?" The question has grown increasingly insistent over the past generation as urban crime rates have grown, but the answer or answers give us little comfort.

There is, in fact, a general answer of sorts to the question. But more specific answers are currently so hedged with technicalities and qualifications that only a scholar can love them. And this unsatisfactory state unfortunately obscures the fact that the general answer, conceived as a kind of baseline, the point to which—but not beyond which—there is currently widespread agreement, represents a considerable scholarly achievement.

Ten years ago, when it was still in controversy, it was necessary to describe that achievement in some detail; today it is possible to run it through more quickly. In brief, the modern historical study of crime was begun a generation ago, in response to what were then relatively new public concerns about rising levels of urban crime in the streets. The politically easiest explanation then was that "they"—recent black migrants to the city—were responsible for the apparent upsurge. One scholarly response—long since discredited—was that there was no upsurge at all, that cops and FBI men were inflating the statistics for political effect. But the dominant one, with the oldest and best credentials, was that growing urban crime rates were as natural and inevitable as urban growth itself.

Earlier histories and sociologists both living and dead combined to reinforce this assumption. Urban historians, reading municipal reports from the previous century, were struck by the continued insistence— often by mayors or police chiefs looking for bigger appropriations— that crime was rising, an assertion often backed by statistics showing growing arrest totals. The Germanic founders of sociology, with their nostalgic concern for the loss of "primary" or village contacts in big contemporary cities, the passage from gemeinschaft to gesellschaft, gave these impressions a theoretical framework. They were further strengthened in this country by Robert E. Park, Ernest Burgess, and their followers in the Chicago school of sociology, who combined to give a powerful antiurban bias to the social sciences generally.

My own equally powerful impression, however, having just emerged during the mid-1960s from something like total immersion in the records of nineteenth-century Boston, was that the small commercial city of the 1820s was a far more violent and crime-ridden place than the great metropolis of the 1880s (Lane 1967). The unmistakable conclusion was that urban growth in itself did not cause crime. On analyzing rising arrest totals over most of the nineteenth century for the state of Massachusetts as a whole, I went on to argue that they really represented just the opposite of what they suggest at first, not more crime but rather more intolerance of crime, as the surge in aggregate totals was wholly the result of arrests for relatively minor offenses such as drunkenness, while the proportion of serious felonies was actually declining (Lane 1968).

A variety of other studies, meanwhile, across the Atlantic, pointed quite independently and unmistakably in the same direction. The first Industrial Revolution, followed by massive urbanization, had occurred in late eighteenth- and nineteenth-century England. And although British scholars were bitterly divided about the course and costs of these events—the continuing basis of the nation's economic and political divisions—they were united in agreeing that the preindustrial rural population was far more violent than the largely urbanized, more fully industrial population of later years (Lane 1974). Throughout the 1970s, meanwhile, studies of various American jurisdictions, many of them more careful and sophisticated than my original article of 1968, disagreed with some of its details but confirmed its outlines. And by the end of the decade or shortly after, two landmark publications, incorporating a number of recent findings, helped put the basic point beyond doubt.

Ted Robert Gurr, with the help of Peter Grabosky and Richard C. Hula, first published the *Politics of Crime and Conflict* (Gurr, Grabosky, and Hula 1977); Eric Monkkonen followed with *Police in Urban America* (1981). What Gurr and his associates found was that serious crime was declining in the nineteenth century, according to official statistics, not only in London but in the very different cities of Stockholm and Sydney as well. Monkkonen, on reviewing the work of eleven scholars covering fourteen jurisdictions in thirteen quantitative studies, ancient and modern, found overwhelming agreement on the same kind of decline. But what he and Gurr also found is that, following this decline, there was also a rise, at least equally strong, dating (usually) from sometime around the middle of our own century. This latter finding—confirmed by official FBI statistics, innumerable scholarly works, and our simple experience as citizens, completes the picture as we now know it.

What we know now is, in fact, quite impressive, as compared with what we knew a generation ago, and directly or implicitly supplies answers to a number of questions of the kind that citizens rightly raise. Rates of serious or violent crime, in short, have not risen steadily with urban growth. They have instead followed what may be described as a kind of gigantic U-shaped curve, down for most of the nineteenth century, and after bottoming out, up since. That this is an international phenomenon suggests that most of the usual parochial explanations for rising crime, whether of the left or right, do not apply. It is important to stress that neither the decisions of the Supreme Court of the United States, the increasingly black complexion of American cities, nor our national gun culture have much to do with rising rates in Scandinavia or Australia. That the curve was down during the previous century suggests also that neither massive economic change, the disruption of traditional society, nor waves of immigration, all modern phenomena first experienced during the nineteenth century, can explain the upsurge either.

But with all of this established, we still do not know what we would like to. If many of the older explanations can be shown not to work, it is harder to find agreement on new ones that will explain the U-shaped curve as a whole. In fact, only three scholars, Ted Robert Gurr, James Q. Wilson, and I, have attempted a comprehensive interpretation of its shape at both ends. We have each used different methods—while I have concentrated on intensive study of individual American jurisdictions, Gurr has correlated studies and official statistics from many different times and places, while Wilson, reflecting on many of the same works that Gurr and I have used, has also projected his understanding of modern studies of criminal psychology (Gurr, Grabosky, and Hula 1977; Gurr 1979, 1989; Wilson and Herrnstein 1985; Lane 1989).

With some oversimplification, it may be said that we all begin with much the same historical sources, use the same definitions, and describe substantially the same U-shaped curve. We all concentrate wholly on the common-law crimes of theft and violence, minimizing the problems of definition and social tolerance described in Section III; we agree further that most of these actions are fundamentally impulsive or irrational (in contrast to white-collar crime, or entrepreneurial vice). We all find, too, that virtually from the time that criminal statistics were first bureaucratically recorded in Western jurisdictions, sometime in the first half of the nineteenth century, the trend for serious offenses was down. The fundamental reason, as most broadly defined by Gurr, is "modernization." In the United States, most clearly in the second quarter of the nineteenth century, the decline in crime was accompanied and at least partly caused by creation of a number of new institutions designed to produce a more orderly population: cops and prisons, public schools and insane asylums, a drive toward reducing formerly very high levels of drunkenness. All of these, with some ups and downs dependent on local factors—the disruption caused by Irish immigration into Eastern cities, for example—took hold at some point in the mid-century decades and helped to create the kind of disciplined environment characteristic of the industrializing cities of the nineteenth century. After many further decades of downward movement, then leveling off sometime during the twentieth century, in more recent decades crime and violence have risen again in the United States and across the Western world as the older institutions of control, those cited above, have lost their effectiveness.

But agreement among the three of us stops with this sketch, for which we have substantially different explanations. And these are especially marked for the right side, the modern upsurge in the U-shaped curve, the part of naturally greatest concern to our late twentieth-century contemporaries.

My own explanation is based on fundamental economic change, which, in turn, creates changes in social psychology. The urban industrial revolution of the nineteenth century simply demanded more orderly, rational, cooperative behavior than the previous economic system, in which farmers, craftsmen, and small merchants operated in relative independence. In a preindustrial society, high levels of drunkenness, and erratic or violent behavior hurt only those most immediately involved. In an industrializing society, in contrast, they were intolerable, as the work of each, in mill or office, was dependent on the predictable behavior of others. The state was called in then, and cops in part created to help tame a formerly unruly population—with special emphasis on drunkenness, the kind of victimless crime that private citizens did not prosecute on their own. The new public schools taught not literacy so much as discipline, as youngsters preparing for regimented lives in factory or bureaucracy learned to sit still, take turns, mind the teacher, hold their water, and listen for the bell. The literally "civilizing" institutions of the nineteenth century, from temperance societies to a variety of incarcerating institutions, worked to make the industrial city function smoothly as far as they did because they were going with the flow, reinforcing the felt needs of the new economic order, helping to create an appropriately new kind of mass social psychology.

The recent upsurge in the U-shaped curve, then, reflects the decay of that economic order, the move out of an industrial into a postindustrial society. The new society makes educational and technical demands unprecedented in the history of the species, leaving millions behind. Good blue-collar jobs were once open to most who would fit themselves to the discipline of industrialism, but no longer. It was never easy to get young people—especially young males—to go along with that discipline, and now that there is little room for those who do not take to purely academic achievement, it is nearly impossible. The result is that the schools and cops, the injunctions to stay clear of the prevailing drugs, no longer work because they are no longer serving their former economic function, and much of the population, suffering from structural un- or underemployment, no longer accepts the kind of social psychology that built the industrial city. In some ways, here at the right end of the U-shaped curve, many citizens have reverted to the free-swinging preindustrial psychology of the left end.

I have pursued this thesis over the years mostly but not entirely through the history of Philadelphia, which, during the nineteenth century, boasted probably the most varied and skilled manufacturing work force in the world, and today, having lost much of its industrial base, is facing bankruptcy. In trying to avoid the inevitable problems associated with criminal statistics, I have incorporated other indices of social behavior, using the appropriate psychological theories to illumine the connections among various forms of *Violent Death in the City*, including suicide and accident (Lane 1979). Partly to show the effects of deliberate exclusion from the urban-industrial revolution on the criminal behavior of one key subgroup, I have worked to uncover *The Roots of Violence in Black Philadelphia* (1986). Some of the same issues, with greater emphasis on the history of the modern underclass, are illuminated further in *William Dorsey's Philadelphia and Ours: On the Past and Future of the Black City in America* (1991), which shows why the economic history of the black population has made it especially—although far from uniquely—vulnerable to postindustrial change. But alas, despite all this effort, it is vain to expect that my colleagues, including Wilson and Gurr, have been convinced. And I can only try, very briefly and equally in vain, to describe their alternatives fairly.

Gurr's interpretation of nineteenth-century developments, across the

Western world, although its broader concept of modernization involves less emphasis on either specific economic requirements or social psychology than mine, is at least roughly compatible with it. For the twentieth century rise in crime rates, however (although he sees it as I do, dating from after World War II and most apparent in the 1960s), Gurr abandons the largely economic-structural explanation that we both apply to the previous century. His explanation, instead, lies in a loss of moral authority by the state and other socializing institutions. This is a loss occasioned in part by the selfishly aggressive hedonism promoted by a consumer society—a position I can easily endorse. But he also insists on the import of such specific political events as the Vietnam War, and the resulting antiauthoritarianism of the young—a position with which I cannot concur. The argument seems to me both parochially American, ironic in the leading cross-national student of crime rates, and too heavily concerned with the attitudes of middle-class youngsters not usually associated with street crime.

James Q. Wilson, meanwhile, deals almost exclusively in moral authority, to the virtual exclusion of economic or other structural influences. His explanation for the nineteenth-century drive against social disorder is that it was inspired by a contemporary religious revival. The resultant improvements in social behavior, describable in terms of an increased ability to delay gratification and curb impulsively violent or larcenous impulses, thus rested on a firmly Christian foundation that held for the rest of the century and beyond. Once that foundation was weakened—a development he ascribes above all to Sigmund Freud and the kind of moral relativism associated with Margaret Mead and other cultural anthropologists—all was lost. Parents could no longer socialize their children with the authority conferred by absolute moral standards, young folks lost the ability to control their impulses, the state, in effect, lost its nerve and will to punish effectively, and the result was and has been higher crime. All of these developments are described wholly without reference to other, nonmoral, kinds of social or economic change. Wilson focuses, as does Gurr, for more recent developments on the attitudes of the middle class, and it seems here his hypotheses do not fit the actual timing of the left-side downswing or more especially the right-side upswing of the U-shaped curve.

But these interpretative disagreements among Gurr, Wilson, and me—differences that could, of course, be easily multiplied were it possible to count the innumerable studies that have covered shorter historical time spans—represent only the first of the problems that make it hard to carve useful answers to contemporary questions out of the U-shaped curve itself. The simple fact is that the historical record is very uneven at best. The curve is, of course, not a smooth and simple line but a gross oversimplification of many different and zigzagging lines, a composite made of the statistics of many different criminal jurisdictions, problematic in many unfathomable ways.

To begin with, virtually all continuing statistical series date only from the second quarter or so of the nineteenth century, by no coincidence the period when the urban-industrial revolution began obviously to take hold. We have only tantalizing glimpses, based on fragmentary records, for the preindustrial period. Two studies based on English coroners' inquests, for example, suggest that medieval villagers and Londoners lived in very dangerous worlds, in which the simple brutality of making a living combined with the utter lack of reliable medicine to make violent death quite common (Given 1977; Hanawalt 1979). To the extent that rates can be estimated—and although the inquests provide a numerator of sorts, the actual population denominator remains quite unknown—it appears that homicides were proportionately ten or twenty times what they are in comparable English jurisdictions today. This suggests to Ted Robert Gurr, quite reasonably, that the U-shaped curve is only the latter end of a kind of huge reverse J-shaped curve, and that the modernization process, involving, among other things, a kind of continuous growth in humane values, has been going on for centuries with various blips, dips, and short-term reverses (Gurr 1989). This is not an unreasonable hypothesis, and the existing evidence does at least put to rest the vision of an idyllically peaceful rural past. But the record for England remains shaky, with gaps some centuries wide, and we simply do not know whether either levels or trends can be extrapolated to Russia, Italy, or Germany.

Even for the nineteenth century, this kind of cross-national comparison is nearly impossible. Governments generally adopted some kind of police institutions during the first half of the century, partly in imitation of the more advanced and admired nations, and began to turn out relatively long runs of criminal statistics. The fact that, when collated, these tend (despite great variations) to show the U-shaped curve pattern—Ted Robert Gurr's great achievement—is powerful evidence for the reality of that curve. But it is composed of a mélange of numbers, sometimes arrests, sometimes court cases, sometimes appeals to the highest authorities, which are simply not equivalent to each other. The timing of the left-hand downturn of the U-shaped curve, if it clearly occurred at all, is different for each national or other jurisdiction, partly because each had a distinctive economic experience and was at any given moment in a different stage of development. Add to this that each police force had its own traditions and missions—the Austro-Hungarians, for example, continually sniffing out sedition, with the British quite relaxed about political crimes not involving Irishmen—throw in often mysterious and idiosyncratic changes in reporting procedures, and it is easy to sympathize with Eric Monkkonen's plaint that the state of early criminal statistics is enough to drive a historian into hysteria.

Even if, for simplicity's sake, we stay within a single nation—our own—we must contend with virtually all of these problems. The preindustrial past, to begin with, remains murky despite the fact that the time span is comparatively short. Even where colonial governments were relatively stable, the surviving records are haphazard and hard to interpret. There were a variety of precursors to cops, but no arrest totals. We have accounts of some courts—how representative?—but not others. Slavery was legal everywhere—did violence done by (certainly not done to) slaves get into the record? How about servants? Are there missing cases handled by church courts? Contemporary terminology obscures much, and in one infamous case, a historian interpreted the category "crimes against public order"—actually disorderly conduct such as drunkenness—to mean treasonable behavior and, so, had colonial New York awash in revolutionary activity. Impressionistic evidence makes it seem unlikely that there was any straight-line trend in the settled New England colonies toward public order, that among themselves the white settlers of eighteenth-century Massachusetts were more peaceable than those of the seventeenth, but there is no possibility of truly statistical comparison. And it would be rash to compare the experience of New Englanders in either century with that of contemporary South Carolina, for example. There, as Michael Hindus (1975) has shown, the whole purpose of law enforcement well into the nineteenth century was entirely different, aimed less at protecting commercial property than at protecting against slave revolt, and "patrol" meant not watchmen or constables but heavily armed horsemen, something between a volunteer militia and a lynch mob, with little concern for recording their activities for posterity.

These differences help remind us that the variety of experience within the United States was quite as great as it was across Europe, that the Boston of Henry James was contemporaneous with the Arkansas of "Hanging Judge" Parker. Each of these regions had its distinctive institutions of criminal law enforcement, and each of the ethnocultural subgroups within them had its own standards of order and morality in ways that make it impossible to recreate behavior out of the record. The problem of the "dark figure"—the number of wholly unknowable criminal acts—haunts all attempts to estimate crime rates even in the present; for the past it is multiplied enormously. What qualifies as assault, for example, and whether or not it ever gets into the legal record, differs in practice not only with the status of actor and victim but with neighborhood, group, or jurisdiction—all variables subject to change over time.

And even if—again for purposes of simplification—the effort to compare is confined to settled late nineteenth-century American cities, in the Northeast or West, with established police forces and recording procedures, the process is full of traps. This was the golden age of municipal statistics; it was part of the very process of civilization for the authorities in most of these cities to keep neatly elaborate columns of figures for miles of streets paved and sewers laid, births, deaths, marriages, smallpox inoculations, and criminal arrests—the latter all in neat rows from "abortion" to "weapons, carrying concealed deadly." But this apparent richness of detail is deceptive, and the figures do not yield easily to a historian's questions.

While arrest totals, for example, are often broken down by native and foreign, male and female, black and white, the individual offenses usually are not, so that it is impossible to say which groups were most at risk of arrest for which crimes. The prose accompanying the totals only rarely helps interpret them. Do rising totals for drunk arrests mean more drunks or—more probably—more public intolerance and, in fact, fewer drunks? How many drunk and other public order arrests did cops make on their own, how many at the insistence of indignant citizens? Do rising totals for larceny mean more larceny or simply more reliance on cops or public prosecution for offenses earlier handled by the victims in other ways? The use of unfamiliar words—for example, arrests for "violence"—reminds us that a different era is also a different culture. The point is underlined even more dramatically by the use of the same word to describe quite different things. "Robbery" in an eastern city during the late nineteenth century usually meant purse snatching, or perhaps drunk-rolling in the vice district (Lane

1986). And while some forms of criminal activity, for example, "robbery from the person" or pickpocketing, have faded over time, others—such as kidnapping for ransom—were just being invented.

Differences in the standard of living and culture of the working classes also complicate comparison. During the previous century, crimes of theft usually increased in hard times as the result of simple economic desperation—the traditional image of the man who steals bread for his family had then much basis in reality. During most of the twentieth century, however, when warm clothing and calories have been more easily taken for granted, crimes of theft have typically soared during prosperity, when goods are temptingly displayed for the taking, and many feel the relative deprivation that results from lacking the expensive consumer goods the whole culture insists that they must have. The very opposite cycle, meanwhile, has operated for crimes of violence. During the twentieth century, hard times appear simply to make people mean and likely to strike out. But during the nineteenth, assaultive crimes usually went down, not up, during depressions—my own guess being that people were simply unable to afford the alcohol that is so heavily associated with impulsive aggression (Lane 1989).

Differences, too, in the operations of the justice system make it hard to mine the past for simple lessons applicable to the present. Criminologists argue about what causes recidivism, about the size of the "professional" class of criminals, about the deterrent effect of swift and sure justice and capital punishment. But in the nineteenth century, there was little systematic exchange of information and no fingerprinting, social security cards, or other means of identification. Anyone arrested outside of his or her home jurisdiction, then, and sometimes in it, was essentially operating on the honor system when asked, "Have you ever been arrested before?" To trust the official figures on recidivism drawn from prison dockets, then, is akin to believing in Santa Claus. And while the nineteenth century generally was marked by quick justice—Philadelphia homicide cases often came up within a month, sometimes a week, of the event—it was hardly sure. Primitive detective work left many homicides unsolved, and the fact that most cases resulted from fights, in which a defendant could plead self-defense, meant that proportionately far more cases than today resulted in acquittals. And although capital punishment was usual in law, the road to the gallows was marked in its own way by as many detours and roadblocks as nowadays the road to the chamber or chair, with judicial decisions routinely overturned by gubernatorial clemency or even pardons (Lane 1986).

Homicide still remains the one offense whose definition was least problematic (although differences in degree were not usually admitted until the midcentury decades), which was never dealt with "off the books" by the victim (although perhaps by the survivors), and almost always taken seriously by the public authorities (except perhaps in interracial cases in the South and West). For purposes of comparison across time and jurisdictions, then, homicide statistics are the best we have—but even the best is none too good.

What we call the "murder rate" is nowadays based first on "crimes known to police," as the numerator, based on police figures for the city or other jurisdiction involved. Since the early 1930s, in addition, these or similar local reports, as of arrests, have been centrally compiled by the FBI to yield a national figure. The aggregate number is then divided by the population of city or nation to produce a rate. Breakdowns by sex, race, and other variables are also available to make it possible to calculate the rate for, say, young black males.

But for the nineteenth century, it is hard to find breakdowns of aggregate statistics to use for the numerators, as I have found in researching the rate of black homicide. And the denominators—population statistics—are also slippery, as modern scholars have found wide census errors—averaging in the double figures, probably—even for white male voters. Such errors were doubtless far greater among those marginal groups, blacks and immigrants, most likely to commit homicide and also most likely to resist being counted by strangers representing the government.

For the nineteenth century, too, the available aggregate figures are not the same as for the late twentieth. There are neither crimes known to police nor national figures of any trustworthiness. Instead of crimes known there are arrests—most commonly used but by no means always available—indictments, convictions, or imprisonments. Basically, we use what we can get or trust—for nineteenth-century Philadelphia I found indictments the best—but as Eric Monkkonen has complained, rates based on different stages in the judicial process are not comparable with each other (Monkkonen 1981). Even the same stage poses problems: before modern constitutional safeguards, police behaved in contradictory fashion. Lacking specialized detectives, they ignored or simply missed far more offenses than they do now but in ways impossible to balance statistically. In notorious or well-publicized cases they often went to the other extreme, arresting dozens of people for a single murder. Jurisdictions differed greatly in this respect, with late nineteenth- and early twentieth-century New York cops booking homicide suspects at a rate several times greater than that for other big cities. All figures for the early twentieth century are complicated by the invention of the internal combustion engine and the fact that automobiles, new to city streets, caused a major rise in what we would call involuntary manslaughter but what contemporary authorities called homicide. The City of Detroit, in the Henry Ford era around World War I, was, by this definition, proportionately the "murder capital" of the United States on paper sixty years before it earned the same title in reality (Lane 1989).

The best source of comparative figures is then, ideally, a true "body count," in which, for the nineteenth century, a researcher examines coroners' inquests case by case to find the number of labeled homicides. Eric Monkkonen is now engaged in such a landmark study for New York City (1990). But it will not surprise readers patient enough to have waded through all the foregoing caveats to learn that long runs of inquests are rare in this country, where the coroner was traditionally an independently elected official responsible to, and thus reporting to, no one else. And there is much evidence of two complications that affected the labeling of such an apparently simple offense as homicide. One was that, as a result of a lower threshold of tolerance for violence, over time, what had been accidents early in the nineteenth century were later called murder, with individual agents held responsible for boiler explosions, fires, and the like. The other is that the coroner was always under a natural pressure, especially in deaths involving the kind of marginal people most often victims of homicide, not to burden a primitive detective system with unsolved cases and, so, often labeled victims of violence as having died of unknown causes, accident, or suicide—the latter even for men pulled out of the river with empty pockets and hands tied behind their backs (Lane 1979).

How then, finally, to answer the question: "Was there more theft, robbery, assault, rape, or murder then than now?" It should be clear by this time that there is no way to reply with certainty, and that, while of some use, the kinds of statistical data and even the concepts and models used by students of modern criminal behavior are not generally reliable guides to past criminal behavior. I can only begin to answer by restricting the question to what I know best, comparing crime rates in the settled eastern and midwestern United States in the late nineteenth century with those in the same places today. And the answers are tentative, informed guesses, based on a traditional historian's sense of the social context as much as on harder numerical evidence.

My guess as to theft is that there was then less than now. Certainly this is true of theft from commercial places; when shops were small, there was little display of abundance, no self-service, and much careful scrutiny of goods and customers. The guess is less sure as to theft from private persons and rests principally on the fact that most people simply had far fewer possessions of which to be robbed. The great majority of reported thefts in the late nineteenth century were of small consumer items, mostly clothing. Some forms of theft, such as professional pickpocketing, were then more common than now, but outside of professionals it was not only the people who stole who were often poor and fiercely in need but also the victims, often neighbors, landlords, or fellow boarders, who guarded what they had with equal ferocity.

Simple assault was then more common. Alcohol consumption was very high, and people who lived in cramped and unattractive quarters spent far more time than we do in public, out in the world, whether working, traveling, or drinking together. Friction was common, fighting a fact of life, and many groups, notably the Irish, quintessential nineteenth-century urbanites, not only valued toughness but thought of physical combat as a form of sport, whether as spectators or participants. Although handguns were already fairly common, they were not as deadly as today's weapons, and strangers were not as commonly suspected of carrying them, making it perhaps a little easier to pick a fight.

Robbery is very hard to call. In nineteenth-century cities, robbery in the modern sense—that is armed robbery—was quite rare, as noted earlier, so that, in one case, news of a holdup in the Bronx ran in the Philadelphia papers for a week (the New York cops blamed it on a person unknown but probably in town with Buffalo Bill's Wild West troupe). Many other kinds of theft from the person were, however, quite common: transient visitors to the semisanctioned red-light district were liable to be rolled by prostitutes or their confederates, and if they found it hard to tell it to the judge next morning, the cases never got into the record (Lane 1986).

The modern women's movement has taught us how unreliable are the official statistics for rape, and the constraints against reporting the offense in the late twentieth century must have been even more powerful in the late nineteenth century, still the Victorian era. Again a qualitative distinction must be made. What we used to define, almost exclusively, as rape—that is violent rape by strangers, or perhaps gang rape—was often front-page news a century ago, while rarely making it out of the police briefs in the 1990s. There was then, too, no common equivalent of date rape because there was little activity that could be classified as dating, among most classes, while among the middle class there was little male expectation of directly genital sex and few unobserved opportunities to indulge in it. But sex forced on unwilling women or girls by authority figures of all kinds was surely very common. Death and desertion created large numbers of truly helpless orphans. As the same two scourges broke marriages as often as divorce does now, and families were generally larger, more children were raised by stepfathers, while large numbers were sent out quite young to work as maids in still other households commanded by strange men. The great majority of single women and widows worked simply because they had to, there was no welfare system of any kind, and with wages barely enough to sustain life those without strong family support were extremely vulnerable to sexual advances by employers.

What, finally, of homicide? Despite the absence of comparable statistics across the century, some firm judgments may be made about the relative contribution of various groups within the two periods. While urban blacks now have homicide rates many times higher than whites, it is important to note that this was not true in the late nineteenth century. Full citizens at last, they were making impressive educational and, among the middle class, economic gains. In Philadelphia and, I am confident, elsewhere, they had lower homicide rates than the desperate "Wild Irish" during the midcentury years and far lower than the Italian immigrants of later decades, mostly single young men. The effects of a prejudiced exclusion from the modern economic sector, jobs in factories or offices, were fully felt only later, intensifying during the twentieth century. Left to do only the worst preindustrial jobs, many responded by leaving the straight economy entirely, living in an inherently violent underworld of vice. Many more continued to behave in the old free-swinging preindustrial fashion that had marked all city dwellers earlier, at the time when the left side of the U-shaped curve was still high, just as their old immigrant competitors were pulling away economically and settling down socially (Lane 1986).

The experience of women, meanwhile, was quite different, as over the past century they have moved modestly to close the still great gap between their official homicide rates and those of men. The two apparent reasons are technological and racial. The growth in the availability of guns, often stashed in the bedrooms or kitchens where men and women traditionally find reasons to argue, has somewhat evened the physical odds. Nineteenth-century domestic fights were overwhelmingly settled in favor of the physically stronger party, but firearms, as Thomas Hobbes noted centuries ago, are great equalizers. The fact that proportionately more urban women are now black is also important. Black women have always enjoyed more sexual equality than their white counterparts in virtually all aspects of life; among other things, this has made them more dangerous domestic opponents, both now and then, a condition reflected in relative homicide rates.

The effort to make statistical comparisons across rather than within periods is complicated by a number of variables in addition to those already cited. Most of them—the difference between indictments, arrests, and "crimes known," the (relative) rarity and weakness of nineteenth-century firearms, the primitive character of detective work—work to make nineteenth-century official figures lower, relative to the "dark figure" of actual homicides committed, than those of the late twentieth century. Another one—relatively primitive medical resources—worked in the opposite direction, as many victims of stabbing and gunshot wounds who died a hundred years ago would survive today. My own estimate—discounting all these complications—is that the murder rate for white adults was then roughly of the same order of magnitude as now—and probably was higher in the 1850s and 1860s, before the U-shaped curve began decisively to point down. Overall, however, increases in both the black population and the black murder rate mean that, for all adults, it is now considerably higher.

But this estimate leaves out the great "wild card"—infanticide—that finally defeats all comparison. Nowadays it is headline news when a dead infant, victim often of suffocation, is found in an alley or dumpster. In the late 1860s, such finds were made two or three times a week in a Philadelphia less than half the size it is now. Children were born not in hospitals but at home, the poorest women were unattended by any but family, and many had no one. Literally thousands of newborns were listed, each year, as dying of causes that could easily have been homicide, allegedly suffocated accidently, or "overlaid," by mothers who rolled over on them while sharing a bed, or allegedly dying of "weakness," "malnutrition," "inanition," and "unknown causes." The justice system was extremely reluctant to investigate these cases; unable either to cure the fundamental economic situation that brought the most desperate of mothers to the dock or to try the heartless seducer who was in contemporary eyes the real villain. An inquest or trial, when absolutely unavoidable, typically ran a predictable course, with a woman's miserable story of abandonment and destitution winning acquittal on grounds of temporary insanity (Lane 1986).

How many of these infanticides were there? It is impossible to say—but quite probably enough to push the real murder rate of the late nineteenth century well past its modern equivalent. And to complicate the matter further, many and perhaps most of them were in effect ex post facto abortions, a fact that opens another set of problems and mysteries.

James Mohr's (1978) path-breaking history of abortion in America contains both good news and bad news for both sides of the contemporary debate over the issue. In the first place, he shows that, following English common law, abortion before "quickening," generally the sixth month or so, was quite legal from the colonial period through the early Republic and on to about the Civil War. Legality is then, in some sense, traditional—and based on contemporary doctors' reports. Mohr estimates that perhaps 20–25 percent of all conceptions in the midcentury decades were aborted. Conversely, the drive to outlaw the practice at any stage of pregnancy was led not by religious leaders, certainly not the still-embattled Catholic minority, but by the most up-to-date physicians, confident that science had determined that human life begins at conception.

Most states, then, criminalized abortion about the 1860s. And once it was criminal, its history as well as its practice went underground. Neither the criminal nor the health statistics are reliable guides to abortion's incidence. In Philadelphia, there were only a handful of prosecutions when the law was new and the practice still presumably common among many quite respectable women and doctors. Thereafter, as the incidence of criminal abortion declined, the number of prosecutions picked up—although they never averaged as many as ten per year. Throughout the late nineteenth century, there was virtually no publicity given to the resulting trials, and there were many acquittals. There seems little aggressive prosecution, and most cases resulted, apparently, when women who had suffered some damage at the hands of illegal practitioners reported it to regular doctors. Deaths, meanwhile, were listed sometimes under "abortion," sometimes under "peritonitis," "sepsis," or other heads, making it very hard to guess the number of either ordinary or fatal cases. And of course once the practice was outlawed, reputable physicians no longer offered reliable estimates.

In Chicago, however, Leslie Reagan in a prize-winning article (1991) has found a very different situation. Although her records date mostly from the early twentieth century, they could probably be read farther back. And there she has found very aggressive prosecution, directed not only at criminal amateurs but at regular physicians and the aborted women themselves.

Abortion, then, is one crime at whose historic incidence I will not even hazard a guess. Its history involves changing definitions from noncriminal to criminal and, more recently, back again, with statistics that probably must be read upside down, with fewer cases prosecuted when the new crime was common, more as it was becoming rarer. Two studies have shown an apparent conspiracy of silence in one big city and a very different situation in another, raising the possibility that not only the official statistics but the actual incidence of abortion may have differed substantially in every major jurisdiction. And although the present-day passions that surround the issue have not—as they have so often—skewed research into the past, there seems no way in which to fill the rather contradictory informational void.

Historians can offer some insight into the issues surrounding some of the current controversies but not the most fundamental ones. Neither numbers, social science concepts, nor a historian's insight offer much help, meaning that the difficulties confronting historical studies of abortion sum up, in extreme form, virtually all of the problems involved in the historical study of crime.

REFERENCES

Banton, Michael. 1964. *The Policeman in the Community*. New York: Basic Books.

Courtwright, David T. 1982. *Dark Paradise: Opiate Addiction in America before 1940*. Cambridge, Mass.: Harvard University Press.

Fogelson, Robert M. 1977. *Big-City Police*. Cambridge, Mass.: Harvard University Press.

Gilje, Paul. 1987. *The Road to Mobocracy: Popular Disorder in New York City, 1763–1834*. Chapel Hill: University of North Carolina Press.

Given, James B. 1977. *Society and Homicide in Thirteenth-Century England*. Stanford, Calif.: Stanford University Press.

Gurr, Ted Robert. 1979. "On the History of Violent Crime in Europe and America." In *Violence in America: Historical and Comparative Perspectives* (rev. ed.), edited by Ted Robert Gurr and Hugh Graham. Beverly Hills, Calif.: Sage.

———. 1989. "Historical Trends of Violent Crime." In *Violence in America*, vol. 1, *The History of Crime*, edited by Ted Robert Gurr. Newbury Park, Calif.: Sage.

Gurr, Ted Robert, Peter N. Grabosky, and Richard C. Hula. 1977. *The Politics of Crime and Conflict: A Comparative History of Four Cities*. Beverly Hills, Calif.: Sage.

Gurr, Ted Robert, and Hugh Graham, eds. 1969. *The History of Violence in America: Historical and Comparative Perspectives*. New York: Frederick A. Praeger.

Haller, Mark. 1971. "Organized Crime in Urban Society: Chicago in the Twentieth Century." *Journal of Social History* 5:210–34.

———. 1985. "Bootleggers as Businessmen: From City Streets to City Builders." In *Law, Alcohol, and Order: Perspectives on National Prohibition*, edited by David E. Kyvig. Westport, Conn.: Greenwood Press.

———. 1990. "Illegal Enterprise: A Theoretical and Historical Interpretation." *Criminology* 28:207–35.

———. 1991. "Policy, Gambling, Entertainment, and the Emergence of Black Politics: Chicago, 1890–1940." *Journal of Social History*, June.

Haller, Mark, and John V. Alviti. 1977. "Loansharking in American Cities: Historical Analysis of a Marginal Enterprise." *American Journal of Legal History* 21:125–56.

Hanawalt, Barbara A. 1979. *Crime and Conflict in English Communities, 1300–1348*. Cambridge, Mass.: Harvard University Press.

Handlin, Oscar. 1951. *The Uprooted*. Boston: Little, Brown.

Harring, Sidney. 1982. *Policing a Class Society: The Experience of American Cities, 1865–1915*. New Brunswick, N.J.: Rutgers University Press.

Hindus, Michael. 1975. "Crime, Justice, and Authority in Massachusetts and South Carolina, 1767–1878." Ph.D. dissertation, University of California, Berkeley.

Johnson, Bruce. 1976. "Taking Care of Labor: The Police in American Politics." *Theory and Society* 3:89–117.

Johnson, David R. 1979. *Policing the Urban Underworld: The Impact of Crime on the Development of the American Police, 1800–1887*. Philadelphia: Temple University Press.

———. 1991. "Crime and Power: Counterfeiters, the Secret Service, and the Nation State, 1865–1900." Ph.D. dissertation, Harvard University, Department of History.

Kennett, Lee, and James LaVerne Anderson. 1975. *The Gun in America: The Origins of a National Dilemma*. Westport, Conn.: Greenwood Press.

Kerner, Otto, ed. 1968. *Report of the National Advisory Commission on Civil Disorders*. New York: National Advisory Commission on Civil Disorders.

Lane, Roger. 1967. *Policing the City: Boston, 1822–1885*. Cambridge, Mass.: Harvard University Press.

———. 1968. "Crime and Criminal Statistics in Nineteenth Century Massachusetts." *Journal of Social History* 2:156–63.

———. 1974. "Crime and the Industrial Revolution: British and American Views." *Journal of Social History* 7:287–303.

———. 1979. *Violent Death in the City: Suicide, Accident, and Murder in Nineteenth Century Philadelphia*. Cambridge, Mass.: Harvard University Press.

———. 1980. "Urban Police and Crime in Nineteenth-Century America." In *Crime and Justice: An Annual Review of Research*, vol. 2, edited by Norval Morris and Michael Tonry. Chicago: University of Chicago Press.

———. 1986. *Roots of Violence in Black Philadelphia, 1860–1900*. Cambridge, Mass.: Harvard University Press.

———. 1989. "On the Social Meaning of Homicide Trends in America." In *Violence in America*, vol. 1, *The History of Crime*, edited by Ted Robert Gurr. Newbury Park, Calif.: Sage.

———. 1991. *William Dorsey's Philadelphia and Ours: On the Past and Future of the Black City in America*. New York: Oxford University Press.

Laurie, Bruce. 1973. "Fire Companies and Gangs in Southwark: The 1840s." In *The Peoples of Philadelphia: A History of Ethnic Groups and Lower Class Life, 1790–1840*, edited by Allen F. Davis and Mark Haller. Philadelphia: Temple University Press.

Liebman, Robert, and Michael Polen. 1978. "Perspectives on Policing in Nineteenth Century America." *Social Science History* 12:346–60.

Maier, Pauline. 1970. "Popular Uprisings and Civil Authority in Eighteenth-Century America." *William and Mary Quarterly* 27:3–35.

Miller, Wilbur R. 1977. *Cops and Bobbies: Police Authority in New York and London, 1830–1870*. Chicago: University of Chicago Press.

Mohr, James C. 1978. *Abortion in America: The Crises and Evolution in National Policy, 1800–1900*. New York: Oxford University Press.

Monkkonen, Eric. 1981. *Police in Urban America, 1860–1920*. Cambridge: Cambridge University Press.

———. 1989. "Diverging Homicide Rates: England and the United States, 1850–1875." In *Violence in America*, vol. 1, *The History of Crime*, edited by Ted Robert Gurr. Newbury Park, Calif.: Sage.

———. 1990. "Homicide in London, New York, 1823–1989." Paper read at Social Science History Association Meeting, Minneapolis.

———. 1991. *Hands Up: American Policing, 1920–1960*. (Forthcoming.)

———. In this volume. "History of Urban Police."

Morn, Frank. 1982. "The Eye That Never Sleeps." *A History of the Pinkerton National Detective Agency*. Bloomington: Indiana University Press.

Platt, Anthony. 1977. *The Childsavers: The Invention of Delinquency*. New York: Oxford University Press.

Radzinowicz, Leon. 1948–68. *A History of English Criminal Law and Its Administration from 1750*. 4 vols. London: Stevens.

Reagan, Leslie T. 1991. "About to Meet Her Maker: Women, Doctors, Dying Declarations, and the State's Investigation of Abortion, Chicago, 1867–1940." *Journal of American History*, June.

Richardson, James F. 1970. *The New York Police: Colonial Times to 1901*. New York: Oxford University Press.

———. 1974. *Urban Police in the United States*. Port Washington, N.Y.: Kennikat Press.

Rosen, Ruth. 1982. *The Lost Sisterhood: Prostitution in America, 1900–1918*. Baltimore: Johns Hopkins.

Rudé, George. 1959. *The Crowd in History: A Study of Popular Disturbances in France and England, 1730–1848*. New York: Oxford University Press.

Schneider, John C. 1980. *Detroit and the Problem of Order, 1830–1880: A Geography of Crime, Riot, and Policing*. Lincoln: University of Nebraska Press.

Silberman, Charles E. 1978. *Criminal Violence, Criminal Justice*. New York: Random House.

Skolnick, Jerome. 1966. *Justice without Trial*. New York: Wiley.

Steinberg, Allen. 1989. *The Transformation of Criminal Justice: Philadelphia, 1800–1880*. Chapel Hill: University of North Carolina Press.

Sutherland, Edwin. 1937. *The Professional Thief*. Chicago: University of Chicago Press.

Walker, Samuel. 1977. *A Critical History of Police Reform: The Emergence of Professionalism*. Lexington, Mass.: Lexington Books.

Westley, William A. 1970. *Violence and the Police: A Sociological Study of Law, Custom, and Morality*. Cambridge, Mass.: MIT Press.

Wilson, James Q. 1968. *Varieties of Criminal Behavior: The Management of Law and Order in Eight Communities*. Cambridge, Mass.: Harvard University Press.

Wilson, James Q., and Richard J. Herrnstein. 1985. *Crime and Human Nature*. New York: Simon & Schuster.

Wood, Gordon S. 1974. *Revolution and the Political Integration of the Enslaved and Disenfranchised*. Washington, D.C.: Enterprise Institute for Public Policy Research.

Albert J. Reiss, Jr.

Police Organization in the Twentieth Century

ABSTRACT

Despite some continuity with past forms and functions, police organization in the twentieth century has evolved in response to changes in technology, social organization, and political governance at all levels of society. Major developments in police organization have occurred in the areas of command organization and mobilization of patrol officers, the organization and work of patrol officers, and the access and use of information systems by all levels of personnel. While there have been some efforts to consolidate law enforcement, police organizations generally remain resistant to this goal. Bureaucratization of the police has produced numerous changes within departments and has been strongly influenced by changing conditions from outside of departments. Community-based and problem-oriented policing are reshaping the way in which some police organizations conduct their business. However, there is an equally strong focus by many departments directed at crime events and their control.

Traditional policing was localized in neighborhoods and local communities of large cities. The beat officer served to prevent, ferret out, and respond to crimes and civil disputes on his beat. The patrol car, the telephone, and the two-way radio changed all of this by giving rise to a reactive strategy of patrol policing. With the widespread availability of phones, citizens could mobilize the police patrol to respond to their "calls for service," as the police came to dub them. The police, through a central communications center, reacted to these calls by two-way radio dispatches of an available one-officer mobile patrol car. Two

Albert J. Reiss, Jr., is William Graham Sumner Professor of Sociology at Yale University.

one-officer patrol cars were dispatched to the more serious incidents. Gradually, the system became more sophisticated with the availability of hand-held radios so that officers could remain in contact with the communications center at all times. When computers became available, communications center personnel were aided in making resource allocation decisions by the development of software based on resource allocation and queuing models (Larson 1972). The goal of rapid response to every citizen "call for service" soon dominated police service delivery. The capacity of citizens to mobilize the police and other emergency services was enhanced with the development of centralized 911 phone communication, and it soon led to the overload of police resources in many police departments.

Early organizational casualties of this technology were the walking beats and the station house—the basic units of a decentralized command system with the walking beats organized around station houses or police precincts. With the closing of station houses, citizens could no longer lodge complaints and adjudicate matters in their neighborhood. These could be handled only by the dispatch of officers to phoned mobilizations or travel to a central station. Officers no longer were needed to patrol a walking beat since a single officer could handle a number of walking beats from the dispatched patrol car.

The demise of the functional role of the station house in large cities was replaced by area commands as the span of technological control widened the span of administrative control. Gone were the station books in which police activities were recorded, and gone was the patrol officer's log of his work as the communications center tape and computerized record keeping replaced them. Detention and booking likewise were centralized as prisoners were more rapidly moved and processed at central locations. Families and friends of the jailed must now travel to a central detention or jail facility. Specialized tactical and investigative mobile units were developed, and they too soon came under central command as the radio provided for their mobilization on request.

Perhaps the major impact that technological inventions had was to solidify the bureaucratic centralization of command and control. The separation of the working police from the communities policed was organizationally complete. The era of the dial-a-radio-active-rapid-response-cop was by the seventies the dominant model of American policing.

Those who developed this model of policing had not, however, calculated the trade-offs. Soon, owing in part to research, the costs appeared to outweigh some of the gains. It became apparent that the volume of calls for service grew at a greater rate than did department resources to handle them, particularly at times of peak demand. An initial response to this was to build decision models that set response priorities for types of calls—from emergency response to wait time. Soon research would undermine the major premise of the response time model—that by responding rapidly more criminals would be apprehended because they would still be at the crime scene. A major study of response time to calls for service by the Kansas City Police Department (1978) and its replication in other cities (Spellman and Brown 1984) undermined this premise by disclosing that the bulk of calls were for "cold crimes," those, like residential burglaries, that had taken place before their discovery. Moreover, in most cases of victimization, the time a citizen took before calling the police was greater than the police response time. Rapid response seemed to pay off only when the victim was a business where employees were rapid mobilizers.

The model had miscalculated what citizens expect of their police. Many, it turned out, did not expect a rapid response time and were willing to wait until the police could handle their problem (McEwen, Connors, and Cohen 1984). More important, the insulation of the police from their public came at a high price. The patrol officer in his air-conditioned and heated car no longer got out of the police vehicle to do preventive patrol or to learn more about the community being policed. The insulation of the police from the public to control corruption and to respond rapidly to their calls had served primarily to insulate the police from the public they were to serve. No longer did the public have confidence that the police were handling, or could handle, their problems, and many, particularly minority groups, felt alienated from the police. On transgressing and perhaps reaching the boundaries of bureaucratic rationality, police organizations appear now to be at the crossroads of a return to traditional modes of policing or pressing forward into rational, bureaucratic administration with the new symbolic forms of communication and problem solving.

This essay attempts to characterize the major ways in which policing changed during the twentieth century while maintaining continuity with the past structures and forms. Determining whether and in what ways police departments have changed is no simple matter, especially since the serious and systematic study of police organization and behavior developed only in the last half of this century, and it remains for the most part a cottage industry.

The focus of this essay is on changes in the structure and behavior of police organizations rather than on the culture and institutions of policing and police behavior. Accordingly, I do not discuss police exercise of force and authority (e.g., Bordua 1968; Reiss 1968; Westley 1970; Bittner 1974, 1980; Klockars 1985, p. 12), their behavior as members of police organizations (Reiss 1971, 1974a; Van Maanen 1974; Manning 1977; Muir 1977; Ericson 1982), occupational effects on their daily lives (Van Maanen 1973, 1980; Punch 1983), changes in police subcultures (Wilson 1968; Reuss-Ianni and Ianni 1983), and the basic legal institutions of policing.

Here is how this essay is organized: Section I identifies the major transitions that have occurred in police organizations during the twentieth century. Section II traces the emergence and consequences of bureaucratization in urban police organizations. Section III examines how police organizations have adapted their use of discretionary authority and accountability in this century and how they have responded to internal corruption of authority and practice. The internal organization of police work is considered in Section IV with respect to how changes in the dynamic internal and external environments have influenced it. The essay concludes with some observations and predictions about the direction of change in police organizations.

I. Police Organizational Transitions in the Twentieth Century

It is surprising how little systematic knowledge we have of changes in police organizations in this country. For much of the century we vastly overestimated their numbers. The President's Commission on Law Enforcement and Administration of Justice (1967, p. 1) estimated that there were approximately 40,000 separate agencies; within a decade the first major census of police organizations reduced that number by about two-thirds. The question of what counts as a police organization continues to bedevil scholars. Most scholarly studies of police organizations and policing represent disproportionately the large metropolitan police departments from the eastern region of the United States and describe only the organization and behavior of police patrol.[1] There

---

[1] The popular and media fascination with detectives has no parallel in the scholarly literature. There are only a few excellent studies of vice detectives (Skolnick 1966; Manning 1980).

are few systematic accounts of even short-run changes in organization. A cursory reading of the literature of police practitioners discloses, not surprisingly, that scholars and practitioners have quite different literatures. Although the practitioner literature provides snapshots that are broadly representative of police organizations and glimpses into the ways that they may be changing, the organization and its environment are rarely described. Rather, the practitioner author focuses on topics of interest to technical specialists within police departments or specialist managers or chief administrators. New technologies, especially, command attention.[2] Besides being notable for general inattention to broader structural and dynamic features of police departments, the absence of some subjects is conspicuous in practitioner writings. Topics such as controlling corruption within the police department or managing police misconduct are rarely treated.

A. The Changing Organization of Law Enforcement

As we approach the twenty-first century and ponder changes of the century almost past, it would be easy to conclude that the basic structural organization of policing today resembles rather closely that in place at the beginning of this century. At its core, policing in the United States consists of a large number of politically autonomous police organizations with overlapping jurisdiction. For all practical purposes, the personnel system of each police department is closed to lateral mobility and open only through recruiting the untrained. Likewise, each department remains at its core a quasi-military organization. Yet even a casual Martian visitor with a century scanner would remark on changes.

Characterizing those changes in police organization and policing in the twentieth century is a formidable task, however, because they are intimately linked with fundamental changes in American society. Principal among these are changes in the growth and composition of the population in cities, in the social organization and political governance of urban communities and neighborhoods, and in technology.

[2] Almost all of the major articles published in recent years in the *Police Chief*, the official publication of the International Association of Chiefs of Police, deal with technocratic themes in policing. A few illustrative titles from November 1989 to March 1990 are "A Strategic Planning Approach to Law Enforcement Training"; "Computer Based Training at the Federal Law Enforcement Training Center"; "The Police Dispatcher as Hostage Negotiator"; "Staff Inspection: Enhanced Systems through Internal Auditing"; "DETERS: Integrating Today's Technologies in Tomorrow's Emergency Response System"; "Artificial Intelligence, Expert Systems, Microcomputers, and Law Enforcement"; "Computer Assisted Report Entry: Toward a Paperless Police Department"; and "Art Theft: A Need for Specializing."

At the turn of the century, American cities were entering a metropolitan phase of growth that was fed by the immigration of young Europeans with high birth rates. Unlike earlier European immigrants who populated rural America, these newer waves from southern and eastern Europe settled disproportionately in the cities. Central cities of this period were a mosaic of ethnic neighborhoods under the control of a political patronage system. The closing of immigration in the 1920s stifled this source of urban growth, but throughout this century our metropolitan central cities continued to receive new populations. In the decades around midcentury, they were fed by the migration of poor whites and blacks who gradually replaced the ethnic settlements of the central city. More recently, the populations of our major metropolitan cities are changing with the arrival of diverse streams of Hispanic and Asian immigrants, giving many of our central cities a new mosaic of ethnic communities and languages.

Throughout the century, urban police organizations have been pressed to adapt to these changing patterns, but the pace was considerably slowed by institutional barriers to changing the ethnic composition of the police force. Police officers, alien in language and culture to the new arrivals, consequently came to be perceived as alien to many of the people living in the ethnic neighborhoods and ghetto communities they policed. Police departments were challenged for their resistance to demands for linguistic and ethnic representation and for equal treatment under the law. Adaptation to the patterns of immigrant settlement seems to have occurred more rapidly in the nineteenth century when the patronage system controlled police hiring and promotion.

As cities grew, so did the size of their police forces, and the number of police per capita increased markedly. Los Angeles, for example, the second largest city in the United States in 1988 with an estimated 3,402,342 inhabitants, had only 102,479 inhabitants in 1900. Their police force in the 1890s numbered fewer than 100 officers (Hale 1893, p. 302). By 1988 the city had 7,533 sworn officers and 2,470 civilian employees (Federal Bureau of Investigation 1989, table 72). Around 1900, there was roughly only one sworn officer for every 1,300 inhabitants. By 1988, that ratio had fallen to about one officer for every 460 inhabitants. Chicago provides another example. The substantial growth of Chicago from 1890 to 1900 made it the second largest city at that time with a population of 1,698,575. With 2,696 sworn duty officers, detectives, and supervisors, it had one officer for every 630 inhabitants. By 1988, with 12,163 sworn officers, the rate was one officer for every 275 inhabitants. The rate for New York City in 1988 was one officer per 280 inhabitants.[3]

Similar comparisons for other cities disclose a seeming paradox. Although the manpower requirements of a foot-beat system of police patrol seem considerable, the personnel requirements for policing today's centralized patrol cities requires at least twice as many police officers per capita. Much of this difference can be attributed to the specialized squads and bureaus in today's bureaucratic police departments. There are proportionately fewer officers assigned to patrol today than in 1900. The patrol officer has given way to officers in specialized units.

The history of urban police in the early part of this century is so closely entwined with the political history of the city that often it is difficult to determine what changes are peculiar to police organization. Corruption, for example, was endemic to the political organization of cities and its "machine politics," as Lincoln Steffens (1931) chronicles so well in his autobiography. Municipal and police corruption scandals profoundly affected police departments as reformers attempted to neutralize the police from political patronage and to curb police protection of rackets and organized criminal activity. This neutralization took two major forms.

The first step was to transform the quasi-military bureaucracy of police organizations into a legalistic and technocratic bureaucracy whose members are committed to an occupational community with norms of subordination and service that set it apart from the community that it policed (Bordua and Reiss 1966, p. 68). This was a crucial step for several reasons. It was a way to hold police accountable to bureaucratic rather than political authority. Some municipalities even went so far as to insulate the chief from being accountable to political authority by making that position a civil service or life tenure position. Prior to these changes, police chiefs in cities were appointed by elected municipal officials or bodies and therefore subject to their demands for loyalty and performance. Moreover, bureaucratization was a means of insulating the appointment and promotion of police officers from political patronage by requiring standards of merit. Additionally, it gradu-

---

[3] The source for the population sizes of these cities in 1900 is the U.S. Bureau of the Census (1942). The 1990 population counts are preliminary estimates from census counts that are still under challenge. The counts of police at the turn of the century are based on Hale (1893). The 1988 counts of sworn officers and civilian employees of police departments are taken from Federal Bureau of Investigation (1989).

ally substituted the rational allocation of police service for its allocation in response to political demands.

The second step, taken somewhat later as the result of technological inventions, was to centralize policing territorially. Whereas policing at the turn of the century was organized into walking beats that made up precincts under a local commander, toward the end of the twentieth century many police departments now operate either from a single headquarters command or, in many of our largest cities, from substation or area commands.

Technological inventions in the twentieth century instituted many social changes (Ogburn 1950). That, not surprisingly, also affected the organization of policing in the United States. More than anything else, technology made possible the demise of foot patrol and the substitution of motor patrol. In no other modern country has the automobile had as substantial an effect on policing. Major cities such as Amsterdam, Copenhagen, London, Paris, Rome, Moscow, and Tokyo still rely heavily on foot patrol in their central cities, whereas foot patrol is uncommon in the core of our cities, except for certain business, transportation, and public housing areas.

Changes in the technology of communication likewise exerted a major effect, especially on the centralization of command and control. At the turn of the century, officers could be centrally commanded only by means of a flashing light atop a call box—a signal to which the officer could respond when in view of a call box located at the intersection of beats. Chicago, for example, installed the Gamewell Police Telephone and Signal Company's Police Signal System in October 1890. In 1893, the department reported that it had 715 call boxes. In 1892, it reportedly handled 4,689,860 duty calls, 61,479 wagon calls, and 2,639 ambulance calls (Hale 1893, p. 222). The turn-of-the-century officer could be supervised only by a corporal or sergeant on foot, bicycle, streetcar, horse-drawn wagon, or mounted on a horse— relatively ineffective means of supervisory contact. With the advent of the radio, officers could be commanded in the field. The invention of the two-way radio and later the hand-held radio enhanced communication not only with a central command but also among officers.

Technological means of communicating and recording information have had major effects on other aspects of policing as well. Today's undercover police officers are "wired" to obtain emergency assistance as well as to communicate and record activity observed undercover. The communication technology currently available to officers facilitates police work. It gives officers with computer terminals in their patrol cars access to information systems. For example, officers can make quick checks to identify stolen motor vehicles or to see if citizens have outstanding warrants. In some departments, officers can file their case reports from a car terminal. Computers have substantially enhanced police capability to solve crimes, especially with recent developments in computer matching of fingerprints and gene typing.

A few contrasts in organization and style of policing may sharpen the difference between today's urban police departments and those in 1900.

1. *There have been substantial changes in command organization and in mobilization of patrol officers.*   The precinct station house was the center of command at the beginning of this century. Citizens frequently mobilized the police by appearing in person at the station house or by phoning the signal office which in turn mobilized officers through their beat call box. Beat officers responded on foot. For emergencies there were horse-drawn ambulances that were operated by the police department. The police surgeon provided emergency treatment at local stations.

By 1990, most police departments had a 911 computer-aided system for allocating calls for service to police patrol units. Many had civilian employees who screened citizen phone complaints and civilian employees who selected police vehicles to be radio-dispatched to calls; some used resource allocation and queuing models to assist in allocating officers to calls for dispatch. Officers responded by radio and were in contact at all times through car or hand-held radios. The more technocratic departments had computers in police vehicles to assist them in accessing and inputting information. Most cities had emergency medical services units to respond to emergency calls.

2. *There have been major changes in the organization and work of patrol officers.*   Patrol in 1900 was organized around foot beats and an officer assigned to the beat for each shift. Among the routine tasks required of the foot-beat officer were those of being "perfectly acquainted with all parts of his route and with the streets, thoroughfares, courts, and houses within it," "to examine in the night-time all doors, gates, and windows of dwellings of stores to see that they are properly secured, and if not, give notice to the inmates, if any," "to see that the sidewalks are not obstructed by persons loitering thereon to the inconvenience of other passengers," and to "strictly watch the conduct of all persons of known bad character" (Boston Police Department 1893). Foot-beat

officers were supervised by roundsmen who were responsible to a precinct patrol sergeant.

There were few specialized bureaus or divisions, even in the larger departments. Detroit in 1893, for example, reported having 3 captains, 18 sergeants, 27 roundsmen, 215 patrolmen, and 21 doormen for assignment to street patrol (Hale 1893, pp. 259–61). This force was apportioned to a central division and three precinct stations. Of the 215 patrol officers, 57 were assigned to day patrol, and 158 to night patrol. Additionally, there were eight detectives assigned to the central division and seven as acting precinct detectives. There were no special units as most departments know them today, although a substantial number of officers were assigned to duties at courts, for inspections, and as truant officers. A single officer was in charge of the Bertillon system, a method of criminal identification based on anthropometric measures. Eleven persons were assigned to the Gamewell Signal and Telephone System as supervisors, operators, or timekeepers—the predecessor to today's central communications center.

By 1990, motorized patrol had replaced foot patrol. Although officers were nominally assigned to beats for proactive and preventive patrol, they were centrally dispatched over a much wider territory as the first car available to respond to a priority call. Except in high-crime-rate areas where officers were assigned to two-person cars, most patrol cars were assigned to a single officer. Where a call required more than one officer, one was assigned as the primary person to handle the call and the other as a backup or cover on the assignment.

Large urban departments today have many specialized units. Detectives are specialized in divisions according to the type of vice or crime to be investigated or monitored. There are specialized teams such as hostage negotiation teams to handle the taking of hostages and special weapons and tactical (SWAT) teams to handle potentially violent or collective behavior incidents. Stationary traffic enforcement often is delegated to civilian employees, and moving traffic may be handled by a special division. There is considerable functional differentiation by task within a modern police department.

3. *There has been a movement from an elementary information system with informal practices to highly formal and complex information systems to which officers routinely have access and to which they contribute information.* At the turn of the century, each station house had a station book in which all incidents and events that the desk sergeant deemed important were entered. Arrests and lodging in the station lockup were duly noted. Individual officers were not saddled with recording information as that

fell to the desk sergeant, superior officers, lockup officers, or signal clerks.

By 1990, all major police departments had a central communications center that handled all incoming phone complaints and almost all internal communications, including dispatch. Communications today are tape-recorded and available for a period of time as evidence. Much police business must be made a matter of record. Officers are obliged to be acquainted with and use many different report forms. The Kansas City, Missouri, Police Department, for example, has 356 different forms for reporting police matters. For some reports, a complaint case number is assigned; others simply require the completion of a report, for example, a field information form, that is turned in at the station. All other reporting is done by radio to central communications.

4. *The occupational basis of policing has been transformed.* At the turn of the century, policing was an exclusively male occupation of sworn officers (except for police matrons in charge of women prisoners). Almost all tasks, including clerical and menial labor, were performed by sworn police officers. Officers were largely organized in brotherhoods. Although a few major departments were under civil service, most were not. There was no collective bargaining, although within a decade police strikes would become more common.

The advent of equal opportunity employment in the last half of the century opened the ranks of police departments to minorities and women who were theretofore excluded from sworn employment. Perhaps as important was the introduction of civilian employees in the department to perform many of the more technical as well as clerical tasks in information processing and for all routine work that was not enforcement related. The Los Angeles Police Department, for example, had 10,023 employees in 1988, one-fourth of whom were civilians. By 1990, police officers in almost all large urban departments were organized to bargain collectively with their municipal employers under state collective bargaining legislation.[4] Police strikes were less common.

B. *Organizational Fragmentation of Law Enforcement and Consolidation*

Responsibility for law enforcement in the United States is divided among federal, state, and local governments. The bulk of police protec-

---

[4] The last major survey was in the early 1970s (Juris and Feuille 1973, table 2-1). At that time most urbanized states mandated municipalities to bargain collectively with their police department organizations. Many had separate organizations for different ranks, e.g., patrol, sergeants, detectives, and various senior officer ranks.

tion is provided by local governments, however. In 1988, 77 percent of the 784,371 employees in police protection were local government employees. Municipalities accounted for just over three-fourths of this local police protection, and counties for the remaining 24 percent. State employment accounted for an additional 15 percent of all police protection and the federal government for 8 percent (Bureau of Justice Statistics 1990, table 7).

A consequence of our tradition of local government and of their proliferation with population growth and urban settlement is that public policing in the United States is highly fragmented among a large number of relatively small autonomous federal, state, county, and municipal organizations. Many of these departments, especially county and municipal departments, have only a few sworn officers. These autonomous law enforcement agencies are only loosely integrated in a law enforcement system of overlapping federal, state, and local jurisdiction (see Geller and Morris, in this volume).

There are a number of reasons for this fragmentation. The system of public law enforcement in the United States is fragmented, first of all, because the adoption of our federated system of national government left the organization of law enforcement to the various states. States, in turn, were bound by tradition to local governing authority and their claims to local law enforcement. Consequently, as the state chartered each county, township, or municipality, each appointed or employed a local law enforcement officer. For counties, these were sheriffs who could deputize others with the powers of law enforcement. Other localities designated citizens as peace officers or watchmen. The first new nation thus maintained continuity with the basic pattern of local law enforcement laid down by its colonial administrators (Bacon 1939; Greenberg 1974, pp. 154–87). State policing did not emerge until early in the twentieth century,[5] and, although it maintains overlapping jurisdiction with local law enforcement in most states, it has not for the most part displaced it.[6]

---

[5] Legislation creating the first state police system in the United States, the Pennsylvania State Police, resulted from recommendations of President Theodore Roosevelt's Anthracite Strike Commission and Governor Pennypacker (Pennypacker 1918). The commission was created in 1902 to investigate violence between miners in their protracted strike with the anthracite coal producers and their private police, the Coal and Iron Police (Mayo 1917; Shalloo 1933, p. 86).

[6] In some states, the state police offer a contract service to local communities. In others, such as Connecticut, the state assigns a state police officer to provide police service to a local community, but these are exceptions rather than the rule.

A second major reason for the fragmentation of law enforcement into many local departments in the United States is that there remain substantial limits on the growth in size of any law enforcement body. Because law enforcement organizations are the creatures of governing bodies, as the population of our cities grew, they soon spilled over their territorial bounds into other jurisdictions of local government, such as a township or county. For a number of reasons, most local governments in the United States were unable to expand the territorial reach of their governing authority. As a consequence, local governments sprang up outside central cities. Soon, the expansion of the central city and its police jurisdiction was choked off by a ring of suburban political communities, each of which usually created its own police department as it grew.

Although aggregate statistics are lacking on the relative employee size of all law enforcement agencies, some sense of the predominance of small police departments can be gleaned from reporting on sworn officer employment for all incorporated cities.[7] By way of illustration, of the 281 city police departments in North Carolina, 56 percent have fewer than 10 sworn police officers. An additional 21 percent have between 10 and 20 sworn officers (Federal Bureau of Investigation 1989, table 72). If we assume that providing a sworn officer on duty for three tours of duty seven days a week—and taking into account vacation and sick leave days—requires the rough equivalent of five officers, then a majority of these departments has fewer than two full-time sworn officers available for protection at any one time.

Even in a highly urbanized state such as New Jersey, there were 486 city police departments in 1988. The modal department of fewer than 10 officers in North Carolina is replaced by the modal department of 10–20 officers in New Jersey. Of the 486 city police departments in New Jersey in 1988, one-fifth had fewer than 10 sworn officers and 49 percent had fewer than 20 officers; 77 percent of all departments had fewer than 40 officers. Although neither New Jersey nor North

[7] The Uniform Crime Reports (UCR) report full-time law enforcement employment separately for each incorporated city but only aggregate law enforcement employment for suburban counties of metropolitan statistical areas for unincorporated places and in rural areas of counties. In 1988, rural county departments served 14 percent of the U.S. population (Federal Bureau of Investigation 1989, p. 322). Employment for sheriffs' departments include those employed in administering jails and some civil process functions so that they lack comparability with data for city departments. Additionally, law enforcement employment is reported for full-time law enforcement employees of college and university police departments.

Carolina have one of the larger police departments in the United States, only 3 percent of all New Jersey departments and 2 percent of all North Carolina departments had 200 or more officers in 1988 (Federal Bureau of Investigation 1989, table 72).

Given the preponderance of small police departments, it is not surprising that from time to time there are pressures to consolidate small local police departments with larger ones, to develop more coordination among them, and to develop a more integrated system of law enforcement in the interest of efficiency and economy of management and of making professional decisions. There have been no movements to consolidate local police into a regional or state system of law enforcement comparable to that in the United Kingdom, and any conception of a national system of law enforcement is anathema to the American citizenry. Pressures toward consolidation, coordination, and integration of local law enforcement encounter substantial resistance as they run counter to the prevailing ideals of local government in the United States. The decentralization of power, authority, and decision making within organizations conforms to the ideals of democratic government and remains the dominant ideology in law enforcement.

There is very little formal integration among public police agencies, which is not surprising given the constitutional division of authority among the various states and with the federal government (Geller and Morris, in this volume). Coordination is largely voluntary with only occasional formal arrangements among local governments through the institution of contract policing, the setting of minimum standards for policing, or the institution of state-mandated training.

Public police organizations also vary in the nature and scope of their jurisdictional authority. We are inclined to think of federal agents and state and municipal police. But these vary considerably as to who is the appointing authority and to whom the police organization is responsive. There likewise are an uncounted number of special police authorities such as those for public housing and transportation and special regional or interstate compacts, for example, port authority police. Moreover, there are at least several hundred campus police departments in the United States that either appoint their own sworn officers or whose officers are appointed as supernumerary officers in an organization with sworn authority.[8]

---

[8] The 1988 UCR received reports of the number of law enforcement officers from 394 universities and colleges (Federal Bureau of Investigation 1989, table 73). Fewer universities and colleges reported the number of offenses known to their police in 1988.

Overlapping jurisdiction and low integration of law enforcement units are not confined to the public sector. There is a fragmentation of policing between private and public sectors as well (Shearing, in this volume). The private investigation and security industries and private organizations' employment of security personnel further divide and fragment policing in America. Currently, the size of the private policing sector, made up largely of unarmed guards and of investigative and security officers, is greater than that of our public police. Yet increasingly, private investigation and security company employees secure law enforcement powers of arrest and the right to use deadly force through state and local legislation. Potentially, private-sector policing with full sworn police powers could exceed that of the public sector. Because private police enforcement is less visible than that of public police and because they administer a private system of justice that is not currently accountable to democratically constituted authority (Shearing and Stenning 1981), substantial issues arise about their role in a democratically organized and integrated police system.

There is almost no formal integration of public- and private-sector policing, and few vehicles exist for doing so. Legislation mandating licensing of private security employees and their selection and training have a minimal effect on their integration. Additionally, increasingly both private- and public-sector organizations either contract for or employ public police officers in off-duty employment (Reiss 1991).

The complexity of this network of law enforcement agencies has thus far precluded a full description of its nature and extent for any major metropolitan jurisdiction in the United States. Lacking also is information to document changes in complexity, coordination, and integration among law enforcement organizations.

During this century, there has been some consolidation of police organizations, and there have been attempts to coordinate and integrate them. There have been two major forms of consolidation. One is the coalescence of departments into a metropolitan police department

---

The two lists of reporting organizations are not identical because a number of states, such as Florida and Kentucky, did not report offenses known but did report the number of law enforcement employees. Only 43 of the 50 states are represented in the voluntary reporting system for college and university police departments. Some colleges and universities known to have campus police departments with sworn officers do not voluntarily report to UCR. The level of underestimation is unknown but appears to be substantial. The largest number of law enforcement employees in 1988 is reported for the University of California Lawrence Livermore Laboratory with 348 employees, only 17 of whom were designated sworn officers.

when a metropolitan county form of government is adopted. Davidson County (Nashville), Tennessee, is an example. The other is the consolidation of police service through the institution of contract policing. This usually takes the form that small departments contract with a county sheriff's department or a large municipality to provide police service. California law facilitates contract policing. The Los Angeles County Sheriff's Department, for example, contracts with 40 of the 87 incorporated cities in the county to provide all police services. Additionally, 36 other cities contract for some type of police service such as search and rescue, arson and explosives, or homicide investigation. All 87 municipalities contract for jail service. There also has been some functional integration of departments, particularly the integration of 911 communication systems that consolidate emergency services for a number of governments. Nevertheless, overall it appears that the forces among law enforcement organizations are toward fragmentation and loose coordination. There has been far less consolidation of police services than has occurred at all levels of public education, health, welfare, and emergency services.

Just why this should have been the case is not altogether clear since some of the same forces are operating on the provision of police services. Indeed, since public prosecution, jail, and court services typically are countywide, it may seem somewhat paradoxical that the movement has been at such a slow rate for police services. A number of factors may account for this slower rate of consolidation and integration.

Examination of the consolidation of local police departments through the adoption of county governments makes it abundantly clear that police departments took no initiative for consolidation and usually resisted such efforts. Indeed, no single constellation of forces accounts for consolidation of local police and other services through the formation of metropolitan county government. Correlatively, it is apparent that there is no movement among police organizations toward consolidation. Where consolidation or integration occurs, it is at the initiation of a county government movement or through contracting by municipal corporations. Police organizations, if anything, actively resist consolidation.

Perhaps a second major factor accounting for the slow rate of change is the fragmentation of both police and public constituencies for consolidated police service. Local government traditions are firmly entrenched, and the belief that local control of police is an essential ingredient of local government is more firmly so. Yet there is evidence that such resistance existed also in the United Kingdom and in Australia prior to the consolidation of their police services. The major difference in the United Kingdom appears to have been that Parliament provided fiscal incentives to the consolidation of police service on a regional basis. Although such fiscal incentives have worked in other areas of public services in the United States, proposals for federal support of local police services, to be politically viable, must insure their autonomy from federal intervention and control. They must not be regarded as incentives to organizational change but as means of improving the resources and capability of local police organizations. Public fears about a Big Brother system of federal control when coupled with organizational resistance to a loss of autonomy seem sufficient to thwart the use of federal or state incentives to integrate or consolidate police organizations.

A factor contributing to both the proliferation and sometimes curbing of small local departments is that police services are provided by county sheriff's departments and some state police organizations as populations grow beyond incorporated territorial boundaries. Yet as municipal organizations emerge in these newly developed suburban and county areas, it appears more common for them to create a local police department than to continue service by county or state police organizations. Rapid growth of small municipal and town corporations associated with the suburbanization of America in the nineteenth century has further compounded the problem of coordinating and integrating police services. The political and territorial limitations on expanding the territorial jurisdiction of central city government to encompass the areas of population growth has thus contributed to the fragmentation of police domains. Correlatively, where municipal governments have extended their jurisdiction over a large territory—as was the case for Colorado Springs, Colorado, or for Dallas and Houston, Texas, or when county sheriff's departments have rapidly extended the range of services to unincorporated county areas, as in Dade County, Florida, or Nassau, New York—there has been less proliferation of local police departments. In 1988, Dade County had 3,352 police employees, and Nassau County, 3,792, ranking them among the larger law enforcement organizations in the United States.

Police departments are part and parcel of a fragmented law enforcement system, especially for municipal code enforcement. Police organizations have little authority to enforce the many code violations that occur within their communities. The twentieth century has witnessed not only a fragmentation of the investigation of violations of municipal codes but also a decline in the ability of the police and other agencies to enforce warrants and insure compliance with them. The investigation of code violations, some of which were at one time the responsibility of the police, now lies with special investigation agencies for each type of code violation (Costello 1885; Bacon 1938). Housing, sanitation, health and safety, fire, and zoning violations, for example, and their enforcement through licensing now lie with separate agencies. Where the service of warrants for failure to comply with enforcement mandates falls on the police, they are ill equipped to do so. More to the point, perhaps, is that this fragmentation is most apparent to the police who must daily encounter its cumulative consequences. It is paradoxical that movements such as problem-oriented and community policing fail to take into account the relative powerlessness of both the police and their citizenry to deal directly with fragmented municipal code enforcement.[9]

II. Bureaucratization and Centralization

A bureaucracy, according to Max Weber (1947), establishes relations between a legally constituted and legitimate authority and its subordinate officials. Bureaucratic organizations are characterized by several relations (Bendix 1960; 1968, p. 207). There are definite and written rights and duties for each position in the organization. Each position has a fixed monetary salary. The office or position in the organization is separated from the incumbent so that no official owns the means of administration. Administrative work is a full-time occupation. Appointment and promotion to positions are based on contract, with technical training prerequisite for appointment and experience and training for promotion. Authority relations between positions are systematically ordered in a formal hierarchy.

[9] The lack of such coordination and integration can have tragic consequences. The March 25, 1990, New York City fire that killed 87 people at a social club documents the consequences of fragmented code enforcement. On April 6, 1990, the New York City Corporation Counsel's Office, which prosecutes building code violations, disclosed that there were 42 outstanding arrest warrants on Alex Di Lorenzo III, described by the *New York Times* as an heir to a real-estate fortune and owner of more than 200 buildings in New York City. Warrants had been issued for failure to correct violations at the Happy Land Social Club, where the tragedy occurred. Some of the warrants had been outstanding since 1980. The New York City Police Department reported that it did not execute the warrants because it has more than 140,000 warrants outstanding in the city and that it was concentrating on executing warrants against violent criminals (*New York Times* 1990).

Modern, urban bureaucratic police organization emerged in England early in the nineteenth century under conditions where the ruling and middle classes were aroused by the threat of rising urban crime and criminality and by the threat that urban riot and disorder from the "dangerous classes" posed to civil society. Fearing that the military, whose ranks were filled by recruitment from the dangerous classes, might side with the urban masses and turn against the ruling elites of the day, the English Parliament created a civil police in London whose political neutrality in civil disorder was guaranteed. Moreover, as Silver maintains, the police served to deflect the hostility of the dangerous classes onto themselves (Silver 1967).

Police departments in the United States became centralized public bureaucracies only in the late nineteenth and early twentieth centuries. Levett (1975, chap. 2) argues that policing in American cities in the first half of the nineteenth century had a distinct organizational form, one that he designates "entrepreneurial policing." The organization of entrepreneurial policing had certain minimal features of rational-legal authority. In particular, legally defined offices were based on contractual relations that were subject only to the authority inhering in the office. But it was entrepreneurial in that relations among officers had minimal hierarchy and members competed with each other for a maximum of individual rewards. It was entrepreneurial also in that a concern for the protection, security, and recovery of property dominated police work, and many tasks were on a fee-for-service basis.

Despite the availability of the organizational model of the London urban police as early as 1829, policing in American cities was not unified until midcentury when all of the diffusely controlled police roles were centralized under a single command and all private police were required to license with city authorities (Levett 1975, p. 59). New York City (the borough of Manhattan) was unified in 1845. Thirty years later most city departments had unified policing under a central command (Levett 1975, chap. 3).

Why was there this lag in creating unified police forces under a central command after the London model? Levett (1975, pp. 97–99), not unlike Silver (1967), contends that unification came about only when urban middle- and working-class coalition politics emerged in our major cities with demands to control the dangerous classes. The American dangerous classes differed from those in England, however. They were immigrants who threatened the middle- and working-class status quo. These immigrants were regarded as the source of urban riot and disorderly behavior.

The political sources of this unification created an organizational form that was only partly bureaucratic—what Levett (1975, p. 106) terms "politicized bureaucracies"—because patronage was the main basis for appointment and promotion. Loyalty to political patrons rather than to superior officers or to units of the police department dominates police work in this bureaucracy. Accountability is to the political party rather than to bureaucratic and governing authority. Levett's basic argument (1975, p. 108) is that the police were centralized primarily to be a major force against behavior that was politically problematic and secondarily because systemic deployment provided more effective control of offenses against property than did the entrepreneurial form of police organization. Maniha (1972), while emphasizing political fealty and the lack of independence of police from political elites, characterizes police departments in this period as facing additional barriers to bureaucratization. Among those he mentions (p. 8) are the alleged strong reliance on nepotism and ethnic affiliation in appointment and promotion, administration by civilian police commissioners who knew little about how large organizations are administered and nothing about policing, the absence of lateral entry into the department's command and staff positions, the short tenure of high police officials, personal ratings of supervisors for promotion, and the recalcitrance of police work to classification for supervision. Some of these remain late in the twentieth century as barriers to full bureaucratic organization and control.

The next stage of police bureaucratization comes late in the nineteenth century and the beginning of the twentieth century as corruption scandals increasingly disclosed the singular role of political patronage in policing. Reform movements succeeded gradually in the twentieth century to establish a *police civil service bureaucracy*. The essential consequences of this bureaucratization of the police were several.

Bureaucratization in the twentieth century had a number of consequences. First, it insured the *political neutrality and legal reliability* of the police by developing a hierarchical system of command and control. That system neutralized the political power of political authorities and made police officers loyal to the police command rather than to ethnic and political groups. Their allegiance is to a community organized around an occupation that sets itself apart from the larger society (Bordua and Reiss 1966). To a substantial degree, day-to-day decision making has been removed from direct political influence of governing parties and authorities and from the arbitrary exercise of power by the chief. Yet local bureaucracies, as contrasted with state and federal police bureaucracies, are less insulated from political authority, and the position of the commander is far less secure. Police chiefs who lack civil service tenure are beholden to political administrations for their appointment and continuation in office, which makes them responsive to external pressures from the ruling administration. The elected ruling administration in turn runs the risk that the response of their constituents to police policies and operations is critical to their continuation in power.

A second consequence of police bureaucratization is that it led to major changes in hierarchical work organization and job mobility. A bifurcation of staff and line occupational roles in an hierarchically organized command became a dominant feature of police departments. The development of the staff is especially noteworthy as an aspect of its bureaucratization. The first half of the twentieth century witnessed a dramatic growth in staff officers. Maniha (1972, p. 49) reports that, as late as 1899, the St. Louis Police Department had only a handful of staff. By 1927, there was one staff officer above sergeant rank for every 2.9 line officers, and by 1949 that ratio had changed to one staff officer above sergeant rank for only 1.4 line officers. Administrators and sworn staff specialists had clearly come to dominate the police bureaucracy.

Bureaucratization has had far fewer consequences for an officer's mobility within a department, however. Bureaucratization had its greatest effect on officer recruitment, selection, and initial training. The political patronage system of recruitment was gradually replaced by a merit system based on test qualification and a rank-based system of promotion. On-the-job training now follows academy-based classroom training during the period of probationary status. Unlike most police departments in the Western world, however, American departments do not recruit separately for the staff and command positions, and there is relatively little training required to qualify for promotion to staff positions. Consequently, junior and senior officers as well as heads of police departments move by promotion and examination from the rank of patrolman to the chief officer position.

Bureaucratization carries with it a third consequence of the growing complexity of organizational structure. There is increasing task specialization and specified areas of jurisdiction for employees. Specialization in the division of labor comes to dominate the organization. Specialization in turn increases the necessity for coordination that increases the power of staff over line officers and leads to the emergence of staff coordinators. In large departments, deputy positions proliferate. An anomalous consequence of bureaucratization of police departments is that, although there ordinarily is only a single deputy for patrol, patrol is the largest operating unit. The deputy for patrol of necessity spends a great deal of time coordinating with other functional deputies rather than being in command of patrol. Specialties such as communications, vehicle maintenance, and records intersect patrol operations and come to dominate its administration. Most of these specialties require technical rather than professional expertise and have implications for the development of a police profession. Increasingly, therefore, these come to be dominated by civilian employees. The consequence of this dependence on technology and technical specialists, however, is a further bifurcation in policing—between sworn officers and civilian employees. This bifurcation has emerged only in the last half of this century, and its full impact is yet to be realized in any department. Potentially, for example, the detective division can be dominated by civilian employees who are experts in specialties of crime analysis.

A final consequence of bureaucratization is the codification of personnel policies, basing appointment and promotion on merit rather than affiliation. To a growing extent, merit was based on expertise rather than solely on past performance, especially in promotions to the staff. In recent years, these criteria, identified in public bureaucracies with a civil service, have been modified somewhat because of equal opportunity employment legislation and court decisions. Initially, testing procedures for recruitment and promotion were challenged at the recruitment level, with contentions that recruitment was biased against minorities and women. More recently, such challenges have applied to promotions as well, especially to the nonexempt supervisory ranks.

There are limits to bureaucratization of police organizations and their centralization of authority. Like many public and private bureaucracies, local police departments have undergone only selective and partial bureaucratization. Below I examine some of the ways in which the bureaucratization of police departments is restricted or limited or where trace beginnings have been truncated. I first examine ways that the external environment of police departments limits their bureaucratic adaptation and then turn to ways that their internal environment restricts adaptation. This separation is somewhat of an artifact since I focus primarily on how the bureaucratic organization of police departments adapts to changing conditions inside and outside the department.

III. Adaptation to the Environment

Noted repeatedly throughout this essay is the fact that all organizations engage in transactions with their environment and are vulnerable to its penetration of their integrity. But the police seem especially so. Initially, the "citizen watch" was an almost indistinguishable part of the community. The watch was an organization of civic obligation. All able-bodied adult males were obliged to perform that service. Gradually, as police organizations emerged and were centralized, they bureaucratized to limit penetration and control by their environment. The functional internal organization of police departments can be seen as an adaptation to this necessity for penetration of its environment and protection from it. Proactive police units, such as narcotics and organized crime, and some reactive units, such as traffic and patrol, are specifically organized to penetrate the civic environment. Others, such as records, are designed to preclude penetration by the larger society. Still others, such as communications, functionally link the two communities. And, finally, internal intelligence is that very special unit designed to penetrate the internal environment of the department while sealing it from civic penetration.

The features of ritualistic organization of policing, such as those of secrecy, personal identification, and the separation of uniform and undercover, can also be understood in terms of environmental penetration. Elsewhere I have pointed out that the police uniform functions to identify police in their environment, while plain clothes are the uniform of penetration. To penetrate illegal behavior successfully and counter civic resistance in their environment, police must go undercover and occupy a citizen role rather than a police role—either as infiltrators or agents provocateurs or as plainclothes officers passing as a particular kind of citizen (Reiss 1974*b*, p. 59). The emphasis on secrecy in police organizations can be seen similarly as a means of closing off its core to civic penetration.

Modern police organizations seem to want closed systems while searching for means to penetrate other systems that, to a growing degree, are closed to them in democratic societies.

A. Discretionary Authority

Bureaucracies are grounded in rules and the legitimate exercise of hierarchical power in their application. Employees are expected to make decisions by a universal application of the rules in their domain of power. In theory, they have no discretion in their application, and all decisions are open to review by superiors to whom they are accountable. The dilemma created by this bureaucratic prohibition on discretion is beautifully stated in a minor literary classic, *Catch-22* (Heller 1961). To paraphrase the military wisdom of its central character: When faced with a decision, find a rule; when a rule cannot be found, make a rule!

Although the foundation of policing is the legal order and its rules, police officers, nevertheless, have enormous discretionary powers to apply the law. Consequently, there is considerable variability among police officers. What is more, discretionary decisions are of low public visibility because often only police officers and those accused of violating the criminal law are present. Especially invisible are the decisions not to invoke the criminal law (Goldstein 1960). Particularly invisible, as Bittner (1967*a*, 1967*b*) points out, is the enormous discretion police officers exercise over citizens in their peacekeeping role. Most decisions, moreover, are unsupervised so that the exercise of discretion not to invoke the law cannot be monitored and reviewed. What is more important, discretionary decisions can be reviewed only when they are directly supervised or a matter of record. Because the police bureaucracy does not require that many discretionary decisions be made a matter of record, those choices cannot be subject to internal review. Correspondingly, only decisions of record are ordinarily subject to external review (Reiss 1974*a*).

Because police officers' decisions have low visibility to supervisory and command officers, the misapplication of rules and misuse of authority are particularly problematic. Most problematic is whether physical force is exercised legitimately (Reiss 1968; Chevigny 1969). Complaints about misapplication of rules and misuse of authority ordinarily are subject only to internal bureaucratic review. Dissatisfaction with bureaucratic internal review has led to demands for external review by civilian review boards (see next subsection).

The exercise of discretion is highly institutionalized in the American system of criminal justice (Reiss 1974*a*) in a way that is inconsistent with the bureaucratization of decision making. Bureaucracies preclude officials from making decisions under conditions of low visibility and without systematic hierarchical review and limit individual discretion in the selection and application of rules. Yet none of these constraints is institutionalized in contemporary police bureaucracies in America. What is particularly striking is that the greatest discretionary powers are lodged with the lowest-ranking officials in the system and that most discretionary decisions are not made a matter of record (Reiss 1974*a*).

The retention of these discretionary powers of law enforcement by patrol officers is an effective limit on bureaucratic police power. They stand in marked contrast with hierarchical review of at least some patrol officer decisions in European countries as, for example, the provision in Germany that magistrates and not the patrol officer determine whether a citizen is to be arrested.

B. Organizational Accountability

Public organizations in democratic societies are accountable to the political authority of elected officials. In the United States, municipal police organizations are held accountable largely through the appointment of the chief by elected public officials or their appointed boards. Except for a minority of civil service chiefs, chiefs of municipal police departments serve subject to the pleasure of those who appoint them. They are vulnerable to dismissal when incumbents fail to be reelected or vacate their office. Municipal chiefs are held accountable by reason of their authority for the conduct of their department and its members and are subject to dismissal for organizational corruption and officer misconduct. Sheriffs, by contrast, are elected officials who normally run on a party platform and are directly responsible to the electorate.

To reduce vulnerability in office, police chiefs developed organizational ways to hold their employees accountable. Chiefs operate on the sound organizational, but misleading civic, principle that a system of internal investigation and discipline is the way to reduce the organizations' vulnerability to scandal and reform. Complaints from external sources are investigated by an internal affairs unit that reports directly to the chief. The chief decides whether to bring charges before an internal review board or an externally appointed and co-opted board of police commissioners. In any case, the organization insures that, at most, individual officers will be charged with misconduct and that the organization will not be held accountable for their misconduct. These operating principles have led chiefs to offer the so-called rotten apple in a barrel of good apples explanation of police misconduct. Unless the individual responsible is punished, the whole barrel will spoil. Most organizational misconduct hence is assured low public visibility, and the organization need not fear charges of misconduct. Only under unusual circumstances is organizational misconduct at risk of public exposure, and that is when newspapers are able to bring charges of organizational scandal and exert pressures to reform. As Sherman (1978) concludes, this results in a cycle of scandal and reform in which only the individual police department scandalized is reformed. Reform, more often than not, is cosmetic and begins with the dismissal of the chief, who, remarkably, normally is free of any taint of corruption. The maxim seems to be that a corrupt department needs an honest chief who can be held responsible and dismissed. Altogether, individuals rather than organizations are held accountable for organizational failures. Institutionally, then, police departments remain invulnerable to reform except through political pressure and a media-generated scandal. The American system of accountability provides no means for holding a system accountable, and organizations in that system are infrequently held publicly accountable.

With the advent of civil rights complaints against the police, there is increasing pressure for some review independent of the police department's internal review and hearings on charges. Pressures are exerted on political authorities to appoint civilian review boards. These pressures have mixed success, but rarely has any governing organization appointed a review board that is entirely independent of police participation in the review process.

Recent work by Brodeur (1989) and others makes clear why the civilian review board is a limited means for holding police officers and their organizations accountable. In reviewing the Canadian experience with civilian review boards, Brodeur draws attention to the fact that there generally is a large gap between the powers of any accountability agency, such as a police review board, and its willingness and capacity to exercise those powers. He draws attention to three different kinds of power that affect civilian control remedies. They are investigative power, that is, the power to ascertain the facts; disciplinary power, which is the power to impose sanctions; and structural power, the power to make and implement policies that remedy situations that lead to misconduct (Brodeur 1989, p. 9). Brodeur contends that the greatest gap between possession and exercise of review board powers occurs with regard to investigative powers. This disjuncture has a structural explanation.

An important reason for this disjuncture is that review boards face the dilemma that they cannot carry out most investigations without the cooperation of the police department. This remains so even if they have their own investigators, which is rarely the case. Typically, a review board must call on the police department's investigators for evidence. Even when they have their own investigators, they must still rely on the department for its internal files on the matter, and they are dependent on individual police officers to cooperate openly and without deception. The blue curtain of police culture can readily subvert such inquiry.

Many investigations must remain indeterminate because there are contradictions in testimony that is the primary evidence available on investigation. Not uncommonly, the only testimony in addition to that of the complainant is that of one or more police officers who are either implicated in the incident or presumed to have witnessed it. Their testimony is constrained and may be compromised. Presented with testimony that on its face must be regarded as credible, no means for resolving the contradictions are available. Lacking independent and impartial witnesses, most complaints cannot be sustained.

At the heart of the review board organizational form, then, is a tenuous presumption that misconduct can be controlled by investigating incidents of misconduct and sanctioning those who are found in violation. Investigation and oral testimony are thin reeds with which to sanction officer misconduct and cannot reach the organizational and systemic sources of that misconduct. As of the close of this century, the only vehicle for processing police organizational misconduct is a government appointed commission. That is an even thinner reed as it also relies largely on blaming persons for the misconduct rather than on transforming organizations and the system of which they are a part.

During the last half of the twentieth century, police departments have had to attend both to the legality of police behavior in carrying out the organizational mandate to enforce the law and to the conformity of the department as an employer to legislative and judicial mandates that it be an equal opportunity employer and be evenhanded in enforcing the law.

Quite clearly, police organizations are adapting to the legislative and judicial mandates that it be nondiscriminatory both in enforcing the law and as an employer. To conform requires major changes in personnel selection, in recruitment and promotion procedures, and in police training. Perhaps no part of the department is left unchanged by this mandate. Departments conform at varying rates, however, some electing to litigate how and in what ways they will be required to change, while others assume less of an adversarial posture. Litigation continues, nonetheless, over essentially local department conformity to statutory and regulatory mandates. The litigation often involves qualification for promotion through legal challenges to the testing procedures and selection from among those certified as eligible for promotion. A major constitutional issue remaining is over the establishment of minority quotas.

The evidence is clear that there has been a substantial increase in the employment of both minorities and women in police departments. Where there is a substantial minority population within a jurisdiction, such as Hispanics in Los Angeles or Miami, minority representation on the force has increased at a greater rate than in most departments. Women and minorities, nevertheless, remain underrepresented in all departments relative to their proportion in the labor force. This disproportion may be owing, in part, to the age-cohort structure of departments. Yet even the younger cohorts display selection effects. Despite gains, in 1988 women constituted only 7.9 percent of all sworn officer employment in all UCR-reporting police agencies while accounting for 64.7 percent of all their civilian employees (Federal Bureau of Investigation 1989, table 69).

The recruitment of minorities has been accelerated by court-mandated hiring quotas. Lacking, however, are statistical assessments of the success of judicial legal strategies on changing minority and gender representation in police agencies. Because either the police department of most medium and large cities or its municipality is under judicial orders to change its policies of recruitment and promotion, the presumption remains that judicial orders will exert a substantial influence to change traditional organizational practices of employment and promotion.

Evidence regarding the effects on police practice of U.S. appellate and Supreme Court decisions concerning the Fourth, Fifth, and Sixth Amendments to the U.S. Constitution is less compelling. There is substantial agreement that defense lawyers and judges utilize the lack of conformity to these decisions as grounds for dismissal of charges, especially concerning illegal searches and seizures, involuntary confessions, and failure to advise accused of their rights. Likewise, there is evidence that detective divisions have altered practices to insure the admissibility of evidence. What is less clear is the extent to which police patrol officers alter their behavior to conform to these decisions.

The organization of intelligence gathering within police departments has changed substantially since the nineteenth century. Police patrol originally was the major source of community intelligence for the department. With the emergence of detective divisions, the intelligence-gathering function of patrol officers was neglected by commanders, even though they remained strategically placed to gather and report intelligence. The control of police corruption now falls largely to internal intelligence units that investigate all allegations of police corruption. An inspections division has gradually been given the role of gathering intelligence on whether and how management's goals are implemented by internal operations. The decline of community intelligence inputs to police organizations has led in some departments to assigning intelligence-gathering functions to existing and newly created units, so-called community relations units. These units often serve almost exclusively to gather intelligence on police relations with minority persons.

Central to this development of intelligence units within police departments has been the development of undercover policing (Marx 1988). Since the 1930s, a major organizational innovation in undercover intelligence gathering in local police departments has been the development of secret intelligence units. The extent to which this development paralleled and was encouraged by Hoover's FBI secret domestic intelligence organization is moot. Within the largest police departments these secret intelligence units operate apart from the detective division. Some departments, in New York City, for example, even secretly recruit and train these intelligence agents so that its members are known only to those who manage them. As Marx (1988, p. 88) observes, the advantage of secret intelligence units is that investigations may last a long time because there is an organizational stake in continuing investigations.

C. Corruption of Police Organizational Authority and Practice

Police organizations, as noted previously, are organized around transactions with people and organizations in their environment (Reiss and Bordua 1967). Police officers occupy boundary-spanning roles. They are the major links through which information and behavior flow to and from the police department (Thompson 1962; Aldrich and Reiss 1971). One consequence of this functional organization of policing is that police departments risk subversion of their mandate by the environment. A central problem for police administrators is to prevent corruption of the department by these links to its environment (Shearing 1981).

Even prior to the establishment of modern police organizations, the deviance of "the watch" was notorious (Bacon 1939). Later descriptions of early nineteenth-century police departments are replete with accounts of discharging chiefs as well as officers for engaging in illegal acts arising from the misuse of their occupational authority (Maniha 1972). Of particular concern was the corruption of their authority by criminal interests and political organizations (Steffens 1931).

A major solution to the problem of police corruption was the adoption of the bureaucratic form of rational administration. The introduction of a hierarchical system of command and control with supervision and discipline of individual officers was regarded as a solution to the problem of corruption. Almost all police departments therefore adopted the basic hierarchical rank organization of the military to insure internal discipline and control.[10]

The bureaucratic solution tended to disregard the fact that bureaucratic administration creates an internal organization of administrative and operating units. These units vary in their vulnerability to corruption. Some units are particularly vulnerable to subversion because they police organized illegal behavior in the community. Much of their work requires undercover investigation and organizational secrecy that is not open to direct hierarchical control—a problem general to all espionage organizations. Accordingly, police departments are particularly vulnerable to the corruption of their vice units because vice detectives engage in secret undercover policing of organized criminal activity.

Police departments also are vulnerable when the hierarchical command is locally organized territorially. Local commanders and their officers are open to penetration by criminal organizations in their precinct or substation. Widespread corruption of detectives and patrol consequently is quite common in precincts where there is considerable organized crime. Hierarchical command both within the police department and within organized crime facilitates that corruption since those at the lowest levels of the organizations operate the payoffs between the organized crime and the police department hierarchies (Cressey 1969). The linchpins in that exchange are the "bagmen" and their supervisors who distribute payoffs to the command (Landesco 1968). Corruption of a territorial police command is unlikely unless at least the supervisory command is implicated in the illegal gain. The hierarchical organization of payoffs in police departments makes it difficult to pene-

---

[10] There is a common misperception that police departments always operated with a quasi-military structure of command. Most departments did not do so until late in the nineteenth century and then usually to introduce discipline to control police behavior and the corruption of officers. Maniha (1972, p. 49) reports that the St. Louis Police Department did not give in to a military hierarchy and organization of staff functions until the Police Reorganization Act of 1899.

trate the corruption of the command and to hold higher officers accountable for the corruption in their district.

In the twentieth century, some police administrators (Wilson and McLaren 1972) concluded that a decentralized territorial organization of policing into beats and precincts made departments vulnerable to widespread corruption by fostering close contacts that could not be monitored. Accordingly, police administrators sought to further insulate the organization from its environment. One way of doing so was implemented in the 1950s by O. W. Wilson in Chicago (see Wilson and McLaren 1972). The general strategy is to remove officers insofar as possible from other than work contacts with the public. They are removed from foot-beat patrol, which provides too many opportunities for corruption by close personal contacts with residents and businesses on their beat. Removed to a motorized beat patrol in one-person cars, officers are permitted little opportunity to congregate. Supervisors are placed in vehicles and closely monitored as to the kind and level of supervision. The station house is downgraded as a place for handling criminal matters, and station commanders are responsible to an area commander. To restrict opportunities for corruption of command officers by bribes and payoffs from illegal activities operating in their command area, commanders are rotated quite frequently to other precincts or commands. In brief, under this strategy, there is a substantial restructuring of the territorial and command organization of policing to insure stricter control over the opportunities of corrupting officers, their supervisors, and their commanders. This model was adopted fairly widely, in part because of its reputed capacity to control corruption. In all but the largest cities, the adoption of the Wilson model of rational police administration has led to the elimination of all station houses and to centralization of command and control in a single headquarters command.

The corruption of detectives by their environment remains problematic. There have been only a few other innovations designed to minimize their corruption. One is to organize a dominant coalition to control corruption following a corruption scandal (Sherman 1978, pp. 247–50). The major control efforts have been premonitory, that is, interventions to control deviant acts prior to their occurrence (Reiss, cited in Sherman 1978, p. 20). One of these premonitory innovations has been to utilize the internal intelligence division to penetrate detective units for early detection of their organized subversion. Another has been to rotate the assignment of detectives across territories so that they have less opportunity to become enmeshed in an organized transaction system of bribery and payoff. There is little evidence to evaluate the effectiveness of these organizational strategies for controlling corruption. On the whole, the twentieth century has witnessed few organizational changes designed to control the subversion of the organization's goals by illegal activities. It remains a concern of all police administrators.

IV. The Internal Organization of Police Work

The bureaucratic organization of police departments experiences considerable turbulence from its own environment. This is partly due to the fact that its external environment is turbulent and far from predictable. Changes in the external environment invariably have repercussions for its internal organization. But police departments also experience considerable flux as internal composition and organization change. Police departments' responses to changes in their external and internal environments often impose limits on bureaucratic organization and control.

A. *Emergence of a Legalistic and Technocratic Bureaucracy*

Since Max Weber (1947) propounded his theory of bureaucracy, organizational studies commonly focus on the internal structure of organizations and on task differentiation within the organization. Among the first to challenge this emphasis were Reiss and Bordua (1967, pp. 25–55). The production of the police, they noted, lies primarily in relations with their environment and its boundary transactions. The modern metropolitan police exist only because communities are legally organized and the fundamental organizational task of the police is to mediate between the urban community and the legal system. The police are, in their words, "a fundamental representative of the legal system and a major source of raw material for it" at the same time that "the police adapt the universalistic demands of law to the structure of the locale by a wide variety of formal and informal devices" (1967, pp. 26–27).

At the same time, Thompson (1967, p. 19) concluded that under norms of rationality, organizations seek to seal their core technologies (specific actions that produce a desired outcome) from environmental influences. The *core technology* of police organizations is the *production and processing of information* (see Manning, in this volume). That this is the core technology of policing should not be confused with the observation that the distinguishing property of the police is that they are empowered to use coercive means by the threat or actual use of force, provided it is exercised legally. Bittner (1974, 1980) and Klockars (1985) fail to separate the core technology of police organizations from the legitimation of the right of its members to use force against others.

Unlike most organizations, however, police departments cannot readily seal their core from external intrusion. The fundamental task of a police organization is to manage and respond to external demands from people and other organizations. They must create, maintain, respond to, and participate in external relationships more than the prototypical corporate organization. The municipal police as an organizational system may be thought of, then, as moving from environment to organization rather than the reverse.

As the twentieth century wanes, it has become clear that the transactions of police organizations with their environment are substantially determined by the goals and means of a legalistic and technocratic bureaucracy. Police organizations have transformed their operations by increased emphasis on management by technology and technical specialists. Of necessity, they have adapted the practice of policing to the legalistic demands of the formal legal system. Nowhere is this more apparent than in the role that technology plays in the production of police evidence.

Each technological change—from the telephone, patrol car, and two-way radio transmission to the computer—has had a significant impact on internal organization and operation of police departments. These inventions and their technologies have affected the organization of police command and control, especially of police deployment and response, and they have affected how information is received, transmitted, and processed. Adaptations to social technologies, such as those of organizational behavior and risk analysis, while less pervasive, are becoming characteristic modes of rational technocratic administration in police departments.

Easily neglected in understanding police organizations are the myriad ways that technocratic management is linked to the production of evidence for the legal system. Technology and technical experts have pervasively altered both proactive and reactive policing. Detectives and police evidence technicians are the major consumers of technology since theirs is the closest link to formal trials. Certainly today's detectives are far more given to technology than logical deduction in dealing with crimes. Their role is less that of solving particular crimes by deduction than of producing evidence for arrested or suspected persons. The narcotics division detective must collect samples of apparent controlled substances and submit them for verification by laboratory test to make a charge stick. Increasingly, they may also seek blood and hair samples. The many narcotics detectives who make buys to secure a search warrant, moreover, are "wired" with sophisticated recorders and transmitters not only for their protection but also for use as evidence. Homicide and sex crime detectives have come to rely on blood, tissue, and hair samples. More recently, they rely on gene typing to determine whether a suspect is the offender in rape cases.

The use of technology in the control of crime is by no means limited to detectives. Radar has become the major means of patrol enforcement of traffic violations. Patrol officers are linked to mainframe computers permitting on-line checks for outstanding warrants, stolen vehicles, and the status of motor vehicle registrations and licenses. They are trained in identifying intoxicated drivers and in the use of Breathalyzers. In some cities all patrol cars are equipped with fingerprint kits, and police are taught how to use the Automated Finger Print Identification System, a computerized system for matching fingerprint specimens. Police evidence technicians now work more closely with fire department specialists in arson investigation. Like the employees of all emergency service organizations, police officers are taught emergency survival techniques, including the Heimlich maneuver of resuscitation.

The technocratic aspects of policing are not limited to the use of material technologies. There are parallel developments in the development and use of social technologies. Perhaps the two that have gained widest adoption in police departments are those of hostage negotiation and SWAT units. Police share with emergency medical services units the development and use of social and psychological technologies for dealing with suicide attempts.

Much of the technocratic emphasis in policing derives from a model of proactive and reactive crime control. Although institutionalized to a lesser degree, police departments also have crime prevention units and programs. By the 1990s, metropolitan police departments not only had community-based prevention programs like Crime-Watch (Skogan 1986, pp. 203–29) but also drug education programs in schools like Drug Abuse Resistance Education (Kleiman and Smith 1990, pp. 69–108).

The technocratic managerial emphasis in police departments contributes to the further development of a rational bureaucratic organization. A characteristic of Weberian bureaucracy (Weber 1947, pp. 329–58) is that it substitutes routine and rational procedures for traditional practices. The information exchange and processing technology of the twentieth century has displaced many of the traditional forms and practices of police departments. Indeed, a major consequence of the technology is that it has changed the very nature of rational discourse within and by organizations. In most police departments, the symbolic forms of communication of the police with the public have been transformed by the telephone and 911 dispatch and, among the police, by two-way radio communication. Manning (1989, in this volume) has drawn attention to the ways that the technology of communication leads to the transformation of communications into an organizational processing language. The language of dispatch and response, for example, becomes cryptic. Often numerical codes are substituted for ordinary speech, thereby eliminating not only the redundancy integral to a language but also significant portions of speech communication. Records are stored as digital codes, thereby freezing information in time and rendering it as obsolete communication for reprocessing in the future. Computerized information is gradually transforming the ways a department is managed. Management decides what information is to be collected routinely as a basis for decisions. The more modernized departments feed computerized information into case management decision models such as the queuing models setting dispatch priorities (Schaack and Larson 1988), resource allocation models for manpower and tactical deployment (Larson 1972), and modus operandi models for solving crimes.

Faced with a turbulent environment and often rapid social changes, police organizations generally adapt the organization to perturbations and fluctuations in demand for police service rather than intervene directly in their environment (Reiss 1982). They are unlikely to forecast changes in their environment and plan adaptations to them. One reason why police organizations appear to be recalcitrant in forecasting future changes in their environment is that typically they operate under norms of organizational rationality that permit them to adapt to their changing environment. As Thompson (1967, p. 22) observed, ordinarily organizations do not forecast when they can successfully control inputs to and outputs from the organization. Owing to the enormous discretionary power of the police over inputs and outputs, they ordinarily can successfully buffer their operations from any turbulence in their environment. They level or smooth their input and output transactions (Thompson 1967, p. 21). They do so in a variety of ways, such as allocating manpower and resources to approximate peak demand. In emergency situations, they can resort to rationing their supply, reallocating officers to crisis demand.

When the environment of the organization becomes too turbulent for these adaptations, police managers take other measures to protect the organization and its core functioning. The main way to do so is temporarily to augment manpower either from supernumerary officers or by drawing on other police or even military organizations. The state police, the National Guard, and even paratroopers have been used in the United States to handle the turbulence of major urban riots.

Research and development units are the major units within organizations that seek to shape their transactions with internal and external environments. Research is empirical investigation that describes and explains how things behave and how that behavior can be changed. Development is the implementation of models that demonstrate that an intervention works in a predictable way. Police organizations essentially lack research and development units. The research unit of most police organizations typically is responsible for providing a statistical description of the organization and its inputs and outputs. Rarely does it undertake research that might lead to intervention. Police organizations satisfy research and development needs primarily by looking to universities for research that may lead to intervention models and to private industry for their development.

Research and development is not yet a core technology of police departments. Adaptive organizations generally rely on research and development as a core technology either to solve problems that fall within the organization's mandate or to adapt the organization to its changing environment. Goldstein (1979) has argued for a problem-oriented police, one that seeks to define and find solutions to police and community problems. A problem-oriented approach to policing requires minimally that its core technologies include research. Perhaps even more important, the applied research of engineering sciences, including social engineering, must become part of that core technology. Yet more is required in a genuine research and development model. Implementation of research requires model development and testing under field conditions. The implication for police organizations is that they must alter their relations with their environment to allow for model testing as well as provide for research and development units within the organization.

B. Third-Party Limitations on the Exercise of Bureaucratic Authority

There has been a substantial increase in the number of police unions since midcentury. Most are local organizations. State or national bodies play only a minor role in police employee relations (Juris and Feuille 1973, p. 27). The main reason for this is that the terms and conditions of municipal police employment are determined primarily by exchanges among local city officials, local police management, and local police union leaders (Juris and Feuille 1973, p. 27). This local locus of control of the employment relationship accounts also for the general failure of centralized national police organizations or of national labor organizations either to enroll large numbers of police officers as members or to develop strong local affiliates (Juris and Feuille 1973, p. 27). Thus, although a majority of local governments must bargain collectively with police unions, the lateral organization of unions is weak. There is considerable variation among local departments, however, in how their employees are organized for collective representation. Police unions may cover all ranks in the department, but ordinarily at least some ranks are organized separately from patrol (Juris and Feuille 1973, table 2-1).

Police management, then, often must deal with two or more police unions and other third-party organizations that pose limits to their bureaucratic authority. This limitation is most evident in collective bargaining and the settlement of employee grievances and public complaints. Matters for collective bargaining and employee grievances are rarely resolved by bilateral negotiations between management and employees. Not only are management and workers represented by third parties in collective bargaining—the municipal corporation and the police unions representing different ranks, respectively—but each also mobilizes and involves other agents in the process of negotiation and settlement. Moreover, the negotiators often must seek ratification for their settlement. Municipal negotiators, for example, must seek budgetary and often legislative approval for proposed settlements, and unions are able to divide the municipal managers. Parenthetically, it is worth noting that municipal organizations may also be subject to pattern bargaining with public safety unions. The settlement of police and fire department contracts may be linked.

The process of collective bargaining therefore is one of multilateral bargaining (McLennan and Moskow 1969, pp. 31–40) in which there may be considerable infringement of bureaucratic authority for at least some of the parties to the settlement. Moreover, as Juris and Feuille

(1973, p. 44) observe, settlement in the public sector of policing occurs primarily in a political rather than an economic context—as does most private-sector bargaining or public-sector bargaining when there is a private-sector alternative source for the service. Policing is a monopolistic service financed from revenues that have little connection with the service provided. Additionally, the settlement is often determined by political rather than rational calculation of costs and benefits.

Third parties are also involved in grievance and complaint processes. Police managers, not uncommonly, find their decisions in employee grievances are appealed to third parties such as a municipally appointed police board, the courts, or, in some states such as Connecticut, to state arbitration. Additionally, unions, not uncommonly, delay the settlement of grievances so that their settlement may be an additional bargaining chip in collective bargaining. The prerogatives of bureaucratic managers likewise can be infringed when civilian complaints are referred to civilian review boards for settlement. It is not surprising that not only police officers but also police managers resist the creation of such boards as each regards it as an infringement on autonomy.

Until early in the twentieth century, the line organizations of police officers were "benevolent and protective associations" dealing with matters that later were handled by municipal insurance and pension funds. Gradually in this century, local organizations of municipal police departments began collective bargaining as state laws and local ordinances permitted. Because of the perceived importance of maintaining law enforcement services without disruption, statutes typically prohibit police officers from striking. Despite this restriction, police unions and brotherhoods use other formal and informal powers to win concessions in collective bargaining. Where they have been denied the legal right to strike, police resort to exercising informal powers. Tactics such as restrictions of output by writing fewer traffic warrants that provide municipal revenue or calling in sick—the "blue flu"—coupled with issue and candidate electoral politics often achieve the same goal (Juris and Feuille 1973, p. 101).

Although police unions generally are limited to bargaining over wages, hours, and benefits, that too is changing. Where off-duty employment is contracted by the municipality, the union may bargain over conditions of off-duty assignment and wages. There are growing demands to control assignments and conditions of work, promotion, and discipline. Most municipal authorities still resist such demands on grounds that they infringe on the legitimate discretionary powers of the police commander. Yet they are not always successful. When the principal line union of the New York City Police Department failed to secure control over hours of assignment from New York City, they were able to obtain such concessions from the state legislature.

Police unions are powerful organizations quite apart from their power in collective bargaining. They exert political power in controversial issues affecting policing. Police unions have mounted successful campaigns against civilian review boards. They support litigation expenses on challenges to promotion procedures, and they maintain active lobbies in legislative assemblies. Additionally, they are a major source of financial support for the defense of police officers who are charged in criminal matters.

C. Transforming the Organization of Police Work

As modern policing emerged through the consolidation of inspection services with the day and night watches (Bacon 1939), a career police emerged. In the early years, however, policing was often a transitory occupation. Moreover, corruption was endemic in many police departments, and policing had a fairly low status as departments experienced repeated cycles of scandal and reform. A quasi-military form of organization was adopted in the post–Civil War period to deal with these problems. What seems to be meant when policing often is referred to as a quasi-military organization is that it rationalized hierarchical authority by adopting the basic military form of hierarchical organization. Several elements made for a relatively easy transition to a command bureaucracy and a higher status police occupation. They included the institution of an hierarchical command based on military ranks, adoption of a cadre system of training and deployment, the institution of strict discipline with strict penalties for nonconformity, and a closed system of promotion from within the ranks.

Traditionally, all members of a police department were sworn employees with full law enforcement powers. Sworn officers performed all administrative, technical, and clerical functions. In recent decades, civilians have been employed in many administrative, technical, and clerical positions. The number of sworn officers and their proportion of total employment has declined in many large departments in recent decades, partly owing to the demand for technical expertise not possessed by sworn police officers but primarily because of the relatively lower investment required for training civilians and their lower continuing cost compared with the cost of a sworn employee. In 1978, the

New York City Police Department, for example, had 28,012 employees, of whom only 17 percent were civilians (Federal Bureau of Investigation 1979, table 60). A decade later, in 1988, it had 36,027 employees, of whom 26 percent were civilians (Federal Bureau of Investigation 1989, table 72). Thus, while the department grew by 29 percent, sworn officers increased at a lesser rate than did civilian employees.

Although the extent to which police departments have been bureaucratized varies by size and governing authority, police departments have been affected by a movement to develop organizations based on a professional model of policing. As Gross and Grambusch (1974) have pointed out, there are certain inherent contradictions between an ideology that emphasizes autonomy of professional practitioners with minimal bureaucratic control and an ideology of bureaucracy in which the professional is subject to hierarchical authority that infringes on autonomy. The contemporary resolution of this contradiction in policing appears to have two parts: first, the emergence of organizations whose goal is to develop professional specialties by retraining officers in specialist police academies to behave as professionals; second, to employ semiprofessional technical specialists whose training and experience is gained outside police organizations but who are expected to operate under a hierarchical command.

Whatever the police profession may turn out to be, it is at present a far cry from an elective profession based on police professional control of police education. Although a junior college or four-year college degree is a requirement in a growing number of police departments, especially West Coast police departments, academic training for police is dominated by general criminal justice program education based in colleges and universities. Police appear less likely than in earlier times to seek legal training at a night law school. They are underrepresented in public and private management programs in comparison with members of other public bureaucracies. The implementation of a professional educational program for a professionalizing ideology is barely under way. Police work is one of the few occupations that qualifies for professionalization; police work satisfies all of the core elements that define a profession: making decisions that involve technical and moral judgments that affect the fate of people (Reiss 1971, pp. 122–23).

Police departments in America, unlike those in most other countries that adopted a quasi-military form of organization, failed to adopt a significant feature of military organization—a bifurcated system of entry equivalent to officer and commandeered ranks in the military.

American police departments soon made a virtue of an open mobility system in which individuals could enter at the lowest rank and conclude their career at a high rank, even though few could do so because there are few positions at high ranks. Appointment to ranks above sergeant is usually based on performance ratings by superior officers. There are no generally adopted national standards of test performance or experience ratings for entry or promotion to any rank, although advisory groups have repeatedly developed such standards.

The failure of police departments to institutionalize the equivalent of a separate officer and line corps has had profound implications for the development of a professional police in America. A single set of recruitment standards for all entrants coupled with an open system of mobility based on minimal standards of education and achievement is unlikely to produce a professional police. Departments are instead likely to continue to meet organizational demands for professional and technical specialties by civilian employment, by expert consultation, or by "outside contract."

The idea of a professional police encompassing all members of an organization is at striking odds with what we know about organizations with professional employees. Professionals constitute only a single occupation within service organizations, whether those given to health care, education, welfare, or civil and criminal justice. Normally, service organizations include different kinds of professionals and a substantial and diversified cadre of nonprofessionals. Indeed, modern organizations, including police departments, must depend substantially on technicians as well as on professionals. Perhaps police departments will become even more professionalized through bifurcation of the sworn and civilian cadres with the latter supplying the knowledge and skills of the different professions that contribute to the tasks a police department must accomplish.

V. Conclusion

Police organizations do not stand still. They undergo continuous, often imperceptible, change. As the twentieth century draws to a close, the twin ideologies of community-based and problem-oriented policing are reshaping at least the way some police organizations do their business. Community policing may be viewed as a reaction against the centralization of command and control in a police bureaucracy. Gone are the local community roots of policing and its symbolization in a community police station. In its place is a central police station and lockup far removed from the citizens who, as suspects or victims, required its services. A consequence has been their alienation from a police they know only by their resort to 911 or who come to fetch them for their misdeeds. Although the centralization of command was accomplished with the goal of a more efficient delivery of police services—by rapid mobilization of citizens and police response to their calls for service—they often appeared only to alienate those who were served. Moreover, to the degree that centralization sought to neutralize the police department from subversion of its goals and authority by political constituencies and organized criminal groups, it at the same time neutralized civic power over the local police. Citizens experienced impersonality in their contacts with the police and abandonment of their local community and its problems. These feelings were both fed and exacerbated by the fact that most other city services also became more centralized and less responsive to local preferences. It is expected that community policing will not only bring police closer to the citizens they serve by reinstituting foot patrol but also by making police develop new policing strategies through citizen participation. A new position has been developed for either police or civilian employees of police departments—the community service officer who performs many citizen contact functions and links local citizens to other urban service organizations. Their participation and that of citizens more generally are expected to reduce their social isolation and in turn make citizens less alienated and enhance their sense of power. Paradoxically, the movement toward a community police with greater local political and citizen participation threatens the very political neutrality of the police, for local rather than universal standards of legality may easily prevail and political power may again become the basis for allocating what are after all scarce police resources.

Problem-oriented policing may be seen as a reaction against what are regarded as the preoccupations of a centralized command—preoccupation with management, internal procedures, and efficiency. Absent is institutionalized concern for the wide range of problems that constitute police business (Goldstein 1990, p. 15). Like community policing, problem policing is concerned with a community and its problems and with engaging the citizenry in overall problem solving. Problem-oriented policing begins with the grouping of police incidents as problems and then moves to disaggregating them into their problem-solving elements. As such it is amenable to a research strategy and would seem highly dependent on research and development as its core technology. Sherman has advanced a special model of research and development for problem-solving policing—the location of "hot spots"—an elaboration of an earlier model of location-oriented policing. The general idea is to concentrate police resources at locations that are repeatedly victimized (see Sherman, in this volume).

The implementation of the programmatics of either ideology faces enormous hurdles in the face of the underdevelopment of research and development capacities and community service units in police departments. Little consideration has been given to the organizational capability required for the implementation of either program or to the limited capability of any single police organization to problem solve. Research and development generally requires more resources than a single police organization—even the largest ones—can command for the wide variety of problems the organization faces. A problem-solving police will have to find collective research and development models of problem solving.

Some cities are building substations around which a community-based policing system will rise again, like a phoenix from its ashes. Mixed models of centralized and decentralized command and control are being tried. In these mixed models, some officers are assigned to community police work and are given substantial discretionary powers to deal with community problems, while others are centrally commanded and deployed to respond to victimization complaints and emergencies. The role of specialized units, whether of vice or traffic, is unclear in these mixed organizational models of policing as new strategies are tried and old ones are modified. I will hazard a guess that police departments are entering a new period of organizational transformation in which material technology will be reduced to the role of an equal player with social technologies—social technologies that are both underdeveloped and under-utilized in the police organizational context. These are the social technologies of research problem solving, of engineering social relationships, and of organizational techniques for managing human problems.

The contrast in rhetorics of community and problem-oriented policing is overdrawn. Yet the rhetorics of contemporary policing characterize the dilemma of police organizations and administrators at the close of the twentieth century. The dilemma of modern policing seems to lie in determining whether to continue opting for rational, bureaucratic administration centering on crime events and their control or, rather, to transform policing into a community and social problem-centered bureaucracy that is accountable to localized groups.

REFERENCES

Aldrich, H., and A. J. Reiss, Jr. 1971. "Police Officers as Personnel." In *Police in Urban Society*, edited by Harlan Hahn. Beverly Hills, Calif.: Sage.

Bacon, Selden D. 1938. "The Early Development of American Municipal Police: A Study of the Evolution of Formal Controls in a Changing Society." Ph.D. dissertation, Yale University.

Bendix, Reinhard. 1960. *Max Weber: An Intellectual Portrait*. Garden City, N.Y.: Doubleday.

————. 1968. "Bureaucracy." In *International Encyclopedia of the Social Sciences*, vol. 2. New York: Macmillan, Free Press.

Bittner, Egon. 1967a. "Police Discretion in the Emergency Apprehension of Mentally Ill Persons." *Social Problems* 14:278–92.

————. 1967b. "The Police on Skid Row: A Study of Peace-keeping." *American Sociological Review* 32:699–715.

————. 1974. "Florence Nightingale in Pursuit of Willy Sutton: A Theory of the Police." In *The Potential for Reform of Criminal Justice*, edited by H. Jacob. Beverly Hills, Calif.: Sage.

————. 1980. *The Functions of Police in Modern Society*. Weston, Mass.: Oelgschlager, Gunn & Hain.

Bordua, David. 1968. "Police." In *International Encyclopedia of the Social Sciences*, vol. 12. New York: Macmillan.

Bordua, David J., and Albert J. Reiss, Jr. 1966. "Command, Control, and Charisma: Reflections on Police Bureaucracy." *American Journal of Sociology* 72:68–76.

Boston Police Department. 1893. *Manual of the Police of Boston*. Boston: Police Department.

Brodeur, Jean-Paul. 1989. "Remarks on Police Accountability." Paper presented at the annual meeting of the International Society of Criminology, Hamburg.

Bureau of Justice Statistics. 1990. *Justice Expenditure and Employment, 1988*. Washington, D.C.: U.S. Government Printing Office.

Chevigny, Paul. 1969. *Police Power: Police Abuses in New York City*. New York: Pantheon.

Costello, Augustine E. 1885. *Our Police Protectors: History of the New York Police from the Earliest Period to the Present Time*. New York: Published for the benefit of the police by the author.

Cressey, D. R. 1969. *Theft of the Nation*. New York: Harper & Row.

Ericson, R. V. 1982. *Reproducing Order*. Toronto: University of Toronto Press.

Federal Bureau of Investigation. 1979. *Uniform Crime Reports for the United States, 1978*. Washington, D.C.: U.S. Department of Justice, Federal Bureau of Investigation.

———. 1989. *Crime in the United States, 1988*. Washington, D.C.: U.S. Department of Justice, Federal Bureau of Investigation.

Geller, William, and Norval Morris. In this volume. "Relations between Federal and Local Police."

Goldstein, Herman. 1979. "Improving Policing: A Problem-oriented Approach." *Crime and Delinquency* 25:236–58.

———. 1990. *Problem-oriented Policing*. New York: McGraw-Hill.

Goldstein, Joseph. 1960. "Police Discretion Not to Invoke the Criminal Process: Low-Visibility Decisions in the Administration of Justice." *Yale Law Journal* 69:543–94.

Greenberg, D. 1974. *Crime and Law Enforcement in the Colony of New York: 1691–1776*. Ithaca, N.Y.: Cornell University Press.

Gross, E., and P. W. Grambusch. 1974. *Changes in University Organization, 1964–1971*. New York: McGraw-Hill.

Hale, George W. 1893. *Police and Prison Cyclopaedia: Newly Revised and Enlarged Edition*. Boston: W. L. Richardson.

Heller, Joseph. 1961. *Catch-22*. New York: Simon & Schuster.

Juris, Harvey A., and Peter Feuille. 1973. *Police Unionism: Power and Impact in Public Sector Bargaining*. Lexington, Mass.: Lexington Books.

Kansas City, Missouri, Police Department. 1978. *Response Time in Analysis*, vol. 2. Kansas City, Mo: Police Department.

Kleiman, Mark A. R., and Kerry D. Smith. 1990. "State and Local Drug Enforcement: In Search of a Strategy." In *Drugs and Crime*, edited by Michael Tonry and James Q. Wilson. Volume 13 of *Crime and Justice: A Review of Research*, edited by Michael Tonry and Norval Morris. Chicago: University of Chicago Press.

Klockars, Carl B. 1985. *The Idea of Police*. Beverly Hills, Calif.: Sage.

Landesco, J. 1968. *Organized Crime in Chicago*. 2d ed. Chicago: University of Chicago Press.

Larson, Richard C. 1972. *Urban Police Patrol Analysis*. Cambridge, Mass.: MIT Press.

Levett, Allen E. 1975. "Centralization of City Police in the Nineteenth Century United States." Ph.D. dissertation, University of Michigan.

McEwen, J. Thomas, E. F. Connors, and M. I. Cohen. 1984. *Evaluation of the Differential Police Response Field Test*. Alexandria, Va.: Research Management Associates.

McLennan, K., and M. Moskow. 1969. "Multilateral Bargaining in the Public Sector." Paper presented at the twenty-first annual meeting of the Industrial Relations Research Association, Madison, Wisconsin.

Maniha, J. Kenneth. 1972. "The Mobility of Elites in a Bureaucratizing Organization: The St. Louis Police Department, 1861–1961." Ph.D. dissertation, University of Michigan.

Manning, P. K. 1977. *Police Work*. Cambridge, Mass.: MIT Press.

———. 1980. *The Narcs' Game: Organizational and Informational Limits on Drug Law Enforcement*. Cambridge, Mass.: MIT Press.

———. 1989. "Occupational Culture." In *Encyclopedia of Police Science*, edited by William Bailey. New York and London: Garland.

———. In this volume. "Information Technologies and the Police."

Marx, Gary T. 1988. *Undercover: Police Surveillance in America*. Berkeley and Los Angeles: University of California Press.

Mayo, Katherine. 1917. *Justice to All: The Story of the Pennsylvania State Police*. New York: Putnam.

Muir, W. K. 1977. *Police: Streetcorner Politicians*. Chicago: University of Chicago Press.

New York Times. 1990. "42 Warrants for Owner of Fire Site." (April 7), pp. 27–28.

Ogburn, W. F. 1950. *Social Change, with Respect to Culture and Original Nature*. New ed. New York: Viking.

Pennypacker, S. W. 1918. *The Autobiography of a Pennsylvanian*. Philadelphia: John C. Winston.

President's Commission on Law Enforcement and Administration of Justice. 1967. *Task Force Report: The Police*. Washington, D.C.: U.S. Government Printing Office.

Punch, Maurice. 1983. "Officers and Men: Occupational Culture, Inter-rank Antagonism, and the Investigation of Corruption." In *Control in the Police Organization*, edited by Maurice Punch. Cambridge, Mass.: MIT Press.

Reiss, Albert J., Jr. 1968. "Police Brutality: Answers to Key Questions." *Transaction 1968*, pp. 10–19.

———. 1971. *The Police and the Public*. New Haven, Conn.: Yale University Press.

———. 1974a. "Discretionary Justice." In *Handbook of Criminology*, edited by Daniel Glaser. Chicago: Rand McNally.

———. 1974b. "Citizen Access to Criminal Justice." *British Journal of Law and Society* 1:50–74.

———. 1982. "Forecasting the Role of the Police and the Role of the Police in Social Forecasting." In *The Maintenance of Order in Society*, edited by Rita Donelan. Ottawa: Canadian Police College and Minister of Supply and Services, Canada.

———. 1991. "Private Employment of Public Police." In *Privatization and Its Alternatives*, edited by W. T. Gormley, Jr. Madison: University of Wisconsin Press.

Reiss, Albert J., Jr., and David J. Bordua. 1967. "Environment and Organization: A Perspective on the Police." In *The Police: Six Sociological Essays*, edited by David J. Bordua. New York: Wiley.

Reuss-Ianni, E., and F. A. J. Ianni. 1983. "Street Cops and Management Cops: The Two Cultures of Policing." In *Control in the Police Organization*, edited by Maurice Punch. Cambridge, Mass.: MIT Press.

Schaack, C., and R. C. Larson. 1988. "An N Server Cutoff Priority Queue Where Arriving Customers Request a Number of Servers." *Management Science* 35:614–34.

Shalloo, J. P. 1933. *Private Police: With Special Reference to Pennsylvania*. Philadelphia: American Academy of Political and Social Science.

Shearing, Clifford D. 1981. *Organizational Police Deviance: Its Structure and Control*. Toronto: Butterworth.

———. In this volume. "The Relationship between Public and Private Policing."

Shearing, Clifford D., and Philip C. Stenning. 1981. "Modern Private Security: Its Growth and Implications." In *Crime and Justice: An Annual Review of Research*, vol. 3, edited by Michael Tonry and Norval Morris. Chicago: University of Chicago Press.

Sherman, Lawrence W. 1978. *Scandal and Reform: Controlling Police Corruption*. Berkeley and Los Angeles: University of California Press.

———. In this volume. "Attacking Crime: Police and Crime Control."

Silver, Alan. 1967. "The Demand for Order in Civil Society: A Review of Some Themes in the History of Urban Crime, Police, and Riot." In *The Police: Six Sociological Essays*, edited by David J. Bordua. New York: Wiley.

Skogan, Wesley. 1986. "Fear of Crime and Neighborhood Change." In *Communities and Crime*, edited by Albert J. Reiss, Jr., and Michael Tonry. Vol. 8 of *Crime and Justice: A Review of Research*, edited by Michael Tonry and Norval Morris. Chicago: University of Chicago Press.

Skolnick, Jerome H. 1966. *Justice without Trial: Law Enforcement in Democratic Society*. New York: Wiley.

Spellman, William, and Dale Brown. 1984. *Calling the Police: Citizen Reporting of Serious Crime*. Washington, D.C.: U.S. Government Printing Office.

Steffens, Lincoln. 1931. *The Autobiography of Lincoln Steffens*. New York: Chautauqua Press.

Thompson, James D. 1962. "Organizations and Output Transactions." *American Journal of Sociology* 68:309–24.

———. 1967. *Organizations in Action*. New York: McGraw-Hill.

U.S. Bureau of the Census. 1942. *Sixteenth Census of the United States: 1940*, vol. 1, *Number of Inhabitants*. Washington, D.C.: U.S. Government Printing Office.

Van Maanen, J. 1973. "Observations on the Making of Policemen." *Human Organization* 32:407–18.

———. 1974. "Working the Street." In *The Potential for Reform of Criminal Justice*, edited by H. Jacob. Beverly Hills, Calif.: Sage.

———. 1980. "Beyond Account: The Personal Impact of Police Shootings." *Annals of the American Academy of Political and Social Science* 425:145–56.

Weber, Max. 1947. *The Theory of Social and Economic Organization*. Translated by A. M. Henderson and Talcott Parsons. Edited and with an introduction by Talcott Parsons. Oxford: Oxford University Press.

Westley, W. 1970. *Violence and the Police*. Cambridge, Mass.: MIT Press.

Wilson, J. Q. 1968. *Varieties of Police Behavior*. Cambridge, Mass.: Harvard University Press.

Wilson, O. W., and R. C. McLaren. 1972. *Police Administration*. 3d ed. New York: McGraw-Hill.

Mark Harrison Moore

Problem-solving and Community Policing

ABSTRACT

Problem-solving and community policing are strategic concepts that seek to redefine the ends and the means of policing. Problem-solving policing focuses police attention on the problems that lie behind incidents, rather than on the incidents only. Community policing emphasizes the establishment of working partnerships between police and communities to reduce crime and enhance security. The prevalent approach that emphasizes professional law enforcement has failed to control or prevent crime, has failed to make policing a profession, and has fostered an unhealthy separation between the police and the communities they serve. Although adoption of these new organizational strategies presents risks of politicization, of diminished crime-fighting effectiveness, and of enhanced police powers, possible gains in strengthened and safer communities make the risks worth taking.

Recently, much fuss has been made about "problem-solving policing" and "community policing." Proponents herald them as important new concepts that bid to replace "professional law enforcement" as the dominant paradigm of modern policing (Kelling 1988). Critics are more skeptical (Greene and Mastrofski 1988). To some, the ideas are nothing but empty slogans—the most recent public relations gimmicks in policing, devoid of substantive content, and lacking in operational utility (Klockars 1988). Others find attractive content to the ideas but judge them utopian—their popularity rooted in nostalgia. Still others see these new conceptions as distractions from the most urgent challenges

Mark H. Moore is Daniel and Florence V. Guggenheim Professor of Criminal Justice Policy and Management at the John F. Kennedy School of Government, Harvard University, Cambridge, Mass.

now facing policing; against the urgent need to control a rising tide of violence, the interest in problem solving and community relations seems a dangerous avoidance of the real business at hand (Bayley 1988).

This essay explores what is known or might reasonably be surmised about the value of problem-solving and community policing. It is necessary, first, to understand what these concepts mean and how they intend to change the practice of policing. These concepts are best understood not as new programmatic ideas or administrative arrangements but as ideas that seek to redefine the overall goals and methods of policing. In the literature on business management, these concepts would be characterized as "organizational strategies" (Andrews 1971). As such, the strengths and weaknesses of the concepts must be considered not only in achieving the traditional operational objectives of police forces such as reducing crime but also in guiding the future development of police departments and enhancing their public support and legitimacy.

My basic claim is that these ideas usefully challenge police departments by focusing departmental attention on different purposes to be achieved by them and different values to be realized through police operations. These ideas also encourage police to be more imaginative about the operational methods that might be used to achieve police department goals and the administrative arrangements through which these departments are guided and controlled. More particularly, the ideas emphasize the utility of widening police perception of their goals beyond the objectives of crime fighting and professional law enforcement to include the objectives of crime prevention, fear reduction, and improved responses to the variety of human emergencies that mark modern urban life. They also suggest the importance of bringing careful analysis and creative thought to bear on the problems citizens nominate for police attention and to find the solutions to those problems, not only in police-initiated arrests, but instead in a variety of responses by police, communities, and other municipal agencies. They suggest the wisdom of shifting from very centralized command-and-control bureaucracies to decentralized professional organizations.

This essay examines the promise of problem-solving and community policing as a means to reduce and prevent crime, to protect and enhance the quality of life in urban America, to secure and strengthen police acceptance of legal and constitutional values, and to achieve heightened accountability of the police to the communities they serve. Section I introduces problem-solving and community policing by describing and distinguishing them, by contrasting them with "professional law enforcement," and by discussing well-documented efforts of individual police departments to adopt them as organizational strategies.

Section II presents the findings of evaluations of early applications of problem-solving and community policing approaches. Of the former, only a handful of evaluations are available. A sizable number of evaluations of recent innovations are pertinent to community policing; these include work on team policing, community relations units, community crime-prevention programs, and various patrol and fear-reduction experiments.

Section III introduces and assesses a variety of objections that have been raised to adoption of these new organizational strategies for policing. These include claims that new policing strategies will unwarrantedly distract police from the core responsibilities of crime prevention and law enforcement, that weakened central authority threatens to politicize the police in bringing them into closer contact with partisan and community political pressures, and that the police will become too powerful and intrusive, to the detriment of both their commitment to constitutional values and their accountability to the public.

Section IV examines problems of implementation. These include problems of limited financial resources, the inherent uncertainties and potential lack of support that discourage innovation, and the police culture's resistance to change. Section V, the conclusion, argues that the promise of these new strategies is bright, even with respect to seemingly intransigent crime problems such as drug dealing and related widespread violence.

I. Defining Problem-solving and Community Policing

Scholars approach new ideas about policing from three different perspectives. The oldest tradition and, in many ways, the richest, tries to explain why the police behave as they do (Wilson 1968; Bittner 1970; Reiss 1971; Rubinstein 1973; Black 1980). These studies seek to give as accurate and general an account of police behavior as is practically possible and then to lay bare the historical, social, political, and organizational factors that give shape to that behavior.

A second, more recent, tradition relies on scientific methods to assess the impact of police operations on particular objectives—usually reduced crime (Skogan 1977). Some of the most important of these studies have looked generally at the effectiveness of such widely used police methods as random patrol (Kelling et al. 1974), directed patrol (Pate, Bowers, and Parks 1976), rapid response to calls for service (Spelman and Brown 1984), and retrospective investigation (Greenwood, Chaiken, and Petersilia 1977; Eck 1983). Others have looked more narrowly at programs devised to deal with particular problems the police encountered such as domestic assaults (Sherman and Berk 1984), armed robberies (Wycoff, Brown, and Peterson 1980), or burglaries (Clarke 1983).

A third tradition has sought to offer advice to police executives and leaders about how police departments ought to be organized and administered (Wilson 1950; Goldstein 1979; Geller 1985). The goal of such studies has been to define the functions of the police and to recommend particular administrative arrangements for ensuring that the police perform their mandated functions efficiently and effectively.

How problem-solving and community policing are evaluated depends a little on the intellectual tradition within which evaluation is attempted. Scholars from the first tradition might imagine that these concepts were intended as descriptions of how police now behave and measure their worth in terms of the accuracy of that portrayal. Scholars from the second tradition might think of these concepts as new operational programs whose worth could be assessed by gauging their impact on crime or rates of apprehension. Scholars from the third tradition might view these concepts as new ideas about how to manage police forces whose value could be weighed by considering whether the implied structures and managerial processes could be relied on to produce a professional, law-abiding, and law-enforcing organization.

The problem is that the concepts of problem-solving and community policing do not fit neatly into any of these traditions. They are certainly not offered as descriptions of how the police now behave. Indeed, no police departments in the United States can today be accurately characterized as community policing or problem-oriented policing departments.

These ideas could be considered more plausibly as ideas in the second tradition: that is, as new operational approaches to the tasks of policing that may be evaluated in terms of their operational results. This seems reasonable because particular operational programs have been closely identified with community or problem-oriented policing.

For example, foot patrol and the establishment of neighborhood ministations have been linked closely to the concept of community policing, while directed patrol operations, dispute resolution, and the use of other agencies of city government to help eliminate conditions that give rise to crime have sometimes been associated with problem-solving policing. These operational programs become "signature programs" of community or problem-solving policing because they reflect the particular influence of some of the important ideas that are contained in these concepts.

Still, the ways that proponents talk about community and problem-solving policing and the ways that practitioners put them into action do not suggest that the concepts are fully captured by any particular operational program. The ideas suggest a far more general approach to policing than can be captured by reference to any particular operational program.

Perhaps the concepts come closest to being managerial ideas that seek to instruct police executives about the best ways to define their purposes or structure their organizations. They are, after all, offered as advice to executives. Moreover, they seem to entail some important organizational and administrative changes in police departments. For example, community policing seems closely associated with shifts by police organizations from centralized, functional, organizational structures to decentralized geographic structures that encourage closer ties with local communities (Moore and Stephens 1991). Problem-solving policing is associated with the decentralization of responsibility to the lowest possible level in the organization with the encouragement of lateral rather than vertical communications, not only across the department, but also outside the department to other agencies of government (Eck and Spelman 1987).

But, again, these ideas seem quite different from the usual kinds of managerial devices that are studied by police researchers partly because they seem large and fundamental and partly because they do not entirely exhaust the set of managerial ideas that could be associated with problem-solving or community policing.

A. Community and Problem-Solving Policing as "Organizational Strategies"

If the concepts of community and problem-solving policing are not accounts of police behavior or tests of operational programs or managerial recommendations to police executives, what are they? The answer is that they are best understood as new organizational strategies that seek to redefine the mission, the principal operating methods, and the key administrative arrangements of police departments. In this respect, they are ideas more akin to ideas that have emerged from the private-sector management literature than to any of the traditions of police scholarship outlined above.

An important part of that literature is concerned with defining (and redefining) an organization's goals and developing suitable organizational capabilities in the light of environmental demands and opportunities (Andrews 1971). The completion of that task is signaled by the development of something called an "organizational strategy."

An organizational strategy is a declaration of goals to be achieved by a given organization along with detailed plans for achieving them. It is also an account of the principal values that animate the organization's efforts and that regulate the organization's internal administrative relationships and external client relationships. The strategy is justified as a whole by explaining why the particular course of action chosen is a beneficial and feasible one in the light of current environmental challenges and opportunities.

Sometimes the concept is used retrospectively and descriptively to give a coherent account of a past set of actions taken by an organization. For example, the concept might be used to explore the past behavior of an organization and to discover that the organization had an *implicit* strategy that guided its operations and determined its success even if that strategy was never fully articulated by its leaders. Often these historical analyses of the implicit strategies of organizations resemble sociological analyses of the factors that shape the development of particular social institutions.

More often, though, the concept is used prospectively and prescriptively as a device that leaders of organizations might use as an instrument of leadership and organizational development. An organizational strategy is offered as a vision of what the leader of the organization would like the organization to achieve or become. The visions contained in organizational strategies are often cast in terms of "new" purposes that the organization is asked to achieve, or "new" values that the organization is asked to express. For example, a police department might be challenged to assume responsibility for the quality of its responses to calls for service as well as its crime-fighting effectiveness or to embrace the values of promoting tolerance and protecting individual rights as well as ensuring that those who commit crimes are brought to justice.

Commonly, as the example suggests, the new purposes or values being advanced are not really new. They have long been part of the organization's conception of its purposes and goals or an important constraint on its performance. What is new is usually the weight or significance that the old values are given in the new regime. In this respect, the value statements contained in organizational strategies are usually declarations of the direction in which the organization's values should now begin to change *at the margin*. They are not necessarily complete accounts of the whole set of values being advanced by the organization. As statements about how the values should change at the margin, the descriptions of organizational strategies can often be understood only against the backdrop of the organization's past history. Without that perspective, it is difficult to understand in what directions the organization is being encouraged to adjust.

It should be clear by now that there is nearly always some discrepancy between the rhetoric that leaders use to explain and justify their organization's performance and the performance of the organization, but the discrepancy can be viewed in two different lights. Sometimes these discrepancies exist because the leader is using the rhetoric of his organizational strategy cynically to deceive and mystify those whose task it is to oversee the organization's performance. He thereby preserves some continuing scope for the organization to misbehave without penalty and allows a subculture of deceit to arise in the organization. This use of rhetoric is hardly foreign to police departments and leaders.

At other times, leaders use the rhetoric of an organizational strategy to challenge and guide their organization toward new purposes. The rhetoric that goes into defining an organizational strategy is potentially useful in this endeavor because it can expose organizations to increased accountability by openly defining the terms by which the organization is prepared to be held accountable. In this view, a leader's rhetoric about organizational purposes and values establishes an implicit contract with the organization's overseers, clients, and employees to which the organization can be held accountable.

What use leaders make of the rhetoric associated with a particular organizational strategy can ultimately be discovered only by observing the extent to which they establish their accountability to overseers, clients, and employees in terms that are consistent with their avowed aims and by whether they use their administrative tools to nudge the organization toward the purposes and kinds of performances envisioned in their strategy.

Obviously, leaders of organizations can be more or less bold in defining their organizational strategies. A conservative approach defines an organizational strategy in terms of familiar purposes and values that the organization is already organized and trained to achieve. A more radical approach defines a strategy in terms of some new and unfamiliar values and purposes that the organization does not now know how to achieve. This is radical because it exposes the leader to criticism from within and outside the organization and to the possibility of operational failure (Moore 1990).

In principle, even the most radical organizational strategy must encompass an explanation not only of its value but also of its feasibility; otherwise it is disqualified as an appropriate organizational strategy. Indeed, that is what is required of the analyses that go into developing an organizational strategy. A strategy is developed by searching for and finding a "fit" between the organization's capabilities and its environmental opportunities. That, in turn, depends on a simultaneous analysis of two key factors: the challenges and opportunities that are present in the firm's market environment and an assessment of the firm's distinctive capabilities for producing particular products or services that can be used to establish its market niche and identity.

The concept of organizational strategy needs to be modified to some degree to be of use to public sector executives. The environment that concerns them is not only the task environment they encounter (e.g., the level and nature of crime in the society) but also the political and legal environment that supplies them with money and resources to accomplish their goals (e.g., the willingness of budget authorities to provide increased automobiles and equipment and the tolerance of the courts for particular police tactics). Moreover, the "value" they create is not profits to be distributed among shareholders, but the achievement of a set of collectively valued purposes, such as reduced victimization or enhanced security, that justify the public investment in their activities.

The challenge of developing an organizational strategy in the public sector, then, is to find some characterization of the organization's overall mission that will be more or less enthusiastically supported by the political and legal authorizing environment; that, if accomplished, is plausibly of value to the community; and that can be accomplished by the organization's existing (or properly enhanced) operational capabilities.

The concepts of community and problem-solving policing are best understood as proposed new organizational strategies of policing because they seek to redefine the overall purposes of policing, to alter the principal operating programs and technologies on which the police have relied, and to found the legitimacy and popularity of policing on new grounds (Andrews 1971; Moore and Stephens 1991). They aim to do this not only in the minds of police leaders and executives but also in the minds and actions of police officers on the street and in the expectations and evaluations of political leaders and the broader citizenry.

B. The Current Strategy of Policing: Professional Law Enforcement

There is great variety in American policing (Wilson 1968). With 17,000 individual departments, each with different histories, operational challenges, and leadership, a great deal of variation is inevitable (Bayley, in this volume). Yet, the surprising fact is that, despite these conditions that favor variety, the basic strategy of policing is remarkably similar from one city to the next. Viewed at a sufficiently high level of abstraction, many things that are significantly different can be made to appear similar. There is, however, a way to describe modern American policing that is sufficiently general to capture much of what currently occurs and yet sufficiently particular to reveal choices not taken in organizing and using police departments. And it is against the backdrop of what has been the dominant strategy of modern American policing—the concept of "professional law enforcement"—that the claims of these new concepts of problem-solving and community policing can be most easily seen, understood, and evaluated.

The essential uniformity of American policing is most immediately obvious in organizational structures. Typically, American police departments are divided into a patrol force that constitutes 60 to 70 percent of the department's personnel, and a detective bureau that makes up another 8 to 15 percent (Farmer 1978). Police departments also often have special squads devoted to specialized activities such as narcotics investigations, juvenile offenses, traffic, and special weapons and tactics. An administrative bureau is responsible for ensuring that the organization is supplied with automobiles, police stations, operational funds, and manpower and accounts for the use of such resources to municipal authorities.

The administrative style of the organization is formally hierarchical, and quasi-military (Bittner 1970). Each officer has a rank and is obliged to take orders from those who outrank him. Elaborate policies and procedures are encoded as standing orders and regulate the conduct of officers. One of the most important jobs of superior officers is to see to it that junior officers' conduct accords with the standing orders. Policies typically flow from the top down, and obedience is expected. The person in command is the person who is responsible for the performance of the unit.

This formal structure guides activity in a working environment quite different from the military organizations and classic production lines for which it was originally created (Wilson 1989). Actual working conditions involve one or two officers working alone without close supervision (Rubinstein 1973). The situations they encounter fall into patterns but it is difficult to describe them as routine. Unusual aspects of the situations that arise often require initiative and invention. In short, the work more closely resembles a hospital emergency room than a military organization at war or a manufacturing production line.

What really determines how police departments operate is not the formal organizational structure or chain of command but the principal operational tactics or programs on which the police rely (Wilson 1989). There are essentially three such tactics: patrol (both random and directed), rapid response to calls for service, and retrospective investigation of crimes. By and large, the patrol division is responsible for the first two, the detectives for the third. Patrol units may differ in how much of their time is committed to directed patrol operations and in what they do when they are not responding to calls for service, but all are connected to the citizenry through telephones, radios, and automobiles that allow police to reach a serious crime call from anywhere in the jurisdiction in under five minutes. Similarly, detective bureaus may differ in their degree of reliance on informants, intelligence files, undercover operatives, and other active methods of investigation, but for the most part, they go to work after a crime has been committed and reported. Their job is to identify the likely culprit and develop evidence to be used at trial.

In most departments, it is taken for granted that the most important responsibility of the police is to control crime and that the most powerful instrument for achieving that objective is to make arrests under the criminal law. Police believe in the power of deterrence and incapacitation to control criminal offenders and keep crime rates low. They also believe strongly in the justice of holding criminal offenders to account for their crimes. They understand that they will be called on by citizens to perform other duties, but the heart of their enterprise is simply "putting bad guys in jail." That is what counts when promotions are handed out and in the locker rooms where "high fives" are given for achievements.

The police also understand that they are creatures of municipal governments, and are, to some degree, accountable to them and through them to the citizenry at large. But police cling to a strong sense of their own independence. They know from their past history that close political ties risk corruption (Fogelson 1977). Moreover, they feel strongly a need for aloofness and authority to do their job. They resist close oversight of their conduct both in individual cases and overall (Geller 1985). They establish popular support in the communities they police by stressing the importance of crime control as an important social objective and by claiming a substantial and distinctive professional competence in achieving that objective. They maintain their legitimacy to use force and the authority of the state by rooting their actions in the obligations of the law.

This can be described as a coherent organizational strategy because it does successfully find a fit between the organization's purposes, its operational capabilities, and its external support. The objective is the successful control of serious crime. Its principal operational capabilities consist of patrol, rapid response, and retrospective investigation. And it finds its support and legitimacy in the popularity of crime control as a purpose and in its commitment to lawfulness in arrests and investigations.

Of course, among police there has always been a certain ambivalence about the role of the law and of legal (as opposed to instrumental) values in controlling the operations of police departments. That ambivalence is reflected to some degree in the distinction between "professional law enforcement" and "crime fighting." When the police take the high road in search of professional autonomy and status, they tend to talk in terms of professional law enforcement rather than crime-fighting, thereby rooting police legitimacy in the law rather than in its instrumental purposes or in politics. Consistency requires that this strategy commit the police to enforcing not only the criminal laws but also those laws that protect citizens from arbitrary action by government agencies—including the police.

At other times, when the police pursue political popularity, they are more apt to talk about themselves as crime fighters, which implies subtly different values that guide and legitimate police departments. The instrumental value of controlling crime and punishing offenders is emphasized; the importance of the law as a constraint on police operations is diminished. The professionalism the police claim changes from a professionalism rooted in legal values and knowledge to one rooted in the technical skills and values associated with putting bad guys in jail.

Police ambivalence about these matters has long been sustained by a similar ambivalence among citizens about the kind of police force they want. The Philadelphia Police Study Task Force (1987) discovered that the citizens of Philadelphia approved strongly of their police force despite believing that officers slept on the job, were rude to citizens, took bribes, and physically abused defendants. One interpretation of these puzzling findings is that the citizens of Philadelphia agreed with the attitude expressed by one police officer who explained: "Look, if we're going to do the hard work of shoveling society's shit and keeping the good folks safe from the bad guys, we ought to be indulged a little bit."

In many American cities, two different deals may have been struck between police departments and their political and legal communities: the public deal—the one that is discussed at Rotary Club meetings—is the commitment to professional law enforcement. The subterranean, implicit deal—the one that is discussed informally and covertly—is the commitment to crime fighting. Insofar as that is true, the distinction between professional law enforcement and crime fighting signals the incompletion of the reform project that sought to internalize legal norms within police departments as important values to be pursued in their operations rather than as constraints on crime-fighting operations. These values remain largely outside the culture of the police.

Still, with the exception of this continuing contradiction, professional law enforcement has been embraced and developed as a coherent strategy of policing. It is often hard for those within and outside the profession to imagine any other style of policing. If, however, one stands back from this dominant strategy of policing, important limitations become apparent—even when evaluated against the announced objectives of controlling serious crime (Neustadt and May 1986; Kelling and Moore 1988). The strategy seems even more limited when one asks the broader question of how municipal police departments might best be used to enhance the quality of life in today's cities. That necessarily involves dealing effectively with crime and violence. But it also means finding ways to deal with drugs, fear, and the unraveling of family and community networks of obligation. Such purposes may not now be defined as police business. They are close enough to current police objectives, however, and the capabilities of the police are sufficiently valuable in addressing them, to make it valuable for the police to redefine their operations to create a greater contribution to their solution.

C. The Limitations of Professional Law Enforcement

An assessment of professional law enforcement as a strategy of policing should begin by observing that it has not so far had a great record in controlling crime. That observation has often been made, and (quite properly) seems to the police to be a cheap shot. They argue that they have done their part well but that they have been let down by the rest of the criminal justice system that has been unable or unwilling to prosecute, convict, and jail those whom police have convincingly accused of crimes. Some, in policing and elsewhere, also argue that adverse changes in society—increasing poverty and unemployment, continuing racism, an increase in the size of crime-prone age groups, the collapse of families, the decay of moral values—tend to increase levels of crime, and that the police and the criminal justice system have done well to keep crime at current levels.

Such finger pointing may well be appropriate and accurate. But if the police are but one factor (and apparently not a very important one) in controlling crime, then that should undermine claims by police that their funding and authority should be increased when crime increases. It should also suggest to police executives the wisdom of founding the popularity and legitimacy of their institutions on some grounds other than effective crime control. Yet these implications have not been widely accepted in policing. The police would like to have it both ways: to be thought to be important, even fundamental, in the nation's attack on crime, and yet not to be held accountable for increasing crime rates.

1. *Weakness in Operational Methods.*   But there is worse news for the strategy of professional law enforcement. Two decades of research have cast doubt on the operational effectiveness of the principal tactics on which the police now rely. We can no longer be confident that patrol deters crime (Kelling et al. 1974), that detectives, working only from evidence at the scene of the crime, can often solve crimes (Greenwood, Chaiken, and Petersilia 1977), or that rapid response results in the apprehension of offenders (Kansas City Police Department 1977–79; Scott 1981; Spelman and Brown 1984; for an alternative view, see Larson and Cahn 1985). Nor can we be sure that arrests, even when

followed by successful prosecutions, convictions, and jail terms, produce general deterrence, specific deterrence, or rehabilitation (Blumstein, Cohen, and Nagin 1978). We can still rely on incapacitation to control some crimes by some offenders (Cohen 1978; Greenwood with Abrahamse 1982). And it is certainly too much to claim that these tactics have no effect on levels of crime. Nonetheless, the confidence we had a decade ago in the professional strategy of policing as a set of operational crime-controlling programs has now eroded.

2. *The Limits of Reactiveness.*   Strategists now recognize that the reactive nature of current police strategy sharply limits its crime control potential. Reliance on patrol, rapid response to calls for service, and retrospective investigation virtually guarantees that police efforts to control crime will be largely reactive. Police on patrol cannot see enough to intervene very often in the life of the community. If they wait to be called, they are, by definition, waiting until an offense has occurred. That is particularly true if they view the calls as discrete incidents to be examined for serious law breaking rather than as signs of an underlying problem that has a past and a future (Goldstein 1979).

Being largely reactive has some important virtues. It insures that the police operate at the surface of social life and do not intrude too deeply; vast spaces of privacy are maintained. When the police do intrude, they have clear reason to do so and at least one citizen who supports their intervention—the person who called. In these respects, a reactive strategy of policing protects privacy and liberty and economizes on the use of state authority by keeping the state's agents at a distance.

The vices of the reactive strategy have been more apparent than its virtues. To many, it is simply common sense that preventing crimes is better than waiting for them to occur. What this position ignores, however, is that, in waiting, privacy and liberty are protected; and further, that insofar as specific deterrence and incapacitation discourage current offenders from committing future crimes, the current strategy produces future crime prevention. But there are two better arguments about the weakness of the reactive approach than the argument that it is not sufficiently preventive.

First, the reactive strategy is systematically unable to deal with crimes that do not produce victims and witnesses. This has long been obvious in trying to deal with so-called victimless crimes such as prostitution, gambling, and drug dealing. It has recently become clear, however, that many other crimes do not produce victims and witnesses ready to come forward (Moore 1983*a*). Sometimes people have been victimized and know it but are reluctant to come forward because they are afraid or they are closely related to the offender and reluctant to see him or her arrested, or some combination of the two. It is hard for the reactive strategy to reach systematic extortion or wife battering or child abuse, for the victims do not give the alarm. It may even be hard to get at robbery in housing projects where the victims and witnesses fear retaliation.

It is also difficult for the reactive strategy to reach criminal offenses that produce victims who do not know they have been victimized. Many white-collar crimes ranging from insurance frauds to dumping of toxic waste fall into this category of producing delayed harms. Because such offenses are essentially invisible to a strategy that depends on victims or witnesses raising alarms, such crimes cannot be handled well by a purely reactive strategy.

Second, the reactive strategy weakens the sense of police presence in a community and makes citizens unsure that they can rely on the police to come when they call or to handle the situations that bother them with any kind of responsiveness to their objectives and concerns. Police operating reactively rarely have time to visit victims and witnesses in the days or weeks following their involvement in criminal offenses. Detectives may show up to obtain statements, and prosecutors may call to notify of court appearances, but patrol officers will seldom call again to offer comfort and reassurance.

Similarly, the police for the most part will not get out of their cars to talk to citizens (Sherman 1986, p. 356). And, if called, police will often cut short the encounter if there is no legal action to be taken. Indeed, George Kelling has pointed to the irony that the abrupt end of many encounters with citizens is justified by the desire of the officers to get back "in service"—in service to a dispatcher who may need a car to be dispatched (Moore and Kelling 1983). Finally, the police know little about the people or situations they encounter. In Sherman's words, reactive policing becomes ahistorical, and without a context (1986, p. 356). Taken together, this means that the police feel distant from a neighborhood's citizens: being distant, they seem both unreliable and uncontrollable. The price is that citizens, and particularly those who are afraid, do not call the police and, instead, absorb their losses and live with their fears.

3. *Insufficient Preventiveness.*   Closely related to the charge that professional law enforcement is too reactive is the claim that the current strategy is not sufficiently preventive. Indeed, to some critics, and

particularly those who emphasize the failure of the reactive strategy to prevent the crime to which the reactive strategy reacts, the criticisms are identical (Brown 1989). But the argument goes beyond the simple claim that police must wait until a crime occurs before swinging into action to arrest the offender. It emphasizes that there may be factors other than offenders' evil intentions that occasion crimes and that these might be the focus of police interventions. Some commodities (such as guns, alcohol, and drugs) may be criminogenic (Moore 1983*b*). Some situations (such as festering domestic disputes or dark exits from subway stations or crowded streets with many check-cashing facilities) may facilitate the commission of crimes (Clarke 1983). Perhaps the police could more effectively control crime by reducing the availability of criminogenic commodities or by ameliorating criminogenic conditions than by waiting to apprehend criminals when crimes occur.

A focus on preventive action eventually leads to a concern that police pursuing the strategy of professional law enforcement ignore the potential contributions of many individuals and organizations outside the police department who could contribute to crime-prevention and control objectives. This has long been obvious to police chiefs who urged citizens to support their local police by calling, and many departments have made an effort to enlist citizens in efforts to prevent burglaries through devices such as property marking and security surveys. But the critics argue that the police do not think often enough or carefully enough about how to mobilize individual and collective efforts of citizens or the capabilities of other government agencies such as schools, licensing boards, and recreation departments to take actions that would eliminate some criminogenic conditions (Goldstein 1979).

4. *Citizens' Demands for Police Services.*   Note that these criticisms of professional law enforcement are made within a conception of policing that establishes crime control as the most important, perhaps the only, objective of policing. In essence, these criticisms seek more effective and more far-reaching methods of controlling crime. But other criticisms of the current strategy of policing begin to break out of this frame (Moore and Trojanowicz 1988). They are rooted in observations of what actually happens in police departments and raise troubling questions about whether the police *should be* single-mindedly focused on reacting to serious crimes.

Most calls for police service do not report serious crimes; even fewer report serious crimes in progress (Wycoff 1982). Instead, they request a variety of services. A large portion of them involve emergencies that could deteriorate rapidly and lead to bad consequences unless someone responds quickly with help. But these are rarely crime emergencies. More often, they are social emergencies such as domestic disputes that have not yet become knife fights or children on the street alone at night or the sudden fears of an elderly woman who hears noises or health emergencies like drug overdoses or miscarriages.

To a great degree, a police department pursuing the strategy of professional crime fighting is inclined to see these calls as "garbage calls" that waste their resources and special capabilities and distract them from the main job of being ready to deal with serious crime whenever and wherever it occurs. The only reason the police get these calls is that they work twenty-four hours a day, seven days a week, and are linked to citizens through phones and radios. They must work that way to be able to deal with crime. But police who are committed to professional law enforcement believe it is wrong for them to waste much time with these nonmission-related calls.

There is a different way to look at such calls. Some might be harbingers of future crimes and, if taken seriously now, would prevent a crime later. That is certainly true for domestic assault cases (Wilt et al. 1977). Alternatively, responses to such calls might be important ways for the police to establish a trustworthy presence in the community. That, in turn, might lead to an enhanced flow of information from the community and greater crime deterrence (Skogan and Antunes 1979). In both respects, an improved response to garbage calls might actually improve police crime-control capabilities.

An even more radical way to view such calls is to see them as appropriate claims on the police, and as clues to how *citizens* (as opposed to the police themselves) think the police might best be used. Perhaps the garbage calls should be regarded as falling well within the police mission. If citizens call because they are afraid or because they need help dealing with health and social emergencies, perhaps the police should think of such calls as central to their mission rather than peripheral.

The point becomes sharper when police arrange meetings with citizens to mobilize their assistance; police often discover that citizens are less interested in talking about robbery and burglary than the police expected (Sparrow, Moore, and Kennedy 1990). Instead, they seem to focus on "quality of life" problems such as noisy kids, visible drug dealing, graffiti, and dangerous-looking, rotted-out buildings. In short, citizens keep nominating problems for police attention different from those the police have taken for themselves as their principal purposes.

This raises questions about the continuing viability and value of a strategy that assigns these citizens' concerns to the periphery of police consciousness and operational attention.

5. *Incomplete Professionalization.* The existing strategy of policing has also disappointed citizens and police by failing to establish the legitimacy of the police or to elevate its professional status. Policing continues to be rocked by intermittent scandals and is the continuing object of mistrust and suspicion. While pay has increased and educational standards have been raised, policing remains largely a blue-collar occupation. This is disappointing because enhanced legitimacy and professional status were among the principal objectives of the recent wave of police reform that sustained professional law enforcement as a concept of policing. In retrospect, two factors seem to have thwarted the reformers' purposes.

One is the continuing inability of the police to establish appropriate mechanisms of accountability linking them to the overall structure of city governance and to the citizens. A central idea in professional law enforcement is that the police should be independent of political influence and should take their guidance strictly from the law and the standards of their profession. As noted above, their commitment to the law as a basis of legitimacy has been undermined to some degree by their continued criticism of constitutional restrictions and by the evidence of ongoing (but diminishing) corruption and brutality. They have preferred to base their legitimacy on their own professional standards—hence the popularity of higher educational standards, more training, even the movement to accredit law enforcement agencies (Williams 1989).

The effort to base police legitimacy on their own professionalism (rather than on lawfulness or political responsiveness or a combination of all three) was intrinsically problematic. It makes the police responsible only to themselves and to no one else—always a suspect position in democratic governance. But the police compounded that strategic error by invoking the principle of professional autonomy and independence to defeat all mechanisms of external control, even in situations where strong evidence indicated that the police had failed in their professional duties. Civilian review boards were, for the most part, defeated and probably for good reason (*Civilian Review of the Police* 1980). They were flawed mechanisms of accountability since they focused far too much attention on individual incidents of brutality or corruption, gave far too much power to individual complainants against the police, and failed to hold police departments accountable for improvements in their overall performance. But having defeated these initiatives, the police offered no satisfactory alternatives.

The absence of continuing external accountability may have seemed a real advantage to the police since it spared them the daily pressures of responding to the oversight and criticism of outsiders. It also made them feel in control of their own destiny. But the reality was that, over time, the absence of ongoing accountability weakened police departments. Without any continuing, formal dialogue between the police, their political overseers, and the community about the overall goals and performance of the police, the police lacked any way of advancing their status. They could avoid criticism, but it was hard for them to win praise. As a result, their standing tended to stagnate.

Without ongoing aggregate measurements of their performance, police became extremely vulnerable to the damaging effect of individual incidents that became the focus of intensive news coverage. A shooting or instance of negligence loomed large in the public mind when the public lacked a larger context in which to understand and evaluate an individual incident.

The police gradually became cut off from the aspirations, desires, and concerns of citizens. Increasingly, the important work to be done was defined by the police rather than by the taxpayers who paid their salaries and bought them their equipment. True, the police remained responsive to the citizenry by responding to their calls for service. But in each case, whether a call was important was subjected to police judgments about its urgency. By tying themselves operationally to citizens only through 911 systems, police could neither see nor hear from citizens about problems that were not embodied in particular incidents. Since there were many such problems, the police were increasingly seen as irrelevant to the concerns of citizens.

Finally, from the vantage point of police executives and leaders, insulation from external accountability made it harder for them to challenge their own organizations to perform. In the traditional imagery of professional independence and strong leadership, the insulation of a police chief from political pressures was supposed to enhance his stature and control over the department and to give him the freedom to chart the organization's future. In reality, however, the effect was to make him more vulnerable to the demands of his own troops. That was particularly true in a world in which many chiefs came from inside their departments, already mired in ongoing obligations to departmental friends, and in which police leaders felt obligated to support their own troops, lest morale decline. These powerful informal influences often made chiefs defenders of their own organizations and personnel rather than managers of the organization for the benefit of the public at large. Stronger external accountability would, it seems, have strengthened their hands vis-à-vis their own organizations and made it more likely that the values pursued through the organization's operations actually reflected the values that citizens would have liked to see reflected.

The second major impediment to legitimacy and enhanced professional standing for policing was that the police never seemed fully to embrace the constitutional values that were the only sure path for accomplishing these goals. In society's hierarchy of values, crime fighting is important, but it is less important than the rule of law. As long as the police embraced the former as their principal raison d'être, some avenues of advancement were cut off. Constitutional values were lawyers' values, not police values. As long as the police failed to embrace them (and sometimes even when they did), prosecutors and judges viewed police as suspect. They were also suspect in the eyes of reporters who covered their operations. And they were vulnerable to outside attacks whenever an incident occurred in which legal values seemed to have been sacrificed to crime-control expediency or to individual officer's desires for money or revenge. In short, even with the reform strategy, the police were standing for the wrong values.

The absence of effective accountability mechanisms and police reluctance to embrace constitutional values undermined the efforts of the reform strategy to enhance the legitimacy and professional stature of the police. Attempts to base legitimacy on educational standards and professional accreditation have not filled the gap. As a result, the foundations of policing seem shaky, individual organizations quite vulnerable to scandal, and police leaders vulnerable to scapegoating.

6. *The Growth of Private Self-Defense.*   A last criticism of the professional strategy of policing is that it has not allowed public police departments to hold onto their share of the market for security services. There has been a dramatic growth in private security that has occurred over the last two decades (Shearing and Stenning 1981; Cunningham and Taylor 1985; Shearing, in this volume). Increasingly, American citizens rely on mechanisms other than public policing to protect them from criminal victimization, and allay their fears (Lavrakas and Lewis 1980; Lavrakas et al. 1981; Skogan and Maxfield 1981; Lavrakas and

Skogan 1984). They buy locks, guns, and dogs in increasing quantities. They patrol their own neighborhoods in increasing numbers. And they band together to buy private security services from commercial firms—sometimes even from public agencies (Reiss 1985).

This has occurred even as the overall popularity of public policing has remained high and even risen. Although Americans seem to like public police forces, they apparently find them increasingly irrelevant to their security concerns. Insofar as one of the important tests of a corporate strategy is its ability to maintain a competitive advantage for an enterprise, professional law enforcement has not performed well.

The eroding position of public policing can be evaluated from two quite different perspectives. Viewed from the perspective of those in public policing, the loss of competitive position is unfortunate because it means less money, status, and opportunity for them and their colleagues. That may be important to police, but it is less important to the general citizenry, particularly if citizens are benefiting from lower taxes and the opportunity to buy security more neatly tailored to their individual desires.

But the decline of public policing can also be viewed from the vantage point of citizens who are interested in the overall quality of justice delivered by the society. Viewed from that perspective, the demise of public policing and the growth in private security portends several significant problems: a more unequal distribution of security; less respect for the rights of defendants; less professional competence overall to be drawn on in times of trouble (Reiss 1988). Thus the decline of public policing is a problem for society at large, not just for those who make careers in public policing.

These weaknesses in the current strategy of policing do not necessarily mean that it is wrong. It may be the best strategy available or the proper one for this stage of the development of policing in American society. Nor do the weaknesses necessarily mean that the strategy will quickly change to something else. Many forces operate to sustain commitment to any orthodoxy—including its familiarity and wide acceptance. What the weaknesses do mean is that there might be room to consider alternatives.

It is in that fertile ground that the ideas of community and problem-oriented policing have taken root. They give different answers to the questions, how might police departments best be used to confront crime, fear, drugs, and urban decay, by redefining the purposes of police departments, their principal operational methods, and even their bases of legitimacy. They have also sought to redefine the working relationships among the police, the community, and the other agencies of local government.

D. Problem-solving and Community Policing as Alternative Organizational Strategies

To see problem-solving and community policing as alternatives to the current strategy of policing requires that they be seen as more abstract than any particular program or set of organizational arrangements. They define general approaches to policing rather than a definitive set of activities. Moreover, the particular programs that reflect a problem-solving or community-oriented style of policing in a particular locality might well differ. The problem-solving approach to domestic assault in Kansas City might be quite different than in San Francisco or Seattle. The community approach to drug dealing in Detroit might be quite different than in Phoenix (Police Executive Research Forum 1989).

Indeed, one common idea across these concepts is that there may be no one best way to deal with each of the problems facing policing. The best response will often depend on local circumstances. Thus the mark of an effective police department will not be how successful it is in implementing the most recent national model of a successful program but instead in how thoughtfully it crafts a local solution to a local problem, taking into account the local character of the problem and the local means of dealing with it.

What makes these concepts distinctive, then, is neither that they embody a particular set of activities nor that they give particular guidance to operations. Instead, they orient the thoughts and actions of police officers and managers in ways that differ characteristically from traditional ways of thinking about police work and, to a certain degree, from one another.

1. *Problem-solving Policing.* Fundamental to the idea of problem solving, for example, is the activity of thought and analysis to understand the problem that lies behind the incidents to which the police are summoned (Goldstein 1979; Eck and Spelman 1987; Sparrow, Moore, and Kennedy 1990). This is not the same as seeking out the root causes of the crime problem in general. It is a much shallower, more situational approach. It takes seriously the notion that situations might be criminogenic and that crime can be prevented by changing

the situations that seem to be producing calls for service (Clarke 1983). The problem-solving challenge is to imagine and design a plausibly effective response to solve the underlying problem. That can and often does include arresting troublemakers or assigning officers to patrol in certain places and times (Eck and Spelman 1987, pp. 43–44). But the important point is that the response is not necessarily limited to these traditional police responses. The challenge is to use mechanisms other than arrests to produce resolutions and to look outside the department as well as within for usable operational capacity.

Some concrete examples taken from Eck and Spelman's pioneering work will make these abstract points clearer (Eck and Spelman 1987; Spelman and Eck 1989):

In 1984, thefts from vehicles parked near the Newport News Shipyards constituted about 10 percent of all index crimes reported in Newport News. An officer assigned to analyzing and resolving this crime problem discovered that most of the crimes occurred in a few parking areas. By interviewing patrol officers, detectives, and officers from the Shipyards' private security force, and those already caught and convicted of thefts in the area, the officer was able to identify a small number of suspects for the ongoing crimes. This information was given to patrol officers patrolling the area who became more aggressive in interviewing suspects when they were seen in the area, and succeeded in making on-view arrests. In addition, the officer gained valuable information from the convicted offenders about what made the autos attractive targets. That information is being used by the workers and the private security force to develop and implement a theft prevention strategy. Thefts have decreased by 55 percent (from 51 per month to 23 per month) since the field interrogations and arrests of repeat offenders began. [Eck and Spelman 1987, pp. 73–77]

The solution to this problem rested on traditional police methods, and relied principally on departmental sources of information. What was unique was the sustained effort made by the officer assigned the responsibility to deal with the problem as a whole to tap and collate previously untapped information and use that information to give co-herence and impetus to what otherwise would have been a fragmented effort.

Here is a second example:

In the spring of 1985, Gainesville, Florida, was hit by a rash of convenience store robberies. The police thought the robberies were the work of one or two repeat offenders. A review of suspect descriptions proved otherwise: many different offenders were suddenly knocking over convenience stores. Officers assigned to analyze this problem observed that the convenience stores that were being robbed differed from the others in that their interiors (and particularly their cash registers) were less visible from the street, tended to hold more cash in their registers, and were staffed by only one person during the late night hours. They then interviewed offenders who had been convicted of convenience store robberies and learned that robbers always avoided convenience stores staffed by more than one clerk.

These findings were presented to an association of local merchants that had been formed to help deal with the problem. The police were surprised by the fact that the merchants rejected the police requests to change their practices to make their stores less vulnerable. Undeterred, the police designed a local ordinance requiring the owners to remove window advertising that blocked the view of the store's interior from the street, to place cash registers in full view of the street, to install security cameras in the store and outside lighting in the parking lot, to limit the amount of cash in the registers, and to staff the stores in late night hours with two employees trained in crime prevention techniques. Despite continuing opposition from the merchants, the City Commission approved the ordinance. Following the implementation of the ordinance, robberies fell 65 percent overall, and 75 percent at night. [Eck and Spelman 1987, pp. 5–6]

Exactly what caused the robbery rates to fall remains controversial. Some claim that the arrests of a small number of offenders who were committing these crimes was the principal explanation (Sherman 1990). From the point of view of those interested in problem solving, however, what is important is that it remains plausible that the particular features of the situation that became the focus of interventions were important causes of the robberies and that the police force was able to persuade the city government to shift some of the burden of dealing with the problem from the police to the merchants through the force of their analysis. But for that, the police would still be responding to robbery calls and explaining to everyone else in the city why they could not supply more police services for them.

2. *Community Policing.* The fundamental idea behind community policing, by contrast, is that effective working partnerships between the police and the community can play an important role in reducing crime and promoting security (Skolnick and Bayley 1986; Sparrow, Moore, and Kennedy 1990). Community policing emphasizes that the citizens themselves are the first line of defense in the fight against crime. Consequently, much thought must be given to how those efforts might best be mobilized. One important technique is for the police to open themselves up to community-nominated problems.

Opening the department to community-nominated problems often affects the police understanding of their ends as well as their purposes, for the communities do not always nominate serious crime problems as their most important concerns. In expressing their concerns, citizens' fears become as important as their actual victimization. The factors that trigger fears often turn out to be things other than serious crime (Skogan 1986). Thus community policing changes one's vision of the ends of policing as well as its means.

The concept of community policing also changes thinking about the bases of police legitimacy. In community policing, the justification for policing is not only its capacity to reduce crime and violence at a low cost while preserving constitutionally guaranteed rights but also its ability to meet the needs and desires of the community. Community satisfaction and harmony become important bases of legitimacy along with crime fighting competence and compliance with the law. Politics, in the sense of community responsiveness and accountability, re-emerges as a virtue and an explicit basis of police legitimacy.

Thus community policing sees the community not only as a means for accomplishing crime control objectives but also as an end to be pursued. Indeed, as an overall strategy, community policing tends to view effective crime fighting as a means for allowing community institutions to flourish and do their work rather than the other way around (Stewart 1986; Tumin 1986). Community policing also seeks to make policing more responsive to neighborhood concerns.

None of this is intended to make the police entirely subservient to communities and their desires. The police must continue to stand for a set of values that communities will not always honor. For example, the police must defend the importance of fairness in the treatment of offenders and the protection of their constitutional rights against the vengeance of an angry community. The police must stand for and seek to produce fairness in the allocation of publicly financed protective services across the population of a city rather than cater to the most powerful neighborhoods. And police executives must retain control over such things as the assignment of particular personnel and the establishment of departmentwide policies and procedures, lest the enterprise cease to operate as a citywide institution and become instead a mere compilation of several independent departments. Under a strategy of community policing, police departments should become more responsive and accountable to the demands of citizens.

An example of community policing in action may usefully illustrate these abstract ideas (Vera Institute of Justice 1988):

> In New York in April 1987, a representative of a tenants'
> association called a Community Patrol Officer with specific
> information about drug dealers and locations in the housing
> project in which he lived. The informant complained that the
> building was inundated with dealers and purchasers who occupied
> apartments and loitered in the halls making deals. The building's
> residents were frightened and frustrated, as were other members
> of the community. . . . The officer's first move was to call a
> meeting with the tenants' association. There was a good turnout of
> the residents, and the officer initiated a discussion in which
> conditions in the building were described clearly. He insisted that
> no specific details be given or accusations made, however, since
> some of the building's drug dealers were attending in order to
> observe and intimidate the others. . . . The meeting showed
> clearly that most of the building's residents shared a common
> attitude toward the problem, but that, because drug dealing is
> illegal, it is the responsibility of the police department to eliminate
> it. Their demand was clear; they wanted the police to clean up the
> building by more frequent patrolling and evictions or arrests of the
> drug dealers.
>   The officer believed it essential that he convince the tenants
> they could not wait passively for the problem to be solved for
> them, but had to become active participants in the solution. He
> argued that the police could not possibly devote to one building as
> much time and attention as these tenants were requesting. He
> explained that the building's residents needed to act not only as
> reporters of the problem, but also to take some responsibility for
> eliminating it. The officer suggested the formation of a tenants'
> patrol. . . to supplement police activity and promised his support

of the patrol. The tenants came around; they formed their own patrol unit.

Within two weeks the tenants' association had been transformed from a rather limited and fragmented organization to a far more cohesive and powerful group. The association established an around-the-clock patrol of the building which monitored and recorded the presence of every person who entered it. . . . The officer conducted vertical patrols of the building five or six times a day . . . and regularly informed special narcotics units in the Police Department about the situation. In addition, he met with representatives of the Department of Housing Preservation and Development, the local City Councilman, the Bureau of Family Services . . . these different resources collaborated in providing information to the tenants, worked on renovating apartments, and assisted in responsibly choosing future tenants in order to assure that the problem would not simply begin again with new faces when the present dealers were evicted. [Pp. 11–12]

3. *Police Strategies Compared.*   When the concrete examples offered above are compared and contrasted in light of the abstract characterizations of police strategies, several important observations emerge. The differences between good professional policing, on the one hand, and problem-solving and community policing, on the other, seem less sharp. As one participant in a management-program class exclaimed when these illustrations were offered, "But we've always done things like that! That is not professional policing, or problem-solving policing, or community policing, that is simply *good* policing."[1]

Other members of the class pointed out, however, that while actions that were presented as problem-solving and community policing had always occurred in police departments, they were seldom acknowledged by supervisors or the managerial systems of the organization as effective policing. They remained covert and unacknowledged. Therefore they were rarer than they could or should have been.

Even though these methods and techniques had long been part of a resourceful patrol officer's operational repertoire, they were different from the standard, acknowledged methods of the organization. The scope of the problems addressed was unusual. They were larger than incidents to which the police were summoned but smaller than city-

[1] Comment made to author during Senior Managers in Policing Program sponsored by the Police Executive Research Forum, Andover, Mass.

wide crime problems for which the police were held accountable. The way data were used to define problems and analyze possible solutions, while not unheard of, are, nonetheless, rare in police circles. The extent to which the community and other governmental agencies were involved in identifying and resolving problems was also unusual. In these respects, then, the concrete examples do reveal a different approach to policing that is characteristic of problem-solving and community policing.

To a great extent, problem-solving and community policing are overlapping concepts (Moore and Trojanowicz 1988). A commitment to problem solving leads quite naturally to the invention of solutions that involve the broader community. Moreover, while problem solving often begins with police-nominated problems, many of the departments that have committed themselves to problem solving have also developed mechanisms to consult with local communities to discover what the problems are. If both occur as a routine matter, then problem-solving policing becomes virtually indistinguishable from community policing. Community policing is designed to let the community nominate problems and focuses on what the police can do in partnership with the community to deal with the nominated problems. That generally requires thought and imagination and is therefore often indistinguishable from problem-solving policing.

Despite the overlaps, each concept has its own distinctive thrust (Moore and Trojanowicz 1988). Problem solving emphasizes thoughtfulness and analysis over community cooperation. Community policing seeks to rivet the attention of the organization not on its own internal operations but instead on how its cooperation with the community seems to be developing. As a matter of emphasis, a problem-solving police department could err by becoming too focused on problems that the police thought were important and by not being responsive enough to community-nominated problems. A community-oriented department might become so focused on maintaining its relationships with the community that it forgot that it was supposed to mount operations that reduced crime, victimization, and fear.

So at abstract and strategic levels and at a concrete operational level, the concepts of problem-solving and community policing seem to differ both from professional law enforcement as an operational philosophy and from one another. While the concrete examples are here presented as a way of revealing the differences in approach, they also remind us that, in the end, these abstract and strategic levels are important not simply as abstractions but as devices that can be used to influence the conduct of police officers in the field.

The most important ways in which these new strategies are supposed to influence police conduct is by authorizing individual officers to gather data about the situations that lie behind incidents so that their underlying causes might be understood; to be thoughtful about the design of police operations to deal with the problem; to construct measures to determine whether one has been successful; to acknowledge the important role of the community in nominating problems for solution, in designing effective solutions, and in executing the solutions; to see that the goal of crime fighting might best be pursued by establishing more trusting relations with the communities that are policed; and to acknowledge that the police have broader opportunities to prevent and control crime and to promote security and ease some of the danger and pain and frustration of living in today's cities than is acknowledged in the conception of professional law enforcement.

To accomplish these things, however—to make these abstract ideas work to provide useful guidance to operational officers—requires important changes in the ways that police departments are structured and managed as well as in the ways that their purposes and operating philosophy are understood. It is not enough to have the general idea. It is not enough even to have the general idea translated into operational realities on an intermittent basis. The organizations must be structured and operated to produce that result day in and day out. That is an organizational and managerial task as well as a conceptual task. It is in this complicated sense that problem-oriented and community policing must be evaluated as organizational or corporate strategies rather than as operational programs, or even as discrete activities undertaken by officers.

II. Evaluating Problem-solving and Community Policing

If problem-solving and community policing are viewed as strategic concepts seeking to redefine the overall mission of policing, how might they be evaluated? This question becomes urgent as more and more police departments consider changing their basic strategies. After all, there is far more at stake in changing the overall strategy of policing than in changing particular programs or administrative arrangements. A much larger fraction of the organization's resources is involved. And changes, once initiated, may be quite expensive to reverse.

Unfortunately, it is far more difficult to evaluate strategic ideas than programmatic ones. Because changes in the basic strategy of policing take years, even decades, to implement successfully, it is difficult to say at what moment the new strategy became operative. This makes pre- and postevaluations that compare performance before and after implementation of innovations difficult to conduct.

Even worse, because a change in strategy often involves a redefinition of purposes as well as means, it is by no means clear what criteria should be used to evaluate success. Obviously, it is important to know whether the new strategy is more or less successful than the old in controlling crime. But the issue is whether, in changing the basic strategy of policing, new criteria such as reducing fear or restoring the quality of life also become important, and if so, how they might be measured. It may also be important to evaluate a strategy in terms of its long-run institutional consequences as well as its operational effectiveness: for example, whether the police become more or less law-abiding over time; whether they become more or less important relative to private security in supplying security services in the nation's cities; and whether the occupational status of policing rises or falls.

Finally, no police department in the United States has as yet fully made the transition to these new styles of policing and operated long enough to produce a convincing record of performance. Consequently, there is little experience to rely on in estimating the value of these new strategies, let alone their long-run institutional consequences.

This leaves an evaluator in an awkward position. The most important claim is that these new styles of policing represent an important shift in the overall strategy of policing. But the available evidence is not really up to assessing this claim. What one can do is more modest. First, lay out the principal arguments that supporters of these styles of policing make for the value of their approach and examine empirical evidence on the success of particular "signature programs" associated with the different ideas. Then, because this evidence is too thin to allow a complete evaluation (and because the empirical evidence would, in any case, be insufficient for a proper normative assessment of the long-run institutional consequences of a fundamental shift in strategy), turn to a close consideration of the principal criticisms of these new strategies of policing.

A. The Effectiveness of Problem-solving Policing: Empirical Evidence

The theoretical justification for problem-solving policing was set out by Herman Goldstein in a pioneering article in 1979. The fundamental notion was that much of the real knowledge about what worked in policing lay in the operating experience of police officers. Goldstein emphasized the importance of representing problems in much more specific, hence local, terms (1979, pp. 244–45). For example, arson was not a single category of offense; it included fires set by "firebugs," pranks by juvenile delinquents, and efforts to defraud insurance companies. Each element of the arson problem demands a separate solution. Similarly, in seeking out information about how problems are actually handled, it is not enough to learn the policies and procedures of the department, one had to observe how resourceful and experienced police officers dealt with individual cases. Only then would the "rich resource" represented by individual officers' practices be well used (Goldstein 1979, pp. 248–49).

The value of problem solving in practice has now been demonstrated anecdotally in operations carried out by police departments in such places as Newport News, Virginia; Santa Ana, California; Baltimore County, Maryland; and New York City, New York. The stories presented above are similar to scores of others from around the nation. Such stories are satisfying mostly because they describe a set of concrete activities that seem to produce attractive concrete results. In this, they have the persuasive power of anecdotes.

But there are at least three risks in relying on anecdotes as evidence for the success of problem solving as an overall strategy. First, the anecdotes may not be accurate descriptions of what occurred. Without outside auditing, there is no way to be sure that the successes are real or that they resulted from police operations rather than from some other factor. For example, debates continue about the real causes of the reduced number of convenience store robberies in Gainesville, Florida, described above (e.g., see Wilson 1990).

Second, the anecdotes may not be significant enough to count for much, even if they are accurate. The worst fear is that the problems are not really solved but are simply displaced to new locations. Even if that were not true, the solution of one or two small problems could hardly justify the operations of an entire police department.

Third, the success of one or two operations is not enough to demonstrate that the department as a whole can engage in this kind of activity repeatedly across the range of problems the police face. If the police cannot do this, then the claim that problem-solving efforts are doing something more than displacing local problems to new areas, or that they are producing something more valuable than what the police are now doing is substantially weakened.

The most sustained and rigorous test of problem solving as a strategy for policing a city is contained in an evaluation of the Newport News police department (Eck and Spelman 1987). The investigators identified precisely these two issues as being important to resolve: first, whether the problem-solving efforts eliminated or abated the problems attacked; and, second, whether the department was capable of carrying on such activities on a widespread, continuing basis—that is, as a routine way of operating (Eck and Spelman 1987, p. 65).

To answer the first question, the researchers examined three of eighteen problems that the organization defined as problems to be solved. One began as a police operation to reduce residential burglaries in a housing project but gradually became a multiagency effort to improve living conditions in the project. The second was the previously described effort to reduce thefts from automobiles in the Newport News shipyards. The third was an effort to reduce prostitution and associated robberies on a particular street.

Many of these problem-solving efforts began essentially as directed patrol operations designed to identify patterns of offending or known offenders and to deploy police to catch the offenders. All gradually evolved into quite different efforts that involved activities other than arrests and agencies other than the police. The attack on burglaries in the housing project involved surveying tenants, cleaning the projects, creating a multiagency task force to deal with particular problems in the housing project, and organizing the tenants not only to undertake block watches but also to make demands on city agencies. The attack on thefts from cars eventually involved the inclusion of police officers in the design of new parking lots to make them less vulnerable to theft. The attack on prostitution and robbery involved enhanced code enforcement against hotels and bars that provided the meeting places for prostitutes and their customers as well as decoy operations against the prostitutes.

The investigators concluded that these problem-solving efforts largely succeeded in achieving their objectives: burglaries in the housing project dropped by about 35 percent and there was no evidence of displacement (Eck and Spelman 1987, p. 72); the number of thefts from automobiles in the shipyards declined by more than 50 percent (p. 76); the number of prostitutes working the particular street dropped from twenty-eight to six, and the number of personal robberies committed in the downtown area of which this street was a part declined by 43 percent (p. 80).

With respect to the second question, the investigators looked at the overall volume and pattern of problem-solving efforts that the department had launched. There were eighteen such problems in the research period. Some were short-lived, local problems; others were local but more durable; still others had citywide significance. It would be nice to know how much of the department's overall efforts over the research period was committed to problem solving as opposed to reactive approaches to crime, what fraction of the department's personnel was engaged in such efforts, and what fraction of the city's overall crime problem came within the scope of problem-solving efforts. Unfortunately those data are not supplied. What the authors conclude, however, is that "police officers can solve problems as part of their daily routine; they enjoy problem solving; and their efforts are often successful" (Eck and Spelman 1987, p. xxv).

The evaluators also observed an important relationship between the depth of the analysis that went into the design of a problem-solving approach and the sort of response that was selected. The more extensively a problem was analyzed, the more likely it was to lead to an approach that did not rely exclusively on police resources or police methods. Changing police officers' views of the sources of the problem changed the nature of the response that seemed appropriate.

B. Evaluating Community Policing

In many respects, the concept of community policing is as old as policing itself. Indeed, many think it is redundant to add the word community to policing since policing, by definition, assumes the existence of a political community with shared norms codified in laws and enforced with day-to-day support from citizens (Cain 1973, pp. 21–25).

To others, adding the word "community" to policing serves to remind the police that the community is an important resource to tap in pursuing the goals of crime reduction and that the cultivation of community support must be an operational goal of policing, influencing decisions about the priority given to certain kinds of activities and about the overall structure of the organization.

To still others, adding the word "community" to policing redefines the ends as well as the means of policing. In this view, the goal of policing is not just to reduce crime but also to reduce fears, restore civility in public spaces, and guarantee the rights of democratic citizens; in short, it is to create secure and tolerant democratic communities. In both these latter cases, advocates of community policing think it is important to add the word to the enterprise of policing because it focuses the attention of police departments on their relationship to the communities they police, and that is an important corrective to the style of policing that had emerged under the professional model of policing.

1. *Team Policing.* The urgency of maintaining a close connection between the police and the community was brought home to professionally oriented police departments toward the end of the 1960s when they confronted large-scale urban unrest. Disciplined, competent, professionalized police forces found themselves unable to deal with this problem. One despairing member of the Los Angeles Police Department now recalls the experience of the Watts riot: "Everything we believed would be effective didn't work. We withdrew officers; that didn't work. We put more officers in; that didn't work. We used our black and liaison officers; that didn't work" (Kennedy 1986, p. x). On review, the Los Angeles Police Department concluded that it had failed because it had lost touch with the communities it policed, and with that, it had lost a crucial capacity to enforce the laws of the state.

Why the police had lost touch was not hard to understand. Like most professional police departments, the Los Angeles Police Department had shifted away from an organizational structure based on local neighborhoods. Geographically based precincts had given way to functional or programmatic units. And while the patrol division retained a geographical structure, centralized dispatching systems had made all the patrol cars available for dispatching throughout the city. The focus of the department had become citywide rather than local.

The solution to this problem, initiated by Chief Edward Davis in 1970, was to reestablish a sense of territorial responsibility in the basic structure of the police department's operations (Kennedy 1986). Davis divided his patrol force into two different kinds of patrol unit. One unit (called the "X car") was available to be dispatched throughout the city as needed. The other unit (called the "basic car") was to be kept in a given geographical area. The dispatchers were instructed to give the "basic car" the first crack at calls within its own service delivery area, and to refrain from dispatching it to other parts of the city except in dire emergencies. In addition, Davis established the position of "senior lead officer" to be assigned to the basic car. In return for greater rank and higher pay, this officer assumed a broader set of responsibilities for establishing and maintaining liaison with local communities.

Davis went further several years later. In 1973, he committed his organization to a concept called "team policing" to give the organization an even stronger sense of geographic accountability. The city was divided into seventy geographic units, each consisting of three to five basic patrol cars. A lieutenant was placed in charge of each area. In an important innovation, the lieutenant commanded not only patrol units but also detectives and representatives of specialist units such as traffic, narcotics, and juveniles, depending on the area's problems. In effect, the lieutenants became minichiefs of small territories. They were told that they were accountable for only one thing: "Whether conditions improved in their areas of responsibility or did not deteriorate." Here was the first modern model of what is becoming community policing.

At this stage, by the mid-1970s, many departments were experimenting with team policing. What evaluations were completed showed generally positive results: when the programs were fielded and sustained, they seemed to enjoy popularity with citizens and police and to produce some improvements in neighborhood conditions, including reductions in crime (Sherman, Milton, and Kelly 1973; Koenig, Blahna, and Petrick 1979).

Other studies, however, documented the enormous difficulty of introducing and sustaining team policing in police departments committed to professional crime fighting. In Dallas, a skilled police executive, supported by substantial outside resources, was unable to implement a reform program (Kelling and Wycoff 1978). In many other cities, successful team-policing programs were unaccountably abandoned despite their apparent success (Sherman, Milton, and Kelly 1973). Even Los Angeles eliminated team policing in 1979 (Kennedy 1986, p. 8).

Why team policing seemed to disappear despite its apparent successes remains obscure. Some blame declining police resources and the dramatic increase in calls for service that made it impossible for large city police departments to sustain the commitment to maintain geographic responsibility. Others see the culprit in the determined opposition of midlevel managers who resented the increasing independence and autonomy of the sergeants and patrol officers who worked on the teams (Sherman 1986, p. 365). Still others think that the schemes fell to the power of the police culture, which preferred professional isolation to close engagement with the community. Whatever the exact reason, it gradually became clear that team policing could not be introduced and sustained within organizations whose dominant purpose was something else and whose culture would not support it. As long as the organization's most important task was getting to calls on time, and as long as the organization remained a steep hierarchy of commanders, it would be hard to fit team policing into existing police organizations.

2. *Community Relations Units.* A different effort to restore strong working relationships between the police and the community lay in the creation of community relations units. These units have had a long but checkered history (Geary 1975; Walker 1980).

Some were created in the mid-fifties as part of a concerted program undertaken by chiefs to develop public support for policing and overcome "the attitudes of contempt that middle-class citizens held toward the police" (Geary 1975, pp. 373–74). These units arranged for police officers to visit schools and speak at meetings of civic associations in order to communicate the police perspective.

Other community relations units, created in response to riots in the 1940s and 1960s, were designed to help the police shore up relations with minority communities and to help prevent riots. Goldstein (1990) has described the activities and significance of these units: "The units sponsored Officer Friendly programs, maintained contacts with civil rights activists, monitored demonstrations, attended meetings of militant groups, and advised command staff on rising tensions. . . . The value of these units . . . was, in my view, a major factor alerting police chiefs to the potential of what has now emerged as community policing."

Still other community relations units sought to enlist direct citizen participation in specific crime-control efforts (Bickman et al. 1976). At first, they concentrated on encouraging citizens to call the police when suspected crimes were occurring. Later, they emphasized crime prevention. They helped citizens analyze their own vulnerabilities through security surveys. They encouraged citizens to mark their property to make it easier for the police to identify property as stolen in investigations and to facilitate its return. They sought to form citizen block watches in which citizens agreed to watch one another's homes.

Unfortunately, these latter efforts were not successfully evaluated. The exact nature and scale of police efforts in this area remains obscure, as are their effects on levels of crime and attitudes toward the police. Consequently, we do not really know whether these police initiatives reduced crime or calmed fears.

What these varied uses of community relations units reveal, however, is how confused the police are about the functions that improved community relations are supposed to serve, and how the units should organize to secure whatever benefits are associated with performing this function well. Many police continue to think that the most important purpose of improved community relations is to build support for policing: community relations units should be megaphones for the department and its purposes rather than antennae tuned into neighborhood concerns. Many police remain skeptical about the operational utility of mobilizing citizens to help them prevent and control crime—particularly when those citizens seem to have little respect or affection for the police.

Even worse, they succumb to the common police tendency to deal with particular problems by forming special squads. (As a saying in the London Metropolitan Police puts it, "When in doubt, form a squad and rush about" [Sparrow, Moore, and Kennedy 1990].) Four adverse consequences flow from concentrating the responsibility for effective community relations in a special squad.

First, by isolating the function in a specialized unit, it becomes vulnerable to organizational ridicule. This often occurred. The community relations units became known as the "grin and wave" or "rubber gun" squads.

Second, once a special squad is formed, everyone else in the department is seemingly relieved of responsibility for enhancing the quality of community relations. That has become the responsibility of the community relations unit.

Third, if the community relations unit should obtain important information about community concerns or ways in which the community might be able to help the department, it is difficult to make those observations heard inside the police department—particularly if what they have to report is bad news or imposes unwelcome demands on the rest of the organization. Goldstein (1990) described the dilemma for officers charged with maintaining liaison with racial minorities: "Officers were often caught in a double-bind, expected by department personnel to stamp out any sign of unrest and expected by minority communities to achieve changes in police practices affecting them."

Fourth, the organization no longer looks for other ways to improve community relations. It does not consider the possibility that the right way to improve community relations is to make every patrol officer a community relations officer, or to make special efforts to ensure that its organizations are representative of the best from the neighborhoods it polices.

In short, while the establishment of community relations units reveals the continuing vitality of the important idea that the police must
stay close to the communities they police, it also indicates how difficult
it is for that idea to begin to influence the operations of the entire
department. The units operate to insulate most of the department from
the continuing challenge of sustaining links to the community that can
serve not only as a basis of support for policing but also as a conduit
for community demands on police agencies and an opportunity to enlist
community groups in operational efforts to control crime and improve
the quality of life.

3. *Community Crime Prevention Programs.*   Team policing and community relations units were largely police-initiated responses to the
sense that there was an untapped potential in the community for dealing more effectively with crime problems. At the same time that the
police were experimenting with these approaches, a series of field experiments was undertaken to test crime prevention programs initiated
by communities themselves—sometimes in alliance with the police. In
many respects, these programs resembled the activities that were being
carried out by police departments through their community relations
units. As one commentator described them: "The fundamental philosophy of community crime prevention is embodied in the notion that the
most effective means of combating crime must involve residents in the
proactive interventions and participatory projects aimed at reducing or
precluding the opportunity for crime to occur in their neighborhoods.
In practice, this involvement translates into a wide range of activities
including resident patrols, citizen crime reporting systems, block
watch programs, home security surveys, property marking projects,
police community councils, and a variety of plans for changing the
physical environment" (Rosenbaum 1986, p. 19). The most important
difference was that these programs were usually designed, executed,
and evaluated outside of police departments.

Rosenbaum (1986) summarized four significant experiments in
community-based crime prevention efforts: the Seattle Community
Crime Prevention Program conducted in the early 1970s; the Portland
Burglary Prevention Program;[2] the Hartford Community Crime Prevention Program; and the Urban Crime Prevention Program in Chicago. These particular programs were selected because the methodol-

---

[2] This was managed by the Portland Police Department Community Relations Unit,
but the unit was staffed by civilians.

ogy for evaluation was particularly strong; the program designs and execution apparently were also strong.

The two programs directed at burglary (the Seattle and Portland programs) seemed to achieve reductions in burglary in the impact areas. The Hartford program, which relied on community mobilization and physical arrangements, also seemed to produce short-run effects on robbery and burglary and citizens' sense of personal security. Moreover, the effort and its effects might have been extended, had the police not stopped supporting the effort. The only effort that seems to have failed is the broad community organization effort that was undertaken in Chicago. Thus these studies suggest that narrowly targeted, well-designed and executed programs that seek to mobilize citizens to produce crime preventive effects can reduce the incidence of important crimes such as robbery and burglary.

4. *Fear Reduction and Foot Patrol.* Beginning in the early 1980s, the concept of community policing began once again to gather momentum within the world of policing. This time, however, both the ends and the means of policing were redefined.

The initial spark came from the findings of experiments with foot patrol in Newark, New Jersey, and Flint, Michigan. These experiments concluded that added foot patrols did not reduce property and violent crime but that, unlike the use of motorized patrol, the efforts were noticed by citizens and succeeded in reducing citizens' fears (Police Foundation 1981; Trojanowicz 1982). The Flint experiment was sufficiently popular to lead to passage of a special tax to support the program; the total number of calls to central dispatching stations for service declined (Trojanowicz 1982).

In the usual course of things, these findings would have fallen on deaf ears because they did not report any significant impact on crime. But in the mid-eighties, when these reports were published, attention was shifting from preoccupation with crime to a growing concern over fear about crime as a problem in its own right. Fear began to claim this status partly because its costs were increasingly being recognized as a major, if not the single largest, component of the overall social costs of crime (Cohen, Miller, and Rossman 1990, pp. 64–79), and partly because it was becoming clearer that fear of crime was curiously disconnected from objective levels of victimization (Skogan 1987). Once fear was recognized as a problem in its own right, the foot patrol experiments became much more important because they suggested that the fear-reducing effect of foot patrol was potentially quite valuable.

This line of thought was boosted when Wilson and Kelling (1982) published "Broken Windows" in the *Atlantic Monthly*, which argued that fear was not only a problem in its own right but also a cause of both crime and neighborhood degradation. They argued that the minor events and incivilities that frightened people, far from being a distraction for police departments, should be identified as key targets of police action. The ongoing disorder, if left unattended, would lead to still more disorder, crime, and neighborhood degradation. More recently, these arguments have been supported with some empirical evidence (Skogan 1990).

Impressed by these arguments, police agencies began altering their operations to see if they could influence levels of fear in the community and, in turn, halt cycles of more fear, crime, and decline. The Los Angeles Police Department conducted fear-reducing efforts in the Wilshire District (Sparrow, Moore, and Kennedy 1990). The Baltimore County Police Department decided to respond to some frightening murders not with more police patrols but with more sustained efforts to discover and alleviate the sources of fear (Taft 1986; Kennedy 1990). The National Institute of Justice sponsored two major experiments in Houston, Texas, and Newark, New Jersey, to determine whether the police could reduce levels of fear by such activities as increasing foot patrol, establishing neighborhood ministations, publishing newsletters, or cracking down on disorderly conditions in public transportation (Pate et al. 1986).

The conclusions of the fear reduction experiments were basically encouraging—at least with respect to the police capacity to still fears. James Q. Wilson summarized the results of the two experiments: "In Houston . . . opening a neighborhood police station, contacting the citizens about their problems, and stimulating the formation of neighborhood organizations where none had existed can help reduce the fear of crime and even reduce the actual level of victimization" (1989, p. ii). As to the more complex question of whether fear reductions will stimulate neighborhood responses that reduce crime and prevent urban decline, the jury is still out (Greene and Taylor 1988).

III. Criticisms and Cautions

The basic logic of problem-solving and community policing, the anecdotal successes, and the positive evaluations of operational programs offer reasons to believe that problem-solving and community policing can be effective in dealing with crime and enhancing security in the general population. But even if the empirical evidence were more complete, the case for adopting these new strategies of policing would still be insufficient, for, in evaluating an overall strategy, other, broader considerations come into play.

To evaluate an organizational strategy in the public sector, one must consider whether the new strategy is well founded as well as effective. A well-founded strategy should honor historical experience, operate in accord with important public values, and be properly accountable to the public. Also of concern are long-run institutional effects of the change in strategy on such things as the future lawfulness of policing, its standing vis-à-vis other public agencies, and its importance relative to private security. In this domain, problem-solving and community policing encounter sharp criticisms (Greene and Mastrofski 1988).

Bayley (1988) identifies a dozen serious threats to the quality of policing that could result from a shift in strategy toward problem-solving and community policing:

1) reduced crime-control effectiveness;

2) deteriorating will to maintain order in the face of violence;

3) an unseemly escape from accountability for crime control;

4) increased grass-roots political power for police departments and their leaders that threatens to distort the proper political processes of cities;

5) increased bureaucratic power for police departments and their leaders that threatens to distort proper governmental processes;

6) increased police/governmental involvement in community affairs and private lives to the disadvantage of liberty and privacy;

7) increased risks that the law will be enforced in discriminatory, unequal ways that vary from one neighborhood to another;

8) erosion of constitutional rights through the encouragement of street-level justice and the encouragement of vigilantism by citizens;

9) increased unfairness in the allocation of police services across neighborhoods, with wealthier, more powerful communities claiming more than their fair share;

10) losses in effective managerial control as a consequence of decentralization;

11) loss of citywide accountability and control as a consequence of decentralization; and

12) diminished professionalism among officers.

A. The Power of the Values of Professional Law Enforcement

Taken individually and as a whole, this list is a serious indictment of the foundations of problem-solving and community policing. To help in addressing these objectives, however, it is worth noting that much of their power derives from the belief that any relaxation of the commitment to the fundamental values and beliefs that have guided police reformers over the past generation threatens to lead the police astray. In effect, the criticisms assume that the past strategy of policing, including the values and assumptions that guided it, was the appropriate one, and any deviation from the orthodoxy must be suspect. To see the grip that the image of professional law enforcement has on our imagination and orientations to policing, consider Bayley's particular criticisms at one higher level of abstraction than the one at which they are presented.

The first three criticisms (loss of crime-control effectiveness, loss of will to maintain order, and escape from accountability for crime control) express the continuing conviction that crime control is the primary—even exclusive—focus of the police. Given this perspective, one would quite naturally be concerned that any broadening of police responsibilities to include fear, urban disorder, and the variety of emergencies that prompt citizens' calls will weaken policing by diluting its focus on serious predatory crime.

Points 4–6 (increased political power, increased bureaucratic power, and increased governmental influence over private affairs) reflect the continuing concern of a liberal democratic society that the police might become too powerful and intrusive a governmental institution. They help to remind us that one of the reasons the sharp focus on serious crime seemed so appropriate in the strategy of professional law enforcement was not only to help the police become successful in that enterprise but also to keep them out of many other social affairs narrowly focused on that task. Since any growth in police power could be viewed as a long-term threat to freedom, it was important to keep the police narrowly focused on serious crime, and reliant primarily on reactive methods of patrol and investigation.

Points 7–9 (discriminatory enforcement, erosion of civil liberties, and unequal distribution of police resources) focus on the possibility that the determined efforts of the last generation of reformers to make the police conform to important legal values such as fairness, impartiality, and respect for the constitutional rights of suspected criminals will be undermined by bringing the police into contact once again with politics—the old enemy of these values. Politics threatens these values because the unequal distribution of private power and privilege is believed to work through politics to shape the enforcement of the law

(Black 1980). To the extent that the police are once again brought into a close embrace with communities, some of the most important successes of past reforms are threatened.

The last triad of criticisms (loss of managerial control, loss of city-wide accountability and control, and loss of professionalism) reflects the conviction that tight, centralized control was the only way to ensure that the police performed competently in their jobs and complied with the important legal values that should guide them. Since problem-solving and community policing encourage decentralization, both control and efficient citywide allocations are threatened by any shift in this direction.

The fears that we have about community and problem-solving policing are the natural fears associated with moving away from a powerful set of beliefs and assumptions that have guided us in the past. Arguably, such fears are characteristic of any "revolutionary" period in which powerful values and beliefs that have long lighted the path toward improvement are challenged by new ideas. To say that the criticisms are psychologically powerful because they are closely aligned with our prior beliefs and assumptions, however, is not to disparage their substantive content. Indeed, there *are* enduring social values embedded in the strategy of professional law enforcement that *do* continue to define important virtues of police organizations. It is simply to remind us that it is sometimes difficult to be fully objective about new possibilities when the grip of past commitments holds us so tightly that we can hardly find the room to imagine how things could be different.

So, to defend problem-solving or community policing against these powerful criticisms it is necessary to consider once again the arguments that are made for community and problem-solving policing in terms of the values that were so important to the strategy of professional law enforcement: namely the sharp focus on crime control as the predominant objective of the police; the interest in limiting the power of the police; the promotion of legal values such as fairness, nonintrusiveness, and constitutionalism; and the reliance on centralized control to achieve these objectives.

B. Emphasizing Crime Fighting

Initially, the sharp focus on crime fighting as the dominant objective of the police is justified on practical grounds. It is an urgent public problem. The police are uniquely qualified to meet the challenge. It makes sense that crime should be the primary focus of police attention.

But, as noted above, the focus on crime fighting is also linked to concerns about keeping the police from becoming too powerful and too intrusive in society. If the police were to use all of their capabilities to help society deal with its problems, they might become too powerful a force in the community and stunt the development of other less coercive social institutions. Or if the police were to intrude in areas where the law offered little guidance or control of their activities, they might well behave badly. Thus, the concern about keeping the sharp focus on crime fighting is closely tied to concerns about controlling the police as well as using them effectively.

I consider below whether community and problem-solving policing threaten to increase the power of the police and weaken their commitment to legal values. At this stage, it is worth addressing the narrower question of whether crime control, *particularly as it is now performed*, is the most important or only valuable use of police resources.

Initially, it seems that there is a great deal of weight behind the critics' concerns that crime-control effectiveness might be diluted. After all, it is impossible to argue that crime is not now an urgent problem for urban communities. And it seems difficult to argue that effectiveness in combating crime would not be diluted if the police were asked to shoulder additional responsibilities.

What advocates of problem-solving and community policing argue, however, is not that crime control should be deemphasized. They agree that crime-control effectiveness must remain the principal touchstone against which police strategies should be evaluated. Instead, they argue that there may be better ways of controlling crime than the techniques common to professional law enforcement. In particular, they are interested in techniques that focus less on reacting to crimes and more on prevention and that rely less on the police themselves and more on the capacities of communities and other public agencies.

They also argue that many activities that do not look like direct crime-control activities may, nonetheless, help build relations with communities that will increase crime-control effectiveness in the future and are, in any case, valuable in reducing fears and improving the quality of neighborhood life. For example, dealing with instances of minor disorder may not only still fears in the community and enhance the neighborhood's morale but also increase the likelihood that citizens will help the police solve crimes (Wilson and Kelling 1982; Skogan 1990).

Thus the real target of those who advocate problem-solving and community policing is not the central focus on crime control as the dominant purpose of the police; it is, instead, the equation of an *exclusive* focus on crime control pursued through a *particular set of operational tactics* with effective crime control. In their view, a somewhat more indirect approach may hold more potential for controlling crime than the direct methods of professional law enforcement, and may, in addition, achieve other valuable benefits such as reducing fears and enhancing citizens' confidence in the police.

C. Limiting the Power of the Police as an Institution

As the police become more responsive to community concerns and more skilled in using crime-prevention and problem-solving techniques, there is the risk that they will become politically and bureaucratically more powerful, and that they will intrude more deeply into the affairs of citizens and other government agencies. As noted above, this conflicts with the desire to keep the police from becoming too powerful an institution in the society.

The desire to limit the power of the police is a patently important objective in a liberal society. Yet, advocates of community and problem-solving policing would argue that slavish adherence to this principle would prevent the police from making important contributions to the solutions of today's urban problems. Most current analyses of conditions in cities indicate a significant breakdown in the important mechanisms of informal social control including responsibilities to family and community. The collapse of these intermediate institutions allow disorder, crime, and fear to flourish.

In this situation, several scenarios are possible. If formal controls are not increased (e.g., if the police remain indifferent to drugs and violence on city streets), the quality of life may continue to deteriorate for many living in the distressed communities. If formal controls are expanded to fill the void (e.g., if police establish curfews and street sweeps), then conditions may improve, but only at the expense of further weakening informal control mechanisms and increasing the dependence and vulnerability of the local communities to state control.

Better than either of these approaches would be one in which the formal social controls were used in ways that were designed to strengthen informal social control (e.g., if the police were to engage in joint problem-solving efforts with those elements of the community that were concerned about alleviating the problems). It is precisely this latter approach that is recommended by problem-solving and community policing. So while these approaches may use the police more intensively in dealing with social problems than would be ideal, they may be appropriate in the relatively desperate circumstance in which we now find ourselves.

There is one additional reason to be interested in increasing rather than holding constant or diminishing the overall strength of policing as a community institution. That reason has to do with the ominous growth of private policing and private security efforts. The reason these are growing is that citizens are losing confidence in the police. The consequence of that growth is potentially disastrous since private policing, even more than politicized public policing, will be sure to be marked by both unfairness and contempt for the rights of the accused.

Indeed, this point reminds us that one of the main reasons public police forces were initially established was not only to increase the overall level of social control but also to produce an alternative to private vengeance and enhance the overall fairness of control efforts. In this respect, the police are a bastion of democratic values rather than a threat to them, and their enhanced standing in the community could become a celebration of these values rather than an attack.

D. Promoting Fairness, Restraint, and Other Legal Values

Critics are also right to focus attention on the possibility that important legal values might be sacrificed by shifting away from the strategy of professional law enforcement to a strategy of community or problem-solving policing. Once policing is cut loose from an obsessive focus with enforcing law and brought back in touch with community concerns, it is entirely possible that the corruption, discrimination, and brutality that once shamed policing will return with new vigor or become an even more exaggerated feature of policing than it is now.

If this were likely, it would be an important reason in itself to resist pressures to change the strategy, for no one would quarrel with the importance of promoting compliance with the legal values of fairness, impartiality, and respect for individual rights. Surely one of the proudest accomplishments of the last generation of policing has been the wider embrace of these values as defining characteristics of quality policing. The strategy of professional law enforcement had a great deal to do with this.

How the commitment to these values would be affected by a shift to problem solving or community policing, however, remains unclear. To critics, a serious danger appears to be that both strategies seek to establish closer, more intimate connections with those being policed. Such intimacy threatens police fairness and impartiality. In individual incidents, the police might be tempted to side with those whom they have come to know well or those who are locally influential. In deploying forces across a city, the police may be tempted to provide better service to those with whom they identify or those who are politically powerful. Such fears seem particularly apt for departments that never embraced the legal values in the first place. Hence, there are reasons to be concerned.

In assessing the magnitude of the risks associated with the change, however, several things are worth noting. At best, the achievement of professional law enforcement in promoting legal values within police departments has been incomplete. In many departments, legal values are still seen as burdensome constraints rather than as important goals to be expressed in, and protected by, police operations.

Part of the reason may be that these values have been imposed from the outside rather than championed from the inside. It seems significant, then, that many of the chiefs who have committed their departments to problem-solving or community policing have spent time developing explicit value statements to guide the operations of their departments, and that the protection of constitutional values figures far more prominently in these statements than it has in the explicit statements of many other police departments (Wasserman and Moore 1988). Of course, words on paper are not the same as cultural commitment, but it is one of the ways that a culture supporting these values is created.

It may also be important that police departments that engage in problem-solving and community policing will frequently find themselves in situations in which they will be pressured to take actions by some groups that abridge the rights of others or asked to resolve disputes among citizens each of whom has reasonable claims. In dealing professionally with such situations, the police may discover for themselves the reasons why they cannot behave illegally. They may also end up communicating to citizens why they, too, must develop tolerance for the rights of others. In short, in the experience of negotiating solutions to problems among several interested parties, the police will learn to rely on legal principles. That, in turn, may encourage them to become "street-corner judges" as well as "street-corner politicians" (Muir 1977). They might also rediscover why it was once considered plausible that they should be part of the judicial branch of government rather than the executive and might thereby discover a commitment to legal values that has so far eluded them.

It would be wrong to be too optimistic about these possibilities. And it is right to be concerned about the threat that district and neighborhood politics pose for the fairness of police operations. But it can reasonably be argued that a relentless police focus on crime-control effectiveness encourages the police to view legal values as constraints rather than as goals. If police were more responsible for ordering relationships in the community, they would more often find legal values a useful guide to proper conduct than they now do.

In any case, the concerns about legal values remind us that problem-solving and community policing must be seen as strategies that build on the past successes of professional law enforcement rather than on abandonment of these principles in favor of a return to the "good old days." The accomplishments of several decades of reform efforts in creating legal culture in the police departments should be preserved and enhanced rather than overturned.

E. Maintaining Central Control

The view that centralized control is essential for making the police law abiding and competent also now seems more suspect than it once did. It has long been apparent that centralized control cannot reliably control police conduct since some amount of irreducible discretion always remained to officers (Elmore 1978). Yet police continued to develop these methods since no other ways to control discretion seemed available.

More recently, other control mechanisms have become more apparent. The threat of civil liability, for example, may be doing more to control misconduct than any amount of effective supervision (McCoy 1985). Some police departments are looking to administrative methods used by industry that rely on the promotion of organizational values, worker participation, and mutual responsibility to promote quality in products and operations rather than continuing to rely on close supervision and "defect finding" (Hatry and Greiner 1986). Others are looking to peer review and other methods of accountability common in professional organizations such as hospitals and law firms for new models of assuring responsible professionalism (Couper and Lobitz 1991). While it is not clear whether these methods will work in policing, they have helped expand current thinking about other kinds of administrative arrangements that can assure quality and integrity in police operations at least as well as even closer supervision.

F. Summary

An advocate of problem-solving and community policing could make a response to the principal criticisms of skeptics. Whether skeptics or advocates will ultimately be proven right remains unclear.

The criticisms do, however, make three key points. First, problem-solving and community policing must be seen and managed as an advance, not as a retreat. Crime-control effectiveness remains an important goal. Lawful arrests remain an important operational tool. Commitment to the law and professionalism remain important bases of professionalism. None of these hard-won goals of the reform era should be abandoned.

Second, the important reform project of integrating the commitment to the law and to constitutional rights into the ideology and operations of the police department remains incomplete. Under community or problem-solving policing, with their emphases on officer and local discretion, the need to embrace these values fully increases rather than decreases. Exactly how to encourage police commitment to legal values remains unclear, but it may be advanced by articulating those values from inside police departments rather than by imposing them from the outside and by asking the police to undertake tasks where legal principles will help them rather than restrain them.

Third, the mechanisms of external and internal accountability need a great deal of work to ensure that the police are pursuing appropriate goals using appropriate means. One of the key ideas of both problem-solving and community policing is that external accountability to the community and to the agencies of municipal government should increase rather than decrease. Both strategies call for experiments with new methods for promoting internal and external accountability including after-the-fact peer evaluations of performance.

Fourth, standards for recruiting and training officers are both raised and changed under problem-solving and community policing. These new strategies are much more dependent on the initiative and resourcefulness of individual officers than is the current strategy that treats all patrol officers as employees who must be continuously supervised. The strategies' effectiveness depends on the officer's knowledge of his local community and government. It is not so much that commitment to professionalism is ending as that it is changing its focus and accelerating. Much more will be expected of officers in the future than was true in the past.

Nobody wants to be too Pollyannaish about the ease with which these ongoing problems of policing may be overcome. But there are so many attractive trends occurring that it is hard to resist encouraging them a little—particularly if we recall both the virtues and the shortcomings of the reform era of policing. Even David Bayley agrees that it would be advisable to continue experimenting with these new concepts, as long as we remain alert to the hazards.

IV. Problems in Implementation

For a new policing strategy to be attractive, it must be feasible for police departments to shift from their current strategy to a new one. It is not enough that there be evidence that the strategy could successfully control crime and promote security. Nor is it enough that the concept withstand skepticism about its value.

It is not easy to change the overall strategy of an organization (Sparrow 1988; Brown 1989). That no police organizations in the United States have successfully made this change is powerful evidence of how hard it is. Many police executives have begun this process, however, revealing that the foreseeable obstacles are not entirely insurmountable and providing clues to what particular methods might be useful in overcoming the problems (Sparrow, Moore, and Kennedy 1990).

A. Limited Resources

The most common practical objection is that there are simply not enough resources available in the department to meet simultaneously the demands of responding rapidly to calls for service, interrupting and solving crimes, and engaging in the crime-preventive, fear-reducing activities associated with problem-solving and community policing. Something has to give. In a world in which both citizens and police look to rapid responses to calls for service as a mark of quality police services, proactive policing methods will always be the thing to give. If this is true, problem-solving and community policing will be consigned to the status of attractive luxuries.

Such observations seem to doom prospects even for *programs* in problem-solving and community policing, let alone entire shifts in organizational strategy. Skilled police executives are discovering, however, that there are ways out of this apparently unresolvable dilemma.

First, the new strategies of policing—first introduced as add-on programs—may prove sufficiently popular to justify additional resources for police departments. It is one thing for citizens and mayors to pour money into police departments pursuing the traditional strategy of policing; it is quite another for them to pay for a strategy of policing that seems more responsive to their concerns. Citizens of Flint, Michigan, an economically distressed community, were opposed to general tax increases but were, nonetheless, willing to support a tax increase to expand foot patrols (Trojanowicz 1982). Similarly, in New York City, the Community Patrol Officers Program has been sufficiently popular to have, to some degree, insulated the police department from absorbing the full share of budget cuts that they would otherwise have been expected to take.

Second, even if resources are not available from the outside, aggressive managers can often free up additional resources inside the organization. Using civilian personnel for some functions and reorganizing shifts to fit manpower more to demands for work beckon as potential sources of additional resources. So does the elimination of special squads that have emerged as a consequence of the tendency to create new squads to solve new problems (Kennedy 1987). Dissolving such squads has the additional virtue of spreading the accumulated expertise of the special unit more widely through the force. Other reallocation possibilities include reducing the number of layers of management and thinning ranks of headquarters personnel (Philadelphia Police Study Task Force 1987). These are radical and difficult steps, but some managers have taken them.

Third, proven technologies can alleviate pressures that come from unmanaged calls for service (Farmer 1981). Calls can be ranked in order of priority, thereby eliminating a large fraction of the need for an emergency response to incoming calls. Citizens can be educated to accept a certain delay in the police response. They can be asked to fill out the reports that officers would complete if they arrived on the scene and to deliver reports to a police station. These innovations reduce pressure for emergency responses and restore some opportunities to the police for proactive methods of policing.

Fourth, strategies are available for addressing needs before incidents occur that lead to calls. There is a structure to the calls for service received by a police department (Pierce, Spaar, and Briggs 1984; Sherman et al. 1987; Spelman and Eck 1989). A small fraction of locations and people account for a very large proportion of calls. It is possible, then, that overall calls for service might go down if the police designed effective responses to the problems underlying the repeat incidents. At a minimum, the proactive police might intercept calls from citizens that would otherwise reach police dispatchers.

It is by no means clear, then, that police executives are without resources for implementing community policing. Some are finding ways to do it.

B. Uncertainty and Accountability

A second difficulty is that there will be turmoil and confusion in the process of transition. Moreover, at the end, there is no guarantee that things will be better. To many police executives, it seems irresponsible and dangerous to plunge into this process of change with uncertain payoff. Indeed, as one chief explained when asked about how he felt when he committed his organization to a strategy of community policing, "I felt like I had just jumped off a cliff" (Sparrow, Moore, and Kennedy 1990). They fear, quite reasonably, that they will be held accountable to standards and images from the past and that their performance in running the organization will look bad.

That is certainly a problem, but it has a solution. It consists of creating an outside constituency for change that will hold the commissioner and the police department accountable to new standards, not the old ones (Moore 1990). Kevin Tucker did this in beginning to turn the Philadelphia Police Department around, and that has been what has allowed Sir Kenneth Newman in London, England, and John Avery in New South Wales, Australia, to advance as far as they have in shifting the course of their organizations (Sparrow, Moore, and Kennedy 1990). Mobilizing an outside constituency for change is also consistent with the goal of attracting additional outside resources, for the outside constituency is often a route to new resources.

C. Changing the Culture of Policing

Probably the biggest obstacle facing anyone who would implement a new strategy of policing is the difficulty of changing the ongoing culture of policing (Sparrow, Moore, and Kennedy 1990). That culture is deeply entrenched in the minds and souls of people now doing the work (Manning, in this volume). It is sustained by current administrative arrangements.

Three approaches are available for changing the culture. First, the organizations should be opened to many more external pressures than they now feel. This means embracing openness as a value and changing the organizational structure so that everyone in the organization is exposed to much more contact with relevant communities than they now are (Sparrow, Moore, and Kennedy 1990). This requires that police executives take steps to get officers out from behind the wheels of their cars and midlevel managers out from behind their desks and reports. Close contact with communities must be made at these levels as well as at the chief's level.

Second, the dominant values of the organization must be articulated (Wasserman and Moore 1988). Such a step is critical for establishing terms of accountability and inviting a partnership with outside groups. It is also critical for announcing to those inside the police department what is expected and what important values they must serve. It is especially critical in police organizations in which direct supervision cannot control behavior because much of the work takes place beyond the eyes of the supervisors.

Third, aspects of existing administrative systems that are inconsistent with new values must be changed. This includes changing from centralized, functional organizations to decentralized, geographic organizations. It means attracting personnel moved by the spirit of service rather than the spirit of adventure and rewarding them for maintaining peace on their beats rather than making numbers of arrests. It means changing performance evaluations from those that emphasize levels of crime, volumes of arrests, and speed of response, to those that measure victimization and fear and community satisfaction with the quality of police service. Unless these systems are lined up to communicate a message to individual officers and managers that is consistent with the overall strategy of problem-solving or community policing, the strategy will not be successfully implemented.

V. Conclusions

Problem-solving and community policing represent interesting new concepts in policing. Evaluated as alternative strategies of policing, they show both promise and hazards. These hazards, though daunting, must be compared not with some ideal but with the current operational reality of policing as it now occurs. Against that standard, the benefits begin to look a little greater and the hazards a little smaller.

Key to the successful implementation of either of these ideas as an overall strategy of policing are efforts to build an outside constituency, and broaden the terms of police accountability. Key to that is articulating a set of values that can serve as a basic contract to guide the working partnership of the police and the community as they seek together to define and resolve the problems of crime and fear.

There is one further point worth making as one thinks about community and problem-solving policing as possible future strategies of policing. That has to do with the question of how the current drug crisis and the looming threat of more widespread violence will affect the potential success of these strategies. To many, the urgency of these problems constitutes an important reason to stand with the tried and true and resist any experimentation.

I tend to think the opposite. If there are any areas in which the strategies of problem-solving and community policing are likely to be most needed, it is in dealing with these particular problems. Surely, an important part of dealing with drugs is learning how to mobilize communities to resist drug dealing. Surely, an important part of dealing with random violence is dealing with rational and irrational fears. Surely, an important part of controlling riots is having networks of relationships that reach deeply into ethnic communities. If anything, then, these problems give impetus to further developments in problem-solving and community policing. It is an interesting time to be a student or manager in policing.

REFERENCES

Andrews, Kenneth R. 1971. *The Concept of Corporate Strategy*. Homewood, Ill.: Dow Jones-Irwin.

Bayley, David H. 1988. "Community Policing: A Report from the Devil's Advocate." In *Community Policing: Rhetoric or Reality*, edited by Jack R. Greene and Stephen D. Mastrofski. New York: Praeger.

———. In this volume. "Comparative Organization of the Police in English-speaking Countries."

Bickman, L., P. J. Lavrakas, S. K. Green, N. North-Walker, J. Edwards, S. Barkowski, and S. Shane-DuBow. 1976. *Citizen Crime Reporting Projects—National Evaluation Program—Phase 1: Summary Report*. Washington, D.C.: National Institute of Law Enforcement and Criminal Justice.

Bittner, Egon. 1970. *The Functions of the Police in Modern Society: Background Factors, Current Practices, and Possible Role Models*. Chevy Chase, Md.: National Institute of Mental Health.

Black, Donald. 1980. *The Manners and Customs of the Police*. New York: Academic Press.

Blumstein, Alfred, Jacqueline Cohen, and Daniel Nagin, eds. 1978. *Deterrence and Incapacitation: Estimating the Effects of Criminal Sanctions on Crime Rates.* Washington, D.C.: National Academy of Sciences.

Brown, Lee P. 1989. "Community Policing: A Practical Guide for Police Officials." *Police Chief*, August, pp. 72–82.

Cain, Maureen E. 1973. *Society and the Policeman's Role.* London: Routledge & Kegan Paul.

Civilian Review of the Police—the Experiences of American Cities. 1980. Hartford, Conn.: Hartford Institute of Criminal and Social Justice.

Clarke, Ronald V. 1983. "Situational Crime Prevention: Its Theoretical Basis and Practical Scope." In *Crime and Justice: An Annual Review of Research*, vol. 4, edited by Michael Tonry and Norval Morris. Chicago: University of Chicago Press.

Cohen, Jacqueline. 1978. "The Incapacitative Effect of Imprisonment: A Critical Review of the Literature." In *Deterrence and Incapacitation: Estimating the Effects of Criminal Sanctions on Crime Rates*, edited by Alfred Blumstein, Jacqueline Cohen, and Daniel Nagin. Washington, D.C.: National Academy of Sciences.

Cohen, Mark A., Ted R. Miller, and Shelli B. Rossman. 1990. "The Costs and Consequences of Violent Behavior in the U.S." Paper prepared for the Panel on the Understanding and Control of Violent Behavior, National Research Council, National Academy of Sciences, Washington, D.C.

Couper, David C., and Sabine H. Lobitz. 1991. *Quality Policing: The Madison Experience.* Washington, D.C.: Police Executive Research Forum.

Cunningham, William C., and Todd H. Taylor. 1985. *The Hallcrest Report: Private Security and Police in America.* Portland, Oreg.: Chancellor.

Eck, John E. 1983. *Solving Crimes: The Investigation of Burglary and Robbery.* Washington, D.C.: Police Executive Research Forum.

Eck, John E., and William Spelman. 1987. *Problem Solving: Problem-oriented Policing in Newport News.* Washington, D.C.: Police Executive Research Forum.

Elmore, Richard F. 1978. "Organizational Models of Social Program Implementation." *Public Policy* 26:185–228.

Farmer, Michael T. 1978. *Survey of Police Operational and Administrative Practices.* Washington, D.C.: Police Executive Research Forum.

———, ed. 1981. *Differential Police Response Strategies.* Washington, D.C.: Police Executive Research Forum.

Fogelson, Robert M. 1977. *Big-City Police.* Cambridge, Mass.: Harvard University Press.

Geary, David Patrick. 1975. "The Impact of Police-Community Relations on the Police System." In *Community Relations and the Administration of Justice*, edited by David Patrick Geary. New York: Wiley.

Geller, William A., ed. 1985. *Police Leadership in America: Crisis and Opportunity.* New York: Praeger.

Goldstein, Herman. 1979. "Improving Policing: A Problem-oriented Approach." *Crime and Delinquency* 25:236–58.

———. 1990. Personal communication with author, July 27.

Greene, Jack R., and Stephen D. Mastrofski, eds. 1988. *Community Policing: Rhetoric or Reality*. New York: Praeger.

Greene, Jack R., and Ralph B. Taylor. 1988. "Community-based Policing and Foot Patrol: Issues of Theory and Evaluation." In *Community Policing: Rhetoric or Reality*, edited by Jack R. Greene and Stephen D. Mastrofski. New York: Praeger.

Greenwood, Peter, with Allan Abrahamse. 1982. *Selective Incapacitation*. Santa Monica, Calif.: Rand.

Greenwood, Peter W., Jan M. Chaiken, and Joan Petersilia. 1977. *The Criminal Investigation Process*. Lexington, Mass.: Lexington.

Hatry, Harry P., and John M. Greiner. 1986. *Improving the Use of Quality Circles in Police Departments*. Washington, D.C.: U.S. Department of Justice, National Institute of Justice.

Kansas City Police Department. 1977–79. *Response Time Analysis*. 3 vols. Kansas City, Mo.: Board of Commissioners.

Kelling, George L. 1988. "Police and Communities: The Quiet Revolution." *Perspectives on Policing*, no. 1. Washington, D.C.: National Institute of Justice and Harvard University.

Kelling, George L., and Mark H. Moore. 1988. "The Evolving Strategy of Policing." *Perspectives on Policing*, no. 4. Washington, D.C.: National Institute of Justice and Harvard University.

Kelling, George L., Anthony M. Pate, Duane Dieckman, and Charles E. Brown. 1974. "The Kansas City Preventive Patrol Experiment: A Summary Report." Washington, D.C.: Police Foundation.

Kelling, George L., and Mary Ann Wycoff. 1978. *The Dallas Experience: Vol. 1: Organizational Reform*. Washington, D.C.: Police Foundation.

Kennedy, David M. 1986. "Neighborhood Policing in Los Angeles." Case no. C16-86-717.0. Cambridge, Mass.: Harvard University, Case Program of John F. Kennedy School of Government.

———. 1987. "Neighborhood Policing: The London Metropolitan Police Force." Case no. C15-87-770.0. Cambridge, Mass.: Harvard University, Case Program of John F. Kennedy School of Government.

———. 1990. "Fighting Fear in Baltimore County." Case no. C16-90-938.0. Cambridge, Mass.: Harvard University, Case Program of John F. Kennedy School of Government.

Klockars, Carl B. 1988. "The Rhetoric of Community Policing." In *Community Policing: Rhetoric or Reality*, edited by Jack R. Greene and Stephen D. Mastrofski. New York: Praeger.

Koenig, David J., John H. Blahna, and Richard L. Petrick. 1979. *Team Policing in St. Paul, Minnesota: An Evaluation of Two Years of Implementation*. St. Paul, Minn.: Team Police Evaluation Unit, Police Department.

Larson, Richard C., and Michael F. Cahn. 1985. "Synthesizing and Extending the Results of Police Patrol Studies." Research report. Washington, D.C.: U.S Department of Justice, National Institute of Justice.

Lavrakas, Paul J., and Dan A. Lewis. 1980. "Conceptualization and Measurement of Citizens' Crime Prevention Behaviors." *Journal of Research in Crime and Delinquency* 17:254–72.

Lavrakas, Paul J., J. Mormoyle, W. G. Skogan, E. J. Herz, G. Salem, and D. A. Lewis. 1981. *Factors Related to Citizen Involvement in Personal, Household, and Neighborhood Anti-crime Measures.* Washington D.C.: U.S Department of Justice, National Institute of Justice.

Lavrakas, Paul J., and Wesley J. Skogan. 1984. *Citizen Participation and Community Crime Prevention, 1979 Chicago Metropolitan Area Survey.* Evanston, Ill.: Northwestern University Center for Urban Affairs and Policy Research.

McCoy, Candace. 1985. "Lawsuits against Police: What Impact Do They Really Have?" In *Police Management Today: Issues and Case Studies*, edited by James J. Fyfe. Washington, D.C.: International City Management Association.

Manning, Peter K. In this volume. "Information Technologies and the Police."

Moore, Mark H. 1983a. "Invisible Offenses: A Challenge to Minimally Intrusive Law Enforcement." In *ABSCAM Ethics: Moral Issues and Deception in Law Enforcement*, edited by Gerald M. Caplan. Washington, D.C.: Police Foundation.

———.1983b. "Controlling Criminogenic Commodities: Drugs, Guns and Alcohol." In *Crime and Public Policy*, edited by James Q. Wilson. San Francisco, Calif.: ICS Press.

———. 1990. "Police Leadership: the Impossible Dream?" In *Impossible Jobs in Public Management*, edited by Erwin C. Hargrove and John C. Glidewell. Lawrence: University Press of Kansas.

Moore, Mark H., and George L. Kelling. 1983. " 'To Serve and Protect': Learning from Police History." *Public Interest* 70:265–81.

Moore, Mark H., and Darrel Stephens. 1991. *Police Organization and Management: Towards a New Managerial Orthodoxy.* Washington, D.C.: Police Executive Research Forum (forthcoming).

Moore, Mark H., and Robert C. Trojanowicz. 1988. "Corporate Strategies for Policing." *Perspectives on Policing*, no. 6. Washington, D.C.: National Institute of Justice and Harvard University.

Muir, W. K., Jr. 1977. *Police: Streetcorner Politicians.* Chicago: University of Chicago Press.

Neustadt, Richard E., and Ernest R. May. 1986. *Thinking in Time: The Uses of History for Decision Makers.* New York: Free Press.

Pate, Anthony M., Robert A. Bowers, and Ron Parks. 1976. "Three Approaches to Criminal Apprehension in Kansas City: An Evaluation Report." Washington, D.C.: Police Foundation.

Pate, Anthony M., Mary Ann Wycoff, Wesley G. Skogan, and Lawrence W. Sherman. 1986. "Reducing Fear of Crime in Houston and Newark: A Summary Report." Washington, D.C.: Police Foundation.

Philadelphia Police Study Task Force. 1987. *Philadelphia and Its Police: Toward a New Partnership.* Philadelphia: Police Department.

Pierce, Glen L., Susan A. Spaar, and LeBaron R. Briggs IV. 1984. "The Character of Police Work: Implications for the Delivery of Services." Report to the National Institute of Justice. Boston: Northeastern University Center for Applied Social Research.

Police Executive Research Forum. 1989. "Taking a Problem-oriented Approach to Drug Enforcement." Interim Report. Washington, D.C.: U.S. Department of Justice, Bureau of Justice Assistance.

Police Foundation. 1981. *The Newark Foot Patrol Experiment*. Washington, D.C.: Police Foundation.

Reiss, Albert J., Jr. 1971. *The Police and the Public*. New Haven, Conn.: Yale University Press.

————. 1985. *Policing a City's Central District: The Oakland Story*. Washington, D.C.: U.S. Government Printing Office.

————. 1988. *Private Employment of Public Police*. Washington, D.C.: U.S. Department of Justice, National Institute of Justice.

Rosenbaum, Dennis P., ed. 1986. *Community Crime Prevention: Does It Work?* Beverly Hills, Calif.: Sage.

Rubinstein, Jonathan. 1973. *City Police*. New York: Farrar, Straus & Giroux.

Scott, Eric J. 1981. *Calls for Service: Citizen Demand and Initial Police Response*. Washington, D.C.: U.S. Department of Justice, National Institute of Justice.

Shearing, Clifford D. In this volume. "The Relation between Public and Private Policing."

Shearing, Clifford D., and Philip C. Stenning. 1981. "Modern Private Security: Its Growth and Implications." In *Crime and Justice: An Annual Review of Research*, vol. 3, edited by Michael Tonry and Norval Morris. Chicago: University of Chicago Press.

Sherman, Lawrence W. 1986. "Policing Communities: What Works?" In *Communities and Crime*, edited by Albert J. Reiss, Jr., and Michael Tonry. Vol. 8 of *Crime and Justice: A Review of Research*, edited by Michael Tonry and Norval Morris. Chicago: University of Chicago Press.

————. 1990. Personal communication with author, April 13.

Sherman, Lawrence W., and Richard A. Berk. 1984. "The Minneapolis Domestic Violence Experiment." *Police Foundation Reports*. Washington, D.C.: Police Foundation.

Sherman, Lawrence W., et al. 1987. *Repeat Calls to the Police in Minneapolis*. Washington, D.C.: Crime Control Institute.

Sherman, Lawrence W., Catherine H. Milton, and Thomas V. Kelly. 1973. *Team Policing—Seven Case Studies*. Washington, D.C.: Police Foundation.

Skogan, Wesley G. 1977. "The Promise of Policing: Evaluating the Performance, Productivity, and Potential of Local Law Enforcement." Paper presented at Workshop on Policy Analysis in State and Local Government, Stony Brook: State University of New York.

————. 1986. "Fear of Crime and Neighborhood Change." In *Communities and Crime*, edited by Albert J. Reiss, Jr., and Michael Tonry. Vol. 8 of *Crime and Justice: A Review of Research*, edited by Michael Tonry and Norval Morris. Chicago: University of Chicago Press.

————. 1987. "The Impact of Victimization on Fear." *Crime and Delinquency* 33:135–54.

————. 1990. *Disorder and Decline: Crime and the Spiral of Decay in America's Neighborhoods*. New York: Free Press.

Skogan, Wesley G., and George E. Antunes. 1979. "Information, Apprehension, and Deterrence: Exploring the Limits of Police Productivity." *Journal of Criminal Justice* 7:217–42.

Skogan, Wesley G., and Michael G. Maxfield. 1981. *Coping with Crime—Individual and Neighborhood Reactions.* Beverly Hills, Calif.: Sage.

Skolnick, Jerome H., and David H. Bayley. 1986. *The New Blue Line: Police Innovation in Six American Cities.* New York: Free Press.

Sparrow, Malcolm K. 1988. "Implementing Community Policing." *Perspectives on Policing,* no. 9. Washington, D.C.: National Institute of Justice and Harvard University.

Sparrow, Malcolm K., Mark H. Moore, and David M. Kennedy. 1990. *Beyond 911: A New Era for Policing.* New York: Basic.

Spelman, William, and Dale K. Brown. 1984. *Calling the Police: Citizen Reporting of Serious Crime.* Washington, D.C.: U.S. Department of Justice, National Institute of Justice.

Spelman, William, and John E. Eck. 1989. "Sitting Ducks, Ravenous Wolves and Helping Hands: New Approaches to Urban Policing." *Public Affairs Comment,* pp. 1–9. Austin: University of Texas, Lyndon B. Johnson School of Public Affairs, Winter.

Stewart, James Q. 1986. "The Urban Strangler: How Crime Causes Poverty in the Inner City." *Policy Review* 37:2–6.

Taft, Philip B., Jr. 1986. *Fighting Fear: The Baltimore County C.O.P.E. Project.* Washington, D.C.: Police Executive Research Forum.

Trojanowicz, Robert C. 1982. *An Evaluation of the Neighborhood Foot Patrol Program in Flint, Michigan.* East Lansing: Michigan State University.

Tumin, Zachary. 1986. "Managing Relations with the Community." Working Paper no. 86-05-06. Cambridge, Mass.: Harvard University, John F. Kennedy School of Government. Program in Criminal Justice Policy and Management.

Vera Institute of Justice. 1988. *CPOP: Community Policing in Practice.* New York: Vera Institute of Justice.

Walker, Samuel E. 1980. "The Origins of the American Police–Community Relations Movement: The 1940s." In *Criminal Justice History: An International Annual,* vol. 1, edited by Henry Cohen. New York: Crime and Justice History Group, Inc., in association with John Jay Press.

Wasserman, Robert, and Mark H. Moore. 1988. "Values in Policing." *Perspectives on Policing,* no. 8. Washington, D.C.: U.S. Department of Justice, National Institute of Justice and Harvard University.

Williams, Gerald L. 1989. *Making the Grade: The Benefits of Law Enforcement Accreditation.* Washington, D.C.: Police Executive Research Forum.

Wilson, James Q. 1968. *Varieties of Police Behavior.* Cambridge, Mass.: Harvard University Press.

———. 1989. *Bureaucracy.* New York: Basic.

Wilson, James Q., and George L. Kelling. 1982. "Broken Windows: The Police and Neighborhood Safety." *Atlantic Monthly* 249(3):29–38.

Wilson, Jerry. 1990. "Gainesville Convenience Store Ordinance: Findings of

Fact, Conclusions and Recommendations." Report prepared for the National Association of Convenience Stores. Washington, D.C.: Crime Control Research Corporation.

Wilson, Orlando W. 1950. *Police Administration*. New York: McGraw Hill.

Wilt, G. Marie, James Bannon, Ronald K. Breedlove, John W. Kennish, Donald M. Sandker, and Robert K. Sawtell. 1977. *Domestic Violence and the Police: Studies in Detroit and Kansas City*. Washington D.C.: Police Foundation.

Wycoff, Mary Ann. 1982. "Role of Municipal Police—Research as a Prelude to Changing It." Technical Report. Washington, D.C.: Police Foundation.

Wycoff, Mary Ann, Charles Brown, and Robert Peterson. 1980. "Birmingham Anti-robbery Unit Evaluation Report." Washington, D.C.: Police Foundation.

Lawrence W. Sherman

Attacking Crime: Police and Crime Control

ABSTRACT

Growing experimental evidence suggests police actions can reduce crime, increase it, or make no difference, depending on a wide range of conditions. Growing epidemiological evidence suggests police can focus their crime-control efforts much more sharply on high-risk places, times, offenders, and (to a lesser extent) victims. These twin findings suggest the value of a more intensive and sustained program of research and development for testing current and innovative police efforts to control crime. Less than 3 percent of street addresses and 3 percent of the population in a city produce over half the crime and arrests. There has been little testing of alternative police tactics for addressing these high-risk targets. Improving police strategy and tactics for crime control requires much more empirical evidence to specify the conditions under which they succeed or fail. It also requires hard choices about resource allocation and more ideas for how to attack specific crime targets.

Can police efforts reduce crime? The answer is in the eye of the beholder. In the "get-tough" climate of the 1980s, victims' advocates and their lawsuits increasingly demanded more of the police actions they were certain would help reduce specific types of crime, such as more arrests for drunk driving (Jacobs 1988, p. 173) and domestic violence

Lawrence W. Sherman is professor of criminology, University of Maryland, and president of the Crime Control Institute. Appreciation is expressed for the work of Dennis Rogan, Janell Schmidt, Robert Velke, and Nancy Beatty, and for the comments of David H. Bayley, Alfred Blumstein, Gary T. Marx, Sheldon Messinger, Mark H. Moore, Norval Morris, Albert J. Reiss, Jr., Michael Tonry, and Franklin E. Zimring on an earlier draft of this essay. Parts of the research discussed in this essay were supported by grants 89-IJ-CX-0033 and 89-IJ-CX-0058 from the National Institute of Justice to the Crime Control Institute.

(Lempert 1984; Sherman and Cohn 1989). At the same time, sociologists and social reformers reacted with increasing stridency about the inability of police to control crime in the face of the "root causes" of crime: family structure, unemployment, and poverty (Currie 1985; Gottfredson and Hirschi 1990). Police themselves partially embraced that view, placing renewed emphasis on the importance of voluntary action by citizens to supplement police efforts at crime control (Brown 1989). A 1989 Gallup poll reported 48 percent of the respondents confident and 50 percent not confident of the ability of the police to protect them from violent crime (Flanagan and Maguire 1990, p. 133).

Within this contentious historical context, police research on crime control has moved forward rapidly. Police have cooperated with unprecedented and powerful research methods, developed massive data bases revealing new insights, and brought research results more explicitly into policy-making. While the sum of the research is no more than a drop in an ocean of unanswered questions, it has provoked major strides in police thinking about crime control. Most important, it has fostered debate on major questions of police strategy, stimulating new ideas and innovations in police attempts to control crime.

The new research has made two specific contributions. One is to focus more attention on the *epidemiology* of specific crime problems, especially the concentrations of problems in small proportions of offenders, places, and victims. This has stimulated new ideas about strategies for setting police priorities among potential targets for crime-control efforts. The other contribution of the research is to probe more precisely the *results* of police work in relation to specific crime-control objectives. This has stimulated new debate about police tactics in reacting to crime and attacking crime problems.

What the research has not done is to settle the debate about the possibility of police efforts reducing crime. Those predisposed against that possibility read the mixed results of this research as evidence for their position. Those predisposed in support of it read the same results as proving the need for more policing. Those employed in doing the research, like most employees, argue that their work has value and should be continued, if only to discover when police work can *increase* crime as well as reduce it. But all would agree that the results so far are scant in relation to the complexity of the questions. If research is ever to make any contribution to crime control, it will come from a painfully slow process of accumulating and replicating results from hundreds of policy experiments and epidemiological studies, the way of the tortoise and not the hare (Zimring 1976). For police policy research after two decades, the race has only just begun.

This essay examines what has been learned so far about the epidemiology of crime-control targets and the crime-control results of police work. Section I considers the strengths and weaknesses of the primary methods of police research on crime control, as viewed from the perspectives of opposing camps in the crime-control debate. Section II examines the new choices of *strategy* in attacking crime raised by crime-control research. It then considers those strategic options, with appropriate tactics, in a crime-specific manner with four kinds of targets: offenders, places, times, and victims.[1] Section III examines police efforts to control stranger violence, finding diverse evidence that field interrogations and directed patrol may reduce robbery, but that place-oriented and victim-oriented problem solving remains underdeveloped. Section IV reviews the evidence on police control of soft crime, with more specific findings about the conditions of deterrence versus escalation in offender-oriented strategies. Section V reviews recent research on the prediction and control of domestic violence. Early evidence of the predictability of domestic homicide by place was seriously flawed; and such homicides appear unpredictable from currently available police data. Minor domestic battery, in contrast, is highly predictable among chronically violent couples, but reactive arrest has not deterred it in most experiments and has even made unemployed suspects more violent in one. Section VI provides briefer overviews of police efforts to control street-level drug marketplaces, burglary, auto theft, and drunk driving. Section VII concludes by suggesting how further research could help identify harmful, helpful, and wasteful police practices in their efforts to control crime.

I. Crime-Control Research: Methods and Perspectives

Three methods dominate modern crime-control research. One is essentially epidemiological, examining the variations, distributions, and concentrations of crime problems in the population. A second is quasi-experimental, examining the before-after differences in crime rates in a target population subjected to a new policy intervention. The third method is fully experimental, randomly assigning alternate tactics or

---

[1] Police strategies for a fifth kind of target, communities, are reviewed in Sherman (1986) and (1990a). The major crime-control evaluations of policing communities published since the 1986 review are found in Rosenbaum (1986); Skogan (1988, 1990); Pate (1989); and Uchida, Forst, and Sampson (1990).

sanctions across a large sample of equivalent units.[2] Each of these methods has different uses, strengths, and weaknesses. All of them make certain philosophical, empirical, and theoretical assumptions about the police role in crime control and what can realistically be expected from research at this stage in its development.

A. Methods—Epidemiology

The epidemiological method helps identify crime-control targets with the greatest potential yield, by showing where the risk of future crime is greatest. Many credit Wolfgang, Figlio, and Sellin (1972) with establishing the model for this kind of criminal epidemiology, by showing that a small proportion of all young males and a somewhat larger proportion of male offenders in a birth cohort produced the majority of all official police contacts. But the approach goes back at least two centuries, to Fielding (1751) and Colquhoun (1795), both of whom identified high-risk locations, victims, and offenders. Fielding stressed gambling houses and gin parlors and proposed to prevent crime more effectively by tighter regulation of those establishments. Colquhoun (p. 25) proposed the creation of a comprehensive registry of criminals as a tool for selecting the most dangerous for ongoing surveillance.

The strength of this method is that it helps distinguish between low-risk and high-risk units in the jurisdiction, whether people, places, or activities. It points, in theory, to targets yielding the "biggest bang for the buck," or the highest return on an investment of resources. It provides a more rational alternative to equal allocation of police resources across the community, without regard to extreme variations in risk. In a military analogy, it identifies key military targets for precision bombing as an alternative to indiscriminate bombing of an entire city.

One major difficulty with using epidemiological data for policy purposes is the risk of false positives, or incorrect predictions of future criminality. A National Academy of Sciences report on criminal careers, for example, shows the dangers of using this method to determine the length of prison sentences (Blumstein et al. 1986). Yet this

---

[2] A fourth method, cross-sectional correlations among large samples of cities, has been used very little in recent policy research, with the exceptions of Wilson and Boland (1978) and Sampson and Cohen (1988) discussed below (see Phillips and Votey 1972; Tittle and Rowe 1974; Logan 1975). Most of that research, however, fails to adjust for interactions between crime levels and measures of police activity that are hypothesized to affect crime levels (Nagin 1978; Sampson and Cohen 1988). Continuing difficulties of interpreting such models have limited their use and impact, and they are not considered further here.

problem is less severe where the costs of error are also less severe. It is remarkable, for example, how little difficulty false positives pose for public health policy. When the prediction is the basis for telling people to use condoms or to stop smoking cigarettes, few critics object that most unprotected sexual encounters do not transmit AIDS or that most smokers never contract "smoking-related" illnesses. When the prediction is the basis for sentencing people to longer prison terms, the problem of false positives becomes far more serious. Since most police strategies are far less intrusive than prison, however, it can be argued that false positives with crime-risk targets are not a serious problem. Performing surveillance and conducting investigations, for example, should not cause irreparable harm to individual liberty, as long as they are done legally and properly.

A more serious difficulty is that the crime distributions do not really identify targets very efficiently. High-risk units often cannot be identified in advance, especially those in the highest risk levels. This objection, where true, is sound, but the evidence presented below shows it is hardly universal. A second problem is that the distributions are not always skewed enough to make high-risk targeting strategies very profitable. If the top 2 percent of the units only account for 10 percent of the crime, then why bother? The answer, of course, is that a successful strategy could reduce crime by 10 percent, a substantial achievement by our current modest standards of success.

The most serious difficulty has been the cost of examining vast amounts of data on large populations. But recent technological advances in police record keeping have diminished this problem in most communities. Where offense and arrest reports were once kept on paper records and filed chronologically, they are now entered directly on computers. While few police departments have used these data sets to conduct their own epidemiological analyses, it is now relatively easy for them to do so.

B. Methods—Quasi Experiments

Police culture thrives on anecdotal evidence, with an epistemology driven by case-by-case analysis. Quasi experiments fit this mold perfectly but offer considerably more rigor for interpretations of cause and effect. Their major tool is a standard list of alternative hypotheses to examine whenever someone claims that "x" made crime go down. The archetype is the Campbell and Ross (1968) analysis of a Connecticut police crackdown on speeding. This analysis examined whether the decline in traffic accidents immediately after the crackdown could have been due to regression to the mean, general changes in weather or road conditions, changes in methods of recording accident statistics, or other factors besides deterrence of speeding from stricter enforcement. These analyses can be made more rigorous by comparing the target jurisdiction to a similar jurisdiction subject to the same historical trends but lacking the specific policy intervention—such as other New England states.

The strengths of such quasi experiments include their relatively low cost and the speed with which they can indicate the success or failure of a new policy. Moreover, accumulations of similar cases over time provide a basis for beginning to draw more general policy conclusions, such as in the case of uniformed patrol crackdowns (Sherman 1990a). The limitations include their vulnerability to misinterpretation or misrepresentation. Klockars (1980), for example, shows how a quasi-experimental analysis misrepresented the effects of sting operations in reducing crime. Sherman (1991) suggests that failure to consider rival hypotheses in general will limit police efforts to solve crime problems, allowing self-deception about police effectiveness. Most important, because each quasi experiment is still essentially an anecdote, it is not possible to generalize very far from the results. Yet policymakers unschooled in the cautions required of such research are sorely tempted to draw fairly broad conclusions from a single anecdote, as the state of Florida is now considering doing with statewide regulation of convenience stores based on one quasi experiment in robbery preventions in a single city (Clifton 1987). Quasi experiments are not nearly as powerful a basis for drawing conclusions as are randomized experiments with large samples, yet they are often given equal weight in policy deliberations as having "proven" something does or does not work.

C. Methods—Large-Sample Randomized Experiments

This most powerful method in police research merits special consideration since it has provided more concrete answers about the effects of policing on crime than any other method. It assesses evidence of cause and effect from equal probability (random) assignment of alternative treatments to a large sample of target units (Pocock 1983). The logic is elegantly simple: equalizing most characteristics of two groups prior to giving them different treatments creates high *internal validity* (whether a change in one variable really caused a change in another) by eliminating most rival hypotheses about the cause of any differences in outcomes (Farrington 1983, p. 260). In this respect the method stands far above quasi experiments, which may always suffer unknown and undetected validity threats from rival hypotheses (Cook and Campbell 1979).

Randomized experiments were invented for testing agricultural strategies and quickly spread to medicine (Fisher 1935). They were first applied to criminal justice policy in the Cambridge-Somerville project, which found (thirty years later) that assigning a "big brother" social worker to high-risk youth had many negative effects on their future lives (McCord 1978). Their first major policy impact came from the Vera Institute's release on recognizance experiment, the Manhattan Bail Project (Ares, Rankin, and Sturz 1963; Botein 1965), an unreplicated 730-case study that became the basis for national adoption of pretrial release without bail on the basis of community ties.

The bail experiment model heavily influenced the board of directors of the Police Foundation, established by the Ford Foundation in 1970 to foster innovation and improvement in American policing. After some initial battles over how best to accomplish that mission, the board decided to spend most of its initial funding of $30 million on a series of what it called policy experiments. The most visible of these was the Kansas City Preventive Patrol Experiment (Kelling et al. 1974), which found no difference in crime from assigning increased and reduced patrol to fifteen different patrol beats. But there were other Police Foundation policy experiments: the San Diego Field Interrogation Experiment (Boydstun 1975), the Cincinnati Team Policing Experiment (Schwartz and Clarren 1977), the San Diego one- versus two-officer patrol car experiment (Boydstun, Sherry, and Moelter 1977), and the Newark Foot Patrol Experiment (Police Foundation 1981). These experiments created a strong model for federal research funding, especially by the National Institute of Justice.

These experiments were not, however, large-sample randomized experiments (Farrington 1983). They were really small-sample quasi experiments, with some attempt to build randomization into the samples of two to fifteen units, usually patrol beats or districts. The randomization did little to improve on the internal validity problems from the many rival hypotheses associated with before-and-after case studies. Nor did it help to increase the weak statistical power associated with the small sample sizes. Not until the Minneapolis Domestic Violence Experiment (Sherman and Berk 1984) did the Police Foundation conduct a medical-style, large-sample randomized experiment in police crime-control tactics, by randomly assigning arrest and no arrest in 314 cases of minor domestic assault. The finding that arrest produced the lowest recidivism was widely publicized, contributing to policy changes and support for further research (Sherman and Cohn 1989).

Randomized experiments in police crime control had actually been pioneered (Dennis 1988) in 1974, with National Institute of Mental Health funding, by Klein (1986); 306 moderately serious juvenile offenders were randomly assigned to postarrest release versus three other increasingly serious dispositions. That the experiment remained unpublished for so long limited its influence on police policy research, despite its striking finding that released juveniles had the lowest official recidivism rate (with no difference in self-reported delinquency). The lack of national publicity about the study may also have limited its impact on police policy in juvenile arrests and its likelihood of replication.

As the first randomized experiment in arrest, it is fortunate that the Minneapolis Domestic Violence Experiment was replicated in six other cities, with varying degrees of similarity to the original experiment. Three of those experiments have reported findings at this writing (Dunford, Huizinga, and Elliott 1990; Hirschel et al. 1990; Sherman et al. 1991). None of them found a deterrent effect of arrest in the main experimental analyses. This pattern raises major substantive questions about arrest policies addressed in Section V. Equally important is the effect of these mixed results on the future of police policy experiments.

The issue of replication constitutes the major difficulty with policy experiments. In most cases, results go unreplicated, which leaves unaddressed the question of *external validity*, or generalizability to other populations beyond the experimental sample. Randomized experiments are valued for strong *internal* validity; external validity is largely unexplored, even in medical research. For example, a drug found effective in treating AIDS among white males may not be effective among blacks and Hispanics (Kolata 1991). Similarly, arrests for domestic violence in Minneapolis appear to be more effective than arrests for domestic violence in Omaha.

The consequences of this first and only program of replications of a promising result in police crime-control research are still unknown. But the pattern of inconsistent replication results has predictably exposed the methods of policy experiments and crime-control research for police to some attack. These attacks derive not just from the method but from more basic perspectives and assumptions about the roles of police and research in crime control.

D. Perspectives on Crime Control and Research

Police research on crime control has two basic premises. One is that it is a good thing for police to try to control crime. The other is that research results are in some sense portable from the setting in which they are produced to other settings where they can be applied. Both premises provoke considerable debate.

In recent years, many scholars and police executives have suggested that it is not, in fact, a good thing for police to try to control crime, as distinct from apprehension of offenders and provision of reactive peacekeeping services. They suggest that the police *can*, *do*, and *should do* little about reducing crime. Many crime victims and their advocates, however, claim that police have great powers, opportunity, and moral duty to prevent crime but often fail to do so out of negligence or ill-chosen priorities. These arguments, then, are respectively theoretical, empirical, and philosophical, with views on the replicability of crime-control programs as a corollary.

1. *Theoretical Perspectives.*   The theoretical argument against police controlling crime is that the causes of routine "street" crime—interpersonal violence, property offenses, and illegal vices—are far too complex for an agency like the police to address. More basic institutions of social bonding, such as the economy, family, schools, and churches, are the primary crime-control forces in society. The effects of police on crime are only marginal in relation to these master institutions, the argument suggests. These institutions, not punishment, control the "root causes" of crime (Currie 1985). This sensible assessment of the relative capacity of social and governmental institutions breaks down, however, when it gets to the subject of the police. It leads otherwise careful scholars into extreme and dogmatic claims about what "cannot be" (Klockars 1991, p. 542). As Gottfredson and Hirschi (1990, p. 270) conclude: "no evidence exists that augmentation of police forces or equipment, differential patrol strategies, or differential intensities of surveillance have an effect on crime rates." This claim is made without even discussing or citing the relevant literature (except to miscite Sherman [1983], which actually discusses three separate experiments showing police effects on crime control).

In making the same point, but with more emphasis on the "demystification" of crime control as mere police marketing rhetoric, Klockars (1991, p. 537) claims that "despite the fact that for the past 50 years police have been promoting themselves as crime fighters . . . the best evidence to date is that no matter what they do they can only make marginal differences in it." The use of the term "marginal" provides ample room for debate. A 10 percent reduction in robbery, for example, would be marginal to some, but substantial to others. Nonetheless, the thrust of the theoretical argument that police methods are essentially irrelevant to the crime rate is that research on such methods is pointless.

2. *Empirical Perspective.* Until recently, the preceding argument was bolstered by the empirical claim that police actually spend very little time on crime (Cumming, Cumming, and Edell 1965; Wilson 1968; Goldstein 1977). This claim arose from descriptions of police calls for service and observations of police activities, using categories that define much police work as unrelated to crime. This led many others to the conclusion that the "real" role of the police is provision of a wide range of community services rather than primarily the control of crime. An agency committed to helping people who lock their keys inside their cars cannot accurately claim to be engaged solely, or even primarily, in crime control. The unstated corollary was that that is how it is, so that is how it must be.

As Greene and Klockars (1991) observe, these descriptions were somewhat misleading and may now be very out of date. They were somewhat misleading because they only examined patrol work and not other police units. They also classified events that could potentially turn into violence, such as "disturbances," as not crime related. They are out of date because they preceded the adoption of 911 and computer-aided dispatch (CAD) systems around the United States, both of which appear to have expanded the volume of calls for service handled by patrol officers on a typical tour of duty. Analyzing CAD data for the city of Wilmington for a one year period ending May 31, 1986, Greene and Klockars (1991, p. 281) concluded that patrol officers "spend nearly half the time they are doing police work in dealing with criminal activity." Similarly, Sherman (1989) found over half the dispatched calls for service in Minneapolis in 1986 to be clearly crime related. While most of the work they actually do in relation to crime may have little connection to its control, the best evidence is that urban police actually do deal with crime, and not cats up in trees, most of the time.

3. *Philosophical Perspective.* Underlying these theoretical and empirical arguments may be a more basic philosophical distaste for coercive institutions and punishment as a tool of social policy. Police policy research is inescapably linked to values and perspectives on core issues of authority, liberty, democracy, and order. The old joke about the greatest safeguard of American liberty being the incompetence of the police summarizes one position. The joke about America's internationally high crime rate making it the land of the brave, if not necessarily of the free, suggests another. The view that crime control and liberty (or at least legality) are mutually exclusive values has dominated much of the debate about the police. Packer (1968) is the most influential writer on that view, posing crime control and due process as polar opposites. Periodic scandals over police excesses tend to reinforce that view, such as the nationally broadcast videotape of California police brutally beating a restrained suspect in early 1991 (Mydans 1991).

This view leads to a preference not to develop research on more effective crime-control strategies, for fear that police may adopt them. This view is attractive to both left-wing and right-wing libertarians, who distrust the authority of the state. It may also be attractive to those who see the police as an important institution of social service and fear the effects of a crime-control focus in limiting police service activities (Goldstein 1977, 1990; Sparrow, Moore, and Kennedy 1990).

4. *Program Replication.* These three arguments lead critics to oppose more police efforts at crime control and more research to evaluate those efforts. This conclusion easily leads to a second premise: that what works in one experiment is not very portable to other populations. The complexity of social life is too great for positivistic methods to discover any general laws of behavior, especially across the great diversity of American cities (Marx 1990). And if the external validity of police research is so poor, then policy experiments may be the wrong method to use. Clinical case studies of police practices seeking wisdom, not quantification (cf. Marx 1988), may be more appropriate. The failure of the Minneapolis replications to confirm the initial results seems to support this view.

A more sensitive position is that policy experiments are important but should be carefully replicated before their results are publicized (Lempert 1984, 1989). This position holds that, because the question of external validity is unanswered, it is better not to have police change what they are doing until at least some replications have been completed.

5. *Crime Victims' Perspective.* Crime victim advocates, in contrast, offer many counterarguments. They take on faith the proposition that police can control crime if they want to and that they have many opportunities to do so. Advocates have a strong philosophical preference for policing and punishment as a tool of social policy, fusing retributivist demands for just deserts to offenders with empirical claims that punishment deters. Through legislation, litigation, and lobbying, they have pressed police for almost two decades to take a more punitive approach to crime or at least to make crime control a higher priority. Advocates for victims of drunk drivers and domestic violence have been particularly effective in redirecting police resources toward those offenses and in provoking more punitive action. They have also argued that the results of police experiments are highly portable, at least where they support the more punitive position. Some domestic violence victims' advocates, for example, opposed the replications of the Minneapolis experiment on the grounds that it was unethical to create new control groups after arrest had already been found to be effective in one site—a position consistent with much medical research practice (Sherman and Cohn 1989).

6. *Policy Research Perspective.* Police policy research takes a different view on each of these arguments. *Theoretically*, it views the police as a central social institution, less powerful than the family and economy but perhaps as powerful as schools. While no reasonable theory would claim police alone determine crime rates, it is just as unreasonable to write police off as irrelevant without better evidence than we have now. *Empirically*, most work of urban police is already devoted to crime prevention and reaction, including the management of drunks (as potential robbery victims), noise and disputes (as potential assaults), and traffic violators (as potential suspects—see Wilson and Boland 1978, 1981–82). The nature of the work is all in the eyes of the beholder, and most of it can be justified as crime related. *Philosophically*, it is not necessary to like punishment or disvalue due process to value the development and testing of police crime-control strategies. Many of the most innovative police approaches to crime control (Goldstein 1990) employ methods other than punishment, and even police tactics implying the threat of punishment carry no obligation or inherent propensity to violate due process (but see Sherman 1990*a*, p. 41).

Most complex is the question of portability and replications. The research position on this is that it is indeed a matter for research. It is not a matter to be resolved by theoretical fiat or philosophies of science. The extent to which findings from one jurisdiction, or one offense, or one type of offender can be generalized to others is simply unknown. Only hundreds of experiments and replications with diverse samples can even begin to answer that question. Where results differ from one type of sample (such as cities or offender types) to another, that is not reason to give up the effort to test police strategies. It is merely a challenge to discover what specific aspects of the differences in the samples (or methods) may account for differences in the results. When such characteristics can be specified, the results may appear to be more robust than they first appear. The proposition that "arrest deters spouse abusers in high-employment neighborhoods but not in low-employment neighborhoods," for example, may be far more robust than the less precise proposition that "arrest deters domestic violence."

The question of whether to publicize research results without replication is more difficult, given the concerns about external validity. Three factors argue in favor of doing so. One is that not announcing results creates a bias for the status quo in police practices, for which there is usually no empirical support; one experiment is arguably better than none. A second factor is that a steady stream of these results will only help make police more sophisticated consumers of research, rather than treating policymakers as if they cannot be trusted until findings have received a scientific seal of approval. Policymakers in all fields misuse research to comport with their biases, which is no argument to stop doing research. The most important factor, however, is that publicizing policy experiments helps to foster their replication, the essential but usually ignored step in the process. There is little reason to believe, for example, that the Minneapolis Domestic Violence Experiment (Sherman and Berk 1984) would have been replicated had it not received substantial publicity (Sherman and Cohn 1989).

The basic questions are what to expect from police crime-control research and how quickly it can be produced. For some, this research is little more than "rearranging the deck chairs on the Titanic" as center-city violence becomes more terrible (Marx 1990). For others, the central problem is that insufficient funds have been invested to speed the process along (U.S. Attorney General's Task Force on Violent Crime 1981, p. 73; Zimring 1990). Inconsistent results are an inherent part of scientific investigation. It is impossible to cite any field that made major breakthroughs in curing a social problem within two decades after starting from scratch. From any perspective, however, research has clearly succeeded in stimulating police debate and innovations in crime-control strategy (Goldstein 1990), for better or worse.

II. Crime-Control Strategy: Hard Choices

The past two decades of research have sharpened several key questions. What is the optimal balance of proactive and reactive police effort? Should police strategies focus on specific crimes or on crime in general? Should police target offenders, victims, times, or places? Should priorities be set within or across types of crime? Every police department answers each of these questions on a daily basis. The answers are often shaped by organizational and political factors. Less often, perhaps, they are also shaped by a concern for crime-control effectiveness.

A. Balancing Proactive and Reactive Strategies

In the quarter-century since Reiss and Bordua (1967) first raised the question of who mobilizes police in any given action, the terms "reactive" and "proactive" have achieved widespread use. The language has helped clarify the hardest strategic choice police face. The choice concerns both philosophical questions of how police can best serve democratic values (Black 1973) and empirical questions about how police can most effectively control crime.

When police action is self-initiated, or proactive, police select their own targets. When police mobilization is initiated by a specific citizen demand, or reactive, police allow citizens to select police targets. All municipal police agencies use both forms of mobilization. The difficult choice is how to allocate personnel time between the two strategies.

Most police patrol time is devoted to reactive mobilizations (Reiss 1971). In recent years, however, there is increasing evidence of new emphasis on proactive strategies, such as decoy units to catch robbers (Wycoff, Susmilch, and Brown 1981), sting operations to catch burglars (Marx 1988), special units to watch repeat offenders (Martin and Sherman 1986), problem-solving strategies to attack high burglary locations (Eck and Spelman 1987), and intensified patrol crackdowns in retail drug marketplaces (Sherman 1990a). There is also more evidence that police agencies vary widely in the extent of their proactivity in patrol tactics generating citizen encounters (Wilson and Boland 1978; Sampson and Cohen 1988). Scholars are increasingly pressed to consider whether a far more proactive police would be good for both democracy and crime control.

1. *Democratic Philosophy.* The philosophical choice is deceptively simple, with reactive policing appearing to be far more democratic than proactive policing. What could be more egalitarian than to give all citizens an equal right to pick the targets of police crime control? Yet absent an equal willingness to use that right, reactive policing becomes anything but egalitarian.

Enormous "selection bias," as statisticians call it, afflicts every choice of police targets by citizens. Many crime victims never call the police, for example, for reasons ranging from fear of retaliation to lack of homeowner's insurance (Flanagan and Maguire 1990, p. 226). Other people falsely accuse enemies and relatives, using police as a tool for private disputes. Reactive policing is completely vulnerable to racial, class, religious, sexual, and ethnic prejudices in citizen decisions to complain about other citizens (Black 1973).

Proactive policing is equally vulnerable to such prejudices on the part of the police. It has the added disadvantage of potentially systematic discrimination against certain ethnic or political groups. Such biases, when they occur, are compounded by the imprimatur of state action. Yet unlike reactive policing, proactive policing has great potential for controlling such selection bias. Using objective criteria for target selection, proactive strategy can come far closer to egalitarian policing, giving all similarly situated individuals equal odds of being selected as targets. Whether using the principles of random selection from a list of congressmen for corruption investigations (Sherman 1983), rank-order targeting of street addresses by frequency of prior police problems (Sherman, Gartin, and Buerger 1989), or some other logic, police can attempt to reduce bias in target selection. While research shows some persistence of selection bias even with fairly objective targeting criteria (Martin and Sherman 1986; Sherman et al. 1989), the result is arguably less biased than purely reactive target selection.

More troubling to democratic philosophy may be any attempt to eliminate citizen power to mobilize police about certain problems. Even if proactive target selection is more egalitarian, it may do less to defuse citizen conflict that may cause crime. Shifting resources from reactive to proactive policing could foster increased vigilantism or "self-help" (Black 1983; Weisburd 1989), which can in turn cause a breakdown of democracy.

Democracy may also break down, however, with the anarchy of high crime rates. Crime control is merely another aspect of serving democratic values, rather than a contradiction of those values. While control of "street" crime may appear to be easier in nondemocratic regimes, there is little systematic evidence supporting that proposition (but see Greenhouse 1990). Even dictatorships must decide how proactive police should be and answer the same questions about crime-control effectiveness.

2. *Crime-Control Effectiveness.* Is proactive policing more effective than reactive policing in controlling crime? The available evidence permits no definitive answer. Each distinct type of crime may be more or less susceptible to proactive crime attacks, depending in large measure on how predictable in time and space the crime may be. Police have historically used proactive strategies most often with the most obviously predictable crimes, such as street prostitution, public intoxication, drunk driving, gambling, and (recently) street-level drug dealing. More recent analyses in the spirit of Goldstein's (1979) problem-oriented policing have revealed less obvious patterns of predictability in a wider range of offenses, such as burglary concentrated in a single apartment complex (Eck and Spelman 1987) and robbery concentrated in less than 2 percent of all addresses in a city (Sherman, Gartin, and Buerger 1989).

Predictability alone, however, does not necessarily make a proactive strategy more effective than a reactive one. It is also necessary to have tested and effective tactics available for attacking predictable crime. When confronted by 125 commercial addresses with highly predictable crime problems, for example, a specially selected group of five Minneapolis police officers (the Repeat Call Address Policing [RECAP] unit) was unable to develop effective ways to reduce repeat calls for service at those addresses (Sherman et al. 1989). They succeeded in closing down two high-crime taverns, reorganized security at a bus station, had fences built around a high-crime parking garage, and tried to install better access control at a YMCA. But overall, they could not reduce total calls compared to a control group. The team was more successful at reducing multifamily residential calls for service by working with the property managers on tenant problems (including evictions), but only temporarily; after six months of reduced calls, the effects of proactive intervention withered away.

To the extent that experiments in proactive strategy employ a wide range of tactics (Wycoff, Susmilch, and Brown 1981; Martin and Sherman 1986; Sherman et al. 1989), they may obscure a key point. Effectiveness at crime control may depend more on specific tactics than on general strategy. There may be a substantial crime-control difference between two proactive tactics, such as robbery stakeouts and target hardening with bulletproof enclosures. There may also be great differences between two reactive tactics, such as hidden robbery alarms or use of 911. Yet there is no difference between two ineffective tactics, regardless of whether they are reactive or proactive.

On empirical grounds, then, the balance between proactive and reactive strategies should depend on the availability of proven specific tactics. If more tactics are proven effective, then more proactive effort may become justified. And the evidence of effectiveness may become even clearer when specific tactics are linked to specific offenses.

B. Specific or General Strategies?

Police strategies are usually expressed in general terms. One strategy is often presumed to work for all offenses. The threat and delivery of apprehension and charging of criminals is implicitly applied across the board. Uniformed patrol and postcrime investigation are the master strategies—both reactive—for every crime from noise to homicide (Colquhoun 1795; Wilson 1963). Just as criminological theory makes few distinctions among types of crimes in explanations of crime (Wilson and Herrnstein 1985; Gottfredson and Hirschi 1990), police have historically made few distinctions among offenses in strategies for controlling crime.

To some, crime-general strategies may be justified by the apparent lack of offense specialization among offenders (Blumstein et al. 1986). To others, police could control crime better if they targeted the specific situations creating opportunities for specific offense types to occur (Clarke 1983). The judgment hinges in part on the choice between a "hydraulic" pressure model of crime causation or an opportunity model (Clarke and Mayhew 1988). Hydraulic models presume that the supply of offenses is determined largely by the supply of offenders and their innate rates of offending (e.g., Merton 1968, chap. 6). Opportunity models presume that the supply of offenders (given their predisposed rates of offending) is only one factor determining crime rates, with the supply of suitable victims and capable guardianship also necessary elements (Cohen and Felson 1979). Hydraulic models logically imply a need for general strategies. Opportunity models imply a need for specific strategies. This strategic choice relates, in turn, to the choice of targets for police strategy.

C. Offenders, Places, Times, or Victims as Targets

Reactive policing deals with incidents, which generally feature victims and offenders intersecting in time and place (Cohen and Felson 1979). It makes little strategic distinction among types of incidents, although this is changing. "Differential police responses" to calls for service are increasingly being used, such as taking a telephone report of a crime or making an appointment for a police car to visit the next day on a low-priority call. These responses explicitly vary by call type and are accepted by callers when they are clearly told what to expect (McEwen, Connors, and Cohen 1986). Such call-screening only delays or rechannels, however, a single strategy of response (investigation), regardless of the elements of the offense. Proactive policing, in contrast, can target any element of a given *pattern* of incidents, especially the most predictable ones (Eck and Spelman 1987). The question then becomes which elements are most predictable.

1. *Places.* Police have long focused on offenders as the most predictable element in any incident. Yet the places—defined as street addresses or intersections—where crime occurs may be far more predictable than the people who commit crimes. In Minneapolis, for example, our analysis of 323,000 calls to the police in 1986 found that a small number of hot spots produced most of the crime in the city (Sherman, Gartin, and Buerger 1989). Only 3 percent of the places produced 50 percent of the calls to which police were dispatched. This concentration was even greater for the predatory crimes of robbery, criminal sexual conduct, and auto theft. Only 5 percent of the 115,000 street addresses and intersections in the city produced 100 percent of the calls for those usually stranger offenses. These findings have subsequently been replicated in Kansas City (Sherman, Rogan, and Velke 1991; see also Pierce, Spaar, and Briggs 1988).

One cause of that concentration, of course, is the small number of those crimes relative to the large number of places. Even without any repeat locations, for example, all of the robberies could only have occurred at 3.6 percent of all places. But the fact is that with repeat occurrences, they occurred at only 2.2 percent of all places, a 40 percent reduction from the hypothetical number with no repeat locations. If the analysis were restricted to commercial establishments or other high-risk places, the concentration would not be as great, but the identification of targets would still be just as clear. Only 297 addresses, for example, produced over half of all dispatched calls to the Minneapolis police in 1986.

Domestic violence is even more concentrated by place of occurrence than robbery. While 21 percent of the places in Minneapolis could have had a domestic disturbance call if no place had more than one, only 8.6 percent of addresses actually produced one or more calls—a 59 percent reduction. While it is probably true that multifamily housing units comprised the bulk of those locations, and that much of the city (such as industrial areas) would be unlikely to have such calls, the identification of the 161 addresses with fifteen or more calls per year might stimulate some useful ideas for a proactive strategy against such violence.

Further examination reveals possible routine activities heavily implicated in causing hot spots (Sherman, Rogan, and Velke 1991). For example, analyses of taverns and surrounding areas in Milwaukee and Kansas City shows that, in 1986–89 in Milwaukee, 4 percent of homicides, 5 percent of aggravated assaults, 3 percent of robberies, and 3 percent of all serious violent offenses combined occurred in taverns—which constituted only 0.5 percent of all places in the city. Kansas City showed a similar pattern, with 3 percent of homicide, 6 percent of robbery, 4 percent of aggravated assaults, and 4 percent of total serious violence in its taverns, which constituted 0.3 percent of the places. These crime risks are also connected to violent crime on the block. In Milwaukee, *the location of a tavern on a block increases the relative risk of the block being violent (defined as 20 or more such offenses in four years) by a factor of 3*. Only 15 percent of 5,672 blocks without taverns met the criteria for violent blocks. Some 29 percent of the 625 blocks with nonviolent taverns were violent blocks, but 51 percent of the 170 blocks with at least one violent tavern (defined as four or more violent offenses in four years) were violent blocks. In Kansas City, the comparable ratios for the same time period were 11 percent for no-tavern blocks, 24 percent for nonviolent tavern blocks, and 44 percent for violent tavern blocks.

The fact that most taverns do not have these risks, however, shows the importance of analyzing all factors in each hot spot. Only 12 percent (132) of Milwaukee taverns produced over half of all 2,019 violent offenses in 1986–89, with 40 percent of taverns reporting no violence at all and 85 percent with one or less violent offense per year. The maximum was twenty-three violent offenses in four years. In Kansas City, only 10 percent of the taverns produced half of the 2,757 violent offenses in 1985–89, with 31 percent of the taverns reporting no violence and 68 percent with one or less violent offense annually. The maximum was seventy-five violent offenses in five years.

Police once gave substantial attention to high-crime bars, with frequent field interrogations of customers. Current practices appear more limited to answering calls for service. The continuing connection of some taverns to concentrations of violent crime suggests they should be a central part of any proactive crime-control strategy.

2. *Offenders.*   Annual distributions similar to those for places can be found among all arrestees in a city as an indicator of the active offender population. In Kansas City, Missouri, for example, the 2.7 percent of the estimated 500,000 city-user (as distinct from resident only) population that was arrested two or more times in 1990 produced over 60 percent of all arrests that year (Sherman, Rogan, and Velke 1991). The most frequently arrested 642 persons produced over 10 percent of all 71,461 "body arrests," defined as each event of taking a person into custody regardless of the number of charges, victims, or co-offenders. One hundred persons were arrested fifteen or more times that year, and ten persons were arrested thirty-two times or more. The distributions for nontraffic arrests only are virtually identical.

More important is the predictability of these offenders' levels of activity, assuming that their frequency of arrests has something to do with their frequency of crime commission. Once a nontraffic offender was arrested three times in 1990 (as over 5,000 persons were), the conditional probability (odds) of yet another arrest hit 55 percent. After seven arrests, the 751 offenders who qualified had a 71 percent chance of a further arrest. The curve of the probability of recidivism rises to 93 percent at the nineteenth arrest that year, with an unstable plateau thereafter as the available time at risk to be arrested declines (because most of the year has been used up by the time one has been arrested nineteen times). On a year-to-year basis, the 426 (less than 1 percent of total) offenders who had ten or more arrests (7 percent of all arrests) in 1989 had, as a group, an 82 percent likelihood of being arrested at least once in 1990. Whether this is a high level of predictive accuracy or a high level of false positives depends, of course, on what kind of proactive policing program is being considered. Nonintrusive surveillance, for example, or listing the person on a "most active" list to be considered by investigators would seem to entail little or no cost for false positives or suffering needlessly inflicted on a person from an inaccurate prediction.

Epidemiological analysis of this type can produce startling results. In 1989, for example, Kansas City police arrested by citation one individual 345 times for false alarm violations. While one could discount this problem as a false indicator of repeat criminality, one can also ask the question of why 345 separate citations were written without the problem being solved. The case is similar to a Philadelphia noise problem generating over 500 police calls in six months (Goldstein 1990, p. 81). Both examples indicate the inherent lack of coordination of reactive effort across the hundreds of patrol officers who can be assigned to each call and the value of proactive strategy based on epidemiological data solely from the standpoint of conserving police resources.

For all the emphasis police have placed on serious offenders, however, there have been remarkably few efforts to develop strategies targeting them. Incidents still drive police actions far more than any analysis of the offenders repeatedly involved in those incidents. Even a unit explicitly aimed at repeat offenders, like the Washington, D.C., Repeat Offender Project (ROP) was highly subjective, and minimally analytical, in its procedures for target selection (Martin and Sherman 1986). Prior to the Kansas City analysis cited above (Sherman, Rogan, and Velke 1991), no police agency ever (to my knowledge) rank ordered all offenders arrested in the past year by total or crime-specific arrest frequency. While such a ranking alone may not be sufficient as a targeting strategy, it would at least provide a check on the subjective tips and leads. This would help insure that targets selected for proactive investigation, or even extra reactive investigation, would be "worth" that effort in potential reduction of offenses.

3. *Times.*   Both places and offenders are highly time-sensitive targets. The concentration of all criminal events by time of day (Barr and Pease 1990, p. 296) may be even more marked within specific targets. For example, a recent analysis of some 1,200 violent crimes over four years in the Georgetown area of Washington, D.C., found that 65 percent of them occurred within a 1,000 foot radius of the "hot spot" intersection of Wisconsin and M Streets, a small portion of the total area. Of those crimes, however, fully half, or about one-third of the total violent crimes in the area, were reported to have occurred between midnight and 3:00 A.M. (Sherman et al. 1991c). Other hot spots, however, are not quite so time sensitive. A one-year analysis of all calls for service in 100 Minneapolis hot spot address clusters (with an average of over 100 calls for service each) found that they were all quite inactive between 3:00 A.M. and 11:00 A.M. Their prime times of high activity in the remaining sixteen hours, however, varied widely across locations.

Places may also become temporarily "hot," as in the immediate aftermath of a burglary. Canadian evidence cited by Barr and Pease (1990,

p. 297), for example, shows that the expected rate of burglary of an address during the first month after it has been burglarized is twelve times the rate without the first burglary. Bars and the immediate vicinity around them are typically hottest around closing time.

Time may also be important for specific offenders. Any offender with ten or more arrests can be analyzed for prime times of day for criminal activity. The times may vary widely across individuals, but that may be irrelevant once a specific person has been targeted for investigation.

The strategic question is the use to which police are willing or able to put these facts. The concentration of calls for service from 7:00 P.M. to 3:00 A.M. is widely known, for example, yet few police departments match that peak load period with peak assignments of personnel. The obvious inconvenience of these hours for police officers leads their unions to fight against making a standard shift to match them. Most agencies persist in using the traditional three eight-hour shifts starting at 7:00 or 8:00 A.M., many with equal numbers of personnel on each shift. This strategy would seem to be impossible to justify on a crime-control basis.

4. *Victims.*   Compared to places and offenders, the individual victims of crime are substantially less predictable. In Kansas City in the five-year period 1985–89, for example, 3 percent of the city "user" population produced only 20 percent of all 231,714 victimizations of persons, as distinct from businesses (counting each person as victimized separately by each crime event, even with multiple victims, offenses, or offenders for a single event). All of the individuals with two or more victimizations in that period contributed only 38 percent of the total, in contrast to all persons with two or more *arrests* producing 62 percent of total arrests (Sherman, Rogan, and Velke 1991).

The fact that victims are not as predictable as arrestees does not rule them out as viable targets for crime prevention efforts, however. If the 3,452 people with an average of one or more Kansas City victimizations per year could be successfully "cured" of victimization, for example, it would reduce the number of victimizations by 7 percent. While this gain may appear "marginal" in percentage terms, it would still prevent 22,314 victimizations over a five-year period, or almost 4,500 victimizations per year. The 269 people with ten or more victimizations alone produced 3,372 of those problems, each of which may involve medical costs, lost days at work, and police investigative time (Sherman, Rogan, and Velke 1991).

We know little about how police might intervene effectively with repeat victims. But there is good reason to believe that victimizations are strongly related to "lifestyle." This perspective on routine activities (Hindelang, Gottfredson, and Garofalo 1978) suggests that some people manage their lives in ways that place them at much higher risk of being victimized. The number one victim in Kansas City in 1985–89, for example, suffered thirty-five offenses in 3.5 years: ten burglaries, ten larcenies, four robberies, two assaults, and nine other offenses, including attempted suicide. A white male in his 60s living in a poor black area, he had six home addresses and fourteen arrests (all minor) in the same time period. One of the arrests was for soliciting for prostitution, one for carrying a weapon, and several for violation of the animal leash law. This pattern may be consistent with any of the five reasons Sparks (1981) offered for multiple victimization: victim provocation, victim inability to defend, victim provision of criminal opportunities, victim attractiveness, or criminal impunity because victims are themselves breaking the law.

One of the helpful aspects of an official records repeat victim analysis (which police can now easily do), as distinct from national victimization surveys (which is all scholars have analyzed in the past), is the insight it offers into particular aspects of the victim's lifestyle. The overlap with the victim's arrest record is one example. A more surprising result is that eleven of the top fifty repeat victims in Kansas City for a five-year period were police officers, primarily victimized by assaults presumably committed by persons they were arresting. This may lead some to discount the value of the analysis. But if these officers are in fact suffering at least three (or more) assaults a year for five years, that should be an important flag for a personnel inquiry. Even in a high-crime area, this seems to suggest some problem in the officers' conduct (Toch 1975).

While there is no precedent for police targeting of high-risk victims, the computer systems needed to identify them are rapidly spreading throughout American policing. Once a citywide ranking of victims by frequency can be produced, as Kansas City has done, the only bar to effective intervention strategies will be inadequate ingenuity and lack of resources for testing them with controlled experiments.

D. Priorities Within or Across Crime Types?

The enormous overreach of the criminal law (Morris and Hawkins 1970) beyond the resources available for its enforcement always requires some triage among offenses: discretion not to invoke the criminal justice process. But the conventional triage criterion of offense seriousness has substantial limitations. Police may well achieve better crime control by setting priorities within, rather than across, offense types.

The main limitation with using only a seriousness criterion is that it can virtually legalize less serious offenses. Such de facto legalization can have serious consequences, possibly undermining any general deterrence of the problem. The maintenance of at least token levels for every type of offense may help to make some deterrence a part of a rational choice to commit the offense. How much enforcement is sufficient to accomplish that goal is an empirical question. But it is clearly possible to provide some enforcement for both homicide and minor assaults, speeding and parking violations, shootings and unscooped dog feces, and burglary and jaywalking. With limited enforcement efforts for the less serious offenses, the question becomes how to set priorities within those offense types.

Seriousness alone may also be a bad guide to setting priorities within offense types. Consider the value-of-goods-lost criterion for burglary investigations, which some departments employ. The not unprecedented threshold of $5,000 value may have the effect of decriminalizing burglary in poorer areas. Yet the arrest of a burglar for a $5,000 theft may have no better crime-control effect than arresting a burglar for a $50 theft. If burglary rates are higher in poorer areas already, then a crime-control perspective might concentrate burglary investigation among low-value theft losses, where greater crime control may be possible from each arrest.

Discretion to make arrests—or not—both within and across offense types has been left largely to street officers as individuals, with little structuring of that discretion by management. But there is no reason why guidelines could not be used to set criteria for high- and low-priority arrests. The same logic could even be used to *limit* arrests, especially where arrests compete with patrol presence. Until we know that arrests are better for crime control than police patrol presence in hot spots, it may be quite important to seek nonarrest alternatives to curbing minor disorder. In agencies with substantial time costs for booking each offender, too many arrests can deplete the street of patrol and possibly encourage more offenses than the arrests deter. The evidence reviewed below suggests all the more reason to have management attempt to structure discretion far more clearly, using criteria based on crime-control effectiveness as well as offense seriousness.

Police managers could, for example, establish an annual arrest "budget," projecting and limiting the number of arrests to be made for each offense type in each area on each watch (Sherman 1990b). Officers would then be given goals, limits, and standards for arrests to use whenever there is an evidentiary basis for making an arrest. Such budgeting would help to reveal tradeoffs between offense types, as well as resource choices between preventive patrol and enforcement. Patrol officers, of course, would certainly resist such attempts to restrict their discretion, but they might come to support the idea if they were given some power in the planning process.

III. Controlling Stranger Violence

There is good reason to apply these strategic perspectives first to stranger violence. Citizen rankings of crime severity (Rossi et al. 1974) suggest that stranger violence is the top priority for crime control. It is also the problem police may be least able to control. It is far rarer than other kinds of crimes and therefore much less predictable. The specific chains of causation are harder to identify, and vulnerable links are harder to find. While stranger violence offenders may be deemed most worthy of long-term incapacitation, very few offenders can actually be controlled by that strategy.

Stranger violence encompasses some, but not all, of the legal categories of homicide, rape, robbery, assault, and arson. Applying the estimates of the proportions of each offense committed by strangers (Flanagan and Maguire 1990, p. 247) to the FBI data on the relative frequency of these offenses (Federal Bureau of Investigation 1989), we can estimate the proportion of stranger violence each offense type produces (table 1). The majority of the problem is aggravated assault, which is fairly difficult to predict by place of occurrence, victims, or offenders. Only 24 percent of all 1989 assaults in Kansas City occurred at the 336 addresses with more than one assault, for example. Almost half of all stranger violence is robbery, which is somewhat (but not much) more predictable by place of occurrence. Almost half (44 percent) of the 1989 Kansas City robberies occurred at the 503 addresses (0.31 percent of all addresses) with two or more robberies. These epidemiological data suggest the potential, if modest, value of proactive police strategies aimed at places as targets. Other data suggest the potential

TABLE 1

Distribution of Stranger Violence by Offense Type, 1988

Offense	Total	Crime by Stranger (in Percent)	Stranger Violence (in Percent)
Robbery	542,968	77	40
Rape	92,486	42	4
Aggravated assault	910,092	63	55
Homicide	20,675	12	1
Total	1,566,221		

Sources.—Federal Bureau of Investigation (1989); Flanagan and Maguire (1990).

value of field interrogations aimed generally at all "suspicious" persons on the streets. Perhaps the most effective strategy would be a combination of the two, with strict attention paid to proper methods of field interrogation.

A. Offender-oriented Strategies

A major issue in criminology is the extent to which offenders specialize. Whatever the evidence over a criminal career, it is relatively hard for police to identify currently active robbers from current year arrest data. Only seventy-nine persons had two or more robbery arrests in Kansas City in 1990. Those seventy-nine, in contrast, accounted for 20 percent (173) of all 879 robbery arrests and may have accounted for even more than that proportion of all robberies (for which the clearance rate is only about 10 percent). The question is what effects on crime would result from giving *legal* special attention to such offenders. Previous efforts have not always met that standard.

In the 1930s, when automobiles were still relatively rare, New York police operated "Strong Arm Squads" against violent criminals (Behan 1990), just as other jurisdictions operated "Goon Squads." The target "goons," or offenders, were probably contract workers who committed stranger violence against people who had broken business deals or failed to pay extortion money. They were a very different type of offender from the modern robber or rapist, if only because they were more readily identifiable through criminal networks. Their known faces allowed police squads to roam the streets by the carful, stopping to jump out if they passed by a known goon. The preventive action consisted of beating the goon up, taking his gun away, and telling him to leave town or at least watch his step. By some accounts, this was an effective way to attack stranger violence.

Detroit maintained a similar tradition well into the 1960s with the "Cruiser" unit (Reiss 1990), also a car full of uniformed officers. Its demise was followed shortly by the creation of the STRESS unit (Stop the Robberies—Enjoy Safe Streets), a group of plainclothes officers that attempted to put stress onto robbery suspects. Its record of killing black suspects (and nonsuspects), if not of reducing crime, made the unit a central issue in the next mayoral campaign (Milton et al. 1977). The results included the election of Detroit's first black mayor and abolition of the unit.

Contemporary attacks on suspected active stranger assailants suggest they are relatively hard to find. The seventy-officer Washington, D.C., Repeat Offender Project began with the goal of focusing constant surveillance on stranger robbers but could not identify enough of them to stay busy. The ones they did identify had the unfortunate habit of going home at night and staying there for 12 to 16 hours, which made surveillance extremely expensive and very boring. ROP officers wound up making more "serendipitous" arrests while watching their targets than actual arrests of the targets. Citing the theory of frequent offense switching among repeat offenders, the unit eventually concentrated on making arrests of reportedly active property offenders, on any charges they could find. The target selection was based almost entirely on tips, with no systematic analysis of repeat arrest patterns like those described for Kansas City. Using informants to lure offenders into burglarizing locations where the officers were waiting, or raiding a home full of stolen property, the Washington ROP unit arrested about half of its targets within one week of being targeted (Martin and Sherman 1986). Whether the active offenders they arrested for property crimes were also the highest risk offenders for robbery and rape, however, is unknown.

One major problem with offender-oriented strategies may be the failure to recognize important patterns of co-offending. While the lone offender model may be generally correct for adult robbers, juvenile robberies are more often committed by groups of two or more (Reiss 1988). Locking up one offender who participates in one or several groups may do nothing to reduce the total number of crimes, given the continuation of the co-offending groups. The one offender, one crime assumption is clearly inadequate as a causal model for stranger violence.

Both juveniles and adults may also be vulnerable to the suggestive influence of "Typhoid Marys," or people who accumulate high numbers of co-offenders (Reiss 1988). These "carriers" are not ringleaders of an ongoing group as much as idea men in a social network, people whose presence in any particular group may tip the balance of action toward committing a violent offense. While the evidence for the existence of these spreaders of criminality is not strong, it can be readily assembled in any police agency with computer systems linking individual rap sheets to arrest reports naming co-arrestees. Rank ordering of all rap sheet subjects by total numbers of co-offenders could reveal enormous disparity, with a small number of offenders being linked to over half of all other offenders. Such persons could just as easily be the unlucky ones who are always talked into crimes resulting in arrests by smarter ringleaders who do not get caught. But the possibility of their being true recruiters warrants closer examination.

If a police department could identify Typhoid Marys of stranger violence in this fashion, they would clearly become a high priority target for proactive investigation. Given the same number of offenses by two different offenders, one a lone wolf and the other a Typhoid Mary, there could be far greater crime reduction from incarcerating the latter. This could occur from the spinoff effects of the carrier's recruitment of new offenders into a first offense of stranger violence. Given that experience, the co-offender could go on to commit other offenses without the carrier, with or without other co-offenders. The lone wolf, in contrast, does not seem to spread crime around, making less contribution to the total volume of stranger violence.

Field Interrogations.   Not all offender-oriented strategies that reduce robbery are focused on specific names or even on that specific crime of stranger violence. Indeed, there is substantial evidence that a police department's level of proactive traffic and disorderly conduct enforcement can affect its robbery rate. Wilson and Boland (1978), using a simultaneous equation model across thirty-five U.S. cities, first reported an inverse relation between the number of moving violations per officer and the rate of robbery victimizations per capita. They theorized that aggressive traffic enforcement was an indicator of the general level of active surveillance with which police patrolled the streets in any given city, which in turn was a function of municipal culture and predictable by various characteristics of local government.

They hypothesized that more intensive watchfulness by police on the streets was an effective deterrent to robbery, either indirectly by apprehending more actual or would-be robbers, or directly by affecting community perceptions of the likelihood of arrest. While admitting their evidence was not as conclusive as a randomized experiment, Wilson and Boland still found strong support for the theory.

Further research has refined and extended the conclusion. Jacob and Rich (1981) challenged the conclusion on the grounds that it could not be replicated with longitudinal data *within* cities on traffic citations and robbery rates. Wilson and Boland (1981–82) replied that, among other things, changes over time within cities did not approximate the differences across cities in patrol style and that Jacob and Rich failed to use the traffic citations per officer as a measure of proactive patrol. More important was the replication and extension of Wilson and Boland by Sampson and Cohen (1988), using a more complex design with the much larger sample of 171 cities. They combined traffic enforcement and disorderly conduct enforcement per officer as a single indicator of "aggressive policing," defined as a tendency to invoke the law even for minor offenses. They also employed elaborate controls on the urban social structural characteristics most highly correlated with street crime rates—the only cross-sectional police and crime study to do so. Police aggressiveness was inversely related to both robbery offenses per capita (but not burglary) and the prevalence of robbery offenders in the cities. Police behavior was almost as powerful an influence on crime as the city's divorce rate.

Sampson and Cohen (1988) also found complex effects of police aggressiveness on robbery offending rates by age and race. Citywide aggressiveness had more powerful effects in reducing black robbery rates than white rates, for both juveniles and adults. Yet further analysis showed that police aggressiveness toward whites (drunk driving and disorder enforcement rates per capita whites), who comprise the majority population in most of the cities, had an independent effect in reducing both white and black adult robbery offending rates. Similarly, police aggressiveness toward blacks had an independent negative effect on adult robbery offending rates among whites and blacks. But black adult robbery rates are more strongly associated with proactive policing of *whites* than of blacks. Thus police aggressiveness has a "pervasive effect" in reducing robbery rates, at least among adults. The effects are generally weaker among juveniles but show more impact on black juveniles than on whites.

The troublesome aspect of these findings is that they run directly contrary to the "friendly policing" thrust of current police innovations (Skolnick and Bayley 1986), designed in part to counteract the kind of aggressive policing Sampson and Cohen find to be so effective in reducing robbery. Proactive field encounters with suspicious persons received very bad press in the 1960s and early 1970s, in large part because of overtones and evidence of racial discrimination and harassment (Rossi, Berk, and Eidson 1974). Field interrogations and traffic stops clearly have a high potential for officer rudeness and racial slurs. Even worse, the police culture associated with proactive patrol has been blamed for causing extreme cases of brutality (Nazario and Jefferson 1991).

Yet there is no reason why legalistic traffic and disorder enforcement needs to be offensive or insensitive to persons stopped and questioned. With proper training and supervision in a community relations–conscious police culture, field interrogations need not provoke community hostility, as the San Diego Field Interrogation Experiment suggests (Boydstun 1975, pp. 54–55). This 1973–74 quasi experiment compared three patrol areas: one area where all field interrogations were suspended for nine months and then reinstated, one area where field interrogations were only conducted by officers specially trained to reduce friction with citizens they stop, and one area where there was no change in field interrogation practices only. Total reported crime was virtually unchanged in the two areas retaining field interrogation, but it rose significantly from seventy-five "suppressible" crimes a month in the baseline period to 104 per month in the experimental period, dropping again to eighty-one crimes per month in the follow-up period. Suppressible crimes were defined as those in theory most sensitive to field stops: robbery, burglary, theft and auto theft, assault, sex crimes, malicious mischief, and disturbances. Citizen surveys in the three areas found that reducing field interrogations had no effect on community attitudes toward police. Interviews with interrogation subjects found most favorable attitudes toward officers who had been given special training in field interrogations, although observations of trained and untrained officers found no differences in their behavior.

The results suggest that, with proper organizational development, it should be possible to do proactive field stops without alienating those persons stopped, with the benefit of controlling suppressible crime by a margin of about 20 percent. The cost of doing so is about 5 percent of a patrol officer's time. The difference across areas in dosage, as

reported in police logs, was 22 minutes of field interrogations per officer per shift in the control area compared to 0 minutes in the experimental area. There may also be community relations costs in such a
practice. The U.S. Supreme Court's subsequent ruling (*Kolender v.
Lawson*, 46 U.S. 352 [1983]) that the San Diego Police had collectively
and discriminatorily harassed a black man with a "dreadlock" hair style
who liked to walk around town suggests the potential difficulty with
any proactive policy aimed at "suspicious" persons as targets. But this
is again a problem that might be solved with more specific guidelines,
especially if they are race-neutral in design and effect.

An unmeasured aspect of the experiment was the kinds of places in
which the field interrogations were conducted. Any guidelines for the
selection of a "suspicious" person must entail a judgment about persons
in relation to the places where they are found. In that sense, field
interrogations may also be seen as a place-oriented strategy for crime
control.

B. Place-oriented Strategies

Some stranger robberies are highly predictable by place over a one-
year period, but most robbery locations have had no recent prior robberies. Even where robbery is predictable, it is impossible to predict
when, in the short run, robbery will occur, absent an informant's tip.
Of the 161 addresses with three to six robberies in Kansas City in
1988, for example, 116 of them (72 percent) had at least one robbery
in 1989. This compares, however, to 1,947 addresses robbed in 1989
that had no robberies in 1988. While the latter group was only 1
percent of the places with no 1988 robbery, it was also 77 percent of
all 1989 robbery locations. Thus, only 5 percent of those locations
were highly predictable as robbery targets.

The most common place-oriented antirobbery strategy has been
stakeout units, which were discredited in many cities for the high rate
of shootouts with and deaths of robbers they produced (Milton et al.
1977). They also seem fairly inefficient in their consumption of police
time, even with informant tips, although this question has not been
examined systematically; epidemiological data alone are clearly inadequate, with a one-year time period covered by the prediction. One
unintended consequence of stakeout units was to reveal an unknown
portion of the robbery rate as fraudulent cover-up of employee theft.
On several occasions in Kansas City in the 1970s, for example, off-site
stakeouts of commercial premises were conducted without notification

of the store clerks. While plainclothes police sat observing no one go into the store, the clerk phoned in a robbery at the premises. When the uniformed officers responded to investigate, the stakeout squad came in. Searches of the clerks revealed the money missing from the register (Joiner 1990). Similar discoveries were made in Washington, D.C., with robberies of both convenience stores and dry-cleaning delivery trucks (Wilson 1990a).

This phenomenon is important to interpreting the effects of more recent innovations in robbery control through situational crime prevention. Cash control devices in stores, bulletproof barriers for lone gas station attendants, and the requirement of two clerks after dark in certain stores may all defeat *fraudulent* robbery as well as real robbery. Where unwitnessed robbery is at stake, it will be difficult to determine how much of it is real or fraudulent. But where environmental design makes it much harder to lie credibly about the occurrence of a robbery, any reduction in reported robbery should not be uncritically accepted as evidence of control of stranger violence.

One of the most influential recent place-oriented strategies to reduce robbery (Goldstein 1990, p. 80; Moore, in this volume) falls victim to this kind of interpretive problem, among others. In Gainesville, Florida, police attacked a rapid rise in convenience store robberies in the mid-1980s by a thorough analysis of the epidemiology of the problem, including its prevalence and frequency across all stores in the community. They analyzed the situational features of the crime and concluded that robbers prefer to wait until they are alone with a clerk before committing the robbery. This conclusion, of course, was based on lone clerks' accounts of how the robberies occurred. It was also supported by a University of Florida survey of imprisoned convenience store robbers the police department commissioned, which found that robbers took the number of clerks (as well as their size and gender, even if alone) to be very important factors in their decision to rob a store.

The police chief used this extensive analysis (Clifton 1987) to support a recommendation to the city council for requiring convenience stores to employ two clerks in each store open after dark. After it was passed, the department claimed a 65 percent reduction in convenience store robberies was attributable to the law. Problem-oriented police officers in other cities, such as Minneapolis, accepted the results as valid, and the *New York Times* cited it on the editorial page as a success story (Anderson 1990). The Florida Legislature was scheduled in 1991 to consider adopting a statewide two-clerk requirement, and other jurisdictions have considered adopting the law based on the success of the Gainesville results (Richman 1990).

Unfortunately, closer inspection by a former Washington police chief retained by the National Association of Convenience Stores (Wilson 1990*b*) found little compelling evidence for the effectiveness of a two-clerk rule, which took effect four months *after* the robberies had already dropped precipitously. He also found several plausible rival hypotheses explaining the reduction in convenience store robberies. Chief among these is an almost identical pattern of rise and fall in convenience store robberies in the Alachua County Sheriff's jurisdiction surrounding Gainesville, even though the county passed no requirement for using two clerks. County police do report, however, that three convenience store robbers, highly active in both the city and county, were apprehended and continuously incarcerated four months prior to and long after the two-clerk rule took effect. The date of their arrests corresponds exactly to the sudden drop in convenience store robberies in both jurisdictions. The robberies merely continued at the same low rate in both areas after the two-clerk rule took effect, with no additional drop in rate.

Additional rival theories for the drop include legislative requirements for a set of additional security features, such as cameras and cash control, which went into effect the same month the robbers were apprehended (by stakeout methods) and robberies declined. The difficulty of concocting a fraudulent robbery claim with a co-employee present is another rival theory, as is simple regression to the mean after a sudden eighteen-month peak (Campbell and Ross 1968).

A more effective place-oriented approach to robbery reduction may be bulletproof booths, which have been widely adopted in gas stations, subway change booths, banks, and liquor stores. In 1987, the Maryland legislature enacted a law requiring their use at all gas stations. The governor vetoed the law, however, and appointed a task force on retail security to study the matter. The task force could find no evidence that the booths were effective and did uncover evidence of pouring and igniting gasoline in the cash hole as a technique for injuring clerks. Examples of robbers taking customers hostage have also been found. The question awaits careful experimentation for resolution.

1. *Preventive Patrol.* The most basic police strategy against public stranger violence has been preventive patrol. This strategy has been given little credence since the Kansas City Preventive Patrol Experiment found increases in patrol ineffective at reducing crime (Kelling

et al. 1974). This quasi experiment in a relatively low-crime area attempted to double patrol car presence in five patrol beats, eliminate it altogether (except for answering calls) in another five, and hold it constant in a third group of five beats. No *statistically significant* changes were observed in crime rates, although there were ample differences of magnitude that the small sample size lacked statistical power to test (Sherman 1986). Moreover, Larson (1976) has suggested that the volume of calls answered in the no-patrol area gave it virtually as much patrol presence as the regular patrol area. Hence the frequent conclusion that "it makes about as much sense to have police patrol routinely in cars to fight crime as it does to have firemen patrol routinely in fire trucks to fight fire" (Klockars and Mastrofski 1991) is not supported by the Kansas City experiment and is contradicted by numerous other quasi-experimental results (Sherman 1990*a*).

Perhaps the most compelling evidence for the preventive effects of patrol on stranger violence is the increase in such crime during the major police strikes for which good data are available. The mayhem during the Liverpool (Sellwood 1978) and Boston (Russell 1975) police strikes in the late summer of 1919 included looting, armed robbery, and (in Boston) numerous rapes and gang rapes (Russell 1975, p. 137).

Admittedly, this increase might be written off to the general political instability of that period rather than to a loss of deterrence from police patrol. Yet, the political instability argument is weaker when used to explain away the crime increase during the seventeen-hour Montreal police strike of October 7, 1969 (Clark 1969): 13.5 times the normal hourly rate of burglaries, 50 times the normal hourly rate of bank robberies, and widespread looting by "ordinarily disciplined, peaceful citizens," although there were no reported rapes (Clark 1969, p.176).

The political instability argument completely fails to explain away the 50 percent increase in store robberies and 42 percent increase in hospital admissions for violent injuries at a large Helsinki clinic during the seventeen-day Finnish police strike of February 1976 (Makinen and Takala 1980). The Finnish "experiment," in an era of long-term political stability, is even more compelling because of very cold weather, a major national fixation on the televised Winter Olympics, and the fact that the data evaluating crime rate changes came from sources independent of the police. Even without the looting and collective behavior of the more famous strikes, Finland's loss of 86 percent of its police force and virtually all of its uniformed patrol force was accompanied by a clearly documented increase in the rate of violence and stranger violence. Similarly, the Nazi arrest of the entire Copenhagen police force in 1944 was followed by a tenfold increase in both robberies and larcenies reported to insurance companies (Andenaes 1974, p. 51).

Drawing conclusions from Kansas City is also inappropriate because traditional preventive patrol in automobiles has been widely dispersed, even along the main commercial arteries police prefer to frequent. Yet as I noted earlier, stranger violence and crime in general are highly concentrated in a small number of addresses (Sherman, Gartin, and Buerger 1989). The odds of a widely dispersed police patrol encountering stranger violence in progress are so low that it appears unreasonable to expect it to have much deterrent effect. Over 6,000 hours of evening observations of high-crime intersections in Minneapolis, for example, found a mean frequency of patrol cars driving by only once in every 23 hours (Sherman and Weisburd 1990).

2. *Hot Spots Patrol.*   Given the concentration of stranger violence in hot spots of crime, the same dosage of patrol can be applied much more intensely where it may do the most good. Police have increasingly employed such a "directed patrol" strategy over the past two decades, with open-air drug markets providing a wealth of targets in recent years. Privately owned premises have also expanded their use of such patrols by off-duty police officers, in such locations as shopping center parking lots, fast-food restaurants, and garden apartment complexes. Until recently, however, there has been little systematic evidence on the effects of such focused patrols at deterring stranger violence, or any other kind of crime.

The Minneapolis Hot Spots Patrol Experiment (Sherman and Weisburd 1990) begins to fill that gap. From December 1988 through November 1989, the Minneapolis Police Department, Crime Control Institute, and Rutgers School of Criminal Justice conducted a randomized experiment in directed patrol in marked automobiles by uniformed police at 110 specially selected hot spots of crime. These locations were clusters of an average of fifteen street addresses selected on the basis of high frequencies of calls for police service for "hard," or predatory, crimes, as well as high volumes of calls about "soft" crime and disorder. Only hot spots that were highly active two years in succession were eligible, to minimize regression to the mean. The average number of calls about both types of crime in the baseline year before the experiment was 188, or about one every forty-six hours. The typical hot spot extended for several addresses, or up to half a block, in all four directions from an intersection, while others were centered on multiple dwellings. All of them were visually independent of the others, so that a police car in one hot spot could not be seen in another.

The 110 address clusters were randomly assigned to two groups of fifty-five (in five statistical "blocks" based on call frequency), one of which was designated to receive increased patrol. The goal was to provide three hours per day of intermittent patrol presence between 11:00 A.M. and 3:00 A.M., the highest crime period. Officers left the hot spots to answer radio calls, but returned at unpredictable intervals to write reports, talk with pedestrians, or just (in their words) "sit on the hot spot." The actual dosage over the year was about 2.5 hours per day according to official police logs. Some 6,500 hours of independent observations in both the experimental and control groups during the evening hours (7:00 P.M. to 2:30 A.M.) showed that police cars were present in the hot spots for 12.8 percent of the observation time of the experimental group, but only 4.5 percent in the control group. This patrol dosage ratio of 2.83 to 1 does not count police car drive throughs, the addition of which drops the ratio slightly to 2.6 to 1. Patrol time was fairly evenly distributed within each group, with only 9 percent of the addresses overall receiving dosage levels close to the mean of the other group. The greater inconsistency was across groups over seasons. When total calls were down, there was less (reactive) patrol presence in the control group and more (proactive) presence in the experimental group. When calls were up, the pattern reversed. The ratio of observed police presence time between the experimental and control group varied from almost 6 to 1 in March to 1.2 to 1 in August, but exceeded 2 to 1 in all months but August.

David Weisburd's preliminary analysis of the call data for stranger violence suggests that directed patrol had a modest deterrent effect on robbery in the hot spots, although there was no significant deterrence of hard crime calls generally (Sherman and Weisburd 1990). Subsequent analyses will explore the extent to which any crime reduction in the experimental hot spots was attributable to displacement to other locations (Cornish and Clarke 1987; Barr and Pease 1990). Scholars will also need time to reflect on the findings and their implications, just as they have on past experiments. But if displacement and other problems are found to be minor, then directed public (though perhaps not private) police patrol in hot spots may be a viable, if expensive, robbery-control strategy.

C. Victim-oriented Strategies

Police have attempted relatively few victim-oriented strategies against stranger violence, apparently with good reason. There is very little repeat victimization for robbery (including larceny purse snatch) found in official crime reports. Over the period 1985–89 in Kansas City, only 2.72 percent of the robbery victimizations were accounted for by the 127 victims who were robbed three times or more. However, those people had seven times the risk of further robberies of people who had not been robbed before. While it makes sense to devote some attention to such a high-risk group, the crime-control payoff citywide would be very marginal indeed.

The most common victim-oriented strategy for stranger violence is police lectures to concerned groups. Subjects include how to prevent crimes through simple precautions, many of which reflect common sense (such as looking in the back of a car before entering it, and always locking a parked car). More problematic topics include how to respond to a criminal attack once it begins: what to do if a rapist attacks, or if you hear a burglar in your home, or if a gun is pointed at you.

One problem with such lectures is that they are based on questionable beliefs about the consequences of taking the various options recommended or described. Victims of would-be rapists are more likely to escape if they offer nonforceful resistance, for example, but only if they live to answer the survey questionnaire (Skogan and Block 1983). The relative rate of death for resistance and cooperation remains unknown. The consequences of forcefully resisting armed robbers, however, are somewhat clearer, in that it increases risks of physical attack and injury (Skogan and Block 1986), and standard police advice is to cooperate. More subtle points about tone of voice, eye contact, speed of movements, and so on are also made in these lectures, but with questionable empirical foundation.

The major problem with this line of strategy is that it remains virtually unevaluated. No one has any idea whether these lessons reduce injury rates or increase them, and both possibilities are quite plausible. The major obstacle to evaluation, fortunately, is that the base rates of stranger violence victimization after receiving this instruction are so low. Reliable estimates of the impact of such instruction, even with a randomized design, would require a very large sample to be observed for many years.

More controversial, but also better evaluated, is the practice of police in some communities of recommending that potential victims—

especially women—buy guns. Recent public health research (reviewed in Cook 1991) suggests that the presence of guns in a home is a strong factor in firearms deaths, including accidents and suicides. But this does not alter the view many hold about the need for guns in self-protection, as well as the evidence some researchers have mustered to support the hypothesis (see Cook 1991). While police executives are increasingly in favor of regulating gun sales to bar access to criminals, many are of mixed minds about the virtues of honest citizens possessing guns to fight criminals.

As long as there is no strong message from police professionals against keeping guns for self-defense, purchases for that reason seem likely to increase. And as gun density grows, the overall homicide rate goes up, according to increasing evidence (Cook 1991). It should follow that police could fight serious violence by actively discouraging most private ownership of guns as merely throwing oil on the fire, even if the effect is that some crimes cannot be rebuffed by armed citizens.

IV. Controlling Soft Crime

Stranger violence dominates the headlines, but the far more frequently occurring "soft" or minor crimes (Reiss 1985) dominate police work-loads. They also have a dominant role in generating public fear of crime and contributing to residential and large corporate flight from center cities (Skogan and Maxfield 1981). Soft crime may also attract hard crime, by communicating to potential assailants that an area is "out of control" (Wilson and Kelling 1982). One of the strongest correlates of calls about robbery in Minneapolis hot spots is calls about drunks (Weisburd, Maher, and Sherman 1991).

Soft crime embraces a wide range of behavior with similar community consequences. Car break-ins leave shattered glass for all passersby to see. Drunks use foul language, urinate in public, or collapse on the sidewalk. Teenagers use "boom boxes" to disturb a quiet residential block as they walk by late at night. A man beats his wife in a parking lot. Each of these events suggests that anarchy is around the corner and underlines the continuing threat of crime in the local environment.

Police strategies against soft crime are often not explicit because most of the offense categories at stake are not serious enough for priority treatment. Soft crimes are often good examples of how some offenses have been effectively decriminalized, with virtually no police attention. Yet there are some things police do already that can have effects on soft crime.

A. Offender-oriented Strategies

Field interrogations, for example, appear to have substantial impact on soft crime. Boydstun (1975, p. 33) found significant increases in a range of soft crime in the San Diego quasi-experimental comparison of one area where field interrogations were suspended for nine months, compared to two comparison areas where they were continued. The soft crimes deterred during the baseline and follow-up periods, but that increased when interrogations were suspended, included petty theft, grand theft, sex crimes, malicious mischief, and disturbances.

Antiloitering "sweeps," invoking ordinances against obstructing pedestrian traffic, produced a decline in recorded crime (but not surveyed victimization) in an experimental area in Newark, New Jersey (Pate et al. 1986). The procedure of ordering young males to clear the sidewalk, then arresting them minutes later if they fail to leave, has been attacked as unconstitutional by scholarly observers (Skolnick and Bayley 1986, p. 199) but not by the courts. Other police procedures employed in this area during the experimental year, which may also have contributed to the measured crime-reduction effect, included automobile checkpoints, random police inspections of public transit buses, and foot patrol. Which of these, if any, was more important than the others in producing the effect is impossible to tell from the design. But it is instructive that the same crime-reduction effect was achieved with much more positive citizen attitudes in a similar area that received a "community policing" program of a storefront, door-to-door police visits, and a neighborhood cleanup as well as street sweeps and other intensive enforcement (Skogan 1990, p. 119).

Newark was also the site of an unevaluated police effort to combat predominantly soft youth crime through truancy enforcement (Williams 1983). Working in the early 1980s with specially powered truancy officers and a school bus, police officers cruised the city during school hours looking for school-aged children. Those picked up were taken to a special detention center–study hall and kept until school hours ended. Parents were also contacted, although without much optimism. The primary objective was to incapacitate the truants from daytime burglary and shoplifting.

Another youth-focused but unevaluated strategy against soft crime was the Minneapolis RECAP unit's enforcement of the state curfew law. Plagued by frequent soft crime calls at 7-Eleven's and other youthful gathering places, the RECAP unit organized a "sweep" of the entire neighborhood surrounding these locations looking for underage people after 10:00 P.M. While it is not clear that the sweeps reduced calls for service at the repeat call locations, over two-thirds of the apprehended juveniles had prior arrests. It seems plausible that sustained curfew enforcement pressure, where legal, could incapacitate the youths from being out at night, perhaps reducing a wide range of soft crime as well as drug abuse and other evening activities (Buerger 1991).

Foot patrol officers have long used a variety of techniques for managing panhandlers, drunks, the homeless, and the mentally ill on their beats. As Bittner (1970) and Wilson and Kelling (1982) have shown, police effectiveness in controlling the potential for soft crime by these marginal populations depends heavily on knowing them as persons. With verbal orders or persuasion based on trial and error with each local "character" in the officer's repertoire, a great deal can be prevented with minimal effort and very rare use of force or arrest. The conventional strategy of wide-ranging automobile patrol, however, greatly limits the capacity of officers to gain this depth of experience with specific individuals.

The use of arrest and prosecution for soft crime may have different consequences than patrol does and different consequences for individuals than for communities. While Boydstun (1975) and Sampson and Cohen (1988) find deterrent community effects from legalistic policing of soft crime, Klein (1986) found crime-*increasing* effects from legalistic treatment of juveniles arrested for primarily soft crimes. This three-month experiment in 1974 was conducted in nine of the eighteen police stations in an unnamed West Coast metropolis, randomly assigning 306 arrested juveniles to four conditions in the juvenile division office: release with no further action, referral to social services, referral with subsidies to cover the costs of social services, and petition (prosecution) to juvenile court. Initial cheating by police on the random assignment procedures was detected and apparently overcome. Follow-up interviews with the juveniles were conducted nine months later with a 59 percent completion rate. Official data on repeat crime were collected for 100 percent of the sample for twenty-seven months after random assignment.

The more complete data set showed the more startling results. While there were no significant differences across the groups in subsequent self-reported crime, there were significant differences in official recidivism. The prevalence of recidivism at fifteen months varied directly with the formality of the treatment, from 37 percent among those juveniles released to 63 percent among those prosecuted. While this experiment does not show that the *arrests* had a crime-escalating effect, it did show that police decisions to treat juveniles legalistically had a clear effect of increasing crime.

Clearly much more needs to be learned about the effects of offender-oriented patrol and arrest strategies on soft crime, preferably through additional randomized experiments. The possibility that police may be increasing crime or hurting community relations with these methods is too serious to ignore.

B. Place-oriented Strategies

Just as there is more soft than hard crime overall, the frequencies of soft crime in specific locations are much higher than frequencies of hard crime. Targeting police resources at hot spots of soft crime is thus even more efficient than targeting at hot spots of hard crime, although they often turn out to be the same places. Two of the most popular place-oriented strategies are problem solving and directed patrol (Moore, in this volume).

1. *Problem Solving.*   Eck and Spelman (1987) describe the Newport News experience with the general approach of "problem-oriented policing" that has been used in many cities to deal with disorderly places (Goldstein 1990). Based on the concepts of Goldstein (1979), and using a strategy similar to the RECAP model (Sherman 1986), problem-oriented policing tries to diagnose the causes of soft crime concentrations at specific locations, do something about them, and then follow up to see if the strategy has been effective.

In Newport News, for example, the approach was used with prostitution as a cause of the problem of robbery in a four block area of downtown. Diagnosis showed that about half the robberies were linked to the persistent prostitution problem with twenty-eight "regulars" in the same area. The multiple-tactic solution began with showing the local judges the connection between prostitution and robbery and obtaining their agreement to increase the sentence for prostitution to two months. In addition, they agreed to suspend ten more months with the condition that the prostitutes stay away from that area or else go back to jail. Police also put enforcement pressure on area bars and rooming houses, using regulatory statutes aimed at control of prostitution. After six months, only six of the twenty-eight regulars were still found in the area, and robberies (of an unspecified frequency) had dropped by 43 percent (Eck and Spelman 1987, p. 80).

In Houston, problem-oriented policing led to the diagnosis of a park as an open-air drug market due to lax supervision at night (Brown 1989). Mobilizing sufficient resources to close down the park at night, police were able to dry up the local drug market.

In Minneapolis, problem-oriented policing led the RECAP unit to a diagnosis of two taverns as disorderly from serving intoxicated patrons, as well as encouraging drug sales. The solution was to have their liquor licenses suspended; both were later torn down for urban renewal, with no new liquor license granted for another location (Buerger 1991).

All of these examples constitute quasi experiments in problem solving for soft crime. Unfortunately, they suffer from strong selection biases, both in picking the problems to begin with and then in reporting success in the literature. Buerger (1991) reports detailed case studies of about 100 attempts by the Minneapolis RECAP unit to solve soft crime problems at specific addresses selected solely on the basis of high total call volume. There are as many failures as successes in the casebook, with opportunities to reflect on what might have been done differently to insure greater success. Perhaps the leading critique is that there were too many diverse problems and individuals at each address, and too many addresses for each officer (about sixty over one year) to take on successfully, even as a full-time assignment (Buerger 1991).

Whatever the reason, the first controlled experiment in problem solving at high-call locations showed no effect on calls in the experimental group for commercial addresses. This conclusion from the RECAP experiment suggests that "problem solving" as a strategy is probably too general for a meaningful experimental test. More useful may be controlled experiments on homogeneous kinds of places with similar problems, testing identical tactics at all experimental sites. The RECAP experiment in strategy, in contrast, targeted widely diverse kinds of places with widely diverse tactics and levels of police attention. The statistical power of any experiment under such conditions of heterogeneity is understandably quite weak. More important, perhaps, is the weakness of the knowledge base from which police can draw to diagnose and solve soft crime problems. Until there is a better literature to guide them in seeking chains of causation, problem-solving officers may be better off selecting problems subjectively on the criterion of a sound hypothesis for solving the problem.

2. *Directed Patrol.* The evidence on directed patrol shows consistent effects in reducing soft crime. The Oakland experience of the

early 1980s (Reiss 1985), for example, is a striking quasi-experimental success in police control of soft crime through directed uniformed patrol presence. In committing themselves to a complete rebuilding of downtown Oakland, a group of developers wanted to insure that its skid row atmosphere and problems would disappear with the old pawnshops and flophouses. Their solution was to offer $1 million per year to the Oakland Police Department (OPD) for additional patrol officers to be directed to the several block "new" downtown, patrolling on foot, horseback, and scooters. The department accepted the offer on certain conditions guaranteeing total control over the officers to the OPD. The additional presence of some twenty-five police officers was multiplied by fairly close collaboration with many more office building security guards.

The destruction of the skid row physical environment, of course, may have been sufficient to displace large portions of the potential soft crime offenders. Adding the directed patrol at the same time as the environmental change makes it impossible to assess directly the effects of police alone. But the joint result insured the economic viability of the new office center. To the extent that reported crime statistics are a valid indicator of the change, they support the conclusion of a reduction in soft crime (Reiss 1985). Considering the substantial population increase in the area as an increase in the supply of potential victims, soft crime could have increased dramatically, but did not.

The conclusion that uniformed police presence can deter soft crime is strongly supported by the experience of police strikes. In the Boston police strike of 1919, for example, the first widespread lawbreaking to start and the last to end was public dice games (Russell 1975, p. 131). In Finland in 1976, systematic observation by researchers independent of police showed clear increases in public drinking and the size of groups of young males (Makinen and Takala 1980, p. 103), as well as a 50 percent increase in phone booth coin burglaries compared to the periods before and after the strike. To the extent that smashing store windows for looting constitutes "soft" crime, the Liverpool, Boston, Montreal, and Baltimore (1974) strikes all experienced that phenomenon (Russell 1975, p. 242; Sellwood 1978), although some other police strikes have not.

The most systematic evidence for this proposition comes from the Minneapolis Hot Spots Patrol Experiment (Sherman and Weisburd 1990). David Weisburd's preliminary analysis of that experiment found that a 250 percent increase in patrol presence at target hot spots produced a 13 percent reduction (or displacement) in total calls for service about crime, most of which were soft crimes. This effect lasted from the beginning of the experiment on December 1, 1988, until August 1, 1989, six weeks after directed patrol was reduced for the summer. In 300,000 minutes of observations of the hot spots during that period, the controls had disorderly events during 4 percent of the time and the experimentals had disorder for only 2 percent of the time. Measurement thereafter was unfortunately confounded by a change in the CAD system on October 1.

Two interesting observations stand out from Weisburd's preliminary results. One is that the effects of directed patrol were largely consistent at 100 crime calls deterred per month as long as the observed patrol time ratio between experimental and control spots remained in excess of 2 to 1. As soon as this ratio dropped, the deterrent (or displacement) effect disappeared. The other striking finding, consistent with the theory of residual deterrence from police crackdowns (Sherman 1990a), is that the deterrent effect lasted for six weeks after the directed patrol time in the experimental group was officially cut back by 33 percent. From the perspective of the department, this was a free bonus of crime control without the full price of patrol.

The price of patrol, of course, is a key issue in using directed patrol against soft crime. It is often said that directed patrol is effective but too expensive to use on a wide scale (e.g., Schnelle et al. 1977). The Hot Spots experiment provides the first experimentally based estimates of crime-control costs per crime. The price of $1,000 per prevented crime (assuming no displacement) is relatively high, at least compared to responding to a call after a crime occurs.[3] The value of preventing

---

[3] Assuming no displacement, hot spots patrol deterred 101 crime calls per month through July 31. At 2.5 hours per day × 55 hot spots × 30 days per month, the cost of this patrol in one officer cars is 4,125 patrol car/police officer hours. The gross cost per crime call deterred (or displaced) is therefore 41 car/officer hours. The cost of answering 101 crime calls, with an average of two cars per call (a low estimate, given usual backup patterns) for 15 minutes per call (also low) is at least 50 hours. Assuming twice as many officers per call answered, or twice the average length of time involved (more realistic for arrests), the cost to answer 101 calls could be 100 officer hours. For every 41 hours invested in hot spot patrol, the benefit to the city was therefore 1 crime call prevented (or displaced) and 30–60 minutes of officer time saved. Every hour on hot spots patrol saves (or displaces) 1.3–8.8 minutes in patrol officer time. There was no net cost increase per crime prevented (or displaced) by directing existing patrol personnel to target hot spots, with an annualized crime reduction benefit of 1,200 crime calls. The cost per crime call prevented of hiring additional officers to perform hot spots patrol, at $25 per hour cost to the city, is $1,000. Put another way, each officer working 2,080 hours per year would be expected to prevent 51 crime calls per year if permanently assigned to directed patrol at hot spots, and if—a very big if—there was no displacement.

the crime, of course, may be worth the higher price. Depending on how the medical costs, lost wages, and property losses from soft crimes are estimated, the cost of each crime prevented could exceed the $1,000 prevention cost. This analysis depends heavily, however, on the assumption of no displacement, an assumption that still awaits testing.

C. Victim-oriented Strategies

Virtually nothing has been done to identify patterns of repeat victimization in soft crime. The area is ripe for computerized records analysis and a problem-solving strategy (Goldstein 1990). Some repeat victim problems may be alcohol related, while others may be chronic and intractable in other respects. But there may be obvious solutions suggested by other patterns, from improved physical security to changing jobs. The first step is to identify and interview any high rate repeat victims.

V. Controlling Domestic Violence

While police can do more to control hard and soft crime than many believe, they can probably do less to control domestic violence. They can certainly do less than many victims' advocates and attorneys have claimed. The irony is that minor domestic violence is among the more predictable offenses, by places, offenders, and victims. The problem is that serious domestic violence, particularly homicide, is virtually unpredictable, despite preliminary findings suggesting the contrary.

Police may be able to do more proactively than they have done before, although our political culture makes it unlikely. Reactive arrests of on-scene offenders, however, may not be as effective as many had concluded from the Minneapolis Domestic Violence Experiment (Sherman and Berk 1984).

A. Reactive Strategies

Given our cultural preference for reactive policing of domestic violence, it is not surprising that we have embraced a reactive strategy so readily. In the period 1970 to 1980, several states loosened the evidentiary requirements for police to make arrests in cases of minor domestic violence they had not witnessed. From 1984 to 1986, there was a fourfold increase in the proportion of urban police agencies encouraging police to make such arrests; several states made such arrests mandatory (Sherman and Cohn 1989). At least part of this increase may have been due to the findings of the Minneapolis Domestic Violence Experiment (Sherman and Berk 1984).

The 1981–82 randomized experiment in Minneapolis encompassed misdemeanor domestic violence cases within four hours of occurrence in three high-crime areas of the city. Forty-four officers were given prerandomized forms for determining which of three treatments to follow: arrest, ordering the suspect to leave the home for eight hours on pain of arrest, or "advising"—essentially doing neither of the other two responses. Of the 314 valid cases, 82 percent were treated as randomized. The other 18 percent received a different treatment from the random assignment, usually arrest, under procedures agreed to at the outset for such reasons as imminent threat of violence, assault on a police officer, or the suspect's refusal to leave the premises. Follow-up measures included official crime reports and interviews with victims, although the response rate to the interviews was very poor; fewer than a third of victims completed the planned six months of interviews.

The analysis consistently found deterrent effects from arrest using a variety of different models (Sherman and Berk 1984; Berk and Sherman 1988). Both official records and victim interviews indicated that arrest had the lowest prevalence of repeat violence for the same couple over a six-month follow-up period, although the rank order of the two nonarrest treatments was different for the two measures. Linear and logistic regression and time-to-failure models all confirmed the deterrent effect of arrest. The results were the same when analyzed by treatment as randomly assigned as well as in an adjusted model of treatment as actually received (Berk and Sherman 1988).

Numerous questions have been raised about the experiment concerning both its external and internal validity. As Sherman and Berk (1984) and Sherman and Cohn (1989) point out, among other things, the sample size was too small to examine interaction effects: the question of whether the rates of repeat violence varied by suspect or victim characteristics. They also note the lack of control on the screening of cases for eligibility, with the officers knowing what the treatment would be at the time they made the eligibility decision. Finally, they suggest that the effects of arrest could be quite different in cities with different cultures or employment rates.

A central recommendation of the final report, however, was that the experiment should be replicated in other sites, in order to address these questions. A second recommendation was that neither police nor state legislatures should adopt mandatory arrest policies, given the potential for diverse individual reaction to arrest (Sherman and Berk 1984). If arrest would increase violence among some persons, even while deterring it among others, it would make little sense to order arrest in all cases where police discretion had previously employed arrest very rarely.

The second recommendation was widely ignored, in part because of the publicity about the experiment generated by the principal investigator (Sherman and Cohn 1989). But the National Institute of Justice accepted the recommendation to replicate the experiment. Police departments and state legislatures adopted mandatory arrest policies in many states, thereby making replication of the Minneapolis experiment impossible in some locales. But the National Institute of Justice did fund six replications, three of which have now been completed. The replications address the separate questions of reactive strategy when the offender is present at the scene and when the offender has departed on police arrival.

1. *Offender Present.*   None of the three replications to date has reported a deterrent effect, but one (Milwaukee) has reported significant interaction effects. These results begin to show how the effects of arrest may be highly conditioned on the ecological context or offender characteristics, with arrest increasing violence under some conditions and not under others. The Omaha replication (Dunford, Huizinga, and Elliott 1990) was the most similar of all six replications to the original Minneapolis design. Its sample size (330), eligibility, treatments, and measurement closely followed Minneapolis, with improvements in randomization procedures. All patrol officers in the department were asked to screen for eligible cases without knowing the treatment that would be assigned. When they had an eligible case, they called the dispatcher for a randomly assigned disposition generated on the spot by a computer program. The three treatments were then implemented as assigned in 92 percent of the cases, in part because the more troublesome cases were not subjected to random assignment. Follow-up measures included initial and six-month victim interviews with a 73 percent completion rate overall. Both official and victim data were restricted to same-couple violence, as opposed to violence outside the relationship.

The Omaha experiment found no specific deterrent effect of on-scene arrest and no differences at all across the three treatments. This result was robust across the same range of models as in the Minneapolis analysis. A longer-term follow up, with one-year victim interviews, is still in progress.

The Charlotte replication (Hirschel et al. 1990) also found no deterrent effect of arrest, although with a different design and sample. Unlike the Minneapolis and Omaha experiments, the Charlotte sample had a strong majority (73 percent) of blacks. Unlike the Milwaukee sample, which also had a majority (75 percent) of blacks, the Charlotte sample had a majority of employed suspects. Its 686 cases were randomly assigned to three treatments, with 83 percent compliance with the design: arrest, arrest by citation without taking into custody, and no arrest. Six-month victim interviews were completed for 47 percent of the sample. No deterrent effects of arrest were found with any of the now standard models of analysis.

The Milwaukee Domestic Violence Experiment (Sherman et al. 1991b) greatly expanded the sample size (1,200 cases); altered the treatments (arrest with three hours in jail, arrest with overnight in jail unless bond is posted, and a warning of arrest if more trouble occurs); and provided direct experimental control over the randomization procedures by Crime Control Institute staff who were always on duty while the experiment was in operation. The misassignment rate was 2 percent, the six-month victim interview rate was 79 percent, and a systematic measure of prevalence and frequency of violence covered periods both before and after the randomized intervention. The sample was predominantly black males with very high unemployment rates, living in high unemployment neighborhoods.

The experiment found no consistent differences in recidivism across the three randomized treatments. There was some evidence, however, of an initial deterrent effect followed by a long-term escalation in the frequency of violence among those assigned to short custody arrest (Sherman et al. 1991b). More important, there was very powerful and consistent evidence of an interaction effect with suspects' unemployment (Sherman and Smith 1991). For employed suspects, arrest reduced the frequency rate of repeat violence by 16 percent. But for unemployed suspects, arrest *increased* the frequency of repeat violence by 44 percent. It is not clear, however, whether this effect is due to individual characteristics or the ecology of their neighborhoods and the differential shame or stigma those neighborhoods attach to arrest (Braithwaite 1989).

These mixed results suggest that arrest is certainly no proven panacea and that mandatory arrest may not be justifiable on the grounds of crime control. This may not disturb its proponents, who may be more persuaded by a policy argument in favor of vigorous state action in response to alleged domestic violence incidents. But it should concern police agencies not required by state law to make arrests when probable cause is found. Mandatory arrest policies for underclass areas with chronic unemployment, similar to Milwaukee's, may be increasing violent crime and should probably be abandoned (Sherman 1992).

Many issues must be addressed in drawing conclusions across sites, a task best left until the completion of all six replications. A central issue in comparing results across sites, however, is the threshold of seriousness necessary to have a case qualify for the experiment. Observations in different experimenting cities suggest very different interpretations of this question by experimenting officers. If that is the case, the differences in results may reflect different effects of arrest on different kinds of offenses or offenders. If that is not the case, a likely explanation for the differences is that similar police actions have different effects in different cities due to differences in demographics, local culture, and the local context of crime and criminal justice. These are all factors that must be addressed in developing systematic knowledge about the effects of the police on crime.

Moreover, these experiments are limited to the individual effects of arrest on those arrested. No analysis to date has addressed the *general* deterrent effects of a mandatory arrest policy in a jurisdiction. No quasi-experimental analyses of domestic assault reports, for example, have been performed to determine any before-after impact. Nor has the most powerful design of all, a random assignment of mandatory arrest to some cities or areas and not others, even been contemplated. But without such analyses, our understanding of the effects of arrest on minor domestic violence will be incomplete.

2. *Offender Absent.* An additional strategy for improving knowledge about this problem is the development and testing of innovative responses. One extension of reactive strategy tested in the Omaha experiment is the seeking of an arrest warrant when the offender is absent. A 247 case randomized experiment in use of this tactic, backed by a very high rate of issuance and prosecution, produced a clear deterrent effect on repeat violence (Dunford, Huizinga, and Elliott 1989). It is curious that a warrant should have more effect than actual incarceration (from arrest) in the same city. But if that result is replicated elsewhere, it would address a large portion of all domestic violence cases—up to half in some jurisdictions. Its value is enhanced by its relatively low consumption of police time.

Police time poses a larger question about policing domestic violence, however, in the relative priority it merits in relation to the cost. Mandatory arrest laws have been extraordinarily costly to some cities. In Milwaukee, for example, there were over 7,000 reports a year under a mandatory arrest policy. Under a 1989 state law mandating arrest, the net was widened to include intimidation, and reports almost doubled to around 14,000. The arrests consume at least three to four hours of police time (using two officer cars), or as much time as it would take to prevent (or displace) 1,200 crime calls in hot spots of crime.

This is a prime example of how an arrest "budget" could limit the amount of resources expended on each crime, while still avoiding decriminalization of the offense. If, for example, mandatory arrest were employed on selected days on a random sequence basis, the number of arrests could be cut substantially without, perhaps, losing the general deterrent effects of such arrests. The residual deterrence of arrests from one day carrying over to other days may be another consequence of rotating crackdowns (Sherman 1990b).

B. Proactive Strategies

All domestic violence control by U.S. police is now reactive. Nowhere, to my knowledge, do police identify high-risk couples and undertake proactive interventions. Such a strategy could pay off in the reduction of minor domestic violence. But it is unlikely to succeed in preventing domestic homicide, as many scholars had long hoped. It is also unlikely that any American police agency would develop proactive strategies to detect hidden domestic violence, especially among the middle and upper classes.

1. *Predicting Domestic Homicide.* The epidemiological analysis of domestic homicide is a case study in the methodological pitfalls such analysis entails. One of the most influential studies of the police role in crime control is the Police Foundation–sponsored Kansas City Police Department analysis of the precursors of domestic homicide and aggravated assault (Breedlove et al. 1977). The widely cited study, which sparked the design of the Minneapolis Domestic Violence Experiment, reported that in about 90 percent of the domestic homicides police had responded to at least one call for service at the address of the domestic homicide victim or suspect in the two years preceding the homicide and to five or more calls in about 50 percent of the cases (Breedlove et al. 1977, p. 23). Similar findings were reported for domestic aggravated assault. Wilson (1977, p. iv) concluded from these results that, at least in Kansas City, "the police can obtain some early warning of assaults

and homicides" since "any given homicide arrest is likely to be the culmination of a series of police interventions."

A follow-up study conducted by the Kansas City Police Department under a National Institute of Mental Health grant reached a similar conclusion about assaults, if not homicides: "The premise that we may have some kind of 'early warning system' embedded in the relationship of disturbances and assaults is substantiated" (Meyer and Lorimor 1977, p. V-2). No data on risk levels in relation to prior frequency of calls, however, were displayed.

Taken in conjunction with the Kansas City homicide findings, these data have suggested a pattern of escalating frequency of police interventions in domestic violence that might describe a high-risk profile for homicide. The findings raised the possibility of proactive police interventions for preventing domestic homicide, which accounts for anywhere from 8 to 21 percent of all murders nationally (Federal Bureau of Investigation 1989), and even more in specific cities. They also raised expectations about police ability to prevent domestic homicide, including numerous lawsuits when police failed to do so.

These expectations were unrealistic, however, given the major limitations of the research: units of analysis and sample sizes and selection. On the units of analysis, the research confused the criminology of *places* with the criminology of *people*. None of the findings cited above measures the prior behavior of the persons involved in the homicide. All of them merely involve police CAD records of police cars dispatched to events at certain addresses, without any record of the identities of the individuals involved. The first Kansas City study was somewhat sensitive to this issue and therefore decided to omit homicides occurring in "apartment buildings with many tenants" (Breedlove et al. 1977, p. 23). This exclusion implies, however, that two- and three-family houses, not uncommon in Kansas City, were left in the analysis. The question then becomes what percentage of the prior calls involved one of the parties involved in the subsequent homicide. Given the nameless CAD data, there was no way to tell.

On the issue of sample size, it is striking that the published version of the Kansas City study, apparently based on 1970–71 homicides (Police Foundation 1977, p. 5), did not report the exact numbers of homicides included in the analysis. We can, however, estimate the number at less than fifty and no more than seventy-three (Sherman et al. 1991*a*). The small number of homicides suggests that there are probably far more *buildings* with high frequency of domestic calls than there are domestic *homicides*. In Minneapolis, for example, a city then of two-thirds Kansas City's population, there were 1,197 buildings with five or more disturbance calls in 1986. If we assume there were twice as many buildings with that many calls in Kansas City, with no more than one homicide in any one building over two years, we have a predictive ratio of only 73 homicides in 2,394, or only 3 percent of high-risk buildings with a homicide. Predicting domestic homicide on the basis of five or more calls would therefore lead to a 97 percent false positive rate, and that is only at the level of buildings. If we multiply the number of buildings by the number of couples in them, the false positive rate would substantially exceed 99 percent. When cases (and buildings) deleted for multiple tenancy are taken into account, the error rate could be even higher.

A similar analysis in Minneapolis (Sherman et al. 1991a) shows that knowing the prior number of domestic calls at an address provides little increase in ability to predict where domestic homicides will occur, even if it does reduce the number of candidates to about 1,000 buildings. Attempts to intervene for prevention of those homicides would clearly produce substantial overprediction and much wasted effort.

Several of the problems described above can be overcome with data from the Milwaukee Domestic Violence Experiment (Sherman et al. 1991b), one of the six replications of the Minneapolis experiment funded by the National Institute of Justice. These data show that out of 15,537 police reports of domestic battery among named couples citywide from April 7, 1987, to February 8, 1989, only in one couple did a homicide later occur (Sherman et al. 1991a). Even more surprising was that thirty-two of the thirty-three domestic homicide victims during that period had no prior police record of domestic battery. Of the 110 batteries involving guns and threat of death, none led to any serious injury.

It thus appears unlikely that homicides are more likely to occur at the extreme end of a distribution of repeated reports to police of less serious violence, falsifying the "escalating violence" theory of prediction at least in terms of official data if not undetected events. The evidence against this thesis is even more compelling with the 1,113 couples in the experiment, with a twenty-two month surveillance period and a mean follow-up period of 15.8 months from the first report. Seventy couples had five or more reported batteries, but no homicides.

In the absence of the "early warning system" ability to make accurate predictions, there seems to be little hope for a proactive police strategy against domestic homicide.

2. *Controlling High-Risk Couples.*   The ability to predict which couples will have additional minor violence is greater, but still limited. In Minneapolis over a one-year period, 9.1 percent of the addresses with any domestic calls accounted for 39.5 percent of all domestic calls, while *9 percent of all addresses accounted for 100 percent of all domestic disturbance calls* (Sherman et al. 1991*a*). The Minneapolis analysis of crime hot spot addresses also found that domestic disturbance calls had the greatest concentration by address of any of six types of calls examined (including robbery, auto theft, burglary, assault, and criminal sexual conduct). Compared to the number of addresses at which domestic calls would be expected to occur without any repeat call addresses, the actual number of addresses with domestic calls was 59 percent lower than expected due to repeat calls—the largest reduction among call types examined (Sherman, Gartin, and Buerger 1989, p. 41). The building addresses at which domestic disturbance calls occur are fairly predictable, with better than two-thirds accuracy of predicting an additional call at some time within the year once there have already been three such calls.

Nonetheless, police predictions of specific couples likely to experience more minor batteries, or the places likely to have more domestic calls, must suffer some false positives (Sherman et al. 1991*a*). The best prediction Milwaukee Police could make about repeat batteries over an almost three-year period, for example, is that couples with seven or more prior reports will have another one during that time period. This prediction will be wrong in one out of four cases. While this error rate is low for purposes of scientific analysis, it may be too high for intrusive (as distinct from more passive) policing. Depending on the intrusiveness of any prevention measure suggested, it could be fiscally or ethically unacceptable to impose a measure that turns out to be unnecessary in such a large proportion of the cases.

If some powerful "inoculation" against domestic violence were possible, it could certainly be applied to the seven-or-more police-report couples. The problem is imagining what could work. A prosecutorial threat to invoke more serious penalties for recurrence sent by mail or delivered by police is one possibility and could be tested experimentally on this high-risk population. Other low cost ideas might also be tried. The point is to continue to address a pervasive problem in a spirit of trial and error rather than concluding it is "impossible" for police to do anything constructive.

VI. Policing Other Crimes

The development of police research has hardly been systematic enough to test the control of all types of crime. This section considers several of the many remaining types of crime that offer either important research results or promising strategies for crime control: drug markets, burglary, auto theft, and drunk driving.

A. Policing Drug Marketplaces

Policing drug crime has been one of the most innovative areas of American law enforcement in the last decade. It is also one of the most confused areas of strategy, with entirely unclear objectives. The longstanding concern with reducing supply has gradually been supplemented with a desire to restrict demand. In the wake of the crack epidemic, however, both goals took second place to reduction of violence and disorder in the immediate vicinity of drug marketplaces.

The central strategic choice in drug enforcement has been between wholesale and retail level dealers. Through most of the 1970s and 1980s, police focused drug enforcement on drug wholesalers. Drug enforcement was limited to special units conducting fairly complex undercover investigations. But the advent of crack created highly visible street markets and crack houses, putting tremendous pressure on police to control retail-level dealers.

From 1985 to 1989, the national arrest rate for homicide doubled among persons under age eighteen (Federal Bureau of Investigation 1986–90; U.S. Bureau of the Census 1986–90). Much of that increase undoubtedly occurred in center cities near retail drug marketplaces, as it did in Washington, D.C., where the homicide rate rose by over 300 percent (Federal Bureau of Investigation 1986–90). The sounds of gunfire became a daily occurrence in some neighborhoods, and the quality of life deteriorated rapidly (Kotlowitz 1991).

Police responded with crackdowns (Chaiken 1988; Sherman 1990b) of massive numbers of uniformed officers on patrol, raids of crack houses, and innovative tactics: "jump-out" squads intercepting observed drug transactions, condemnation of buildings and landlord fines over drug deals in residential settings, and even using front-end loaders to assault a well-fortified crack house. Kansas City police in early 1989 began raiding about one crack house every day, and local taxpayers approved a referendum for an increase in the sales tax to hire more police and prosecutors dedicated solely to drug enforcement.

Evaluation results on drug crackdowns to date have been mixed (Kleiman and Smith 1990). A Lynn, Massachusetts, crackdown on an open-air drug market reportedly reduced the robbery and burglary rates for two years, without discernible displacement (Kleiman 1988). The Lynn crackdown's use of observation-of-sale arrests was apparently more effective than the warrant arrests made in Lawrence, Massachusetts, where the crackdown resulted in no reduced drug use and an *increase* in violent crime. A massive crackdown in New York's lower east side, "Operation Pressure Point," succeeded in reducing drug use, robbery, and homicide, but the reductions decayed after the first year—a typical pattern found in most crackdowns (Sherman 1990*a*, p. 21).

Uchida, Forst, and Annan (1990) compared intensive drug enforcement alone to intensive drug enforcement plus community oriented "door-to-door" police visits to residences in Birmingham, Alabama, and Oakland, California. The intensive enforcement consisted of street corner buy-and-bust tactics, as well as raids and sweeps. In both cities, the door-to-door tactics were not fully implemented as planned, due to police resistance. But in both cities the only reductions in violent crime were found in the areas where door-to-door visits supplemented the intensive enforcement. Combined with the positive results of door-to-door visits in Houston and Newark (Pate et al. 1986; Skogan 1990), these results suggest that visits may be a far more powerful strategy than most police imagine.

On balance, we still know very little about dealing with the quality of life and soft crime problems surrounding drug marketplaces. But the continuing war on drugs creates both opportunities and a demand for more evaluations. To make further progress, the next stage of drug enforcement evaluations will require large-sample randomized experiments using marketplaces as the unit of analysis.

B. Controlling Burglary

Police strategies for controlling burglary have been highly burglar oriented, minimally victim oriented, and rarely fence oriented (Shover 1991). The burglar-oriented strategies include traditional use of informants and witnesses, as well as two newer strategies. The early 1970s Robert Redford movie, "The Sting," apparently prompted similar methods against burglars. Police set up fake fencing operations and bought stolen goods from burglars to get evidence for prosecution. Despite some favorable evaluations, however, Klockars (1980) found no evidence of a crime-reduction effect. Marx (1988, p. 126) offers strong suggestive arguments that stings can simply increase the supply of burglars by raising the level of demand for stolen goods.

If Marx is correct, then Reiss (1990) may correctly hypothesize that a fence-oriented strategy could do more to reduce burglary than a burglar-oriented strategy. Police have rarely incapacitated major fences, in part because of their skill in avoiding an evidentiary trail. But a thorough diagnosis of the local market structure for stolen goods (which may vary widely by type of goods, from art to computers) could reveal a number of potential fences as targets for proactive, undercover enforcement.

A more valuable burglar-oriented strategy may be police monitoring of previously convicted burglars, in cooperation with correctional authorities. Under a National Institute of Justice grant, for example, Indianapolis police are participating in an experiment to supplement electronically monitored house arrests of juvenile burglars. One comparison is between burglars on house arrest without police surveillance and burglars visited daily at unpredictable times by the local beat car. The theory is that burglars will be less likely to cheat on their house arrest (by going out to commit burglaries, among other things) if they know police may catch them—a testament to the weak technology and correctional follow up of electronic monitoring. An added virtue of this program should be building up police information networks among burglars, which could help to identify more fences.

The advent of automatic fingerprint identification systems may also dramatically increase police capacity to apprehend, and perhaps to deter, burglars. In the past, police had to have a suspect in mind in order to check fingerprint records. In recent years, however, many states have implemented a computerized search process requiring only one good print to produce a match with any prints already in the local system. This development has produced many anecdotal accounts of improved apprehension rates, but no systematic evaluations.

One reason burglar-oriented strategies may not work, however, is the low rate of repeat burglary arrests in any given year, at least in Kansas City (Sherman, Rogan, and Velke 1991). The maximum number of repeat burglary arrests in 1990 was only four. In contrast, only 134 persons had two or more burglary arrests, collectively generating

29 percent of all burglary arrests. Assuming that they commit many burglaries besides those for which they are arrested, it would seem that those people bear watching.

The victim-oriented strategy of the 1970s focused on target hardening. Police became virtual public relations agents for lock manufacturers, alarm companies, and hardware stores. But the evidence that hardware reduced burglary risks was quite mixed. Waller and Okihiro (1978) found no evidence that hardware made a difference, although having someone in the home did. Yet hardware-encouraging community-organizing programs in both Seattle (Lindsay and McGillis 1986) and Portland (Schneider 1986) reported substantial crime-reduction effects. One reason they may have been so successful, however, is the selection bias built into the choice of neighborhoods. Attempting to mount similar neighborhood watch programs in Chicago and Minneapolis neighborhoods that were less eager to implement the programs met with no measured crime-reduction effect (Skogan 1990, chap. 6).

Marking identification on personal property, or "Operation Identification," also shows mixed results. While it has not been found to increase the likelihood of property being recovered, both U.S. (Schneider 1986) and Welsh (Laycock 1986) evaluations have found that it reduces the rate at which homes are burglarized. It is possible, of course, that the act of marking goods creates some greater level of watchfulness by families or that visible stickers indicating participation in the program displace burglars to other locations. But in the absence of any better evidence, the police effort expended in getting the property marked appears to be cost-effective (Laycock 1986).

High-risk victims could also be the focus of special police programs, with a potentially greater crime-reduction effect. In Kansas City in 1985–89, only 1 percent of the population (5,423 people) produced 26 percent of the burglary victimizations (Sherman, Rogan, and Velke 1991). There were 751 people burglarized at the rate of one per year or higher, and one victim reported thirty-six burglaries in five years. These people could be targeted for problem-solving efforts to diagnose the causes of the repeat burglaries and the possible solutions to each individual set of circumstances.

C. Controlling Auto Theft

Big-city auto theft enforcement is often focused on professional "chop shops" for breaking up cars and on professional gangs of car thieves. And in Kansas City, a small number of auto thieves—who may or may not be very "professional"— are repeatedly arrested. In 1990, 209 persons accounted for 502 auto theft arrests, or 32 percent of all such arrests (Sherman, Rogan, and Velke 1991). But the offender-oriented focus has been problematic in the late 1980s, as increased auto theft rates appear to be connected to drug shipments and subsequent abandonment of cars. The problem might be better controlled by increased technology and potential fraud analysis.

The primary new technological solution is the Lo-Jack car locator system, which has been tested in Massachusetts since 1986 (Grable 1991). The commercially marketed system, based in Needham, Massachusetts, works by having a radio transmitter installed in a hidden location in the car by company personnel. If the owner reports the car stolen, duly equipped police agencies are then able to pinpoint the location of the car within a twenty-five mile square, after they activate the transmission device from police headquarters. In the first five years of operation, Massachusetts police recovered 95 percent of the vehicles reported stolen. The average recovery time is two hours, and the fastest was seven minutes. Arrest rates average 20 percent, compared to the national auto theft clearance rate of 5 percent.

The cost of the system to private citizens is about $600. A more expensive system ($1,500) activates a central station alarm if the car is moved without proper authorization codes. The Michigan-based Code-Alarm system avoids the possible delay in reporting associated with Lo-Jack since the owner does not need to discover the theft for the system to be activated. Code-Alarm also gives police a device that enables them to turn off the engine of the stolen car once they are in pursuit of it, avoiding the possible damage of a high-speed chase (Grable 1991).

If either commercial system were universally adopted by police agencies, police could track and arrest a car thief at any time until the car is disassembled and the locator destroyed. This capacity would not create a deterrent effect, however, until the prevalence of the system was so high that thieves would calculate the risk to be unattractive. This could happen more readily with mandatory installation in all new cars, which in the long run could make a big dent in car theft rates. In the short run, however, it would probably just displace theft on to older cars made before the new requirements. That is exactly what happened in England, for example, after the introduction of steering column locks on all new cars (Mayhew et al. 1976). In Germany in

1963, however, auto theft went down 60 percent across the board when all cars—old and new—were required to install steering column locks (Mayhew et al. 1976).

A mandatory locator system would also help to deter insurance fraud in car theft reporting, although smart con artists might still find ways around it. What will be harder to escape is a regional or national registry of car theft victims, which would identify repeat victims by social security number or drivers' licenses. Unusually high levels of car theft would either expose victims as frauds or restrict their access to further car insurance as plain bad risks. In Kansas City, for example, in 1985–89, there were 386 people who reported three or more car thefts in five years, and eighteen people who reported five or more (Sherman, Rogan, and Velke 1991). Whether careless or fraudulent, these people are worth some special attention.

D. Controlling Drunk Driving

Police control of drunk driving has probably been more successful than critics have claimed. H. Laurence Ross (1982), the leading student of drunk driving enforcement, has found fairly consistent evidence of actual or threatened police crackdowns producing immediate deterrent effects on single-vehicle nighttime fatal accidents. But he also finds these effects to wear off, sooner or later. He therefore concludes pessimistically that "deterrence-based policies are questionable in the long run" (Ross 1982, p. 111). As Jacobs (1988, p. 212) points out, this conclusion may be unjustified by the data, which may tap only a small subset of the potential drunk driving population. It also unduly discounts the value of the short-term deterrent effects he so consistently observes in different nations, in different decades, with different police enforcement methods.

As Sherman (1990a) suggests, Ross's consistent finding can be put to more strategic use. The key is the common finding of the short-term crackdowns that the measured deterrent effects persisted after the police efforts had ended. This "residual" deterrent effect lasted in some cases as long as the crackdown itself. In order to obtain twice the deterrence for the same amount of personnel time, police might continually alter targets and tactics of drunk driving crackdowns. Since there are more areas in most jurisdictions than police can cover intensively, constant shifts in geographic targets makes sense in any case.

The difficulty in evaluating some of the newer tactics, like checkpoints, is that few state laws require alcohol testing of drivers involved in accidents, even fatal ones. Most drunk-driving data are based on dead drivers or inferences from overall accident rates. Until wider testing of drivers in fatal accidents is required, even the U.S. Department of Transportation's national FARS (Fatal Accident Reporting System) data on trends in alcohol-related deaths will remain highly speculative. At the local level, it will be difficult to examine the effects of any geographically focused enforcement efforts on drunk driving in the immediate vicinity of those efforts.

These strategies are primarily across-the-board, general deterrent strategies. Relatively little problem-oriented policing has been focused on the more persistent problem of chronic recidivists at high risk of injuring themselves or their passengers in an accident. The situational epidemiology of DWI-related accidents, for example, has not been widely discussed. But a few police agencies have recognized the high prevalence of drunk drivers who have just come from a tavern or pool hall, over 50 percent in one California study of DWI arrestees (Yoder and Moore 1973). Some agencies have responded to this by staking out bars and following cars as they depart, watching for erratic driving. Shaw (1989) suggests that police lobby for barring convicted drunk drivers from even visiting public drinking places as a condition of probation or parole.

Reactive strategies for drunk driving enforcement take on new dimensions with the car phone. While it was once almost impossible for good citizens to call police with the exact whereabouts of a drunk driver, car phones allow citizens to tail the driver until police come. Public relations campaigns to encourage such actions could stimulate them, even with the predictable cost of some rate of false alarms.

VII. Future Prospects

What can police do about crime? One answer to the question might be that we do not know because they never really tried. That judgment would be overly harsh, for despite the preoccupation with answering 911 calls there is much that police do that has some effect on crime. The important question is *what effect* since police efforts can sometimes increase crime as well as control it. A related question is *what else* could they do that they are not now doing, and should it be substituted for some current activities? As little as we know about the effects of current activities, there are probably more legal, constitutional, and morally proper tactics that have not been tried than have been. Therein lies the lesson for future prospects.

It is unlikely that police will achieve anything like medicine's spectacular successes in virtually eliminating certain diseases. There have been some such precedents in crime control: robberies of buses eliminated by eliminating cash, domestic skyjackings almost eliminated by metal detectors. But the police have not yet directly accomplished such results. Nor, given the intractability of most crime problems, are they likely to.

What seems more likely to work is a steady accumulation of results, searching for some with modest success. While this process is necessarily plagued by a "theory gap" in frameworks for organizing and understanding diverse results (Zimring 1978), that problem seems likely to be solved more quickly with more data rather than more dataless theory. Police are more than willing to step up the pace of experimentation with specific tactics against specific crime problems. The major problem is a lack of trained and willing social scientists available to work with them, a shortage linked directly to the dearth of federal and foundation support for research and development for crime control.

This pace will remain sluggish if it is wholly or primarily dependent on federal sources of funding. While police chiefs have called for more research and development on drug enforcement, Congress has ignored their pleas. What may be more feasible is a combination of city and foundation funds for conducting local experiments, with technical support from the national research organizations. The New York City Police, for example, have funded research by the Vera Institute of Justice. But American foundations in the 1990s are almost uniformly uninterested in crime, and the continuing decline of most big cities makes city funding unlikely.

No matter how research is funded, the key resource will still be imagination. Without creative ideas for diagnosing and treating a crime problem with policing, there will be nothing to evaluate. Academics tend to scorn the process of idea generation and to respect rigorous tests. But rigorous tests of bad ideas will make little progress. Police professionals should be emboldened by their own detailed knowledge of the crime problems they face and encouraged to gather even more systematic data on them. There are only 500 active research criminologists in the United States and over 500,000 police. The odds should support more ideas from the rank and file. Anything national and local organizations can do to encourage the "suggestion box" for crime control will increase the stockpile of hypotheses.

Innovative crime-control tests could also revive the office of chief of police, a position now slowly being strangled by police unions, red tape, and 911 calls. Modern police chiefs have relatively little opportunity to exercise leadership in crime control except for bold initiatives, which can be even more valuable if properly evaluated. For despite the quasi-military symbolism of police rank structure, the jurisprudence of policing assumes more of a hospital model. Officers, like doctors, deal with cases and take the primary responsibility for the decisions they make. The police department, like the hospital, is merely a source of organizational support and personnel resources for those decisions, but not the decision maker itself. Police chiefs have become hospital administrators rather than generals.

This essay's reliance on the military concepts of strategy and tactics may seem inappropriate for the hospital model of police work. But it is the hospital model itself that is inappropriate to crime control. Hospitals are reactive organizations, relying on people to come to them when they are sick. The goal of the hospital is to heal the sick, not to control disease. Public health organizations, by contrast, take no patients, but seek to control disease. They employ many doctors, but decision making is an organizational, not individual, responsibility. The strategies and tactics for fighting epidemics like AIDS, or chronic sources of mortality like heart disease, are determined in truly quasi-military fashion. It is no accident that the federal Centers for Disease Control is an arm of the U.S. Public Health Service, which is a uniformed service commanded by a (surgeon) general.

A police chief as "surgeon general" would be far more concerned with crime analysis, especially chains of causation and emerging epidemiological trends. A crime-control chief would strike at those causal chains wherever there is a vulnerable link. Just as the surgeon general speaks out against smoking, a police chief could speak out against divorce and other individual choices that may contribute to community crime rates—even while respecting the rights of people to make such choices. And just as the local health department closes down restaurants for operating unclean kitchens, a crime-control police department can close down taverns or entertainment facilities for operating high-crime establishments.

Police departments cannot escape their responsibilities as "hospitals," of course. But they already do refuse to deal with many kinds of cases, through the exercise of officer discretion. This precedent opens the door to the addition of the public health model to the traditional hospital model of police organization, paying for "disease control" by cutting back on the costs of "patient care" (McEwen, Connors, and Cohen 1986). Indeed, the merger of the two approaches may allow joint strategies that are unheard of in disease control. Hospitals play relatively little role in providing preventive medicine, despite the enormous opportunity they have through direct contact with the sick. Police can use their contacts with victims, places, and offenders to attack causal chains as well as to treat the specific cases.

Given this perspective on the possible future—and to some extent, current—directions for police departments, there is every reason to talk about strategic and tactical choices for crime control. Police chiefs can become both surgeons general and hospital administrators. There is no major legal obstacle to clearer organizational direction of officers' time, including discretion to arrest. This does not mean that the direction must be top-down since policies can be made just as well through bottom-up initiatives and participation. But it does mean that the organization can make coordinated and systematic choices rather than letting the choices emerge topsy-turvy from the individual decisions of each officer.

Approaching strategic choices in this manner can also breathe new life into the concept of community policing (Skolnick and Bayley 1986). In making explicit choices about priorities, strategy, and tactics, police agencies can seek citizen comment before the choices become final. They can also make different choices for different communities, in reflection of local preferences. Interest group pressure can also be dealt with more rationally through clear choices. Rather than seeing the police department as a bottomless well, interest groups could be educated to see it as an organization of finite resources. If there is to be increased attention to one problem, attention to something else must be cut. Getting interest groups to see the broader public interest, rather than making unilateral assaults on police executives, would be much better for democratic policing. It might even foster more effective crime control.

REFERENCES

Andenaes, Johannes. 1974. *Punishment and Deterrence*. Ann Arbor: University of Michigan Press.
Anderson, David C. 1990. "Editorial Notebook: The Tyranny of 911." *New York Times* (September 17, eastern ed.).

Ares, C. E., Anne Rankin, and Herbert Sturz. 1963. "The Manhattan Bail Project: An Interim Report on the Use of Pre-trial Parole." *New York University Law Review* 38:67–95.

Barr, Robert, and Ken Pease. 1990. "Crime Placement, Displacement, and Deflection." In *Crime and Justice: A Review of Research*, vol. 12, edited by Michael Tonry and Norval Morris. Chicago: University of Chicago Press.

Behan, Cornelius J. 1990. Personal communication with author.

Berk, Richard E., and Lawrence W. Sherman. 1988. "Police Responses to Family Violence Incidents: An Analysis of an Experimental Design with Incomplete Randomization." *Journal of the American Statistical Association* 83:70–76.

Bittner, Egon. 1970. *The Functions of the Police in Modern Society: Background Factors, Current Practices, and Possible Role Models*. Chevy Chase, Md.: National Institute of Mental Health.

Black, Donald. 1973. "The Mobilization of Law." *Journal of Legal Studies* 2:125–49.

———. 1983. "Crime as Social Control." *American Sociological Review* 48:34–45.

Blumstein, Alfred, Jacqueline Cohen, Jeffrey Roth, and Christy Visher. 1986. *Criminal Careers and "Career Criminals."* Washington, D.C.: National Academy Press.

Botein, Bernard. 1965. "The Manhattan Bail Project: Its Impact in Criminology and the Criminal Law Process." *Texas Law Review* 43:319–31.

Boydstun, John. 1975. "San Diego Field Interrogation: Final Report." Washington, D.C.: Police Foundation.

Boydstun, John, Michael E. Sherry, and Nicholas P. Moelter. 1977. *Patrol Staffing in San Diego: One- Or Two-Officer Units*. Washington, D.C.: Police Foundation.

Braithwaite, John. 1989. *Crime, Shame, and Reintegration*. Cambridge: Cambridge University Press.

Breedlove, Ronald K., John W. Kennish, Donald M. Sandker, and Robert K. Sawtell. 1977. "Domestic Violence and the Police: Kansas City." In *Domestic Violence and the Police: Studies in Detroit and Kansas City*. Washington, D.C.: Police Foundation.

Brown, Lee P. 1989. "Community Policing: A Practical Guide for Police Officials." *Police Chief*, August, pp. 72–82.

Buerger, Michael. 1991. *Repeat Call Policing: The RECAP Casebook*. Washington, D.C.: Crime Control Institute.

Campbell, Donald T., and H. Laurence Ross. 1968. "The Connecticut Crackdown on Speeding: Time-Series Data in Quasi-experimental Analysis." *Law and Society Review* 3:33–53.

Chaiken, Marcia R., ed. 1988. *Street-Level Drug Enforcement: Examining the Issues*. Washington, D.C.: National Institute of Justice.

Clark, Gerald. 1969. "What Happens When the Police Strike." *New York Times Magazine* (November 16), sec. 6, pp. 45, 176–85, 187, 194–95.

Clarke, Ronald V. 1983. "Situational Crime Prevention: Its Theoretical Basis and Practical Scope." In *Crime and Justice: An Annual Review of Research*, vol. 4, edited by Michael Tonry and Norval Morris. Chicago: University of Chicago Press.

Clarke, Ronald V., and Patricia Mayhew. 1988. "The British Gas Suicide Story and Its Criminological Implications." In *Crime and Justice: A Review of Research*, vol. 10, edited by Michael Tonry and Norval Morris. Chicago: University of Chicago Press.

Clifton, Wayland, Jr. 1987. "Convenience Store Robberies in Gainesville, Florida: An Intervention Strategy by the Gainesville Police Department." Photocopy. Gainesville, Fla.: Gainesville Police Department.

Cohen, Lawrence E., and Marcus Felson. 1979. "Social Change and Crime Rate Trends: A Routine Activity Approach." *American Sociological Review* 44:588–608.

Colquhoun, Patrick. 1795. *A Treatise on the Police of The Metropolis*. London. 7th ed. enlarged 1806, reprinted at Montclair, N.J.: Patterson-Smith, 1969.

Cook, Philip. 1991. "The Technology of Personal Violence." In *Crime and Justice: A Review of Research*, vol. 14, edited by Michael Tonry. Chicago: University of Chicago Press.

Cook, Thomas, and Donald T. Campbell. 1979. *Quasi-experimentation: Design and Analysis Issues for Field Settings*. Chicago: Rand-McNally.

Cornish, Derek, and Ronald V. Clarke. 1987. "Understanding Crime Displacement: An Application of Rational Choice Theory." *Criminology* 25:933–47.

Cumming, Elaine, I. Cumming, and Laura Edell. 1965. "Policeman as Philosopher, Friend and Guide." *Social Problems* 12:276–86.

Currie, Elliott. 1985. "Crimes of Violence and Public Policy: Changing Directions." In *American Violence and Public Policy*, edited by Lynn A. Curtis. New Haven, Conn.: Yale University Press.

Dennis, Michael L. 1988. "Implementing Randomized Field Experiments: An Analysis of Criminal and Civil Justice Research." Ph.D. dissertation, Northwestern University, Department of Psychology.

Dunford, Franklyn W., David Huizinga, and Delbert S. Elliott. 1989. "The Omaha Domestic Violence Police Experiments: Final Report to the National Institute of Justice." Washington, D.C.: U.S. Department of Justice, National Institute of Justice.

Dunford, Franklyn W., David Huizinga, and Delbert S. Elliott. 1990. "The Role of Arrest in Domestic Assault: The Omaha Police Experiment." *Criminology* 28:183–206.

Eck, John, and William Spelman. 1987. *Problem Solving: Problem-oriented Policing in Newport News*. Washington, D.C.: Police Executive Research Forum.

Farrington, David. 1983. "Randomized Experiments on Crime and Justice." In *Crime and Justice: An Annual Review of Research*, vol. 4, edited by Michael Tonry and Norval Morris. Chicago: University of Chicago Press.

Federal Bureau of Investigation. 1986–90. *Crime in the United States*. Washington, D.C.: U.S. Government Printing Office.

Fielding, Henry. 1751. *An Enquiry Into the Causes of the Late Increase of Robbers*. London. Reprinted 1977 at Montclair, N.J.: Patterson-Smith.

Fisher, R. A. 1935. *The Design of Experiments*. Edinburgh: Oliver & Boyd.

Flanagan, Timothy J., and Kathleen Maguire. 1990. *Sourcebook of Criminal Justice Statistics—1989*. Washington, D.C.: Government Printing Office.

Goldstein, Herman. 1977. *Policing a Free Society*. Cambridge, Mass.: Ballinger.

———. 1979. "Improving Policing: A Problem-oriented Approach." *Crime and Delinquency* 25:236–58.

———. 1990. *Problem-oriented Policing.* New York: McGraw-Hill.

Gottfredson, Michael R., and Travis Hirschi. 1990. *A General Theory of Crime.* Stanford, Calif.: Stanford University Press.

Grable, Ron. 1991. "Stolen Car Retrieval Systems." *Motor Trend* (January), p. 106.

Greene, Jack R., and Carl B. Klockars. 1991. "What Police Do." In *Thinking about Police*, edited by Carl B. Klockars and Stephen D. Mastrofski. 2d ed. New York: McGraw-Hill.

Greenhouse, Steven. 1990. "Poles Find Crime Replacing Police State." *New York Times* (March 4, eastern ed.), p. 20.

Hindelang, Michael, Michael R. Gottfredson, and James Garofalo. 1978. *Victims of Personal Crime.* Cambridge, Mass.: Ballinger.

Hirschel, J. David, Ira W. Hutchison III, Charles W. Dean, Joseph J. Kelley, and Carolyn E. Pesackis. 1990. "Charlotte Spouse Assault Replication Project: Final Report." Washington, D.C.: U.S. Department of Justice, National Institute of Justice.

Jacob, Herbert, and Michael J. Rich. 1981. "The Effects of the Police on Crime: A Second Look." *Law and Society Review* 15:109–15.

Jacobs, James B. 1988. "The Law and Criminology of Drunk Driving." In *Crime and Justice: A Review of Research*, vol. 10, edited by Michael Tonry and Norval Morris. Chicago: University of Chicago Press.

Joiner, Larry. 1990. Personal communication with author (former chief of police, Kansas City, Missouri).

Kelling, George L., Tony Pate, Duane Dieckman, and Charles Brown. 1974. *The Kansas City Preventive Patrol Experiment: A Summary Report.* Washington, D.C.: Police Foundation.

Kleiman, Mark. 1988. "Crackdowns: The Effects of Intensive Enforcement on Retail Heroin Dealing." In *Street-Level Drug Enforcement: Examining the Issues*, edited by Marcia Chaiken. Washington, D.C.: U.S. Department of Justice, National Institute of Justice.

Kleiman, Mark, and Kerry Smith. 1990. "State and Local Drug Enforcement: In Search of a Strategy." In *Drugs and Crime*, edited by Michael Tonry and James Q. Wilson. Vol. 13 of *Crime and Justice: A Review of Research*, edited by Michael Tonry and Norval Morris. Chicago: University of Chicago Press.

Klein, Malcolm W. 1986. "Labeling Theory and Delinquency Policy: An Experimental Test." *Criminal Justice and Behavior* 13:47–79.

Klockars, Carl B. 1980. "Jonathan Wild and the Modern Sting." In *History and Crime: Implications for Criminal Justice Policy*, edited by James Inciardi and Charles E. Faupel. Beverly Hills, Calif.: Sage.

———. 1991. "The Rhetoric of Community Policing." In *Thinking about Police*, edited by Carl B. Klockars and Stephen D. Mastrofski. 2d ed. New York: McGraw-Hill.

Klockars, Carl B., and Stephen Mastrofski, eds. 1991. *Thinking about Police.* 2d ed. New York: McGraw-Hill.

Kolata, Gina. 1991. "In Medical Research, Equal Opportunity Doesn't Always Apply." *New York Times* (March 10, eastern ed.), p. E16.

Kotlowitz, Alex. 1991. *There Are No Children Here*. New York: Doubleday.

Larson, Richard C. 1976. "What Happened to Patrol Operations in Kansas City." *Evaluation* 3:117–23.

Laycock, Gloria. 1986. "Property Marking as a Deterrent to Domestic Burglary." In *Situational Crime Prevention*, edited by Kevin Heal and Gloria Laycock. London: H.M. Stationery Office.

Lempert, Richard. 1984. "From the Editor." *Law and Society Review* 18:505–10.

———. 1989. "Humility Is a Virtue: On the Publicization of Policy-relevant Research." *Law and Society Review* 23:145–61.

Lindsay, Betsy, and Daniel McGillis. 1986. "Citywide Community Crime Prevention: An Assessment of the Seattle Program." In *Community Crime Prevention: Does It Work?* edited by Dennis P. Rosenbaum. Beverly Hills, Calif.: Sage.

Logan, Charles. 1975. "Arrest Rates and Deterrence." *Social Science Quarterly* 56:376–89.

McCord, Joan. 1978. "A Thirty Year Follow-up of Treatment Effects." *American Psychologist* 33:284–89.

McEwen, J. Thomas, Edward F. Connors III, and Marcia I. Cohen. 1986. *Evaluation of the Differential Police Response Field Test*. Washington, D.C.: U.S. Department of Justice, National Institute of Justice.

Makinen, Tuija, and Hannu Takala. 1980. "The 1976 Police Strike in Finland." *Scandinavian Studies in Criminology* 7:87–106.

Martin, Susan, and Lawrence W. Sherman. 1986. "Selective Apprehension: A Police Strategy for Repeat Offenders." *Criminology* 24:155–73.

Marx, Gary T. 1988. *Undercover: Police Surveillance in America*. Berkeley and Los Angeles: University of California Press.

———. 1990. Personal communication with author.

Mayhew, Patricia, Ronald V. G. Clarke, Andrew Sturman, and J. Michael Hough. 1976. *Crime as Opportunity*. Home Office Research Study no. 34. London: H.M. Stationery Office.

Merton, Robert K. 1968. *Social Theory and Social Structure*. New York: Free Press.

Meyer, Jeanie Keeny, and Theron D. Lorimor. 1977. "Police Intervention Data and Domestic Violence: Exploratory Development and Validation of Prediction Models." Report prepared under grant Ro1MH27918 from National Institute of Mental Health to Kansas City, Missouri, Police Department.

Milton, Catherine H., Jeanne Halleck, James Lardner, and Gary Abrecht. 1977. *Police Use of Deadly Force*. Washington, D.C.: Police Foundation.

Moore, Mark. In this volume. "Problem-solving and Community Policing."

Morris, Norval, and Gordon Hawkins. 1970. *The Honest Politician's Guide to Crime Control*. Chicago: University of Chicago Press.

Mydans, Seth. 1991. "Tape of Beating by Police Revives Charges of Racism." *New York Times* (March 7, eastern ed.), p. A 18.

Nagin, Daniel. 1978. "General Deterrence: A Review of the Empirical Evidence." In *Deterrence and Incapacitation: Estimating the Effects of Criminal Sanction on Crime Rates*, edited by Alfred Blumstein, Jacqueline Cohen, and Daniel Nagin. Washington, D.C.: National Academy Press.

Nazario, Sonia, and David Jefferson. 1991. "L.A. Law: A Videotaped Beating Highlights Problems of Los Angeles Police." *Wall Street Journal* (March 12), p. 1.

Packer, Herbert S. 1968. *The Limits of the Criminal Sanction*. Stanford, Calif.: Stanford University Press.

Pate, Antony Michael. 1989. "Community Policing in Baltimore." In *Police and Policing: Contemporary Issues*, edited by Dennis Jay Kenny. New York: Praeger.

Pate, Tony, Mary Ann Wycoff, Wesley Skogan, and Lawrence W. Sherman. 1986. *Reducing Fear of Crime in Houston and Newark: A Summary Report*. Washington, D.C.: Police Foundation.

Phillips, Llad, and Harold Votey. 1972. "An Economic Analysis of the Deterrent Effect of Law Enforcement on Criminal Activity." *Journal of Criminal Law, Criminology and Police Science* 63:336–42.

Pierce, Glen L., Susan A. Spaar, and LeBaron R. Briggs IV. 1988. "The Character of Police Work: Strategic and Tactical Implications." Report to the National Institute of Justice. Boston: Northeastern University, Center for Applied Social Research.

Pocock, Stuart J. 1983. *Clinical Trials: A Practical Approach*. New York: Wiley.

Police Foundation. 1977. *Domestic Violence and the Police: Studies in Detroit and Kansas City*. Washington, D.C.: Police Foundation.

———. 1981. *The Newark Foot Patrol Experiment*. Washington, D.C.: Police Foundation.

Reiss, Albert J., Jr. 1971. *The Police and the Public*. New Haven, Conn.: Yale University Press.

———. 1985. *Policing a City's Central District: The Oakland Story*. Washington, D.C.: U.S. Government Printing Office.

———. 1988. "Co-offending and Criminal Careers." In *Crime and Justice: A Review of Research*, vol. 10, edited by Michael Tonry and Norval Morris. Chicago: University of Chicago Press.

———. 1990. Personal communication with author.

Reiss, Albert J., Jr., and David J. Bordua. 1967. "Environment and Organization: A Perspective on the Police." In *The Police: Six Sociological Essays*, edited by David J. Bordua. New York: Wiley.

Richman, Teri. 1990. Personal communication with author (vice president, National Association of Convenience Stores).

Rosenbaum, Dennis P., ed. 1986. *Community Crime Prevention: Does It Work?* Beverly Hills, Calif.: Sage.

Ross, H. Laurence. 1982. *Deterring the Drinking Driver: Legal Policy and Social Control*. Lexington, Mass.: D. C. Heath.

Rossi, Peter, Richard E. Berk, and Bettye K. Eidson. 1974. *The Roots of Urban Discontent*. New York: Wiley.

Rossi, Peter H., Emily Waite, Christine E. Bose, and Richard E. Berk. 1974. "The Seriousness of Crimes: Normative Structure and Individual Differences." *American Sociological Review* 39:224–38.

Russell, Francis. 1975. *A City in Terror: 1919—the Boston Police Strike*. New York: Viking.

Sampson, Robert J., and Jacqueline Cohen. 1988. "Deterrent Effects of Police on Crime: A Replication and Theoretical Extension." *Law and Society Review* 22:163–89.

Schneider, Anne L. 1986. "Neighborhood-based Anti-burglary Strategies: An Analysis of Public and Private Benefits from the Portland Program." In *Community Crime Prevention: Does It Work?* edited by Dennis P. Rosenbaum. Beverly Hills, Calif.: Sage.

Schnelle, J. F., R. E. Kirchner, J. D. Casey, P. H. Uselton, and M. P. McNees. 1977. "Patrol Evaluation Research: A Multiple-Baseline Analysis of Saturation Police Patrolling during Day and Night Hours." *Journal of Applied Behavioral Research* 10:33–40.

Schwartz, Alfred I., and Sumner N. Clarren. 1977. *The Cincinnati Team Policing Experiment: A Summary Report*. Washington, D.C.: Police Foundation.

Sellwood, A. V. 1978. *Police Strike—1919*. London: W. H. Allen.

Shaw, James. 1989. "Reinventing the Police: A New Tactic for Dealing with Driving while Intoxicated Offenders." Unpublished manuscript. University of Maryland, Institute of Criminal Justice and Criminology.

Sherman, Lawrence W. 1983. "From Whodunit to Who Does It: Fairness and Target Selection in Deceptive Investigations." In *Abscam Ethics: Moral Issues and Deception in Law Enforcement*, edited by Gerald M. Caplan. Cambridge, Mass.: Ballinger.

———. 1986. "Policing Communities: What Works." In *Communities and Crime*, edited by Albert J. Reiss, Jr. and Michael Tonry. Vol. 8 of *Crime and Justice: A Review of Research*, edited by Michael Tonry and Norval Morris. Chicago: University of Chicago Press.

———. 1989. "Repeat Calls for Service: Policing the 'Hot Spots.'" In *Police and Policing: Contemporary Issues*, edited by Dennis J. Kenny. New York: Praeger.

———. 1990*a*. "Police Crackdowns: Initial and Residual Deterrence." In *Crime and Justice: A Review of Research*, vol. 12, edited by Michael Tonry and Norval Morris. Chicago: University of Chicago Press.

———. 1990*b*. "An Arrest Budget?" Address before the National Conference on Crime, John Jay College of Criminal Justice, New York, March 6.

———. 1991. "The Results of Police Work: Review of *Problem-oriented Policing*, by Herman Goldstein." *Journal of Criminal Law and Criminology* (forthcoming).

———. 1992. *Policing Domestic Violence: Experiments and Policy Dilemmas*. New York: Free Press.

Sherman, Lawrence, and Richard A. Berk. 1984. "The Specific Deterrent Effects of Arrest for Domestic Assault." *American Sociological Review* 49:261–72.

Sherman, Lawrence, Michael E. Buerger, Patrick R. Gartin, Robert Dell'Erba, and Kinley Larntz. 1989. "Beyond Dial-a-Cop: Repeat Call Address Policing." Report to the National Institute of Justice. Washington, D.C.: Crime Control Institute.

Sherman, Lawrence, and Ellen G. Cohn. 1989. "The Impact of Research on Legal Policy: The Minneapolis Domestic Violence Experiment." *Law and Society Review* 23:117–44.

Sherman, Lawrence, Patrick Gartin, and Michael E. Buerger. 1989. "Hot Spots of Predatory Crime: Routine Activities and the Criminology of Place." *Criminology* 27:27–55.

Sherman, Lawrence, Dennis Rogan, and Robert Velke. 1991. "The Menagerie of Crime: Targets for Police Crime Control Strategies." Unpublished manuscript. Washington, D.C.: Crime Control Institute.

Sherman, Lawrence, Janell D. Schmidt, Dennis Rogan, and Christine DeRiso. 1991*a*. "Predicting Domestic Homicide: Prior Police Contact and Gun Threats." In *Woman Battering: Policy Responses*, edited by Michael Steinman. Cincinnati, Ohio: Anderson.

Sherman, Lawrence, Janell D. Schmidt, Dennis P. Rogan, Patrick R. Gartin, Ellen G. Cohn, Dean J. Collins, and Anthony R. Bacich. 1991*b*. "From Initial Deterrence to Long-Term Escalation: Short Custody Arrest for Underclass Domestic Violence." *Criminology* (forthcoming).

Sherman, Lawrence, and Douglas A. Smith. 1991. "Ghetto Poverty, Crime, and Punishment: Formal and Informal Control of Domestic Violence." Unpublished manuscript. University of Maryland, Institute of Criminal Justice and Criminology.

Sherman, Lawrence, Robert Velke, Carol Bridgeforth, and Danee Gaines. 1991*c*. *Violent Crime in Georgetown: High-Risk Places and Times*. Washington, D.C.: Crime Control Institute.

Sherman, Lawrence, and David Weisburd. 1990. "The General Deterrent Effects of Increased Police Patrol in Hot Spots of Crime." Paper presented to the Academy of Criminal Justice Sciences, Denver, March.

Shover, Neal. 1991. "Burglary." In *Crime and Justice: A Review of Research*, vol. 14, edited by Michael Tonry. Chicago: University of Chicago Press.

Skogan, Wesley G. 1988. "Community Organizations and Crime." In *Crime and Justice: A Review of Research*, vol. 10, edited by Michael Tonry and Norval Morris. Chicago: University of Chicago Press.

———. 1990. *Disorder and Decline: Crime and the Spiral of Decay in America's Neighborhoods*. New York: Free Press.

Skogan, Wesley, and Richard Block. 1983. "Resistance and Injury in Non-fatal Assaultive Violence." *Victimology* 8:215–26.

———. 1986. "Resistance and Nonfatal Outcomes in Stranger-to-Stranger Predatory Crime." *Violence and Victims* 1:241–53.

Skogan, Wesley, and Michael Maxfield. 1981. *Coping with Crime: Individual and Neighborhood Reactions*. Beverly Hills, Calif.: Sage.

Skolnick, Jerome, and David Bayley. 1986. *The New Blue Line: Police Innovation in Six American Cities*. New York: Free Press.

Sparks, Richard F. 1981. "Multiple Victimization: Evidence, Theory and Future Research." *Journal of Criminal Law and Criminology* 72:762–78.

Sparrow, Malcolm K., Mark H. Moore, and David Kennedy. 1990. *Beyond 911: A New Era for Policing*. New York: Basic.

Tittle, Charles R., and Alan R. Rowe. 1974. "Certainty of Arrest and Crime Rates: A Further Test of the Deterrence Hypothesis." *Social Forces* 52:455–62.

Toch, Hans. 1975. *Agents of Change: A Study in Police Reform*. Cambridge: Schenkman.

Uchida, Craig D., Brian Forst, and Sampson Annan. 1990. *Modern Policing and the Control of Illegal Drugs: Testing New Strategies in Two American Cities: Draft Executive Summary*. Washington, D.C.: National Institute of Justice.

U.S. Attorney General's Task Force on Violent Crime. 1981. *Final Report*. Washington, D.C.: U.S. Government Printing Office.

U.S. Bureau of the Census. 1986–90. *Current Population Reports*. Washington, D.C.: U.S. Government Printing Office.

Waller, Irwin, and Norma Okihiro. 1978. *Burglary: The Victim and the Public*. Toronto: University of Toronto Press.

Weisburd, David. 1989. *Jewish Settler Violence*. State College: Pennsylvania State University Press.

Weisburd, David, Lisa Maher, and Lawrence W. Sherman. 1991. "Contrasting Crime-general and Crime-specific Theory: The Case of Hot Spots of Crime." In *Advances in Criminological Theory*, vol. 5. New Brunswick, N.J.: Transaction Press.

Williams, Hubert. 1983. Personal communication with author (former police director, city of Newark).

Wilson, James Q. 1968. *Varieties of Police Behavior*. Cambridge, Mass.: Harvard University Press.

———. 1977. "Foreword." In *Domestic Violence and the Police: Studies in Detroit and Kansas City*. Washington, D.C.: Police Foundation.

Wilson, James Q., and Barbara Boland. 1978. "The Effect of the Police on Crime." *Law and Society Review* 12:367–90.

———. 1981–82. "The Effects of the Police on Crime: A Rejoinder." *Law and Society Review* 16:163–69.

Wilson, James Q., and Richard Herrnstein. 1985. *Crime and Human Nature*. New York: Simon & Schuster.

Wilson, James Q., and George Kelling. 1982. "Broken Windows: The Police and Neighborhood Safety." *Atlantic Monthly* (March), pp. 29–38.

Wilson, Jerry V. 1990a. Personal communication with author (former chief of police, Washington, D.C.).

———. 1990b. *Gainesville Convenience Store Ordinance: Findings of Fact, Conclusions and Recommendations*. Report prepared for the National Association of Convenience Stores. Washington, D.C.: Crime Control Research Corporation.

Wilson, Orlando W. 1963. *Police Administration*. 2d ed. New York: McGraw-Hill.

Wolfgang, Marvin, Robert Figlio, and Thorsten Sellin. 1972. *Delinquency in a Birth Cohort*. Chicago: University of Chicago Press.

Wycoff, Mary Ann, Charles Susmilch, and Charles Brown. 1981. "The Birmingham Anti-robbery Experiment." Draft report. Washington, D.C.: Police Foundation.

Yoder, Richard, and Robert Moore. 1973. "Characteristics of Convicted Drunken Drivers." *Quarterly Journal of Studies on Alcohol* 34:927–36.

Zimring, Franklin E. 1976. "Field Experiments in General Deterrence: Preferring the Tortoise to the Hare." *Evaluation* 3:132–35.

———. 1978. "Policy Experiments in General Deterrence: 1970–1975." In *Deterrence and Incapacitation: Estimating the Effects of Criminal Sanctions on Crime Rates*, edited by Alfred Blumstein, Jacqueline Cohen, and Daniel Nagin. Washington, D.C.: National Academy of Sciences.

———. 1990. Personal communication with author.

William A. Geller and Norval Morris

Relations between Federal and Local Police

ABSTRACT

Although sound constitutional policy supports *some* aspects of federal law
enforcement jurisdiction, there remains a vast ambit of overlapping federal
and nonfederal criminal jurisdiction guided primarily by political fashions.
The lack of a rational basis for delineating these respective jurisdictions
inhibits strategic planning for efficient, effective, coherent anticrime
efforts. The incentives and disincentives to communication, cooperation,
coordination, and collaboration are substantial, with leading contemporary
incentives including the need to combat multijurisdictional criminals
and the lure of equitably sharing assets forfeited by drug offenders.
Considerable progress has been made in fostering a climate of positive
interchange between federal and nonfederal police, from information
exchange to technical assistance to multijurisdictional operational task
forces. Making continued progress in strategic planning remains a
daunting task given the powerful mythology and political realities that
support the persistence of more than 14,000 local and at least fifty federal
police agencies.

It is sometimes argued that, if the overall purpose was to render policing inefficient, it could not be better achieved than by multiplying the
number of independent police forces throughout the land until they
exceeded fourteen thousand, allocating geographically and politically
defined boundaries to each, and then superimposing another several
dozen independent investigative agencies on the whole edifice, these

William A. Geller is associate director of the Police Executive Research Forum.
Norval Morris is Julius Kreeger Professor of Law and Criminology at the University of
Chicago. The authors wish to express their gratitude to Charles Rinkevich, Clifford
Karchmer, Jason Peltz, and Janet Haley for their assistance in assembling information
about federal agencies and joint federal-state-local task forces.

having diverse jurisdiction over the entire landscape. For good measure, one might enhance inefficiency by having more than half the nation's police forces employ fewer than ten full-time officers and, for emphasis, having a thousand of them employ only one officer (Bureau of Justice Statistics 1990*a*, p. 58). Such, they say, is a fair description of the structural impossibility of cost-effective policing in the United States.

But there is a contrary view. One unanticipated consequence of this balkanized structure of American policing is that the modern movement toward community-based, problem-oriented policing—to have preventive, enforcement, and other services closely related to the needs and opportunities of the particular community being served—may be greatly facilitated (see Moore, in this volume; Slahor 1990, p. 51); Monolithic efficiency may not be all that efficient; independence of decision at the peripheries may well be a larger value, particularly where the needs and resources of those at the peripheries differ. But even the architects of the new strategic thrust toward community and problem-solving policing almost certainly would prefer some consolidation of the smallest law enforcement agencies; and they would readily concede that community-based officers are best at combating community-based crime, not multiregional, multistate, or multinational offending.

Potential inefficiency—squandering scarce resources that are desperately needed for other societal problems besides crime and disorder—is not the only cause for concern about the untidy pattern of federal, state, and local police jurisdiction in the United States. Effectiveness considerations arise as well, for poor husbanding of resources and deficient coordination of anticrime and order maintenance assets may make for weak strategic and tactical planning and ineffectual operations. A related issue is that of unmet needs—problems that simply fall between the institutional stools as federal, state, and local law enforcement agencies, unaware of one another's priorities, assume that someone else is taking care of a particular problem. Still another reason to care about the chaotic state of affairs in American police jurisdiction is the possibility that agencies at different levels of government will, as a generality, have different organizational cultures that are not ideally suited to the development of effective countermeasures against the crime and related problems each agency targets. This last concern theoretically could be mitigated somewhat as a byproduct of standardized training offered to police at all levels of government.[1] If the behavioral differences begin to disappear between federal and local police, it may become less important on some dimensions whether a formal structural integration of federal and local operations—or the functional equivalent—is achieved. Such standardization is far from the rule nowadays. Even if it were, it might convey a number of benefits, but reducing inefficiencies probably would not be among them.

Here as elsewhere we are captives of our history, and the present multiplicity and diversity of police forces shows no sign of reducing significantly. And mythology, too, has great force. The justification usually offered for the hodgepodge of American police forces is that freedom, and a healthy system of checks and balances arising out of interagency competition, precludes the creation of a national police force. This is a deeply, one might say passionately, held belief, and it is for the time being politically unassailable. Other federal systems of government—Australian, Canadian, German, Swiss—seem no less free, their citizens no more threatened by police power and their more centralized police no more prone to corruption, excessive force, or other improprieties; but the argument is hardly worth pursuing. We are held by our history and our mythology of freedom and accountability to the present administrative structure of policing, and in this essay we assume the continuance, for a long time, of the current pattern of city, county, state, and federal law enforcement agencies, and we focus not on the wisdom of preserving or modifying that pattern but on matters of collaboration and conflict and on the formidable problem of delineating the proper scope of federal criminal jurisdiction. It is, in large part, an essay about "turf."

Though federal police[2] constitute less than a tenth of all police in

---

[1] See Michelson (1990, p. 57) for discussion of an automated testing system bringing greater standardization to the training of police officers at different academies within California. Modifying an organizational culture is, of course, a daunting enterprise, and we do not suggest that academy training alone will produce significant change in subcultural norms.

[2] See Abrams (1983, p. 781). Abrams observes: "It is noteworthy that in common parlance no one refers to federal criminal law enforcement agencies as federal 'police,' perhaps in implicit recognition that they do not have the principal responsibility for maintenance of public order in the country in the manner of a local constabulary."

Another way of putting the point is that federal agents generally were conceived as *enforcement* personnel rather than as police agents equally responsible for *preventing* crime, regulating human conduct, and helping those who strayed and paid their debts to avoid recidivism. Evidence of this point emerges from comparing the growth of the FBI to the growth of the federal probation function. Between 1934 and 1941, the FBI's total staff the United States (Bureau of Justice Statistics 1988, p. 59), and federal prosecutors, judges, public defenders, correctional forces, and criminal cases are greatly outnumbered by their state and local counterparts, federal practice takes on an increasingly dominant role in public perceptions and in media attention. The campaigns against drugs, political and judicial corruption, organized and white-collar crime, insider trading, pollution of the environment, and the impurity and dangers of our food and medicinal drugs become centerpieces of public interest, and the federal role in all is seen as dominant.

The same point can be made in another way. The largest federal law enforcement agency, the FBI, as of April 1991 had 22,932 employees of whom 10,036 were special agents (Sessions 1991)—yet they are seen as the dominant crime detection force in a country of nearly two hundred and fifty million. The sworn personnel of the New York City Police Department (26,882 in 1990, with budget allocated to hire thousands more in the next several years) number nearly three times the FBI's cadre of field agents.

Questions of jurisdiction tend to excite emotion only in lawyers and in those whose turf is affected. But since federal criminal jurisdiction so often overlaps state and local criminal jurisdiction, the behavior that is criminal being cognizable in each, it is necessary to try to define general principles that can guide each to their proper relative law enforcement spheres. Arguably, the respective *non-law-enforcement* activities of police at each level of government present fewer problems of

---

increased from 772 to 4,370. Between 1932 and 1941, the number of federal probation officers rose from 63 to 239, about half the rate of growth experienced by the FBI (Douthit 1975, p. 331). Some of the federal agencies are, in fact, called police (e.g., the Military Police, the U.S. Park Police, the U.S. Capitol Police, the Supreme Court Police), and, for the most part, those forces do indeed have general security and peacekeeping obligations within their domains.

Another, more contemporary reason for maintaining a semantic distinction between the titles of FBI, DEA, Secret Service, and other federal agents, on the one hand, and local police on the other, might be to avoid in the federal sector the implicit, if unintended, demeaning of the work of line enforcement personnel that often arises within organizations that use a large number of ranks. Meese (1991, p. 11), writing about ways to enhance the professional status of local police first-line officers, observes that the military model's long list of ranks is one among many aspects of modern municipal policing that needs to be critically examined. "Several Federal law enforcement agencies have . . . moved away from the military model in their organization and rank structure," he writes. "The Federal Bureau of Investigation and the United States Secret Service classify their basic officers as 'special agents,' a term used for all nonsupervisory positions from entry level through veteran members." If one must use military analogies, he urges, "police officers on the street should be considered the equivalent of 'commissioned officers' in their own right, with concomitant respect, authority and discretion" (ibid., pp. 10–11).

overlap and role uncertainty. There is much that local police do to keep the peace without invoking the criminal law and hence without directly raising traditional questions of intergovernmental police coordination or conflict (Goldstein 1990). But when enforcement of criminal laws is deemed an appropriate problem-solving tactic, the absence of broad consensus around general principles of federal, state, and local enforcement jurisdiction impedes quality strategic planning and produces costly inefficiencies. Thus, with much-deserved modesty, at the conclusion of this essay we tender some preliminary thoughts concerning the proper delineation of federal criminal jurisdiction. Our approach in this essay to exploring relations between federal and local law enforcement is as follows: Section I chronicles the emergence and history of federal law enforcement and describes the major current federal law enforcement agencies. Section II examines and illustrates incentives and disincentives to cooperation, coordination, and collaboration between federal, state, and local police agencies. Section III examines the mechanisms of federal-local cooperation and coordination, and Section IV, the conclusion, emplasizes the continuing need for and briefly explores some principles that help delineate the federal police role.

I. The Emergence of Federal Criminal Law

There is a direct and obvious federal interest in protecting federal officials and federal property. Likewise, there is a direct federal interest in preventing and, if they occur, punishing crimes committed on federal territory and crimes against federal property. Hence the first and obvious basis of federal jurisdiction, a jurisdiction akin to that in every state, provides for federal law enforcement within the special territorial jurisdiction of the United States. This is a *direct* and uncontested federal jurisdiction. Several federal police forces were early formed to enforce this jurisdiction, for example, the U.S. Marshals and the Immigration and Naturalization Service's border patrol.

Similarly, there are some federal governmental functions, setting aside national defense and the federal government's jurisdiction over the military,[3] which also fall within the direct jurisdiction of the central

---

[3] The federal military jurisdiction has expanded in recent years. In 1987, the U.S. Supreme Court, in *Solorio v. United States*, 483 U.S. 435 (1987), abandoned the requirement of a "service connection" before criminal acts by members of the military may be tried in military rather than civilian courts. In *Solorio*, a Coast Guardsman molested two young women off the Guard base, an offense that would have been tried in the local

government. Abuse of the mail system, smuggling prohibited goods, the illegal entry of aliens into the United States, piracy, treason, and other offenses against national security invoke a direct federal interest and, like jurisdiction over federal property and personnel, create few problems of competition with state and local law enforcement authority. As early as 1790, Congress exercised authority to punish theft of military property and interfering with or obstructing federal judicial processes, and this power has not since been doubted.

It is with the invocation of *indirect* federal jurisdiction that problems arise. The Constitution gives residual powers to the states, but each of the enumerated powers allocated to the central government can and usually does create an indirect federal interest, protectable by federal law enforcement and cognizable in federal courts, often overlapping with similar state authority.[4] The express authority in the Constitution for this ambit of federal jurisdiction is to be found in the "necessary and proper" clause of Article I, Section 8, Clause 18: "The Congress shall have power . . . to make all laws which shall be necessary and proper for carrying into execution the foregoing powers, and all other powers vested by this Constitution in the government of the United States, or in any department or officer thereof."

Since the Supreme Court's decision in *McCulloch v. Maryland*, 17 U.S. (4 Wheat.) 316 (1819), it has been clear that Congress may employ criminal sanctions to buttress the exercise of any federal power. In that case, the Court held that the "necessary and proper" clause gave Congress the power to incorporate a national bank. The Court interpreted the "necessary and proper" clause very broadly, stating "[i]t must have been the intention of those who gave these powers, to insure . . . their beneficial execution. This could not be done by confining the choice of means to such narrow limits as not to leave it in the power of Congress to adopt any which might be appropriate, and

---

civilian criminal courts under prior case law. But, the Court decided, it was sufficient for military court jurisdiction if the offense was proscribed by the Uniform Code of Military Justice and, at the time of the offense, the defendant was a member of the Armed Services. Military law enforcement officials see the *Solorio* decision as significantly affecting the allocation of federal and local enforcement resources in the vicinity of military bases (see, e.g., Conroy and Lockett 1988, p. 36; Wright 1991, p. 73).

[4] An overlap in federal and local jurisdiction does not necessarily mean that identical charges could or would be brought pertaining to the same harmful conduct, although this could be done. For instance, Hausner et al. (1982, p. xv) point out that a bank robbery could be prosecuted as such in either federal or state courts but that a consumer fraud making use of the mails would likely be prosecuted as consumer fraud in state courts but as a violation of postal regulations in federal courts.

which were conducive to that end" (17 U.S. 316, at 415). In other words, the necessary and proper clause enables Congress to make any law that is in the view of Congress useful in carrying out any other congressional power. The potential scope of federal jurisdiction is thus immense.

An overview of the range of these direct and indirect criminal jurisdictions of the federal government may give some idea of the range and diversity of federal law enforcement activities. Federal law enforcement scrutiny extends to all federal property and personnel, the mails, all activities affecting interstate commerce (and in an interdependent market such as the United States that is a formidable array of activities), all interstate movement of criminals, of victims of crime, and of the proceeds of crime, activities affecting interstate communications (again, consider the extent of that power), and all other matters covered by federal statutory and regulatory processes. Such a listing only begins to sketch the reach and complexity of federal jurisdiction; to go further one must plunge into the mysteries of the mail fraud statutes (codified at 18 United States Code Annotated [U.S.C.A.] secs. 1341–43, [1990]) by which any use of the mails in the course of any fraudulent criminal conduct gives jurisdiction to the federal courts; of the Hobbs Act (18 U.S.C.A. sec. 1951 [1990]) by which any interference with commerce by threats or violence attracts federal jurisdiction; of RICO (Racketeer Influenced and Corrupt Organizations; 18 U.S.C.A. secs. 1961–68 [1990]); and a bundle of federal statutory attacks on organized and white-collar crime.

Trying to bring some order to this melange, it may be suggested that federal law enforcement has three principal functions: to inhibit and punish conduct that directly harms or threatens the federal government, its personnel, and property; to inhibit and punish antisocial conduct with which the states are unwilling or incompetent to deal, in particular, conduct reaching beyond their boundaries; and finally to ensure compliance with federal statutes and federal regulatory processes.

A. The History of Federal Policing

Federal law enforcement increased and spread as the role of the federal government in the life of the United States burgeoned. The historical perspective is clear: before the Civil War a modest reach; from the Civil War to the turn of the century a steady expansion into activities that had traditionally been the prerogative of the states; and, then, during this century an acceleration of federal regulatory functions touching very many aspects of the lives of those making up the single market that now characterizes American industry and commerce.

Prior to the Civil War, federal criminal jurisdiction was confined to acts threatening federal governmental processes, misconduct by or against federal officers, and interference with government programs such as the mails. Also, of course, federal law enforcement had exclusive jurisdiction in federal territories, such as the District of Columbia, as well as in the maritime and overseas territorial interests of the United States.

The Civil Rights legislation that followed the Civil War (codified at 18 U.S.C.A. secs. 241, 242 [1990]) was the first expansion of federal jurisdiction to create overlap between federal and state enforcement authority. As the federal government sought to protect the rights of its citizens against the activities of other citizens or of other governmental agencies, the overlap of jurisdictions became inevitable. The abolition of slavery, the prohibition on denial of the civil rights of any citizen, the concepts of due process and equal protection of the laws to constrain deprivations of life, liberty, or property meant that federal law enforcement reached conduct theretofore exclusively within the states' police powers.

A similar expansion of federal power at the expense of the states came in the post–Civil War legislation providing criminal penalties for the misuse of federal governmental services, in particular, misuse of the mails, so that a broad range of fraudulent conduct fell within federal law enforcement jurisdiction. Likewise, penalties for misconduct involving interstate facilities, such as the railroads, expanded federal jurisdiction. But the most luxuriant expansion was attached to the Industrial Revolution, of which the railroads were perhaps the harbinger, which in the late nineteenth century began to turn the United States into a great and unified industrial power. Interstate transportation, interstate commerce, and a booming interdependent market properly attracted federal legislative controls and with them concomitant federal authority.

Constitutional challenges were launched against this intrusion of federal law enforcement into frauds and corruptions previously within the exclusive jurisdiction of the states. By and large, powers exercised under the mail fraud statutes were upheld by the courts whereas criminal punishments based on the commerce clause tended to be rejected (Abrams 1986). But with the turn of the century and the decision of the Supreme Court in the *Lottery Case* in 1903 (*Champion v. Ames*, 188 U.S. 321), these uncertainties were laid to rest, and the commerce clause (Article I, Section 8: "The Congress shall have power . . . to regulate commerce with foreign nations, and among the several States, and with the Indian tribes.") was held to provide criminal jurisdiction for a broad power to control and regulate interstate commerce (see generally Stern 1973).

The unfolding of federal jurisdiction in this century is more familiar. The Food and Drug Act of 1906 (after 1938 renamed the Food, Drug and Cosmetic Act, 9 U.S.C.A. secs. 310 et seq.) was the forerunner of an expansive federal power. The Mann Act of 1910 (18 U.S.C.A. secs. 2421–22) prohibiting the interstate transportation of women for immoral purposes; the Harrison Act of 1914 (codified in 1964 at 26 U.S.C.A. secs. 4701 et seq.) launching a comprehensive federal assault on narcotics; the Dyer Act of 1919 (codified in 1988 at 18 U.S.C.A. secs. 10, 2311–13) attacking the interstate movement of stolen vehicles; and the "Great Experiment" of prohibition between 1919 and 1933 were all testaments to the extending arm of federal law enforcement power (Douthit 1975).

With the New Deal and subsequent federal welfare legislation that reach grew yet further, and the recognition in the thirties of the power of organized crime made the federal government the central force in an effort to eliminate and curtail its corruptive influence.

But by no means is federal law enforcement practice ruthlessly expansive. Though the historical tendency has certainly been toward its steady and sometimes luxuriant growth, there are also forays of expansion in certain areas followed by retractions or abandonments of authority over those same areas. The "Great Experiment" of prohibition is perhaps the leading example, coming as it did after decades of experimentation by individual states with their own versions of prohibition.

Between 1851 and 1863 a majority of the states first tried and then abandoned various forms of alcohol prohibitory legislation. By 1919 and the ratification of the Eighteenth Amendment there were only five dry states, so that from then until 1933 this field of law enforcement was defined by the Volstead Act (chap. 85, 41 Stat. 305), policed by federal agents, and enforced by federal courts—and the convicted criminals it produced were subject to federal incarceration. After 1933 federal law enforcement largely withdrew from the field, and state and local regulatory and licensing systems, locally enforced, resumed their prior aegis (although the Bureau of Alcohol, Tobacco and Firearms of the U.S. Department of the Treasury retained some jurisdiction over regulatory matters and criminal violations).

The Mann Act followed a similar though less dramatic pattern: vigorous federal interdiction of interstate movement of women for immoral purposes superimposed on benign or malign neglect (depending on your view of such legislation) of similar activities intrastate. And for it too enforcement waned though the laws remained on the books.[5]

A similar foray characterizes the Dyer Act's attack on the interstate movement of stolen vehicles; in the 1920s and 1930s, federal prisons were full of car thieves; by the 1960s and 1970s, auto theft was prosecuted extensively in only a few federal circuits; today, car theft legislation and the activities of car thieves not having changed, only those car thieves involved in extensive car theft rings, or running "chop shops," are to be found in federal prisons.

As a last example of this sweep and ebb of jurisdiction, consider bank robbery, finding its federal jurisdictional link in national legislation insuring banks and their depositors against certain types of loss and thus justifying the exercise of federal police power (Douthit 1975). But the burden of other concerns, particularly increased attention to drug offenses, organized crime, and white-collar crime, drove bank robbery to the periphery of federal concern, more and more of its enforcement being left to state authorities. This was in part due to a study by the FBI that revealed that 40 percent of bank robberies during the late 1970s were being solved by local and state police without any FBI involvement, and a further 25 percent by collaboration between local and state police and the FBI. Given increasing pressures on the FBI from other duties, the reduction of its role in bank robbery made good bureaucratic sense (Bureau of Justice Statistics 1988, p. 60).

Fashion and changing political and social interests thus frequently influenced what law enforcement activities would be assumed by federal authorities and what would be left to the states, the limitations of federal resources playing an important role in these decisions.

Nevertheless, by the beginning of the 1990s, in terms of potential reach the federal law enforcement power is almost plenary, subject only to the Bill of Rights but not to many meaningful jurisdictional

---

[5] See U.S. Attorneys Manual, secs. 9–79.100: "Generally, prosecutions under 18 U.S.C. secs. 2421 and 2422 [the Mann Act] should be limited to persons engaged in commercial prostitution activities, even though the element of commercialism is not a legal requirement." There could hardly be a clearer statement of how prosecutorial discretion controls the nonenforcement of criminal legislation.

constraints. Indeed, the federal government began in the late 1980s to devote some investigative and prosecutive resources to federal aspects of certain burglaries and nonbank robberies, premised on the Bureau of Alcohol, Tobacco, and Firearms' role in combating the criminal use of firearms (Moore 1990; Thomas and York 1991). In March of 1991, Attorney General Richard Thornburgh promoted such activity, announcing his "Project Triggerlock," in which U.S. attorneys and federal investigative forces would attempt to target violent offenders, such as armed robbers, who employ guns in their crimes, and to take advantage of federal statutes that impose "stiff mandatory sentences" for firearms offenses (*Crime Control Digest* 1991*a*, pp. 3–4; Gorman 1991). For instance, the Armed Career Criminal Act of 1984 mandates a fifteen-year sentence for gun possession in the case of a person convicted three times previously for violent or drug-related felonies (*Crime Control Digest* 1991*a*, p. 4). In practice, as Triggerlock illustrates, the exercise of a nearly limitless federal law enforcement authority is severely constrained by operational decisions by federal prosecutors and federal agencies as to which activities they will reach out to control— and those decisions are in turn controlled by the political will of the times. No commentator has been able satisfactorily to define those interests of the central government, and of all of us as citizens of the United States, which properly attract federal as distinct from state and local power.

B. The Development of Federal Agencies

The Postal Inspection Service, which exists today, predates the Declaration of Independence by nearly four decades, and as such holds undisputed claim as the first federal police force. Two other eighteenth-century police forces were established by Congress in 1789: the Revenue Cutter Service of the U.S. Customs office, to deal with smuggling (Abrams 1986, p. 6); and the U.S. Marshals Service, to ride circuit with the Supreme Court as it met in the thirteen states and to perform various other tasks at the behest of the president, the attorney general, the Treasury Department, the War Department, the federal courts, and other agencies (Torres 1985, pp. 353, 360). The settlement of the American territories in the "Wild West" produced some of the best known figures in the history of American policing, including U.S. Marshals and Deputy Marshals Wyatt Earp, Bat Masterson, and Wild Bill Hickok (Calhoun 1990). During the nineteenth century, Congress created the Bureau of Indian Affairs' law enforcement apparatus within the Department of Interior (1878). Institutional expansion of federal policing moved into a higher gear in 1919 with the establishment of the Criminal Division within the Department of Justice. Pronounced expansion began in 1924 with J. Edgar Hoover's taking over the Department's Bureau of Investigation, which later became the Federal Bureau of Investigation, the paramount federal police force.

Between the 1930s and the end of World War II, the pattern of federal policing was laid down. Federal crimes increased, and federal police agencies multiplied (see the Appendix). The 1992 budget estimate for federal expenditure on law enforcement was $7,261,000,000, a sum difficult to contemplate. There was a further $2,195,000,000 for federal correctional activities. These sums did not include the $5,314,000,000 budgeted for federal litigative and judicial activities, nor are they easily divisible between civil and criminal, prosecutorial and judicial processes (see Maguire and Flanagan 1991, p. 14, table 1.10).

The FBI, DEA, Customs Service, Internal Revenue Service (IRS), the Secret Service, U.S. Marshals Service, and the Bureau of Alcohol, Tobacco and Firearms are among the more widely known federal enforcement bodies laying claim to the lion's share of the current federal law enforcement budget. They and their lower-profile sister agencies in the federal police family are identified and discussed briefly below as prelude to a consideration of the reasons that incline and disincline these and local police forces to collaborate against the nation's crime problems.

C. Current Federal Law Enforcement Agencies

The American tradition of fragmenting policing responsibilities is reflected at all levels of government. As of 1986, the Bureau of Justice Statistics (1988, p. 63) documented the existence of 11,743 municipal, seventy-nine county, and 1,819 township general purpose police agencies; more than 3,000 county sheriff's departments (in 1991 there were said to be 3,096 sheriffs' agencies [Feldkamp 1991a, p. 3]), most of which provide general purpose police services to at least some portions of their geographical jurisdiction; fifty-one state police and highway patrols; and 965 nonfederal, special purpose police agencies (park rangers, harbor police, transit police, public housing police, campus security forces, and the like).[6]

[6] The general distinction between a county police force and a county sheriff's department lies in the appointment of the police chief by the county government and the popular election of the sheriff.

At the federal level, the precise number of agencies characterized as "law enforcement" depends on which aspects of protective and investigative missions are relevant for any given tabulation. A senior FBI administrator reported that, if one includes all federal bodies (including the dozens of inspectors general offices) possessing any authority to investigate criminal violations of federal statutes, the federal landscape is dotted with approximately 110 law enforcement organizations (Revell 1990). Another senior U.S. Justice Department official noted that, as of 1988, 141 federal law enforcement and regulatory agencies participated in the Regional Information Sharing System (RISS), a federally supported set of seven intergovernmental mutual assistance networks, each targeting multistate criminal enterprise (Abell 1988, p. 58). Still other estimates range as high as two hundred federal agencies "that have some criminal enforcement role" (Abrams 1986, p. 7). The number of federal law enforcement bodies shrinks to an even fifty, however, if only federal agencies are considered that, like all local police departments, have standing authority to carry firearms, conduct searches, and make arrests. This group of fifty is listed in the Appendix. It is further testament to the complexity of sorting out jurisdictional questions both among federal law enforcement agencies and between them and nonfederal police that, after diligent efforts reviewing available publications and contacting a large number of federal agencies, we are still left with only an approximate tally of the federal units possessing standing authority to carry firearms and make arrests.

We do not suggest that the only reasonable way to define federal police forces is by virtue of their arrest and weapons authority. Some would distinguish police from nonpolice federal bodies instead according to whether a given agency has primarily enforcement or regulatory obligations. Bayley (in this volume) presents a three-part typology of national-level police forces, including general purpose, special purpose, and ancillary responsibilities. Both are attractive conceptions. Our purpose in drawing attention in this essay only to agencies whose personnel routinely carry firearms and exercise arrest powers is primarily convenience. Few would contest that at least these fifty organizations should be counted as police; practitioners tell us that the vast majority of the state and local police operational contacts with federal enforcement bodies occur with various of these fifty agencies; and one has to begin somewhere. We leave it to future efforts to explore the utility of casting the classificatory net more widely in the sea of federal agencies, as we necessarily must leave it to others *rigorously* to address the considerably more important questions of the *quality* of federal-

state-local police operational collaboration and the effects of those efforts on the nature and amount of criminal predation in America.

The jurisdiction of many of these fifty agencies is centered around
particular places, problems, or people. For example, some agencies
have broad police powers within restricted geographic areas, such as
national parks, forests, federal office buildings and grounds, airports,
or military installations. Others have narrower subject matter jurisdiction but their beats encompass the entire nation (e.g., evasions of immigration, tax, or drug laws; transgressions of fish and wildlife laws and
treaties; and abuse of the U.S. mail system). Still others exist primarily
to safeguard limited numbers of "protectees" or supervise large numbers of probationers and parolees. A few of the fifty, such as the FBI,
DEA, Secret Service, Customs, Bureau of Alcohol, Tobacco and Firearms, and the U.S. Marshals Service, have widespread and frequent
contact with the vast majority of local police departments in the nation.
Local police in communities that contain or lie near military bases,
nuclear power plants, national forests, Native American reservations,
foreign consulates, or certain other federal protectorates also have
higher levels of contact with specialized federal enforcement agencies.
Similarly, police in border communities (and, increasingly as part of
drug enforcement efforts, police located far from national borders) have
frequent contact with Customs and Immigration and Naturalization
Service personnel.

A few of the federal agencies (principally the FBI, DEA, and U.S.
Marshals Service) are discussed more fully later in this essay. The brief
descriptions of agencies in the Appendix illustrate the dispersion of
federal police authority among the federal government's labyrinth of
departments and agencies. Obviously, some of these fifty policing bodies account for many more arrests and prosecutable cases than others,
primarily a function of agency mission and size. A study by the Institute for Law and Social Research a decade ago reported that, in 1979,
five federal enforcement agencies—the FBI, DEA, Bureau of Alcohol,
Tobacco and Firearms, Postal Inspection Service, and Secret
Service—accounted for "72 percent of the cases brought by investigative agencies for federal prosecution" (Hausner et al. 1982, p. v).

We can illustrate a pattern of slow but steadily growing responsibilities by considering one agency—the Treasury Department's Secret
Service. The U.S. Secret Service's dignitary protection responsibility
has expanded over the years, typically in response to successful assaults
on unprotected officials. But the Service did not originally have official

protection duties. The agency was founded in July 1865, three months after President Lincoln was assassinated, to stem rampant counterfeiting since as much as a third of the currency in circulation in 1860 was estimated to be bogus (Torres 1985, p. 370). Not until after President William McKinley was assassinated, in September 1901, did Congress authorize the Secret Service to protect the president. In 1917, Congress extended this protection to the president's immediate family. Shortly after Robert Kennedy was assassinated on the presidential campaign trail in June 1968, Secret Service protection was further extended to major presidential candidates during election years. Currently, Secret Service responsibility includes eighteen "permanent protectees," including the president and family; former presidents and their families; the vice-president and family; the president- and vice-president-elect; major presidential candidates; and foreign heads of state visiting the United States (Torres 1985, pp. 370–71).

The thousands of armed federal agents employed by the enforcement bodies enumerated in the Appendix are, by the most recent federal estimate, just 8 percent of the national total of sworn police—77 percent are employed by municipal or county agencies; state police constitute 15 percent (Bureau of Justice Statistics 1988, pp. 59, 63).[7] Much federal criminal jurisdiction is exclusive, but concurrent jurisdic-

---

[7] In October 1988, there were 572,633 full-time-equivalent employees (including sworn personnel and civilians) in nearly 14,000 municipal, county, and township general purpose police agencies in the United States; 108,005 full-time-equivalent employees in the state ploice forces; and 65,297 full-time-equivalent "police protection" employees in the federal government (Maguire and Flanagan 1991, p. 18). Among the largest federal law enforcement organizations are the FBI, the DEA, and the U.S. Marshals Service, which employed the following numbers of personnel as of 1991: FBI—22,932 total, of whom 10,036 were sworn agents (Sessions 1991; see also *Crime Control Digest* 1990c, p. 9; *Crime Control Digest* 1990e, p. 8); DEA—6,286 total, of whom 3,312 were special agents (Tauber 1991; see also *Crime Control Digest* 1990c, p. 9); U.S. Marshals Service—approximately 3,300 total, of whom about 2,300 were marshals and deputy marshals (Dempsey 1991). Federal antidrug initiatives in recent years have increased the federal law enforcement cadre (Office of National Drug Control Policy 1990, p. 105; Office of National Drug Control Policy 1991, pp. 136, 140) and seek to do so further (e.g., the Administration's fiscal year 1992 budget request seeks the addition of 1,516 new FBI positions, including 409 new agents, and the expansion of the Bureau's overall "direct funding" from $1.7 billion in 1991 to approximately $2 billion in 1992 [*Crime Control Digest* 1991a, p. 4]). By contrast, some tallies indicate that many local police agencies have either remained at about the same staffing levels or shrunk (Recktenwald 1990). Attempting to arrive at a reliable tally of all publicly funded, full-time sworn police officers in the United States, despite the efforts of the FBI each year in its *Crime in the United States* publication, is as daunting a task as trying to enumerate the federal agencies empowered to use lethal force in the apprehension and arrest of criminal suspects. Neither the Justice Department, the Labor Department, nor the U.S. Census Bureau is able to provide a complete count of America's police.

tion exists over a considerable array of crime. This concurrent jurisdiction, combined with interest at both the federal and local levels in tapping one another's policing expertise and resources, has produced numerous and widely disparate types of operational and administrative contact between federal and local enforcement bodies. Our discussion of the resulting mechanisms of interaction later in this essay is limited by an absence of pertinent data that would be required to assay with any rigor either the quantity or quality of intergovernmental law enforcement contact and cooperation. What is possible, however, is an exploration of the reasons why joint policing ventures seem to be on the increase and of the impediments that remain to even closer collaboration.

II. Factors That Shape Collaboration and Isolation

An elaboration of the assorted conditions that induce and impede intergovernmental law enforcement cooperation best begins with a reminder of the dynamic interaction between our Constitutional architecture, which allocates power among levels of government, and the operational needs of a nation whose communities and states are highly interdependent. The interdependence of geographically remote communities and sovereigns makes what the Supreme Court termed "cooperative federalism" (*Murphy v. Waterfront Commission of New York Harbor*, 378 U.S. 52 [1964]) essential for the execution of local, state, and national police powers.

It is perhaps no accident that the Supreme Court was moved to utter a phrase such as "cooperative federalism" in a case concerning criminal activity in New York City. That city, with dense concentrations of the drug and organized crime problems that are the principal current targets of formalized law enforcement partnerships, is also perhaps "exhibit one" concerning the structural obstacles to interagency collaboration. Ronald Goldstock (1987), head of the New York State Organized Crime Task Force, noted one type of structural impediment— the multiplicity of institutional players whose differing priorities, skills, and work styles must be accommodated to find common ground for effective collaboration: "In the New York City metropolitan area, there are two organized crime strike forces, three United States Attorney's Offices, two drug task forces, the Internal Revenue Service, the Federal Bureau of Investigation, the Drug Enforcement Administration, the Immigration and Naturalization Service, the Customs Service, two state prosecutor's offices, more than fifteen District Attorneys, and a variety of state and local police forces, all of whom presumably have jurisdiction to investigate an organized crime syndicate dealing in drugs" (Goldstock 1987, pp. 96–97).

As the seat of government, the District of Columbia presents a different kind of extreme illustration of the potential for interagency rivalry. A federal park police official with whom we spoke some years ago suggested that, at the right kind of criminal event in Washington, D.C.—say, international narcoterrorism directed at the vice-president and a foreign dignitary on the grounds of a national monument—twenty-six separate federal and local law enforcement agencies could plausibly claim entitlement to investigate the incident.

Despite a number of structural impediments to intergovernmental law enforcement cooperation, we sense, from conversations with an unscientifically drawn sample of experienced law enforcement executives at all levels of government, a striking consensus on one point: Even though there remains ample room for further progress, over the past two or three decades there has been a substantial improvement in relations between federal and local agencies.[8] The same observation was not made, however, about relations *within* the federal law enforcement family. (For accounts of illustrative turf wars among federal agencies, see Abrams 1986, p. 135; Abrams 1988, p. 1; Stoll 1989; *Crime Control Digest* 1990*a*, pp. 5–6; Bentley 1991*a;* Feldkamp 1991*a*, p. 2; Mackenzie 1991.) Since this essay's mission is to focus on *intergovernmental* law enforcement relations, the question posed for present purposes about reported feuding—at least at operational levels (see, e.g., O'Connell 1990, p. 3)—among federal agencies is how, if at all, these squabbles may affect federal-local interaction. The short answer for most in law enforcement seems to be that the incentives for federal-

---

[8] Although our respondents cited an improved rapport and respect over the decades between the preeminent federal investigative body—the FBI—and nonfederal enforcement organizations, several practitioners and policy analysts expressed the view that some federal agencies traditionally have fared better than others in establishing a smooth working relationship with local police. For example, Lupsha (1990) reports that local police departments generally have had an easier time over the years working with the Bureau of Alcohol, Tobacco, and Firearms (ATF) than with the FBI, perhaps because of different work styles and traditions at ATF, perhaps partly because of the narrower focus of ATF and a consequent perception among local police that ATF agents were able to offer more specialized assistance than FBI agents. Whatever the reasons, the manifestation of cooperativeness by ATF most often mentioned by local police in our conversations was ATF's willingness to share credit generously with local agencies when investigations bore positive results. The differences in ATF's and the FBI's reported relationships with local officials may also have been influenced by the FBI's investigatory responsibility concerning local police illegalities. We return to this last point later.

local cooperation would be strengthened considerably by better strategic planning (Office of National Drug Control Policy 1990, pp. 49, 51) and better budgetary support (Special Committee on Criminal Justice in a Free Society of the American Bar Association Criminal Justice Section 1988, pp. 5, 39–44)—both of which generally are impeded to the extent that federal agencies improperly hoard intelligence or other assets.[9] Infighting within the federal law enforcement apparatus produces inefficiencies a fearful nation can ill afford and provides ready objects of ridicule for congressional factions reluctant to allocate the funding and enforcement authority needed for a comprehensive, strate-

[9] One effort to enhance relations among the federal enforcement agencies is the federal Office of Personnel Management's development of "a model performance standard which encourages and facilitates interagency cooperation on drug issues" (Office of National Drug Control Policy 1990, p. 116). Another is the Federal Law Enforcement Training Center's (FLETC) multifaceted efforts to improve understanding, communication, and collaboration among the sixty-eight federal agencies it serves (Rinkevich 1991a). Founded by Congress in 1970 as a consolidated national training center for a large number of federal agencies, the FLETC was expected to produce economies of scale and greater consistency in the quality of basic and advanced training than previously had been achieved when each federal law enforcement agency separately trained its own personnel. An important benefit obtained by the integration of different agencies' personnel in basic training courses has been the growth of rapport and trust that would have been much more difficult to achieve in the absence of joint training (Federal Law Enforcement Training Center 1990b, pp. 4–5). Among the uniformed police who receive at least some joint training at the FLETC are personnel from the Border Patrol, U.S. Capitol Police, the General Services Administration's Office of Physical Security and Law Enforcement, the National Park Service, the U.S. Park Police, and the Secret Service Uniformed Division. Among the criminal investigators who are intermingled for entry-level instruction are those from the Naval Investigative Service, the Bureau of Alcohol, Tobacco and Firearms, the U.S. Customs Service, the IRS, the U.S. Marshals Service, the Secret Service, and the various Inspectors General Offices (Federal Law Enforcement Training Center 1990b, p. 5). The FBI's absence from this networking experience (the FBI runs its own highly respected academy, although it does have some participation in FLETC activities) may help explain some of the lingering friction between its agents and other federal enforcement personnel, but broader structural issues and overlapping jurisdictional responsibilities for different agencies very likely produce most of the strains.

Still another mechanism already in use for fostering better coordination among federal agencies with concurrent jurisdiction is the cross designation of personnel. For example, DEA in 1990 cross designated 1,000 Customs agents so they would have increased authority to investigate drug smuggling (Office of National Drug Control Policy 1991, p. 26). Still, the competitive pressures on the various federal agencies are suggested by the inability of the federal Bureau of Justice Statistics, in its *Drugs and Crime Facts, 1989*, to produce a meaningful total on the tonnage of drug seizures. This disability results from the fact that each agency (DEA, FBI, Customs Service, Coast Guard, etc.) takes credit for the full tonnage taken during seizures in which it participated, without distinguishing single- from multiagency efforts (Bureau of Justice Statistics 1990b, p. 8). With plans to begin recording at least the antidrug activities of federal enforcement units in the Departments of Justice, Treasury, Defense, and Interior in the FBI's new National Incident Based Reporting System, an enhancement of the Uniform Crime Reporting program, there is some chance that it will become easier to sort out the differential contributions of the various federal agencies participating in joint efforts (Office of National Drug Control Policy 1991, pp. 109–10).

gically sound campaign against crime, disorder, and pervasive feelings of insecurity.

International Association of Chiefs of Police past-president Charles Gruber, asked whether he thinks relations between federal and local law enforcement agencies have changed at all over the past twenty years, typified the perceptions of many knowledgeable practitioners:

> Yes, there has been a great improvement. The main problems today are not federal-local; they're federal-federal. Within the federal government, there is a great deal of in-fighting among the agencies involved in drug enforcement. They fight over turf and budget, and they are extremely reluctant to share intelligence. Supposed allocations of responsibility, such as the FBI focusing strictly on high-level drug trafficking, often are not respected in practice. The operational relationships between any given federal agency, on the one hand, and state and local police agencies, on the other, are considerably better. The intergovernmental efforts suffer budgetarily, however, because of the inability of the federal bureaucracies to reach consensus on critical questions concerning the organization and management of the nation's so-called war on drugs. [Gruber 1990]

Thus, while hard data illustrating the quantity and quality of federal-local cooperation and coordination are not available, anecdotal evidence and expert opinion generally support the notion that, under the circumstances, the reported improvement in these intergovernmental efforts is a notable accomplishment. In the balance of this section of the essay, we discuss the factors that seem to carry the most weight when federal and local practitioners make key decisions about whether to collaborate across bureaucratic boundaries—first the incentives, then the disincentives.

A. Incentives to Cooperation, Coordination, and Collaboration

One powerful incentive for federal-local affiliation arises when an individual or group of criminals operates in multiple jurisdictions. Federal agencies, for their part, can coordinate simultaneous multistate investigations (Abrams 1983, p. 780; Conly 1989, p. 42). Thus, looked at from the point of view of the local police detective, joining forces with federal investigators means an opportunity to cross state lines and make arrests and seizures outside the local officer's jurisdiction (Klockars 1990)—even overseas; an opportunity to be deputized as a federal special agent; and the right to "board aircraft with weapons" (Bocklet 1991, p. 276). Local police, in turn, can contribute particularized intelligence about acts committed locally by the suspects and can tap informants they have spent a great deal of time cultivating. A state police investigator assigned as a supervisor to a multijurisdictional drug task force summarized what for him were clear advantages of federal-state-local task forces over individual agency investigations: "the marshaling of resources and expertise from street-savvy city cops, . . . DEA agents with national contacts, . . . legally astute federal attorneys working hand-in-hand with attentive judges" (Bocklet 1991, p. 273).

Avoidance of collisions among enforcement personnel unknowingly working the same or related cases provides another powerful invitation to communication and coordination. Interagency relationships are seriously strained and the public's already shaky confidence in the efficiency and effectiveness of government is further eroded by revelations that officials from different jurisdictions have been using tax dollars not merely duplicating effort but actually working at cross purposes. When one agency unwittingly arrests or shoots another's informants or undercover agents or in some way impels another to take precipitate action in arresting or prosecuting suspects without adequate preparation, the public interest in safety and peace of mind is bound to suffer. The *New York Times* recounted a situation in which a drug dealer who single-handedly sent a Boston neighborhood into a downward spiral of instability and fear turned out to be an FBI informer about whom local police had not been told (1990, p. A7). Chaiken, Chaiken, and Karchmer (1990, p. 44) cite the White House's 1972 street-level drug enforcement initiative, administered by the Office of Drug Abuse Law Enforcement (ODALE), as an unhappy object lesson concerning the importance of interagency coordination. They report:

> The ODALE strategy was to position federal investigators at the same street levels where local police were also increasing their enforcement response. Because of the federal intrusion into what had been a local police effort ["*a sweeping federalization of drug enforcement*"], conflicts between local police and ODALE agents surfaced. Local and federal investigators realized they were often targeting the same dealers, but without effective communication.
>
> After a few years of operation, it was rare indeed to find anyone in law enforcement willing to speak out in favor of the ODALE approach to federalizing street-level drug enforcement.
> Throughout government and in the press, ODALE was viewed as a strategic and operational disaster. But an important lesson had

been learned. ODALE was the first failed experiment in simply throwing more investigators at a local drug problem. [For discussion of the weak strategic foundation for such an approach at the local level, see Eck and Williams 1991; Karchmer and Eck 1991.] Quite possibly, the failure can be traced to the rapid implementation of ODALE without first carefully planning a strategy or convening all the agencies involved to hammer out a mutually agreeable course of action.

Cognizant of the ODALE debacle and other less publicized inter-agency miscues, the national law enforcement agency accreditation effort calls upon every police agency to adopt written directives establishing "procedures for maintaining liaison with other law enforcement agencies in adjoining jurisdictions or agencies having concurrent authority in the agency's service area" (Commission on Accreditation for Law Enforcement Agencies 1987, p. 4).

Among the undercover and overt operational activities requiring tactical coordination between enforcement organizations with concurrent authority is the especially delicate situation in which, occasionally, police attempt to influence the outcome of turf wars between competing criminal groups. Authorities, after consideration of the public policy mine field they are entering, may decide that the best way to minimize injury to their communities is differentially to target the rivals so as to tip the balance of power toward the less violent enterprise (Edelhertz 1987, p. 195). There is a wide variety of opinions concerning the legitimacy of such a tactic;[10] passing on that question is beyond

[10] Marx (1988, pp. 146–47) explores the similar drawbacks of another phenomenon—the expenditure by police of increasingly large amounts of "buy money"in some jurisdictions. Such tactics may be wittingly or unwittingly inducing criminal infighting that otherwise would occur less frequently. Covert drug buys, Marx suggests, may increase

retaliatory attacks on informers (or those perceived to be informers). Part of the increased homicide rates in the 1970s, particularly among minority youth, has been attributed to the vastly augmented amounts of federal buy money for drugs and information that became available. This increased the opportunity for persons to become informers, some of whom were subsequently attacked or killed as a result. Violence and competition among groups involved in contraband trafficking may also have increased. The self-protective actions of undercover agents (whether police or civilians) to cast suspicion away from themselves and onto others by accusing them of being informers may also lead to criminal assaults as a result of mistaken identity.

Improved interagency communication and joint strategic and tactical planning perhaps could help reduce the bloody unintended consequences of police deployment of large amounts of "buy money" and of disinformation techniques used to conceal undercover operatives' true identities.

the scope of this inquiry. The purpose here is to explore the situations in which intergovernmental communication and coordination will be important, assuming *arguendo* the legitimacy of the police mission at hand.

Not only is good communication across enforcement agencies needed if police intend to manipulate criminal turf wars, it is essential also so that police will not be surprised when *criminals* attempt to manipulate the *police* to influence the outcome of criminal turf wars. That an informer might be motivated by considerations other than helping to establish law and order is not new. Miller (1989, pp. 197, 204), writing of the federal revenuers' assault on moonshiners in Mountain Country during the last part of the nineteenth century reports: "While the five- or ten-dollar reward for information, a substantial sum, motivated some informers, 'ginerally,' summarized an old mountaineer, 'hit's jest somebody who has a gredge agin the blockader fer family reasons, or business reasons, and turns informer to git even.'[11] The arrival of an outside power in the mountains allowed angry mountaineers to use arrest and imprisonment by federal officers as weapons of vengeance. . . . In the famous Hatfield-McCoy feud, Roseanna McCoy warned her Hatfield lover of her own brothers' scheme to capture him by having him arrested for moonshining."

Averting abuse of the state's police power and intergovernmental law enforcement collisions or gaps in coverage provides an incentive for close attention by prosecutive as well as investigative and enforcement authorities (see Hausner et al. 1982). For instance, writing fifteen years ago, the then–assistant attorney general in charge of the U.S. Justice Department's criminal division called for the creation of communications and information management systems to alert federal, state, and local prosecutors when one sovereign might affect another's criminal investigation by an impending grant of immunity to compel a witness' testimony. "Federal authorities may often be unaware of a state grant of immunity and the compulsion of testimony," he observed (Thornburgh 1976, pp. 160, 163). Supreme Court Associate Justice Harlan noted that clarifying the rules governing use by state and federal prosecutors of immunized testimony secured in each other's jurisdictions would, in the long run, "probably make joint programs for crime prevention more effective" (*Murphy v. Waterfront Commission*, 378

---

[11] "Moonshiners were often called 'blockaders' by their neighbors because they 'ran the blockade' of federal officers to sell their 'mountain dew'" (Miller 1989, p. 197).

U.S. 52, 92 [1964]). Gaps in coverage—worthy cases being declined by both federal and state prosecutors—can also come at times from ambiguous guidelines concerning the prosecution priorities and conditions of different jurisdictions. Hausner et al. (1982, p. xiv) reported that "ambiguity with respect to whether the offender should be prosecuted federally or otherwise often causes . . . concurrent jurisdiction offenses not to be prosecuted at all." Thus, the need to have costly investigations result, when appropriate, in prosecutions provides a strong incentive for federal and local police jointly to urge federal and local prosecutors to establish clear, workable guidelines for prosecution of cases cognizable in both venues.

The complexity of some crime is another reason local police team up with other agencies to acquire additional investigative skills. Where local police accept responsibility for investigating business crime (see First 1990) and where their concern over syndicate gambling or drug operations requires their grappling with money laundering schemes, police commonly seek federal agency support. That is, they often seek such support when they overcome the initial hurdle of getting local agency approval to address such problems at all. If local police attempt to attack syndicate crime, they soon realize that organized crime's lawyers, accountants, and other business advisors generally are able craftsmen—whose successful challenge calls for high levels of police and prosecutorial proficiency of a sort generally best obtained in intergovernmental task forces (Blakey 1983, p. 1108; Conly 1989, p. 41; Bocklet 1991, p. 273). Similarly, where local police are inclined to tackle high-technology crime (involving computers, telecommunications, etc.), they often find it important to combine available expertise and investigative resources (Bequai 1987; Conly 1989, pp. 38–41, 46–48; McEwen 1989, pp. 7–10, 85–91). Sometimes local agencies possess formidable talents concerning computer-related crime, as in the case of the Lakewood Police Department in Colorado (Conly 1989, p. 41), but the vast majority of nonfederal police would require federal assistance to move against this variety of high-tech offense.

Intelligence about changing organized crime and drug markets is crucial for short- and midterm antidrug planning at all levels of law enforcement, and opening channels of access to pertinent intelligence is an important incentive for local and federal agencies to cooperate. Some of the critical information will be conventional tips about trafficking organizations and operations. Some might concern patterns of unusual cash transactions in a community indicative of money laundering (Office of National Drug Control Policy 1990, p. 61). Still other types of intelligence, such as public health information, can also contribute to police planning. For example, medical information on the behavioral effects of different drugs can help various units of local, state, and federal government anticipate and attempt to prepare to address certain types of drug use epidemics. Medical experts warn that a stimulant epidemic (as with cocaine) is likely to be followed by a depressant epidemic (perhaps involving heroin) as drug abusers seek to reduce "unpleasant post-euphoric 'lows' " (Office of National Drug Control Policy 1990, p. 46).

Local involvement with federal task forces also pays other kinds of mid- and long-term dividends for the local agencies. For instance, local investigators receive on-the-job training in advanced investigative techniques (including sophisticated undercover methods; Marx 1988) during the course of their task force activity and thus become more valuable assets to their home departments (Chaiken, Chaiken, and Karchmer 1990, p. 48; Bocklet 1991, p. 278). Among the skills often developed by local detectives participating in interagency task forces are "report writing, testifying before grand juries, use of court authorized electronic surveillance, working closely with an experienced prosecutor from the inception of a case, and seeking hidden assets through financial investigations" (Chaiken, Chaiken, and Karchmer 1990, p. 48). The morale boost that local detectives may obtain from the prestige of helping to make inroads against particularly resistant targets and from the admiration that their own agencies may feel for their newly acquired investigative acumen is a related incentive for cooperative arrangements.

Similarly, the local agency stands to gain in public reputation not only on the heels of successful joint task force operations but simply by virtue of prominent federal officials (the U.S. attorney, the agents in charge of the local FBI and DEA offices) treating the local police as worthy partners in challenging and sensitive investigations.[12] The impact on city hall, local media, police, and the public at large of having the U.S. Attorney General stand beside the local police chief praising his or her agency's role in producing major federal organized crime or drug indictments may be difficult to measure on some objective scale

---

[12] As in most things, esteem and salary often are not linked. Federal legislation was introduced in 1990 aimed at upgrading the starting salaries of federal police to bring them more in line with the starting salaries of local police in large metropolitan areas where many federal agents are based (*Crime Control Digest* 1990m, p. 1).

but is nonetheless real and important—certainly to the police chief and the participating investigators. Moreover, enhanced local police reputation—both in the general public and within the law enforcement policy community—can often translate into a range of tangible benefits, including greater public cooperation with police and better fiscal support from local, state, and national funding sources.

Fiscal considerations may also provide other kinds of incentives for local agencies to work with intergovernmental task forces. For instance, complex cases often call not only for a critical mass of investigative talent lacking in any one agency but for lengthy prosecutions that local jurisdictions can ill afford (Abrams 1983, p. 783). Thus, in some instances even when local police are fully competent to conduct an investigation, the county prosecutor presses for an intergovernmental effort to shift the prosecution costs to the federal government. Where federal authorities will not accept a case (because, for instance, it does not meet the U.S. attorney's criteria for prosecution) and local caseloads prohibit taking it on, crimes may simply fall between the prosecutorial stools (Conly 1989, pp. 41–42).

An inability to stem the tide of street violence also impels a number of police organizations to seek comfort and strength in affiliation. When assault weapons being used by criminals on a given city's streets have been transported from other states or nations, local police authorities are powerless acting alone to choke off the supply of arms. As Morris (1989a) observed, "The nation's drug and violence problems are forcing federal, state, and local police to cooperate, just as they are forcing local police and previously distrustful community members to work together."

Having a common enemy is a strong incentive for law enforcement alliances. Even a common adversary does not always help avert infighting over tactical matters, of course. The point was put well more than twenty years ago by Chicago Conspiracy Trial defendant Abbie Hoffman: "Conspiracy?" he asked incredulously, "We couldn't agree on *lunch*!" It is captured as well in the Arabian proverb: "The enemy of my enemy is not necessarily my friend." Federal-local affinity born of a common foe is laudable, of course, so long as the enemy is nefarious. But camaraderie may also stem from shared bigotry, as happened at times during the civil rights conflicts of the 1950s and early 1960s in both southern and northern locales.[13] In this sense, the costs and

[13] Morgan (1983, p. 772) reports that, prior to the FBI's investigation of the killing of three civil rights workers in Mississippi by the Ku Klux Klan in 1964, a number of FBI

benefits of better bonding and coordination among law enforcement personnel across agencies are comparable to the issues one encounters within a given police agency. There need not and should not be, but often is, a trade-off between building solidarity within the ranks, and building the bridges of trust and collaboration between police and their service populations that are crucial to effective policing. Thus, in thinking about the various contemporary incentives to mutual assistance between federal and local law enforcement, one should keep in mind the importance of strengthening these incentives in ways that also foster other crucial relationships. The current movement in local police administrative thinking toward value-driven leadership and management provides what many observers and practitioners believe is a promising approach to boosting the morale and expertise of officers through the enhancement of their satisfactory working relationships both within the police organization and with the rest of the citizenry (Kelling, Wasserman, and Williams 1988; Wasserman and Moore 1988; Brown 1991*a*, 1991*b*; Couper and Lobitz 1991; Geller 1991).

Where local police excel, clearly, one of the most potent incentives for federal agencies to join forces with locals is the acquisition of additional, talented personnel (federal task force standard agreements call for the participating local investigators to be "experienced"). The federal law enforcement cadre is small compared to the nation's publicly funded municipal, county, and state sworn police complement. The private security industry, numbering roughly three times the entire cadre of federal, state, and local public police in America, typically would not be seen as competing with publicly funded police in competence; yet some communities and companies will invest in quantity over quality and purchase supplementary private security protection when they no longer find the public police service to suffice. In this circumstance, an additional incentive arises for public police at all lev-

---

field offices evinced a pattern of sacrificing the enforcement of civil rights in the interests of protecting "working relationships with local law enforcement agencies. To intervene on behalf of blacks or 'outside agitators' when local police were looking the other way might generate ill will; in extreme cases, doing so would have involved FBI agents in investigating their local counterparts."

Just as civil rights issues provided the basis early on for some undesirable bonding (to put it less politely, *unlawful* bonding) among federal and local officials, they also created tensions when different agencies with concurrent jurisdiction adopted conflicting enforcement postures. For instance, the enforcement of school integration and related school busing by U.S. Marshals and other federal agents strained intergovernmental law enforcement relationships in communities where local police, reflecting local government preferences, adopted informal segregationist policy (Morris 1989*b*).

els to collaborate with one another: the maintenance of "market share" as against the private security industry. Clearly, we do not suggest that communities will employ private security to attack organized crime or governmental corruption, but increasingly private security are being hired to help communities reduce retail drug trafficking and associated violence.

As federal and local police think about the mutual benefits of collaboration on complex crime problems, they often conclude that what the federal government lacks in domestic troops,[14] many local and state governments lack in investigative and prosecutive tools. Thus, federal authority to eavesdrop on participants in suspected criminal conspiracies is often a prime incentive for local participation on federal task forces (Abrams 1986, p. 811). More favorable rules for obtaining other types of search warrants may also exist in the federal forum than under particular states' laws (Abrams 1986, p. 793; Goldstock 1987, p. 97). Moreover, the statute of limitations for many federal offenses is five years, longer than the limitations periods available in many state court systems (Hausner et al. 1982, p. x). While multijurisdictional teams thus often benefit from being able to operate under the statutory and case law of the jurisdiction providing the greatest legal advantage, great care must be taken to avoid overlooking legal obligations that may eventually become relevant depending on the prosecutorial strategy adopted and judicial interpretations of the rules governing joint law enforcement efforts. For example, investigators must realize when they obtain a search warrant satisfying one jurisdiction's rules but violating another jurisdiction's that they are foreclosing certain prosecutorial options down the road. Additional incentives for local enforcement authorities to use the federal forum stem from the fact that federal rules are often more lenient toward prosecutors than are state rules concerning the proof needed to secure conspiracy indictments and convictions (also see Bocklet 1991, p. 275), and concerning eliciting testimony from grand jury witnesses without granting them complete immunity. Naturally, to preserve the possibility of any prosecution, authorities must take steps to ensure that any immunized testimony bearing on the

---

[14] Sometimes the local agency participants in a joint task force benefit as much as do the federal agencies from the infusion of additional personnel into a joint task force. Especially in the case of a small police force, their vehicles and officers may be reasonably easy for local drug dealers to identify after a short while, and the opportunity to bring fresh faces and cars into undercover operations in the area can restore a tactical advantage to the police (Bocklet 1991, p. 279).

subject matter of their investigation does not taint their current investigation (Abrams 1986, p. 793).

With due care taken, however, the incentives for local use of federal investigative tools are powerful. Wiretapping and other investigative techniques are particularly important in efforts to identify and move against offenses, such as many aspects of organized crime operations (e.g., gambling, extortion, and narcotics transactions), that are unlikely to arrive on the police blotter through victim complaints (see H. Schwartz 1969, 1977; Blakey and Goldstock 1977; Fishman 1983; Marx 1983, p. 1156; Marx 1988; Felten 1991, p. 27). The most effective use of electronic surveillance often requires the involvement of prosecutors during the early stages of investigations, an arrangement that task forces can facilitate (Blakey 1983, p. 1108). Federal investigative and prosecutorial participation on task forces also expedites the processes of subpoenaing and securing the presence of out-of-jurisdiction witnesses and of consolidating scattered defendants for trial (Abrams 1983, p. 780).

Another crucial tool, available in organized crime cases, that draws local authorities to work with their federal counterparts is the federal capacity to induce witnesses to testify by granting them not only legal immunity from prosecution (where the witness is an offender) but physical immunity from assassination. The federal Witness Security Program was established by Title V of the Organized Crime Control Act of 1970 and is managed by the U.S. Marshals Service. This program facilitates prosecution of racketeers by protecting government witnesses (whether law-abiding civilians, criminal suspects, or federal or state prisoners) and their families—prior to, during, and following prosecutions. Although the concept of witness protection is not without opposition on policy grounds (Marx 1988, pp. 147, 158, 198, 207, articulates some of the concerns), most law enforcement practitioners give this program extremely high marks. Former U.S. attorney for the Southern District of New York Rudolph Giuliani reported: "Because of organized crime's demonstrated use of murder and other acts of violence over the years, were it not for the Witness Security Program the Government would have few if any witnesses available for its organized crime prosecutions. . . . The testimony of protected witnesses has resulted in a 78 percent conviction rate in significant organized crime cases which would never have been brought at all but for the Program" (1987, pp. 115–16). The most widely known aspect of the Witness Security Program is its relocation of witnesses and any members of their immediate families who wish to participate.

Between 1971, when the Witness Security Program commenced operation, and April 1991, a total of 5,693 witnesses came under the protection of the program; counting protected family members, the number of individuals relocated since 1971 exceeds 13,000 (Dempsey 1991). The U.S. Marshals Service further reported that 173 new witnesses were added to the program during the fiscal year ending September 30, 1990, bringing the total number of "active" funded witnesses as of that date to 766 and the total number of active funded program participants (witnesses plus participating family members) to 1,609 (U.S. Marshals Service 1991; see also Maguire and Flanagan 1991, p. 60, for data covering the fiscal year that ended September 30, 1990). Legislation sought by the Bush administration would provide the death penalty, under certain circumstances, for persons convicted of attempting to kill federal witnesses, members of their families, federal jurors, or certain federal officials (Office of National Drug Control Policy 1990, p. 23; Office of National Drug Control Policy 1991, p. 34).

Not only federal investigative and prosecutive tools but federal remedies are also more potent than local ones in many instances. Asset forfeiture and stringent sentences under federal statutes may exceed what is easily attainable under state or local provisions (Office of National Drug Control Policy 1990, p. 23; Bocklet 1991, p. 276).[15] Federal pretrial detention options—used by some enforcement officials as de facto punishment—also give joint task forces authority not always available under state law. A joint task force effort in Philadelphia—the "Violent Offender Project"—made extensive use of federal pretrial detention. The project, as of March 1991, had arrested 441 violent offenders who had been preying on Philadelphia neighborhoods, and had thus far enjoyed a 100 percent conviction rate (Feldkamp 1991b, p. 5).

Since strategy in organized crime and drug trafficking control has begun to shift in recent years away from arresting and incarcerating key players to disrupting and dismantling criminal organizations

---

[15] In some circumstances, state sanctions will prove more attractive, and the capacity of a multijurisdictional task force to "forum shop" can be an aid to successful investigations. For instance, at times task forces have been able to secure cooperation with ongoing investigations from upper-class suspects by proposing to charge them under state law, where sentences may be shorter but the accommodations in state prisons would be considerably less comfortable than what the offender might get in a federal institution. In other instances, state penalties (such as for drug dealing) may be more severe than federal penalties and thus provide a useful tool in securing the cooperation of investigative targets (Goldstock 1987, p. 97).

(Goldstock 1987; Stier and Richards 1987, p. 77; Office of National Drug Control Policy 1990, pp. 51, 54, 65; Bocklet 1991, pp. 272–73), asset forfeiture and such related remedies as divestiture, corporate dissolution, and reorganization available under RICO have grown enormously as law enforcement weapons (Abrams 1983, p. 783; Office of National Drug Control Policy 1990, pp. 59, 60; but see Crovitz 1990, p. A15, for a view that the RICO statute is unconstitutionally vague). Arresting "Mr. Big," while still an objective for many agencies, generally has taken second chair as a control technique since mature criminal organizations have shown a remarkable capacity to regenerate leadership and, at times, to continue taking direction from incarcerated bosses (Edelhertz 1987, p. 198; Stier and Richards 1987, pp. 77–78; Office National Drug Control Policy 1991, p. 28).

The prospect of disabling ongoing criminal enterprises is obviously only part of the attraction of asset forfeiture. Another element—the super glue of interagency task forces—is the ability of law enforcement agencies at all levels of government to supplement their budgets by sharing the forfeited assets that their investigators helped to identify and confiscate. Asset forfeitures secured by all federal agencies in 1989 were valued at nearly $1 billion ($973.9 million) by the DEA (*Crime Control Digest* 1990*b*, p. 7). The Office of National Drug Control Policy (1990, p. 17) projected 11,000 new drug-related asset seizures in 1990 and payment to state and local agencies of roughly $238 million from an established asset forfeiture fund (*Crime Control Digest* 1990*c*, p. 7; Trojanowicz and Bucqueroux 1990, pp. 267–68).[16] The drug czar's

---

[16] The DEA's budget office reported that, typically, "40 percent to 50 percent of the total [forfeited assets] is cash or other liquid instruments that can go directly into the federal fund. The remaining portion is property that typically nets 10 percent to 20 percent of its retail dollar value." This property includes both items used to conduct drug trafficking (cars, boats, airplanes, buildings) and valuables acquired by offenders with their drug profits (Trojanowicz and Bucqueroux 1990, p. 268). DEA officials also reported, however, that record forfeitures, seizures of cocaine (81.7 tons in 1989, three times the 1986 tonnage taken), and arrests (25,618 total federal drug arrests in 1989, of which 15,097 were for cocaine trafficking) still had not observably disrupted the cocaine market in the United States (*Crime Control Digest* 1990*b*, p. 7). By the time the President's 1991 *National Drug Control Strategy* report was released in February 1991, drug officials were beginning to note a decrease in both occasional and frequent cocaine use in the nation, as detected in household surveys conducted every few years by the National Institute on Drug Abuse (NIDA), Department of Health and Human Services. Occasional users (use less than once-per-month in the past year) were said to have numbered approximately 8.6 million in 1985, 5.8 million in 1988, and 4.1 million in 1990. Frequent cocaine users (use weekly or more frequently in the past year) were estimated at 431,000 in 1985, 862,000 in 1988, and 662,000 in 1990, although NIDA cautioned that these figures were based on relatively small numbers of household survey respondents who

1991 report indicated that fully $240 million in assets were transferred to state and local law enforcement agencies during the preceding year (Office of National Drug Control Policy 1991, p. 28). Typically, when asset forfeitures have been accomplished by DEA State and Local Task Forces, the DEA retains ten percent of the forfeited amount for administrative costs, with the balance being distributed amongst the jurisdictions whose law enforcement agencies participated—in proportion to their investigative involvement (Bocklet 1991, p. 276). Forfeited assets returned to state and local police agencies by the federal government typically are earmarked for drug-control activities (enforcement as well as prevention—Office of National Drug Control Policy 1991, p. 28), although these activities in some jurisdictions are broadly defined to cover a variety of crime-prevention efforts, such as design and implementation of problem-oriented policing and gun buy-back programs. By contrast, sometimes *state*-administered civil and criminal asset forfeiture programs do not share drug proceeds with police agencies in a manner that the police consider equitable, thus providing incentives for police to use federal rather than state forfeiture mechanisms (Trojanowicz and Bucqueroux 1990, p. 268). Chaiken, Chaiken, and Karchmer (1990, p. 48) observe that, with federal asset sharing, often "the agency's cost for the loss of an investigator to a task force is made up out of forfeiture proceeds."

Asset forfeiture is not universally greeted with enthusiasm among the law enforcement policy community. There are some who worry, for example, that competition for forfeiture funds risks undermining cooperation among local departments and also risks distracting local police from "a proper focus on street-level [drug] sales" (Trojanowicz 1989). Even ardent proponents of asset forfeiture as a weapon in the drug war readily concede the need to fashion safeguards to protect the interests of "third parties"—those "not involved in narcotics trafficking but whose property may be subject to forfeiture because it was either used in or derived from a drug transaction" (Goldsmith and Lenck 1990, p. 7).

In the case of both DEA state and local task forces and organized crime drug enforcement task forces (both described in a later section of this essay), formal interagency agreements typically provide other

fall within the frequent user category (Office of National Drug Control Policy 1991, pp. 8–10). The Drug Czar's Office also reported "strong secondary evidence of recently reduced drug availability: significantly higher wholesale cocaine prices, and significantly lower wholesale cocaine purity" (Office of National Drug Control Policy 1991, p. 15).

financial incentives for local agencies to contribute personnel to the teams. It is common, for example, for the federal government to cover the cost of investigative overtime (the local police officer's home agency pays his or her regular salary). This overtime can amount to a substantial sum annually (Chaiken, Chaiken, and Karchmer 1990, p. 45). Further, the DEA provides funds and equipment needed to support the activities of the assigned officers (office space and supplies, travel funds, funds for the purchase of evidence and information, and investigative equipment). When local investigators join forces with their federal counterparts (in DEA or other task forces), often the local personnel gain access to communications equipment of a sort they normally lack (e.g., radios with ranges covering multistate regions instead of their usual radios, which may be effective only over a fifteen-mile area—Klockars 1990). The DEA also underwrites the cost of any training it decides to provide for the detailed officers. The sharing of forfeited assets and other financial assistance provided by the federal government for task forces have parallels in bilateral and multilateral international treaties that the United States has signed in hopes of stemming the production and transportation of narcotics that have strong markets in this country (Office of National Drug Control Policy 1990, pp. 48, 57).

Another incentive for local police to operate under the umbrella of a federal task force is that that umbrella can help them weather any storm of civil litigation. A San Diego Police Department member of the DEA state and local task force cited "freedom from liability in all federal tort cases" as a powerful attraction of the task force. "If a lawsuit comes in against any of our agents," he continued, "the DEA handles it. This is especially important for many of our small police departments because a major legal action could strain their resources, if not ultimately bankrupt them" (Bocklet 1991, p. 276).

Despite numerous incentives for intergovernmental law enforcement cooperation and coordination, certain circumstances, such as widespread, systemic corruption in a particular agency, could effectively blackball that agency as a full partner in joint investigations. Indeed, during the 1950s and 1960s the FBI generally took the position that it could not work closely with local police because of the possibility that the bureau might have to investigate them if concerns arose about police illegalities (Morris 1989a). This position gradually shifted over time, partly in response to the generally improved reputation for integrity and other aspects of professionalism that many local police agencies have enjoyed over the past two decades (Delattre 1989; International Association of Chiefs of Police 1989a; Murphy and Caplan 1991). Although the FBI maintains responsibility for investigating official misconduct in local police agencies, the general pattern nationwide in which city, county, and state agencies more actively attend to self-policing responsibilities—and, when necessary, work jointly with the FBI to ferret out and remove corrupt police—has enabled a more trusting and respectful relationship generally between the FBI and nonfederal agencies. It will be interesting to watch whether new interagency strains set in as a result of the FBI's stepped-up attention to police use of excessive force following the videotaped beating of motorist Rodney King by Los Angeles Police Department members in March 1991 and other documented instances of police brutality in other police agencies.

It is especially noteworthy that concerns about corruption—as distinguished from concerns about brutality and other abuses of authority—are not the substantial hurdles to intergovernmental mutual assistance that they were at one time in light of the perception of some that police corruption, if anything, is on the increase. One West Coast police manager argued that local police integrity problems, stemming directly from the corruptive efforts of drug traffickers, are "more widespread now than at any time since Prohibition" (McCown 1988, p. 4). Where this perception prevails, continued joint enforcement efforts by federal and local agencies are made possible principally by two factors: the belief by federal authorities that most local officials take seriously their responsibility for searching out and attacking corruption in their own ranks; and the capacity to avoid tainting task force efforts with local police corruption by carefully screening candidates for task force participation and, where necessary, by using informal lines of interagency communication that circumvent the normal chain of command.

Another consideration bearing on integrity may provide a further incentive for intergovernmental cooperation. Police executives who subscribe to the theory that familiarity almost inevitably breeds corruption could find that placing some of their investigators on interagency task forces might lessen the likelihood of collusive dishonesty and abuse of authority because there are "no longstanding personal ties" among members of the multiagency team (McCown 1988, p. 39). Some would contest the logic or at least the wisdom of this incentive, arguing, as Trojanowicz and Bucqueroux (1990) do in the context of promoting the community problem-solving movement, that effective policing depends on powerful bonding both among co-workers and between police and their service community (also see Goldstein 1990; Couper and Lobitz 1991). Indeed, Trojanowicz and Bucqueroux (1990) and other commentators and practitioners believe that the informal accountability systems inherent in a reinvigorated police-community partnership will help prevent and detect traditional forms of police corrupt practices, as well as police brutality (Trojanowicz 1991).

Just as many believe that over the past two decades integrity concerns have decreased as an inhibition to interagency collaboration, even if the frequency of drug-related corruption has risen, others observe that changing societal tensions have relieved some of the irritants to intergovernmental law enforcement cooperation. A former head of the U.S. Marshals Service reported that a number of local police agencies, as extensions of their local governments, disliked the Marshals Service when it moved into their communities to enforce court-ordered school desegregation or school busing (Morris 1989a). Some sources of interagency tension have diminished not only because of reductions in institutionalized community racism but because of a radical shift in many police agencies' conceptions of their responsibilities, as attested to by their aggressive minority recruitment/retention personnel efforts, their strong moves against "hate" or "bias" crime (see National Organization of Black Law Enforcement Executives 1991; Scott 1991; Stewart and Fisher-Stewart 1991), and their strides over the past two decades in reducing the use of lethal force to apprehend suspects (Geller and Scott 1992). To be sure, many would argue that racial tensions in America are growing worse, not better. Our perception is that, in most communities where this is true, the *police*, albeit with occasional headline-producing exceptions and with ample room for improvement in low-visibility conduct, display less institutionalized racism in their dealings with others (and with their own personnel) than is displayed by the average citizen. If such performance is inspired as much by the career risks associated with misconduct as by personal decency, so be it. The result is that most local police forces are less likely to find themselves at odds with federal bodies responsible for enforcing civil rights laws than was true some years ago and, hence, more able to imagine and carry off collaborations. In part, such progress may stem from substantial advances over the past two decades in African Americans rising to CEO positions in municipal police departments. As of July 1991, blacks held the top post in over 250 American police agencies, including in a number of the largest cities—progress which has eluded Hispanics and other racial and ethnic minorities thus far and which has eluded black law enforcement professionals in the federal police community (Williams 1991, p. 3).

Reducing irritants to intergovernmental cooperation often requires imaginative attention to the structural and infrastructural elements of interagency interaction. Chief among the positive developments—and a strong impetus for more and higher quality joint endeavor—has been the clarification of each party's roles, often accomplished through formal interagency agreements. For instance, opportunities for misunderstanding and mistrust are reduced by the DEA state and local task force standard agreement (discussed later in this essay), which specifies, among other matters, that nonfederal officers will be assigned to the task force for at least one year, during which they are under the "direct control and supervision of DEA Task Force supervisory personnel" and must adhere to both DEA and their home agency's policies and procedures. The agreement provides that any inconsistencies in these obligations is to be resolved by designated senior officials from both the DEA field office and the police agency. Further, DEA supervisors are obligated by the contract to make special reports concerning assigned officers' job performance to the officers' home departments (and to provide copies of all task force activity reports depicting the officers' activities). In turn, the home agency still bears the responsibility of evaluating these personnel under applicable state and local law (Chaiken, Chaiken, and Karchmer 1990). Given the difficulty most police agencies have had framing meaningful performance evaluation criteria for officers working on *familiar* types of problems (Mastrofski and Wadman 1991; Moore 1991), the capacity of local departments appropriately to assess the conduct of their personnel on complex, multijurisdictional problems may be low; but at least the respective agencies' areas of responsibility for performance appraisal are clearly staked out under the DEA agreements.

Besides the benefits of specifying joint task force members' respective roles, some inhibitions to collaboration have almost certainly been curtailed over the years through general professional education—at the FBI's National Academy, at the interagency Federal Law Enforcement Training Center, and in many other settings. Most such curricula these days stress the importance of pooling knowledge and effort for more efficient, better-conceived crime control and peacekeeping in a nation of diminishing public resources and rising predation. The intermingling of police from all levels of government at such training produces benefits that can have long-term operational significance.

Following trends in private-sector strategic thinking about leadership and management style, attention to interpersonal and management skill questions related to multijurisdictional task forces has also reportedly motivated more and higher quality joint action by law enforcement agencies. Chaiken, Chaiken, and Karchmer (1990, p. 49) report: "Many of the problems . . . stem from local reaction to the federal agency's selection of a task force commander with limited experience in dealing with nonfederal investigators. Hence, plans to prevent or reduce task force problems need to incorporate a process of careful leadership selection."

According to many practitioners and observers, the historic pattern in which federal agencies, such as the FBI, were principally information takers but not information providers when working with local law enforcement authorities (Morgan 1983, p. 770; Lupsha 1990)—a traditional hurdle to respectful collaboration—has changed considerably in recent years. Today, although room for progress clearly remains, we are told there is a much better mutual exchange of pertinent intelligence.[17] Similarly, the efforts of task force management to keep local agencies' senior executives informed of the progress of cooperative investigations has helped to mollify distrust and foster more generous resource sharing.[18] Under DEA's standard task force interagency contract, the police chief (or his or her designee) whose personnel are detailed to the task force is briefed at least monthly on task force activity and may request special briefings as they are deemed useful. During all such briefings, the state or local department is afforded an opportunity to provide written input concerning "the establishment, modification or refinement of Task Force goals and objectives as well as identification of specific criminal targets" (Chaiken, Chaiken, and Karchmer 1990, p. 116).

Some incentive for formal and informal cooperation and collabora-

[17] U.S. Court of Appeals (Seventh Circuit) Judge William Bauer, a former U.S. Attorney and county prosecutor in the Chicago metropolitan area, reports that fairly rapid and observable improvements in federal information sharing with local law enforcement entities were produced under U.S. Attorney General Robert Kennedy, who issued certain directives on the subject (Bauer 1990).

[18] Lupsha (1990) offered the view that former U.S. attorney for the Southern District of New York, Rudolph Giuliani, by being especially sensitive to the information and other needs of the New York City Police Department, was able to succeed where predecessors had failed in making cases against organized crime leaders, drawing on years of work by the New York City Organized Crime Bureau and the New York State Organized Crime Task Force. Giuliani's style was such that he reportedly left a good feeling among the New York City Police hierarchy in the wake of celebrated federal court convictions and the attendant flurries of media attention.

tion may also be provided by efforts to frame feasible strategies for law enforcement action against difficult problems (such as organized crime) (Stier and Richards 1987, pp. 76–77). Strategic planning occurs both at the national level (within agencies' headquarters and within coordination and oversight bodies) and at the level of each individual task force. Although serious attention is beginning to be devoted by many parties to strategic planning, by most accounts high-caliber strategic planning remains a rarity in federal-local law enforcement efforts (Goldstock 1987; Moore 1987). If comprehensive planning improves, the already powerful incentives to intergovernmental cooperation and coordination should be strengthened considerably.

Finally, an essential part of the infrastructure of effective and efficient collaboration is the growing body of useful policy and operational research on crime control, order maintenance, and community problem solving. Much of this research over the past several decades has been sponsored by the U.S. Department of Justice agencies (the Law Enforcement Assistance Administration and, in recent years, the National Institute of Justice, the Bureau of Justice Assistance, the Bureau of Justice Statistics, and others that operate under the department's Office of Justice Programs). Further, by establishing research review mechanisms that assemble practitioners from all levels of government (together with researchers having pertinent subject matter expertise), important informal liaison is established between agencies that is conducive to more rational planning and operational cooperation over time. The subject matter of government sponsored research fostering better interagency cooperation is as diverse as the crime problems facing the nation. National police leaders have quite rightly observed what professional researchers say all the time—that much remains to be studied—and the practitioners recently have called for the appointment of a Presidential commission bringing to bear on crime and disorder problems the best current thinking from a wide array of disciplines (Brown 1990, 1991c). Such a call for greater integration of disparate knowledge and the creation of a more comprehensive national strategy against crime and fear need not demean progress to date. It does, however, point out how much remains to be done to improve the incentives for, and the strength of, partnerships for public safety in this nation.

B. Disincentives to Cooperation, Coordination, and Collaboration

Some of the disincentives to joint federal-local action lie at the core of our federalism. The tradition of self-governance, reflected in the

Constitution's reservation to the states of powers not granted to the federal government, has given rise to a pervasive pattern of local police departments in America. Some cherish the independence of municipal departments; others cite the fragmentation of policing into thousands of municipal, county, township, and special police agencies as a major obstacle to professional growth (e.g., Murphy 1989, p. xv). For better or worse, the desire of communities for local control over policing generates varying levels of reticence concerning hands-on federal involvement in addressing local manifestations of crime.[19]

Law enforcement agencies' obligations to different sovereigns and different political interests naturally compels their allegiance to different missions, enforcement priorities, and directions, thus limiting the subjects around which intergovernmental task forces can coalesce (Goldstock 1987, p. 96). Various policy statements generated by both the U.S. Justice Department's criminal division in Washington, D.C., and the ninety-four U.S. attorney's offices offer guidance on current federal criminal enforcement priorities. The policies are embodied in such documents as the "Principles of Federal Prosecution," first issued in 1980 by Attorney General Benjamin Civiletti (cf. Levi 1976) and later incorporated in the U.S. Attorneys' Manual, and the individual U.S. attorneys' "written guidelines for the declination of alleged violations of federal criminal laws" (Frase 1980; Abrams 1986, pp. 139, 149). Among the most common criteria used to determine the acceptance of a crime for federal prosecution is the dollar value of the harm involved.

Thus, even where common interests are identified, sometimes cooperation is precluded. Federal statutes, U.S. Department of Justice Criminal Division edict, or U.S. attorney policy on case acceptance may bar the federal government from assisting local agencies with certain complex cases, for instance, even though the investigation and prosecution of those cases is often beyond the capacity of local officials. In the area of computer crime "federal prosecution standards limit federal involvement in many of the computer-related offenses that

[19] Local control over policing is a part of the mainstream of the community policing movement. Sometimes, as in Santa Ana, California, during the early 1980s, efforts by local police to secure crucial community support for public safety efforts have placed local officials in direct conflict with federal officials. Chief Raymond Davis, attempting to serve a community whose population was predominantly Chicano—many of whom were recent arrivals in America—waged a highly visible public relations campaign against the enforcement of immigration laws by the INS within his city's borders (Davis 1985).

come to the attention of state and county investigators. U.S. Attorneys decline to prosecute juveniles, which eliminates many 'hacker' cases from their consideration, because the federal criminal justice system is not designed to handle juvenile matters. Cases involving adults are also declined if the dollar loss is not sufficient to meet federal prosecution requirements" (Conly 1989, p. 39).

Congress's penchant for giving federal agencies more enforcement obligations than enforcement resources makes case selection extremely difficult within federal investigative and prosecutorial offices. In an environment where some cases deemed crucial by *federal* law enforcement are neglected, it is no surprise that many cases deemed important by *local* police are not docketed for joint task force activity (Abrams 1983, p. 784).

This is not to suggest, however, that federal prosecutorial enforcement priorities at any given time are immutable in the face of local pleas for modification. Indeed, incorporating local police and prosecutorial thinking in the framing of federal enforcement policies is the very purpose of many of the mechanisms for intergovernmental communication, however well-administered they may be, which are discussed in the next part of this essay. Besides such bodies as the law enforcement coordinating committees (Abrams 1986, p. 151), the Justice Department's office of liaison services was established by Attorney General Edwin Meese and has been maintained by his successors to facilitate efficient communication between local enforcement authorities and the attorney general—communication that otherwise might have been encumbered by labyrinthine communications protocols. How well such mechanisms of communication have attained their intended purposes is a topic on which experienced practitioners differ (Forst 1990).

Disincentives for federal-local coordination stem not only from resource constraints but from lingering skill and integrity deficits in some locales. A lack of pertinent investigative training in some local agencies prevents them from providing personnel who can serve as effective partners in complex cases. For instance, in the area of computer crimes, "even when investigators are willing to cooperate with each other, there is no guarantee that they will know enough about warrant preparation and evidence collection to prepare a good computer-related case" (Conly 1989, p. 39).

Information processing constraints in some instances also limit interagency mutual assistance (Gruber, Mechling, and Pierce 1991). For example, where federal, state, or local investigators cannot respond to inquiries from one another in a timely fashion because pertinent data cannot be efficiently retrieved from either paper or automated files, cooperative and coordinated operations are forestalled. One step planned to address this problem in the antidrug arena—which can be emulated for attacking nondrug crime as well—is the automation of DEA's extensive intelligence files so that the data contained in them can be "built on by other law enforcement agencies" (Office of National Drug Control Policy 1990, pp. 17–18, 84; Office of National Drug Control Policy 1991, pp. 121, 136, 139). Another step is a new Treasury Department agency, the Financial Crimes Enforcement Network (FinCEN), which was designed to share financial crime data bases (O'Connell 1990a, p. 2; Office of National Drug Control Policy 1991, p. 117; Rinkevich 1991a). Other efforts at automated data processing, and linking automated systems so they can communicate, are enumerated in the 1991 national plan of the Office of National Drug Control Policy (1991, pp. 120–22).

There are, of course, various necessary and proper constraints on the efficient collection and dissemination of information pertinent to crime control, and these are sometimes significant and proper impediments to greater interagency collaboration. Among the constraints are protecting the individual's privacy rights and criminal procedural rights, "legal and policy restrictions on sharing information among agencies, the protection of confidential informants, intelligence sources, and methods, as well as avoiding the premature disclosure of potential evidence" (Office of National Drug Control Policy 1991, p. 120). The Central Intelligence Agency (CIA) is an example of an agency constrained by law from sharing various types of information with other federal policing organizations. Thus, although the CIA has expanded its role in gathering intelligence relevant to antidrug enforcement activities, "statutory limitations and Executive Order restrict the sharing of certain types of information related to foreign topics" (Office of National Drug Control Policy 1991, p. 117)—a shield whose occasional unnecessary use one might expect to be a powerful temptation for intelligence operatives jealous of their prerogatives.

Such considerations as protecting informant identities and safeguarding operational plans will very likely arise as substantial impediments to multiagency cooperation and knowledge sharing where organizations doubt the integrity of key managerial personnel in other agencies. In such a circumstance, joint investigations are undertaken only with great caution to avoid compromising the effectiveness of operations and the safety of assigned investigators. Since organized crime can hardly flourish in the absence of powerful mechanisms for political corruption (Abrams 1983, p. 780; Stier and Richards 1987, p. 78; Lupsha 1991), concerns about sharing intelligence necessarily continue to pervade interagency collaboration against organized crime.

Even where agencies trust one anothers' integrity, the continuing obligation of federal agencies (principally the FBI) to scrutinize alleged corruption, brutality, and other official misconduct within state and local police agencies can provide occasional irritants to interagency cooperation on a broad range of crime problems. Whether such inter-agency contacts produce friction often is a function of the judgment and sensitivity with which both federal and local officials carry out their respective responsibilities. Mutual recriminations, posturing, and failure of the investigating agency to give the subject agency due credit for helping to clean its own house are prescriptions for interagency friction.[20]

Sometimes a local agency's reticence to release personnel for task force activities arises from a perception that task force procedures will complicate the agency's efforts to monitor its loaned workers' integrity. The International Association of Chiefs of Police, in a federally funded effort to develop safeguards to prevent recurrences of the widespread drug corruption experienced by the Miami Police Department in the late 1980s, observed:

---

[20] In beginning to step up its attention to state and local police brutality and to provide enhanced technical assistance for preventing brutality in the wake of notorious misuses of police force in several jurisdictions (the Los Angeles Police beating of Rodney King in March 1991 being the most widely publicized), the FBI has taken great care to treat self-remediation efforts by nonfederal agencies with respect (Major City Chief Administrators 1991). An aspect of the police corruption problem not discussed in the text deserves mention, for it reflects a different dimension of disincentive for some local police forces to bring federal agents into their cases. Even though over recent years police agencies have become much more proactively engaged in efforts to foster integrity (Murphy and Caplan 1991), the large federal role in this domain has, arguably, unwittingly impeded the development of these strengths within local agencies.

In much the same fashion, federal de facto preemption of other areas of crime control—organized crime, white-collar or business crime (embezzlement, price-fixing, etc.), computer fraud, political corruption, and others—without the federal resources to investigate or remediate more than a smattering of such crimes, has exacted a high price. Local police have failed to develop sufficient capacities for addressing these problems. Bittner (1982, p. 5) has suggested that, in some instances, what has impelled local police to refrain "from developing enforcement capacities in these areas of criminal conduct [is that] special enforcement agencies were created when the various crimes were defined in legislation."

Drug cases investigated cooperatively by several agencies—
either permanent task forces or ad hoc groups—can also present
difficulties for supervisors and auditors. The involvement of
another agency should never preclude a thorough review of all
case documents and an accounting of funds. In cases involving the
cooperation of federal agencies, for example, the informant might
be an individual developed by the local police department. When
the case is terminated, the informant may be placed in the Federal
Witness Protection Program for safety. But the department's
informant records may show that the informant has been paid
substantial sums of money for information and activities during
development of the case. It is important that the U.S. Marshals
Service verify payments by formally interviewing the informant.
A written memorandum of understanding between investigating
agencies spelling out these authorities and responsibilities can
reduce problems in future cooperative cases. [International
Association of Chiefs of Police 1989a, p. 63]

At times, the sheer number of federal, state, and local enforcement
personnel working different aspects of a complex investigation can
present formidable challenges to supervisors in each participating
agency responsible for attesting to the continuing legitimacy of the
joint venture. Consider, for instance, the January 14, 1990, indictment
in Boise, Idaho, of Los Angeles street gang members on federal drug
trafficking charges, which reportedly "culminated seven months of
work that at one time involved more than 160 federal, state, county
and local law enforcement officers" (*Crime Control Digest* 1990d, p. 7).

Turf jealousies between agencies also discourage cooperation and
coordination at times. Historically, a common view among local police
was that the federal-local law enforcement relationship consisted primarily
of "the Feds stealing our snitches, cases, and headlines" (Wadman 1990). By most accounts this situation has improved dramatically,
although parochial self-interest and resentment over past headline grabbing
or more serious usurpations undoubtedly still contribute occasionally
to strained interagency relations and concomitantly meager resource
sharing. In a sense, the unwillingness to share power
productively that is manifest in some interagency contacts parallels the
strains that historically have appeared in local police dealings with the
private security industry and with such citizen volunteer patrol efforts
as the Guardian Angels (Rosenbaum, Hernandez, and Daughtry 1991).
Gray (1983, p. 370) observes: "Frequently . . . private security firms

and the police duplicate each other's efforts. Moreover, the cooperation between the two is occasionally strained because of a confusion of roles and because of the lower hiring, training, and retention standards of most private security firms" (cf. Cunningham and Taylor 1985).

One of the techniques that may sometimes help overcome competition over turf is to locate new, as yet unclaimed, real estate. For example, Guyot and Martensen (1991) argue that where the Law Enforcement Assistance Administration (LEAA) found success in attempting to foster intergovernmental law enforcement coordination in programs it funded was primarily "in new areas, such as sting programs and strike forces, [which] thus did not threaten traditional working arrangements."

Yet, turf concerns persist as a disincentive to information sharing and joint operations. Many local investigators have seen that there are trade-offs to joint investigations, one being that they may lose some or even most control over their cases and credit for eventual arrests to federal authorities. Moreover, local detectives may lose some of their informants, who learn during assistance to a task force investigation that federal agencies often pay more for tips than do local police (Klockars 1990). It may also be true, however, that local police can cultivate informants they would never have been able to control without access to federal information funds. As a DEA supervisor in the Phoenix Drug Task Force put it, "While the police departments may develop contacts and informants, someone has to pay them to risk their necks" (Bocklet 1991, p. 277).

Other obstacles to coordination and cooperation may arise in the context of asset forfeiture under RICO and other statutes. Federal officials report that efforts are underway to streamline what has become a notoriously slow process used by the federal government to forward equitable shares of forfeited assets to participating local agencies (Carvino 1989; *Asset Forfeiture Bulletin* 1990, p. 2; Office of National Drug Control Policy 1990, p. 17). These efforts include reducing the number of layers of review required before dispensing forfeited funds to nonfederal police agency applicants, empowering U.S. attorneys in the field to authorize local sharing when the assets at issue in the forfeiture proceeding were worth less than $1 million, and providing training and informational literature to help nonfederal law enforcement agencies better prepare their paperwork concerning the seizure and the request for equitable sharing (*Asset Forfeiture Bulletin* 1990, p. 2). Given the depth of dissatisfaction among local police participants in multijurisdictional task forces over the long waiting periods for equitably sharing in forfeited assets (e.g., Bocklet 1991, p. 276), it may be some time before federal efforts to speed up the processing of the equitable sharing system succeed in changing generally held perceptions in the field. Sometimes, competition arises between different levels of government over who should control forfeited assets. For example, tempers flared between state governments and localities concerning "adoptive forfeitures" in the 1980s, finally being resolved by Congress in 1989 in favor of the localities. The result was to allow localities to reap the pecuniary benefits of asset forfeiture by bringing suitable cases to the federal government for federal prosecution (International Association of Chiefs of Police 1989*b*, p. 1).

Some observers have worried that, although the prospect of sharing forfeited assets may be providing incentives for individual local agencies to collaborate with the FBI and DEA, the quest for confiscated assets may be deterring cooperation *among* local and state agencies, who wish, through limiting the number of partners in an investigative venture, to reduce the number of shares into which the spoils of victory will be divided. Similarly, the assets of middle- and upper-echelon operatives in a drug distribution chain may serve as magnets for police resources that would accomplish more good—and, in the long run, might represent a more cost-effective deployment—if targeted at street-level retail operations that, left unchecked, erode a neighborhood's morale and capacity for self-defense (Trojanowicz 1989; cf. Office of National Drug Control Policy 1991, p. 28).

Rudimentary levels of strategic planning (cf. Stier and Richards 1987, pp. 77–78) also inhibit more active collaboration between law enforcement agencies at different levels of government. Goldstock (1987, p. 97) observes that the process of hammering out tolerable interagency agreements can occupy a great deal of agencies' time and substantially preempt the efforts that must be devoted to strategic planning. Some local police chiefs, believing that strategies premised on conventional criminal justice system arrest, prosecution, and incarceration are incapable of ameliorating problems that most affect their communities (see Kelling 1991), are extremely reluctant to remove officers from their own operations and assign them to federal task forces, where they may be sent to Asia and other distant locations pursuing these strategic objectives (Wadman 1990).

The problem of weak strategic planning cannot be overstated as an obstacle to useful concerted action by law enforcement bodies at all levels of government. The problem gets compounded because those most drawn to crime-fighting ideas that can fit on a bumper sticker— elected officials—often succeed in stifling what little institutional commitment the police may have had to searching for strategies and tactics that make a long-term investment in the improvement of their communities. Friel (1990, p. 45) captures nicely the process by which political scapegoating of criminal justice institutions for the bankruptcy of public policy on crime control begins a destructive spiral: "As soon as you introduce increased accountability for a policy gone wrong as a way of covering your backside, what is the response of people running those agencies who can see that accountability coming down? They are going to shift from qualitative objectives, which are very hard to measure, to quantitative ones; from substance to style."

As public policymakers search for valuable anticrime strategies, they will need an essential component of any good strategic planning process—quality intelligence. Its absence can impair the attractiveness of joint operations. What, then, is thought to be the state of the art of strategic intelligence gathering? A National Institute of Justice appraisal of law enforcement intelligence operations targeting organized crime in 1986 painted a dismal picture:

> With a few exceptions, intelligence units have little status, are separated from the operating units of their agencies by a wide gulf, make little input to policy, are used largely to gather evidence rather than to generate cases or support policy planning, and have few resources and little training. There appear to be many reasons for the failure to adequately support and properly use organized crime intelligence. Agency supervisors and staffs, and to some extent intelligence agents, have little understanding of how intelligence can be gathered and used. There is tension between investigators who face the hard, grubbing work of gathering evidence in streets, and desk-bound intelligence units. Investigative and prosecutive agencies tend to focus on near-term demands for information that will support pending investigations and prosecutions, rather than fact-gathering and analyses that will enable them to strike, perhaps far in the future, against major organized crime enterprises. Since little policy planning is done, the potential of intelligence for this purpose is hardly likely to be exploited. Intelligence, as a discipline, has been imprecise and expensive. There is not yet a tradition in intelligence. Finally, intelligence is obviously most useful to agencies that are proactive,

but most law enforcement agencies are reactive—by necessity or choice. [Edelhertz 1987, p. 199]

Efforts to coordinate and strengthen the dissemination of useful intelligence are being planned by the Office of National Drug Control Policy. It would aim to integrate and otherwise facilitate use of disparate intelligence bases by creating a National Drug Intelligence Center (NDIC). The NDIC would report directly to the Attorney General and would be charged with coordinating "the collection and the production of intelligence information regarding drug trafficking" and with consolidating, analyzing, and appropriately disseminating all relevant intelligence gathered by federal, state, and local law enforcement agencies. The intelligence information is sought to help portray "the structure, membership, finances, communications, and activities of criminal drug organizations, in addition to the specific details of particular drug smuggling or money laundering operations" (Office of National Drug Control Policy 1990, pp. 6, 17, 83–84; Office of National Drug Control Policy 1991, p. 118). Such a system can be no better, of course, than the intelligence that agencies can acquire.

Even where individual agencies develop quality intelligence, they may hesitate to share it freely among networks of law enforcement authorities, not out of parochialism but out of concern over losing the capacity to safeguard its use. Lupsha (1991, p. 232) observes:

The basic safeguards [to ensure the fairness and integrity of police intelligence efforts] include collection only of information that is justified by reasonably suspected criminal conduct; development of standards for data that are to be included in the system; collation and analysis in a secure environment; purging of information or leads that are unfounded or out-of-date; and dissemination only to criminal justice agencies with a clear need to receive the information. Although these safeguards typically are not difficult for a single department to adopt and follow, they become complicated in regional and other multijurisdictional intelligence-sharing arrangements. For this reason, a formal compact that sets forth explicit criteria and due process safeguards should precede the implementation of any intelligence-sharing arrangements. [See also Godfrey and Harris 1971, pp. 73–91; Martens 1987; New Jersey Department of Law and Public Safety 1975; Office of National Drug Control Policy 1991, p. 120]

Powerful strategic planning depends on the assessment of completed operations to identify the strengths and weaknesses of approaches taken and to "institutionalize the wisdom of experience" (Goldstock 1987, p. 99; see also Cordner, Fraser, and Wexler 1991). Yet, law enforcement agencies at all levels of government far too often view rigorous analysis of investigations—or other police work (Geller 1985, p. 352)—as either an exorbitant exercise or an unwarranted second-guessing of officer decision making. Such denigration of debriefing exercises and performance appraisal generally (see Mastrofski and Wadman 1991) would be viewed as irresponsible management in the military or private industry, Goldstock notes (1987, pp. 98–99), yet in law enforcement lack of genuine planning and analysis is allowed to dominate (Reiss 1991).[21] The National Institute of Justice (NIJ), in the late 1980s, sponsored a pioneering "multi-agency investigative team" research project which, among other objectives, sought to increase the frequency and quality of "post-investigation follow-up and critique" in serial murder investigations (Brooks et al. 1987, p. 42). More recently, Chaiken, Chaiken, and Karchmer (1990) produced a report for NIJ that examines what does and does not work in organizing and coordinating multijurisdictional antidrug efforts. The Police Executive Research Forum, with NIJ support, in the late 1980s and early 1990s launched a series of innovative case studies of police administrative decision making, which employed analytically skilled practitioners from other jurisdictions in the appraisal of the subject agency's work. Such appraisals are a promising source of information on how single agencies and networks of

---

[21] An interesting technological tool has been developed by the FBI that holds great potential for post hoc analysis in a related area—critical incident management—and that might find adaptations for creating institutional memory about the relative merits of different investigative approaches. The Bureau's Strategic Information Operations Center, a command post linked through telecommunications to field posts and used to coordinate information among all affected agencies during domestic terrorism incidents, prison riots, or other critical situations, makes use of a "continuous time-line." This plotting system displays events and FBI responsive actions by time of occurrence. As such, it "provides a continuing narrative of all significant events. The preparation of a time-line begins as soon as possible after a crisis occurs in order to plot initial field events, and it is continued as part of the monitoring process. Separate time-lines also can be made to track events related to the crisis in such areas as public affairs and logistics" (Sessions 1989b, p. 10). With data collection commencing early enough in an incident and with care taken to input all key data (in a way that does not impede timely and effective operational decision making), the electronic narrative could be used subsequently in calmer times for simulation training exercises and appropriate assessments of tactical decisionmaking and resource management. Similarly, police critical incident management training might benefit from adapting recent Defense Department technological advances in simulated computer war games.

agencies and community groups can more productively identify, target, and overcome public safety problems.

Other efforts to facilitate better strategic planning—to produce the successes that will, in turn, engender further collaborative work—are being made by a variety of practitioners and analysts (see, e.g., Giuliani 1987; Goldstock 1987; Moore 1987; Foster 1989; Office of National Drug Control Policy 1990, pp. 19, 83–88, 125; Office of National Drug Control Policy 1991, pp. 116–18).[22] There is reason for cautious optimism that leadership aiming to alter public policy so that it accepts the interrelatedness of problems (see, e.g., Brown 1990, 1991*b*, 1991*c*; Office of National Drug Control Policy 1991, pp. 2–3) will heighten the incentives for using multidisciplinary and multijurisdictional remedial mechanisms when they are appropriate.

The existing incentives for federal-local police interaction are already reasonably strong. What have been the resulting mechanisms of interaction? They are many and diverse, and we devote the next part of this essay to an overview of their origins, growth, and current variety.

III. The Mechanisms of Federal-Local Cooperation and Coordination

Formal, operational cooperation between federal law enforcement bodies and local police departments—cooperation structured with interagency agreements that enumerate obligations and prerogatives—is primarily a late-twentieth century enterprise. Ad hoc interaction between federal enforcement agencies (notably the Justice Department's U.S. Marshals Service and the Treasury Department's Customs unit) and local peacekeepers dates to the early days of the Republic (Calhoun 1990). But there were not even formal local police agencies as we know them for federal agencies to work with in a routinized way until the mid-nineteenth century. The nation's first modern municipal police organization conducting both day and night watches was established in 1844, when the New York City Police Department was created substantially

---

[22] Among a number of important efforts to upgrade the quality of strategic planning by American law enforcement was a series of meetings during the 1980s and early 1990s among high-level policymakers, titled the Harvard Executive Session on Policing, underwritten by the National Institute of Justice, the Charles Stewart Mott Foundation, and other sources and administered by Harvard's Kennedy School of Government, Program in Criminal Justice Policy and Management. A "sister" Executive Session on Drugs and Community Policing, funded by the Charles Stewart Mott Foundation, was jointly managed by the Kennedy School of Government and the Police Executive Research Forum during 1990–91.

in the image of Sir Robert Peel's 1829 invention, the London Metropolitan Police. Other jurisdictions soon followed suit, and by the 1870s nearly all major cities in the country had organized full-time paid police forces (Fosdick 1920, pp. 66, 82–83, 168–69; Walker 1977, p. 7; Miller 1983, p. 72; Lane, in this volume; Monkkonen, in this volume).

Early operational interaction between federal and local police was limited and often was not very positive. In 1862, Treasury agents assigned to the Internal Revenue Service began enforcing alcohol and tobacco tax laws in the precursor unit to today's Bureau of Alcohol, Tobacco, and Firearms (Miller 1989). The unit would gain major national prominence through the front-page exploits of such Prohibition-era Treasury agents as Eliot Ness, but enforcing Prohibition was primarily a federal undertaking, and such contacts as federal agents had with local police generally could not be characterized as cooperative. Walker (1977, p. 109) paints darkly with a broad brush: "For the municipal police, national prohibition represented a strong continuity with earlier traditions of nonenforcement and corruption."

There are undoubtedly notable examples over history of efforts to streamline and strengthen joint pursuit of mutual goals by local police and U.S. Marshals, Treasury agents working Customs Service and Prohibition-era antialcohol assignments, and other federal agents. But the story of *organizational* as opposed to *individual* interest in establishing and nurturing federal-local police relationships best starts with the founding of the FBI—a relative newcomer in the federal police family. It was 1908, sixty-four years after the creation of the New York City Police Department, before Napoleon Bonaparte's grandnephew, U.S. Attorney General Charles Bonaparte, persuaded President Theodore Roosevelt to create by executive fiat what the Congress explicitly refused to authorize—a national bureau of investigation (Cummings and McFarland 1937; Whitehead 1956; Ungar 1975; Walker 1977, p. 77). Roosevelt's creation of the bureau was not his first close association with law enforcement oversight; eleven years earlier he had finished a two-year term as the most dominant among three commissioners of the New York City Police Department. Nor was this the first time his best intentions concerning police professionalism would be frustrated by ineptness and corruption within a police force. It was not until 1924 that the bureau began to walk a path toward its eventual reputation for integrity and competence, with the elevation by Attorney General Harlan Fiske Stone of an American Civil Liberties Union–backed bureau agent, John Edgar Hoover, to the post of director (Walker 1977, pp. 43–45, 78).

The emergence in the 1930s of an FBI role in collating local crime information and in servicing various technical needs of local departments marks the beginning of institutionalized, routinized, intergovernmental law enforcement dealings as we recognize them today. The emergence of the crime statistics compilation and technical assistance roles for the FBI can be better understood against the backdrop of two developments: a resolute resistance to creating a single, national police force (including by J. Edgar Hoover), in the face of which the feasible alternative was seen as some degree of liaison and cooperation among autonomous enforcement units at each level of government (Rosen 1989, p. 10); and efforts to reform local policing by making it more "scientific," which meant, among other things, that information management, other investigative skills, and certain technological capabilities perceived to be within the expertise of the FBI attained new prominence as objects of professional aspiration (Kelling and Stewart 1991).

The idea of active liaison between local police and the FBI was made more acceptable by a climate in which many of those interested in city police reform, including the crime commissions of the 1920s, urged that local police should be viewed not as extensions of local political administrations but as components of complex state and even national criminal justice systems (Douthit 1975, p. 318; Walker 1977, p. 125; cf. Kelling 1991). By the 1930s, many of the police reformers were ready to concede that the American tradition of local control over policing made the *consolidation* of small departments in a given region into large unified forces politically unfeasible.[23]

August Vollmer in 1934 broached the still somewhat sensitive subject of operational cooperation between local police and *federal* enforcement bodies (Vollmer 1934, pp. 77–79). Many in local policing were then uneasy to see the federal government actively exercising a concur-

[23] Raymond Fosdick a decade earlier presented a series of arguments favoring consolidation (Fosdick 1920, pp. 166–73). The call for consolidation (e.g., of agencies having less than ten officers) was echoed, to little effect, much more recently by the President's Commission on Law Enforcement and Administration of Justice (1968, pp. 301–9) and the National Advisory Commission on Criminal Justice Standards and Goals (1973, pp. 108, 149–50). Although these recommendations were not implemented, they came in the context of recurring emphasis on the value of interagency communication and cooperation—again, setting a tone in which federal-local collaboration emerges as merely another example of sensible intergovernmental relations. In this regard, also see the strong support given to regional criminal justice coordinating councils and the more constrained support given to interagency task forces by the Commission on Accreditation for Law Enforcement Agencies (Commission on Accreditation for Law Enforcement Agencies 1987, pp. 4-1, 4-2).

rent criminal law jurisdiction with local police, evincing the fear of an omnipresent national police force that was widespread among local officials and the general public (Bomar 1934, pp. 435–37; Millspaugh 1937; Douthit 1975, p. 330). The idea of active *collaboration* across federal-state-local lines was anathema, and the belief continued to find expression in the literature well into the 1930s (e.g., *Fortune* 1934; Seagle 1934; Wechsler 1937). But local receptiveness to some forms of support by the federal enforcement establishment, albeit not genuine collaboration, was the news of the day by the time President Franklin Roosevelt's new U.S. attorney general, Homer Cummings, held a national "conference on crime" in 1934 (Douthit 1975, pp. 327, 330).[24] The attorney general surveyed the nation's hodgepodge of local initiatives against what was felt to be a growing crime problem and found it wanting, staking out the beginnings of a strategic policy leadership role and an increased concurrent operational role for federal enforcement organizations that would soon take hold in the public mind as the right way to proceed (Cummings 1934, p. 457).

Cummings's call for local police to begin looking to federal government agencies as models of efficiency in targeting crime problems came at a time when the nation was beginning to marvel at the crime-busting brashness of the FBI. During the Depression, the banner headline crimes across the nation were kidnappings and bank robberies (the latter because, as Willie Sutton would put it so aptly, that's where the money was). J. Edgar Hoover, with characteristic immodesty, recounted recent Bureau successes against the nation's tabloid public enemies in a speech to the 1934 Attorney General's Crime Conference: "John Dillinger, the flagbearer of lawlessness, is dead, killed by federal bullets. 'Pretty Boy' Floyd, who for years laughed at the law—lies in his grave, dead of gunshot wounds inflicted in open battle by our special agents. The career of 'Baby Face' Nelson is over; he died of seventeen bullet wounds while two of the finest men I ever knew gave their own clean lives that they might serve society by ending his filthy one. Wilbur Underhill no longer carries the name of the Tri-State Terror. He, too, is gone, as well as such men as Homer Van Meter, Tommy Carroll, and others. That is progress" (Hoover 1934, p. 25, quoted in Douthit 1975, p. 330).

---

[24] Douthit (1975, p. 331) reports: "One participant in the Attorney-General's Conference [on Crime in 1934] commented on what an 'amazing thing' it was to see state and local officials turn to the federal government for support when three years before they had been so resistant."

Thus, when the FBI spoke about scientific approaches to crime detection, intelligence gathering, armamentation, and other matters, local police, stymied in their own efforts to bring notorious criminals in their midst to justice,[25] increasingly paid at least grudging attention.

Although multifaceted interaction between federal and local police would still take considerable time to emerge, recommendations for a more systemic approach to law enforcement began during the 1930s to stimulate some coordinating efforts *among* local police forces. Thus in some regions local police agencies started to cooperate and pool resources and talents, generally focusing their efforts on the development of communications networks, on forensic laboratory analysis, and on the management of criminal history records (Walker 1977, p. 146; see also Carson and Brown 1970; Layton and Lowery 1989; Lesce 1989; Mastrofski 1989). As yet, however, the principal vehicle for mutually satisfactory routine federal-local interaction was the fledgling national Uniform Crime Reporting (UCR) program.

Another early exemplar of intergovernmental communication on law enforcement issues was the battle against organized crime, but this was a state initiative rather than an illustration of federal leadership. Intergovernmental contact for organized crime control was far more operational in character, however, than was the federal-local relationship through the UCR. During the 1920s and 1930s a number of scholars, study commissions, and legislative committees (e.g., Illinois Association for Criminal Justice 1929, pp. 18–19; U.S. Senate Committee on Commerce, Subcommittee on Senate Resolution 74, 1933, pp. 1–5, cited in Douthit 1975, p. 329; Wigmore 1933, pp. 734–35) cited organized crime as a major societal problem, and in 1935 New York governor Herbert H. Lehman acted to address it. He named Thomas E. Dewey special prosecutor responsible for attacking organized crime and political corruption. The Rackets Bureau concept pioneered in New York served as a model twenty-six years later for

---

[25] We do not mean that local police could not, at times, boast of equal body counts in the war against violent predators. But those attainments were not always motivated by the same principles that impelled the federal crime-busting spree. For instance, on February 14, 1929, Chicago Police wiped out six members of the Moran gang, notorious bootleggers. But instead of a pat on the back from Federal Prohibition administrators, the incident provoked an immediate investigation into whether the police had acted in retaliation for the Moran gang's decision to stop paying protection money to the police, a decision that, in turn, was said to be a reprisal for police complicity six weeks earlier in the theft of 500 cases of whiskey from a Moran gang warehouse (*Wisconsin News* 1929, p. 1).

U.S. Attorney General Robert Kennedy's expansion of the Justice Department's Organized Crime and Racketeering Section (Blakey 1983, p. 1108) and, later, for the development of intergovernmental organized crime strike forces (Goldstock 1987, p. 88; on the New York State response to organized crime generally, see Constantine 1988).

The expansion of a wide array of federal government nonpolice roles during the New Deal in the 1930s also enhanced the nation's receptivity to and demand for a larger federal role in law enforcement—both direct activity and support services for local police systems (Morgan 1983, p. 770). Since 1930, a number of important mechanisms of contact between the FBI (and, more recently, other federal agencies) and local police forces have emerged. The variety and increasing mutuality of these intergovernmental contacts may be illustrated by considering several examples, moving from early federal support efforts, to the enhancement of federal technical assistance and information sharing, to operational partnerships and attempts at strategic coordination efforts.

A. The Early Federal Support Efforts

The development of the FBI-managed Uniform Crime Reports in 1930 provided a crucial "ice-breaker" in the federal-local relationship by establishing the precedent of local police agencies sharing crime information with federal law enforcement authorities. But the move to centralize the nation's crime statistics should not be seen as a *federally* led crossing of the intergovernmental divide. Great legitimacy was attached by local police to the FBI's willingness to accept and compile national crime statistics because the International Association of Chiefs of Police (IACP)—the country's oldest organization of local police department chief executives—had been calling for the development of a national clearinghouse for such data since its earliest conventions in the 1890s and made a rudimentary effort to begin providing this service itself in 1897. By the late 1920s, a strong national consensus had developed—including such influential supporters as police chiefs August Vollmer and William Rutledge, the International City Managers Association, various federal officials, and the Rockefeller Foundation—that some sort of national crime data bank should be established (Walker 1977, pp. 155–56).[26] The early information linkage

---

[26] In a possible modern analog to the development of a national crime reporting system housed in the FBI, the International Association of Chiefs of Police, in 1991, without waiting to see whether the federal government might be willing to bear the burden of

between the FBI and local policing, with the full approval of the IACP, was a powerful precedent for the collaboration to come (Zolbe 1980; Cameron 1990, p. 36).[27]

Crime statistics were but one emblem of the "scientific policing" movement, a powerful reform ideology given voice by Vollmer, Hoover, Raymond Fosdick, and others, whose principal objectives included uncoupling municipal policing from the corruptive influences of partisan politics (Kelling and Stewart 1991). Other elements included scientific crime detection, crime analysis, and fingerprint identification. In the wake of the 1929 Saint Valentine's Day Massacre in Chicago, a broad coalition of police, academics, and business leaders supported the creation of one of the nation's first major crime labs, the Scientific Crime Detection Laboratory, housed at Northwestern University. Within two years, in 1932, the FBI opened its own crime lab, earning the admiration of the local law enforcement community and the general public as well and beginning a long tradition of backup service to local police in cases requiring sophisticated evidentiary analysis (Walker 1977, pp. 155–57). In keeping with this tradition, the FBI lab in 1988 expanded its intergovernmental assistance to include DNA typing (Labaton 1990, p. B10; Bashinski and Peterson 1991), and the DEA and the Secret Service over the past decade have made their respective narcotics and computer labs available to local police confronting cases with complicated drug or computer-fraud evidence (Conly 1989, p. 40; Markoff 1990, p. A21; Bocklet 1991, p. 272). The Bureau of Alcohol, Tobacco and Firearms also makes its laboratory available to local police for analysis of evidence in crimes involving weapons and explosives (Rinkevich 1991a).

Another key FBI response to the expanding investigative needs of

---

attempting to compile national statistics on use of justifiable and unjustifiable force by local police departments across the land, announced an intention to begin searching for ways to establish such a national data base (International Association of Chiefs of Police 1991, p. 10). This initiative, a response to widespread concern about police brutality after the March 1991 brutal beating of an unarmed arrestee, Rodney King, by Los Angeles Police, might be predicted to follow the course of national crime reporting: a sincerely motivated, ultimately unworkable private effort by a police association to collect information, eventually to be taken over by the FBI or some other appropriate unit of federal government—if, that is, sufficiently influential national leaders continue to express a need for the data on a regular basis (see Geller and Scott 1992).

[27] After sixty years of growth, the *Uniform Crime Reports* is in the process of evolving to another level, with the FBI's transition over the next several years to the National Incident-based Reporting System (Clede 1990).

local police during the 1930s was its willingness to maintain a national fingerprint file. The Bureau's fingerprinting initiatives enjoyed the enthusiastic support of local and national leaders. Indeed, Vollmer, Hoover, and others championed a highly visible but ultimately unsuccessful effort for universal fingerprinting of all Americans. During the height of the 1935 "Program for Voluntary Fingerprinting," national newspapers featured front-page pictures of prominent business, financial, political, and sports figures voluntarily being fingerprinted. The celebrity ten-prints came from President Franklin Roosevelt, John D. Rockefeller, Jr., Jack Dempsey, and many other notables. In Berkeley, where August Vollmer was chief of police at the time, 52,000 community residents (nearly half the population) submitted fingerprints at "fingerprint service stations" located in schools, libraries, and firehouses. Local businesses gave discounts to those who submitted fingerprints to the government, and civic-minded participation in the program was urged by churches, newspaper editorials, patriotic organizations, and youth groups (including the Boy and Girl Scouts; Walker 1977, pp. 157–58).

In the fifty years following J. Edgar Hoover's ascendancy to the bureau's directorship in 1924, the FBI's fingerprint collection grew from 810,188 sets to approximately 159,000,000 sets (Walker 1977, pp. 157–58), and in 1991 the FBI had what it estimated to be 193,482,106 fingerprint cards on file,[28] 55 percent of which pertained to criminal and 45 percent to civil matters—the civil purposes including use by the federal government, including the military, for identification of personnel (Federal Bureau of Investigation 1991; for earlier data, see Torres 1985, p. 137). These records have been relied on extensively by local police through the decades. In a single *month* (February 1991), the Bureau's Identification Division received 705,636 fingerprint cards, processed 27,515 expungement and purge requests, purged 1,916 offense fingerprint cards in "nonserious offenses," identified 4,379 fugitives through the posting of wanted notices in FBI files, processed latent fingerprints in 1,067 cases, received and processed 1,441,355 name check requests and 328,161 record requests, and sent (primarily by U.S. mail) 505,067 communications (replies to various information

[28] Since many of these records are not automated, obtaining an actual count would be impossibly expensive. Estimating techniques include measuring the linear feet of files and other methods.

contributors) (Federal Bureau of Investigation 1991).[29] In a typical *day* in 1989, the Bureau processed about 15,000 criminal fingerprint cards, about a third of which formed the basis for new records, with the remaining two-thirds being used to update existing information (Slahor 1989, p. 85). If one measured the activity of the FBI's Identification Division only on the basis of communications sent, based on February 1991 monthly counts—and February is a slower month than many for the Identification Division (Federal Bureau of Investigation 1991)—it would tally a mind-boggling 26,582 items of correspondence per day and 6,060,804 items per year. The name check and record requests received and processed for 1991, again based on activity levels for the month of February, can be estimated to total over twenty-one million by year's end.

In a fashion that paralleled the FBI's acceptance of responsibility for managing national crime statistics, conducting forensic analysis, and running fingerprint checks, the Bureau also emerged as an early leader in training local police. In 1934, law enforcement executives and other influentials from throughout the nation, convened in an Attorney General's Conference on Crime, were challenged by President Franklin Roosevelt to develop mechanisms for upgrading and coordinating the administrative and operational features of local, state, and federal law enforcement agencies. The conferees obliged the president by formally recommending the establishment of some form of national police training institute, run by the federal government. Within a year, this idea had taken concrete shape as the FBI's National Police Academy (Walker 1977, pp. 154–55; Thornburgh 1988, p. 10; Rosen 1989).

Although the FBI was by far the most prominent federal source of training assistance for local police in the early days, it was not the only one. In 1935 the IACP asked the Department of Interior for help in developing training materials that could be used in state and local police recruit orientation programs. The resulting 1938 manual, *Training for Police Service*, is credited as one of the first documents to attempt to

---

[29] The FBI, under a director, deputy director, and two associate deputy directors (for investigations and administration, respectively) is organized into ten headquarters divisions, several headquarters offices (public affairs, congressional affairs, etc.), and fifty-six field offices around the nation. Among the headquarters divisions with which local police have frequent contact are the Identification Division, the Training Division, and the Laboratory Division (Torres 1985, pp. 138–39; Office of the Federal Register, National Archives and Records Administration 1990, pp. 361, 381). The field offices have frequent operational contact with local police.

build training around an empirical analysis of police work (Walker 1977, p. 164).

In the decades since, federal training on a wide variety of subjects has been provided to thousands of state and local police officers and executives at the FBI's academy in Quantico, Virginia,[30] and at the multiagency Federal Law Enforcement Training Center (FLETC) based in Glynco, Georgia (its main site), Marana, Arizona, and Artesia, New Mexico (Federal Law Enforcement Training Center 1990a, p. i).[31] The DEA, which, like the FBI, has an academy in Quantico,

[30] The FBI Academy runs three primary training programs for nonfederal personnel: the eleven-week National Academy, for police below the level of executive; the National Executive Institute (NEI), for major city chiefs, who attend in three one-week sessions spaced over a year; and the Law Enforcement Executive Development Seminars (LEEDS), a two-week course for chiefs and executives from medium-sized agencies (Rosen 1989, p. 9). The FBI charges no tuition for these courses and pays each attendee's travel, room, and board expenses (Thornburgh 1988, p. 10), largely, according to then Training Academy Director James Greenleaf, as a way of thanking local law enforcement nationwide for their ongoing operational cooperation with the Bureau (Rosen 1989, p. 9). As of September 1988, the tightly knit National Academy alumni group numbered 21,732 (Thornburgh 1988, p. 10). In addition to these Quantico-based programs, the FBI provides satellite teleconferencing that reaches thousands of police per broadcast and operates a field training program that, during 1988, served more than 212,000 trainees, primarily in smaller departments (Rosen 1989, p. 9). One short course of instruction offered by the FBI covers federal jurisdictional questions, including "identifying the appropriate Federal agencies which handle offenses against the United States" and discussing "crimes in which joint jurisdiction exists" (Federal Law Enforcement Training Center 1990a, p. 23).

[31] The Federal Law Enforcement Training Center, a bureau of the Treasury Department, provides instruction for sixty-eight federal law enforcement organizations (Rinkevich 1991a, p. 10)—armed and unarmed investigative personnel alike—and for state and local law enforcement personnel. About twenty federal agencies maintain on-site training staffs at the Glynco location. The state and local programming is provided by the FLETC's National Center for State and Local Training, established by President Ronald Reagan in 1982, twelve years after Congress established the FLETC for the purpose of upgrading basic training to federal law enforcement personnel (Federal Law Enforcement Training Center 1990b, pp. 4–5, 10). The FLETC now trains more than 20,000 students annually (cf. Marx 1988, p. 43), including nearly 4,000 state and local officers, "making FLETC the largest law enforcement training organization in the country" (Rinkevich 1991a, p. 2). State and local police participate in forty training programs which vary in length from a few days to four weeks. State and local programs serve various levels of organizational personnel, from line investigators and patrol officers to training academy instructors to planning personnel to top-level and chief administrators. State and local training is provided at the FLETC's three sites and at various other locations around the country. Some but not all courses are free. Trainees have the advantage of instruction by subject matter experts from the federal agencies with principal operational responsibility for the topic taught. For example, the U.S. Marshals Service runs a Court Security Seminar, emphasizing the need for proactive security risk assessments and countermeasures in the wake of the assassination of a judge and a shooting confrontation in a federal courtroom in 1970 (Federal Law Enforcement Training Center 1990a, p. 84). Similarly, Postal Inspectors and IRS Criminal Investigators provide instruction on fraud and financial investigations. The DEA runs drug law en-

also provides narcotics enforcement training to drug investigators from various federal, state, local, and foreign police departments (Bocklet 1991, pp. 272, 278). In a twelve-month period during 1989 and 1990, for example, the DEA provided instruction to 8,100 American police at all governmental levels and 1,700 foreign police (Office of the Federal Registrar, National Archives and Records Administration 1990, p. 388).[32] In 1990, the Department of Defense stepped up its training to state and local police concerning "intelligence analysis, detection and monitoring [of drug trafficking], use of ground sensors, and photo recon" (*Crime Control Digest* 1990e, p. 10). Such training, if well done, fosters professional development, cross-fertilization, and friendship among the law enforcement cadre and a spirit of respect by attendees toward the sponsoring federal agencies (Torres 1985, p. 131; Conly 1989, p. 47; Rosen 1989; International Association of Chiefs of Police 1990, p. 6).

The provision of federal training to local police on a tuition-free basis (not the universal practice but a common one) always has been a significant element in the federal side's courtship of local police support and cooperation, and this inducement to interaction assumes a larger importance in recessionary times, when advanced training is often one of the first items to be jettisoned from local budgets. The long-standing support role of the federal government exemplified in the FBI's, FLETC's, and DEA's training programs, in the FBI's national fingerprint record system, and in various federal agencies' crime lab services has done much over the past six decades to smooth the way to joint operations, by providing tangible evidence that federal-local interaction could mean more than local giving and federal taking.

---

forcement training; the U.S. Forest Service and the National Park Service teach law enforcement personnel how to investigate wildland fires caused by arson; and the U.S. Secret Service offers instruction on investigating forgery of documents and on interagency protocols and responsibilities for safeguarding traveling federal protectees.

As with the FBI's training programs, cross fertilization and networking are important benefits of the FLETC (Rogers 1990, p. 30). In the words of the FLETC's director: "An important outgrowth of the commingling of students and agencies at Glynco is the cooperative spirit which develops in such an environment. This spirit promotes the exchange of ideas and skills to enhance the training offered and establishes relationships which contribute to more effective law enforcement at all levels" (Rinkevich 1990).

[32] Among the subjects on which the DEA offers to train state and local narcotics enforcement officers are "interdiction, search and seizure procedures, undercover operations, clandestine laboratory investigations, money laundering, drug gang profiles, diversion control, forensics, and cannabis eradication procedures" (Bocklet 1991, p. 272).

B. The Blossoming of Technical Assistance and Information Sharing

Although not, strictly speaking, a federal law enforcement agency in the sense of having agents with whom local police could potentially collaborate on joint investigations, the Law Enforcement Assistance Administration merits at least brief discussion. Established at first as the Office of Law Enforcement Assistance, LEAA was a centerpiece of President Lyndon Johnson's war on crime—a war declared because of rising public concern about "crime in the streets" and that problem's exploitability by such political adversaries as Senator Barry Goldwater. During the height of LEAA's activity in the 1970s it funded a mass of hardware, technical assistance, training, college education (through LEEP, the Law Enforcement Education Program), and research on crime and justice—most of it geared to upgrading local policing in one way or another (see generally Hudnik 1984). LEAA, and the crime commissions, federal and state, of the 1920s and 1930s, helped to create an atmosphere in which federal-local law enforcement cooperation and coordination was deemed important. Moreover, LEAA's funding spree represented a milestone in federal-nonfederal law enforcement relations, for it was the first time that substantial federal funds were spent on upgrading local crime control (Friel 1990, p. 38). Indeed, LEAA backed its call for greater intergovernmental coordination with funds during the 1970s to launch the first federal-state-local task forces organized to work with federal agents on drug-related crimes. LEAA's encouragement of intergovernmental law enforcement communication and cooperation was echoed by President Johnson's Commission on Law Enforcement and Administration of Justice, convened in 1965, and by the National Advisory Commission on Criminal Justice Standards and Goals (1973), a predominantly police panel brought together under President Richard Nixon in 1971 with LEAA funding (also see Advisory Commission on Intergovernmental Relations 1971). The American Bar Association's *Urban Police Function Standards* in 1973 represented another important declaration of the operational and administrative value of police agencies sharing information and expertise (Walker 1985, pp. 355–57).

The capacity of and demand for federal law enforcement agencies to provide technical assistance to local police—and to conduct research bearing on local enforcement issues—have been promoted significantly by these and other blue-ribbon commissions and by the work of LEAA and its successor agencies—the National Institute of Justice, the Bureau of Justice Assistance, the Bureau of Justice Statistics, the Office of Juvenile Justice and Delinquency Prevention, and the Office for Victims of Crime. These agencies are all housed organizationally within the Justice Department and coordinated by its Office of Justice Programs.

Another nexus between LEAA and its successor agencies and nonfederal law enforcement bodies has been standard setting. For example, LEAA, pursuant to the 1973 Omnibus Crime Control Act's requirements, set standards governing data quality for all fifty states' criminal history records, standards enforced by the threat to withhold federal funding from noncomplying jurisdictions (Kaplan 1990, p. 47). Although sometimes the federal government takes considerable and, occasionally, well-deserved, abuse for its support of ever-more powerful criminal intelligence data networks, it is important to remember the positive role of LEAA in helping states attend to data quality issues in the mid-1970s, shortly after computers came into use by law enforcement agencies and following the marriage of information and automation that forever changed the lives of Americans. Before LEAA's regulations on criminal history data quality were promulgated in the mid-1970s, questions of accuracy, completeness, and disclosure to public or private users typically were answered in the unfettered and widely differing discretion of the chiefs of the nation's 14,000 odd police departments (Kaplan 1990, p. 47).

In some instances, federal technical assistance has come in the form not of mandatory standards but of model policies and specifications on various subjects that state and local officials are free to adopt, adapt, or ignore as they see fit. Over the past decade, for instance, the National Institute of Justice has devoted considerable resources to developing consumer protection standards for the manufacture of soft body armor—a standard-setting exercise that has embroiled NIJ in a multiyear battle with the association of body armor manufacturers. Another example of federal support for model policies is the Bureau of Justice Assistance's grant in the late 1980s to the International Association of Chiefs of Police to develop a national policy center, which issued model police agency policy statements on a wide range of pressing administrative and operational concerns. And the Joint Federal Task Force on Clandestine Labs, created by the Anti-Drug Abuse Act of 1988 (Public Law [P.L.] No. 100-690, codified at 21 U.S.C. sec. 1504), has prepared guidelines to help nonfederal police and environmental officials safely dispose of hazardous materials seized during raids on illicit drug processing labs (International Association of Chiefs of Police 1989c, p. 4).

Besides other federally funded efforts to write model policies on a wide range of operational and administrative matters, the operating policies of some federal agencies de facto become models for many local police agencies. A prime example is the FBI's "defense-of-life" policy governing use of deadly force to apprehend suspects. The FBI's longtime adherence to this strict shooting policy helped stimulate many police departments to tighten their own firearms policies years before civil rights pressures, accreditation commission standards, and the Supreme Court's ruling in *Tennessee v. Garner*, 471 U.S. 1 (1985), moved other agencies in this direction. If the FBI succeeds in relaxing its deadly force policy, as it announced a desire to do in 1990, sparking immediate controversy within the police community, this move, too, can be expected to be cited as a model by numerous local agencies unhappy with their current defense-of-life policies (Geller and Scott 1992). A practical, if unintended effect of the selection of certain vendors to provide equipment to highly regarded law enforcement agencies is that the vendors' products tend to proliferate throughout the law enforcement field—this despite the policy of the FBI and other federal agencies of "not endorsing any vendor's equipment except for [the federal agency's] own use" (Nemecek 1990, p. 33).

Another important role for federal agencies in technical assistance has been their support of clearinghouses and crime analysis units to serve the immediate needs of local police in connection with patrol or investigative operations. Five federally funded programs illustrate this area of activity: the FBI's National Crime Information Center and its Violent Criminal Apprehension Program, the DEA's El Paso Intelligence Center, the Regional Information Sharing System, and INTERPOL.

1. *The National Crime Information Center.*   The National Crime Information Center (NCIC), established by the FBI in 1967, is a criminal justice information teleprocessing network, accessible to all U.S. police agencies, the Royal Canadian Mounted Police, and the Police of the Commonwealth of Puerto Rico. Access to NCIC and other law enforcement data bases (e.g., the National Law Enforcement Telecommunications System and data bases maintained by the DEA, the Federal Aviation Administration, the Immigration and Naturalization Service, and the Department of State) is provided for many agencies worldwide through the Customs Service's Treasury Enforcement Communications System (TECS II; Office of National Drug Control Policy 1991, p. 121).

NCIC enables law enforcement authorities to make immediate checks for stolen property, wanted persons or warrant information, criminal history data, and missing children (Morgan 1983, p. 774; Torres 1985, p. 141). When the NCIC system was founded, it was the first "automated information operationally useful" to most local police departments, whose lack of computerization prevented them from having access even to their own records rapidly enough to meet the needs of their field personnel (Cameron 1990, p. 36).

As of April 1, 1991, the NCIC data bank contained 7,444,386 records, in the following categories: stolen securities (1,929,718); stolen and recovered guns (2,133,719); miscellaneous stolen articles (1,237,692); stolen and felony vehicles and stolen vehicle parts (1,021,819); stolen license plates (673,065); stolen boats (27,370); wanted persons (347,569); missing persons (70,712); foreign fugitives (633); and unidentified persons—primarily unidentified bodies, amnesia victims, and infants (2,089) (McKee 1991).[33] By 1989, NCIC's computer system was capable of searching its data bases, then containing approximately 11 million records (including 24 million names and aliases), for name checks in about one-fourth of a second (Slahor 1989, p. 86). By 1990, the NCIC data base exceeded 20 million records, its authorized users numbered 59,362 agencies, and the center handled as many as one million transactions per day (Nemecek 1990, p. 30; see also O'Connell 1990b, p. 6). Even at that, NCIC could not keep up with demand for its services.

On the horizon for NCIC is the two-way transmission between police patrol cars and NCIC of mug shots and fingerprint images of wanted persons and the virtually instantaneous analysis at NCIC headquarters of fingerprints transmitted from the field (Nemecek 1990, pp. 30–31). A bit further over the horizon is a system that will permit prompt responses to field officers from NCIC headquarters, based on nothing other than a visual image of a questioned individual—for example, a person stopped for a traffic violation. The individual's picture could be captured by a dashboard mounted video camera during questioning, digitized and transmitted almost instantly to NCIC headquarters through a base station in the region, compared by an automated system to images of wanted persons stored on optical disks, and a "hit/

---

[33] For NCIC data base tallies from a decade earlier, before the FBI transferred the maintenance of more than two million computerized criminal histories from NCIC to the Bureau's Identification Division, see Torres (1985), p. 142.

no hit" response could be transmitted back to the field officer before the detained driver has a chance to become aggravated by the duration of the stop (Nemecek 1990, pp. 32–33; O'Connell 1990*b*, pp. 1–6).

Data quality control has been a prime objective of NCIC. Some, mostly outside of law enforcement, believe that the maintenance of acceptable levels of data quality is impossible, citing the risk that "incorrect or out-of-date data may find their way into the system from one local police force and then be supplied to another halfway across the country" (Morgan 1983, p. 774). Other critics tell horror stories of individuals detained in jail for several months based on mistaken data obtained through an automated criminal history system (Gordon 1990, p. 43). The FBI itself discovered in 1985 that every day police agencies around the nation were sending NCIC more than 12,000 "inaccurate or invalid reports on wanted persons" (Gordon 1990, p. 43). A General Accounting Office (GAO) report in March 1990 found that the computerized data base used by Customs agents at border crossings and airports "contains highly incomplete and inaccurate information" and faulted the Customs Service, which maintains the TECS II communications network used to access the national data base, for defects that produced "an increased risk that known or suspected law violators may enter the United States undetected, and that innocent persons may be stopped and intensively inspected at the borders for offenses they did not commit" (Shenon 1990, p. 1). In response, Customs Service officials faulted the GAO audit for having selected an excessively narrow sample of criminal history records to study and for not giving the Customs Service credit for having previously identified and begun corrective measures to deal with some of the data accuracy problems (Shenon 1990, p. A14). The Customs Service, of course, is only one of many federal, state, and local agencies contributing information to the data base, although Customs came in for special criticism by the GAO because the accounting report discovered that Customs personnel had failed to enter data into the system on criminals it discovered during border screenings conducted a year earlier (Shenon 1990, p. A14).

In an effort to reduce the risks associated with false criminal history information, the FBI validates NCIC records by sending them for review to the states at least twice each year (Slahor 1989, p. 86). At times NCIC has had expansionist aspirations that have been squelched for civil liberties and political reasons. For instance, in March 1989 the FBI dropped a proposal "to provide police and other investigators with information on individuals suspected but not convicted of serious crimes" (*Law Enforcement News* 1990, p. 5).

2. *The Violent Criminal Apprehension Program.*   Of more recent vintage than NCIC is the FBI Academy's Violent Criminal Apprehension Program (VICAP). Begun in May 1985, VICAP exists to collect, collate, analyze, and disseminate under appropriate circumstances information about specified categories of violent crime.[34] These categories include solved or unsolved homicides, missing person cases (where the subject may have been killed), and cases in which unidentified decedents have been found and homicide is or may be the cause of death (Brooks et al. 1987; Sessions 1989*a*, p. 10). With data furnished by state and local agencies on a continuing basis, VICAP crime analysts have been able to link serial murderers to victims and alert local police to noteworthy crime patterns and homicidal styles. In 1990 the FBI began developing standards to assist local police in detecting potential serial killers (*Crime Control Digest* 1990*f*). Besides continuing to operate VICAP, the Bureau as of mid-1989 was providing technical assistance to several states that were establishing their own crime analysis centers comparable to VICAP (Sessions 1989*a*, p. 10).

3. *DEA's El Paso Intelligence Center.*   The need to process and efficiently disseminate criminal intelligence bearing on multijurisdictional crime has given rise to other mechanisms of cooperation and coordination. In the drug enforcement arena, the DEA's El Paso Intelligence Center is one such clearinghouse.[35] Described by federal drug officials as "the drug control community's principal tactical interdiction intelligence processing and analysis facility," the center's automated data processing capabilities are currently limited, but significant upgrades are planned to equip the center to serve a wide variety of federal, state, and local enforcement bodies (Office of National Drug Control Policy 1990, pp. 125–26). As the Office of the National Drug Control Policy's 1991 report makes clear, most of the federal departments or agencies participating in antidrug *enforcement* operations or intelligence analysis—the Justice Department's DEA and FBI, the Treasury Department's Customs Service and other Treasury intelligence units, the CIA, the Department of Defense, and the Department of Transporta-

[34] VICAP should not to be confused with ICAP, the Integrated Criminal Apprehension Program, a series of several dozen local experiments in crime analysis and directed patrol funded by the Law Enforcement Assistance Administration starting in 1975.

[35] The CIA also has established a "center to integrate intelligence and law-enforcement efforts against narcotics producers and traffickers" (Wines 1991, p. A13).

tion's Coast Guard—have separate intelligence collection and appraisal capabilities. But these capabilities and the information they examine are not shared in a fashion that permits the development of a comprehensive strategy making efficient and effective use of the nation's federal, state, and local enforcement resources (Office of National Drug Control Policy 1991, pp. 116–18). The wherewithal to "improve coordination and cooperation among [the various federal antidrug intelligence centers] so that a full understanding of the structure and infrastructure of trafficking organizations and their allied enterprises may be developed" (Office of National Drug Control Policy 1991, p. 118) remains elusive. Thus, although DEA's El Paso center is beginning to meet law enforcement's needs for *tactical* and *operational* intelligence on drug trafficking (e.g., information on changing transportation methods and routes; Office of National Drug Control Policy 1991, p. 118), *strategic* intelligence management of the sort needed to identify and target the Achilles heels of drug trafficking enterprises lags far behind (*Crime Control Digest* 1990g, p. 8).

4. *The Regional Information Sharing System.*   A more fully realized information networking and technical assistance program is the Regional Information Sharing System. The RISS program's objective is to "enhance the ability of local, state, and federal criminal justice agencies to identify, target and remove criminal activities and conspiracies spanning jurisdictional boundaries" (Hughes 1989, p. 6). Established with funding by the Omnibus Crime Control and Safe Streets Act of 1968 and initially coordinated through LEAA, RISS was launched with the creation in 1973 of the first of seven regional networks: the Regional Organized Crime Information Center (ROCIC), located in Nashville and, as of 1990, serving 350 agencies in fourteen states (Abell 1988, p. 58; *Crime Control Digest* 1990h, p. 7). The other six RISS programs—and the number of agencies they served as of 1990—are the Rocky Mountain Information Network, founded in 1977, headquartered in Phoenix, and serving 600 agencies in eight states; the Leviticus Project, founded in 1978, headquartered in Richmond, Virginia, which is a network of twenty-nine law enforcement and regulatory agencies convened to focus exclusively on combating criminal activity in the coal, oil, natural gas, and gold ore industries; the New England States Police Information Network, founded in 1979, headquartered in Randolph, Massachusetts, and serving 184 agencies in six states; the Mid-States Organized Crime Information Center, founded in 1980, headquartered in Springfield, Missouri, and serving 542 agen-

cies in nine states; the Western States Information Network, founded in 1981, headquartered in Sacramento, and serving 768 agencies in five states; and the Middle Atlantic/Great Lakes Organized Crime Law Enforcement Network, founded in 1981, headquartered in West Trenton, New Jersey, and serving 211 agencies in eight states (Abell 1988, p. 58; Middle Atlantic/Great Lakes Organized Crime Law Enforcement Network 1989, p. 41; *Crime Control Digest* 1990*h*, pp. 7–8).

Together, the seven RISS networks include participating agencies from every state and two Canadian provinces. RISS funding ($14 million in federal funds during 1991) is administered by the Justice Department's Bureau of Justice Assistance.

Each RISS program offers somewhat different services to member agencies, although there are several common elements. The core function of every RISS network is information sharing, typically through automated data bases. Through each program's clearinghouse, member agencies can furnish and receive "intelligence on major criminal conspiracies, narcotics networks, organized crime groups and white-collar crimes" (Abell 1988, p. 58). Some of the programs' data bases "permit searches for unknown subjects and [analysis of] trends in criminal activity." RISS programs also typically assist member agencies with analysis of intelligence data (e.g., preparing visual aids illustrating the links between coconspirators, discrepancies in statements provided to investigators, or "gaps in the chronology of events"; Abell 1988, pp. 58–59).

Some of the RISS networks emphasize training. For example, the Middle Atlantic/Great Lakes Organized Crime Law Enforcement Network cosponsors several information sharing conferences per year, in concert with different combinations of federal, state, county, and local police agencies in its eight-state region. Topics range widely and have included stemming the spread and organizational evolution of violent street gangs, intelligence analysis, use of surveillance equipment, and investigating child sexual exploitation as well as handling the stress that police working these cases commonly experience (Abell 1988, p. 59; *Crime Control Digest* 1990*i*, pp. 4, 6). The Western States network is the only one dedicated solely to a single type of criminal enterprise (narcotics trafficking; Abell 1988, p. 58).

In addition to training and criminal intelligence sharing, some RISS programs loan member agencies state-of-the-art investigative equipment, make WATS telephone lines available to facilitate member agencies' networking, and even provide "buy money" and funds for the purchase of confidential information for police departments that cannot cover these items out of their own budgets (Abell 1988, p. 59).

The Bush administration's 1991 budget request sought a reduction of $3.6 million in federal funding for RISS, calling for joint federal, state, and local funding that together would give RISS an annual budget of $13 million (*Crime Control Digest* 1990c, p. 10; *Crime Control Digest* 1990b, p. 7). Congress, as it had done in earlier years when the Carter and Reagan administrations sought to reduce or eliminate federal funding for the RISS program, reiterated its support for RISS, appropriating $14 million for the program in 1991. But RISS remains a target of federal budget slicers, and the Bush administration's 1992 budget request sought to eliminate funding altogether for the RISS program (*Crime Control Digest* 1990c, p. 8; *Crime Control Digest* 1991b, p. 5).

5. *INTERPOL.*   A final example of a federally supported information clearinghouse used operationally by state and local police departments is INTERPOL. INTERPOL, as chartered, is an association of nearly 150 countries "dedicated to promoting mutual assistance among law enforcement authorities in the prevention and suppression of international crime" (Office of the Federal Registrar, National Archives and Records Administration 1990, p. 385). The general secretariat is in St. Cloud, France. United States participation began in 1938, took a hiatus during World War II, and resumed in 1947.

Each nation participating in INTERPOL establishes a "National Central Bureau" of INTERPOL, hence the formal name of the U.S. Justice Department's unit: "United States Central Bureau— International Criminal Police Organization." Through a voluntary state liaison program, coordinated by the Illinois State Police, thirty-eight American states have established offices within a state criminal investigative body to serve as informational conduits between law enforcement organizations in their states and the U.S. National Central Bureau.

Without any police powers of its own, INTERPOL functions as a channel of international communication (through telecommunications networks and conferences) on crime problems and the movement of identified criminals or suspects, witnesses, weapons, or other contraband. Since the 1980s, INTERPOL has been very active with state and local police forces in the United States (Rinkevich 1991a), facilitating information sharing on international criminal investigations and on the use of American airports and seaports in connection with terrorist threats and other illegal transnational activity. Another INTERPOL communications linkage allows for American and Canadian police departments to query each others' automated national records systems concerning drivers' licenses, vehicle ownership, wanted persons, and weapons and explosives that might be moving across international borders (*National Directory of Law Enforcement Administrators, Correctional Institutions and Related Agencies* 1989, p. 445; Office of the Federal Registrar, National Archives and Records Administration 1990, p. 385).

Article 3 of the INTERPOL constitution specifies that the organization's information-sharing network cannot be used to support police action in any country targeted at political, religious, racial, or military foes of the subject police agency or the government it serves (*National Directory of Law Enforcement Administrators, Correctional Institutions and Related Agencies* 1989, p. 445). The use of such international data bases as those facilitated by INTERPOL is subject, of course, to all the concerns that surface in connection with the use of American criminal history data bases—and probably additional concerns stemming from the differential respect for the privacy of individuals that is manifest in different countries. Concerns about improper disclosures and inaccuracies in disclosed information apparently are addressed (how well, we do not know) by the establishment of protocols for the dissemination of information and the use of audit teams to track the use of information provided through INTERPOL (*National Directory of Law Enforcement Administrators, Correctional Institutions and Related Agencies* 1989, p. 445).

C. Full Operational Partnerships and Efforts to Coordinate Law Enforcement Strategy

As federal support for local policing, mutual information sharing, and other formal and informal contacts between federal and local agencies from the 1930s through the early 1960s began to build a base of understanding and respect on which genuine operational collaboration would be possible, the resilience and complexity of certain crime problems provided the common interest around which such joint action could be forged.

1. *Organized Crime Strike Forces.* One of the earliest and most important formal mechanisms for multilateral federal-local operational collaboration was the organized crime strike force initiated by the Justice Department in 1966 as the "Buffalo Project." This effort in upstate

New York assembled federal and local prosecutors and investigators from the FBI, IRS, Bureau of Narcotics, Customs, Secret Service, Department of Labor, local police, and other agencies to pool their talents for the collection, analysis, and tactical use of intelligence about organized criminal enterprises. Strike forces were implemented in other metropolitan areas, consonant with recommendations of the President's Commission on Law Enforcement and Administration of Justice (1967, 1968), after the Buffalo group succeeded in indicting more than thirty individuals for organized crime activities under applicable federal, state, and Canadian laws (Comment 1970; Blakey 1983, p. 1109). Typically, state or local participants were involved as "informal" members of strike forces, while the formal members were assorted federal agencies (Kelley 1975; Abrams 1986, p. 10).

The strike forces were established to serve disparate objectives: reduction of duplicative organized crime investigations by U.S. attorneys in adjoining districts who were targeting the same criminal organizations or acts; stimulation of needed investigations (sometimes U.S. attorneys, typically serving for four-year terms, had insufficient incentives to mount long-term investigations); creation of a critical mass of enforcement talent capable of engaging and defeating a savvy enemy; and enhancement of voluntary cooperation by local law enforcement agencies with federal investigative and prosecutorial units (Abrams 1983, pp. 782, 784; Morgan 1983, p. 772; Abrams 1986, p. 10; *Crime Control Digest* 1990*j*, p. 4). By 1981, the strike force program had major units in fourteen large cities and suboffices in another twelve and had registered significant convictions of the leading organized crime figures in New York City, Kansas City, and Los Angeles (Blakey 1983, pp. 1110–11).[36]

But the strike force program had detractors from its earliest days, notably J. Edgar Hoover (Morgan 1983, p. 772) and many U.S. attorneys (including, in the 1970s, then–U.S. attorney in Pittsburgh Richard Thornburgh). Hoover expressed characteristic opposition to having FBI agents supervised by anyone other than Bureau personnel. U.S. attorneys objected to the competition of strike forces for cases (Abrams

[36] The major strike force units were located in Boston, Brooklyn, Buffalo, Chicago, Cleveland, Detroit, Kansas City (Mo.), Las Vegas, Los Angeles, Miami, Newark, New Orleans, Philadelphia, and San Francisco. The suboffices were located in Atlanta, Fort Lauderdale, Tampa, Camden (N.J.), Houston, Honolulu, Rochester (Minn.), Milwaukee, Providence (R.I.), New Haven, Rochester (N.Y.) and Syracuse (N.Y.) (*Crime Control Digest* 1989, p. 3).

1986, p. 135; *Law Enforcement News* 1989, p. 3). Over the years, three audits by the U.S. General Accounting Office supported the notion that the strike forces were weak on strategic planning and had not produced expected higher levels of cooperation and coordination among federal and local law enforcement agencies in combating organized crime (U.S. General Accounting Office 1977, 1981, 1989; see also U.S. General Accounting Office 1985).

The U.S. attorneys won a partial victory in their quest for "absorption of the strike forces into the U.S. attorneys offices" when, in 1988, Attorney General Edwin Meese "ordered strike force chiefs throughout the country to begin reporting to the U.S. attorneys in their respective districts" (Abrams 1988, p. 20). Effective January 1, 1990, their victory was made complete when U.S. Attorney General Richard Thornburgh reorganized the Justice Department's efforts to challenge organized criminal enterprises, abolishing the twenty-six organized crime strike forces and distributing most of their 115 lawyers and seventy-one support personnel among the U.S. attorneys' offices. The step, announced some months earlier, was predictably controversial, despite the GAO's and others' misgivings about the performance of the strike forces (*Crime Control Digest* 1990*j*; Lupsha 1990). Vigorous objections were made that "the U.S. Attorneys' offices . . . lack the continuity of leadership and experience necessary for fighting entrenched organized crime" (*Law Enforcement News* 1989, p. 3). In response, the attorney general cited the success of Rudolph Giuliani, former U.S. attorney for the Southern District of New York, in spearheading the interagency team work that, following the demise of strike forces in New York City in 1976, convicted high-level Cosa Nostra figures (Abrams 1986, p. 135; *Law Enforcement News* 1989, p. 3).

Under the Department of Justice's (DOJ) revamping of its organized crime fighting apparatus, special attention to questions of coordination among law enforcement agencies is to be provided by a new Organized Crime Council[37]—based in Washington, D.C., chaired by the deputy attorney general, and comprising representatives of DOJ's Criminal Division, U.S. attorneys' offices, and various federal law enforcement

[37] Related efforts of earlier vintage include the National Council on Organized Crime, established in 1970, chaired by the attorney general, and tasked with developing "a strategy to eliminate organized crime" and the National Organized Crime Planning Council (NOCPC), formed in late 1976, chaired by the Justice Department's Organized Crime and Racketeering Section chief, and responsible for facilitating "detailed planning and coordination between the strike forces and federal law enforcement agencies" (U.S. General Accounting Office 1981; Abrams 1986, p. 135; Goldstock 1987).

bodies (*Crime Control Digest* 1990*j*, pp. 3–4). In January 1991, Attorney General Richard Thornburgh announced that the Justice Department during the 1990s would have a dual strategic focus on traditional and emerging organized crime groups. The efforts, he reported, would be designed to continue removing traditional mob bosses from circulation and to keep new leaders—from "Japanese crime gangs, Jamaican Posses, Chinese Triads, motorcycle gangs, and Sicilian Mafia" (*Crime Control Digest* 1991*b*, pp. 6–7)—from stepping in to fill the more traditional syndicate leadership slots. Critics of the attorney general's earlier decision to disband the organized crime strike forces, some of whom resigned as federal prosecutors to protest the move, reacted to the more recent announcement by saying they saw little in it that represented an innovation in strategy or programming. Moreover, Justice Department spokespersons conceded that the latest plan to, as the attorney general phrased it, "put out a contract" on the mob hierarchy in major American cities, would not devote any additional FBI agents to the investigation of syndicate cases (*Crime Control Digest* 1991*b*, p. 7).

Two principal vehicles exist today for formalized operational collaboration between local, state, and federal agencies targeting drug problems.[38] The one which makes the most extensive use of state and local police, and is considerably older, is the DEA State and Local Task Force ("DEA Task Force," for short). The other mechanism is the Organized Crime Drug Enforcement Task Force (Office of National Drug Control Policy 1990, pp. 70, 94; Office of National Drug Control Policy 1991, pp. 27–28).

2. *Drug Enforcement Administration Task Forces.* Drug Enforcement Administration Task Forces serve to "promote cooperation between DEA and State and local law enforcement officials, with the goal of immobilizing local drug trafficking groups" (Office of National Drug Control Policy 1990, p. 96). Thus, they focus at both ends of the distribution chain, from major importers to street retailers (Abrams 1986, p. 10; Chaiken, Chaiken, and Karchmer 1990). In general, how-

[38] *Informal* cooperation and collaboration occurs as well, on an ad hoc basis. In the drug arena, for example, DEA or FBI agents team up with local or state investigators who realize they can help each other move against common targets in the drug trade. Although seized assets can be shared by both collaborators' agencies in the wake of such informal collaborations, the local or state investigators' expenses will remain entirely the responsibility of their employing agency. This financial consideration makes *formal* interagency cooperation comparatively more attractive, although reportedly the sharing of seized assets between federal and local agencies remains a strong enough inducement to collaboration that informal, ad hoc joint investigations are "a popular and increasingly frequent phenomenon" (Chaiken, Chaiken, and Karchmer 1990, p. 48).

ever, these task forces have enjoyed their greatest success against mid-level traffickers (Office of National Drug Control Policy 1991, pp. 27–28). It is not uncommon for DEA Task Forces to feed cases that become highly complex to the Organized Crime Drug Enforcement Task Force (OCDETF) responsible for the region in which the DEA groups are functioning. As of early 1990, approximately a fourth of all DEA Task Force investigations had been forwarded for further investigation to OCDETFs (Office of National Drug Control Policy 1990, p. 97).

The DEA task forces are created and supervised by DEA personnel and involve state and local police assigned on a relatively long-term basis (at least a year) pursuant to formal interagency agreements. The DEA was established on July 1, 1973,[39] and has developed divisional field offices in nineteen U.S. cities and foreign offices in forty-seven other countries (Torres 1985, p. 129; Office of the Federal Registrar, National Archives and Records Administration 1990, p. 388). By 1991, there were seventy-one formal DEA task forces nationwide and plans for more (Chaiken, Chaiken, and Karchmer 1990, pp. 45, 46; *Crime Control Digest* 1990*b*, p. 7; Office of National Drug Control Policy 1990, pp. 16, 96–97; Office of National Drug Control Policy 1991, pp. 27–28, 129). The DEA's estimated 1991 budget was $694 million, and the Administration sought to raise it to $748 million for fiscal year 1992, $55 million of which would fund DEA State and Local Task Forces (Office of National Drug Control Policy 1991, pp. 28, 140).

The federal drug task force approach to intergovernmental collaboration was pioneered by DEA's predecessor agency within the Justice Department, the Bureau of Narcotics and Dangerous Drugs, which

---

[39] The DEA drew personnel from its predecessor agency (the Department of Justice's Bureau of Narcotics and Dangerous Drugs), from the Treasury Department's U.S. Customs Service, and from the Food and Drug Administration's Bureau of Drug Abuse Control, which had been created in 1966. Drug enforcement responsibility has been centered in the Department of Justice only since 1968, when the Treasury Department's Bureau of Narcotics was disbanded in the wake of a scandal in which agents were caught selling confiscated drugs (a problem from which the DEA has not been entirely exempt; see *New York Times* 1991, p. A9). When the Bureau of Narcotics was transferred to the Department of Justice and renamed the Bureau of Narcotics and Dangerous Drugs in 1968, the unit had only 300 special agents (Torres 1985, p. 127; Chaiken, Chaiken, and Karchmer 1990, p. 44). In 1991, DEA had 6,286 total employees, of whom 3,312 were special agents (Tauber 1991). In January 1982, the attorney general gave the FBI concurrent jurisdiction with the DEA over drug offenses enumerated in the Controlled Substances Act (21 U.S.C. sec. 801). Moreover, the director of the DEA reports to the attorney general through the director of the FBI (Office of the Federal Registrar, National Archives and Records Administration 1990, p. 381).

established a New York metropolitan area task force in 1970. In the early days, no formal interagency agreements had yet been devised, and efforts to implement the vague mandate for cooperation and coordination among task force participants challenged the patience and ingenuity of many dedicated personnel (Chaiken, Chaiken, and Karchmer 1990, p. 44; on early interagency narcotics enforcement units generally, see Faughnan and Gilroy 1979). Steps were taken, however, to make full partners of the local and state agencies in task force policymaking and operational supervision. In the New York task force, an executive committee of agency heads "developed policies on such major issues as personnel selection, targeting, and investigative supervision" (Chaiken, Chaiken, and Karchmer 1990, p. 45). Moreover, task force investigative group supervisors were drawn from the ranks of all the participating agencies (ibid.). In April 1991, the New York City DEA task force, the "largest and most formally structured task force sponsored by the DEA" (Bocklet 1991, p. 272), had 190 sworn personnel, of whom forty-nine were DEA agents, seventy-five were New York City Police Department detectives, and sixty-six were New York State Police investigators (Bocklet 1991, p. 274; Hannon 1991). This pattern of staffing DEA task forces primarily with nonfederal personnel is standard throughout the nation (Chaiken, Chaiken, and Karchmer 1990, p. 46). Indeed, DEA directives "stipulate that federal personnel contribution to a state and local task force cannot exceed one agent for every four local agency officers" (Bocklet 1991, p. 279). (The New York City task force balance of personnel in 1991 was nearly within this guideline.) This requirement can create problems of inadequate staffing in sparsely populated but drug-afflicted areas of the country, where local police departments are too small to detail very many officers to the federal task force.

As reflected in DEA's standard interagency contract and its deputization form, after proper clearance participating nonfederal investigators are granted federal investigative and arrest authority, under 21 U.S.C. section 878. The powers they acquire are identical to those of DEA agents (Chaiken, Chaiken, and Karchmer 1990, p. 46). This grant of federal "enforcement personnel authority" is a departure from an earlier, controversial practice, commenced by the Bureau of Narcotics and Dangerous Drugs in 1970 and continued by DEA until passage in 1986 of the Anti-Drug Abuse Act. Under the earlier approach, state and local police assigned to DEA task forces were deputized as U.S. Marshals (the Marshals Service being a sister agency to DEA within the Department of Justice), thus technically acquiring enforcement authority over matters outside the jurisdiction of DEA agents (see the Appendix for a summary of the key responsibilities and powers of the U.S. Marshals Service).

The working relationships today among DEA Task Force members probably represent the high-water mark thus far in American history in genuine, federal-local police teamwork (Bocklet 1991), although many local police are quick to cite their dealings with the Bureau of Alcohol, Tobacco and Firearms as another instance of exemplary intergovernmental sharing of burdens and benefits. The DEA task forces' focus on retail and local wholesale activities would be all but impossible without the active participation on the task forces of local police officers, whose knowledge of the local community—and its offense patterns, offenders, informants, and geography—provides crucial intelligence for strategic and tactical decisionmaking. Moreover, the local investigators on the task forces provide essential liaison to their home departments, both to avoid having those departments and the task force duplicating efforts or working at cross purposes and to elicit supplementary personnel when needed for "major raids or long-term surveillance" (Chaiken, Chaiken, and Karchmer 1990, p. 46).

The Drug Enforcement Administration pays overtime salaries for the local and state investigators assigned to the task forces and also provides "buy money," funds to pay informants, vehicles, radios, and surveillance and other equipment needed for task force operations (Torres 1985, p. 129; Chaiken, Chaiken, and Karchmer 1990, p. 45). Under federal asset forfeiture and sharing provisions, assets forfeited by drug offenders (funds, vehicles, and other items) are shared equitably between the DEA and the state and local agencies whose personnel contributed to the successful operation (Chaiken, Chaiken, and Karchmer 1990, p. 47; Bocklet 1991). The general view among law enforcement practitioners is that despite the many difficulties of federal-state-local police collaboration in drug law enforcement, a high level of efficiency has been achieved by the DEA Task Forces (Chaiken, Chaiken, and Karchmer 1990, p. 49).[40]

3. *Organized Crime Drug Enforcement Task Forces.* The other principal current, formal mechanism for intergovernmental law enforcement operational collaboration is the series of Organized Crime Drug En-

---

[40] Walton and Murphy (1981) give similarly high marks to FBI–local police task force cooperation in New York City.

forcement Task Forces. The OCDETFs had their genesis in then Vice-President Bush's "South Florida Task Force," in which state and local agencies, starting in 1982, played a significant investigative role in concert with federal law enforcers (Mackenzie 1991, p. 17; Rinkevich 1991*a*). Since their designation in 1982 as "presidential drug task forces," the OCDETFs have operated out of U.S. attorneys' offices in large cities, and have targeted primarily "multinational or multistate organized criminal enterprises" which "organize, direct, and finance large-scale drug-related and money laundering" operations (Abrams 1986, p. 10; Office of National Drug Control Policy 1990, pp. 15, 70, 96; Office of National Drug Control Policy 1991, p. 27). In this way, at least by charter they are more narrowly focused on high-level operatives in drug distribution networks than are the DEA Task Forces. Also in contrast to the DEA groups, the OCDETFs are principally *federal* interagency teams whose use of state and local police is the exception rather than the rule (for an account of the successes of the Philadelphia police working with the FBI Organized Crime Task Force against syndicate leaders, see Friel and Guinther 1990). The reason typically given for infrequently drawing on nonfederal officers to staff these task forces is that the upper-level drug traffickers targeted usually have not been the focus of investigative attention by state and local police agencies in the region and, accordingly, their investigators are unlikely to have pertinent informants or other expertise to contribute to the task force (Chaiken, Chaiken, and Karchmer 1990, p. 47).

The OCDETFs are staffed with personnel from the Bureau of Alcohol, Tobacco and Firearms, DEA, FBI, Immigration and Naturalization Service, IRS, U.S. Coast Guard, U.S. Customs Service, U.S. Marshals Service, and Justice Department prosecutorial and managerial personnel (U.S. attorneys and staff from DOJ's Criminal Division and Tax Division) (Office of National Drug Control Policy 1990, p. 16). The intensive, continuing involvement of prosecutors in all OCDETF operations is reflected in the Justice Department's 1991 budget request, which, among other items, sought the hiring of more prosecutors to allow OCDETFs to "maintain a 1:4 ratio of prosecutors to investigators" (*Crime Control Digest* 1990*b*, p. 9). Case investigations by the OCDETF can be initiated by any one of the participating federal agencies (the FBI initiates most), and the initiating agency has the prerogative of selecting any state or local personnel who may work the particular case (Chaiken, Chaiken, and Karchmer 1990, p. 47).

Like the DEA Task Forces, OCDETFs pay local and state investigators' overtime costs, provide other investigative support, and share with task force members' agencies assets forfeited by drug offenders (Chaiken, Chaiken, and Karchmer 1990, p. 47). The Bush administration for fiscal year (FY) 1991 sought increased funding to provide additional "resources for state and local participation" in OCDETFs (*Crime Control Digest* 1990*b*, pp. 7–9; Office of National Drug Control Strategy 1990, p. 16). Its fiscal year 1992 budget request was for a total of $402 million to fund the OCDETF program; the FY 1991 allocation was $335 million (Office of National Drug Control Policy 1991, p. 27); and the FY 1990 allocation was $215 million (Office of National Drug Control Policy 1990, p. 96).

In 1990, there were 13 OCDETFs covering specific regions of the United States, each headquartered in a major city: Florida-Caribbean (Miami), Southeast (Atlanta), Mid-Atlantic (Baltimore), New York–New Jersey (New York), New England (Boston), Gulf Coast (Houston), South Central (St. Louis), North Central (Chicago), Great Lakes (Detroit), Mountain States (Denver), Southwest Border (San Diego), Los Angeles–Nevada (Los Angeles), and Northwest (San Francisco) (Office of National Drug Control Policy 1990, p. 15). Data current through 1988 indicated that, from the time the OCDETFs were launched in 1982, they were collectively responsible for nearly 2,500 investigations—and for an organized crime drug enforcement task force, an investigation often is a lengthy and complex undertaking (Bocklet 1991, p. 272).

4. *Other Intergovernmental Collaborations.*   Besides the concentration of intergovernmental collaborative energies on drug problems, there are also noteworthy examples of ad hoc task forces and less formal interagency investigative assistance against other types of multijurisdictional crime. For instance, every year the U.S. Marshals Service apprehends thousands of federal fugitives; most of these cases have been worked jointly with local police as part of a Marshals Service program titled Fugitive Investigation Strike Team (FIST; Commission on Accreditation for Law Enforcement Agencies 1987, standard 4.1.2; Morris 1989*b*, p. 11; Federal Law Enforcement Training Center 1990*a*, p. 85). Operations by FIST reportedly succeeded in arresting more than 14,000 fugitives over a several-year period in the late 1980s. To place that number in context, FBI National Crime Information Center data revealed that, during 1988, "there were approximately one quarter of a million Federal, State, and local fugitive warrants on file" (Federal Law Enforcement Training Center 1990*a*, p. 84). The 14,000 figure

also gives significance to the results of a ten-*week* interagency fugitive manhunt during the fall of 1990 that was led by the Marshals Service and dubbed Operation Southern Star: 3,743 fugitives arrested, over 90 percent of them wanted on state drug charges, eleven wanted for murder. In all, the operation entailed joint effort by twenty-eight state and local law enforcement agencies, plus U.S. Marshals Service offices in five of the metropolitan areas designated by the Office of National Drug Control Policy as "High Intensity Drug Trafficking Areas"—Miami, Houston, San Antonio, San Diego, and Los Angeles (*Crime Control Digest* 1990*k*, p. 6).

As another example of less formal interagency collaboration, the U.S. Secret Service,[41] Postal Inspectors, and the FBI assist local agencies with certain types of computer crime investigations. The Secret Service has "a general policy of assisting local investigators in the investigation of computer-related crimes, even if the case results in a local prosecution, as long as the crime violates a federal law" (Conly 1989, p. 39; Conly and McEwen 1990, p. 5). If a computer fraud is prosecutable federally under U.S. attorneys' guidelines, then the Secret Service very often will assist with an initial local prosecution of the offenders. The FBI, whose caseload entails only a small amount of computer-related matters, typically will help local investigators on such cases only when a violation is likely to be accepted by the appropriate U.S. attorney for federal prosecution. Even if the Secret Service or FBI cannot help a local agency investigate a computer-related crime, their financial crimes supervisors generally are able to refer police to helpful computer experts (Conly 1989, pp. 40–41).

Some of the Secret Service–led ad hoc task force operations targeting computer fraud in the 1990s are fairly complex exercises. In one effort, named Operation Sun Devil, on May 8, 1990, "more than 150 Secret Service agents, plus state and local law-enforcement officers, served . . . 28 search warrants in 14 cities" (Markoff 1990, p. A21).

---

[41] The Secret Service, besides its dignitary protection responsibilities, is charged with investigating violations of Title 18 U.S.C. sec. 1029 (dealing with credit card and telephone access code fraud and other matters). The FBI, in accordance with a 1985 agreement between the attorney general and the secretary of the treasury, has joint jurisdiction with the Secret Service over these matters and "primary" jurisdiction, under the Computer Fraud and Abuse Act of 1986 (18 U.S.C. sec. 1030), over cases involving "bank fraud, organized crime, national security, or terrorism" (Conly 1989, pp. 38–39; see also Markoff 1990, p. A21). We saw earlier that another memorandum of understanding between the attorney general and the secretary of the treasury sought to settle turf claims concerning the leadership of the United States' participation in INTERPOL.

Their targets were members of a computer hackers group, including teenagers, who named their loose affiliation the Legion of Doom and were charged with using national computer bulletin boards to exchange technical information on how to break into computer systems (Markoff 1990, p. A21).

More formal task forces, entailing written agreements, are also convened by various federal and local agencies to address computer-related offenses. Generally, these task forces form to handle single cases and disband when an investigation has been completed (Conly 1989, p. 41; Conly and McEwen 1990, p. 5). For example, an ad hoc task force of federal, state, and local investigators was assembled in the late 1980s in Arizona to investigate a computer crime that spanned several jurisdictions. The Greater St. Louis Major Case Squad, based on one established earlier by then-chief Clarence Kelley in Kansas City, since 1965 has fielded teams of specialized homicide investigators at the request of city and county agencies within a 4,500 square mile area in Missouri and Illinois. It operates under an established board of directors and clearly delineated policies and procedures (Layton and Lowery 1989; also see Lesce 1989).[42] A contemporary "network"-oriented rather than case-oriented multijurisdictional task force involving a large number of local agencies is in the Regional Organized Crime and Narcotics Task

---

[42] Another interesting example of mutual assistance among local agencies is the "investigative consulting team," which was pioneered in Atlanta during the early 1980s as that city suffered through the apparent serial murders of fifteen children over a sixteen-month period. Under this approach, five experienced homicide detectives (one each from the police departments in Oakland, New York City, Detroit, and Stamford, Connecticut, plus a recently retired West Coast police executive who was widely esteemed as an investigator and who headed the team) went to Atlanta, at the invitation of then Atlanta Public Safety Director Lee Brown. The team was not asked to participate directly in the investigations, nor was its arrival in Atlanta intended to send a message to local investigators that their superiors lacked confidence in their abilities. Rather, the team was to observe the investigative process and provide counsel, in the manner of consulting physicians or lawyers on a complex medical or legal case. The investigator who headed the team was Pierce R. Brooks, who later would be the first head of the FBI's VICAP program. The Police Executive Research Forum prepared a case study of this effort, which, the report observed, had melded two traditions—mutual assistance pacts among neighboring police departments and informal detective to detective brainstorming sessions at regional homicide investigators' conferences or other meetings (Brooks 1982; also see Layton and Lowery 1989; and Lesce 1989). There may be interesting adaptations of this novel effort that could foster better cooperation—and better results—in the context of federal-state-local concerns. Indeed, the mutual assistance represented in the Atlanta child murder cases was an important step in the expansion of ad hoc federal assistance to state and local police, for the experience with these cases resulted in the Department of Justice's Bureau of Justice Assistance being granted authority to provide substantial technical assistance grants to help with high-profile local criminal investigations (Rinkevich 1991a).

Force in the Portland, Oregon, area (Chaiken, Chaiken, and Karchmer 1990, p. 3; Coyle and Coldren 1991). Some federal-local computer fraud investigative collaborations are open-ended efforts. For instance, Philadelphia city police investigators are assigned full-time to the Secret Service field office to handle computer fraud cases that violate federal statutes but will be prosecuted by county or state prosecutors (Conly 1989, pp. 40–41).

Besides joint investigative exercises, there are numerous examples throughout the past several decades of federal, state, and local police teaming up for a short period to handle security and associated intelligence tasks for major events—a presidential summit conference, a papal visit, the visit of Nelson Mandela to several cities in America during 1990 (Kifner 1990, p. A12), the Olympics in Los Angeles during the 1980s, the Goodwill Games in Seattle in 1990. Most such events have important national and international security aspects and typically include the establishment of a task force and command center staffed by FBI counterterrorism experts, the Secret Service, the State Department's Office of Diplomatic Security (which mounted its largest protection effort in the agency's history for the Mandela New York City visit in June 1990—Kifner 1990, p. A12), as well as municipal, county, and state police (*Crime Control Digest* 1990*l*).

Other mechanisms of intergovernmental collaboration include emergency response systems that are set in motion during crises pursuant to previously established protocols. One such mechanism is the FBI's recently established Strategic Information Operations Center (SIOC), a national headquarters-based command post "capable of carrying out a full range of crisis management functions," including the provision of critical information to state and local law enforcement agencies. The SIOC became fully operational in conjunction with the presidential inauguration on January 20, 1989. Since sometimes multiple critical incidents with major national implications occur simultaneously (as happened in November 1987 when prison uprisings occurred in Oakdale, Louisiana, and Atlanta, Georgia), the Operations Center has multiple work stations, each fully equipped to provide the command post's complete range of services (Sessions 1989*b*, p. 10).

Just as the SIOC attempts to coordinate strategy in individual emergencies, other mechanisms exist whose purpose is to frame regional or national strategies for multiagency assaults on continuing problems of common interest. Some such problems are of indefinite but relatively limited duration. One example was the creation of a twenty-four-hour

FBI command post in its Washington, D.C., headquarters to receive, process, and disseminate information about possible terrorist assaults on American targets during the "Operation Desert Storm" war in the Persian Gulf in 1991 (Bentley 1991*b*, p. 2).

Two other mechanisms, intended to help shape regional and national strategies on what are seen as long-term crises, are the Law Enforcement Coordinating Committees and the Office of National Drug Control Policy. Created by the U.S. Justice Department at the recommendation of the 1981 *Report of the Attorney General's Task Force on Violent Crime*, the Law Enforcement Coordinating Committees (LECCs) were designed to help alleviate some of the problems that otherwise might be encountered in organized crime investigations and prosecutions involving several jurisdictions (Abrams 1986, p. 137; Goldstock 1987, pp. 97–98). LECCs are chaired by U.S. Attorneys with a view to providing a forum for leadership concerning federal and state cooperation against both organized crime and drug problems (Fines and Smith 1985; Bureau of Justice Statistics 1988, p. 60; Office of National Drug Control Policy 1990, p. 16). As described by the 1983 annual report of the Attorney General, "The LECC's have spawned a wide variety of cooperative law enforcement activities, ranging from bank robbery task forces to cross-designation of prosecutors to sharing law enforcement intelligence. The committees are designed to facilitate assistance from the federal government, and have been received with enthusiasm by state and local law enforcement officials" (Abrams 1986, p. 137).

A central objective of the LECCs, which frames the potential subject areas for federal-local collaboration, is coordinating priorities among the federal investigative and prosecutorial field offices within each federal district to ensure that scarce resources are used to maximum effect. These priorities are expressed in federal district law enforcement plans, which may vary from district to district but "generally reflect national law enforcement priorities as established by the Attorney General" (ibid.). Not all reviews of the track record of the law enforcement coordinating committees are as positive as the foregoing. Forst (1990), for example, reports that a number of local police officials and district attorneys are less sanguine about the accomplishments of the LECCs.

The Office of National Drug Control Policy (the drug czar's office) was established by the Anti-Drug Abuse Act of 1988 (P.L. No. 100-690, codified at 21 U.S.C. sec. 1504). Like the Organized Crime Drug Enforcement Task Forces, the drug czar's office (hereafter, ONDCP) evolved out of Vice-President Bush's "South Florida Task Force" in the early 1980s (Rinkevich 1991*a*). The ONDCP represents the latest of "16 significant proposals to reorganize the federal drug control programs" since 1966 and has among its chief purposes fostering improved coordination and cooperation among law enforcement agencies at all levels of government. The ONDCP has sought to address its mandates by establishing several coordinating mechanisms, including the supply reduction working group; the demand reduction working group; the research and development committee; the drug-related financial crimes policy group; and a process of designating "lead agencies" to provide operational coordination on different control programs (Office of National Drug Control Policy 1990, pp. 108–12). Each working group or committee, including its standing and ad hoc subcommittees, is composed of representatives from federal agencies and departments and, in some cases, from state and local public agencies and the private sector (ibid., pp. 109, 114, 127).

The coordinating mechanism of immediate interest for purposes of this essay on enforcement-related interaction between federal and non-federal police organizations is the supply-reduction working group. This working group's committees are charged with addressing four major policy areas: "interdiction (Border Interdiction Committee), high intensity drug trafficking areas, the Southwest border, and State and local drug enforcement" (ibid., pp. 71, 108, 112). The purpose of the state and local drug enforcement working group committee is to "ensure that national policy decisions include the concerns of our state and local agencies and their respective national organizations" (ibid., p. 108).

For the five "high intensity drug trafficking areas" designated by the ONDCP in 1989 under its statutory authority (they are multicounty regions surrounding New York City, Los Angeles, Miami, and Houston, plus a multistate area along the nation's southwest border), various mechanisms of coordination have been created. In each of the areas, a lead agency coordinator has been designated (from the U.S. Department of Justice for the four metropolitan areas, from the U.S. Department of the Treasury for the southwest border area). The mission of these coordinators is to "conduct all necessary coordination with State and local officials, Federal investigators and prosecutors, OCDETF and DEA State and Local task forces, and jail and prison administrators." The Treasury official responsible for the multistate Southwest Border Area is charged with coordinating the efforts of all these entities plus a Department of Defense team called "Joint Task Force 6" and is responsible for directing "Operation Alliance," an intergovernmental interdiction support network (ibid., pp. 69–71, 95). "Operation Alliance" has been replicated under the project title "North Star" in Buffalo, New York (Rinkevich 1991a).

Another subunit of the Supply Reduction Working Group, the Drug-related Financial Crimes Policy Group, has among its principal objectives fostering cooperative intra- and intergovernmental relationships to counter money laundering (Office of National Drug Control Policy 1990, p. 58). Among the specific objectives having implications for federal-state-local relations are strengthening state money laundering laws; improving state regulation and monitoring of nonbank financial institutions that are licensed by state and local governments; and intensifying multiagency investigations that use a range of federal and state government resources and expertise to uncover money laundering activities (ibid., p. 58).

In drug enforcement and in other areas of concurrent federal, state, and local police jurisdiction, the prospects for really efficient and valuable use of scarce law enforcement resources are limited, as we noted at the outset of this essay, not only by flawed ideas about how to ameliorate crime and disorder but by the lack of clear principles for delineating the respective jurisdictions of federal, state, and local law enforcement. Fully articulated principles have eluded many before us and are beyond us as well. But we close this essay with some thoughts that may assist others, as more is learned about the value of different anticrime strategies and tactics and about the relative strengths and weaknesses of enforcement bodies at different levels of government, in forging a more functional delineation of intergovernmental policing responsibilities than exists currently.

IV. Toward Principles for Delineating the Federal Police Role

A leading academic commentator on these matters, Professor Norman Abrams of UCLA, suggests that "insofar as the federal system has a significant responsibility for pursuing criminal activity that does not injure direct federal interests and that might as easily have been prosecuted by state and local authorities, it is still a system in search of a rationale" (1983, p. 785).

Though that is true, those who direct police and prosecutorial practices in the states and in the federal system seem well contented with the present division of responsibilities—not so contented with allocations *within* the federal system but with apportionments between federal and nonfederal authorities. Nor are state and local police content with the amount of federal *funding* devoted to the support of enforcement, prevention, and rehabilitative efforts at any level of government. But budgetary assistance is a separate question, we think, from whether the allocation of policing *authority* as between federal and nonfederal organizations makes sense in the view of incumbent practitioners. As we have seen, there are occasional tensions between federal enforcement agencies and local police departments, but overall a high degree of intergovernmental collaboration and cooperation has been achieved. One reason for this is the high regard in which the most active federal investigative agencies generally are held and also the training opportunities, technical services and funds, such as they are, which flow to the states and cities from the federal government. Nevertheless, it cannot be denied that a haphazard patchwork of responsibilities has been created, and over the past twenty years there have been steady and diligent efforts to slice the pie of police and prosecutorial responsibilities in a more principled fashion.

The most important reformative effort was the work of the Brown Commission, a commission appointed in 1966 by President Lyndon Johnson under the chairmanship of then-governor Edmund G. Brown of California and the directorship of Professor Louis Schwartz of the University of Pennsylvania, charged with the task of drafting a federal criminal code.

Since production of the American Law Institute's Model Penal Code in 1962, three-quarters of the states have brought order and principle to their statute books on crime by adopting a modified version of that code; but not Congress. The Federal Criminal Code is not a code at all; it is a collection of disparate statutes, based on no agreed general principles of the substantive criminal law other than those that federal judges can unearth from the Common Law of crime and borrow from the Model Penal Code. It is incoherent also in the sense that there are no agreed jurisdictional principles undergirding the various statutes bound together into Title 18 of the U.S. Code.

The Brown Commission—formally, the National Commission on Reform of the Federal Criminal Law (1971)—based its recommendations for a federal law of crime on the Model Penal Code and the work of the courts, federal and state, which had interpreted various provisions of that code, adapting that learning to federal needs. The twelve-member commission and its staff had no established federal blueprint, comparable to the Model Penal Code, as they confronted the jurisdictional patchwork of federal criminal law. As regards federal property and personnel and other direct federal interests, their task was not challenging—retain jurisdiction and draft a modern substantive code to give it shape. As regards the indirect federal jurisdiction where federal and state interests overlap, where each has a good claim to the police power, the task was much more challenging.

It is not unfair criticism to say that the commission avoided the issue of trying to define the proper ambit of federal jurisdiction. Instead, it recommended bringing order to federal jurisdiction by defining the jurisdictional basis for each crime and further allowing, in its recommended "piggyback" jurisdiction, federal authority over any subsidiary offenses committed or attempted in pursuit of the offense for which federal jurisdiction had been provided.[43] They suggested how to bring some degree of order to federal law enforcement jurisdiction, but offered no principles to delimit that jurisdiction (L. Schwartz 1977; Abrams 1986, p. 67). And, in the result, one of the impediments to the passage of a federal criminal code in the intervening two decades has been some opposition in Congress to what is seen as a potential expansion of federal jurisdiction. Whether what the Brown Commission recommended would in practice expand the federal law enforcement role is an almost metaphysical question. What now exists is limited by little more than prosecutorial convention and by the scarcity of federal investigative resources—and those powerful limitations would continue were the Brown Commission's recommendations to receive Congressional acceptance.

For many years there has been an on-again off-again effort, always supported by the Department of Justice no matter which party was in power, to achieve legislative passage of a federal criminal code. The codification movement has foundered on the penchant of special interests to insist on their expression in the proposed code and on Congress's receptivity to their concerns (L. Schwartz 1977; Abrams 1986, p. 67). Thus, pro and contra handgun control factions fight desperately for their views to find expression in the code, as do those favoring or disfavoring legislation to criminalize abortion, and so on. In 1984 the penalties provisions of the federal statute book were refashioned when the United States Sentencing Commission was established; but the

---

[43] The proposed piggyback jurisdiction is set forth in sec. 201(b) of the Brown Commission's recommended code (National Commission on Reform of the Federal Criminal Laws 1971; see also Abrams 1986, pp. 59–60, 66–67).

substantive and jurisdictional recommendations of the Brown Commission remain as recommendations only (Joost 1986; Abrams 1988, p. 6; Nagel 1990).

Perhaps if we consider one area of overlapping jurisdiction and reflect on what principles should guide balance between federal and state jurisdiction there, we might better be able to grope toward such principles generally. Consider the problem of governmental corruption. There is no lack of illustrative cases to draw on at either the federal, state, or local levels. The complex web of charges and convictions in the ABSCAM investigations in Philadelphia (Marx 1988) and recent wholesale indictments of sitting legislators in South Carolina and Arizona are merely the more celebrated of numerous recent public corruption cases. For purposes of illustration, we arbitrarily draw our example from the Greylord prosecutions in Chicago involving corruption among some in its city council, among some county judges, and among some of the city police.

Surely there can be no downside to such supremely successful undercover police exercises. But there is, and it is to be found in the "leave it to the Feds" attitude that characterizes too much of city law enforcement in relation to these types of crimes (see generally Ruff 1977), certainly if they have impact on the state legislature, the city government, and the state and local judiciary.

Prior to Greylord, the names of several of those later convicted as corrupt were widely known in the Chicago legal community as being corrupt. Nor was this the product of any particular inside information. Their names, particularly of those practicing in the traffic court, were known to very many Chicago lawyers (including the prosecutors) and to Chicago police. Yet nothing whatsoever had been done by city law enforcement authorities to bring them to book for thinning the traffic court docket through bribery of presiding judges. When the question of locally investigating these corrupt practices would be raised prior to Greylord, we would be advised that it would be impossible to keep the necessary undercover investigation confidential; somehow it would leak between the police, prosecutors, and courts and would come to naught. And further, we were assured, the more ample wiretapping powers possessed by federal law enforcement authorities gave them the necessary tools for the investigation. Well, the state legislature could change that, we replied. Don't be ingenuous, came the response, do you think they would allow such a weapon to be fashioned against themselves?

In our view, none of these obstacles to local initiative are impervious. Legislative reluctance to arm their potential inquisitors has a long and dishonorable tradition; entrenched congressional opposition to the creation of a national bureau of investigation under President Theodore Roosevelt was animated in no small measure by federal prosecutions of two members of Congress for fraudulent dealings in western lands (Walker 1977, p. 77). Yet the FBI *was* born and, over time, equipped with powerful implements of investigation. There is no good reason why the city of Chicago and the county of Cook could not, even conceding existing legal constraints on investigative methodology, have put together an efficient task force of police and prosecutors to run its own "Greylord"—and they should have.

But despite the theoretical opportunities for such local initiative, the pattern of actual practice remains clear. The "leave it to the Feds" attitude spawns a widespread abdication of local criminal law enforcement power across the nation (cf. Bittner 1982, p. 5); local attacks on any substantial and deep-seated local corruption—with the important exception of *police* corruption, where genuine progress has been made in local acceptance of house-cleaning responsibilities (Delattre 1989; Murphy and Caplan 1991)—are less common than hen's teeth.

Such a development, by which federal law enforcement should have in effect exclusive jurisdiction over governmental corruption when undercover investigation is required, would not be intolerable were federal resources adequate to the task. It would still be undesirable for the atmosphere it creates in which local police and communities alike come to feel powerless to alter traditions of dishonesty that affect their daily lives. But, as we have seen, the federal resources are so scant that pervasive corruption in several cities must be effectively exempt from attack.

Greylord could have been pursued in many cities of this country; Chicago certainly had no monopoly on the forms of corruption entailed, nor was it the worst offender. Likewise ABSCAM and Philadelphia. If we are seriously to reduce such corruption in our cities—and to fill the dishonesty vacuum with homespun and therefore more palatable structures to foster governmental integrity—state and city law enforcement will have to shoulder more of the burden. Unless the local enforcement apparatus is used to bolster local efforts to upgrade professionalism and responsibility in municipal service, those efforts are likely to be viewed as platitudinous.

That city corruption can be supplanted with integrity is made clear by the successes of a few city police forces in weeding out the corrupt and venal from their own forces and establishing higher objects of aspiration for their members than simply doing no wrong (Delattre 1989; Delattre and Behan 1991; Murphy and Caplan 1991). An FBI–local police discussion of initiatives to stem police brutality urges law enforcement supervisors to watch their subordinates and endeavor to "catch them doing something right" (Major City Chief Administrators 1991, p. 5). When necessary, city police know how successfully to use undercover investigation against their own personnel (Marx 1988). Given decent political and judicial support they could responsibly aim these weapons in those directions. But, so far, the "leave it to the Feds" attitude seems dominant.

A counterargument would be this: the FBI has developed a much larger competence at such investigations than have local police, and coming in from outside they have other natural advantages. Among these advantages, the FBI is not as beholden to local prosecutors, courts, and other executive and legislative bodies or officials as are local police for the success of investigations and prosecutions. The rise of multijurisdictional task forces targeting drug and other offenses in recent decades and the interdependence of their participants mitigates this argument, of course, but it remains the case that the FBI is far freer than a local police force to target a powerful local governmental official without suffering subtle organizational reprisals that inhibit further investigations. Thus, the argument runs, leave the politically delicate local corruption investigations to the Bureau, and increase its resources to that end.

One might offer a similar argument on behalf of an enlarged role for *state* police in investigating local governmental corruption, with the exception of local *court* corruption, since these courts, within their respective geographic jurisdictions, hear criminal cases generated by the state police. Reiss (1990) reports that in Connecticut the tradition for some years has been for the state police to investigate local police corruption without awaiting the intervention of federal authorities. The argument for FBI or state preemption of local government corruption investigations is not without appeal, but what should be realized, putting aside the disincentives created for local craftsmanship in integrity maintenance, is the extent of increased resources that would be required.

What might we learn from this consideration of de facto jurisdiction over governmental nonpolice corruption concerning the proper allocation of law enforcement responsibilities to the federal system? To move from description of the existing federal law enforcement role to cautious prescription of its recommended role is no easy task, but earlier in this essay we said we would attempt this task—not, however, without the safety net of acknowledging both its difficulty and our sense of uncertainty. As we attempt to frame the beginning of helpful working principles, let us first clear the ground of those aspects of the federal role that are obvious.

Given the multiplicity of police jurisdictions, state and local, to which the work of the FBI and the DEA and other federal police forces relate, it is obvious that slippage, overlap, and inefficiencies can result. A relatively recent development has been the creation of collaborative task forces, focused on a particular type of criminal activity in a defined region, bringing to bear the combined skills of federal, state and local police forces. Such task forces are to be encouraged; they raise no problems of conflicting jurisdictions and have had some success in relation to drug offenses, political corruption, insider trading, and other crimes.

Similarly, where federal personnel, property, or agencies are the targets of conduct defined by federal or state statutes as criminal, there is little doubt that that conduct is appropriately within the purview of the federal law enforcement, prosecutorial, judicial, and correctional authorities. The applicable law if a federal statute applies to the conduct is that statute; if the conduct is defined as criminal by a state statute, then the assimilative jurisdiction of the federal courts is invoked and the state or local law is applied by the federal court. Again, there is little argument about the appropriateness of this jurisdiction, though sometimes the assimilative jurisdiction raises difficult technical problems.

Likewise, conflict between state and federal jurisdictions does not arise in those many situations where federal statutes apply to conduct that is not otherwise defined as criminal. A mass of federal regulatory statutes impinge on conduct not regulated by the states.

It is in the broad area where the same conduct is a crime against both federal and state laws, capable of being prosecuted by either, or indeed both levels of government, that difficult problems of allocation of resources arise. In these situations of overlapping jurisdiction, what is the proper scope of federal jurisdiction? All we can offer in response to this daunting question are some notes, some ideas, some reflections relevant to an answer.

Where criminal conduct was pursued in several states, or when the crime because of its complexity or scope exceeded the investigative capacities of state law enforcement authorities, the wisdom of invoking federal rather than state or local enforcement seems obvious. To a degree, but only to a degree, these principles help to characterise the types of crime over which federal jurisdiction has been preemptive of state jurisdiction. A brief historical excursus in this area of overlapping jurisdictions will reveal, however, that political concerns, one might almost say in vote-attracting fashion, have been the dominant force rather than the logic of superior efficiencies.

In the early decades of this century, the Mann Act brought many convicts to federal prisons for behavior—pimping and running brothels—that is now rarely punished by either the federal or state authorities, but was then punishable by both, even when economic sexual exploitation was not involved. Transporting a female across state lines for immoral purposes was the lever of federal dominance of this jurisdiction. Federal prisons no longer contain those so trespassing morally. In the thirties and forties the Dyer Act flooded federal prisons and youth correctional institutions with car thieves and joyriders who indulged their passions for the motorcar and illicit gain by driving someone else's car across state lines. This jurisdiction is now left almost exclusively to the states, the exception being extensive car theft rings, and "chop shops" where federal jurisdiction still plays a role. Federally insured banks became the next jurisdictional concentration of federal authorities, and though this still remains a federal concern there is increasing effort to persuade state authorities to bear the primary burden. Federal courts and federal prisons are now flooded with drug cases, the jetsam of the series of "drug wars" launched by successive federal administrations. And, as we write, a new federal initiative is planned by which the greater severity of federal laws and federal sentencing for those criminals who carry guns is to be brought to bear.

One cannot look coldly at this list of the ebb and flow of federal criminal jurisdiction without being aware that current fashions of political concern play a determinative role.

To point to this ebb and flow of federal initiative is not really to offer a criticism; it may well be that the national government *should* respond nationally to what are seen from time to time as national criminal problems—Communists, pimps and seducers, car thieves, bank robbers, those who trade in prohibited drugs, and criminals who carry guns—whether state authorities are or are not pursuing such matters. But there are difficulties in this since the political lure of being "tough" on whatever is for the moment perceived nationally as particularly opprobrious may inefficiently skew a rational allocation of resources between the states, the localities, and the federal government to handle that currently fashionable evil.

Hence, though it is not inappropriate for the national government to respond to current national concerns about particular types of crime, the danger is that the response is too often a simple invocation of federal jurisdiction rather than an effort to buttress state and local instrumentalities, which is often the more efficient and effective technique. Of course, the disadvantage of that sometimes more appropriate technique is obvious—it gains no votes for the federal Congressperson and is welcomed only by those very few who are informed on these matters.

Federal authorities have a substantial advantage over state and local authorities in investigating cases of state and local governmental corruption. Greylord, the investigation of judicial corruption in Chicago, would not have been easy to run as a state investigation, though selected state police and judicial officers did know that the Greylord investigation was being pursued. How to phrase this in a nondefamatory manner? It would be highly desirable for state and local authorities to investigate and prosecute and convict criminality in those same state and local authorities; the reality is that for this desirable initiative we have to look for the time being to federal authorities.

Two reasons are often advanced for this: first, the obvious point of the suspicion turning to certainty that some local and state authorities will protect their own; second, because it is alleged that the federal police forces, in particular the FBI and the DEA, have developed skills at undercover investigative work, necessary for this type of investigation, which are, by comparison, lacking in local and state forces. We are not so confident of this. Several excellent undercover sting operations have been effectively mounted by state and city police forces. Nevertheless, this second point does have some validity in that for such undercover work new faces, faces not previously seen on the local scene, have an advantage.

Trying to draw together these speculations on principles that should guide the relationship among federal, state, and local policing of those types of crime which fall within the jurisdictions of each (which, in practice, covers a great deal of serious criminality), three tentative propositions can be advanced.

First, it is entirely appropriate that federal police see as their primary duty the protection of federal officers and federal property. Second, subject to a concern that the police, prosecutorial, judicial, and correctional forces of the nation be effectively deployed, it does not seem objectionable that federal concern should predominate in relation to those types of crime that are from time to time seen as nationally significant. Finally, that being said, the third principle that may prove helpful in allocating the tasks of repressing crime and punishing criminals is that federal authorities should devote themselves primarily to those areas where they have an operational advantage over state and local authorities, where their investigative techniques are sharper, their resources more ample, and their courts less clogged. That the locus of operational advantage may shift between police organizations at the several levels of government over time and across geography, necessitating reallocation of responsibilities, merely underscores the importance of continual progress in constructive interjurisdictional communication and in principled and strategically sound decision making by the leadership of the criminal justice policy community.

TABLE A1

Federal Agencies with Authority to Carry Firearms and Make Arrests

Department/Agency	Year Established	Predecessor Agency/Agencies	Key Responsibilities
A. Executive branch: Department of Agriculture: Forest Service	1905		Protect land and animals in national forests from criminal acts; protect campers from assaults; prevent timber thefts; enforce traffic laws; prevent arson and accidental forest fires (initiated Smokey the Bear symbol in 1945); eradication of marijuana grown in U.S. forests
Office of Inspector General	1962, 1978	When established in 1962 this was the first OIG in federal government; re-organized under IG Act of 1978	Investigate fraud, criminal allegations against USDA employees; one of the two Federal OIGs (the other being the OIG attached to the General Services Administration) granted *statutory* law enforcement authority
Department of Commerce: National Oceanic and Atmospheric Administration, National Marine Fisheries Service	1970	Bureau of Commercial Fisheries, Department of Interior	Enforcement of federal laws and international treaties on hunting/fishing and possession/importation of illegally taken fish and wildlife

Department of Defense: Defense Criminal Investigative Service, Office of Defense Inspector General	1982		DCIS is the investigative arm of the Defense Inspector General; it provides oversight of the activities of the Army Criminal Investigative Service Command, the Naval Investigative Service Command, and the Air Force Office of Special Investigations and coordination of their activities among one another and with the Defense Criminal Investigative Service; DCIS is one of two OIGs (the other being Department of Justice's OIG) granted law enforcement authority via a blanket deputation by the Department of Justice
Air Force: Office of Security Police	1975	Air provost marshal; Air Force inspector general (1948)	Patrol unit; full police services on Air Force bases
Army: Criminal Investigation Division Command	1971	1915–19; deactivated after World War I; reactivated in 1944; renamed U.S. Army Criminal Investigative Agency; established as a major Army Command in 1971	Investigation of serious crimes within the military; wartime missions are logistical security, management of criminal and terrorist-related intelligence, and law and order operations
Intelligence and Security Command	1977	Counterintelligence Corps (during World War II); Intelligence and Security Branch (1962)	Intelligence investigations
Military Police Corps	1919	Provost Marshal of Army (1776); Army Deputy Chief of Staff, Personnel; Army Deputy Chief of Staff, Operations	Full-service police agency at military facilities; investigate minor offenses; wartime role includes prisoner of war operations, traffic and circulation control, and general law and order missions

TABLE A1 (*Continued*)

Department/Agency	Year Established	Predecessor Agency/Agencies	Key Responsibilities
Marine Corps: Criminal Investigation Division	1945		Investigate misdemeanors and minor military offenses and assist Naval Investigative Service (the Marine Corps is part of the Department of the Navy) by loaning investigative personnel; during wartime and "combat contingencies," assume full investigative power with deployed forces
Military Police	1945, 1970	Military Police were reduced in size in 1950s, with MP duty becoming a rotating assignment of Marine Corps personnel; Marine Corps Military Police reestablished as full-time enforcement police force in 1970	Full-service police agency at military facilities; investigate minor offenses
Navy: Naval Investigative Service	1966	Office of Naval Intelligence (1916)	Investigate major offenses involving Naval personnel and property; exclusive jurisdiction within Navy over espionage, sabotage, subversive activities
Shore Patrol			Police patrol duties analogous to those of the Military Police in other branches of the military

Department of Interior:		
Bureau of Indian Affairs, Division of Law Enforcement Services: Uniformed BIA officers Tribal police officers Bureau of Land Management:	1878	During French and Indian Wars, two superintendents of Indian Affairs assigned to Department of War. Full-service police agency enforcing both federal and tribal law on reservations; involved in eradication of domestically grown marijuana
Law Enforcement and Resource Protection Operations	1974	Special agents and uniformed rangers investigate violations and enforce federal laws and regulations relating to public lands or their resources; jurisdiction in 1974 was limited to protection of wild horses and burros on public land; jurisdiction expanded in 1976
Fish and Wildlife Service	1940	Game wardens under Department of Commerce (1871). Enforce commercial and private laws on hunting, fishing, environmental protection (similar to Department of Commerce National Marine Fisheries Service)
National Park Service: Division of Ranger Activities	1972	Division of Ranger Activities and Protection (1916). Law enforcement activities at national parks throughout the United States, other than those in Washington, D.C., San Francisco, New York City (including riot control—e.g., Yosemite Valley National Park riot in 1974); eradication of marijuana grown in national parks; investigation of arson (setting wildfires)

TABLE A1 (*Continued*)

Department/Agency	Year Established	Predecessor Agency/Agencies	Key Responsibilities
U.S. Park Police	1919	Park Watchmen on federal park lands (1791); Park Watchmen transferred from Department of Interior to Army Corps of Engineers (1867); name changed to U.S. Park Police (1919); responsibilities transferred back to Department of Interior (1933)	An urban uniformed and plainclothes police unit providing protection for all U.S. parklands, but historically only servicing parklands and key federal grounds in Washington, D.C., and parklands in San Francisco and New York City (crowd control at demonstrations, etc.); authorized to provide police services at any U.S. park, regardless of location
Department of Justice: Administrative Office of the U.S. Courts, Division of Probation	1870		
	1930	Probation officers appointed by judges	Supervise persons on probation and parole; arrest violators
Bureau of Prisons: Corrections officers	1930		Control and transport prisoners; arrest fugitives
Drug Enforcement Administration	1973	Bureau of Narcotics (Treasury Department, 1930); Bureau of Narcotics and Dangerous Drugs (DOJ, 1968)	Investigation of major narcotic violators who operate at interstate and international levels; enforcement of regulations governing legal manufacture and dispensing of controlled substances; management of a national narcotics intelligence system; coordination with federal, state, and local law enforcement authorities and cooperation with counterpart agencies abroad; training, scientific research, and information exchange in support of drug traffic prevention and control; DEA administrator reports to the Attorney General through the FBI director

Agency	Year	Predecessor / Department	Responsibilities
Federal Bureau of Investigation	1935	Bureau of Investigation (1908)	Broad, general investigative responsibility concerning more than 250 federal crimes; since January of 1982, the attorney general has given the FBI concurrent jurisdiction with the DEA over drug offenses in the Controlled Substances Act (21 U.S.C. sec. 801)
Immigration and Naturalization Service (five "programs"):		INS under Department of Labor (1933); previously under Departments of State, Treasury, Labor, Commerce	
1. Border Patrol	1924		Interdiction of aliens, narcotics and other contraband *between* (not *at*) ports of entry; until 1990 INS Act, INS agents in all five law enforcement programs had authority to make arrests and carry weapons under the Attorney General's interpretation of existing law—the 1990 Act grants Congressional authority to agents in the first four INS law enforcement programs to carry weapons and make arrests
2. Criminal Investigations	1933		Investigation of alleged crimes within jurisdiction of INS
3. Detention and Deportation	1955		Custodial and deportation responsibilities
4. Intelligence	1955		Uniformed and plainclothes intelligence functions related to INS responsibilities
5. Inspections	1891		Law enforcement inspectional responsibilities *at* ports of entry (in contrast to Border Patrol's work *between* ports of entry); can be cross-designated with U.S. Customs Service (Department of Transportation) to perform inspectional functions under U.S. Customs laws; Inspections unit's authority to make arrests and carry weapons is currently an implied authority approved by the attorney general and will be determined by further development of regulations

TABLE A1 (*Continued*)

Department/Agency	Year Established	Predecessor Agency/Agencies	Key Responsibilities
Marshals Service	1789	Until 1861 reported to Secretary of Treasury and other top officials	Security in federal courts; protect federal judges, prosecutors, jurors; enforce federal court orders; execute federal warrants (including fugitive warrants); execute "unlawful flight" fugitive warrants issued by state and local courts; transport federal prisoners; maintain custody of all federal pretrial detainees; arrest some indictees; manage Witness Security Program; riot control on federal lands or reservations, in federal prisons and in connection with federal court orders (e.g., school desegregation); escort missile convoys; administer DOJ's program for management and disposal of property subject to judicial and administrative forfeiture
Office of Inspector General	1989	Bureau of Prisons has had Office of Inspection since 1930	Investigate violations of fraud, abuse, and integrity laws which govern operations financed by DOJ, and develop such allegations for criminal prosecution and civil or administrative action; one of two federal OIGs (the other being in the Department of Defense) granted law enforcement authority via blanket deputation by the Department of Justice

Department of State:			
Bureau of Diplomatic Security— Diplomatic Security Services	1985	Bureau of Secret Intelligence (one-man office established in 1916, later called Office of the Chief Special Agent); Division of Security (1948)	Dignitary protection (foreign diplomats, official visitors other than heads of state, who are protected by Secret Service); embassy security; visa/passport enforcement; protection of foreign missions (resident foreign officials or facilities in United States); provide security to U.S. embassies overseas
Department of Transportation:			
Coast Guard, Intelligence and Law Enforcement Branch	1967	Coast Guard initially under authority of Department of Treasury (1790)	Principal enforcement responsibility for federal laws on high seas and navigable waters of U.S. (including narcotics interdiction); Intelligence and Law Enforcement Branch provides investigative support
Federal Air Marshals	mid-1970s	Washington National Airport Police (1940) (Washington National and Dulles Airports are no longer policed by federal personnel; in 1987 this responsibility was turned over to the Metro-Washington Airport Authority, similar to a regional Port Authority Police) Sky Marshals (early 1970s)	Armed in-flight intervention
Department of Treasury:			
Bureau of Alcohol, Tobacco and Firearms	1972	1862–1972 was subunit of IRS within Treasury	Reduce criminal use of firearms and explosives (including bombings and arson-for-profit schemes); enforcement of tax and other federal alcohol and tobacco regulations

TABLE A1 (*Continued*)

Department/Agency	Year Established	Predecessor Agency/Agencies	Key Responsibilities
Bureau of Engraving and Printing Office of Security, Police Services Branch, Police Force Unit	1973	Bureau Watch (guards) (1880), which had District of Columbia Special Police powers beginning circa 1900; U.S. Secret Service Uniformed Force (1937); Bureau of Engraving and Printing Guards (1953)	Enforce federal and District of Columbia laws as well as Department of Treasury and Bureau of Engraving and Printing rules and regulations on Bureau property
Customs Service (three component law enforcement operations): 1. Office of Enforcement 2. Office of Internal Affairs 3. Office of Inspectional Control	1789	Prior to establishment of the three component operations, these functions were performed (since 1789) by Special Agents	Interdict and seize contraband, including counterfeit merchandise, narcotics, firearms entering U.S.; process persons, baggage, cargo, mail entering U.S. at 239 ports of entry; administer certain navigation laws; revenue fraud investigation; can be cross-designated with Immigration and Naturalization Service, Department of Justice, to perform inspectional services under the Immigration and Naturalization laws; Customs agents process cargo and people according to Customs laws, whereas INS agents process people according to Immigration and Naturalization laws; responsible for the enforcement of 412 laws, although the agency concentrates on narcotics

Internal Revenue Service:			
Criminal Investigation Division	1919	Agents assigned to prevent revenue fraud (1863)	Tax fraud investigations
Office of Assistant Chief Inspector (internal security)	1952		Handle internal affairs matters within IRS
Mint:			
U.S. Mint Police Force	1979	Guard Force under General Services Administration (1973), subsequently U.S. Mint Special Police	Guard the Mint at West Point (Philadelphia), Denver, and San Francisco, and bullion in Fort Knox; provide protection for Mint employees and visitors, monetary and bullion assets, plant, facilities and equipment and Mint property against abuse, disorders, and all other unsafe or illegal practices
Secret Service:			
Special agents	1865		Dignitary protection—president, vice-president, major candidates for president, former presidents, visiting foreign heads of state (e.g., at United Nations meetings); investigate threats against protectees; counterfeiting and computer fraud enforcement (since 1984 Secret Service has been the primary federal agency enforcing computer fraud laws); Uniformed Division provides security at Treasury Buildings in Washington, D.C.
Uniformed Division		Uniformed Division includes the previous Treasury Police Force, which in turn was preceded by Treasury Guard Force and Treasury Security Force	
Environmental Protection Agency: Office of Criminal Enforcement—special agents	1989	Office of Criminal Investigations (1982), part of EPA National Enforcement Investigative Center	Plainclothes unit, enforces the criminal penalty provisions of the environmental statutes administered by the EPA

TABLE A1 (*Continued*)

Department/Agency	Year Established	Predecessor Agency/Agencies	Key Responsibilities
General Services Administration: Federal Protective Service	1949	Federal Works Agency and Federal Works Administration	Security for federal buildings and property nationwide; administer security guard contracts
Office of Inspector General	1978		Investigates fraud; one of the two federal OIGs (the other being in the Department of Agriculture) granted *statutory* law enforcement authority
Postal Service: Postal Inspection Service	1737		Plainclothes personnel enforce approximately 100 laws pertaining to the mails (e.g., frauds, use of mails to transport injurious materials, crimes against postal employees or property, theft of mail); internal audit arm of Postal Service responsible for safety and security of 750,000 employees, 40,000 facilities, and $35 billion in operating revenues (1991 figures)
Smithsonian Institution: National Zoological Park Police	1951	Watchmen (1882); National Zoo Police Officers (1890); Zoo protected by Metropolitan Police (1891)	Full police services at National Zoo and perimeter grounds in Washington, D.C.; authorized to protect all Smithsonian Institution buildings (separate from the unarmed Smithsonian Protection Services)
Veterans Administration Department of Medicine and Surgery Security Service			Security services at Veterans Administration property

B. Legislative branch:			
Capitol Police	1851	One guard in 1801	Full police service for U.S. Capitol grounds and buildings
Government Printing Office:			
Government Printing Office Police	1860		Security of GPO facilities; police powers concurrent with those of local police in jurisdictions where premises located
Library of Congress:			
Library of Congress Police	1897	When Library of Congress was housed in the Congress building, security services were furnished by the U.S. Capitol Police; in 1897 when the Library's own building was built, a new police force was established under the administration of the Library of Congress	Uniformed personnel protect life, property, and civil rights of Library of Congress staff and patrons by maintaining law and order and assisting in the protection of library collections and property
C. Judicial branch:			
U.S. Supreme Court Police	1949	Prior to 1949 Supreme Court met in Capitol Building and was protected by U.S. Capitol Police	General police services for Supreme Court buildings and grounds
D. Independent establishments:			
Amtrak:			
Amtrak Police Department	1970		Patrol and investigation pertaining to all nationwide Amtrak facilities and equipment
Tennessee Valley Authority:			
Public Safety Service	1936	Security force when TVA established (1933)	Police and fire fighting services for TVA facilities and lands (including nuclear and conventional power plants in Tennessee River Region)

TABLE A1 (Continued)

Note.—Consistent with the view of senior federal law enforcement officials (e.g., Rinkevich 1991*a*), this table does not count the Metropolitan Police Department of Washington, D.C. as a federal law enforcement agency. The department does, of course, provide general police services to the District of Columbia. The choice not to include the Metropolitan Police among federal agencies is one with which some might differ. As documentary support for our decision to omit it, the official *United States Government Manual, 1990/1991* (Office of the Federal Register, National Archives and Records Administration 1990) does not include it or other units of the District of Columbia government under its listings of Federal government entities.

We have also omitted the Office of Security of the Central Intelligence Agency, which some in federal law enforcement positions suggested to us was an armed security force protecting CIA headquarters facilities and employees and which is indeed trained at the Federal Law Enforcement Training Center in Glynco, Georgia, along with apparently similar forces, such as the U.S. Capitol Police, Supreme Court Police, and others (Rinkevich 1991*b*). We omitted the Office of Security because, when we contacted the CIA, we were told that the CIA has no armed security force with arrest powers protecting its grounds and personnel. We remain somewhat skeptical of this assertion, although we did not place ourselves in the position of second-guessing the subject agency's own statements when compiling this table. Moreover, the *United States Government Manual, 1990/1991*, consistent with our respondent at the CIA, does state: "The Agency has no police, subpoena, or law enforcement powers or internal security functions" (p. 534). It seems to us that this statement, and the insistence by the Agency staff that the Office of Security does not belong on our table confuses a uniformed police guard force, similar in kind to others included above, with the central function of the CIA. Our best guess is that the table above should in fact include the CIA's Office of Security.

Nor are most of the twenty-five statutorily created federal Inspectors General Offices listed in this table. Among other duties, the Offices of Inspector General (OIGs) have responsibility to investigate possible frauds that violate federal criminal law, but OIG investigative personnel (commonly called agents or special agents) do not generally in the course of those investigations have arrest powers or authority to possess firearms. As part of basic training, agents (investigators) employed by Inspectors General Offices in various agencies generally receive firearms training but are only authorized to carry firearms in most OIGs on a case-by-case basis. That authorization comes in the form of deputation by the Department of Justice (Bosen 1991; Terjesen 1991). How often OIG agents receive such deputization from the Department of Justice varies. For instance, the Department of State's OIG employs a total of 240 staff, 18 percent of whose workload in 1990 was devoted to investigations (the balance being divided evenly between audits and inspections). Special agents trained to conduct criminal investigations are a small percentage of this OIG's 240 employees. From approximately September 1988 through October 1990, eleven of the State Department OIG's special agents were deputized, usually for short investigations, by the Justice Department (Bosen 1991). In some instances, OIG agents may also be deputized by the Department of Justice to provide armed security services to the head of the agency within which the OIG office is housed, but that is an exceptional practice (Office of the Inspector General, Dept. of Agriculture 1991). Most of the Inspectors General staffs receive criminal investigative training at the Federal Law Enforcement Training Center in Glynco, Georgia (Rinkevich 1991*b*).

334

Of the twenty-five statutorily established Inspectors General offices, the four that are included in the table above are the Department of Agriculture OIG and the General Services Administration OIG (both of which have "statutory law enforcement authority" [Terjesen 1991]), the Department of Defense OIG (its investigative branch is called the Defense Criminal Investigative Service), and the Department of Justice OIG. The latter two do not have statutory law enforcement authority but instead have been granted "blanket deputation law enforcement authority—for all agents, renewable on an annual basis" (Terjesen 1991).

Under the Inspector General Act of 1978, P.L. 95-452, October 12, 1978, 92 Stat. 1101, as amended by a series of laws, the most recent being 103 Stat. 393, 415 (August 9, 1989), the following federal departments or agencies (formally titled generically as federal "establishments") have offices of inspector general: the Departments of Agriculture, Commerce, Defense, Education, Energy, Health and Human Services, Housing and Urban Development, the Interior, Justice, Labor, State, Transportation, Veteran's Affairs, and the Treasury; the Agency for International Development, the Environmental Protection Agency, the Federal Emergency Management agency, the General Services Administration, the National Aeronautics and Space Administration, the Nuclear Regulatory Commission, the Office of Personnel Management, Railroad Retirement Board, the Resolution Trust Corporation, the Small Business Administration, and the United States Information Agency (Inspector General Act of 1978, sec. 11(2), as amended through August 9, 1989, 103 Stat. 393). These twenty-five statutory OIGs constitute the "members" of a body called the President's Council on Integrity and Efficiency (PCIE) (Bosen 1991). The PCIE, appointed in March 1981, in addition to the statutory Inspectors General, includes FBI and Department of Justice officials, and a representative of the Office of Management and Budget. The PCIE is charged with ensuring that resources are applied in a way that minimizes fraud, waste, and abuse (Gosseaux and Curran 1988, p. 61).

Besides the twenty-five OIGs established by the Inspectors General Act of 1978 (as amended), thirty-three additional federal agencies have established their own offices of inspector general by executive initiative. These thirty-three are referred to within the inspectors general community as "small agency IGs" and, although not full-fledged "members" of the President's Council on Integrity and Efficiency, they are members of a Coordinating Conference of the PCIE. The thirty-three small agency inspectors general, who also apparently could be granted law enforcement authority by being deputized on a case-by-case basis, are attached to the following federal establishments: ACTION, Amtrak, the Appalachian Regional Commission, Board for International Broadcasting, Commodity Futures Trading Commission, Consumer Product Safety Commission, Corporation for Public Broadcasting, Equal Employment Opportunity Commission, Farm Credit Administration, Federal Communications Commission, Federal Deposit Insurance Corporation, Federal Elections Commission, Federal Housing Finance Board, Federal Labor Relations Authority, Federal Maritime Commission, Federal Reserve System, Federal Trade Commission, Government Printing Office, Interstate Commerce Commission, Legal Services Corporation, National Archives and Records Administration, National Credit Union Administration, National Endowment for the Arts, National Endowment for the Humanities, National Labor Relations Board, National Science Foundation, Panama Canal Commission, Peace Corps, Pension Benefit Guarantee Corporation, Securities and Exchange Commission, Smithsonian Institution, Tennessee Valley Authority, United States International Trade Commission, and the United States Postal Service. Nonstatutory Inspectors General also loosely affiliated with the President's Council on Integrity and Efficiency but not members of the coordinating conference include those in the Administrative Office of the U.S. Courts, the District of Columbia Government, Merit Systems Protection Board, National Gallery of Art, and the Selective Service System (Bosen 1991).

Many of these small agency inspectors general have extremely limited staffing, in some cases making arrangements with some of the statutorily established Offices of Inspector General to borrow staff for audits and other activities (Bosen 1991).

335

REFERENCES

Abell, Richard B. 1988. "Effective Systems for Regional Intelligence Sharing." *Police Chief* 55(11): 58–59.

Abrams, Norman. 1983. "Federal Criminal Law Enforcement." In *Encyclopedia of Crime and Justice*, edited by Sanford H. Kadish. New York: Free Press.

———. 1986. *Federal Criminal Law and Its Enforcement*. St. Paul, Minn.: West.

———. 1988. *Federal Criminal Law and Its Enforcement (1988 Supplement)*. St. Paul, Minn.: West.

Advisory Commission on Intergovernmental Relations. 1971. *State-Local Relations in the Criminal Justice System*. Washington, D.C.: U.S. Government Printing Office.

Asset Forfeiture Bulletin. 1990. "Thornburgh Makes Asset Forfeiture a Top Priority." *Asset Forfeiture Bulletin* (a bulletin produced for the Justice Department's Bureau of Justice Assistance by the Police Executive Research Forum) (May), pp. 1–5.

Bashinski, Jan, and Joseph Peterson. 1991. "Forensic Sciences." In *Local Government Police Management* (golden anniversary edition), edited by William A. Geller. Washington, D.C.: International City Management Association.

Bauer, William. 1990. Personal communication by William A. Geller with U.S. Court of Appeals (Seventh Cir.) judge, formerly U.S. attorney for the Northern District of Illinois, February 6.

Bayley, David. In this volume. "Organization of Police in English-speaking Countries."

Bentley, S. Woodruff, Sr. 1991*a*. "DOD Kills Proposal to Consolidate Military Criminal Investigative Organizations: Gives Greater Power to Defense Criminal Investigative Service." *Crime Control Digest* 25(1):4.

———. 1991*b*. "Desert Storm: Law Enforcement Agencies Can Upgrade Preparations for Terrorist Activity." *Crime Control Digest* 25(4):1–3.

Bequai, August. 1987. "Technocrimes—Why the Cops Can't Cope." *Law Enforcement Technology* (March/April), p. 28.

Bittner, Egon. 1982. "Emerging Police Issues." In *Local Government Police Management*, 2d ed., edited by Bernard L. Garmire. Washington, D.C.: International City Management Association.

Blakey, G. Robert. 1983. "Organized Crime: Enforcement Strategies." In *Encyclopedia of Crime and Justice*, edited by Sanford H. Kadish. New York: Free Press.

Blakey, G. Robert, and Ronald Goldstock. 1977. *Electronic Surveillance: Two Views*. Ithaca, N.Y.: Cornell Institute on Organized Crime.

Bocklet, Richard. 1991. "DEA State and Local Task Forces: A Body for Law Enforcement." *Law and Order* (January), pp. 272–79.

Bomar, Horace L. 1934. "The Lindbergh Law." *Law and Contemporary Problems* 1(October):435.

Bosen, Becky. 1991. Personal communication and written memorandum to William Geller from administrative aide Becky Bosen, Office of the Inspector General, U.S. Department of State, May 14, 16.

Brooks, Pierce R. 1982. *The Investigative Consultant Team: A New Approach for*

Law Enforcement Cooperation. Washington, D.C.: Police Executive Research Forum.

Brooks, Pierce R., Michael J. Devine, Terence J. Green, Barbara L. Hart, and Merlyn D. Moore. 1987. "Serial Murder: A Criminal Justice Response." *Police Chief* 54(6):37–45.

Brown, Lee P. 1990. "Call to President Bush: Establish a Commission on Crime and Violence." *Police Chief* 57(11):8–10.

———. 1991*a*. "Values and Ethical Standards Must Flow from the Chief." *Police Chief* 58(1):8.

———. 1991*b*. "Foreword." In *Local Government Police Management* (golden anniversary edition), edited by William A. Geller. Washington, D.C.: International City Management Association.

———. 1991*c*. "The National Commission on Crime and Violence— Redoubling Our Efforts." *Police Chief* 58(3):6.

Bureau of Justice Statistics. 1988. *Report to the Nation on Crime and Justice.* 2d ed. Washington, D.C.: U.S. Department of Justice, Bureau of Justice Statistics.

———. 1990*a*. *BJS Data Report, 1989.* Washington, D.C.: U.S. Department of Justice, Bureau of Justice Statistics.

———. 1990*b*. *Drugs and Crime Facts, 1989.* Washington, D.C.: U.S. Department of Justice, Bureau of Justice Statistics.

Calhoun, Frederick. 1990. *The Lawmen.* Washington, D.C.: Smithsonian Institute Press.

Cameron, Jerry. 1990. "Intelligence, Expert Systems, Microcomputers and Law Enforcement." *Police Chief* 57(3): 36–41.

Carson, Dale, and Donald K. Brown. 1970. "Law Enforcement Consolidation for Greater Efficiency." *FBI Law Enforcement Bulletin* 39(10):11–15.

Carvino, James. 1989. Personal communication with the Boise, Idaho, police chief, formerly deputy director of the U.S. Justice Department's Office of Liaison Services, responsible for facilitating communication between local law enforcement and the attorney general, December 13.

Chaiken, Jan, Marcia Chaiken, and Clifford Karchmer. 1990. *Multijurisdictional Drug Law Enforcement Strategies: Reducing Supply and Demand.* Issues and Practices series. Washington, D.C.: U.S. Department of Justice, National Institute of Justice.

Clede, Bill. 1990. "NIBRS: The National Incident-based Reporting System." *Law and Order* (March), pp. 100–101.

Comment. 1970. "The Strike Force: Organized Law Enforcement vs. Organized Crime." *Columbia Journal of Law and Social Problems* 6:496–523.

Commission on Accreditation for Law Enforcement Agencies. 1987. *Standards for Law Enforcement Agencies.* Fairfax, Va.: Commission on Accreditation for Law Enforcement Agencies.

Conly, Catherine H. 1989. *Organizing for Computer Crime Investigation and Prosecution.* Washington, D.C.: U.S. Department of Justice, National Institute of Justice.

Conly, Catherine H., and J. Thomas McEwen. 1990. "Computer Crime." *NIJ*

Reports (January/February), pp. 2–7. Washington, D.C.: U.S. Department of Justice, National Institute of Justice.

Conroy, Edward D., and Carl L. Lockett. 1988. "Implications of *Solorio v. United States* to Military and Civilian Law Enforcement." *Police Chief* 55(8):36–37.

Constantine, Thomas A. 1988. "Organized Crime: The New York State Police Response." *Police Chief* 55(1):36–43.

Cordner, Gary, Craig Fraser, and Chuck Wexler. 1991. "Research, Planning, and Implementation." In *Local Government Police Management* (golden anniversary edition), edited by William A. Geller. Washington, D.C.: International City Management Association.

Couper, David C., and Sabine H. Lobitz. 1991. *Quality Policing: The Madison Experience*. Washington, D.C.: Police Executive Research Forum.

Coyle, Kenneth R., and Chip Coldren. 1991. "Case Studies in Multijurisdictional Task Force Implementation and Operation." Report prepared for the National Institute of Justice. Washington, D.C.: Criminal Justice Statistics Association (forthcoming).

Crime Control Digest. 1989. "Thornburgh Decides to Merge 26 OC Strike Forces into U.S. Attorneys' Offices." 23(25):2–3.

———. 1990a. "In Cleveland . . . DEA Accused of Blowing Drug Case Involving Other Agencies." 24(43):5–6.

———. 1990b. "Record Drug Busts Fail to Dent Market." 24(7):7.

———. 1990c. "Bush Budget Seeks $10.6B for Drug Control; Includes $492M for State/Local Aid." 24(5):1.

———. 1990d. "Los Angeles Gang Members Charged in Idaho Drug Case." 24(3):7.

———. 1990e. "DOD to Provide More Anti-drug Training to State and Local Police." 24(11):10.

———. 1990f. "FBI Developing Standards to Help Police Detect Potential Serial Killers." 24(8):6–7.

———. 1990g. "DOJ Establishing National Drug Intelligence Center." 24(24):8–9.

———. 1990h. "No Budget Cuts, RISS Directors Tell Bush Administration." 24(15):7.

———. 1990i. Announcements of Information Sharing Conferences co-sponsored by the Middle Atlantic/Great Lakes Organized Crime Law Enforcement Network. 24(7):4, 6.

———. 1990j. "DOJ Now Merging Organized Crime Strike Forces into U.S. Attorneys' Offices." 24(1):3–4.

———. 1990k. "Security Is a Massive Project for Seattle's Goodwill Games: Undermanned, Underfunded, Overwhelmed." 24(25):3–4.

———. 1990l. "USMS, State and Local Police Nab 3,743 Fugitives in Massive Nationwide Operation." 24(43):6–7.

———. 1990m. "Senate Bill Would Aid in Recruiting, Retaining Federal Law Enforcement Officers: Implements NACLE Recommendations." 24(11):1–3.

―――. 1991a. "Project Triggerlock: A.G. Orders U.S. Attorneys to Get Tough on Violent Felons Who Use Guns." 25(14):3–4.

―――. 1991b. "New Report: U.S. to Target Mafia Bosses, Emerging Crime Groups." 25(6):6–7.

―――.1991c. "DOJ Seeks FY 1992 Budget of 10.2 Billion, with Most Money for Law Enforcement." 25(6):1–5.

Crovitz, L. Gordon. 1990. "Some RICO Knee-Slappers and One That Isn't Funny at All." *Wall Street Journal* (October 24), p. A15.

Cummings, Homer. 1934. "Lessons of the Crime Conference." In *Attorney General's Conference on Crime*, edited by U.S. Department of Justice. Washington, D.C.: U.S. Department of Justice.

Cummings, Homer, and C. McFarland. 1937. *Federal Justice*. New York: Macmillan.

Cunningham, William C., and Todd H. Taylor. 1985. *The Hallcrest Report: Private Security and Police in America*. Portland, Oreg.: Chancellor.

Davis, Raymond C. 1985. "Organizing the Community for Improving Policing." In *Police Leadership in America: Crisis and Opportunity*, edited by William A. Geller. New York: Praeger.

Delattre, Edwin J. 1989. *Character and Cops: Ethics in Policing*. Washington, D.C.: American Enterprise Institute for Public Policy Research.

Delattre, Edwin J., and Cornelius J. Behan. 1991. "Practical Ideals for Managing in the Nineties: A Perspective." In *Local Government Police Management* (golden anniversary edition), edited by William A. Geller. Washington, D.C.: International City Management Association.

Dempsey, William. 1991. Personal communication by William A. Geller with U.S. Marshals Service Public Information Officer Dempsey (May 9).

Douthit, Nathan. 1975. "Police Professionalism and the War against Crime in the United States, 1920s–30s." In *Police Forces in History*, edited by George L. Mosse. Beverly Hills, Calif.: Sage.

Eck, John E., and Gerald L. Williams. 1991. "Criminal Investigations." In *Local Government Police Management* (golden anniversary edition), edited by William A. Geller. Washington, D.C.: International City Management Association.

Edelhertz, Herbert. 1987. "Overview of Symposium Issue Papers and Deliberations." In *Major Issues in Organized Crime Control: A Compendium of Papers Prepared by Experts in the Field*, edited by Herbert Edelhertz. Washington, D.C.: U.S. Government Printing Office.

Faughnan, Joseph, and Joseph Gilroy. 1979. "Interagency Narcotics Enforcement Unit." *Police Chief* 46(7):26–27.

Federal Bureau of Investigation. 1991. Monthly activity report for February 1991 of the Identification Division, furnished by Statistics Unit staffer Frank Smith.

Federal Law Enforcement Training Center. 1990a. *The National Center for State and Local Law Enforcement Training: Catalog of Local Law Enforcement Training Presented by Federal Agencies*. 8th ed. Glynco, Ga.: U.S. Department of Treasury, Federal Law Enforcement Training Center.

————. 1990*b*. *Department of the Treasury, Federal Law Enforcement Training Center: Organization and Operations.* Glynco, Ga.: U.S. Department of Treasury, Federal Law Enforcement Training Center.

Feldkamp, Robert H. 1991*a*. "Key Agency for Funding Criminal Justice Programs Given Generally Good Marks." *Crime Control Digest* 25(8):1–3.

————. 1991*b*. "In Philadelphia: Violent Traffickers Project Deemed Highly Successful." *Crime Control Digest* 25(11):4–5.

Felten, Eric. 1991. "An Older, Wiser FBI Hesitates to Sting the Hand That Feeds." *Insight Magazine* (February 4), pp. 26–27.

Fines, Gerald D., and L. Lee Smith. 1985. "Law Enforcement Coordinating Committees: One District's Experience." *FBI Law Enforcement Bulletin* 54(10):18–20.

First, Harry. 1990. *Business Crime: Cases and Materials.* Westbury, N.Y.: Foundation.

Fishman, Clifford S. 1983. "Wiretapping and Eavesdropping." In *Encyclopedia of Crime and Justice,* edited by Sanford H. Kadish. New York: Free Press.

Forst, Brian. 1990. Memorandum to William Geller and Norval Morris, April 11.

Fortune. 1934. "The Marines Are Coming" (August 10), pp. 56–63.

Fosdick, Raymond B. 1920. *American Police Systems.* Montclair, N.J.: Patterson Smith. (Reprinted 1969.)

Foster, Thomas W. 1989. "Implications of U.S. Border and Immigration Incidents for Federal and State Law Enforcement Agencies." *American Journal of Police* 8(2):93–122.

Frase, Richard S. 1980. "The Decision to File Federal Criminal Charges: A Quantitative Study of Prosecutorial Discretion." *University of Chicago Law Review* 47:246.

Friel, Charles M. 1990. "Intergovernmental Relations: Correctional Policy and the Great American Shell Game." In *Criminal Justice in the 1990's: The Future of Information Management: Proceedings of a BJS/SEARCH Conference,* edited by Bureau of Justice Statistics. Washington, D.C.: U.S. Department of Justice, Bureau of Justice Statistics, April.

Friel, Frank, and John Guinther. 1990. *Breaking the Mob.* New York: McGraw-Hill.

Geller, William A. 1985. "Introduction to Part 8: Whither Professionalism?" In *Police Leadership in America: Crisis and Opportunity,* edited by William A. Geller. New York: Praeger.

————. 1991. "Preface." In *Local Government Police Management* (golden anniversary edition), edited by William A. Geller. Washington, D.C.: International City Management Association.

Geller, William A., and Michael Scott. 1992. *Deadly Force: What We Know—a Practitioner's Desk Reference on Police-involved Shootings in the United States.* Washington, D.C.: Police Executive Research Forum.

Giuliani, Rudolph W. 1987. "Legal Remedies for Attacking Organized Crime." In *Major Issues in Organized Crime Control: A Compendium of Papers Prepared by Experts in the Field,* edited by Herbert Edelhertz. Washington, D.C.: U.S. Government Printing Office.

Godfrey, E. Drexel, and Don R. Harris. 1971. *Basic Elements of Intelligence.* Washington, D.C.: U.S. Government Printing Office.

Goldsmith, Michael, and William Lenck. 1990. *Asset Forfeiture: Protection of Third-Party Rights.* Washington, D.C.: U.S. Department of Justice, Bureau of Justice Assistance and Police Executive Research Forum.

Goldstein, Herman. 1990. *Problem-oriented Policing.* New York: McGraw-Hill.

Goldstock, Ronald. 1987. "Operational Issues in Organized Crime Control." In *Major Issues in Organized Crime Control: A Compendium of Papers Prepared by Experts in the Field,* edited by Herbert Edelhertz. Washington, D.C.: U.S. Government Printing Office.

Gordon, Diana R. 1990. "Someone to Watch over Me." *Criminal Justice* 5(1):7–46.

Gorman, John. 1991. "Street Crimes Involving Guns to be Federal Cases." *Chicago Tribune* (April 11), sec. 2, p. 6.

Gosseaux, Joseph S., and Daniel J. Curran. 1988. "The Team Approach to Curtailing White-Collar Crime." *Police Chief* 55(8):60–68.

Gray, Thomas C. 1983. "Crime Prevention: Police Role." In *Encyclopedia of Crime and Justice,* edited by Sanford H. Kadish. New York: Free Press.

Gruber, Charles. 1990. Personal communication by William A. Geller with the president of the International Association of Chiefs of Police and then–chief of police for Shreveport, Louisiana, February 23.

Gruber, Charles, Gerald Mechling, and Glenn Pierce. 1991. "Information and Law Enforcement." In *Local Government Police Management* (golden anniversary edition), edited by William A. Geller. Washington, D.C.: International City Management Association.

Guyot, Dorothy, and Kai Martensen. 1991. "The Government Setting." In *Local Government Police Management* (golden anniversary edition), edited by William A. Geller. Washington, D.C.: International City Managament Association.

Hannon, Mark. 1991. Personal communication by William A. Geller with Public Information Officer Hannon of the Drug Enforcement Administration's New York City Field Division, May 13.

Hausner, Jack, Barbara Mullin, Amy Moorer, and Brian Forst. 1982. "The Investigation and Prosecution of Concurrent Jurisdiction Offenses: Executive Summary." Report prepared for the Office of Legal Policy, U.S. Department of Justice. Washington, D.C.: Institute for Law and Social Research, January.

Hoover, J. Edgar. 1934. "Detection and Apprehension." In *Attorney General's Conference on Crime,* edited by U.S. Department of Justice. Washington, D.C.: U.S. Department of Justice.

Hudnik, John K. 1984. *Federal Aid to Criminal Justice: Rhetoric, Results, Lessons.* Washington, D.C.: National Criminal Justice Association.

Hughes, William. 1989. "What Can be Done to Stop the Crips and Bloods Advance across the United States? National Coordination Needed." *Crime Control Digest* 23(49):3–7.

Illinois Association for Criminal Justice. 1929. *Illinois Crime Survey.* Chicago:

Illinois Association for Criminal Justice and Chicago Crime Commission. (Reprinted 1968. Montclair, N.J.: Patterson Smith.)

International Association of Chiefs of Police. 1989a. *Building Integrity and Reducing Drug Corruption in Police Departments.* Arlington, Va.: International Association of Chiefs of Police.

———. 1989b. "Section 6077 Prohibitions Dropped, Major Victory Declared for Law Enforcement." *IACP News* 3(12):1–4.

———. 1989c. "Legislative Alert: Joint Federal Task Force on Clandestine Labs Asks Input from IACP Membership." *IACP News* 3(6):4.

———. 1990. "Dedication Ceremony at FLETC Artesia Facility." *IACP News* 4(3):6.

———. 1991. "IACP Addresses Police Brutality Concerns: 'Project Response' Underway." *Police Chief* 58(5):10.

Joost, Robert H. 1986. "Simplifying Federal Criminal Laws." *Pepperdine Law Review* 14:1–38.

Kaplan, Carol G. 1990. "In the Beginning: A Review of Federal/State Information Law and Policies." In *Criminal Justice in the 1990's: The Future of Information Management: Proceedings of a BJS/SEARCH Conference,* edited by Bureau of Justice Statistics. Washington, D.C.: U.S. Department of Justice, Bureau of Justice Statistics, April.

Karchmer, Clifford, and John E. Eck. 1991. "Local Drug Control." In *Local Government Police Management* (golden anniversary edition), edited by William A. Geller. Washington, D.C.: International City Management Association.

Kelley, Clarence M. 1975. "Mutual Cooperation in the Fight against Organized Crime." *Police Chief* 42(2):24–26.

Kelling, George L. 1991. "Crime and Metaphor: Toward a New Concept of Policing." *New York: The City Journal* 1(5):65–72.

Kelling, George L., and James K. Stewart. 1991. "The Evolution of Contemporary Policing." In *Local Government Police Management* (golden anniversary edition), edited by William A. Geller. Washington, D.C.: International City Management Association.

Kelling, George L., Robert Wasserman, and Hubert Williams. 1988. "Police Accountability and Community Policing." No. 7 in the *Perspectives on Policing* series, published jointly by the National Institute of Justice, U.S. Department of Justice, Washington, D.C., and the Kennedy School of Government, Harvard University, Cambridge, Mass.

Kifner, John. 1990. "New York Readies Mandela Welcome." *New York Times* (June 20), p. A12.

Klockars, Carl. 1990. Personal communication by William A. Geller with University of Delaware at Newark criminal justice Professor Klockars, April 12.

Labaton, Stephen. 1990. "DNA Fingerprinting Is Facing Showdown at an Ohio Hearing." *New York Times* (June 22), pp. A1, B10.

Lane, Roger. In this volume. "Urban Police and Crime in the Nineteenth Century."

Law Enforcement News. 1989. "DOJ Looks to Scrap OC Units." (April 15), p. 3.

————. 1990. "The Year in Review." (January 31), p. 5.

Layton, Lawrence B., and Robert G. Lowery, Sr. 1989. "Investigative Cooperation St. Louis Style." *FBI Law Enforcement Bulletin* 58(5):3–6.

Lesce, Tony. 1989. "Between Small Agencies Cooperation Is the Key." *Law and Order* 37(6):26–31.

Levi, Edward. 1976. "Department of Justice Guidelines—Four Critical Areas." *Judges Journal* 15:5.

Lupsha, Peter. 1990. Personal communication by William A. Geller with University of New Mexico organized crime specialist, January 3.

————. 1991. "Organized Crime." In *Local Government Police Management* (golden anniversary edition), edited by William A. Geller. Washington, D.C.: International City Management Association.

McCown, Lee C. 1988. "What Will Be the Extent of Drug Related Corruption within California Law Enforcement by the Year 2000?" California Law Enforcement Command College, Commission on Peace Officer Standards and Training, Independent Study Project, Paper No. 6-0099. Sacramento: California Commission on Peace Officer Standards and Training.

McEwen, J. Thomas. 1989. *Dedicated Computer Crime Units*. Washington, D.C.: U.S. Department of Justice, National Institute of Justice.

McKee, Monte. 1991. Personal communication by William A. Geller with staff member McKee in the FBI's National Crime Information Center User Services unit, May 13.

Mackenzie, Richard. 1991. "Borderline Victories on Drug War's Front Line." *Insight Magazine* (January 14), pp. 8–17.

Maguire, Kathleen, and Timothy J. Flanagan, eds. 1991. *Sourcebook of Criminal Justice Statistics—1990*. Washington, D.C.: U.S. Department of Justice, Bureau of Justice Statistics.

Major City Chief Administrators, National Executive Institute Associates, Federal Bureau of Investigation. 1991. *Use of Unauthorized Force by Law Enforcement Personnel: Problems and Solutions*. Quantico, Va.: Federal Bureau of Investigation.

Markoff, John. 1990. "Drive to Counter Computer Crime Aims at Invaders: Legitimate Users Voice Worries over Rights." *New York Times* (June 3), pp. A1, A21.

Martens, Frederick. 1987. "The Intelligence Function." In *Major Issues in Organized Crime Control: A Compendium of Papers Prepared by Experts in the Field*, edited by Herbert Edelhertz. Washington, D.C.: U.S. Government Printing Office.

Marx, Gary T. 1983. "Police: Undercover Tactics." In *Encyclopedia of Crime and Justice*, edited by Sanford H. Kadish. New York: Free Press.

————. 1988. *Undercover: Police Surveillance in America*. Berkeley and Los Angeles: University of California Press.

Mastrofski, Stephen D. 1989. "Police Agency Consolidation: Lessons from a Case Study." In *Police Practice in the '90s: Key Management Issues*, edited by James J. Fyfe. Washington, D.C.: International City Management Association.

Mastrofski, Stephen D., and Robert C. Wadman. 1991. "Personnel and Agency Performance Measurement." In *Local Government Police Management* (golden anniversary edition), edited by William A. Geller. Washington, D.C.: International City Management Association.

Meese, Edwin, III. 1991. "Community Policing and the Police Officer." Paper prepared for the Executive Session on Policing, Harvard University, John F. Kennedy School of Government, Program in Criminal Justice Policy and Management, February 28.

Michelson, Richard S. 1990. "The POSTRAC System: A High-Tech Computer System for Police and Sheriff's Academies." *Law and Order* 38(3): 55–58.

Middle Atlantic/Great Lakes Organized Crime Law Enforcement Network (MAGLOCLEN). 1989. *MAGLOCLEN 1989 Annual Report*. West Trenton, N.J.: MAGLOCLEN.

Miller, Wilbur R. 1983. "Cops and Bobbies, 1830–1870." In *Thinking about Police—Contemporary Readings*, edited by Carl B. Klockars. New York: McGraw-Hill.

———. 1989. "The Revenue: Federal Law Enforcement in the Mountain South, 1870–1900." *Journal of Southern History* 55:195–216.

Millspaugh, Arthur C. 1937. *Crime Control by the National Government*. Washington, D.C.: Brookings Institution.

Monkkonen, Eric. In this volume. "History of Urban Police."

Moore, Mark H. 1987. "Organized Crime as a Business Enterprise." In *Major Issues in Organized Crime Control: A Compendium of Papers Prepared by Experts in the Field*, edited by Herbert Edelhertz. Washington, D.C.: U.S. Government Printing Office.

———. 1990. Personal communication by the authors with Mark H. Moore, Daniel and Florence Guggenheim Professor of Criminal Justice Policy and Management, Harvard University, Kennedy School of Government, April 12.

———. 1991. "Police Accountability and the Measurement of Police Performance." Working paper written for the Harvard Executive Session on Policing, Cambridge, Mass., December 5–7.

———. In this volume. "Problem-solving and Community Policing."

Morgan, Richard E. 1983. "Federal Bureau of Investigation: History." In *Encyclopedia of Crime and Justice*, edited by Sanford H. Kadish. New York: Free Press.

Morris, Stanley E. 1989a. Personal communication by William A. Geller with the deputy director for supply reduction of the Office of National Drug Control Policy, who previously headed the U.S. Marshals Service, November 30.

———. 1989b. "The Importance of Cooperative Enforcement Programs." *Police Chief* 56(11):11.

Murphy, Patrick V. 1989. "Foreword." In *Character and Cops: Ethics in Policing*, by Edwin J. Delattre. Washington, D.C.: American Enterprise Institute for Public Policy.

Murphy, Patrick V., and Gerald Caplan. 1991. "Fostering Integrity in Police Agencies." In *Local Government Police Management* (golden anniversary edition), edited by William A. Geller. Washington, D.C.: International City Management Association.

Nagel, Ilene H. 1990. "Structuring Sentencing Discretion: The New Federal Sentencing Guidelines." *Journal of Criminal Law and Criminology* 80:883–943.

National Advisory Commission on Criminal Justice Standards and Goals. 1973. *Task Force on Police Report.* Washington, D.C.: U.S. Government Printing Office.

National Commission on Reform of the Federal Criminal Law. 1971. *Final Report.* Washington, D.C.: U.S. Government Printing Office.

National Directory of Law Enforcement Administrators, Correctional Institutions and Related Agencies, 1989. 1989. Stevens Point, Wis.: National Police Chiefs and Sheriffs Information Bureau.

National Organization of Black Law Enforcement Executives. 1991. *Hate Crime: A Police Perspective.* Washington, D.C.: National Organization of Black Law Enforcement Executives.

Nemecek, David F. 1990. "NCIC 2000: Technology Adds a New Weapon to Law Enforcement's Arsenal." *Police Chief* 57(4):30–33.

New Jersey Department of Law and Public Safety. 1975. *New Jersey State Police Intelligence Manual.* West Trenton, N.J.: Department of Law and Public Safety.

New York Times. 1990. "Boston Journal: Neighbors' Nuisance Locked Up (So Is Spy)" (May 28), p. A7.

———. 1991. "Ex-U.S. Drug Agent Is Guilty in Narcotics Conspiracy Case." (national ed.) (April 17), p. A9.

O'Connell, Richard J. 1990. "Once Again, Sportsfans, We Look at What Next Year Will Bring—Crash and Burn, So Far. . . ." *Crime Control Digest* 24(7):1.

O'Connell, Rick. 1990*a*. "FinCEN: Treasury Inaugurates Financial Crime Intelligence Anti-Drug Network System." *Crime Control Digest* 24(21):2–3.

———. 1990*b*. "Budgetary Woes: NCIC 2000 Ready to be Built, but FBI Doesn't Have the $17 Million Needed—New System Would Provide Instant Photo, Fingerprint IDs." *Crime Control Digest* 24(23):1–6.

Office of the Federal Register, National Archives and Records Administration. 1990. *United States Government Manual, 1990/1991.* Washington, D.C.: U.S. Government Printing Office.

Office of National Drug Control Policy. 1990. *National Drug Control Strategy* (January). Washington, D.C.: U.S. Government Printing Office.

———. 1991. *National Drug Control Strategy* (February). Washington, D.C.: U.S. Government Printing Office.

President's Commission on Law Enforcement and Administration of Justice. 1967. *Task Force Report: The Police.* Washington, D.C.: U.S. Government Printing Office.

———. 1968. *The Challenge of Crime in a Free Society.* New York: Avon.

Recktehwald, William. 1990. "City Police Ranks Hit 20-Year Low." *Chicago Tribune* (February 25), pp. 1, 8.

Reiss, Albert J., Jr. 1990. Personal communication by William A. Geller with William Graham Sumner Professor of Sociology, Yale University, April 12.

———. 1991. "What Is 'R & D' Really?" In *Local Government Police Management* (golden anniversary edition), edited by William A. Geller. Washington, D.C.: International City Management Association.

Revell, Oliver B. 1990. Personal communication by William A. Geller with the then–associate director for investigations of the FBI, January 27.

Rinkevich, Charles F. 1990. "Foreword." In *Catalog of State and Local Law Enforcement Training Presented by Federal Agencies*. 8th ed. Glynco, Ga.: U.S. Department of the Treasury, Federal Law Enforcement Training Center.

———. 1991*a*. Correspondence to William A. Geller from the director of the Federal Law Enforcement Training Center, February 15.

———. 1991*b*. "The Experiment Called FLETC." Photocopy. Glynco, Ga.: U.S. Department of Treasury, Federal Law Enforcement Training Center.

Rogers, Richard H. 1990. "FLETC's Law Enforcement Training Partnership." *Police Chief* 58(11):30

Rosen, Marie Simonetti. 1989. "James W. Greenleaf: Assistant Director in Charge of the [FBI] Training Division." *Law Enforcement News* (April 15), pp. 9–14.

Rosenbaum, Dennis, Eusevio Hernandez, and Sylvester Daughtry, Jr. 1991. "Crime Prevention, Fear Reduction, and the Community." In *Local Government Police Management* (golden anniversary edition), edited by William A. Geller. Washington, D.C.: International City Management Association.

Ruff, Charles F. C. 1977. "Federal Prosecution of Local Corruption: A Case Study in the Making of Law Enforcement Policy." *Georgetown Law Journal* 65:1171–1228.

Schwartz, Herman. 1969. "The Legitimization of Electronic Eavesdropping: The Politics of 'Law and Order.'" *Michigan Law Review* 67:455–510.

———. 1977. *Taps, Bugs, and Fooling the People*. New York: Field Foundation.

Schwartz, Louis. 1977. "Reform of the Federal Criminal Laws: Issues, Tactics, and Prospects." *Law and Contemporary Problems* 41:1.

Scott, Elsie. 1991. "Bias Crimes." In *Local Government Police Management* (golden anniversary edition), edited by William A. Geller. Washington, D.C.: International City Management Association.

Seagle, William. 1934. "The National Police." *Harpers* 169(November):751–61.

Sessions, William S. 1989*a*. "Violent Criminal Apprehension Program: Essential Link to Joint Investigations." *Police Chief* 56(6):10.

———. 1989*b*. "The FBI's Strategic Information Operations Center." *Police Chief* 56(12):10.

———. 1991. Personal communication by William A. Geller with staff in the office of FBI Director William S. Sessions, May 6.

Shenon, Philip. 1990. "Border Screening against Criminals Is Seen as Flawed." *New York Times* (May 10), pp. A1, A14.

Slahor, Stephanie. 1989. "Triple Eye (III): A Resource Worth Using." *Law and Order* (October), pp. 85–86.

———. 1990. "Leading the World's Largest Force." *Law and Order* (April), pp. 51–54.

Special Committee on Criminal Justice in a Free Society of the American Bar Association Criminal Justice Section. 1988. *Criminal Justice in Crisis: A Report to the American People and the American Bar on Criminal Justice in the United States—Some Myths, Some Realities, and Some Questions for the Future*. Washington, D.C.: American Bar Association.

Stern, Robert L. 1973. "The Commerce Clause Revisited: The Federalization of Intrastate Crime." *Arizona Law Review* 15:271–85.

Stewart, Robert, and Gayle Fisher-Stewart. 1991. "Managing Diversity." In *Local Government Police Management* (golden anniversary edition), edited by William A. Geller. Washington, D.C.: International City Management Association.

Stier, Edwin H., and Peter R. Richards. 1987. "Strategic Decision Making in Organized Crime Control." In *Major Issues in Organized Crime Control: A Compendium of Papers Prepared by Experts in the Field*, edited by Herbert Edelhertz. Washington, D.C.: U.S. Government Printing Office.

Stoll, Clifford. 1989. *The Cuckoo's Egg*. New York: Doubleday.

Tauber, James. 1991. Personal communication by William Geller with program analyst James Tauber, Statistical Analysis Unit, Planning and Evaluations, Drug Enforcement Administration, Washington, D.C., May 9.

Terjesen, Robert. 1991. Personal communication by William A. Geller with the assistant inspector general for investigations, U.S. Department of State, May 13, 16.

Thomas, Pierce, and Michael York. 1991. "Area's Gun Store Thefts Soar with Demand for Firepower." *Washington Post* (May 23), pp. A1, A14, A15.

Thornburgh, Richard L. 1976. "Reconciling Effective Federal Prosecution and the Fifth Amendment." *Journal of Criminal Law and Criminology* 67:155.

———. 1988. "The FBI National Academy—a Symbol of Excellence." *Police Chief* 55(11):10.

Torres, Donald A. 1985. *Handbook of Federal Police and Investigative Agencies*. Westport, Conn.: Greenwood.

Trojanowicz, Robert. 1989. Draft program announcement for April 1990 "Drugs and Community Policing" Conference at Michigan State University (photocopy).

———. 1991. "Community Policing and Accountability: A Proactive Solution to Police Brutality." Working paper written for the Harvard Executive Session on Policing, Cambridge, Mass., December 5–7.

Trojanowicz, Robert, and Bonnie Bucqueroux. 1990. *Community Policing: A Contemporary Perspective*. Cincinnati: Anderson.

Ungar, Sanford. 1975. *The FBI*. Boston: Little, Brown.

U.S. General Accounting Office. 1977. *War on Organized Crime Faltering: Federal Strike Forces Not Getting the Job Done*. Report to the Congress by the comptroller general of the United States. Washington, D.C.: U.S. General Accounting Office.

———. 1981. *Stronger Federal Effort Needed in Fight against Organized Crime*. Report to the Congress by the comptroller general of the United States. Washington, D.C.: U.S. General Accounting Office.

———. 1985. *Coordination of Federal Drug Interdiction Efforts*. GGD-85-67. Report to the Congress by the comptroller general of the United States. Washington, D.C.: U.S. General Accounting Office.

———. 1989. *Organized Crime: Issues concerning Strike Forces*. Report to the Congress by the comptroller general of the United States. Washington, D.C.: U.S. Government Accounting Office.

U.S. Marshals Service. 1991. *The Director's Report: A Review of the U.S. Marshals Service in FY 1991*. Washington, D.C.: U.S. Department of Justice.

U.S. Senate Committee on Commerce, Subcommittee on Senate Resolution 74. 1933. *Crime and Crime Control*: 1–5. Washington, D.C. (cited in Douthit 1975, p. 329).

Vollmer, August. 1934. "Police Administration." In *Municipal Year Book, 1934*, edited by International City Managers Association. Washington, D.C.: International City Managers Association.

Wadman, Robert. 1990. Personal communication by William A. Geller with the then–chief of police of Aurora, Illinois, and former chief of Omaha, Nebraska, January 12.

Walker, Samuel. 1977. *A Critical History of Police Reform: The Emergence of Professionalism*. Lexington, Mass.: D.C. Heath.

———. 1985. "Setting the Standards: The Efforts and Impact of Blue-Ribbon Commissions on the Police." In *Police Leadership in America: Crisis and Opportunity*, edited by William A. Geller. New York: Praeger.

Walton, Kenneth P., and Patrick V. Murphy. 1981. "Joint FBI/NYPD Task Forces: A Study in Cooperation." *FBI Law Enforcement Bulletin* 50(11):20–23.

Wasserman, Robert, and Mark H. Moore. 1988. "Values in Policing." No. 8 in the *Perspectives on Policing* series, published jointly by the National Institute of Justice, Washington, D.C., and the Kennedy School of Government, Harvard University, Cambridge, Mass., November.

Wechsler, Herbert. 1937. "A Caveat on Crime Control." *Journal of Criminal Law and Criminology* 27:629–37.

Whitehead, D. 1956. *The FBI Story*. New York: Random House.

Wigmore, John H. 1933. "The National Menace of Organized Predatory Crime: How to Combat It." *Journal of Criminal Law and Criminology* 23:734.

Williams, Willie. 1991. "Today's Challenges Become Tomorrow's Success: Remarks to the 15th Annual Conference of the National Organization of Black Law Enforcement Executives." *Noble Actions Newsletter* (Fall), pp. 3–4.

Wines, Michael. 1991. "C.I.A. in Search of a Role: Webster Has Given Agency a Better Image But Successor Needs to Chart New Course." *New York Times* (May 9), pp. A1, A13.

Wisconsin News. 1929. "Federal Dry Chief Expects Slayers Named Today, Calls Chicago Police Killers of Gangmen: Call Civic Leaders in Grand Jury Quiz." (February 15), pp. 1–2.

Wright, Donald K. 1991. "The Cab Driver Killer and the Case of *Solorio v. United States*." *Law and Order* (May), pp. 73–74.

Zolbe, Paul. 1980. "The Uniform Crime Reporting Program: 50 Years of Progress." *FBI Law Enforcement Bulletin* 49(9):2–7.

Peter K. Manning

Information Technologies and the Police

ABSTRACT

The police have long hoped that technology would ease their most vexing problems. The most important recent innovations in technology involve computers and related software. The police are information dependent and rely on the public as a primary source of information; how the police obtain, process, encode, decode, and use information is critical to understanding their functions. There are at least three types of police *information* (primary, secondary, and tertiary), *intelligence* (prospective, retrospective, and applied), and *operational strategies* (preventive, prospective, and reactive), each of which interacts in a complex fashion with technology. These processes are importantly patterned by police work, especially the role of the patrol officer, and the occupational cultures of policing. Technology is embedded in social organization; it shapes organizations and is shaped by them.

The American urban police have long hoped that technology would enhance their status as professionals and ease the growing burdens of policing urban areas. The most influential early twentieth-century police reformers, August Vollmer, Bruce Smith, Harry Fosdick, and O. W. Wilson, held high hopes for police work (Ericson and Shearing 1986) and police management (Leonard 1938; Fuld 1971; Stead 1977) becoming more scientific. Since the first major technological innovation—the use of a telegraph by police and fire departments in Albany, New York, in 1877—each major innovation—including the tele-

Peter K. Manning is professor of sociology and psychiatry at Michigan State University. He thanks Albert Blumstein, David Bayley, Brian Forst, Steve Mastrofski, Craig Uchida, Oliver Revell, and James K. Stewart for comments on an earlier draft, and Albert J. Reiss, Jr., for discussions about the general problems addressed here.

type used by the Pennsylvania State Police in 1923, the one-way radio in Detroit in 1928, the two-way radio in Boston in 1934, the widespread use of the automobile in the 1930s, centralized call collection, and computer-assisted dispatching—has been envisioned as a solution to chronic, vexing policing problems (Kelling 1978). The President's Commission on Law Enforcement and Administration of Justice (1967) argued for improved police technology as a means of crime control, asserting that technology would reduce processing time, speed the police to crime scenes, and increase arrests. There was also a belief that such innovations might save money.[1]

The Law Enforcement Assistance Administration (LEAA) took these recommendations seriously, and by the early 1970s was funding computer-driven command and control systems and urging centralized communications. The present widespread use of computers in Britain and in this country is in large part a result of Home Office and federal funding and support, respectively (Hough 1980a).

These innovations produced significant changes. The two-way radio and the automobile vastly increased the capacity of the urban police to allocate resources and respond to citizens' calls. New technologies are stimulating new approaches to management (Goldstein 1990). Current and ongoing research suggests that information technologies, the most important and influential kinds of technology, have been constrained by the traditional structure of policing and by the traditional role of the officer.

Innovations in computing and related software technologies that appeared in the corporate world in the 1980s are now making their way into large police departments. A new wave of information technologies has the potential to shape policing well into the next century. The question is, How will this take place, and what facets of policing will it shape?

This essay seeks to identify foreseeable effects of interactions between police organizations, practices, and traditions and new information technologies and outlines the new technologies' potential assets and liabilities for transforming police work. One can then better ask what might be done to facilitate adaptation of these tools by the police,

---

[1] Policing costs taxpayers more than $20 billion a year (Moore and Trojanowicz 1988). Most police costs are relatively fixed: the cost per year of maintaining a patrol car 24 hours a day is estimated to be $500,000–700,000. About 90 percent of police budgets are devoted to salaries, pensions, and fringe benefits (Larson 1989, p. 28). Cost savings would be welcome.

and how their effectiveness might be evaluated in light of current practices and structures.

This essay assesses the role of information technology as used by American urban police forces, with some attention to federal agencies insofar as they cooperate and share technology with local forces. I have sought and reported systematic studies on information technology that report some assessment or evaluation component rather than rely on anecdotal reports from single police departments. Many technologies doubtless have capacity to solve more crime, provide better links to the public, and expand the analytic skills or managerial competence of police, but as they are still new and experimental, their current effects cannot easily be established.

Because my focus is on *information technologies*, I do not discuss many interesting and important technological changes of the last twenty years: *crime solving and evidential matters* such as the use of DNA typing, biochemical assay, automated computer data-base fingerprint matching, accident reconstruction, and traffic and arson analysis; *weapons and force innovations* such as the introduction of 9 mm and 10 mm semiautomatic weapons into police departments, the development of nonlethal weapons such as "stun guns," training in the martial arts, laser-guided weapons and night scopes, coercion and control techniques (disaster and crowd and riot-control training), and SWAT teams and tactics; *noncoercive persuasive techniques* such as mediation, rape counseling, and hostage negotiation; and a host of means of *enhancing the primary data-gathering capacity* of the police such as surveillance devices, miniaturized tape recording and transmitting machines, drug and alcohol testing kits, video cameras for recording traffic stops, and more systematic tools for crime-scene analysis and data storage and retrieval.[2]

Technology is an apparatus, or the means by which work is accomplished, and it may be material, logical, or social in its manifestations. Technology is embedded in social organization and has social meanings attributed to it; it changes organizations and occupations and is shaped by them. The focus here on information, its use, and processing requires that several important connections be drawn between information, the social organization of policing, the occupational culture of policing, and technology.

[2] I thank Steve Mastrofski for clarifying my thought on this and suggesting many of the items in the list.

Policing is a service occupation whose central "input" and basis for action is information. The central issue in police technology is the use, processing, and application of *information* and the meanings that are attributed to information as it is transformed within police organizations. Information is a critical feature of modern societies and is the essential and central feature of policing.[3]

Since the police are information dependent and must rely on the public as a primary source of information, the ways in which the police obtain, process, encode, decode, and use information are critical to understanding their mandate and function. Police gather diverse types of information and use it to different ends. They are guided by commonsense assumptions about their work, their core role, and the expectations of their publics. The police gather *primary* information or "raw data" that is then processed within policing for crime solving or closing the events to become *secondary* information. When processed twice, gathered, and formatted, it can move up the organization to become *tertiary* or "managerial" information. These forms of information and *intelligence* (information gathered for anticipated events, rather than gathered in response to an ongoing event) are realized and interact with police operational *strategies* (the allocation of resources to obtain a preventive, prospective, or reactive end).

These processes are embedded in and importantly patterned by police work and the occupational cultures of policing. Technology differentially shapes policing, altering the gamelike interactions between upper and middle management, low-level supervisors, and the lower participants (Crozier 1972). Although there is little question that the shape of policing will change in the next ten years, the precise roles that information technology will play in this transformation remain unclear.

Here is how this essay is organized. Section I introduces recent major technological innovations by police, with particular emphasis on information technology. Section II discusses police decision making and ways in which different kinds of information are obtained, re-

---

[3] Information has been seen as key to police operations (e.g., Willmer 1970) and to explanations of the number, nature, and quality of police "outputs." Virtually all such theories have assumed that the basis for police actions is information, and stated explanations for outcomes are based on this assumption (Skolnick 1966; Reiss and Bordua 1967; Wilson 1968; Black 1980). Information, however, is only as good as a theory that defines its meaning and use since only in perspective or context is a difference important (Rappaport 1971; Leaf 1972; Klapp 1978, 1986).

corded, processed, transmitted, and transformed within different components of police organizations. Section III examines traditional police strategies and interactions among strategies, organizational modes, and different forms of information. In Section IV the content of information in various organizational contexts and the forces that give it shape and meaning are examined. Sections V and VI, respectively, provide an overview of police adoption of new information technologies in recent decades and of evaluations of the effectiveness of new technologies. A brief conclusion is presented in Section VII.

I. Technology and the Police

Webster's Collegiate Dictionary (ninth ed.) defines *technology* as a technical language, an applied science, and a technical means for achieving a practical purpose. This glosses the concept by referring to technology as the totality of means employed to provide objects necessary for human sustenance and comfort.[4] Academics differ in their definitions of technology (Zey-Ferrell 1979; Pennings and Buitendam 1987). A working definition is required: technology can be defined as the means by which raw materials are converted into processed outputs (Winner 1977; Zey-Ferrell 1979, pp. 108 ff). This definition does not restrict "technology" to physical objects yet can accommodate the limiting physical properties of any technology.

Technologies have potential as *sign vehicles*, sources of expressed or given-off meaning (Goffman 1959). In a seminal review of the interrelations of technology and work organization, Barley (1988, p. 47) cautions that, "as one moves away from the 'man-machine' interface to higher levels of analysis, it becomes increasingly untenable to claim that a technology's ramifications are reducible to its physical properties." Technology is not only a physical and material matter, it takes on intersubjective meaning, consequence, purpose, use, impact, direction, or social significance in social and organizational contexts in which collective lines of action are articulated. The symbolization of technology is a social fact that constrains its use and application (Barley 1983, 1986; Perrow 1983).

Technologies, especially the subtle interpersonal decision-making techniques of service occupations such as police, are mutable and am-

---

[4] Several important historical studies of technology and organization suggest the need for careful consideration of the development of technology and its relationship to organizational strategies, e.g., see Chandler (1962) and Stinchcombe (1990).

biguous not only because they are displayed in the context of encounters with the public but also because they are encoded and decoded by the informal rules and principles shaping the occupation's cultures.

A. Police Functions and History

Given this framework, it is essential to place technology in the context of the social organization of the Anglo-American police. Histories of the Anglo-American police (Hart 1951; Radzinowicz 1968–75; Miller 1977) suggest that the general organizational *form* of policing, and perhaps the primary set of tasks of the police officer, has remained remarkably stable for over 160 years in spite of massive changes in the external political environment (Bayley 1985).

This stability is in no small part due to the lack of fit between many technological innovations and the central mandate and tasks of policing (Wilson 1968; Manning 1977, 1980a, 1980b, 1988; Hough 1980a). Analytic features of the *police role* are important to this stability. Although policing has gained and lost clusters of tasks, most of the core tasks assigned to policing since the early nineteenth century have endured, and those that have been lost have not altered its central preoccupations with maintaining order in the interests of those with authority and power and with the management of civility. The *core technology* of the police is situated decision making with the potential for application of violence (Bittner 1990). This is face-to-face work unmediated by technology, even if enhanced by it.

Police organizations differ markedly from other organizations in several important ways that amplify their conservative tendencies (Reiss, in this volume). Police organization is a traditional form of work organization, legitimated in part by charisma and in part by rational bureaucratic authority, and it is closely associated with the central values of society and legitimate authority (Reiss and Bordua 1966). It seeks to manage or decouple from its external environment (Weick 1979) rather than control it, and it is deeply resistant to rapid and overt change. The traditional organization of work and the command bureaucracy have insulated officers from job insecurity, political forces, and to some degree from public accountability and have fostered the characteristic occupational cultures of urban policing in Anglo-American societies. The irony perhaps is that as the police have become the leading edge of the mass-produced service delivery system, officers in cars have lost the capacity to act in the sensitive personalized fashion that is at the core of the role. Police organizations possess and hold in reserve slack resources, primarily personnel (Thompson 1967), that can be mobilized in emergencies, thus altering the number of sources of information (Bordua and Reiss 1967; Reiss and Bordua 1967). Because managing uncertainty is critical to social control, the police concentrate personnel and technology at the bottom of a very flat hierarchy, "on the streets," and in the communications center where messages are received from citizens, screened, and passed on as work assignments to officers. The formal structure of incentives within urban police departments, which rewards those who make arrests and appear in court (they are paid overtime in many departments for court appearances), perpetuates the belief that the work is fraught with danger and risk. Changes in beliefs about the nature and kinds of events requiring attention, and events themselves, can quickly alter the number of officers "on the street."

The evolution of police has shaped their penchant for certain kinds of technologies. Police evolved during the nineteenth century from Sir Robert Peel's reactive principles of policing (Miller 1977), in which police maintain a sustained presence and availability, to attempting proactive styles in which police use investigative and active responses to crime (Klockars 1984). The late twentieth century has witnessed active police involvement and penetration into private relations and events. The police have begun themselves to define, even in advance, what and who requires control (Marx 1988; Sherman, in this volume). Police now believe that they are expected to intervene before or simultaneously with an event, or to create the conditions under which the probability of crime is highly likely, and the probability of apprehension of the offender is high. They have widened their concerns, a subtle but significant expansion of their legal mandate, with little change in their political accountability or skills.

Since the police reform movement of the 1930s (Reppetto 1978), American police departments have become increasingly technologically oriented with respect to their management of citizen demands for service and are faced with a growing number of citizen calls for service. The combination of police dependence on citizen information and police preference to control the dispersal of services and to control corruption creates an ongoing tension (Lipsky 1980; Manning 1989, chap. 1). This tension is one of the primary dramatic themes animating policing in this century.

The radio, the patrol vehicle, and, recently, the computer have fostered the idea that technology will free police of the burdens of directly managing the messy human condition. The problems of concern to policing have until recently, however, been narrowly defined as acute, ahistorical, almost randomly generated events (Goldstein 1990). This reactive "corporate strategy" (Moore, in this volume) increases police work loads and affords little capacity for police to manage their work load above the level of the streets.

B. Claims Made for Information Technology

A series of claims has been made for the information technologies adopted by the police. The relevant 1970s innovations included computer-assisted dispatch (CAD), management information systems (MIS), centralized call collection using three-digit phone numbers ("911"), and centralized integrated dispatching of police, fire, and medical services for large metropolitan areas.

Requests for computers were based on the premise that communications technology will simplify calling for emergency services, facilitate increased "service," lighten work loads, increase potential for rapid response to citizens' calls, and ultimately reduce crime. Other recent innovations included management-oriented attempts to control or routinize patrol and detective work (e.g., to order and rank requests for service and use solvability factors to reduce the caseloads in detective work) or to manage caseloads generally; a few were relevant to crime solution such as the emerging forensic techniques (DNA typing, computer-based fingerprint matching, and elaborate drug testing technologies). It was assumed or explicitly claimed that these technologies enhance efficiency, conserve resources, and mark an advance over high-cost labor-intensive policing (Larson 1989). These goals are now driving a second round of expensive innovations (Boston's computer system cost $20 million in 1985; Detroit's cost $21 million in 1989). Community policing, also partly a reaction to mobilized patrol and the management of demand by computerized dispatch and reactive policing, encourages a wider kind of engagement with "communities" and is based on decentralized information gathering, analysis, and application (Trojanowicz and Buqueroux 1989; Goldstein 1990).

II. Police Decision Making

In order to understand how information technology interacts with police organization, the core technology of the police, situated decision making, must be understood in the context of the social organization of policing. Police decisions and tasks shape definitions, expectations, and uses of technology; decision making, in turn, both shapes the environment and is shaped by it (Reiss, in this volume).

A. Police Decision Making in Organizational Context

Rational decision making based on rules and precedents is a characteristic of modern bureaucratic organizations. Rational decision making incorporates evaluations of facts and values with organizational principles and procedures. Routines are established and standardization is produced. Police officers, however, are charged with the initial, and often unreviewed, responsibility for committing the organization to action. Police are event driven in large part, but this is not simply a function of modern technology.

The events encountered by police shape their decisions and the ways in which information is received. Police-relevant events are sporadic and uncertain in appearance, duration, extent, and potential. It is possible to predict that 100 robberies will take place in a given city in a year, but precise times, perpetrators, property losses, injuries to victims, and political responses cannot be predicted. Situations that are unknown and uncertain may include danger and may be considered "risky." The police possess no general theory of policing that enables them to predict events and to justify fully and rationalize their practices. Thus, the police use a *situational rationality* that takes into account the particular times and places of events, rather than a set of firm rules, regulations, or laws.

Six features of police decision making affect and shape the form of information acquisition and the nature of responses to technology in Anglo-American police organizations. The first feature is that police decisions are extremely consequential for the individuals who are the subject of decision. A second is that police officers screen people and events for further processing; that is, their decisions differentiate between people, leading to either a decision to do nothing or a decision to proceed further. Screening, based on discretion, enables police to manage justice and to conserve organizational resources (Reiss 1974). Third, police decisions, like decisions made in other parts of the criminal justice system (Reiss 1974), involve both case and policy-oriented (precedent-setting) decisions. Fourth, police decision making is variably visible. Most police decisions are virtually invisible or of low visibility (Goldstein 1960). Case decisions—private, immediate, particularistic, and made in reactively mobilized circumstances—are visible to the extent that they occur in the presence of a suspect, a victim, or complainant, while policy decisions are collective, abstract, considered, and taken in private. Fifth, when compared with other kinds of legal decisions, police decision making is marked by great complexity and heterogeneity. The conduct subject to police control varies widely from trivial misconduct to major violations of criminal law. The perceived gravity or triviality of an act or event influences law enforcement judgments. Sixth, a choice to act is followed by the question of how to act (Bayley and Bittner 1985; Bayley and Garofalo 1989). Police can arrest, choose to do nothing, or give advice, warn, threaten, or formally caution. They may refer people to other agencies or, in domestic disputes, engage in social mediation or arbitration (Goldstein 1990, pp. 8–9, 104–14).

The core technology of police, their decision making, is fundamental, not easily altered, and multiply determined, and it is the mode of decision making that determines what information is available to other officers. "Street decisions" are the source of most of the information that the organization knows (and knows it knows) and is in some cases stored in official files and data banks.

B. The Role of Information in Police Organization

Information and meaning differ. *Information takes on meaning through organizational actions.* Information is a difference that makes a difference (Bateson 1972, pp. 201–27), while meaning refers to alterations in the functioning or orientation of actors from among information bits or attributions. Constraints on information gathering include information sources, types of information, degrees of differentiation of organizational units in information terms, message movement and meaning, and horizontal transformations of information (Manning 1980a, 1980b, 1989). These constraints set the stage for an analysis of how changes in information technology might change the meaning of police actions.

1. *Sources of Information.* Sources of information shape meaning. They, either public or police based, are of primary importance. The four principal types of information sources are the general public, organizations and alarm systems, other police sources, and external elites (Manning 1988). The bulk of information arises from the general public (Reiss 1971; Goldstein 1990, pp. 8–10). The general public's propensity to call is constrained by willingness to report generally, social conditions determining access to phones, the number of phones per capita, propensities to use them, and the nature of the event being reported (Spelman and Brown 1981). Citizen-originated information is

least trusted, most diverse, and most severely screened and evaluated at the "front end" of the police organization by operators and dispatchers. The overall aim of police communication systems, given the social conditions that pattern calls, is to reduce the potential overload from citizens' calls (Manning 1989). Internal police business constitutes a very large proportion of the total police information load. Alarm system calls, over 90 percent of which are false, remain an important work-load factor and potential source of information. Little is known about elite influences or communication patterns with police management.

2. *Types of Information.*   Information received (and worked on) by the police can be divided into three types. These reflect two features of policing that constrain message movement and information technology: the social location of the message within the functional divisions of policing and the format within which it is cast. Functional divisions organize information for use and, thus, change its meaning and give it different potential for predicting the future (Stinchcombe 1990). Format changes, especially from individual officers' memories to records or written (or computer-based) files, alter the official capacity of the organization to know what it knows and are fundamental changes in the management potential of information.

Primary information is what first comes to police attention or has been processed by a single unit. An example is the material a patrol officer writes in a car log about a response to a call for service. If he or she talks about this with another officer, even a detective, this remains primary information until it has been altered or transformed in its format and moves location within the organization. Primary information dominates all but a few police functions. Units such as patrol and traffic are most dependent on citizen-derived information and provide the greatest amount of "new information" as a result of their stops, enquiries, and observations and any encounters which they initiate on their own. According to various sources, around 86 percent of police work load, a rough index of information, arises from citizen calls (Reiss 1971, p. 11). Other functional divisions of the police receive less primary information than does patrol. The difference in amount is unknown since records are not kept on the calls made to detective, vice, or juvenile units unless the call results in an investigation (see, e.g., Manning 1980*a*; and Ericson 1981, p. 84, table 3.2).

Secondary information has been once (or more) processed by any two units within the police and has changed in location as well as its format.

An example is the movement of a crime report from a patrol officer to the detective bureau. This information changes its location and format. If a detective works on verbal information provided by a patrol officer, it remains primary information because it is being processed from the organization's official point of view *and* it has not changed format. Variations in this theme become quite complex. Information having made one loop, such as between patrol and detective work and back, is secondary information once processed. Such loops could in theory be endless, producing multiply processed secondary information. Secondary information is present in all functional areas of policing, both staff and line, but it is concentrated in juvenile, vice, and detective work since a large proportion of such casework is based on information received and passed on from patrol or traffic. Previously encoded information (put in police classification or format) is used in internal affairs divisions, although some original or primary information is also gathered.

Tertiary information has been processed by any two functional units and has changed format at least once. Once information has changed formats more than once, and location more than once, it remains processed tertiary information. For example, information processed by a single unit, sent to a second, and on to a third, such as information moving from a patrol division to a detective division, on to internal affairs and back to patrol, would remain tertiary information once processed by internal affairs, although now located in a patrol division. Information cannot, given this perspective, regress in form. Tertiary information is the domain of police management (sergeants and above). Police administration exercises authority based on tertiary information that has been twice processed by the units it claims or is intended to be guiding, commanding, and controlling.

3. *Information Is Differentiated by Focus in the Organization.* The amount of information that exists in and across the units in police organizations varies in part because units differ in their definition of the *focal point* of their work. If the unit's focus or mandate is clear (and enunciated and accentuated by leadership and supervision), then the degree of differentiation of the total information possessed will be low: redundancy will prevail. By contrast, if a unit has little focus, or is given a general brief or assignment, for example, to prevent crime, or to improve community relations, the total information set is likely to be highly differentiated. This implies, of course, that within broad divisional distinctions, given units could be more or less focused. To

some degree, a focus on core knowledge can be created by setting explicit operational strategies—by use of targeting in narcotics units, directed patrol in the patrol division, or specific objectives in community policing.

4. *Dependency among Officers and the Uncertainty of Information.* From an information perspective, externally derived information is linked most closely to tasks and demands arising in the external environment. This is a rough index of uncertainty and degree of dependency on sources of information that are not controlled by the police unit in receipt of the information, but by external social networks. A correlate is that the more tied the officers are to external information, the more dependent they are on their colleagues.

Patrol units are most closely tied to the unpredictable inputs flowing indirectly and directly from the environment. Patrol officers make cases and assemble facts for further processing. They experience varying amounts of uncertainty, depending on the nature of the encounter. In the circumstance of an arrest, case and outcome are the same, but in other circumstances, the outcomes are unknown until review of the case by a sergeant is complete or until further investigative work is undertaken. The traffic unit shares many of these characteristics with patrol. Traffic officers are sometimes housed in a separate unit with separate dispatching and assignment functions, but both traffic and patrol officers screen, with the operators and dispatchers, the external environment. Both are dependent on each other for close teamwork.

The juvenile and detective divisions are less environment dependent than are the patrol and traffic segments and somewhat more autonomous in processing information. These divisions are dependent on information passed on to them by patrol, but through their well-refined procedures for screening, typifying, and selectively investigating and clearing cases, they are able to reduce their dependence (Waegel 1981). Specialized units work with once-processed information that is reduced in complexity (and randomness) by case management and formatting.

Narcotics and vice divisions are less dependent than patrol, juvenile, and detective divisions on external calls or on patrol-produced data because a substantial minority of their information comes from their own efforts, or those of their informants. These divisions create their cases and, thus, produce the facts relevant to further investigative work. They experience the least uncertainty among line units and the greatest capacity to control the facts and outcomes of their work among line units. (They are often placed in the staff side of organizational charts and report in theory to a deputy chief.) Although vice units operate for the most part as individual entrepreneurs (Manning 1980*a*), in respect to their ability to generate original data, they most resemble internal affairs and research-and-planning divisions.

Administrators appear to be loosely coupled to the public at large and to the lower levels of the organization. They rely on primary and secondary information produced and forwarded through channels by patrol and other units and create some unique refined management, personnel, planning, and budgetary knowledge. Although they possess some general, abstract, and synthesized information, the amount of unrefined raw data is small. The capacity further to synthesize, reduce, and order information for decision making lies with administration.

5. *Vertical Transformations of Meaning.* As messages move, the information content decreases, and meaning is transformed (MacKay 1969). This takes place as messages move from "bottom" to "top," and across and through the organization within the police communications system (PCS).[5] Consider the transformations that occur. First, little information moves from the "bottom" to the "top," assuming that information enters the organization at the bottom as a result of citizens' calls or the related activities of patrol officers. Patrol officers respond to events on their own and are also obligated to respond in some fashion to messages relayed by dispatchers from the public. The limited upward flow of information from the street to middle and top managers results from several things. Managers often dislike use of other than normal channels for reporting of events and find communication outside of ordinary channels time consuming (see Goldstein [1990], p. 75, for a rare contrary example of exceptional and creative reporting of a problem). Lower levels of the organization systematically conceal "bad news." There is a general preference not to "rock the boat" (Van Maanen 1975). The inspectorial model gives lower participants the task of scanning the environment and shaping the review and management functions of those at the top (Reiss 1983; Jackall 1988; Manning 1989;

---

[5] The "vertical" locus of information may create conflict. For example, potential conflict exists between the information that officers encounter on the ground or over the radio and the direction and guidance that administrators seek to provide and want to be seen to be providing. Administrators are seen by others as "paper pushers" and irrelevant to police work. Their doubts about information arise from interpreting and interpolating the interpretations already made by officers engaged in case-based police work. Because the work does not require immediate decisions and derives primarily from within the organization, police managers experience decision problems analogous to those encountered by middle management in business (Lawrence and Lorsch 1969; Jackall 1988).

Hawkins and Manning 1991). Most of this information is briefly stored, resides in the memories of officers dispersed in time and space, has no uniform format, and can therefore rarely be retrieved.

Second, when information enters at the middle or top of the organization, it is typically relevant to management or internal staff functions and takes the form of internal affairs reports, investigation of complaints, and supervisory questions. It generally moves only up.

Third, when information enters the organization at the top, coming from city councils, mayors or city managers, or elite members of communities, or as complaints against officers, it is usually in the form either of correspondence or conversation. By tradition complaints against officers directed to top or middle management must be seen to have been responded to (whether they are investigated is another matter). This represents one of the most important sources of management's knowledge about officers' performance. Reports of officers' malfeasance are important symbolic indications of command (Wilson 1968). Questions of compliance with command authority, setting of organizational policy, and changes in the office of chief raise important issues and problems but have been little studied by social scientists (see Reiner, in this volume). There have been no studies of elite communications, and it is not reasonable to speculate either about their content or their flow within the organization. Little is known about how and why information flows "down the line" in police departments (see, however, Mastrofski and Ritti [1991] on management of drunk driving laws).

6. *Horizontal Transformations of Meaning.* When a message moves from the external world of the citizen to the police world, it crosses both symbolic and concrete boundaries and exits through those boundaries when it is transmitted to a unit for response.

The communications systems of most urban police departments include three roles or segments: operators, dispatchers, and officers (Manning 1988, fig. 2.1). As a call from a member of the public moves from the operators' segment where calls are answered and interpreted and entered into the computer, it is formatted and classified into the logic of the police system of categories (which include a number, a priority, and a set of information bits relative to the subsequent management of the message). It changes channel from telephone to computer, is transformed from voice to computer file, screened, and acted on as a potential call for action and becomes, metaphorically at least, police property. In the dispatchers' segment, it is also modified by the technology of radio and computer, by the interpretive work that the dispatcher must provide to make sense of the brief incident passed on from the operator, by the roles and tasks he or she must perform to process the message, and by the police classification system (in this segment and that of the officers, informal priorities are set by the occupational culture). Officers, the third segment, use the communications technology available, normally a two-way FM radio and a hand-held set, interpret the meaning of the message within the occupational culture, act within the limits of their discretion, and provide their own rules of thumb about the meaning of the assignment they have been given. Officers act in terms of their own assessment of the calls within the context and field of their current work and understandings and are given license to act as they understand is needed (Bittner 1970).

The same point can be made about information movement across units as well. If a detective receives information from another officer about his impressions of a series of burglaries, he will evaluate the meaning of the information based on his personal confidence in the officer; if the information comes from a crime analysis unit showing patterns of burglaries on a given street, it is horizontally transformed in a way that collapses sender, message, and channel and alters the confidence question radically. Officers will have more trust in the direct, idiosyncratic information given them by a fellow officer than in the more systematic, reliable, and generalizable information issued by the crime analysis unit.

Information thus has different meaning depending on its organizational context. Technology works differentially on information by source, type, differentiation in focus in an organizational segment or division in the force, the dependency of officers on externally derived information, and its location in a vertical or horizontal flow. However, as long as the power and authority to make decisions remains with the patrol officer, the most significant organizational questions lie in examining the use and response of patrol officers to this technology.

III. Police Operational Strategies and Intelligence

Anglo-American urban police organization results from traditional practices and the differential capacity of the police to know or selectively encounter information (Reiss 1974, 1983, 1984; Langworthy 1986; Slovak 1986). This organizational mode, together with the form and content of decision making and information flow, in turn shapes interactions between information processing and police operational strategies.

A. Strategies

Anglo-American police use rhetorical or presentational strategies to persuade or shape public opinion or to defend or expand their mandate and their operational strategies. An *operational strategy* deploys officers and other resources in time and space and includes consideration of the number of assigned officers at a given position and the distribution of positions.

Anglo-American police use three operational strategies: *reactive*, *proactive*, and *preventive* (Reiss 1971; Manning and Van Maanen 1977, p. 144). Response to events following passive receipt of calls for service, or taking action independently, is termed reactive strategy. When the officer creates the conditions of crime, or solicits or creates the crime, the strategy is termed proactive. Actions on the part of the police to alter, prevent, or intervene in advance of situations are preventive. Police primarily act reactively; this is shown by concentration of personnel in the communications center and the deployment of 90 percent of police resources to patrol. These historically patterned strategies interact and are not mutually exclusive.[6] These three operational strategies are in turn related to police intelligence functions.

B. Intelligence

Police intelligence, or systematized, classified, and analyzed information that has been encoded in police-relevant categories, takes three forms. *Prospective* intelligence is information gathered in advance of a crime or problem on the basis of identifying selected targets and working out some socially grounded "theory" or understanding of the nature, appearance, and frequency of the phenomena to be controlled. An example is the career criminal targeting strategy of the Washington, D.C., police evaluated by Sherman and Martin (1986; see also Sherman, in this volume). Little of such evidence is systematically collected in a form that might be considered "prospective intelligence."

Retrospective intelligence is information that accrues in the normal course of police work; for example, in arrest records, traffic violations, and outstanding warrants. After a robbery or burglary in which suspects are in hand, information may be sought on previous activities for the purpose of investigation or to gather supporting data. Gathering relevant data related to a given offense may be difficult. Although any

---

[6] Correlates of these operational strategies are the time at which intervention is meant to occur, the aim of that intervention, the place or role of the agent in the intervention, the relationship of the agent to the public, and the relevant information technology (Manning and Van Maanen 1977, p. 144).

police department is awash with files, records, evidence, and paper, there is no central "meta-information system" for storing, retrieving, or cross-referencing these diverse data. Use is dependent on an individual officer's good memory, shrewd judgment, and patience.[7] No system articulates, for example, detective cases, juvenile records, vice-narcotics units' files (e.g., nicknames, modus operandi, informants, current or past cases), departmental arrest records, current or past charges, police dispatch tapes, phone message files, and intelligence files.

Applied police intelligence is relevant once evidence on suspects is present. Applied intelligence is used or sought to link previously named suspects with known deeds. Use of applied intelligence may require analytically processed data such as forensic materials and the inferential work of linking suspects to time, place, opportunity, motive, and the like. The creative use of applied intelligence is the basis for great detective films, but it is surprisingly lacking in everyday police work (Greenwood, Chaiken, and Petersilia 1977; Sanders 1977; Ericson 1981).

C. Strategies and Intelligence

The operational strategies of the police at least arguably drive their data collection and analysis (Goldstein 1990). The strategies interact with intelligence needs and shape the sorts of intelligence information that is developed and maintained. Knowing the nature of police, then, allows one to understand the relative degree of development and use of various types of intelligence; the uses of that intelligence could not be predicted by reference to the a priori value of a given type of information. The following discussion is organized by the strategies that drive police conceptions of needed information. Beliefs shape usage: what is believed to be required information shapes police uses of information technology.

When the police employ *preventive strategies*, they require considerable intelligence bearing on the past and potential criminal behavior of individuals or groups. This will mean gathering and analyzing both

[7] Available evidence suggests that most officers do not possess this rich knowledge, in part because they do not seek it; in part because they are not trained to do so; in part because they are not systematically rewarded for being active, observant, and interested; and in part because they rarely—at least in large cities—have the opportunity to spend a great deal of time in the same area, with the same partner, during the same period of the day (Mastrofski 1983).

prospective and retrospective intelligence. However, such intelligence information is often considered tangential to the tacit and unspecified aims of policing. As a result, units that carry out prospective intelligence functions, such as police community relations and crime prevention units, are perceived as having low status and being marginal and ancillary to traditional crime-stopping patrol-based policing (Norris 1979; Radelet 1986). These units function without sustained resources and administrative support or are given very uneven and uncertain resources, thus ensuring that they will be unable to develop and achieve long-term goals, sustain close training and supervision, and maintain a consistent programmatic direction. Little, if any, prospective intelligence is gathered by community relations and crime prevention officers because they possess no focus or theoretical conception of the nature and causes of crime (or, conversely, of social order), and the type of information needed is therefore not defined.

As this intelligence function is more clearly defined and linked to outcomes and rewards, officers' appreciation of the value of this sort of information may be changing (Eck and Spelman 1987). The community policing program developed by Trojanowicz and others is an elaboration and modification of this preventive strategy (Kelling 1988; Moore and Trojanowicz 1988; Moore, Trojanowicz, and Kelling 1988; Kelling and Stewart 1989). Although crime prevention units provide no new primary information, there is promise that they might now be capable, with computer graphics and very large data banks, of performing productive analyses.

When using *proactive strategies*, police in theory rely on prospective intelligence that allows them to predict or plan for events. However, police organizations, on the whole, do not produce long-term plans. This has been changing, and the rise of "sting operations" is certainly suggestive of trends in the development of proactive strategies. Even when police organizations develop such plans, most fail sufficiently to constrain agents' choices by developing and applying organizational rules and procedures concerning the control of money, evidence, informants, and warrants or to expand agents' horizons of choice beyond gathering and immediately acting on readily available and obvious information (Manning 1980a). Information is gathered in an ad hoc manner and stored without much concern for retrieval. In other words, absent close supervision and guidance and organizational controls on the allocation of resources to cases, individual officers will determine the modes of working cases. Left to their own devices, without training or rewards to do so, officers will rarely use expert systems, network analysis, or modeling of drug markets.

Reactive strategies create and arise from retrospective intelligence. Some applied intelligence may be used when the incident is subject to checks via automatic criminal histories, motor vehicle records, and outstanding warrants. Clearly, in the absence of changes in policy or command, the dominance of reactive strategies and retrospective intelligence means that each officer creates his or her data bank or intelligence capacity and operates autonomously.

D. Strategies, Intelligence, and Technology

Any form of information technology will interact with strategies and intelligence functions. Both prospective and preventive strategies can be assisted by information technologies. In the case of preventive strategies in which prospective and retrospective intelligence are used, technologies have great promise for data storage and retrieval and unused potential. Proactive strategies also will require prospective and retrospective intelligence, and such work could be well served by targeting. Clearly, network analysis and computer technology are essential for larger projects involving mapping of members of a drug-dealing group or pornography ring (see Jacoby, Ratledge, and Allen 1988). Little attempt is made to use information in a predictive, preventive, or evaluative fashion (Rheinier et al. 1979), although new computer software programs are increasingly available for this purpose.

The most important strategic use of information technologies is in association with reactive strategies. Reactive strategies use applied intelligence and some retrospective intelligence gathered through informants, confessions, admissions to previously known crimes, or detectives' interviews of suspects. Once a possible crime has been identified and the police have information as to its content, personnel, location, and consequences, both prospective and retrospective intelligence are used. Applied intelligence is clearly enhanced by the automated computerized matching of finger prints, for example. When using a reactive strategy, retrospective intelligence is the dominant mode. Since the purpose of information technology is to organize and systematize existing, accumulated, and stored data and to facilitate retrieval by creating workable formats, it fits well with reactive policing. Reactive policing produces raw statistics gathering: mapping and charting past crimes as to time, location, amount of property involved, and type of crime by district or perpetrator and by unit or persons responsible for investigation. Data on stolen vehicles, license plates, drivers' licenses, out-standing warrants, and criminal records are among the systematized types readily available. For situations where an officer intervenes and is indecisive about the status of the suspect with regard to arrest or detention, such computerized systems may assist decision making. They will provide the necessary information that will allow the police to hold and perhaps charge a person who might otherwise not be questioned or arrested and charged with a crime or violation. These arrests represent small, but important, increments for police depart-ments, and because officers trust these data and they produce visible, immediate, and concrete results, or "hits," they are much appreciated by officers. Traffic warrants, and drunk driving records, once comput-erized, can be used effectively in making arrests and in generating income for municipalities and have thus gained popularity in some cities.

When any one of these three types of operational strategy is used, an information technology that employs sophisticated data processing can contribute to applied intelligence. This is discussed further below.

IV. Information Use in the Police

The previous sections have laid out the constraints and opportunities on information and its *forms* in light of the social organization of polic-ing. Here, the focus shifts to questions of the *content* and use of police information given its form.

Any bit of information is only as good as its theory. Any data sit in a field of meaning or a set of relational forces that are ordered by a perspective, or way of looking. Police patrol officers use a common-sense theory of coherence between setting, actor, action, and agency or purpose. For example, a very clever Detroit officer has retrieved some 1,000 occupied stolen cars in his career (*Detroit Free Press* 1990) by noting anomalies in cars such as broken windows covered with cardboard or repainted old cars with damaged locks, each of which signals that a car may have been broken into, repainted, or the locks changed. These facts suggest that the setting contains incongruous elements. Others have described the use of the incongruity principle for officers on patrol (Sacks 1980). Similarly, a pattern of murders, or bank transactions, or phone calls cannot be indexes of social relations and networks without a theory that connects these data to a problem or a crime and, furthermore, cannot establish motive, opportunity, or intent. Thus, what might be called the commonsense theory of "police information," its acquisition, storage, and use, is a basis for understanding what data will be entered into and retrieved from computers.

Information in police departments can be best characterized as systematically decentralized. Often, primary data known to one officer are not available to other officers because of the personalized practices of data "storage." Most of the information that exists in policing is primary data possessed by aggregated records or files or the information stored mentally by an officer.

Some information is located in officers' case files, private notes, or log books. Only under certain specified conditions does it become universally understood, generally shared, reproducible knowledge held collectively by the records or institutional memory of the organization. The fragmented character of the knowledge possessed by officers is "designed" in part to protect officers from close day-to-day supervision, review, and discipline.

The organizationwide emphasis on the individual officer acting with discretion and judgment, working in a widely dispersed network of invisible colleagues, amplifies the asymmetrical aspects of information flow and processing. Policy flows downward, and yet most decisions and facts are gathered and remain at the officer and sergeant level. The basic and fundamental knowledge of policing is believed by many police to consist of the facts gathered on the scene that only the person there can understand fully and in depth. All essential police knowledge is thought to be contextual, substantive, detailed, concrete, temporally bounded, and particularistic and surrounded by tacit assumptions and meanings. It is believed that police officers should learn and know social life in precisely this detailed and grounded fashion.

Secrecy is emphasized. Often it is worthwhile for the officer to retain information for personal use. Information is rarely shared. There are few individual rewards for shared investigations, cooperation across divisions, or across police units (see Geller and Morris, in this volume).

Themes emphasized in the occupational culture determine what information is viewed as decision relevant. Themes such as individual autonomy and discretion, the craft character of police work, and the socialization pattern for young recruits (see Van Maanen and Schein 1979) add to this emphasis. Pressure to close incidents and return to service, that is, to be out of contact with anyone in need of assistance, also rewards action and not abstract analysis.

The craftlike and clinical definition of police work, as well as its exciting immediacy and the previously described features of police knowledge, are the basis for discrediting paperwork, files, and all forms of bureaucratically ordered information. Much information is entered on forms or transferred to central locations, such as "suspect files." This means that centralized information, of whatever quality, is often viewed as trivial. In fact, the most often stored and used data are of a "housekeeping" nature—payroll, absences, and personnel records. Little referral is done based on such information (Scott 1981).

Authority is personalized. Personalization of authority and information, when combined with secretive guarding of knowledge and an exaggerated emphasis on accomplishing work that terminates immediately and is closed without paperwork, means that police decisions on the street based on primary information are largely unreviewed and unreviewable.

Officers' practices screen and filter information entered into any record-keeping system, thus shaping primary data. This directly affects the amount, quality, validity, and reliability of processed secondary and tertiary data used to rationalize or account for management decisions (Hough 1980a; Manning 1980a, 1989). For example, an officer to whom an incident is assigned by a dispatcher has no obligation to provide a written record on the substance of decisions or of the event, only a formulaic filling in of the log in the car and a verbal report to the dispatcher. In Detroit, for example, officers do not have to say what was done or provide a named result of their decisions. In Boston, officers may call the outcome of their actions in response to an assignment "service rendered" (Peirce 1991). Many such incidents are record free: they neither produce records nor are their particulars recorded if a note is written. If recorded, the calls may be covered by written glosses such as, "all quiet on arrival," "no sign," "all in order (on arrival)," "area searched—no trace," "no trace on arrival," or "no police action required" (Meyer 1974; Ekblom and Heal 1982; Davis 1983). Officers and dispatchers frequently do not agree on the nature of the incident (Peirce, Spaar, and Briggs 1984), but changes in classification are not considered relevant to command and control. The ordering and integration of a layer of information considered command-and-control relevant or "operations relevant," is based on "street knowledge" and decision making, while leaving open the definition of what is relevant to officers on the ground.

Primary data, in raw and unintegrated form, are organized and stored in chunked and coded units in individual officers' memories. When (or because) data are full and rich, they are not entered into the computer in many cases, and when they are entered, they are often construed by those who use the system as trivial. Command officers distrust the system as well and rely instead on their memories, what has happened before in such situations, reports received from inspectors, and personal interviews conducted with those involved.

No formal administrative theory drives information gathering and analysis. Data gathering is shaped by a set of unexplicated common-sense assumptions about the nature of police work (Manning 1982). In an important sense, the quality of the data and an inability to specify in advance what information is needed (and the focus is always on the officer on the street, not the sergeant, shift commander, or chief) means that what is entered into computer records is a severely edited version of the primary reality encountered on the street by officers.

Even if entered, edited primary information must be converted in some fashion and placed within an analytic framework if it is to become useful secondary or tertiary information (Hough 1980a, p. 347). The "administrative model" of policing based on the rational gathering of information for purposes of crime control and ordering (Manning 1977) assumes data are entered validly and reliably; it does not describe the conditions under which primary information will be entered into the system. In short, currently constituted police information systems rarely meet administrative needs.

Information is not the ordering principle on which the existing hierarchy of police organizations is based. Control of officers and internal management are the ordering principles. As has been suggested, the vertical and horizontal processing of information is not based on a rational theory of control of crime rates or the clustering of activities in time or space, but on maintaining traditional patrol work loads by area and time of the day, and on maintaining internal management of the workers (Bittner 1970; Goldstein 1990).

Many of the above features of the occupational culture of policing have been examined elsewhere (Van Maanen 1974; Manning 1977, 1979, 1982, 1989; Mastrofski 1989). The preceding points and themes found in the occupational culture have important consequences for the quality and texture of information, its meaning, and its use. The culture shapes the nature of valued and disvalued information and patterns its flow through the organization. These themes are central to the resistance that police have shown to new information technologies and to the differential success of some other sorts.

V. Technological Innovations in Policing

The intrinsic uncertainty in police decision making, resting on judgment and commonsense reasoning, and difficulties in establishing goals and objectives in police work, mean that policing is difficult to evaluate using measures of "efficiency," "effectiveness," and productivity. It is not possible to evaluate interactions between technology and social organization and practices because little has been written about the practices, constraints, and opportunities associated with the use of new information technologies. Of course, it is not possible to conclude from poorly done evaluations that the technology is a failure, but poorly executed evaluations add to the difficulty in critical review of evidence. There are also confounding effects of implementation problems of the innovations and the integration of the new technologies with current practices.[8]

Since the role of police practice in patterning the use of information has been emphasized in this essay, it is perhaps best to discuss innovations in information technology in respect to the three types of information processed in police organizations. My goal in this section is to note the kinds of innovations reported and the kind of information they process.

A. Primary Information

Modifications in the processing of primary information have been the focus of most innovations in police communications systems. Included here are modifications in the input and throughput capacity of the PCS. These include call collection using a single central number such as 911; computer-assisted dispatching; techniques associated with CAD such as split patrol, call tracing, wider data access or "networking" through the use of the FBI's National Crime Information Center (NCIC); and computer-based linkages for the exchange of information between police departments (Tien and Colton 1979; Stevens 1989).

The following narrative is historical, and points out changing emphases in processing primary information. Although the first full-time

---

[8] Most of the systematic research suggests that the absence of training in new techniques, fear and resistance of officers, and ambivalence of sergeant ranks and above undercut the potential of these innovations. The rewards and supports given for using these techniques seem not well understood. The police are wedded to reactive strategies based on prospective and applied intelligence organized by a case focus, and there are few rewards for acting otherwise.

computer assisted dispatching was installed in the St. Louis police department in the 1960s, and central call collection and dispatching was introduced in Chicago shortly thereafter, it took many years for the innovation to spread. Computer assisted dispatching is restricted to large and middle-sized cities. By the early seventies, as a result of Law Enforcement Assistance Administration funding, a few large departments (New York, Detroit, and Chicago, among them) adopted CAD systems that automatically assigned the call to a beat and were used to relay the call now defined as an incident to dispatchers and then as a job for officers. These transformations are important because they represent changes in location, in roles and tasks, in technology employed, and in the interpretative work done on the message (Manning 1989).

Computer-assisted dispatching has been facilitated by rapid escalation in the use of three-digit (911) emergency systems and the integration of metropolitan services such as police, fire, and emergency medical services. Most large urban departments now collect and queue calls from the public using a computer, and use some form of computer-assisted dispatch. This system of recording and processing has evolved in the last twenty years or so, from systems that depended on an operator, usually a sworn officer, taking notes on the call and caller (name and address of the caller and the nature of the incident) by hand on a card or sheet of paper and relaying it on to a dispatcher or dispatching the call directly (Percy and Scott 1985; Manning 1989, chap. 3). The constraints that this produces vary from highly automated systems like those in Boston and Detroit, to mere "electronic conveyor belts" that simply pass the message through the system (Larson 1989, p. 28).

Computerized message processing aims to gather and store information (in retrievable formats) about the caller, the call (time of day, day of the week), the operator (identification number, time spent processing the incident), the incident (once accepted by the operator) and its routing, assignment, and disposal. It also serves to allocate screened calls to dispatchers responsible for a given area of the city, to record assignments and current work loads of officers, and to permit brief (a few weeks at most) storage of records on the mainframe. Most records are kept in hard copy for a few months and then discarded or put in semipermanent storage. In effect, the processing of these messages functions to screen, evaluate, and assign work to officers. The communications center operates with the notional authority of the chief; that is, once assigned, a job is viewed by command officers as something like a "command" to officers to act or investigate.

The first systematic evaluation of CAD and computerized functions in city government was undertaken in the mid-seventies by Larson and his associates (Colton 1978). Only two in ten systems that adopted integrated systems of centralized call collection were considered operational and successful in an evaluation in the late seventies (Chaiken et al. 1975). Four of five such systems reviewed by Colton and Herbert (1978) failed to achieve acceptance. It is consistently noted that the social context within which the system is installed determines the degree of "success" of the system even when success is defined modestly as functioning for more than five years and merely meeting design specifications (Colton and Herbert 1978).

Around 1980, some departments, among them Tampa-St. Petersburg, Florida, and Wichita, Kansas, developed the capacity to display on a screen the address of the phone from which a caller was calling. Larson (1989) terms this an "enhanced 911" system; eighty-nine of the 125 largest cities in the United States use enhanced 911, and some thirty-six states have or plan laws requiring this system. An enhanced system will allow checks of address and simplified data gathered from distressed callers who are often confused or anxious. Many callers hesitate or are flustered when police operators answer, as in Detroit: "Police, *where* is the problem?" This question and the subsequent algorithm of questioning forces the caller to slot emotional, personal, and cognitive bits into a preset (computer file-based) format (Manning 1989). The Detroit police computer was designed to permit the operator to gain access to a file only on entry of a valid address and is designed to have the operator elicit, one item at a time, a series of answers to complete the file so that it can be sent to the dispatcher. Some of the format-ordered questioning will be reduced by an enhanced system. It is possible using these systems for the operator on receipt of a call to pull up data on the screen for previous calls to the ten block area from which the current call came, features of those calls, and what, if any, police response was made or is being made. This technique is useful in identifying repeat calls about events such as floods, traffic accidents, or neighborhoodwide disputes that affect an area. It can reduce the ahistorical character of police response and could be an integrated aspect of community policing.

A few recurring problems arise in use of such systems. To be used effectively, these primary data must be processed and reduced analytically. Even enhanced 911 does not obviate the principal problem: it only records the *site from which the call was made*, not the location of the incident, or the caller's actual address. It may not assist in locating "hot spots" (see Sherman, Gartin, and Buerger 1989, pp. 34–36). A large proportion of calls for service come from public locations such as courts, city halls, and hospitals; these internal system-maintenance calls ("Taking a break"; "Have 7-92 call in"; "require radio mainte-nance") constitute between 33 and 58 percent of the work load of any 911 system (see Percy and Scott 1985, p. 78, table 5-5). A crime call is a rare event; 50 percent of all calls are screened out by operators (or refused service—around 10 percent in the Fort Worth Study done by Percy and Scott [1985], p. 67), terminated, lost, or referred (Bercal 1970; Percy and Scott 1985). Increasing the information system's ca-pacity and patrol officers' access to it appears to increase the volume of message transmission with no increase in effectiveness (Colton 1978, fig. 2-3). That information is available, or that the system has the capacity to store, retrieve, and analytically reduce data, does not mean that such operations are carried out, or used to reallocate personnel or effort, to alter strategies or tactics, or to describe ongoing operations (Manning 1989, chap. 8).

There was great interest in the seventies, in part because of the enthusiasm of Massachusetts Institute of Technology scientists for its potential, in the use of the hypercube or patrol car allocation model (PCAM) prescriptive decision models for queuing jobs, and dis-patching and assigning cars on the basis of work load, proximity, and time (Larson 1978). These models were not adopted, and their ostensi-ble merits remain untested (Larson 1972; Colton 1978; Colton, Bran-deau, and Tien 1979).

Most large forces have access to lists of outstanding warrants, miss-ing persons, criminalistics information, and FBI wanted lists. The rec-ords of state departments of motor vehicles are now accessible to virtu-ally all large urban departments and state police (Stevens 1989). The use of these information sources has grown steadily. These inquiries are considered by police officers as useful augmentation of their author-ity since they reduce time on the street with persons stopped, can lead to arrests and clearances, and relate directly to enhancement of the officers' crime control function (see Manning 1989, chap. 8).

The possibility of additional precision in classification and control of incidents led to a series of funded research projects. In the seventies, the LEAA sought to reallocate police time on the assumption that reduced response time enhances crime control effectiveness. Reduced response time does under certain circumstances minimally increase arrests and crime control (President's Commission on Law Enforcement and Administration of Justice 1967; Manning 1980*b*; Cordner, Greene, and Bynum 1983; Beick 1989). However, time expended in citizen decisions to call the police proved far greater than time spent by vehicles traveling to the scene (Spelman and Brown 1981). The differences resulting from citizen "delay," which varies closely with types of crime, city size, and population density, always exceeded police processing time. Citizen expectations were more important to their satisfaction with how police responded to incidents than was time lapsed between the call and arrival (Pate et al. 1976; Percy 1980). In terms of arrests or clearances of crime, the nature of the crime, the availability of witnesses, physical evidence, or a victim, and the propensity of citizens to report are always the principal constraints on successful police action (Greenwood, Chaiken, and Petersilia 1977).

Emphasis shifted to efforts to refine the nature of the information received and processed and to alter citizens' expectations of the nature and timing of police responses. The argument was made, though never proven, that careful and systematic call screening coupled with differential police responses (DPR) to different kinds of incidents would free resources to be used in other tasks and operations (Farmer, Sumrall, and Roberts 1979). Larson (1990) suggests that rapid response and community policing can be complementary since the time saved in crime-related actions by improved differential response can be used by officers to develop problem or incident analyses.

The suggestion that such changes in officers' activities would take place "naturally" overlooks patrol officers' control of the distribution of their time among assignments and their ability to patrol from 40–50 percent of the time on duty (Cordner 1979). Moreover, police are not rewarded for other than one-at-a-time servicing of calls for assistance. Based on research in four cities, Farmer, Sumrall, and Roberts (1979) argued that operators working with minimal information can rank potential calls by seriousness and inform callers that a car would come as soon as possible, or within an hour or so, or refer the call, or handle the call directly via phone. Replications of this study produced similar results (McEwen, Connors, and Cohen 1986; Worden 1989), without reductions in citizen satisfaction with police response. Other less systematic approaches to differential response have been tried. Detroit, for example, has assigned a single "garbage car" with city-wide duties to handle low priority calls like taking stolen car reports or verifying the return of missing persons.

Recent research involving a reformulation of primary information has focused on the relationship between spatial location, repeat calls, and police work (Sherman et al. 1987). The hypothesis is that calls for service can be reduced by locating and characterizing high-use areas of the city (defined as addresses from which a high rate of phone calls issue) and placing officers in such spots or having them focus patrol efforts there. This would reduce the work load of operators, dispatchers, and officers; allow officers to attend "serious calls"; save time not spent on "trivial calls"; and further focus officers' attention on "hot spots" of crime. Mapping calls geographically to target these areas has been suggested for drug control and general crime control (Sherman et al. 1987; Maltz and Dada 1990). These attempts to focus police efforts parallel promising, earlier "directed patrol" experiments in Delaware that attempted to set tasks for one-half a shift of officers and thus reduce random patrol and discretion (Tien and Colton 1979). Modified targeting of high-risk areas yielded some success in Oakland (Reiss 1985). These ideas are widely discussed but not yet widely adopted in urban policing.

Car locator and tracking systems (automatic vehicle locators [AVL] and transponders) have been suggested as a means to locate and monitor car location and movements and display them on a video map of the city. This is used in "a handful of cities" (Larson 1989, p. 30), and has been abandoned in others (Detroit, for example). In theory, AVL will allow dispatchers to assign the nearest car to a job by use of software that will calculate point-to-point travel times. Some forces use an automatic computer-based warning that blinks or buzzes at a dispatcher's terminal if a car exceeds a preprogrammed time to complete an assignment. Besides providing a means of worker control and surveillance, such systems are said to enhance officer protection since dispatchers will know if an officer is out of service too long. These systems were a disaster when first introduced in St. Louis in the late 1970s (Larson, Colton, and Larson 1976), in part because officers sabotaged them by "hiding" in areas where multiple radio waves collided with signals bouncing off buildings in ways that misled dispatchers. A warning system activated when an officer pushed a button to inform the dispatcher of potential danger was abandoned because it was unreliable and did not indicate the location of the car.

The most recent information innovations involve hardware. These include laptop computers combined with personal work stations, mobile digital computers in vehicles, and cellular telephones. Some large police departments, including Detroit and Dallas, use mobile miniterminals primarily for running records and warrants checks and for forwarding inquiries to NCIC and state motor vehicle departments (Stevens 1989). Laptop computers can reduce the need for paperwork and permit direct entry of data into the main frame of the police computer. (This is being tried experimentally at the time of this writing in one precinct in Los Angeles.)

Cellular telephones have substantial implications for management, especially in light of the assumption that sergeants and middle management "command and control" officers are on the ground. Cellular phone communications, although monitored for numbers called and frequency of use, may be beyond reach of computer monitors of the tape-recording systems used for other official radio-telephone transmissions. Although police often use public telephones, even to call the police station, cellular phones will bypass records monitoring by supervision.

The potential of cellular phones and laptop computers to augment proactive intelligence in community policing schemes seems great but has not been evaluated (Larson 1990). These technologies have potential because they are consistent with officers' abhorrence of paperwork and their wish to maintain secrecy and autonomy. Many officers believe that crime-related, computer-based information increases their crime-control effectiveness, and shortens transaction times, thus making miniterminals acceptable to them.

B. Secondary Information

A computer-based information system can provide analytically reduced and ordered data to inform modifications of police operations. Larson (1972) has claimed that the most exciting result of "computerization" will be the application of techniques to secondary and tertiary data to assist police management. Significant innovations in creation and use of secondary information include a broad set of software that affects police functions other than patrol or response to citizens' requests for services.

These include systems that identify solvability factors in cases and that prioritize cases in detective work based on the quality or quantity of the available evidence (Greenburg, Yu, and Lang 1973; Eck 1983) and integrated approaches to data processing and sharing such as team policing and the "Rochester model" of integrated investigation (Bloch and Bell 1976). They provide administrative tools for evaluations and for indirect supervision of detectives. Case management in most departments seems still to be handled by decentralized and personalized operations using paper records and files (Ward 1989), but Los Angeles County and other forces are sharing case files on selected crimes with other agencies (Kling, personal communication). Most crimes are solved at the scene or as a result of immediately available clues; improved secondary information makes current practices visible but neither alters nor transforms them (Ericson 1981, 1982; Waegel 1981). Improved screening of cases and use of solvability factors do not address some basic investigative issues. These include the quality of human relations in investigations and how to deal with politically difficult or important "big cases." These techniques do not alter the basic constraints on detectives (Greenwood, Chaiken, and Petersilia 1977).

There is much potential in "crime analysis" units that enable departments to map crime patterns onto beats, city blocks, or census tracts over time and combine them with data on crime methods or other data to create a detailed moral or crime-based cartography (Peirce 1988). These techniques have the potential to be mapped onto other sorts of social data and to create areal maps of what the Chicago school of sociology termed "social disorganization" (Baldwin 1979). Computer graphics and analytics with heuristics for investigation, including modeling and simulation, have been developed, but the results so far have been disappointing (Gay, Beall, and Bowers 1984). Rheinier et al. (1979), in an investigation of crime analysis techniques, found that these new techniques were rarely used. Neither were they used when made available in Strathclyde, Scotland (Hough 1980b). They still hold promise for reducing work loads and increasing the rate of clearance of crimes should they be widely adopted.

C. Tertiary Information

Tertiary information is rarely found in policing and, when available, is rarely used. Most management uses of information technology, other than for control of lower-level police, have been in administration (Stevens 1989); management information, records keeping, and internal management; routinizing work flow or process-control systems; and data storage and retrieval. Very few uses of information technology are analytic, strategic, or tactical. Management information systems potentially can include not only information about "housekeeping functions," but also information that facilitates planning, policy creation, resource allocation and reallocation, management, and intelligence.

The most sophisticated and complex information systems, based on applied artificial intelligence or "metaknowledge" (knowledge about knowledge), expert systems, and their variants, are seen by some as promising. Hernandez (1989), in a typically hopeful entry in the *Encyclopedia of Police Science*, suggests that artificial intelligence can be used to profile villains and networks of associates of criminals in drug cases but notes that no such systems were in use at the time of writing. The National Institute of Justice, however, is funding experimentation with a program entitled "Drug Market Analysis" in four sites—Kansas City, Hartford, Pittsburgh, and Jersey City—to develop computer information systems on drug crimes for use by narcotics officers, patrol officers, and detectives.

Expert systems, the modeling of decision preferences of experts and programmed means of building them into organizational practices, are also said to be promising (Ratledge with Jacoby 1989). An expert system for modeling the solution of residential burglaries is in place in Baltimore County and is being used experimentally in Tucson, Arizona, and Rochester, New York (Jacoby, Ratledge, and Allen 1988). Such techniques are likely to become more popular as police become better able to develop and implement proactive and preventive strategies.[9]

Networks for data sharing and access to information systems are restricted at present to vehicle registrations in state motor vehicle departments' records and computers and warrants and records checks through the FBI's NCIC (Stevens 1989); some western states are sharing fingerprint identification systems.

Evaluations of the application of computerization to forensic evidence and records (Turner 1989), of use of video technology in traffic control (Missonelle 1989), and of profiles and expert systems in the investigation of white-collar crime (Edelhertz and Stotland 1989) are not mentioned in key reviews of developments in this field. Emphasis is on current practices or the potential of selected information technologies.

Complex tasks involving secondary and tertiary information, especially involving investigative work, appear to have been little affected

---

[9] I am grateful to Craig Uchida of the National Institute of Justice for bringing these experimental studies to my attention.

by computer analytic data retrieval and process-control systems. Police investigative functions continue to be shaped by traditional practices. Presumably new information technologies are being used in at least some departments, but no written research evaluations of their effects are available.[10]

D. Why Technology Is Used as It Is

There has not been much research on police adoption and adaptation of information technology. Such research as exists is often inconclusive or suggests that new technologies have less effect on police practices than their proponents predict or prefer. Four fundamental factors shape the uses of information technology in policing.

Organization.   The sequencing of policing tasks is shaped more by organizational practices and contexts than by objective or uniform standards. Police organizations are highly segmented and geographically spread. Information gathering and use are case based and individually organized. Authority is personalized. Police functions (staff and line, investigation and patrol, officers and management) are highly segregated. Information is power and is retained and typically restricted in use to the immediate situation. People present diverse, changing, unpredictable behavior and are suffused with feelings; social events seen in need of control are uneven, unpredictable, discrete, and irregular in appearance. Police tasks are complex and nonstandardized; learning is apprenticeship style and enhances and amplifies the personal bases for policing styles (Van Maanen and Schein 1979; Fielding 1988). Choice and autonomy are valued and protected within the organization. Case-based situated decision making is not easily simulated or stored for retrieval (although expert systems make this increasingly possible). Police are often unwilling to monitor and systematize available data (see Sherman, Gartin, and Buerger 1989).

The traditional division of labor.   An interaction exists between information and the social organization of police work. Each functional unit in the police has tacit objectives and resources. Interactions exist between the type of information, the uses to which it is put and the means by which it is processed, stored, and retrieved. Primary information is used to obtain objectives for a functional unit, and those objectives shape how information is gathered, processed, and applied.

---

[10] I am grateful to Oliver Revell of the FBI for providing a list of the potentialities of computers for case management, fingerprint matching, and network analysis in the FBI.

Information flow and usage.   Information flows into police departments and is employed in operational strategies. Information is of little
importance in preventive strategies because the relevance of various
types of information is not specified, and there is no theory of causation
and efficiency that might determine what is to be gathered, stored,
and applied. Information is critical in proactive strategies, but is not
systematic, centralized, and theoretically applied, and is not guided by
computerized systems (in most police forces, data from detective work,
and cases and records from other secondary information sources such
as juveniles and vice records and files, are never entered in computer
records). Information is most used in reactive strategies where a suspect
is known, a crime is known to have been committed, and a prior record
exists on the suspect. The most important information is retrospective
intelligence, and is differentially useful to the police, given their strategies. Conversely, computer-based information is most relevant and
used in doing routine "housekeeping tasks," such as internal record
keeping, records of payroll, holidays and sick days taken, message
transfer, and data storage for retrieval for review.

Practices and routines.   Procedures and routines pattern the effects of
any new technology. Police users, who are typically both suspicious
of computers and ill-trained in their use, decide what information to
enter into the various systems and thereby determine their use. However, community policing may introduce new routines (Moore, in this
volume). Because community-based policing involves decentralized operations such as local ministations, offices in schools, and foot patrol,
tools such as cellular phones, minicomputers, and personal laptop computers may be extensively used by community-based officers.

VI. Impacts: Roles and Internal Changes in Police
Organizations

Technology threatens to change the balance of power within police
organizations and is a powerful source of organizational destabilization
or differentiation of police culture. The social roles of the police are
shaped by homogeneity in gender and skills. Only about 10 percent
of officers are female; members of various minority groups seldom
exceed 15 percent. Recent research suggests that social factors, such
as education, rank, shift, task differentiation, and crime-fighting orientation, are important divisions within police organizations (Jermeir et
al. 1991). Work takes place in a highly rank-conscious organization, in
which workers are subject to strong authority intended to maintain

control and punish errors. This leads to concealment and lies by officers, as is perhaps true of all organizations (Jackall 1988). Police organizations are stable and hierarchically ordered, command based, and dominated by lower-level participants. Management strives to maintain the external appearance of command and control. These sources of homogeneity and diversity are altered, at least potentially, by technology.

A. Role Changes

It is not clear exactly *how* technology and occupational culture shape information usage and "police outputs." Technology affects police work thorough loosely coupled relationships (Weick 1979; Manning 1989) within and between segments of the police organization and between police organizations and other organizations in the criminal justice system (see Reiss 1974). There is little task specialization in police roles, nor is there a base of highly differentiated knowledge. The impact of technology tends to be filtered and shaped by the social worlds in which it is resident (Barley 1988; Gash 1989).

The impacts of technology appear to vary with context. Social variables—*rank, skills and knowledge base, symbolic capital* (the resources based on deference and status held by the members of a segment in the organization [Bourdieu 1986]) *level of function, and focus of work*—organize the impacts of information technology on police organization.

1. *Rank.* Should police at the highest ranks choose to use new information technologies, they may enjoy increased capacity to govern and to monitor officers and to use sophisticated techniques (based on secondary and tertiary information) in proactive and preventive strategies. They will increase their skills and deepen their knowledge base and will be better able to control the allocation of resources and to administer systematic rather than ad hoc or crisis-driven policies. Some symbolic capital will be increased for higher-level segments of the police organization by association with the symbols and appearances of science and technology and the rationalization of scientific police work.

Police in lower-level segments are in danger of losing discretion and autonomy as on-line monitoring of their activities becomes more common and technological devices permit increased review of their actions and choices. Their skills should increase as they learn simple word processing and master some features of data retrieval as a result of use of laptop computers and remote or car miniterminals.

However, the lower segments within the police organization may lose less freedom if they master techniques for protecting their personal and occupational interests. They can do this in two ways. First, they can manipulate codes used to process information, creating and circumventing them by controlling the entry and quality of data; they can resist controls by refusing calls, remaining out of service, and otherwise controlling their work loads.

A second defensive strategy might be further expression of the lower participants' counterculture (Manning 1979). This could take the form of work stoppages and strikes or increased union strength and bargaining demands. Disaffection might be amplified by new technology, leading to alienation and feelings of powerlessness, withdrawal, and further loss of autonomy.

Actors in organizations can manipulate and circumvent rules and structures to achieve autonomy and power and can use uncertainty to their advantage (Crozier 1972). Cybernetic processes, those that provide information on current states to regulate or modify future states, are partial, limited, and often truncated by organizational structures in order to maintain organizational stability vis-à-vis the external environment (Weick 1979). This "feedback" has previously been based on trust (Cain 1973), and reduced trust will reduce feedback.

2. *Skill.* Some skilled work may be enhanced by new information technologies. Detective work will be increasingly computer based and information will become less personal and individualistic or investigator centered; the shared knowledge base should grow immensely. The question is how the technology will facilitate case management and whether the development of new police strategies will facilitate detective work. The trend toward community policing, for example, appears to de-emphasize the role of detectives by increasing the autonomy of officers to investigate their own cases and to substitute geographically based authority for casework based on organizationally differentiated patrol and investigative functions.

3. *Symbolic capital.* Prestige, deference, and power within police organizations resulting from technological innovation accrue in segments and in rank groups. It is not clear how these changes will play out. Research based on sample surveys of police organizations is much needed. Technology is patterned by the norms and values of the police occupational culture and by the contexts and locations for decision making. Studies that permit statistical controls for dimensions of police subcultures, relations between size of department, and social distance

between social worlds and ranks can be valuable for laying out the moral topography of police cultures (Worden and Mastrofski 1989; Jermeir et al. 1991).

4. *Level of function.* Technology in the police will have greater potential and impact for decision making and crime control strategies at middle and higher levels of police management and in detective work than in patrol. The data reduction and analysis function of computer technology will enhance and change the eroded power and role of police management. Their traditional functions of reviewing and internal supervision will be altered in the direction of more "management." Computers are very useful for storing, processing, and reducing secondary and tertiary information and in storing primary data from patrol.

5. *Focus of work.* Technology will have greater impact on crime-focused work than on order-maintaining work, on reactive rather than preventive or proactive crime-control strategies. Crime-focused work can mobilize public action and support by producing informants, evidence, witnesses, and the rewards of arrest and charge of offenders; preventive or proactive police work lack comparable indices of success.

Innovations in primary-information processing affect most telephone operators and dispatchers. Any alteration in the information-processing capacity of operators directly increases the work load of dispatchers and indirectly that of patrol officers. There is a certain irony in this. Officers believe that operators send everything down indiscriminately; operators and dispatchers fear being sanctioned for refusing to assign calls. Research data show that roughly 75 percent of calls are screened, referred, or terminated by operators without being forwarded to officers (Bercal 1970; Percy and Scott 1985; Manning 1989). Answering and screening, regardless of whether a unit is requested, sent, or arrives, expresses ritual and drama; any response heightens the significance of the police as information processors and maintains police discretion and autonomy (Manning 1982).

Information shapes police classification of incidents and the nature and quality of police response for a small set of "serious" calls. However, the decision about what is to be called "serious" is *dependent* on context and governed by noninformational aspects of message processing. In a study of police dispatchers in Michigan, Payne (1989) found that similar incidents—for example, "man with a gun"—were given as examples of "good" and "bad" dispatching. The operator's response was not determined by the name given the incident, but by good sense used in imagining the context and acting in accord with tacit understandings. Davis (1983) makes the same point that it was not possible to retrieve domestic violence incidents from the classifications given by operators, dispatchers, or officers; the event could have been classified under many official categories. In a Boston study, operators' classification of calls and officers' final classification differed substantially: calls classified originally by operators as serious crime were reduced in number by half to a third by officers after accepting the calls (Peirce, Spaar, and Briggs 1984, p. 39). Officers often use "sponge categories" such as "service rendered" or "investigation" to describe their activities on the scene. These two categories account for some 50 percent of all "clearances" used to report the result of an accepted job (Peirce, Spaar, and Briggs 1984, p. 41).

Those most affected by these innovations will be the traffic, detective, and juvenile divisions and their managers. Work loads should decrease and relevant data should be more likely to be stored and accessible.

B. Internal Reorganization

Changes in information-processing technology may change demands for information and alter the internal structure of policing by decentralizing command and control information and by increasing centralization of other modes of information storage and retrieval.

From an information-systems perspective, there will probably be a sharp initial rise in demand for information and an increase in transaction costs, followed by a gradual lowering of costs. There will initially be an increased potential for centralized monitoring, evaluation, and command and control, with a period of resistance followed by a new emergent equilibrium. This should come as centralized records become more common and better used in supervision and management. Work loads will be altered. Operators' work loads should rise as the use of centralized call collection (911) systems increases. There is some evidence that police work loads in large cities are increasing, due both to increased crime and to improved communications. The work load in patrol should be volatile for a considerable period of time, and work load variations should shift back and forth between dispatchers and officers. These work load consequences of widespread computerization are so closely joined that ironic consequences may result. If centralized call collection and dispatch are introduced, the number of calls to the police increases if other things remain constant (e.g., the number of private phones, the placement of public phones, and the number of police lines). Moreover, centralized call collection and dispatch increase the potential for screening and filtering false or malicious calls, repeat calls by the same caller, and calls made about the same problem by many callers (Manning 1989). Technological filtration and systematic selective control of demand will replace informal bases for demand control. The administrative component of the police should rise in proportion to the size of the organization (if predictions about the differentiation and division of labor within organizations hold for the police).

High technology and increased demand will influence decentralizing forces that are unleashed by laptop and in-car computers and cellular phones. These will be more widely used. Whether this will increase the discretionary powers of the line officer is not known. Record keeping, advanced planning, and evaluation will be easier.

VII. Conclusion

Technology in the workplace is molded and shaped by the environment, the organizational structure, and the occupational culture of policing more than they are shaped by technology. Police operational strategies shape the kinds of intelligence, or systematized information, needed and sought. The social organization of policing amplifies the asymmetrical nature of information flow in which information, mostly primary, concentrates at the "bottom" of the organization. This is because much of the information is personalized and low-level police have discretion about entering data into the management information system. Lower-level participants use the system to protect their interests and deny management access to much information that might be compromising, while higher management uses internal affairs and records for control and discipline purposes.

Innovations carried out in policing in the last thirty years have focused on primary information and on routinization and control of officer discretion. For example, studies of information technology in policing primarily illustrate managerial concerns such as increasing police operational efficiency (mainly "throughput" or reduced transaction costs; see Goldstein 1977; Manning 1980b). Innovations tend to cluster around modifications of communications machinery or control techniques that increase the organization's capacity to shape external demands for service, to identify needs, to monitor responses to incidents, and to adjust responses minimally—but rarely, if ever, to realign resources systematically on the basis of such aggregated and reduced data (Tien and Colton 1979, p. 325). These innovations refine management tools to shape work routines, control operators, dispatchers and patrol officers, and monitor these work tasks rather than transforming work to increase the skills of workers and to enhance the problem-solving capacity of police managers (see Markus 1984; Rule and Attewell 1989).

With the exception of differential response and directed patrol studies and some innovations in expert systems, the innovations are means for managing the environment rather than changing it. They do not focus on events, nor are they "crime focused" or "order-focused" in their intent. They have, for example, no known impact on crime (Manning 1980*b*). Perhaps because of the failure of the claims for technology made in the late seventies but disproven by evaluations, the latest round of innovations claim to increase the quality of policing service or to argue for a combination of enhanced 911 and community policing (Larson 1990).

Innovations in the processing of primary information such as computer-based dispatching, without changes in screening practices, supervision, allocation strategies (such as differential response), and changes in the level and kind of citizen demand, have little impact on what police do, although they modify the forms of how police do it. Innovations in the creation and use of secondary and tertiary information are unusual. Many of the management tools are driven by concern for efficiency and, except for those that shape and control demand, seem to have a brief life. The differential meaning and use of information in vice and detective work as opposed to patrol suggests that *technology* will be more likely to succeed in settings where primary information is used, policing is based on reactive strategies, and intelligence is applied or retrospective. Technological innovation provides symbolic capital for management, even if they do not use it, while technology, with some exceptions, is viewed as a source of loss of autonomy by the lower-level participants.

Some topics and consequences of information technology have not been studied. Research problems in policing are generally premised on a pragmatic, management-oriented, efficiency-tinged perspective that is little concerned with either public satisfaction or response or officer morale and social integration. No cost-effectiveness studies have been done of budgetary profit and loss as a result of innovations in information technology. Research on technology has focused narrowly on the managerial potential of the systems rather than on employee morale or performance, control or management of crime, or delivery of enhanced services that improve the quality of community life and citizens' satisfaction with policing. These matters have been predominantly the focus of community policing programs rather than of technologies.

The computer revolution in policing, fueled in part by federal encouragement and money, and in part a social construction of the media and the computer industry (Kling and Iacono 1989), has yet to take place. The optimistic claims of twenty years ago have not been realized. It is difficult to know the extent or adoption of new information technologies because the drift toward computerization of functions is probably moving more rapidly than the published reports reflect. However, shrinking urban budgets and tax bases suggest that the major changes in computer systems seen in the late seventies will not be widespread in the near future. It is more likely that changes will be modifications and enhancements of the ill-used current capacity and refinements of software and implementation sophistication.

The central assumption of these new technologies, behind the rhetoric of crime control and efficiency, is a belief in the centrality of information and rationality in guiding organizational actions. This takes several guises. First, it assumes incorrectly that the content of messages, files, cases, reports, and records is limited in meaning to its declarative informational content. Informational aspects of messages encoded by operators on computers for processing citizen demands for service are a small but significant determinant of patterns of message processing. Allocation and intervention decisions made by urban police with high-technology computer dispatching systems are governed primarily by conventional practices and interpretations, roles and tasks of organizational members, the classification system into which messages are cast, and other noninformational aspects of the message itself (Manning 1982).

Second, it assumes that the flow of information is the primary basis for organizational structure. The control and display of traditional forms of authority, issues of honor, respect, and dramatization of conventional values, and maintenance of differentiated stratification systems that contain them, lie at the heart of policing.

Third, it denies the active role of organization members in using, shaping, and subjectively constructing technology to maintain a dialectic between objective constraints and individual choices and between the conservative and controlling forces of the organization and their own autonomy. For example, police officers, like other industrial workers, control their output. Assignments handled come under workers' control of output as does any industrial production process and are shaped by shared and sanctioned peer practices governing number of calls handled, speed of response, and reporting return to service. These matters of work load are facets of police culture and vary from department to department.

Fourth, the vague notion that available, even conventionally acceptable, technology will be used and employed without constraint of police practices and local political traditions is naive and untenable. It denies the important role of ignorance and error and of unanticipated consequences of change. As the review of innovations suggests, human actions are not solely error producing and systems error or "glitch" free. Rather, the interactive features of informational systems and actors produce systems of ideology and belief that define and shape "error" (Perrow 1983; Markus 1984; Barley 1986).

All forms of information technology in the police have an indeterminate effect on the organizational structure of policing; technology is used to produce and reproduce traditional practices, yet is slowly modifying them (cf. Kling and Iacono 1989; Rule and Attewell 1989). The social cohesion of the organization and the relevant work groups shapes the uses of technology (Jackall 1988). Theories of social change based on technological advances preceding social changes have grasped a kernel of truth, but they have overlooked the symbolic aspects of technologically driven change. They have perhaps underestimated the ways in which technology is a ploy in games of power and control within organizations, a way of amplifying uncertainty, and a source of symbolic capital for management, independent of its usefulness in achieving stated public goals or objectives (Crozier 1972).

REFERENCES

Baldwin, John. 1979. "Ecological and Areal Studies in Great Britain and the United States." In *Crime and Justice: An Annual Review of Research*, vol. 1, edited by Norval Morris and Michael Tonry. Chicago: University of Chicago Press.
Barley, Stephen R. 1983. "Semiotics and the Study of Occupational and Organizational Cultures." *Administrative Science Quarterly* 28:383–413.

———. 1986. "Technology as an Occasion for Structuring." *Administrative Science Quarterly* 31:78–108.

———. 1988. "Technology, Power and the Social Organization of Work." In *Research in the Sociology of Organizations*, vol. 6, edited by S. Bardach. Greenwich, Conn.: JAI.

Bateson, Gregory. 1972. *Steps toward an Ecology of Mind*. New York: Ballantine.

Bayley, David. 1985. *Patterns of Policing*. New Brunswick, N.J.: Rutgers University Press.

Bayley, David, and Egon Bittner. 1985. "The Tactical Choices of Police Patrol Officers." *Journal of Criminal Justice* 14:329–48.

Bayley, David, and James Garofalo. 1989. "The Management of Violence by Police Patrol Officers." *Criminology* 27:1–25.

Beick, William. 1989. "Crime Analysis." In *Encyclopedia of Police Science*, edited by William G. Bailey. New York and London: Garland.

Bercal, T. 1970. "Calls for Police Assistance." *American Behavioral Scientist* 13:681–91.

Bittner, Egon. 1970. *The Functions of Police in Urban Society*. Bethesda, Md.: National Institute of Mental Health.

———. 1990. *Aspects of Police Work*. Boston: Northeastern University Press.

Black, D. 1980. *Manners and Customs of the Police*. New York: Academic Press.

Bloch, P., and J. Bell. 1976. *Managing Investigations: The Rochester System*. Washington, D.C.: Police Foundation.

Bordua, David, and Albert J. Reiss, Jr. 1967. "Law Enforcement." In *The Uses of Sociology*, edited by P. Lazarsfeld, W. Sewell, and H. Wilensky. New York: Basic.

Bourdieu, P. 1986. *Homo Academicus*. Cambridge, Mass.: Harvard University Press.

Cain, M. 1973. *Society and the Policeman's Role*. London: Routledge & Kegan Paul.

Chaiken, J., T. Crabill, L. Holliday, D. Jaquett, M. Lawless, and E. Quade. 1975. *Criminal Justice Models: An Overview*. Santa Monica, Calif.: RAND.

Chandler, Alvin. 1962. *Strategy and Structure*. Cambridge, Mass.: MIT Press.

Colton, Kent W., ed. 1978. *Police Computer Technology*. Lexington, Mass.: D. C. Heath.

Colton, Kent W., M. Brandeau, and J. Tien. 1979. *National Assessment of Police Command and Control Systems*. Cambridge, Mass.: Public Systems Evaluation.

Colton, Kent W., and S. Herbert. 1978. "Police Use and Acceptance of Advanced Development Techniques: Findings from Three Case Studies." In *Police Computer Technology*, edited by Kent W. Colton. Lexington, Mass.: D. C. Heath.

Cordner, G. W. 1979. "Police Workloads." Unpublished manuscript. East Lansing: Michigan State University, School of Criminal Justice.

Cordner, G. W., J. Greene, and T. Bynum. 1983. "The Sooner the Better: Some Effects of Police Response Time." In *Police at Work*, edited by R. R. Bennett. Beverly Hills, Calif.: Sage.

Crozier, Michael. 1972. "The Relationship between Micro and Macrosociology: A Study of Organizational Systems as an Empirical Approach to Problems of Macrosociology." *Human Relations* 25:239–51.

Davis, Stephen. 1983. "Restoring the Semblance of Order: Police Strategies in the Domestic Dispute." *Symbolic Interaction* 6:261–78.

Detroit Free Press. 1990. "Clever Cops" (editorial). (April 20).

Eck, John. 1983. *Solving Crimes.* Washington, D.C.: Police Executive Research Forum.

Eck, John, and William Spelman. 1987. *Problem-solving.* Washington, D.C.: Police Executive Research Forum.

Edelhertz, H., and E. Stotland. 1989. "White Collar Crime." In *Encyclopedia of Police Science,* edited by W. G. Bailey. New York and London: Garland.

Ekblom, P., and K. Heal. 1982. *The Police Response to Calls from the Public.* Home Office Research and Planning Unit Report no. 9. London: H.M. Stationery Office.

Ericson, Richard V. 1981. *Making Crime.* Toronto: Butterworths.

———. 1982. *Reproducing Order.* Toronto: University of Toronto Press.

Ericson, Richard V., and Clifford D. Shearing. 1986. "The Scientification of Police Work." In *The Knowledge Society,* edited by Gernot Bohme and Nico Stehr. Dordrecht and Boston: D. Reidel.

Farmer, M. T., R. D. Sumrall, and J. Roberts. 1979. *Differential Response Strategies.* Washington, D.C.: Police Executive Research Forum.

Fielding, Nigel. 1988. *Joining Forces.* London: Tavistock.

Fuld, Leonard. 1971. *Police Administration.* Montclair, N.J.: Patterson Smith.

Gash, Deborah. 1989. "Information Technology and the Redefinition of Organizational Roles." Unpublished manuscript. East Lansing: Michigan State University, School of Labor and Industrial Relations.

Gay, W., T. M. Beall, and W. Bowers. 1984. *A Four Site Assessment of the Integrated Criminal Apprehension Program.* Washington, D.C.: University Science Center.

Geller, William, and Norval Morris. In this volume. "Relations between Federal and Local Police."

Goffman, Erving. 1959. *The Presentation of Self in Everyday Life.* Garden City, N.Y.: Doubleday Anchor.

Goldstein, Herman. 1977. *Policing a Free Society.* Cambridge, Mass.: Ballinger.

———. 1990. *Problem-oriented Policing.* New York: McGraw-Hill.

Goldstein, J. 1960. "Police Discretion Not to Invoke the Criminal Process: Low Visibility Decisions in the Administration of Justice." *Yale Law Journal* 69:543–94.

Greenburg, B., O. S. Yu, and K. Lang. 1973. *Enhancement of the Investigative Function.* Springfield, Va.: National Technical Information Services.

Greenwood, P., J. Chaiken, and J. Petersilia. 1977. *The Criminal Investigation Process.* Lexington, Mass.: D.C. Heath.

Hart, Jennifer M. 1951. *The British Police.* London: Allen & Unwin.

Hawkins, Keith, and Peter K. Manning. 1991. *Legal Decision-making.* Oxford: Oxford University Press.

Hernandez, Armand P. 1989. "Artificial Intelligence." In *Encyclopedia of Police Science,* edited by William G. Bailey. New York and London: Garland.

394   Peter K. Manning

Hough, J. M. 1980a. "Managing with Less Technology." *British Journal of Criminology* 20:344–57.

————. 1980b. *Uniformed Police Work and Management Technology.* Home Office Research and Planning Unit Report no. 1. London: H.M. Stationery Office.

Jackall, Robert. 1988. *Moral Mazes.* New York: Oxford University Press.

Jacoby, J., E. Ratledge, and R. Allen. 1988. "Building an Expert System for the Baltimore County Police Department." Unpublished report. Washington, D.C.: Jefferson Institute for Justice Studies.

Jermeir, J. W., L. W. Fry, J. W. Slocum, Jr., and J. Gaines. 1991. "Organizational Subcultures in a Soft Bureaucracy: Resistence behind the Myth and Facade of an Official Culture." *Organizational Studies* (forthcoming).

Kelling, George. 1978. "Police Field Services and Crime: The Presumed Effect of a Capacity." *Crime and Delinquency* 2:173–84.

————. 1988. "Police and Communities: The Quiet Revolution." *Perspectives on Policing*, no. 1. Washington, D.C.: U.S. Department of Justice, National Institute of Justice. (February).

Kelling, George, and James K. Stewart. 1989. "Neighborhoods and Police: The Maintenance of Civil Authority." *Perspectives on Policing*, no. 10. Washington, D.C.: U.S. Department of Justice, National Institute of Justice.

Klapp, O. 1978. *Opening and Closing.* Cambridge: Cambridge University Press.

————. 1986. *Overload and Boredom.* Westport, Conn.: Greenwood.

Kling, R., and P. Iacono. 1989. "The Mobilization of Support for Computerization: The Role of Computerization Movements." *Social Problems* 35:226–43.

Klockars, Carl. 1984. *The Idea of Police.* Newbury Park, Calif.: Sage.

Langworthy, Robert. 1986. *The Structure of Police Organizations.* New York: Praeger.

Larson, Richard. 1972. *Urban Patrol Analysis.* Cambridge, Mass.: MIT Press.

————. 1978. *Police Deployment.* Lexington, Mass.: D. C. Heath.

————. 1989. "The New Crime Stoppers." *Technology Review* 10:28–31.

————. 1990. *Rapid Response and Community Policing—Are They Really in Conflict?* Community Policing Series no. 20. East Lansing: Michigan State University, School of Criminal Justice.

Larson, R., K. W. Colton, and G. Larson. 1976. "Assessment of a Police Implemented AVM System...." Technical report. Washington, D. C.: Law Enforcement Assistance Administration.

Lawrence, P. R., and J. W. Lorsch. 1969. *Organization and Environment.* Homewood, Ill.: Richard Irwin.

Leaf, Murray. 1972. *Information and Behavior in a Sikh Village.* Berkeley: University of California Press.

Leonard, V. A. 1938. *Police Communication Systems.* Berkeley: University of California Press.

Lipsky, M. 1980. *Street-Level Bureaucracies.* New York: Russell Sage.

McEwen, J. T., E. F. Connors III, and M. I. Cohen. 1986. "Evaluation of the Differential Police Response Field Test: Research Report." Washington, D.C.: U.S. Department of Justice, National Institute of Justice.

MacKay, J. 1969. *Information, Mechanism and Meaning.* Cambridge, Mass.: MIT Press.

Maltz, M., and M. Dada. 1990. "Community Dynamics and Hotspots." Grant proposal from the Department of Criminal Justice, University of Illinois at Chicago, submitted to the National Institute of Justice, Washington, D.C.

Manning, Peter K. 1977. *Police Work*. Cambridge, Mass.: MIT Press.

————. 1979. "The Social Control of Police Work." In *The British Police*, edited by Simon Holdaway. London: Edward Arnold.

————. 1980*a*. *Narcs' Game*. Cambridge, Mass.: MIT Press.

————. 1980*b*. "Crime and Technology: The Role of Scientific Research and Technology in Crime Control." In *Five Year Outlook for Science and Technology in the United States*, vol. 2. Washington, D.C.: National Science Foundation.

————. 1982. "Organisational Work: Enstructuration of the Environment." *British Journal of Sociology* 33:118–39.

————. 1988. *Symbolic Communication: Signifying Calls and the Police Response*. Cambridge, Mass.: MIT Press.

————. 1989. "Occupational Culture." In *Encyclopedia of Police Science*, edited by William Bailey. New York and London: Garland.

Manning, Peter K., and John Van Maanen, eds. 1977. *Policing*. New York: Random House.

Markus, Lynne. 1984. *Systems in Organizations*. Boston: Pitman.

Marx, G. 1988. *Undercover Policework in America: Problems and Paradoxes of a Necessary Evil*. Berkeley and Los Angeles, Calif.: University of California Press.

Mastrofski, S. 1983. "Information and Policing." In *Police Work*, edited by R. Bennett. Beverly Hills, Calif.: Sage.

————. 1989. "Improving Explanatory Studies of Police Behavior." Unpublished manuscript. University Park: Pennsyvania State University, Department of Administrative Justice.

Mastrofski, S., and R. Ritti. 1991. "You Can Lead a Horse to Water...." Unpublished manuscript. University Park: Pennsylvania State University, Department of Administrative Justice.

Meyer, J. C., Jr. 1974. "Patterns of Reporting Non-criminal Behavior to the Police." *Criminology* 12:70–83.

Miller, W. R. 1977. *Cops and Bobbies*. Chicago: University of Chicago Press.

Missonelle, Joseph. 1989. "Video Technology." In *Encyclopedia of Police Science*, edited by William G. Bailey. New York and London: Garland.

Moore, Mark H. In this volume. "Problem-solving and Community Policing."

Moore, Mark H., and Robert Trojanowicz. 1988. "The Concept of Community." *Perspectives on Policing*, no. 6. Washington, D.C.: U.S. Department of Justice, National Institute of Justice.

Moore, Mark H., Robert Trojanowicz, and George Kelling. 1988. "Crime and Policing." *Perspectives on Policing*, no. 3. Washington, D.C.: U.S. Department of Justice, National Institute of Justice.

Norris, F. 1979. *Community Relations*. Lexington, Mass.: D. C. Heath.

Pate, T., A. Ferrara, R. Bowers, and J. Lorence. 1976. *Police Response Time: Its Determinants and Effects*. Washington, D.C.: Police Foundation.

Payne, Dennis. 1989. "Contextual Disequilibrium: A Study of Dispatchers' Perceptions of Job Related Training Factors." Ph.D. dissertation, Michigan State University, School of Criminal Justice.

Peirce, G. 1988. "Graphics of Crime." Paper presented at the forty-first meet-
ing of the American Society or Criminology, Reno, November.
————. 1991. "Mapping Crime." In *Domestic Violence*, edited by E. Buzawa.
Boston: Auburn House.
Peirce, G., S. Spaar, and L. Briggs. 1984. "The Character of Police Work:
Implications for the Delivery of Services." Unpublished manuscript. Bos-
ton: Northeastern University, Center for Applied Social Research.
Pennings, J., and A. Buitendam, eds. 1987. *New Technology as Organizational
Innovation*. Cambridge, Mass.: Ballinger.
Percy, S. 1980. "Response Time and Citizen Evaluation of the Police." *Journal
of Police Science and Administration* 8:75–86.
Percy, S., and E. J. Scott. 1985. *Demand Processing and Performance in Public
Service Agencies*. Tuscaloosa: University of Alabama Press.
Perrow, Charles. 1983. "The Organizational Context of Human Factors Engi-
neering." *Administrative Science Quarterly* 28:521–41.
President's Commission on Law Enforcement and Administration of Justice.
1967. *The Challenge of Crime in a Free Society*. Washington, D.C.: U.S. Gov-
ernment Printing Office.
Radelet, Louis A. 1986. *The Police and the Community*. 4th ed. New York:
Macmillan.
Radzinowicz, L. 1968–1975. *The History of English Criminal Law*, vol. 4. *The
Reform of the Police*. London: Stevens.
Rappaport, R. 1971. "Ritual, Sanctity and Cybernetics." *American Anthropolo-
gist* 73(February):59–76.
Ratledge, E. C., with J. Jacoby. 1989. *Handbook on Artificial Intelligence and
Expert Systems in Law Enforcement*. Westport, Conn.: Greenwood.
Reiner, Robert. In this volume. "Police Research in the United Kingdom: A
Critical Review."
Reiss, Albert J., Jr. 1971. *The Police and the Public*. New Haven, Conn.: Yale
University Press.
————. 1974. "Discretionary Justice." In *The Handbook of Criminal Justice*, ed-
ited by Daniel Glaser. Chicago: Rand-McNally.
————. 1983. "The Policing of Organizational Life." In *Control in the Police
Organization*, edited by Maurice Punch. Cambridge, Mass.: MIT Press.
————. 1984. "Selecting Strategies of Social Control over Organizational
Life." In *Enforcing Regulation*, edited by Keith Hawkins and J. Thomas.
Boston: Kluwer-Nijoff.
————. 1985. *Policing a City's Central City: The Oakland Story*. Washington,
D.C.: U.S. Department of Justice, National Institute of Justice.
————. In this volume. "Police Organization in the Twentieth Century."
Reiss, Albert J., Jr., and David J. Bordua. 1966. "Charisma, Bureaucracy and
Leadership in Policing." *American Journal of Sociology* 72:68–78.
————. 1967. "Environment and Organization: A Perspective on the Police."
In *The Police: Six Sociological Essays*, edited by David Bordua. New York:
Wiley.
Reppetto, T. 1978. *The Blue Parade*. New York: Macmillan.
Rheinier, B., M. R. Greenless, M. H. Gibbens, and S. P. Marshall. 1979.

Crime Analysis in Support of Patrol. Law Enforcement Assistance Administration report. Washington, D.C.: U.S. Government Printing Office.

Rule, J., and P. Attewell. 1989. "What Do Computers Do?" *Social Problems* 16:225–41.

Sacks, H. 1980. "Notes on Police Moral Assessment of Moral Character." In *Studies in Interaction*, edited by D. Sudnow. New York: Free Press.

Sanders, W. 1977. *Detective Work*. New York: Free Press.

Scott, Eric J. 1981. "Police Referral in Metropolitan Areas." Report to the National Institute of Justice. Bloomington: University of Indiana Workshop in Political Theory and Policy Analysis.

Sherman, Lawrence W. In this volume. "Attacking Crime: Police and Crime Control."

Sherman, Lawrence W., et al. 1987. "Repeat Calls to Police in Minneapolis." Crime Control Reports no 5. Washington, D.C.: Crime Control Institute.

Sherman, Lawrence W., P. Gartin, and M. E. Buerger. 1989. "Hot Spots of Predatory Crime: Routine Activities and the Criminology of Place." *Criminology* 27:27–55.

Sherman, Lawrence W., and S. Martin. 1986. "Catching Career Criminals." Washington, D.C.: Police Foundation.

Skolnick, Jerome. 1966. *Justice without Trial*. New York: Wiley.

Slovak, J. 1986. *Styles of Urban Policing*. New York: New York University Press.

Spelman, W., and D. K. Brown. 1981. *Calling the Police: Citizen Reporting of Serious Crime*. Washington, D.C.: Police Executive Research Forum.

Stead, J., ed. 1977. *Pioneers in Policing*. Montclair, N.J.: Patterson Smith.

Stevens, J. 1989. "Computer Technology." In *Encyclopedia of Police Science*, edited by William G. Bailey. New York and London: Garland.

Stinchcombe, A. 1990. *Information and Organizations*. Berkeley and Los Angeles: University of California Press.

Tien, James, and Kent Colton. 1979. "Police Command, Control, and Communications." In *What Works?* Law Enforcement Assistance Administration report. Washington, D.C.: U.S. Government Printing Office.

Thompson, James. 1967. *Organizations in Action*. New York: McGraw Hill.

Trojanowicz, R., and B. Buqueroux. 1989. *Community Policing*. Cincinnati: Anderson.

Turner, Ralph. 1989. "Forensic Sciences." In *Encyclopedia of Police Science*, edited by William G. Bailey. New York and London: Garland.

Van Maanen, John. 1974. "Working the Street." In *Prospects for Reform in Criminal Justice*, edited by H. Jacob. Beverly Hills, Calif.: Sage.

———. 1975. "Police Socialization: A Longitudinal Examination of Job Attitudes in an Urban Police Department." *Administrative Science Quarterly* 20:207–28.

Van Maanen, John, and E. Schein. 1979. "Toward a Theory of Organizational Socialization." In *Research in Organizational Behavior*, edited by Barry Staw. Greenwich, Conn.: JAI.

Waegel, W. 1981. "Case Routinization in Investigative Police Work." *Social Problems* 28:263–75.

Ward, Richard. 1989. "Case Management." In *Encyclopedia of Police Science*, edited by William G. Bailey. New York and London: Garland.

Weick, Karl. 1979. *The Social Psychology of Organizing*. 2d ed. Reading, Mass: Addison-Wesley.

Willmer, M. A. P. 1970. *Information and Policing*. Edinburgh: University of Edinburgh Press.

Wilson, James Q. 1968. *Varieties of Police Behavior*. Cambridge, Mass.: Harvard University Press.

Winner, L. 1977. *Autonomous Technology: Technics-Out-of-Control as a Theme in Political Thought*. Cambridge, Mass.: MIT Press.

Worden, Robert. 1989. "Differential Police Response: Response Delays, Telephone Reports and Citizen Satisfaction." Unpublished manuscript. East Lansing: Michigan State University, School of Criminal Justice.

Worden, Robert, and Stephen Mastrofski. 1989. "Varieties of Police Subcultures: A Preliminary Investigation." Paper presented to Law and Society Association, Madison, Wis., June.

Zey-Ferrell, M. 1979. *Dimensions of Organizations*. Santa Monica, Calif.: Goodyear.

Clifford D. Shearing

The Relation between Public and Private Policing

ABSTRACT

Employment by private policing agencies equals or exceeds public police employment in many countries. Reigning conceptions of relations between public police and private policing have changed markedly. A state-centered view of police functions disparaged "private armies" and saw order maintenance as a quintessential function of government. In recent decades, a laissez-faire view has emerged that celebrates "private-public partnerships" and sees private policing as an industry providing both a service and a public benefit. Social theorists question the wisdom and the likely future directions of the privatization of order maintenance.

This essay examines the nature, characteristics, and scope of private policing through a consideration of its relation to public policing. It identifies three conceptions of the relation between public and private policing that have not only described but constituted this interaction. The main focus is on North America, where most of the research and writing on private policing has been undertaken, though some allusion is made to developments in Europe.

The first task is to define private and public policing. Policing, as the term is used here, refers to the preservation of the peace, that is, to the maintenance of a way of doing things where persons and property are free from unwarranted interference so that people may go

Clifford Shearing is professor of criminology and sociology at the University of Toronto. Philip Stenning has helped shaped the definition of policing proposed in this essay. I have benefited from comments made by the editors, the reviewers, Tony Doob, and Nigel South. The assistance and insights of Susan Addario, Mary Condon, Patrick Delhougne, Julia Powditch, and Audrey Sinco are also gratefully acknowledged.

about their business safely. This meaning is evident in the old English word "frith," from which the term "peace" is derived (Keeton 1975, pp. 3–4). The *Oxford English Dictionary* (1989, p. 33) defines frith as "freedom from molestation" and as "security." Just what constitutes security varies across societies, and it is this variation that gives "peace" substantive meaning. As Spitzer (1987, p. 48) observes, citing Gore, "Security always implies the preservation of 'an established order against whatever seems to threaten, disturb or endanger it from without or from within.' " What threatens, disturbs, or endangers depends on the nature of this established order.

In defining policing in terms of peace, I am attempting to avoid the problems of two alternative approaches. First, I am responding to criticism of the very restrictive use of the term to refer to the activities of the public police (Cain 1979). Second, in distinguishing peace from order and policing from ordering, I am taking a stance against my own efforts (Shearing and Stenning 1981) to rectify this deficiency by calling on earlier historical usages that equate policing with governance (Andrew 1989).[1]

In restricting the definition of policing to security, I am seeking to recognize the significance of peace as a "foundation order" on which other orders—for instance, the order of financial markets—depend and policing as an activity that seeks to maintain this foundation.[2] My objective is to salvage the link between policing and crime fighting that the equation of policing with the public police recognizes without being trapped by the institutional limits of this definition.[3]

---

[1] Stenning (1981, p. 10) provides the following example of such an expanded historical usage in a passage cited from the New Municipal Manual of Upper Canada, 1859: "The word 'police' is generally applied to the internal regulation of Cities and Towns, whereby the individuals of any City or Town, like members of a well governed family, are bound to conform their general behaviour to the rules of propriety, good neighborhood, and good manners, and to be decent, industrious and inoffensive in their respective situations."

[2] This conception of peace as a foundation order is identified by Hobbes (1968, p. 186), who describes a state of affairs without freedom from molestation as follows: "In such condition, there is no place for Industry; because the fruit thereof is uncertain; and consequently no Culture of the Earth; no Navigation, nor use of the commodities that may be imported from the Sea; no commodious Building; no Instruments of moving, and removing such things as require much force; no Knowledge of the face of the Earth; no account of Time; no Arts; no Letters; no Society; and which is worst of all, continual feare, and danger of violent death; And the life of man, solitary, poore, nasty, brutish and short."

[3] It is possible to limit the definition of "policing" further in ways that are consistent with an even more restrictive usage, for example, by limiting policing to activities undertaken to respond to *breaches* of the peace in contrast to activities designed to produce or

The expression "peace," from its earliest uses, has referred to more than simply the presence of protection. It also denotes a prediction that this protection will persist over time. Peace refers to a reduction of, or absence of, risk.[4] Thus, Hobbes (1968, p. 186) argued that peace was not simply the absence of war but absence of the threat of war. As Spitzer (1987, p. 47) correctly notes, "Security is said to exist when something *does not* occur rather than when it does. Security in the more restricted sense in which it is used here [i.e., as peace] exists when stores are not robbed, pedestrians are not molested, computer codes not broken, and executives and their families are able to enjoy life free from threats, assassinations or kidnapping."

Such a state of affairs typically requires design and effort. It requires a strategy in Foucault's sense of structured, coordinated practices (Garland 1990, p. 137). Peace is seldom something that simply happens; it requires an *assurance* of security.[5] For example, the Canadian Charter of Rights and Freedoms, in setting out the terms of the Canadian peace, claims that the rights and freedoms it enunciates are "guaranteed." Thus, policing, understood as the preservation of the peace, refers to activities through which an assurance or guarantee is realized or, more accurately, to activities intended to promote such realization.[6]

This idea of a *guarantee* can be traced to another Old English word closely associated with frith, namely, grith (Keeton 1975, pp. 3–4). "Grith" is defined in the *Oxford English Dictionary* (1989, p. 858) as "guaranteed security, protection, defense; safe-conduct." The related

---

create peace, an activity captured by the term "regulation" (Metnick 1980). Although a definition of "policing" as responses to breaches of the peace has certain analytic advantages, these are outweighed by the requirement of having to find another term to refer to "preserving the peace." What is important analytically is that these various distinctions are made. The terminological challenge is to develop a nomenclature that explicitly separates meanings that common usage distinguishes implicitly ("policing" in common usage is read differently depending on the context within which it is used) while at the same time respecting the central features of this usage.

[4] This idea of freedom from worry is captured as Spitzer (1987, p. 44) notes by the term "security." The *Oxford English Dictionary* defines the condition of security in terms of protection from danger; safety; and freedom from doubt, care, anxiety, or apprehension. To be secure is to be assured, confident, and safe.

[5] Herein lies the answer to Spitzer's (1987, p. 44) query as to how it is that "security" can become a "commodity that can be purchased in the market-place?" What is purchased is the protection of a guarantor.

[6] Spitzer (1987, p. 43) cites Marx's comments on the French constitution of 1793 as follows: "*Security* is the supreme social concept of civil society, the concept of the *police*, the concept that the whole society exists only to guarantee to each of its members the preservation of his person, his rights, and his property. . . . Civil society does not raise itself above its egoism through the concept of security. Rather, security is the *guarantee* of the egoism."

term "hand-grith" is defined as "protection under the king's hand" (p. 858) and a "grith-breach" as a "breach of the peace" (p. 858). The notion of grith recognizes that protection or sanctuary was not only guaranteed by the king (Rock 1983). There were other griths as well, for example, "church-grith." In my use of the term "peace" I want explicitly to recognize both an assurance of protection and that there may be multiple guarantees and guarantors of peace.

Ever since the social world has been constituted through a political consciousness that recognized a public and a private sphere (Hobbes 1968, p. 264; Mnookin 1982; Rose 1987), policing has had a public and a private face.[7] This is so because the entities that have had the will and capacity to offer credible guarantees of peace have been located within both these spheres. Over time one of these entities, the nation-state, has obtained supremacy over the definition of both these spheres. It has defined itself as the ultimate guarantor of order within the territorial boundaries defined by the network of states (Giddens 1987).[8] States, in seeking to realize their claims to supremacy, have sought to set limits on what private entities can do to preserve peace.

States that recognize a private sphere, such as liberal democratic states, typically have not distinguished between corporations and individuals in setting these limits. Nonetheless, the variations in capacity that frequently differentiate them have meant that it is corporate entities rather than individuals who, by and large, have been in a position to act to preserve the peace (Spitzer and Scull 1977: Critchley 1978; Rock 1983). Thus, in practice, private peacekeeping has been largely a corporate matter (for exceptions, see Radzinowicz 1948, p. 205).

These corporate entities have varied considerably. There have been voluntary associations such as the seventeenth- and eighteenth-century societies for the "prosecution of felons" (Radzinowicz 1948, p. 102; Shubert 1981). Their contemporary counterparts are groups like the Guardian Angels who have attempted to establish themselves as guar-

---

[7] During the period prior to the nineteenth century, as both Rock (1983) and Robert (1988) suggest, while a private/public distinction was used, it was not associated as closely with the state/civil distinction as it is today, so that what one finds are arrangements that one would, from a contemporary vantage point, think of as semiprivate and semipublic.

[8] The emergence of the state as an entity able to establish its peace as supreme was an uneven and contested process. As recently as the seventeenth and eighteenth centuries England was full of competing peaces and alternative sanctuaries, some legitimate and some illegitimate. As a result, the "boundaries between private licence and public regulation were highly fluid" (Rock 1983, p. 197). Rock cites Rudé as stating that Westminster's government was "for many years a jungle of rival jurisdictions" (1983, p. 208).

antors of peace in a number of American cities, especially in places such as the New York subway system. By contrast, there have been business corporations, including the huge private trading companies like the Dutch and English East India Companies (*Encyclopedia Britannica* 1972, 7:793, 877) and the Hudson's Bay Company (Phillips 1991), as well as contemporary corporations that act to preserve the peace within their domains (South 1988). This corporate predominance does not mean that individuals have not engaged in policing. They have done so, however, principally as the agents of corporate entities—both public (state) and private—rather than as guarantors of the peace in their own right.

This essay attempts to account for the evolution of private policing by developing and illustrating three alternate conceptions—state centered, laissez-faire, and pluralist—of its character and function. Section I offers a brief history of state-centered policing and shows how the use of force was conceived as a state monopoly. Section II examines the origins of private policing; while Section III explores policing from a pluralist perspective. Conclusions are offered in Section IV. They offer caution concerning the effects of blurring of distinction between public and private policing in the "postmodernist" age.

I. State-centered Policing

The creation of the "new police" in London in 1829 is regarded as a symbolic turning point in a gradual but steady transfer of responsibility for policing from private to public hands. Conventional histories of the development of the "new police" depict this assertion of state control over policing as a series of progressive improvements in which private assurances of peace were replaced by public responsibility for peacekeeping (Reiner 1985).

In this state-centered view private policing is presented as a precursor of modern public policing brought about by the absence of a state that was strong enough to provide credible assurances of peace. Thus, as Rock (1983, p. 199) observes, "When the state could guarantee neither physical security nor legal control, effective government passed in large measure to those who were independently powerful." In documenting the problems with private guarantors and private arrangements for maintaining the peace, these histories have identified a host of problematic private initiatives. Examples include corrupt fee-for-service organizations like the Bow Street Runners of London whose "blood money" only the wealthy could afford and scoundrels like the "thief taker" Jonathan Wilde who became wealthy on the fees he obtained for returning goods from crimes for which he was responsible (Radzinowicz 1948; Critchley 1978; Rock 1983; South 1987).

These histories, written from the vantage point of a historical period that accepted the nation-state as the most appropriate location of responsibility for policing (Reiner 1985), trace the emergence of strong states through a slow, irregular process (Rock 1983). This historical understanding of the emergence of modern public policing as the most satisfactory form of policing both expressed and contributed to the creation of a state-centered political consciousness that was suspicious of private peacekeeping and hostile toward it (Rock 1983). Nedelsky (1983, p. 1) summarizes this political consciousness within the United States: "Modern America is characterized by the expanding scope of state power. More and more areas of life once left to the 'private' ordering of individual choice are now considered properly matters of collective control, regulation, and amelioration."

The operation of this consciousness in the United States is evident in the "political spectacles" (Edelman 1988) that took place during the early twentieth century over the continuing presence of private policing as a feature of American life. Among the most dramatic of these, in terms of the rhetorical language employed, were the deliberations of Senate and Congressional committees established in response to criticism of the policing practices of railroad and mining companies, especially in their dealings with labor (Weiss 1979).[9] The concern was that these companies were maintaining private peaces that favored the protection of their assets at the expense of their employees' security and property. These government reports, which constitute a significant part of the American historical record of private policing and its relationship to public policing in the late nineteenth century and the first half of this century, both expressed and constituted a political consciousness that identified and railed against the dangers of private, and especially corporate, policing.

While this consciousness has now begun to lose its grip, its shadow has been long, and it has not readily given way to alternative ways of

[9] The history of spectacular events and accounts of private policing in the United States goes back to the 1870s. One of the most notorious incidents was the 1892 Carnegie Steel Company strike at its Homestead Work in which the Pinkerton contract policing organization was involved in what came to be known as the Homestead Massacre. This incident was the "subject of a House Judiciary subcommittee investigation, which question the propriety of law enforcement by hired police" (O'Toole 1978, p. 27; see also Lipson 1988, p. 19).

seeing policing. As this perspective provides the backdrop against which alternative conceptions are articulated, and as it continues to be taken for granted in many discussions of peacekeeping, especially legal ones (Mewett 1988, p. 16), it is important to understand both its premises and arguments.

The Senate and Congressional reports told a story of railroad and mining corporations that, with the aid of "mercenaries" like the Pinkerton National Detective Agency, sought to promote an order that was at odds with the public peace and the public interest. These reports were particularly critical of the corporations' use of force to establish and maintain an order that promoted their private interests. The committees insisted that only the state was in a position to promote the public interest. They described the activities of the railroad and mining company police as the actions of aggressive "private armies" that were undermining the public peace and challenging the American state. The term "private police" was deliberately employed as an oxymoron to emphasize that corporations in the United States were acting inappropriately as "private governments" (Macauley 1986). It was asserted that policing within a modern state was fundamentally a responsibility of public government. Policing was presented, in essentially Weberian terms, as ultimately dependent on the use of force as a resource. This resource, it was argued, should be monopolized by public government and accordingly should be used only under state authorization and control.

An excerpt from the 1939 report of the United States' Senate Committee on Education and Labor entitled "On Private Police Systems"—part of a series of reports under the general rubric of "Violations of Free Speech and Rights of Labor"—illustrates the outraged governmental response to the activities of these industrial "shock troops" and their "bloodstained history":

> Private police systems cannot be viewed as agencies of law
> and order. . . . When the armed forces of the employer are
> injected into the delicate relations of labor and management, the
> consequences seriously threaten the civil rights of citizens and the
> peace and safety of whole communities. . . . The subjugation of
> one group of citizens to the economic interests of another by the
> use of armed forces saps the very foundation of democracy. . . .
> The utilization of privately paid armed forces to coerce and
> intimidate citizens in the pursuit of their legitimate interests is

foreign to the spirit of free American society. [United States
Committee on Education and Labor 1971, pp. 2–4]

The committee argued that private police existed in the United
States in large numbers as partisan forces that threatened the public
interest and the state. Private police were a salient reminder of the
importance of sustaining a strong state with a monopoly over the use
of coercive force in the maintenance of order. The nature of the relationship between private and public policing was clear; while the public police acted in the public interest, private police acted for private
interests that were often, if not always, at odds with the public interest.

The ultimate reason for the existence of these partisan institutions
was placed firmly at the door of the state in the same way that conventional British histories had analyzed private policing (Critchley 1978).
Private police existed in America because public governments were
unable to fulfill their responsibilities to protect their citizens. This
created a vacuum that private corporate entities filled—indeed were
compelled to fill—by acting as private governments (Shearing and
Stenning 1981, pp. 226–27). The opening paragraph of the Senate
report articulates this way of seeing policing and establishes the context
for the analysis to follow:

Company police systems have a long history, closely related
to the geographic expansion and industrial development of the
United States. In pioneer days, when local, State, and Territorial
governments were still in the early stages of development,
property owners were understood to protect their own domain,
individually, or through hired hands. Private police became
necessary when policing requirements of property owners to
protect their property against thievery and vandalism exceeded
the limits of coverage offered by the public police. Railroads,
for instance, with large amounts of rolling stock and extensive
properties and rights-of-way in open and unprotected country, had
to develop the special services needed by them. Similarly, the
protection of remote and extensive properties, such as those of
mining and lumber enterprises, had to be furnished by the
owners. [United States Committee on Education and Labor 1971,
p. 2]

In other words, the use of force, which should be a capacity exclusive to the state and used by it to promote the public interest, was

extended beyond its proper domain to become a tool of economic competition. "In carrying out even the essential functions of protecting life and property, a private police system is created to defend the interests of the employer, whether an individual or a corporation. Only incidentally does it exercise the nonpartisan function of guardian of the law. Whenever private police expand their activities beyond the protection of life and property they act only as an instrumentality of private economic policy. Thereupon the differences between public and private police systems become particularly significant" (United States Committee on Education and Labor 1971, p. 2). Private entities did not have a right to guarantee peace within their domains because they would not, and as a matter of fact did not, do so in the "public interest."

The solution was obvious. The state should ensure that its police were capable of delivering the assurances of protection that citizens, including corporate citizens, required. There was no room in the modern, postfeudal state for private governance. Wherever private policing was found, it should be replaced with public policing. If there was to be any role for private agents, it was not as police sustaining a private conception of the peace. The only acceptable roles for them were as guards who assisted private entities in a very limited way to protect life and property as an expression of self-defense or self-help.

This distinction between legitimate self-defense and illegitimate private armies has its roots in the public/private dichotomy central to the liberal understanding of governance as located exclusively in the public sphere. Within this view of corporations, while they should not be permitted to govern—that is, to define and keep the peace—they have the same right as any other "individual" to act within the bounds of the private sphere. To remove the possibility of self-protection entirely would be to deny any limit on state power by repudiating a private sphere of individual autonomy. Nedelsky (1989, pp. 15–16) is instructive: "Our political tradition has virtually identified freedom and autonomy with the private sphere, and posed them in opposition to the public sphere of state power. The idea of a boundary between these spheres, a line dividing individual autonomy from the legitimate scope of state power, has been central to the American conceptions of freedom and limited government." Permitting corporations to act as private governments who defined and maintained a peace allowed the private sphere too much autonomy; yet the other extreme of eliminating the possibility of private "watchmen" would destroy the limits on governmental power so critical to the liberal conception of the state.

The understanding of policing as legitimate in its public manifestation and dangerous in its private one promoted a politics of policing as a state monopoly. This politics was so successful that by the middle of this century private policing was considered an anachronistic institution that had withered away in response to the growth of the "new police." Policing was now simply assumed to be public, and this assumption guided research which set about defining the nature, characteristics, and scope of the phenomenon (Cain 1979). Questions about private police and about the relationship between public and private policing simply did not arise. For example, the United States President's Commission on Law Enforcement and Administration of Justice neither acknowledged private policing nor considered how it might contribute to the "war against crime" (President's Commission on Law Enforcement and Administration of Justice 1967a, 1967b).

This view of policing as public was shared by researchers on both sides of the political spectrum. Despite a variety of disagreements about the nature of policy, they agreed that modern policing meant state policing and this, in turn, did and should mean state use of force to preserve the peace (Bittner 1970). Thus, while Marxist scholars were critical of claims that the state used its access to force to promote a general good, they shared the liberal view of policing as a state monopoly and its assessment of private government's inability to police in a nonpartisan fashion.

II. The Emergence of a Laissez-Faire Conception

We now know that during the 1960s, while scholars and policymakers were operating within a framework that recognized only public policing, the structure of policing was experiencing a "quiet revolution." The private provision of protection was expanding exponentially, after what appears to have been a period of decline in response to hostility toward private police in the early part of this century (Weiss 1987a, p. 110).

Figures published in the 1970s and 1980s indicated that the number of employees of private firms in the United States who provided policing on a fee-for-service basis (contract security) doubled during the 1960s; the yearly growth rate was 7.4 percent. This was nearly twice the annual growth rate of the public police that, at 4.2 percent, was itself considerable (Shearing and Stenning 1981, p. 199). Figures for the United Kingdom for the 1970s were not as large, though the proportions were even more striking. Public police strength increased at a yearly rate of 1.6 percent while contract security numbers increased at a rate of 4.2 percent (Shearing and Stenning 1981, p. 203). By 1975 the ratio of public to private police (in-house and contract) was 0.9:1 in the United States (Shearing and Stenning 1983, p. 495), a proportion that by the mid-1980s was reported to have increased to 1:2 (Cunningham and Taylor 1985, p. 112) and 1.1:1 in Canada (Shearing and Stenning 1983, p. 495). In the United Kingdom the comparable proportion in 1978 was 1.09:1 (Shearing and Stenning 1981, p. 203). While serious questions can be raised about the accuracy of the precise proportions and numbers, these figures leave no doubt that private police by the 1970s accounted for a significant part of all police and that the contract policing industry had grown rapidly. Estimates of growth have now begun to appear for Europe. While these statistics are not as dramatic, they have prompted concern about and interest in private policing (see Laitinen [1987] on Finland; Robert [1988] on France; Rosenthal and Hoogenboom [1988] on Holland; and Van Outrive [1987] on Belgium).

In the early 1970s research drawing attention to the existence of private policing emerged in both Britain and the United States (Braun and Lee 1971; Peel 1971; Scott and McPherson 1971; Kakalik and Wildhorn 1972; Wiles and McClintock 1972). These studies challenged the taken-for-granted assumption of the 1950s and 1960s that contemporary policing was exclusively state policing and argued that private policing was an important contemporary phenomenon that needed to be recognized and understood.

American governments at both state and the federal levels were the first to address these questions. An examination of private policing by the RAND Corporation, commissioned by the U.S. Department of Justice, was at the forefront (Kakalik and Wildhorn 1972). This wide-ranging study not only described the extent, scope, and nature of private policing and its relations to the public police but developed an influential policy stance that directly challenged the earlier conception of corporate police as "private armies." In retrospect, RAND's report can be identified as one of the earliest indications of the shift in political consciousness that has promoted the privatization of a whole range of services previously seen as fundamentally public (Weiss 1987b; McConville 1988; Matthews 1989; Ryan and Ward 1989; see also Hoogenboom's [1987] discussion of the Dutch government's 1985 privatization policy). If policing—a quintessentially public service according to the state-centered view—could be privatized, then so could other public services.

RAND not only argued that private policing was alive and well and to be found all over the United States but also that private policing, especially contract security, was an "industry" providing a "service." The image of private policing as private armies challenging state authority was replaced with one of private policing as just another industry providing services to the public. Policing was constructed as a commodity that could be as effectively provided by private enterprise as by the state. RAND's report thus transformed the issue of public or private policing from a question of politics and sovereignty to be responded to in absolute terms to a matter of economics and efficiency to be addressed in terms of balance, proportion, and degree (Landes and Posner 1975; Kraakman 1986). In other words, the issue of the relationship between public and private policing became essentially a question of the most efficient way to provide policing services.

RAND was clearly not unaware of the concerns and reform initiatives of the state-centered view of policing. However, Kakalik and Wildhorn (1972), the authors of the RAND report, established their position by shifting the terms of the debate rather than by confronting the premises of the state-centered view directly. They concluded that the emergence of private policing in the United States was not a cause for alarm since it did not threaten the state's claims to monopoly over the definition of the peace. This position was validated by recourse to the earlier acceptance of the notion of legitimate self-help (Becker 1974) to argue that private policing, as a service, involved primarily the employment of agents to undertake tasks of self-defense. By characterizing private policing in this way, Kakalik and Wildhorn made clear that the industry did not pose a challenge to the state. Private police, it was argued, were inoffensive people employed in simple preventive activities necessary for self-defense that the public police had neither the resources nor the inclination to undertake. "The major functions of private guards are to prevent, detect, and report criminal acts on private property, to provide security against loss from fire or equipment failure, to control access to private property, and to enforce rules and regulations of private employers" (Kakalik and Wildhorn 1972, 1:19).

The rapid development of contract security meant only that self-defense, which had for some time been provided privately (and legitimately) on an in-house basis, was now available from a developing service industry no different in principle from any other service industry. What was changing was not the division of labor between public and private police but the distribution of policing within the private sector. While the state should be apprised of this development and regulate it to ensure that the public interest was not undermined, it was not a matter for concern. Modern private policing was merely a manifestation of the policy of permitting self-defense that the congressional committees had established. Far from being a threat, contemporary private policing was a distinct asset. It was an industry making a useful contribution to the American economy at the same time as it relieved taxpayers of costs they would have to bear if the state were to undertake these tasks.[10]

This transformation of private policing from a threat to an asset was accomplished by conceptualizing private police as junior partners in the business of policing, who were working to assist their senior partners, the public police, in keeping the peace (Shearing and Stenning 1981, p. 220). This interpretation of private policing was accomplished by simultaneously blurring the line between "self-defense" and peacekeeping while mobilizing it to argue that private police were doing no more than engaging in self-defense writ large. The public peace included the protection of corporate property and the protection of corporate customers and staff. If corporations were willing to contribute to this as part of their own self-defense, this was all to the good. RAND made clear that this junior/senior partner scenario was not simply a desirable possibility but already an actuality. American policing, in practice, was a mix of public and private police.

In the mid-1980s the U.S. Department of Justice published a major follow-up study to the RAND report prepared by the Hallcrest Corporation (Cunningham and Taylor 1985). Hallcrest was hired both to assess developments in the decade since RAND reported and to suggest ways in which cooperation between public and private police could be improved through a more complete and effective employment of what was identified as a "massive and under-utilized resource" (Cun-

---

[10] Weiss (1987a, pp. 272–73) describes the sensibility, that Hallcrest both expressed and contributed to, as follows: "In contrast to liberals and traditional conservatives alike, neo-conservatives do not adhere to the philosophical separation between government and business. . . . In a complete reversal of conservative position on policy, government programmes that were once considered a drain on business (because the tax funds could have been better used for capital investment) are now valued as a new market, where entrepreneurs can turn administrative costs into potentially large profits. They argue that the private sector is not only less expensive, but more effective in service delivery. This same argument is currently being applied to criminal justice."

ningham and Taylor 1985). Hallcrest's mandate was thus to advance the reform agenda RAND had initiated. In doing so it accepted and worked within the framework RAND had established in which policing was seen as a commodity and private policing as an important American industry. Its review of the decade since the RAND report took the form of an economic analysis that considered the various aspects of private policing as an industry. Cunningham and Taylor, the Hallcrest consultants responsible for the study, summarized their findings with respect to this industry as follows:

> The popular perception of private security as a fast growing industry is certainly supported by analysis of the available data sources. By 1985 Americans will easily spend $20 billion per year for products and services to protect themselves—more than they'll spend to support all enforcement agencies (federal, state, local) in the U.S. Private security, in the aggregate, is big business—from the one-person private investigators and entrepreneurial alarm installers all the way to multi-national companies. Both large and small firms have been able to successfully carve their own niche out of an ever-expanding marketplace. Continuing technological innovations and product development, crime and fear of crime, and strained public resources will all contribute to sustained and dynamic growth of this important segment of the economy. Private security clearly plays a major protective role in the life of the Nation. [1985, p. 163]

For Hallcrest, much more than for RAND, policing was a "product" and "private policing" was an industry in the business of "servicing" crime and the fear of crime. Cunningham and Taylor sought to cement and extend this conception of policing, as well as the support it generated for the advancement of privatization, in three ways. First, they expanded RAND's idea that public and private police were partners in peacekeeping; second, they responded to concerns raised within the academic literature about the implications of private policing for civil liberties (South 1988); and third, they responded to public police resistance to private policing (Draper 1978, pp. 155–66; Shearing, Stenning, and Addario 1985a).

Cunningham and Taylor expanded on RAND's notion of policing partnerships through a series of interrelated conceptual initiatives. First, they shifted the focus of attention from private policing as self-defense and protection to private policing as crime fighting. This idea was developed by elaborating on RAND's argument that there was little difference in practice between what public and private police did. In support of this they cited favorably Scott and McPherson's (1971, pp. 273–74) claim that the activities of private police were "virtually identical in many respects to those carried out by the public police." However, while this observation had been made by Scott and McPherson in the pre-RAND era to raise concerns about the development of private policing, it was now mobilized, in the post-RAND era, as evidence in favor of promoting privatization. The claim that private police were undertaking the same tasks as the public police to the same ends was used to move from a junior partner to an equal partner conception of private policing's relationship to public police.

This reconception was in turn employed to argue for a policy of enhanced public-private police cooperation that would accelerate the process of privatization RAND had reported and legitimized. The authors did so by advocating "the utilization of their respective talents and resources in a complementary and coordinated attack on crime . . . to maximize protection of American communities" (Cunningham and Taylor 1985, p. 5). The imagery of private armies was now completely silenced and replaced by a call for private-public coordination of crime-fighting efforts in pursuit of the shared value of protection. In addition to greater use of private policing in crime fighting, Hallcrest recommended increased information sharing and interchange of personnel and experience.

In taking this position, Cunningham and Taylor responded to the disquiet of academic researchers, both pre- and post-RAND, about the implications for individual liberties posed by the growth and acceptance of private policing. This literature drew attention to the way in which the very "institutions of privacy" (Stinchcombe 1963) that protected individuals from state-initiated intrusions not only granted corporate entities a sphere of autonomous action but legitimized their intrusions on the privacy of individuals (Flavel 1973, p. 14; Shearing and Stenning 1982, pp. 41–44; Reiss 1987, p. 25).[11] The literature also

---

[11] In developing this point Shearing and Stenning (1982, p. 15) write: "Corporate orders are defended on the grounds that corporations, like any other 'persons,' have a right to a sphere of private authority over which they have undisturbed jurisdiction. Furthermore, this right is sacrosanct, for to encroach upon it would undermine the very freedoms that are definitive of liberal democracy. The irony is that it is the liberal frame itself . . . that has legitimated the development of huge multinational corporations into powerful private authorities whose very existence, and activity, mock the liberal frame."

adverted to the violations of privacy that resulted from exchanges of information between public and private police agencies (O'Toole 1978; Rule et al. 1980; Shearing and Stenning 1982, pp. 12–15; Marx 1987).[12]

Cunningham and Taylor did not interpret these concerns as requiring a bar to privatization but rather as technical problems to be overcome. The position was that regulatory controls needed to be enhanced through both legislative provisions and self- and market regulation (South 1989, pp. 97–100). In responding to civil liberties concerns, Cunningham and Taylor (1985) employed the analyses of scholars who had raised questions about the implications of privatization to support their own position in favor of increased privatization. One example is their use of Scott and McPherson (1971) just noted; another is their mobilization of Shearing and Stenning's analysis of the difficulties of regulating private policing. "We concur with Shearing and Stenning (in their extensive study of governmental regulation in Canada) that effective control and upgrading of private security will occur only when the industry and government cease to rely almost exclusively on legal mechanisms. Shearing and Stenning call for 'careful and selective use' of legislation in conjunction with control mechanisms which can be exerted by three major groups that are in the best position to exercise influence over the nature and operation of private security: the industry itself, clients, and the general public as employers and consumers" (1985, p. 230).

Cunningham and Taylor adopted a three-pronged response to public police resistance to enhanced public-private police cooperation. First, they used Shearing and Stenning's criticism of the "vacuum theory" argument that private policing was a makeshift response to inadequate state response to keeping the peace to assert that private policing was not a result of the underfunding of the public police:

> Shearing and Stenning (1981) correlate the growth of private security with "shifts in property relationships." Whenever one finds a shift in property relationships towards large geographically connected holdings of mass private property one also finds a shift towards private policing initiatives. The private streets and enclosed areas of large industrial, commercial, and residential

---

[12] The issue of information sharing draws attention to the exchange of personnel between public and private policing. There is a long history of public police officers moving into private policing as a second career (O'Toole 1978, p. 121; Shearing, Farnell, and Stenning 1980; Marx 1987).

developments tend to be protected privately whereas public areas are protected by public police. Shearing and Stenning call this a "new corporate feudalism" which has shifted protective resources from the public to the private sector. Thus, the "fiscal crisis of the state" and declining police resources have resulted from this shift; they did not cause it. [1985, p. 171]

If private policing was the result of structural change in the organization of contemporary society, it was pointless for the public police to resist it.

Second, they identified the source of this resistance as the partisan interests of the public police, which were undermining the ability of communities to respond to crime. They argued that much of the resistance to private policing and privatization was simply a "turf war" in which the public police were seeking to maintain their privileged position:

> Law enforcement has enjoyed a dominant position in providing protective services to their communities but now foresees an erosion of their "turf" to private security. Extensive interviews with both proprietary and contract security managers have confirmed that this fundamental shift has already occurred through technological substitution for labor, and it is now simply being manifested in more highly visible human resources. This position was succinctly summarized by a leading police and security educator: "If one were to make a big pie of the protection of the wealth, health, and welfare of a community, law enforcement would be a small part of the pie. Law enforcement, which is basically manpower, is now seeing a manpower shift to the private sector. But manpower is a small part of protection resources. A shift of protection resources to the private sector has already happened: cops only see the change in their turf." [1985, p. 172]

Finally, Cunningham and Taylor followed Shearing and Stenning's use of the gerund "policing" to describe the activities of "private security" (Shearing, Farnell, and Stenning 1980; see also South 1988). They thereby accorded the public police "ownership" of the term "police" while at the same time denying that policing was their exclusive preserve. Since the term "policing" was used by Shearing and Stenning to allow analytic consideration of a variety of activities not undertaken by the public police, this linguistic ploy served Hallcrest's privatization

agenda by undermining the privileged position held by the public police within the state-centered framework (1985, p. 167).

Hallcrest's reform agenda has prompted a growing recognition of
and respect for private police on the part of public police and has
spawned a number of studies, in the United States and elsewhere, to
foster the privatization of policing and enhance public-private police
cooperation. Marx identifies several forms of cooperation between public and private police agencies: "joint public/private investigations,
public agents hiring or delegating authority to private police, private
interests hiring public police, new organizational forms in which the
distinction between public and private is blurred, and the circulation
of personnel between the public and private sectors" (1987, pp. 172–
73). For example, within the United States, the Justice Department
has recently published a report entitled "Public Policing—Privately
Provided" that sets out a framework for greater recourse to the private
policing industry for some functions traditionally provided by the public police (Chaiken and Chaiken 1987). The foreword to this report,
directed to the police community, makes clear just how far RAND
and Hallcrest have reshaped the political agenda since the 1930s with
respect to the privatization and distribution of policing:

> Nearly as much money is now paid by governments to private
> security companies as is spent for public law enforcement by the
> federal and state governments combined. Many police officers
> see these rapidly rising expenditures for private security as a
> disturbing movement towards the privatization of entire city police
> departments. But the authors of this report feel such concerns are
> misplaced. Rather, competent police administrators are recognizing
> the distinctions between functions that can best be performed
> by sworn police officers and other functions that can more
> productively be handled by civilians or private firms under
> contract. . . . The report was prepared to help administrators
> understand and evaluate the current state of provision of
> police-related services by private contractors. It gives concrete
> guidance on the types of police-related tasks that are best suited
> for contracting with private companies and on the advantages and
> disadvantages of private contracting. . . . It gives practical advice
> on the contracting process and gives addresses and telephone
> numbers of experienced municipal and state administrators you
> can contact for further advice. [Chaiken and Chaiken 1987, p. iii]

In assisting public police managers to decide which policing functions can be privatized and in developing Hallcrest's equal partner

conception, Chaiken and Chaiken reject the claim that there are some tasks which belong in principle to the public police and cannot be privatized. They reject, for example, the argument that functions requiring the legal status of "peace officer" cannot be privatized.[13] Instead they insist that the division of labor must be determined on pragmatic grounds. They assert that tasks that require a "multiplicity of skills" should remain with the public police because their training equips them for such tasks, and those that do not require a combination of skills can and should be transferred (1987, p. 6). In making this claim these authors at once confirm the principle that there are no theoretical limits to privatization (as training changes, so will what is transferred) and at the same time allay police opposition to privatization by actually advocating the transfer of tasks that public police officers and managers regard as peripheral (see Fixler and Poole [1988] for a discussion of barriers to privatization).

In a second study commissioned by the National Institute of Justice, Reiss (1988) explores the "private employment of public police." This study was prompted by Hallcrest's (Cunningham and Taylor 1985, p. 200) findings that between 20 and 30 percent of all public police personnel were engaged in "off-duty security employment." These officers were hired both by private businesses (as in-house security) and by private police forces (contract security firms). Hallcrest canvassed a variety of concerns related to the employment of off-duty police officers. Perhaps the most controversial was the concern that what was being bought was not simply an employee but state authority and a state-issued license to use physical force (Stenning and Shearing 1979). Reiss develops this point: "There seems little reason to doubt then that public police officers not only bring to private employers greater formal authority but that they enjoy greater informal power as well. As Shearing and Addario have shown, public police are more likely than private security personnel to be regarded as moral protectors. Accordingly, the public police can lay claim to moral as well as legal authority for

---

[13] The significance of peace-officer status arises because peace officers typically have greater legitimate access to physical force in the preservation of the peace than do ordinary citizens (Stenning and Shearing 1979). Restriction of functions that require peace-officer status to the public police arguably assures that private police do not have special access to physical force. This is symbolically significant, but in defining the legal and political status of private police, it is not of great practical moment as private police have seldom had difficulty getting access to the coercive force available to peace officers through the simple device of "calling the police" (Shearing and Stenning 1982; Shearing 1984).

their actions" (Reiss 1988, p. 75, with reference to Shearing, Stenning, and Addario 1985*b*).

Reiss discovered that, in defending this practice of police moonlighting, chiefs of police drew on the conceptual framework developed by RAND and Hallcrest. They argued that so long as care was taken to ensure that off-duty police officers were being paid to keep the peace, the public was benefiting because off-duty officers were working at private expense to do what the state was required to do anyway (Reiss 1988, pp. 15–24). Reiss explores the extent to which this defense was credible by examining the methods used by public police organizations to ensure that the public interest was being met by off-duty police officers acting privately. He concludes that satisfactory methods of control can exist and argues in support of the employment of off-duty peace officers on the grounds that the private use of such officers contributes to the public good. To facilitate this integration of policing resources, Reiss recommends a contracting system between police departments and private employers to allow for "greater control over private employers and over the officer during off-duty assignment" (1988, p. 77). "If the public police can satisfy a private employer's demand for police services in ways that are both superior to that provided by private security while at the same time increasing the preventive and deterrent capability of the public police, there may be good reasons for organizing to meet at least some of that demand through regular rather than secondary employment of their police officers" (Reiss 1988, p. 80). This statement illustrates just how much "progress" has been made since the 1930s in the acceptance of private guarantors of peace as legitimate features of an integrated structure of public and private policing.

A recent study that advances this idea of an integrated policing structure that fully exploits public and private resources was released by the solicitor general of Canada (Normandeau and Leighton 1990). This report goes beyond the positions adopted by RAND and Hallcrest to recognize that private policing resources are not restricted to specialized security personnel employed as part of private police departments but include anyone,[14] and indeed anything, that contributes

---

[14] See, e.g., Weiss's (1987*a*) discussion of the importance of union discipline in the declining use of private police at the Ford Motor Company, Shapiro's (1987) analysis of the variety of resources used in "policing trust," and Shearing and Stenning's (1982) analysis of the use of employees as police resources.

to the preservation of the peace.[15] Normandeau and Leighton recommend that Canadian policing policy should encourage "new strategic partnerships" that integrate all the policing capacities available within communities to preserve the peace. Policing, they argue, is a community affair in the sense that it is to the community that governments must look for the resources they require to meet their policing responsibilities (see Stenning [1989] for a view that advocates "equal partnerships" that challenge state dominance in the definition of order). In doing so they are arguing for a system of policing that bears a striking resemblance to the ancient English system of frankpledge that required communities to ensure that the king's peace was maintained and to cooperate with the crown's officials in their efforts to do so (Critchley 1978).

One of the most striking features of this report is that the civil liberties disquiet that had so dominated the earlier twentieth-century debate, and that almost all the contemporary American and European studies recognize, is simply not raised. In so completely ignoring these concerns, the Canadian report goes far beyond either RAND or Hallcrest in silencing the civil liberties arguments that were so prominent within the state-centered framework. This implies a loss of both the relevance of the public/private distinction and the importance of private space as a source of liberty (see Nedelsky 1983). More specifically the implication is that if the community and the state are united as a single integrated system then the need for individuals to protect themselves from the state and from state intrusion falls away. The private becomes the public, and the public the private.

Each of the studies reviewed in this section makes clear just how much the political response to private involvement in policing has altered since the 1950s when the state-centered view was virtually unquestioned. This change, as the 1988 convening by the Council of Europe of a criminological research conference on "privatization of crime control" indicates (e.g., McConville 1988), has not been limited to North America. The laissez-faire conception articulated by RAND two decades ago is now the conventional wisdom underlying the political consciousness that guides the relationship between public and private policing.

---

[15] For example, as Shearing and Stenning (1984) note, with reference to Disney World, the Disney characters, such as Mickey Mouse, the park attendants, the flower beds, the transportation vehicles, and the organization of the monorail platform are all resources within an integrated policing enterprise.

The Marxist counterpoint to the liberal version of the laissez-faire way of seeing accepts the essential outlines of this position but disputes the conception of the public interest that is put forward. Critical theorists accept that privatization has occurred and has done so under an umbrella of state control. However, they view this as evidence of the continuing evolution of an exploitative state-corporate alliance promoting "selective policing, biased in favour of wealth and power" (Flavel 1973, p. 15; Spitzer 1987). While this position echoes the concerns of state-centered theorists, it does not share their belief in the possibility of a just and fair state within a capitalist society. The privatization of policing, like that of other aspects of criminal justice, is expressed in metaphorical terms as a "widening of the net" of state control in the interests of capital (Cohen 1979).[16] "Thus, 'tiny theaters' of private control supplement the more centralized state apparatus" (Reichman 1987, p. 261). It is argued that, far from enhancing the quality of life as Hallcrest maintained, privatization has had the effect of bringing more and more of daily life under the control of an oppressive capitalist state (Henry 1987a, pp. 89–90). Privatization, and more specifically private policing, is an ugly specter, an "unholy alliance," to be resisted (Klare 1975a, 1975b; Bunyan 1976; Bowden 1978).

What is required instead are democratic forms of policing controlled by local communities. Popular policing should replace that of an exploitative state-corporate apparatus (Turk 1987, pp. 132–36; West 1987). For these theorists a policing structure that arises out of, and responds to, popular interests should be substituted for the public-private policing alliance (Kinsey, Lea, and Young 1986). In promoting this agenda, these scholars have sought to replace the story advanced by RAND and Hallcrest of an evolution of public-private cooperation in the public interest with revisionist histories asserting that the laissez-faire strategy of privatization is just another stage in the ongoing process of mystification that characterizes capitalist social control (Reiner 1985).

Both the state-centered and laissez-faire conceptions are founded on an understanding of the social world as divided into public and private

---

[16] Philippe Robert observes: "There is no such thing as pure privatization: state action does not disappear. It simply fades into the background in some types of cases, and is combined with various patterns of private management of security. In one sense, privatization does not exist. Private security systems (in-house or contracted out) do not replace public agencies which were previously state-controlled: they are now organs which are added to earlier systems, and are combined with them" (1988, p. 112).

spheres whose boundaries and significance assume the existence of a nation-state that either does, or should, monopolize governance. They both assume a history of conflicts over the sources of governance arising from multiple griths or sanctuaries (Rock 1983) but maintain that this either is, or should be, a thing of the past. The willingness of the laissez-faire framework to accept and countenance privatization and a coordinated system of public and private policing—integrating the activities of state and corporate guarantors of peace to create what O'Toole (1978, p. 227) has termed the "police-industrial complex"—represents a supreme confidence in the existence and persistence of strong nation-states.

III. A Pluralist Perspective

In the course of my analysis of the laissez-faire position, especially as it has been developed by and since Hallcrest, I have drawn attention to the way the reform agenda it embodies contributes to the emergence of a reality that challenges two fundamental assumptions on which the position itself rests. First, the acceptance and promotion of corporate guarantors of order, with their feudal resonances of relatively autonomous nonstate corporate entities, creates a tension within the laissez-faire framework that gestures toward a more fractured conception of policing that denies the state its privileged position. Second, the promotion of an integrated policing system, as my comments on the implications of Normandeau and Leighton's recommendations suggest, undermines the public/private distinction. Within the liberal versions of this framework these tensions are contained both through an assumption of a shared definition of the peace, permitting the coordination of private and state resources, and through a silence with respect to implications for institutions of privacy.

In responding to this conceptual tension a number of scholars have turned to the work of the legal pluralists (see Henry 1983, pp. 47–56; 1987a) as well as the poststructuralist linking of discourse and power (Shearing and Stenning 1984; Cohen 1987; Henry 1987a), in particular Foucault (1977, 1981), for inspiration in developing ideas about the nature of policing which involve an understanding of power as decentered and embedded in relationships. Waltzer (1983, p. 483, cited in Cohen 1987, p. 378) contrasts the centered and decentered conceptions as follows: "Foucault is concerned not with the dispersion of power to the extremities of the political system but with its exercise in the extremities. For the Americans, power was dispersed to individuals and groups and then recentralized, that is, brought to bear again at the focal point of sovereignty. For Foucault there is no focal point but an endless network of power relations."[17]

The replacement of the idea of dispersal of a central power with that of fractured or decentered power, harks back to Rudé's "jungle of rival jurisdictions" (cited in Rock 1983, p. 208) that characterized late seventeenth- and early eighteenth-century England and argues that the triumph of the state was not as complete, nor as secure, as has been believed. Thus, Cohen (1987, p. 378) asserts that what Foucault is proposing—in contrast to critical theorists who have sometimes sought to use him to support their state-centered claims—is that "there is no discernible sovereign state to take over or ruling class to replace. The same micro-physics of power can and will reproduce itself in quite different political systems . . . each micro-system is not quite autonomous but it is 'particular' and has to be challenged on its own terms."

By locating policing within the context of autonomous and semiautonomous sources of ordering that, although coupled to the state in a variety of ways, do not express a delegated authority, Shearing and Stenning (1983) have sought to challenge both the state-centered and the laissez-faire conceptions of policing. They have suggested instead a new corporate pluralism in which corporations cooperate and coordinate with each other and the state as relatively autonomous guarantors of peace, as well as secondary orders that build on the foundation order of peace.

In exploring the implications of these ideas for policing, Shearing and Stenning (1983, 1984; Stenning and Shearing 1991) have argued that privatization has prompted a fundamental shift in responsibility for policing, from state to corporate hands, that is challenging state power and redefining state-corporate relationships. They argue that what appears (when viewed from within a way of seeing that privileges the nation-state) as a widening of the net of state control is revealed (when viewed from a pluralist perspective) as a change in the location of power. This shift, they propose, has not only been accompanied by a thinning of the net of control but has brought with it important

---

[17] This idea is expressed, as Henry (1987a, p. 46) indicates, by the legal pluralists: "Modern legal pluralists such as Pospisil (1971) have . . . captured the essence of horizontal plurality with the notion that 'any human . . . does not possess a single legal system, but as many legal systems as there are functioning groups' (Pospisil 1971, p. 98), and that the multiplicity of these systems forms a mosaic of contradictory controls that simultaneously bear on the individual."

changes in the nature of policing as the objectives and capacities of corporate entities have begun to shape the ordering process.

Not surprisingly the order being promoted by corporations through their policing activities is directly related to their interests as competing entities within a capitalist economy (Shearing and Stenning 1981, 1983; Shearing, Stenning, and Addario 1985c), a feature of private policing that South (1988) captures in the title of his book *Policing for Profit*. The strategies that result are controlled by the profit motive, are more instrumental than moral (for a qualification, see Stenning et al. 1990; for a critique, see Henry 1987b), and are less likely to be performed by specialized police officers. In developing this argument Shearing and Stenning (1984) pointed to Disney World, with its embedded policing strategies which move policing out of the hands of specialized agents, as well as its instrumental focus on prevention rather than moral ordering, as the epitome of the new policing of an emerging "corporate feudalism." Privatization, they argued, involved more than simply a change in the location of a "service" from one set of agents to another. Policing changed as its location changed.

Shearing and Stenning also questioned whether the privatization of policing was driven by the fiscal crisis of the state. Privatization had occurred and was occurring, they claimed, not because of, or not simply because of, a fiscally induced drive by the state to rid itself of costly services but because the corporate environment produced by the emergence of "mass private property" provided corporations with the legal space and economic incentive to do their own policing.

In developing this analysis they accepted Spitzer and Scull's (1977) assertion that a critical reason for state involvement in policing and other social services during earlier periods of the capitalist economy was the "free-rider problem"[18] that discouraged businesses from directly performing community services such as policing. The emergence of "mass private property" had, however, fundamentally altered this cost-benefit equation, now motivating corporations to perform such "services" themselves and to withdraw support from the state as a vehicle for corporations to pool resources in response to the free-rider problem. Ironically, in responding to this new situation, corporations were using the legal institutions of property and privacy guaranteed

---

[18] If a business organization provides a service that competitors will benefit from but do not contribute toward, it provides them with a "free ride" and puts itself at a competitive disadvantage.

by the state to withdraw support from it. This enhancement of corporate power was challenging traditional conceptions of national sovereignty and the role of the nation-state as the primary guarantor of peace.

Cohen (1987, pp. 376–77) in commenting on this development cautions against its enthusiastic acceptance as a move in the direction of community control. In doing so he raises the specter of a return to decentered power but now equipped with a new disciplinary technology of embedded power:

> In a society in which the power to control is invested not just
> in the state but in the commercial market, and in particular
> in the hands of large corporate interests, non-statist forms of
> decentralization cannot be valued in themselves. Nowhere is this
> better illustrated than in the growing critical literature on private
> security. At first sight, what could be better: autonomy from state
> control, decentralization, no positivist notion of disciplinary
> measures aimed at the individual soul, control embedded in a
> structure which appears consensual. But put this into practice,
> under the sole force of commercialism, and we have all the
> horrors that Shearing and Stenning describe in their nice analysis
> of Disneyworld: social control which is ". . . embedded,
> preventative, subtle, co-operative, and apparently non-coercive
> and consensual."

While Shearing and Stenning (1984) did not refer specifically to the economic issues of deregulation, the globalization of markets, and the emergence of worldwide corporations, their arguments resonate with claims by economists that these developments mark "the latest stage in the erosion of the autonomy of the nation state" (Stopford and Turner 1985).

In developing these arguments Shearing and Stenning, like Cain (1979), maintained that the theoretical framework used by scholars such as Bittner (1970) to understand policing was too state centered to allow for comprehension of the implications of corporate policing. To adopt a framework that by definition accorded hegemony to the state was to be captured by the state's claims to be the supreme guarantor of order. This conclusion has prompted attempts (e.g., Henry 1987a) to develop a conception of policing and, more generally, ordering that is consistent with a view of the social world as "irreducibly and irrevocably pluralistic, split into a multitude of sovereign units and sites of authority, with no horizontal or vertical order, either in actuality or in potency" (Bauman 1988, p. 799).

These emerging conceptions conjure up an image of a world in which corporate "private governments" exist alongside state governments (Macauley 1986) in an "integral plurality" (Fitzpatrick 1984) of shifting relations and claims with respect to sovereignty that change over both time and terrains. Such an understanding permits a recognition of giant corporations, which compete in a global market, as sites of governance from which assurances of security and order are sought and relied on (Macauley 1986). This is occurring at the same time as the emergence of global markets is challenging the boundaries of states and the very notion of the state as a basis for political organization (Stopford and Turner 1985).

The pluralist conception confronts the laissez-faire position by rejecting the argument that privatization involves no more than a technical transfer of tasks from one service sector to another. Instead it argues that what is taking place, under the guise of privatization, is a fundamental shift in the location of responsibility for guaranteeing and defining the peace from the state to corporate entities. Together with the state, these corporations constitute a field of interpenetrating and loosely coupled entities that negotiate territories and spheres of autonomy (Macauley 1986). Pluralists dispute a conception of the political and legal spheres as organized vertically with the state at the apex. In its place they suggest a more horizontally organized sphere of linked but autonomous entities with mutual claims over each other, characterized by considerable fluidity and flux (Rock 1983, p. 193; Henry 1987a). Corporate entities, including the state, operate in each other's shadows and in each other's rooms, but no room or shadow is, in principle, more significant than any other (Galanter 1981).

This position identifies policing as a generic function that is not the property of the state (Cain 1979). It accepts that the state is one guarantor of order among others, albeit the primary—though not the exclusive—guarantor of peace for much of the past century. Viewed from within this conception, the centralization of policing that the state-centered view expressed and helped create may simply be a transitional stage from one decentered corporate-based system to another. Pluralism, thus, suggests that we accept Cohen's (1987, p. 378) advice and take decentralization very seriously indeed.

If the pluralist position is correct, the emerging landscape of fractured sovereignty raises fundamental questions about what response should be adopted to this globalization and privatization of policing and governance more generally. Scholars who take the pluralist arguments seriously have expressed an ambivalent response. They are inclined to welcome the shift in governance from the state to the community on the grounds that it enhances local control and autonomy. They are concerned, however, about the emergence of corporate "communities" in which corporations act as private governments with enormous power over their "citizens" (Shearing and Stenning 1982). Cohen (1987, pp. 376–77) captures this ambivalence:

> I would recommend a cautious reaffirmation of the values behind decentralized community control—"cautious" for these do not seem to me absolute values which cancel out all others. And instead of abolition—which is unrealistic—I would advocate attrition: a gradual wearing away of the criminal law, by a process of benign neglect, until it is only used when there is genuinely no alternative. . . . Of course the problem with Disneyworld (and similar examples of shopping complexes, condominium estates and the other "feudal-like domains". . .) is that they represent only a part of the community package. They require no knowledge of the individual, they are authoritarian, and they are not informed by any progressive ideology. These points are obvious—we all understand why Disneyworld is different from a kibbutz—but to be fair to the community vision, we have to take the whole package together and not judge the results of the component parts.

A response that is less ambiguous will require, as Cohen suggests, the more adequate development of a theoretical understanding of power that moves decisively beyond conceptions that take a strong state for granted and accepts the Foucauldian insight that "the king's head has long been cut off; [that] power is not wielded by a single subject, [and that] there is no central source of command, no practical center of political life" (Cohen 1987, p. 378). It is just such a theory that the pluralists are endeavoring to create.

IV. Conclusion

Just what the emerging decentralized world will look like remains uncertain. This uncertainty is reflected in the contemporary use of the prefix "post" to refer to the "post-modern" age. We are a lot clearer about where we have come from than where we are going.

Policing, because it lies at the heart of any order, however, provides a dark glass through which we may be able to catch glimpses of the shape of the world we are tumbling toward. What this peep through the prism of policing reveals is that the emerging social world is unlikely to be one in which governance is monopolized by states. Perhaps as Cohen suggests governance will rest more directly in the hands of local communities. The fear is that the reality might be pervasive and intrusive corporate governance in which the interests of capital are more directly pursued than state-centered theories of capitalism ever dreamed was possible. While the state might wither away this may not mean a lessening of the domination of capital interests (O'Toole 1978; Shearing and Stenning 1983, 1984). If this fear is realized, the political realm will be one in which economy infuses governance more completely than even the most instrumental Marxist theorists have proposed. In such a world definitions of the public interest and the peace will mirror the interests of corporate governments.

Whatever the nature of government, the strategies of governance will likely reflect the capacities of the new governing entities. If the Foucauldian analysis is any guide, force will not be the primary means of policing or ordering more generally (Shearing and Stenning 1984). The hope of "visionary politics" (Cohen 1987, p. 379) is that this might mean more consensually based local control processes; the "realpolitik" fear is that corporate access to information about most aspects of our lives—through the use of computer matching, "computers as informant," and the like—will "routinize the discovery of secrets" (Marx and Reichman 1987) in ways that will eliminate privacy and with it opportunities for resistance (Reiss 1984, 1987). If this fear is realized, a "Brave New World" of unseen, embedded, and pervasive control that eliminates autonomy and privacy may well become our everyday reality (Shearing and Stenning 1984). The net will be widened and thinned, but those fishing will not be exclusively state officials.

What happens will in part be a consequence of emerging material, structural conditions (Spitzer and Scull 1977, 1980), but it will also be a product of the agency of people responding to, and acting within, these structures and the "tiny theaters" of power they make possible. This response will depend on the sensibilities that shape their actions (Garland 1990; Shearing and Ericson 1991). These sensibilities, and the voices they make possible, are the sites of struggle, and it is this struggle that will shape the world we are entering (Petchesky 1987; Weedon 1987). This struggle over political consciousness takes place, as this essay has sought to illustrate, on and through a terrain of discourse (Ericson 1987) that establishes ways of seeing and being that prompt action (Gusfield 1981, 1989; Shearing and Ericson 1991). Much of this terrain is hidden and implicit (Foucault 1977; Bourdieu 1984; White 1984), but much of it—Foucault's comments in *Discipline and Punish* (1977) about our world being a society of surveillance and not of spectacle notwithstanding—will take place through highly visible spectacles (Geertz 1973; Bourdieu 1977; Mathiesen 1987; Petchesky 1987; Edelman 1988; Stenning et al. 1990). Contemporary society is more like the world of the Greeks than Foucault in his "more inflated rhetoric" (Garland 1990, p. 146) would have us believe (Barthes 1972; White 1984). We are in the "panoptic machine," but we are also very much "in the amphitheatre" and "on the stage" (Mathiesen 1987, pp. 59–60).

Discourse, in both its spectacular and nonspectacular forms, has as its focus the "soul" as "the seat of the habits" (Foucault cited in Garland 1990, p. 143; Stenning et al. 1990). The battle between visionary and "realpolitik" versions of pluralism will be fought on the terrain of the "soul." It is in the "poetic logic" and figurative imagery of language (White 1984; Shearing and Ericson 1991) that the future shape of governance will be settled. In this essay I have sought to show how the state-centered and laissez-faire discourses have shaped policing. I have also introduced the burgeoning pluralist discourse and suggested how it is contributing to the emerging public debate over the location of governance. The pluralist perspective provides an alternate way of seeing that, at present, remains on the edges of public debate but will probably move closer to the center as the reform agendas of the laissez-faire conception work to establish the world the pluralist conception is "discovering." Pluralist reform agendas are already beginning to shape political consciousness.

The future scholarly task this essay has identified is the examination of this process through an analysis of how the ways of seeing and the voices of the post-laissez-faire world contest with older meanings, and with each other, through the various logics and mediums available within the contemporary world (Bourdieu 1977, 1984; Foucault 1981). One of the conceptual implications of the pluralist view—to be watched closely, because it challenges the most fundamental premises of both the state-centered and the laissez-faire ways of seeing—is the blurring of the distinction between public and private realms (Rose 1987) and public and private authorities as the state loses its focal position. What we recognize now as a blurring may prove in retrospect to be the earliest stages of a very different conception of social space in which the public realm may come to be equated with the corporate realm. Such a development may well have implications far beyond policing.

REFERENCES

Andrew, Donna T. 1989. *Philanthropy and Police: London Charity in the Eighteenth Century*. Princeton, N.J.: Princeton University Press.

Barthes, Roland. 1972. *Mythologies*. London: Jonathan Cape.

Bauman, Zygmunt. 1988. "Sociology and Postmodernity." *Sociological Review* 36:790–813.

Becker, Theodore M. 1974. "The Place of Private Police in Society: An Area of Research for the Social Sciences." *Social Problems* 21:438–53.

Bittner, Egon. 1970. *The Functions of the Police in Modern Society*. United States Public Health Service Publication no. 2059. Washington, D.C.: U.S. Government Printing Office.

Bourdieu, Pierre. 1977. "Symbolic Power." In *Identity and Structure: Issues in the Sociology of Education*, edited by Denis Gleeson. Duffield, England: Napperton.

———. 1984. *Distinction: A Critique of the Social Judgment of Taste*. Cambridge, Mass.: Harvard University Press.

Bowden, Tom. 1978. *Beyond the Limits of the Law*. Harmondsworth: Penguin.

Braun, Michael, and David J. Lee. 1971. "Private Police Forces: Legal Powers and Limitations." *University of Chicago Law Review* 38:555–82.

Bunyan, Tony. 1976. *The History and Practice of the Political Police in Britain*. London: Julian Friedmann.

Cain, Maureen. 1979. "Trends in the Sociology of Police Work." *International Journal of the Sociology of Law* 7:143–67.

Chaiken, Marcia, and Jan Chaiken. 1987. *Public Policing—Privately Provided*. National Institute of Justice, Issues and Practices. Washington, D.C.: U.S. Government Printing Office.

Cohen, Stanley. 1979. "The Punitive City: Notes on the Dispersal of Social Control." *Contemporary Crisis* 3:339–64.

———. 1987. "Taking Decentralization Seriously: Values, Visions and Policies." In *Transcarceration: Essays in the Sociology of Social Control*, edited by John Lowman, Robert J. Menzies, and T. S. Palys. Aldershot: Gower.

Critchley, Thomas A. 1978. *A History of Police in England and Wales: 1900–1966*. London: Constable.

Cunningham, William C., and Todd H. Taylor. 1985. *The Hallcrest Report: Private Security and Police in America*. Portland, Oreg.: Chancellor.

Draper, Hilary. 1978. *Private Police*. Harmondsworth: Penguin.

Edelman, Murray J. 1988. *Constructing the Political Spectacle*. Chicago: University of Chicago Press.

Encyclopedia Britannica. 1972. Chicago: William Benton.

Ericson, Richard V. 1987. *Visualizing Deviance*. Toronto: University of Toronto Press.

Fitzpatrick, P. 1984. "Law and Societies." *Osgoode Hall Law Journal* 22:115–38.

Fixler, Philip E., and Robert W. Poole, Jr. 1988. "Can Police Services be Privatized?" *Annals* 498:108–18.

Flavel, W. 1973. "Research into Private Security." Paper presented to the second Bristol Seminar on the Sociology of the Police, Bristol, April.

Foucault, Michel. 1977. *Discipline and Punish: The Birth of the Prison*. New York: Pantheon.

———. 1981. "The Order of Discourse." *Untying the Text: A Post-structuralist Reader*, edited by R. Young. London: Routledge & Kegan Paul.

Galanter, Marc. 1981. "Justice in Many Rooms: Courts, Private Ordering and Indigenous Law." *Journal of Legal Pluralism* 19:1–47.

Garland, David. 1990. *Punishment and Modern Society: A Study in Social Theory*. Oxford: Clarendon.

Geertz, Clifford. 1973. "Deep Play: Notes on the Balinese Cockfight." In *The Interpretation of Cultures: Selected Essays*, edited by Clifford Geertz. New York: Basic.

Giddens, Anthony. 1987. *The Nation-State and Violence*. Berkeley and Los Angeles: University of California Press.

Gusfield, Joseph R. 1981. *The Culture of Public Problems: Drinking-Driving and the Symbolic Order*. Chicago: University of Chicago Press.

———. 1989. "Constructing Ownership of Social Problems: Fun and Profit in the Welfare State." *Social Problems* 36:431–41.

Henry, Stuart. 1983. *Private Justice: Towards Integrated Theorizing in the Sociology of Law*. London: Routledge & Kegan Paul.

———.1987*a*. "The Construction and Deconstruction of Social Control: Thoughts on the Discursive Production of State Law and Private Justice." In *Transcarceration: Essays in the Sociology of Social Control*, edited by John Lowman, Robert J. Menzies, and T. S. Palys. Aldershot: Gower.

———. 1987*b*. "Private Justice and the Policing of Labor: The Dialectics of Industrial Discipline." In *Private Policing*, edited by Clifford D. Shearing and Philip C. Stenning. Newbury Park, Calif.: Sage.

Hobbes, Thomas. 1968. *Leviathan*. Aylesbury, England: Penguin.

Hoogenboom, A. B. 1987. "Privatization of the Police Function in the Netherlands." Paper presented at the International Sociological Association Meetings, Montreal, November.

Kakalik, James S., and Sorrel Wildhorn. 1972. *Private Security in the United States*. 5 vols. Washington, D.C.: U.S. Department of Justice, National Institute of Law Enforcement and Criminal Justice, Law Enforcement Assistance Administration.

Keeton, George Williams. 1975. *Keeping the Peace*. Chichester, N.Y.: Barry Rose.

Kinsey, Richard, John Lea, and Jock Young. 1986. *Losing the Fight against Crime*. Oxford: Blackwell.

Klare, M. 1975a. "Rent-a-Cop: The Private Security Industry in the U.S." In *The Iron Fist and the Velvet Glove: An Analysis of the U.S. Police*, edited by the Center for Research on Criminal Justice. Berkeley, Calif.: Center for Research on Criminal Justice.

——. 1975b. "Rent-a-Cop: The Boom in Private Police." *Nation* 221:486–91.

Kraakman, Reinier H. 1986. "Gatekeepers: The Anatomy of a Third-Party Enforcement Strategy." *Journal of Law, Economics, and Organization* 2:53–104.

Laitinen, Ahti. 1987. "The Privatization of the Police Function in Finland." Paper presented at the International Sociological Association Meetings, Montreal, November.

Landes, W. M., and R. A. Posner. 1975. "The Private Enforcement of Law." *Journal of Legal Studies* 4:1–46.

Lipson, Milton. 1988. "Private Security: A Retrospective." *Annals* 498:11–22.

Macauley, Stewart. 1986. "Private Government." In *Law and the Social Sciences*, edited by Milton Lipson and Stanton Wheeler. New York: Russell Sage.

McConville, Sean. 1988. "The Privatisation of Penal Services." Paper presented at the Council of Europe, Eighteenth Criminological Research Conference, Strasbourg, August.

Marx, Gary T. 1987. "The Interweaving of Public and Private Police in Undercover Work." In *Private Policing*, edited by Clifford D. Shearing and Philip C. Stenning. Newbury Park, Calif.: Sage.

Marx, Gary T., and Nancy Reichman. 1987. "Routinizing Secrets: Computers as Informants." In *Transcarceration: Essays in the Sociology of Social Control*, edited by John Lowman, Robert J. Menzies, and T. S. Palys. Aldershot: Gower.

Mathiesen, Thomas. 1987. "The Eagle and the Sun: On Panoptical Systems and Mass Media in Modern Society." In *Transcarceration: Essays in the Sociology of Social Control*, edited by John Lowman, Robert J. Menzies, and T. S. Palys. Aldershot: Gower.

Matthews, Roger, ed. 1989. *Privatizing Criminal Justice*. London: Sage.

Metnick, Barry M. 1980. *The Political Economy of Regulation: Creating, Designing, and Removing Regulatory Forms*. New York: Columbia University Press.

Mewett, Alan W. 1988. *An Introduction to the Criminal Process in Canada*. Toronto: Carswell.

Mnookin, Robert H. 1982. "The Public/Private Dichotomy: Political Disagreement and Academic Repudiation." *University of Pennsylvania Law Review* 130:1429–40.

Nedelsky, Jennifer. 1983. "Individual Autonomy in the Bureaucratic State: Toward a Reconception." Paper presented at the Russell Sage Foundation Colloquium, New York, November.

——. 1989. "Reconceiving Autonomy: Sources, Thoughts and Possibilities." *Yale Journal of Law and Feminism* 1:7–36.

Normandeau, Andre, and Barry Leighton. 1990. *A Vision of the Future of Policing in Canada: Police Challenge 2000: Background Document*. Ottawa: Solicitor General Canada.

O'Toole, George. 1978. *The Private Sector: Rent a Cop, Private Spies and the Police Industrial Complex*. New York: Norton.

Oxford English Dictionary. 1989. Oxford: Clarendon Press.

Peel, John D. 1971. *The Story of Private Security*. Springfield, Ill.: Thomas.

Petchesky, Rosalind. 1987. "Fetal Images: The Power of Visual Culture in the Politics of Reproduction." *Feminist Studies* 13:263–91.

Phillips, Jim. 1991. "The History of Canadian Criminal Justice, 1750–1920." In *Criminology: A Reader's Guide*, edited by Jane Gladstone, Richard V. Ericson, and Clifford D. Shearing. Toronto: Centre of Criminology (forthcoming).

Pospisil, Leopold. 1971. *Anthropology of Law*. New York: Harper & Row.

President's Commission on Law Enforcement and Administration of Justice. 1967a. *The Challenge of Crime in a Free Society*. Washington, D.C.: U.S. Government Printing Office.

———. 1967b. *Task Force Report: The Police*. Washington, D.C.: U.S. Government Printing Office.

Radzinowicz, Leon A. 1948. *A History of English Law and Its Administration from 1750*. Vol. 2, *The Clash between Private Initiatives and Public Interest in the Enforcement of the Law*. London: Stevens & Sons.

Reichman, Nancy. 1987. "The Widening Webs of Surveillance: Private Police Unraveling Deceptive Claims." In *Private Policing*, edited by Clifford D. Shearing and Philip C. Stenning. Newbury Park, Calif.: Sage.

Reiner, Robert. 1985. *The Politics of the Police*. Brighton, England: Harvester.

Reiss, Albert J., Jr. 1984. "Selecting Strategies of Social Control over Organizational Life." In *Enforcing Regulation*, edited by Keith Hawkins and John Thomas. Boston: Kluwer-Nijoff.

———. 1987. "The Legitimacy of Intrusions into Private Space." In *Private Policing*, edited by Clifford D. Shearing and Philip C. Stenning. Newbury Park, Calif.: Sage.

———. 1988. *Private Employment of Public Police*. Washington, D.C.: U.S. Department of Justice, National Institute of Justice.

Robert, Phillipe. 1988. "The Privatization of Social Control." In *Crime and Criminal Policy in Europe: Proceedings of a European Colloquium, July 1988*, edited by Roger Hood. Oxford: University of Oxford, Centre for Criminological Research.

Rock, Paul. 1983. "Law, Order and Power in Late Seventeenth- and Early Eighteenth-Century England." In *Social Control and the State*, edited by Stanley Cohen and Andrew Scull. Oxford: Martin Robertson.

Rose, Nikolas. 1987. "Beyond the Public/Private Division: Law, Power and the Family." *Journal of Law and Society* 14:61–76.

Rosenthal, Uriel, and Bob Hoogenboom. 1988. "Some Fundamental Questions on Privatization and Commercialization of Crime Control, with Special Reference to Developments in the Netherlands." Paper presented at the Eighteenth Criminological Research Conference, Council of Europe, Strasbourg, August.

Rule, James B., Douglas McAdam, Linda Stevens, and David Uglow. 1980. *The Politics of Privacy*. New York: New American Library.

Ryan, Mick, and Tony Ward. 1989. *Privatization and the Penal System: The American Experience and the Debate in Britain*. Milton Keynes: Open University Press.

Scott, Thomas M., and Marlys McPherson. 1971. "The Development of the

Private Sector of the Criminal Justice System." *Law and Society Review* 6:267–88.

Shapiro, Susan P. 1987 "Policing Trust." In *Private Policing*, edited by Clifford D. Shearing and Philip C. Stenning. Newbury Park, Calif.: Sage.

Shearing, Clifford D. 1984. *Dial-a-Cop: A Study of Police Mobilization*. Toronto: University of Toronto, Centre of Criminology.

Shearing, Clifford D., and Richard V. Ericson. 1991. "Culture as Figurative Action." *British Journal of Sociology* (forthcoming).

Shearing, Clifford D., Margaret Farnell, and Philip C. Stenning. 1980. *Contract Security*. Toronto: University of Toronto, Centre of Criminology.

Shearing, Clifford D., and Philip C. Stenning. 1981. "Modern Private Security: Its Growth and Implications." In *Crime and Justice: An Annual Review of Research*, vol. 3, edited by Michael Tonry and Norval Morris. Chicago: University of Chicago Press.

———. 1982. *Private Security and Private Justice: The Challenge of the 80s*. Montreal: Institute for Research on Public Policy.

———. 1983. "Private Security: Implications for Social Control." *Social Problems* 30:493–506.

———. 1984. "From the Panopticon to Disney World: The Development of Discipline." In *Perspectives in Criminal Law: Essays in Honour of John Ll. J. Edwards*, edited by Anthony N. Doob and Edward L. Greenspan. Toronto: Canada Law Book.

Shearing, Clifford D., Philip C. Stenning, and Susan M. Addario. 1985*a*. "Police Perception of Private Security." *Canadian Police College Journal* 9:127–52.

———. 1985*b*. "Public Perception of Private Security." *Canadian Police College Journal* 9:225–53.

———. 1985*c*. "Corporate Perceptions of Private Security." *Canadian Police College Journal* 9:367–90.

Shubert, Adrian. 1981. "Private Initiative in Law Enforcement: Associations for the Prosecution of Felons, 1744–1856." In *Policing and Punishment in Nineteenth Century Britain*, edited by Victor Bailey. London: Croom Helm.

South, Nigel. 1987. "Law, Profit, and 'Private Persons': Private and Public Policing in English History." In *Private Policing*, edited by Clifford D. Shearing and Philip C. Stenning. Newbury Park, Calif.: Sage.

———. 1988. *Policing for Profit: The Private Security Sector*. London: Sage.

———. 1989. "Reconstructing Policing: Differentiation and Contradiction in Post-war Private and Public Policing." In *Privatizing Criminal Justice*, edited by Roger Matthews. London: Sage.

Spitzer, Steven. 1987. "Security and Control in Capitalist Societies: The Fetishism of Security and the Secret Thereof." In *Transcarceration: Essays in the Sociology of Social Control*, edited by John Lowman, Robert J. Menzies, and T. S. Palys. Aldershot: Gower.

Spitzer, Steven, and Andrew T. Scull. 1977. "Privatization and Capitalist Development: The Case of the Private Police." *Social Problems* 25:18–29.

———. 1980. "Social Control in Historical Perspective." In *Corrections and Punishment*, edited by David Greenberg. Beverly Hills, Calif.: Sage.

Stenning, Philip C. 1981. "Legal Status of the Police." A Study Paper prepared for the Law Reform Commission of Canada. Ottawa: Minister of Supply and Services.

———. 1989. "Private Police and Public Police: Toward a Redefinition of the Police Role." In *Future Issues in Policing: Symposium Proceedings*, edited by D. Loree. Ottawa: Minister of Supply and Services.

Stenning, Philip C., and Clifford D. Shearing. 1979. "Search and Seizure: Powers of Private Security." A Study Paper prepared for the Law Reform Commission of Canada. Ottawa: Minister of Supply and Services.

———. 1991. "Policing." In *Criminology: A Reader's Guide*, edited by Jane Gladstone, Richard V. Ericson, and Clifford D. Shearing. Toronto: University of Toronto, Centre of Criminology (forthcoming).

Stenning, Philip C., Clifford D. Shearing, Susan M. Addario, and Mary G. Condon. 1990. "Controlling Interests: Two Conceptions of Ordering Financial Markets." In *Securing Compliance: Seven Case Studies*, edited by Martin L. Friedland. Toronto: University of Toronto Press.

Stinchcombe, Arthur L. 1963. "Institutions of Privacy in the Determination of Police Administrative Practice." *American Journal of Sociology* 69:150–60.

Stopford, John M., and Louis Turner. 1985. *Britain and the Multinationals*. Chichester, N.Y.: Wiley.

Turk, Austin T. 1987. "Popular Justice and the Politics of Informalism." In *Private Policing*, edited by Clifford D. Shearing and Philip C. Stenning. Newbury Park, Calif.: Sage.

United States Committee on Education and Labor. 1971. *Private Police Systems*. New York: Arno Press and the *New York Times*.

Van Outrive, L. 1987. "The Privatization of the Police in Belgium—the Production of a New Private-Public Order." Paper presented at the International Sociological Association Meetings, Montreal, November.

Waltzer, Michael. 1983. "The Politics of Michel Foucault." *Dissent* 30:481–90.

Weedon, Chris. 1987. *Feminist Practice and Poststructuralist Theory*. New York: Blackwell.

Weiss, Robert P. 1979. "An Interpretation of the Origin, Development and Transformation of Private Detective Agency Policing in the United States, 1830–1940." Ph.D. dissertation, Southern Illinois University.

———. 1987a. "From 'Slugging Detectives' to 'Labor Relations': Policing Labor at Ford, 1930–1947." In *Private Policing*, edited by Clifford D. Shearing and Philip C. Stenning. Newbury Park, Calif.: Sage.

———. 1987b. "The Reappearance of the 'Ideal Factory': The Entrepreneur and Social Control in the Contemporary Prison." In *Transcarceration: Essays in the Sociology of Social Control*, edited by John Lowman, Robert J. Menzies, and T. S. Palys. Aldershot: Gower.

West, Gordon W. 1987. "Vigilancia Revolucionaria: A Nicaraguan Resolution to Public and Private Policing." In *Private Policing*, edited by Clifford D. Shearing and Philip C. Stenning. Newbury Park, Calif.: Sage.

White, James Boyd. 1984. *When Words Lose Their Meaning: Constitutions and Reconstitutions of Language, Character and Community*. Chicago: University of Chicago Press.

Wiles, Paul, and Frederick H. McClintock, eds. 1972. *The Security Industry in the United Kingdom*. Cambridge: Cambridge University, Institute of Criminology.

Robert Reiner

Police Research in the United Kingdom: A Critical Review

ABSTRACT

The British police occupy a unique position as the first to be created under representative government, and one which for a long period was regarded as an exemplar of civility. In recent years, however, this image has been undermined by a number of scandals and controversies. The crisis in confidence in British policing has facilitated a huge explosion of police research in the last decade. Whereas earlier policing research had been primarily concerned with issues derived from a variety of social theories, current work is mainly policy oriented and evaluative. A review and assessment of research on the British police demonstrates that much current work is limited in scope to immediate managerial concerns. There is a need for a revival of the broader theoretical conceptions that have been displaced in recent years.

The police in the United Kingdom, or perhaps more specifically and accurately in England, occupy a special place in the history of policing in the world. For many years they were a role model of successful policing, with the Scotland Yard detective and the British bobby representing popular ideals of crime investigation and peacekeeping.

This distinctive historical place was identified by the American historian, Wilbur Miller, in his influential comparative study of the creation of the London and New York City forces. "London's Metropolitan Police, created in 1829, was the first modern police force in a nation with representative government" (Miller 1977, p. ix). Earlier police forces in Europe were clearly instruments of the state (Chapman 1970). The widespread popular opposition to the creation of a modern profes-

Robert Reiner is professor in the law department, London School of Economics.

sional force in England was indeed grounded on the assumption that a police organization would inevitably be a tool of government oppression. It was the distinctive achievement of the policies pursued by the architects of modern British policing, Sir Robert Peel and his appointees as metropolitan commissioners, Rowan and Mayne, to defuse such anxieties (Miller 1977, p. ix). Slowly but surely, with help from the increasing integration of British society generally, the police came eventually to stand as a symbol of national pride, accepted throughout the social structure by the middle of this century (Reiner 1985, chaps. 1, 2).

The result was the construction of an image of ideal policing that had strong resonances around the world. As another American historian of the London police put it: "What people in our own age think of when they hear the words 'English police' is an unarmed police force of constables who are ordinarily courteous to tourists, patient, and restrained in confronting crowds" (Smith 1985, p. 5). This image became an explicit reference point for evaluating policing in other countries (Sherman 1983, p. 233).

The notion of policing by consent in Britain was probably always more a question of image than substance. Its foundation was a hierarchical and deferential social order, rather than the saintly character of all British bobbies. By its nature, the extent of police deviance at any time is an unknown dark figure, with only the occasional cause célèbre casting a brief flash of illumination on it. We do not know how much corruption and abuse of powers lurked beneath the facade of British policing in the golden age of public acceptance. But the fragmentary evidence of police memoirs certainly suggests that the benign image had a harsh Janus face, hidden because of the deference to authority maintained in a rigidly class-stratified society. The following episode, narrated by Sir Robert Mark (later the scourge of corruption when he was metropolitan police commissioner in the 1970s), is telling about the realities of life on the beat in the heyday of the British police:

> Most of us carried, wholly improperly, short rubber
> truncheons. . . . One Friday night an enormous navvy pushed the
> head of a constable through a shop window and started quite a
> battle. . . . I stretched out the left side of my mackintosh for
> cover, drew my rubber with my right hand and gave him a hefty
> whack on the shin. . . . The next morning at court, looking
> sheepish and surprisingly clean, he pleaded guilty, apologised to
> the court, thanked the officers in the case and was fined the

customary ten shillings. As he left the dock my heart stood still.
His right leg below the knee was encased in plaster of Paris. He
had been taken to the Royal Infirmary during the night and
treated for a suspected fracture. . . . Far from there being any
hard feelings he greeted me cheerfully and we went off for a drink
together. Nowadays, of course, it would have meant a complaint,
an enquiry, papers to the Director of Public Prosecutions and a
prosecution or discipline case. [Mark 1978, p. 28]

The decline in public standing since that golden age is as likely to be
due to changing public expectations and decreasing deference and a
toughening of the tasks confronting the police as it is to a fall in the
caliber of the constabulary itself (Reiner 1989*a*). But however the com-
plexly intertwined causes may be analyzed, it is agreed by all commentators that the last twenty years or so have seen a growth of questioning, debate, and controversy about policing (Reiner 1985; Uglow 1988;
Morgan and Smith 1989). By the end of the 1980s, the crisis of legitimacy and confidence in the British police had become a cliché, with
1989 being a vintage year for scandals (Reiner 1990).

This upsurge of concern about policing in the political arena is undoubtedly one source of the explosion of research on the British police
that has occurred in the 1980s (Reiner 1989*b*). It has certainly been a
boom period for police research, with the 1981 riots and the ensuing
Scarman Report acting as a catalyst for funding and access opportunities in much the same way as the U.S. ghetto disorders of the 1960s
(Sherman 1973). Writing in 1979 in the introduction to a representative
collection of essays, Simon Holdaway could claim plausibly that "the
relative dearth of research into the British police has achieved the status
of a cliché amongst sociologists. The British police have remained
largely hidden from sociological gaze" (1979, p. 1).

During the 1980s, the state of British police research has been completely transformed. Police researchers in Britain in 1979 constituted a
cozy club (most of whom are represented in Holdaway's 1979 volume).
In 1989, the Police Foundation (an independent research organization
established in 1980) published its second *New Register of Policing Research*
(Bird 1989); the first had appeared in 1987. This document attempts to
list all "research projects on policing being undertaken in British universities, polytechnics and research institutions at the present time."
Although not fully comprehensive (it is based on voluntary returns by
individual researchers), it provides a good indication of the volume and
range of current work. The register is 207 pages long and lists 184

separate projects being carried out in sixty-nine different institutions. The dimensions of the research explosion on the British police in the 1980s can be graphically illustrated. Whereas in 1979 it was possible for Simon Holdaway to publish a 188-page volume of ten essays representing almost all of the important research of the time, by 1989 it took a 207-page volume merely to provide a partial listing of projects.

The quantitative expansion has been accompanied by a qualitative change (although whether this amounts to progress is a moot point [Holdaway 1989]). All of the researchers in Holdaway's collection were academics, and they were motivated primarily by issues and questions derived from a variety of theoretical traditions, although most were also concerned about the policy and political implications of their work. The projects listed in the Police Foundation compilation are policy oriented in a far more direct and immediate way, much of the research emanates wholly or partly from research institutes outside higher education, and, perhaps most tellingly, much of it involves police officers themselves as researchers.

Complementary institutional necessities have been the mother of the invention of police-oriented research in Britain. On the one hand, the advent of the Thatcher government and the 1980s brought a cold climate for British higher education in general, and social science research in particular. However, the overall cutback of support for social science was accompanied by a reorientation toward those sectors that were relevant to the policy concerns of the government, such as criminal justice. On the other hand, the British police have suffered numerous shocks that have brought about an accumulating crisis of legitimacy. The 1981 Scarman report on the Brixton disorders of that year became the symbol of one direction forward for British policing, an attempt to regain legitimacy by greater openness and professionalism (Scarman 1981). For most of the decade of the 1980s, police forces have been more accessible to outside researchers than in the past. The impact of Scarman and, perhaps even more significantly, the comparatively generous pay levels for the police that have been maintained throughout the decade (due to the Conservatives' implementation of the 1978 Edmund Davies earnings formula) has meant that there are many more police officers with higher educational qualifications. In 1981, there were 2,610 college graduates in the police, but by 1988 this number had risen to 7,409 (although this still amounts to only 6 percent of the police establishment). The increased number of college graduates in the ranks of the police has facilitated greater access for police researchers (about

40 percent of those at chief officer level—metropolitan commander rank or above—are graduates). It has also provided a pool of capable police officers for a growth of in-house research, or projects conducted in collaboration with outside researchers.

The purpose of this essay is to summarize and take stock of the recent explosion in British police research. The examination is organized into four main sections. Section I offers a brief account of research on policing in Britain up to the 1980s. Section II looks at the main constituencies and bodies responsible for generating police research in the 1980s. Section III provides a summary of the themes and results of recent work by answering ten questions: What do police do? Who are the police? What do police think? How are they shaped by training? What does the public want from them, and are they satisfied? Does policing deviate from the rule of law? Are the police fair? Are the police effective? How are the police managed and controlled? How did policing get to its current position? Obviously, given the plethora of recent research, coverage cannot be complete. The selection of studies and issues is intended to provide a clear account of the main lines of development, rather than to be fully comprehensive. The conclusion, Section IV, attempts to assess the current state of play and suggests future directions.

I. Police Research in Britain before 1980

Academic research on the police in Britain has a clear and distinguished genesis in Michael Banton's pioneering study, *The Policeman in the Community*, published in 1964. Until that time, writing on the police had been either works of history, primarily written by enthusiastic amateurs (notably Reith 1938, 1940, 1943, 1956), journalistic pop sociologies (Gorer 1955; Rolph 1962), the memoirs of retired police officers, or officially commissioned research for public inquiries (notably the large-scale opinion surveys of the public and the police concerning their relationship that had been conducted for the 1962 Royal Commission on the Police). Police research was, of course, also in its infancy in the United States at that time, although a series of classic studies appeared in the 1960s (the first few publications are cited in Banton [1964], and, in turn, Banton was clearly influential on much American research of that period).

Banton's 1964 work is a significant starting point for the British police research tradition in a number of ways. It is notable for its firm commitment to ideals of scholarship rather than to sensationalism or "relevance." Although no less scholarly, many of the classic American studies of the 1960s are clearly motivated by or linked to the stirring political and legal conflicts and controversies of the time in which policing played a central role. This seems as true of the work of individual scholars like Skolnick (1966), Wilson (1968), and Bittner (1970) as it does of projects actually originating in commissions formed as an outgrowth of public inquiries, such as Skolnick (1969), Reiss (1971), or Black (1980). Banton's publishers attempted to spice up his work by references in the blurb to relations between the police and the public becoming "a focus of national concern" and to "popular reactions to certain well-publicised incidents." (These are obviously supposed to signal the series of scandals leading to the Royal Commission on the Police report in 1962. While causing a great stir at the time, they seem, by the standards of today, to be "pretty small beer" [Reiner 1985, p. 62].) However, Banton (1964), in his preface, plays down such concerns. He explicitly rebutted the assumption that he "must be examining defects in police organisation and conduct." Rather, he started from "the idea that it can be instructive to analyse institutions that are working well in order to see if anything can be learned from their success" (Banton 1964, p. vii).

Banton's pioneering sociological study is responsible for many ideas and approaches that have been returned to time and again in subsequent work. It initiated what became the central research strategy of most subsequent British work: detailed participant observation. Its account of the police role as primarily consisting of non-law-enforcement "peacekeeping" tasks has been echoed and developed in much subsequent work in Britain and around the world (Cumming, Cumming, and Edell 1965; Wilson 1968; Martin and Wilson 1969; Punch and Naylor 1973; Shearing and Leon 1976; McCabe and Sutcliffe 1978; Punch 1979a, 1979b; Hough 1980; Antunes and Scott 1981; Morris and Heal 1981, chap. 3; Ekblom and Heal 1982; Shearing 1984; Smith and Klein 1984; Bayley 1985, chap. 5; Skolnick and Bayley 1986; Southgate and Ekblom 1986; Shapland and Vagg 1988). The analysis of police culture offered by Banton (although the term is not used by him) identifies characteristics that have been replicated in many subsequent studies, notably the themes of police suspiciousness, internal solidarity, and social isolation (as they are termed in Skolnick's seminal synthesis [Skolnick 1966, chap. 3]). In some respects, Banton's study was ahead of its time. It was based on comparative research on police work in Britain and the United States. While several subsequent studies have compared forces within one country, international comparison has been rare (exceptions are Manning [1977]; and more recently, Bayley [1985]; and Skolnick and Bayley [1988], all of which have contributed to a significant cross-fertilization of British and American research). Banton's key analytic theme, the interpenetration of informal and formal social control, and the greater relative importance of the former, has only recently been reemphasized (Shapland and Vagg 1988).

Banton's work was path breaking for the development of British police research not only through his own scholarly achievements. During the early 1970s he organized three conferences at the University of Bristol on "The Sociology of the Police" (reported in Banton 1971, 1973, 1975). Almost all the police researchers in Britain at that time were present at these meetings and gave papers based on their work (all of which have been published elsewhere: Lambert 1970; Cain 1973; Chatterton 1976, 1979; Holdaway 1977, 1983; McCabe and Sutcliffe 1978; Reiner 1978a; Carrier 1988). There were also some distinguished American visitors (notably, James Q. Wilson in 1971, and Mark Furstenberg and Lawrence Sherman in 1973).

The key themes of British academic police research in the 1970s were laid down at the Banton conferences. The most characteristic type of study was close participant observation of police patrol work, primarily concerned with laying bare the occupational culture of operational policing.[1] Inspired by a variety of theoretical perspectives, several sociologists followed Banton's lead and attempted to immerse themselves in police culture in order to describe and account for the rules and meanings that constitute it. This phase resulted in several key works which, between them, provide a firm basis for understanding the crucial aspects of police culture (notably, Cain 1973; Chatterton 1976, 1979, 1983; Holdaway 1977, 1979, 1983; Manning 1977, 1979 [a study of British policing by a leading American sociologist]; and Punch 1979b, 1985 [observational studies of Dutch police by a British sociologist]). This rich tradition of detailed observational research cannot readily be summed up without distorting somewhat the work of individuals within the group. (Holdaway [1989] offers a recent reassessment by a prominent member.)

The key theme was the exploration of what industrial sociologists

---

[1] Although participant observation was the paramount approach, a few studies of the police occupation and organization used other techniques such as questionnaires (Martin and Wilson 1969), interviews (Reiner 1978), or analysis of statistics and case files (Lambert 1970; Mawby 1979).

would call informal organization. It parallels the importance to early American empirical police research of the discovery of police discretion (Goldstein 1960; La Fave 1965; Skolnick 1966; Bittner 1967*a*, 1967*b*; Wilson 1968; Reiss 1971). Much of the interest lay in demonstrating that the backstage life of the police, who are apparently the acme of a bureaucratic, rule-bound organization, was a fluid world incorporating rule infractions, much spontaneity, and a complex set of informal meanings and understandings. Thus a fascinating aspect of the various studies was the documentation of forms of illicit "easing behavior," of the ingeniously varied interpretations of the "ways and means act" that involved various ways of distinguishing the "law in action" from the "law in the books."

This British work was not explicitly concerned with the obvious policy implications of these discoveries, unlike contemporary American research, which more overtly stemmed from a civil-libertarian perspective (e.g., Skolnick 1966). The political and policy implications of the work were fairly apparent, however (Cain 1979, pp. 144–46). As Holdaway sums it up in the introduction to his collection of essays representing research in the 1970s, "One of the basic themes running through this book . . . is that the lower ranks of the service control their own work situation and such control may well shield highly questionable practices" (1979, p. 12).

As the decade of the 1970s drew to a close, the political aspects and implications of policing and police research in Britain came increasingly to the surface, reflecting a growing politicization of all aspects of national life and public policy. Researchers on police subculture began to underline the problems implied by their pinpointing of the comparative autonomy of the rank-and-file police. "If, in a British society itself pervaded by social inequality, we desire a more accountable police, then we will check police power and we cannot expect the police to do this themselves" (Holdaway 1979, p. 13). Similarly, at the end of a study of police unionism, occupational culture, and attitudes toward work, I pointed to the growing politicization of the police as a pressure group and the problems of containing police power (Reiner 1978*a*, pp. 268–69).

However, there were, in the 1970s, relatively few academic studies of contemporary policing conducted from an overtly critical or Marxist viewpoint (though there were important historical studies such as Storch [1975, 1976]; and Cohen [1979]). A pioneering exception is Brogden's (1977) study of the hidden exercise of power by chief constables over police authorities. Other important radical studies of policing appeared in the late 1970s but did not include an empirical research component. *Policing the Crisis* (Hall et al. 1978), which became a key text for Marxist interpretations of the preconditions of Thatcherism, does offer an account of the police contribution to the creation of a "moral panic" about mugging in the early 1970s. It is not based on research within the police, however, but on media and official reports. (One of the coauthors of *Policing the Crisis*, Tony Jefferson, did begin work on a large-scale observational study of one police force, funded by the Home Office in the late 1970s, but the results were not published until 1987 [Grimshaw and Jefferson 1987].) An influential study by a radical journalist and political activist (prominent in the Greater London Council police committee's research work in 1983), Tony Bunyan's *The Political Police in Britain*, was published in 1976. However, this work was almost entirely a collation of secondary historical sources and media reports. It did stimulate the growing concern with the political dimensions of policing, which was to become a major focus of research and debate in the 1980s. Some researchers who had contributed to the Banton-inspired tradition of sociological studies of policing began to publish more critical theoretical and political analyses in the late 1970s (Cain 1977, 1979; Reiner 1978*b*, 1978*c*).

For the most part, however, the small amount of research on policing that had been carried out in Britain by the end of the 1970s was within the tradition pioneered by Banton: participant observation of the organizational and occupational culture. The research was stimulated primarily by sociological questions rather than by policy or political issues. Toward the end of the decade, however, there were stirrings indicating new approaches that would develop apace in the 1980s. On the one hand, there were the radical studies mentioned above. On the other hand, there were indications of greater interest from official sources in sponsoring research on policing matters as they moved into the political spotlight. The Home Office Research Unit, the Royal Commission on Criminal Procedure, and the London Metropolitan Police all commissioned important research projects in the late 1970s, although these would not be published until the next decade.

In policing and police research, as in all aspects of national life, 1979 and the election of Mrs. Thatcher mark a significant break. The advent of the 1980s is more than just a convenient chronological dividing line. The harbingers of growing conflict, which were already apparent by 1979 (and associated with the development of the new interest in police research exhibited by official agencies and radical groups), presaged an extent of controversy and debate about policing that was unprecedented in recent times (Reiner 1985). In turn, this stimulated a flood of police research that was completely without precedent and is still continuing. The rest of this essay surveys and assesses the fruits of this activity. In the next section, I consider the variety of institutional sources from which this work emanates.

II. The Institutional Sources of British Police Research

There are eight distinct types of institutions supporting research on policing in Britain. The only common element is the fact that each of these institutions has considerably expanded its police research activity during the 1980s. In other respects, they vary widely in scope, resources, aims, and motives, as well as in the style, scale, and methods of the research they support.

A. Academic Institutions

Almost all the serious published research on policing until the 1980s emanated from academic institutions. As indicated above, it was primarily aimed at contributing to the development of academic interests and disciplines and involved small-scale, individual research. Many of the published research works on the police up to 1980 originated as doctoral dissertations. (This includes the studies by Cain, Chatterton, Holdaway, Reiner, and others.)

It remains true that the universities, polytechnics, and other higher-education institutions are the bastions of police research. The Police Foundation's *New Register of Policing Research* lists fifty-five separate institutions of higher education that are currently contributing to police research in some way (Bird 1989, pp. 205–7).

While the individual scholars ploughing a solitary furrow, with their little grey cells aided only by a pen or perhaps a word processor, remain, they have largely been displaced by academics working on large-scale, externally funded team research. Most of the original group of police researchers who began in the early 1970s are still active in the field and are listed in the *New Register*. (There are projects involving Chatterton, Holdaway, Manning, and Reiner; however, all of these researchers are now listed as involved in funded, collaborative research.)

Furthermore, while the 1970s academic police research was the product of individual scholars in traditional discipline-based departments, much of it now comes from centers and institutes of research in criminology, criminal justice, and police studies, which have mushroomed within academe in the 1980s. Some of this work has been located in centers that existed before 1980 (although none had previously pursued police research), notably the Oxford Centre for Criminological Research (e.g., Maguire 1988; Shapland and Vagg 1988; Maguire and Corbett 1989), the Cambridge Institute of Criminology (e.g., Bennett 1983, 1988), the Sheffield Centre for Criminological and Socio-Legal Studies (e.g., Jefferson and Grimshaw 1984; Lidstone 1984; Grimshaw and Jefferson 1987), and the Edinburgh Centre for Criminology (Baldwin and Kinsey 1982). However, during the 1980s, numerous new centers were set up in higher-education institutions, some calling themselves Centres of Police Studies (e.g., Strathclyde, Exeter), but most opting for a broader criminal justice label (e.g., Bristol, Southampton, Reading, Leeds) or ad hoc titles such as the Centre for the Study of Public Order at Leicester University. Many of these centers are based on new degree courses in criminal justice or police studies that have rapidly spread around the country in the 1980s at both undergraduate and graduate levels, largely to cater to the new thirst for higher education (and the promotion it is intended to help) within police forces, stemming primarily from the Scarman report and its impact (Brogden and Graham 1988; Tierney 1989). However, many of those centers, which started as teaching-based institutions, have begun to generate published research, some of it based on studies undertaken as student dissertations by serving police officers.[2]

During the 1980s, then, the police research scene in British higher education was transformed both quantitatively and qualitatively. There was a huge growth of funded, collaborative research, usually with a clear policy orientation, and increasingly emanating from institutions with a base in the education of criminal justice practitioners.

B. Research Councils and Foundations

The main source of funding for police research activity in the 1980s came from government-funded research councils and private charitable

---

[2] The pioneer of this sort of work was the Cranfield Institute of Technology and its Centre for Policy Studies in Public Order, directed by John Brown. Many serving police officers were taught in masters degree courses at the institute in the late 1970s and early 1980s, until the demise of John Brown in 1985. The center was responsible for several volumes of conference papers (e.g., J. Brown 1984; A. Brown 1985), and a number of influential student dissertations (notably, M. Jones 1980).

foundations. In addition, the Home Office directly funded external research through its Research and Planning Unit, as did some other government bodies, but these are considered in Section III.

The Economic and Social Research Council (ESRC) has been an important source of finance for police (and other criminal justice) research in the 1980s. Originally established in 1965 as the Social Science Research Council with a brief to encourage and support social science research, the ESRC renamed itself in 1982 and clearly attempted to move in the direction of supporting more policy-oriented research on issues seen as relevant to government priorities. It has sought to stimulate this by the vehicle of special programs and initiatives focused on specific policy issues. Three of its initiatives in the 1980s have concerned the criminal justice area: the first, on crowd behavior, was established in 1981 (at around the time of the first Brixton riots); the second, on the criminal justice system, was set up in 1984; while the third was launched in 1985 with the aim of evaluating the Police and Criminal Evidence Act (PACE) of 1984. The first two initiatives included several projects that dealt either directly with policing or with closely related issues. (Samples of the results are collected in two edited volumes: Gaskell and Benewick [1987]; and Downes [1991].) The PACE initiative projects all directly concern policing, and most are now beginning to publish their results. These are discussed in Section III.

Private charitable research foundations such as Nuffield and Leverhulme have also begun to support more projects concerned with policing. Since these institutions react to applications submitted by academics rather than actively pinpointing areas of interest, the growth of research funded in this way is a reflection of growing academic interest. Examples of work supported include studies of the Special Constabulary (Leon 1989), international policing (Anderson 1989), and chief constables (Reiner 1988a, 1989c, 1991), all financed by the Nuffield Foundation.

C. Government Organizations

During the 1980s, both central and local government departments have become involved heavily in police research, commissioning external research in higher-education institutions as well as supporting in-house research units.

1. *Central Government.* The most important central government agency by far in this area is the Home Office's Research and Planning Unit (HORPU), which both conducts its own research (it constitutes

the largest body of criminological researchers in the United Kingdom and probably in Europe) and finances outside research in universities and polytechnics.[3]

The Home Office's Research and Planning Unit was established in 1957, realizing the possibility created by Section 77 of the Criminal Justice Act in 1948, which had authorized the Home Secretary to conduct, or support financially, research into "the causes of delinquency and the treatment of offenders, and matters connected thereto." (For its history and impact see Lodge 1974; Clarke and Cornish 1983; Bottoms 1987; Hood 1987; Martin 1988; and Rock 1988.) At first, the Home Office Research Unit (as it was called until 1982) concentrated almost exclusively on research on the causes of crime and treatment of offenders. (Until 1969, its publication series was called "Studies in the Causes of Delinquency and the Treatment of Offenders.") It continued to neglect policing issues until the end of the 1970s. Its series of "Home Office Research Studies" lists only one study on policing out of the forty-seven titles published up to 1979: Ditchfield's (1976) research on *Police Cautioning in England and Wales*. However, matters have changed dramatically since then. Two policing studies appeared in 1979, one on crime prevention and the police (Burrows, Ekblom, and Heal 1979), and one on race, crime, and arrests (Stevens and Willis 1979). Between 1980 and 1985, ten of twenty-eight studies published focused on police, an emphasis shared by the new series of Research and Planning Unit Papers that was launched in 1980 (ten of thirty-four papers published by the end of 1985 concentrated on policing). The priority given to policing research seems to have continued unabated in the second half of the 1980s. Of twenty research studies published between 1986 and 1989, eight concerned policing issues. (A useful collection of examples of the Home Office work on policing is Heal, Tarling, and Burrows 1985.) The externally funded research supported by the Home Office also exhibits this emphasis: about a quarter of projects supported concern policing.

The Home Office is by far the most important department of central government in terms of funding police research. However, some other branches of government have begun to support work in this area. The lord chancellor's department recently financed a major study of access to legal advice in police stations (e.g., Sanders et al. 1989).

2. *Local Government.*   A very significant departure in the 1980s has

---

[3] As Rock has expressed it, "With a staff of just over 45 in 1986, the Research and Planning Unit is the Goliath of the British criminological world" (1988, p. 65).

been the extensive development of local government research on policing. The initial impetus for this was the election in 1981 of several radical-labor local authorities in the major metropolitan centers. The local police authorities in these areas began to exercise a far more vigorous interpretation of their responsibilities for police accountability than their predecessors had, with numerous much-publicized clashes with their chief constables resulting. (See, e.g., Loveday [1985]; and Okojie [1985] for the cases of Merseyside and Manchester.)

In London, where there is no locally elected police authority, the Greater London Council established a police committee that campaigned vigorously for the creation of a local police authority (Greater London Council 1983). Its support unit also sponsored research and published a newsletter, *Policing London*, that regularly carried exposés of police malpractice as a means of furthering its case (Reiner 1985, chap. 7). Following this lead, a number of London boroughs and some provincial authorities established monitoring groups that functioned primarily as campaigning bodies but also disseminated research information on policing through newsletters (like Manchester's *Policewatch*) in the style of *Policing London*. Although primarily of importance in the context of political struggles around the issue of police accountability, these units provided a source of research material on local police developments (Scraton 1985, chap. 8; Brogden, Jefferson, and Walklate 1988, pp. 190–93; Jefferson, McLaughlin, and Robertson 1988). The metropolitan authorities that had been the spearhead of the campaigns for greater local police accountability were all abolished by the Local Government Act of 1985 and replaced by less activist Joint Boards (Loveday 1985, 1987, 1990; Lustgarten 1986, pp. 82–84). This change has undercut dramatically the extent of local research activity and has also diluted local accountability, although several London boroughs have maintained their monitoring work as part of the campaign to establish a local police authority in London.

From a research standpoint, the most overwhelmingly important work has been that supported by Merseyside Metropolitan Council (Kinsey 1984, 1985a, 1985b; Loveday 1985)—one of the metropolitan authorities that was abolished by the 1985 act—and Islington Council, whose police committee support unit generated the very influential Islington Crime Survey (Jones, MacLean, and Young 1986). A second survey has since been completed (Crawford et al. 1990). The Merseyside and Islington crime surveys have had a considerable impact on debates about crime and policing, complementing and, to an extent, challenging the results of the three national British Crime Surveys (BCS) conducted during the 1980s by the Home Office Research and Planning Unit (Hough and Mayhew 1983, 1985; Mayhew, Elliott, and Dowds 1989). Like the national BCS (and other local studies, notably Farrington and Dowds [1985] on Nottinghamshire), the Merseyside and Islington surveys provide a wealth of data on the relation between police statistics and victim experience, on reporting behavior and police recording practices, and on interactions with, and attitudes toward, the police by the public in general and by members of specific social groups.

The Merseyside and Islington surveys have also criticized the Home Office studies in a number of ways. Above all, they have emphasized the "rational kernel" of fear of crime for vulnerable groups of people living in high-crime inner-city areas, while the BCS has tended to minimize the basis of such fears by concentrating on average risks of victimization across a wider range of the population.

The Merseyside and Islington crime surveys have not only been important for the empirical data and policy conclusions they have generated, they have also been the empirical bearers of the most influential and controversial theoretical development in British criminology in the 1980s, "new left realism," which emerged out of the erstwhile "new criminology" of the 1970s (Taylor, Walton, and Young 1973) and is now disavowed by them as "left idealism." The "new realists" argue that crime is a social issue of importance for the most deprived and vulnerable sections of the population, the Left's traditional heartland. Socialists, however, have allowed this issue to be "stolen" by the Right (Downes 1983). Viable policies for preventing and alleviating crime can and should be pursued by the Left as immediate and practical reforms, not relegated to a socialist millennium. Policing is a valid and important social function that must be made more effective, though it must be restricted to dealing with clear infractions of criminal law and subject to local democratic control (Lea and Young 1984; Kinsey, Lea, and Young 1986; Matthews and Young 1986; Young 1988). (For critical comments on this "new left realism," see Scraton 1987; Brogden, Jefferson, and Walklate 1988, pp. 178–90; Cohen 1988.)

D. Internal Police Research

Police research is also conducted in house by national organizations and by local police research units. The research involves the major issues of operation and management.

1. *National Bodies.*   In addition to sponsoring research through the Research and Planning Unit, the Home Office also supports a growing amount of police research primarily directed to and conducted by police forces themselves. The main vehicle for this is the Scientific Research and Development Branch (SRDB) and the Police Research Services Unit (PRSU) which exists within it.[4]

The idea for what became the SRDB came from the 1962 Royal Commission on the Police's *Final Report*. The report argued the need for "a properly conducted programme of research" (Royal Commission on the Police 1962, para. 241) and recommended that a central government unit be established to "help plan police methods, develop new equipment and study new techniques" (Weatheritt 1986, p. 11). This led to the creation in 1963 of a Home Office Police Research and Planning Branch, the precursor of the current SRDB. At its inception, the branch's staff consisted primarily of police officers (five of them, plus two civilian scientists). Its early work looked at central operational issues such as detective methods and the value of foot patrol. It was instrumental in engineering the transition in the late 1960s from foot patrol to the primarily motorized unit beat system, the source of much subsequent controversy (Weatheritt 1986, chap. 6).

Recently, the SRDB has concentrated increasingly on technical issues. In 1984, it employed about ninety technical and scientific staff. About one-quarter of its £5 million-budget goes to computer development, and most of the rest to other technical research. Hardly one-tenth of the resources is used for studies of management or operations of a more social kind.

The Police Research Services Unit is an organizationally separate body within the SRDB, consisting of about twelve middle and senior ranking police officers seconded by their forces. Their function is to liaise between the SRDB scientists and the police service. They also sponsor and coordinate research activity within forces and support individual officers in research projects, some of which are undertaken in liaison with academics and do get published (e.g., Christopher 1990).[5] For the most part, however, the SRDB and PRSU are con-

---

[4] There is also a Home Office Crime Prevention Unit which, since 1983, has conducted research on crime prevention and has also collated information from local force crime-prevention projects. It publishes a series of research papers (now over twenty volumes) that reports its work.

[5] An account of the work of SRDB and PRSU is published in the annual reports of Her Majesty's chief inspector of constabulary. The report also lists examples of the

cerned with providing technical research support to police forces rather than with making a contribution to wider academic or public understanding of or debate about policing. As Mollie Weatheritt (assistant director of the Police Foundation) has assessed it in her definitive study of internal police service research (on which I have drawn heavily in this section), "The Branch has always placed greater priority on developing and nurturing relationships with the police service than on creating for itself any significant public profile or on contributing directly to the quality of public debate on the police. Its reports are not formally published (though they are usually available on request) and their existence is not widely known outside the police service" (1986, p. 12).

2. *Local Police Research Units.* In addition to centrally directed internal police research under the auspices of SRDB and PRSU, most individual police forces have their own research departments. In 1986, nineteen out of the forty-three forces in England and Wales had a named research department, but all have some officers responsible for some kind of planning and research and development function. For the most part, these research departments are small, with less than a half-dozen officers. They are more concerned with administrative issues— collecting and collating statistical information for the chief constable's annual report and other managerial purposes, designing new forms and bureaucratic routines, and running a force-suggestions scheme—than with research in the broader sense. However, a few research departments, usually in the larger forces, are staffed by graduates with research experience and are responsible for developing and evaluating much more far-reaching operational or management initiatives. Mollie Weatheritt has described and analyzed a dozen of these, which were concerned with a variety of experimental schemes for improving patrol operations or crime prevention. Most of the internal evaluations of such innovations she describes critically as "foregone conclusions" research,

projects of individual officers that have been supported since 1987 by PRSU awards. The 1988 edition lists fifteen grants awarded in 1988. Most are on technical subjects such as interactive video systems and lap-top computers. But a few are on more general criminological or management topics (e.g., "the relationship between social stress and crime in Avon" or "the value of custody records as police performances indicators"; see *Report of Her Majesty's Chief Inspector of Constabulary, 1988* [1989, chap. 6]). Very full accounts of the structure and work of in-house police research organizations can be found in the regular "Police Foundation Noticeboards" published in *Policing*, especially the summer 1987 and spring 1989 issues. The Police Staff College at Bramshill has not been a productive source of research, but tutors there have been responsible for two essay collections (Pope and Weiner 1981; Thackrah 1985).

"the seeking out of research information to support a preferred course of action" (Weatheritt 1986, p. 19). However, she also detects several sources of a trend toward much more methodologically rigorous and carefully planned in-house police research of an evaluative kind. First, there has been a growth of expertise available within some police research departments themselves. Second, there has been encouragement from the Home Office and the Home Office Inspectorate of Constabulary for forces to seek expert advice from outsiders in research planning and analysis. Finally, the Home Office emphasis on "value for money" from policing, which has gathered apace during the 1980s as an aspect of its general financial management initiative (Horton and Smith 1988; Reiner 1988*b*; Smith 1989), has stimulated police concern for objective and critical assessment of policing activities. The effect of these factors "should be to raise the status and importance of policing research, to create a demand for research information by police themselves, and to encourage the police to use research-based arguments in place of traditional assertion" (Weatheritt 1986, p. 19).

E. Independent Research Organizations

The establishment, in 1980, of the Police Foundation (explicitly modeled on its American counterpart) was a significant reflection, as well as cause, of the much greater interest in police research that developed in Britain during the 1980s. The foundation is a politically independent registered charity with no government funding. It has firm establishment roots, with Prince Charles as its president and a team of noted industrialists and assorted members of the "great and the good," as well as a number of chief constables, as its trustees. Nevertheless, its director, Barrie Irving, assistant director, Mollie Weatheritt, and all the staff succeed in maintaining a quality of critical independence and objectivity in the foundation's work. The objectives of the foundation are defined in its trust deed as being to promote efficiency and effectiveness in policing, to undertake and promote study and research to that end, to publish useful findings and foster public understanding, and to initiate practical projects in the policing and crime-prevention fields. The income of the foundation is derived from appeals to industry, commercial organizations, grant-giving bodies, and private trusts. This is used to support research done directly by staff members (e.g., Irving et al. 1989) or to fund research done by academics (e.g., Dix and Layzell 1983; Waddington 1988) or police forces (e.g., Blair 1985). The foundation also organizes numerous conferences to publicize the fruits of this research, notably two major conferences based on its research program "Policing and the Public" (which was supported by the ESRC [Morgan and Smith 1989; Weatheritt 1989]). The foundation also publishes a regular research notice board in the quarterly journal, *Policing*, which gives details of the structure of all police research organizations in Britain and their current activities.

The Police Foundation is the major specialist independent police research organization in Britain. However, other research institutions have made forays into the policing area during the 1980s. The most important of these has been the Policy Studies Institute (PSI), an independent organization with a long and distinguished record of research on economic and social policy issues. Its first venture in the police field, the large-scale study of *Police and People in London* (Smith, Gray, and Small 1983), was commissioned by the London Metropolitan Police but emerged as an uncompromisingly critical (albeit constructive) work. It had a great effect on both public debate and police opinion and was an important catalyst for change, influencing Sir Kenneth Newman's reorganization strategy. Smith followed up this seminal study with an action research project (funded by the Home Office) intended to assess the construction and use of performance indicators by police management (Horton and Smith 1988). This same PSI team is currently engaged in an innovative project that is intended to analyze the process of police policy-making in key policy areas (with funding from the ESRC and the Leverhulme Trust). The PSI has also developed research projects, conferences, and publications on community policing (Willmott 1987).[6]

F. Pressure Groups

Pressure groups in the civil liberties field have obviously concerned themselves with policing issues in a decade in which these have been at the center of the political arena. The most prominent has been the National Council for Civil Liberties (NCCL), with its research arm, the Cobden Trust. The NCCL is, first and foremost, an important collator of information about developments in policing that have negative implications for criminal justice and publishes critical documents concerning these (e.g., Hewitt 1982; Franey 1983; Spencer 1985; Thornton 1985). In addition, through the Cobden Trust, it finances research by academ-

---

[6] Other more specialist research organizations with interest in the policing field include the Institute for the Study of Drug Dependence (Dorn, Murji, and South 1991).

ics and others on criminal justice and policing developments. Notable examples include studies of Northern Ireland (Boyle, Hadden, and Hillyard 1975, 1980; Greer 1987), the policing of the 1984–85 miners' strike (Fine and Millar 1985; Percy-Smith and Hillyard 1985), and police accountability (Jefferson and Grimshaw 1984). The research activities of the NCCL were disrupted, however, by an internal dispute concerning an independent inquiry that it undertook in 1984 under the chairmanship of Peter Wallington into the policing of the miners' dispute. The interim report was disowned by the 1985 Annual General Meeting (AGM) of the NCCL, on the ground that it had "exceeded its terms of reference in commenting on the conduct of striking and working miners and setting out civil liberties principles which did not directly relate to the role of the police" (McCabe et al. 1988, p. 5). It is hardly surprising that the panel resigned and went on to publish its findings (and a definitive account of the dispute: McCabe et al. 1988).

Other pressure groups that have supported and published research in the policing field include the Equal Opportunities Commission (on policewomen [Jones 1987]); the Commission for Racial Equality (on ethnic minority recruitment [Oakley 1989]); the Scottish Council for Civil Liberties (Gordon 1980); the Welsh Campaign for Civil and Political Liberties (Davies, Gifford, and Richards 1984); Inquest (on alleged police killings [Benn and Worpole 1986; Ward 1986]); the British Society for Social Responsibility in Science (Ackroyd, Rosenhead, and Shallice 1980); and a variety of single-issue campaigning groups (Scraton and Gordon 1984; Scraton and Chadwick 1987).[7]

G. Journalists

In the past, journalistic work on the police has tended to be sensationalistic and to concentrate on retailing the spectacular exploits of particular detectives (who were their treasured sources). There are, however, some important exceptions to this even before the 1980s, including a well-researched observational study of the London Metropolitan Police (Laurie 1970) and a detailed account of the corruption scandals of the 1970s at Scotland Yard (Cox, Shirley, and Short 1977).

During the 1980s, studies of policing based on systematic research

---

[7] Another important pressure group supporting research in this area was State Research, which was established at the end of 1977 but closed in 1982. This was a vigorous collective of radical journalists and campaigners who published a regular bimonthly *State Research Bulletin* collating developments in policing.

by journalists began to appear regularly. Perhaps significantly, none of this work emanates from specialist crime correspondents whose stock in trade was the retailing of sensational detective exploits (Chibnall 1977). Studies by journalists have contributed significantly in a number of areas of the policing debate. Kettle and Hodges (1982) and Manwaring-White (1983) have produced studies of the policing of disorder and the development of police tactics to counteract it. On the same issue, Northam (1988) wrote an extremely significant account of the secret Association of Chief Police Officers (ACPO) *Public Order Guide to Tactical Options,* which was based on a leaked copy. Northam's account has been rightly criticized for distortions of interpretation arising out of the sensational nature of his "scoop" (Waddington 1989), but it remains an example of how journalists' research has undoubtedly contributed to knowledge of policing in a valuable way.

In the last couple of years there have been two journalistic studies of the London Metropolitan Police, both based on extensive periods of participant observation (Brown 1988; Chesshyre 1989). Chesshyre's study, in particular, is one of the most sensitive and insightful accounts of the practice of policing to appear in recent years, and it is a valuable guide to the current policing scene in London. Another recent study by a journalist based on about 500 interviews with police officers (Graef 1989) offers some valuable accounts of present police perspectives at all levels of the force.[8] It is clear that print and broadcast journalism are important sources of police research now, not only for uncovering information about specific cases but also for sponsoring more systematic studies.

H. Private Enterprise

Until recently, private industry and commercial organizations have not contributed much to policing research (except indirectly through financing independent research trusts and institutions such as Nuffield, Leverhulme, and the Police Foundation). However, the government's general commitment to privatizing public expenditure wherever possible has had some repercussions for police research. A few enterprising

---

[8] Earlier in the 1980s, Roger Graef was also responsible for two fly-on-the-wall documentary series on BBC TV: *Police—Thames Valley* and *Operation Carter*. These offered the most penetrating picture of police practices that a television audience had seen until then, affecting police policy in practical ways (notably, by its celebrated filming of a police interview with a rape victim).

academics have succeeded in tapping the resources of private industry. A comparative study of public order maintenance in English and German cities has been carried out (Weinberger and Reinke 1989), for example, financed by Volkswagen. Joanna Shapland of the Sheffield University Centre for Criminological and Socio-legal Studies has recently obtained funding from Storehouse Pic for research on crime and business, which will include an examination of the policing aspects. It is likely that, in the present climate of government cuts in higher-education spending, private enterprise finance will be sought increasingly for policing studies, as for other social science research.[9]

III. The Results of British Police Research

Previous attempts to summarize the findings of police research in Britain have done so by attempting to collapse the field into a number of distinct approaches to policing. In an influential survey of the police literature, Cain distinguished five broad types: studies of police and civil rights; police organization studies, usually but not invariably based on participant observation; police work and the construction of deviance; the relationship between the police and the community; and studies of the politics of policing (Cain 1979; her typology is also adopted by Tomasic [1985, pp. 82–87]).

Later attempts at a synthetic overview have also recognized some of the same distinctions. In an account of the politics of police research in Britain, I suggested that work had gone through four broadly distinct stages, corresponding to different levels of development of the policing debate in the political arena (Reiner 1989b). The first was a "consensus" stage, in which studies were largely celebratory, lauding the success of the British police in achieving a reconciliation between order and legitimacy. In the early 1970s, as controversies about policing developed, concern grew about police deviance and threats to civil liberties. Research in this period was primarily concerned with mapping the informal organization and culture of police work as a source of deviation

---

[9] There is also a considerable expansion of technological research by private companies on developing equipment and systems for use by police forces. Since 1987, the Association of Chief Police Officers has been hosting the annual International Police Exhibition and Conference in London, which provides a venue for manufacturers of policing paraphernalia to display their wares to a large assembly of British and foreign police organizations. The advent of the single European market after 1992 and the breaking down of barriers in Eastern Europe will undoubtedly add further stimulus to the research efforts of companies geared to supplying police forces with equipment of all kinds.

from the rule of law. As political conflict surrounding the police became increasingly overt and acute in the late 1970s and early 1980s, research began to focus on questions of controlling the police and raised fundamental issues about the role of the police in the social and political structure. Finally, by the mid-1980s, a new mood of "realism" pervaded all sides in the political debate about policing. Research attention began to focus once again on the microprocesses of police work and organization rather than on the macrolevel of the formal framework for police accountability. However, research was now much more overtly concerned with practical policy issues: how could effective policing be accomplished through managerial strategies? More recently, Shapland and Hobbs provided a survey of the field that "roughly divided the studies into three: those largely sociological studies which have emphasised a descriptive approach and the culture of the police; those which have taken a managerial approach; and broader legal and historical analyses" (1989b, p. 3).[10]

The distinctions between broad approaches varying in political orientation, theoretical perspective, and methodological style are clearly discernible in the literature. However, while useful for giving a bird's-eye view of the positions in the field, the implication of hermetically sealed theoretical divisions inhibits the task of presenting the conclusions of research. I therefore organize the presentation of research findings here not according to overall perspectives but according to the concrete issues that are addressed. The key research results relating to ten topics that have concerned police policymakers and academic analysts alike, both in the United Kingdom and the United States are considered. These are: What are the police for? Who are the police? What do police think? How are police shaped by training? What do the public think of the police? Does policing deviate from the rule of law? Are the police fair? Are the police effective? How are

[10] In addition to these essays attempting to summarize the state of police research, the growth of policing research in Britain in the 1980s has stimulated publication of a number of books that provide more detailed overviews. These include Reiner (1985); Bradley, Walker, and Wilkie (1986); Brogden, Jefferson, and Walklate (1988); Stephens (1988); Uglow (1988); and McKenzie and Gallagher (1989). All these texts combine accounts of the historical development of policing, syntheses of the social scientific research on police work and organization, and reviews of the political debates about police accountability and control. Collections of essays that provide a good sampling of the field are Reiner and Shapland (1987); Morgan and Smith (1989); and Weatheritt (1989). Another mark of growth has been the foundation of new journals devoted to police research, e.g., *Policing* and *Policing and Society*.

police managed and controlled? How did policing get to its current position?[11]

There is now so voluminous a body of research in Britain on these issues that complete coverage of findings is impossible. However, an attempt is made to point up the main work that has been done.

A. What Are the Police For?

In her influential review of the sociological literature on the police, Maureen Cain has criticized most studies for not providing "a definition of the object of their analysis . . . it has been taken for granted that we 'know' what the police, as an institution, really is" (1979, p. 143). Her own answer follows: "Police, then must be defined in terms of their key practice. They are appointed with the task of maintaining the order which those who sustain them define as proper" (1979, p. 158). Her definition, then, is a functional one.

At a theoretical level, this attempt at a functional definition of the police has been criticized. It overlooks the variety of tasks that the police are called on to deal with and begs the question of how effectively they accomplish their supposed function(s). It has been cogently argued that police are viewed better (in the sense of a theory capable of encompassing most of their activities) not in functional terms but as the institutional repository of the use of legitimate force, "the capacity for decisive action. . . . The policeman, and the policeman alone, is equipped, entitled and required to deal with every exigency in which force may have to be used" (Bittner 1974, p. 35; see also Klockars 1985, chap. 1).[12]

[11] The approach I am adopting opens itself to the charge of empiricism in assuming that studies from different theoretical perspectives can be compared and synthesized as if they refer to the same concrete object. Nevertheless, it seems a more fruitful way of organizing the presentation of research than the epistemological purism of comparing theoretical problematics that cannot speak to each other. These ten questions are underpinned by an implicit theoretical agenda for the analysis of policing. The prior issue is what are the police *for*, what is the purpose or function of policing? The immediate determinant of police practice is the police culture (question 3), which is itself shaped by the social base of the police (question 2) and their training (question 4). Assessments of the quality of policing can be considered from a variety of standpoints: the public (question 5), the legal system and its standards (question 6), ideals of social justice (question 7) and technical managerial efficiency and effectiveness (question 8). To the extent that policing practice is deemed to have shortcomings from any of these viewpoints, the questions, who can or should change the police and how, are raised (question 9). Finally, the understanding of how the present functioning, culture, and structure of police organizations came into being must be addressed by a theoretically informed history (question 10).

[12] It is arguably possible to synthesize the functionalist and the capacity definitions, as Marenin has suggested in defining the police as "the privately and publicly employed

The question, What is the police function? has been a chestnut of police research from the outset (Shearing and Leon [1976]; Punch [1979a]; and Reiner [1985, pp. 111–16] review the early research). However, it has primarily been addressed in such research themes as, "What do the police *do?*" The fallacious move from observed practice to notions of the police function is precisely what attracted Cain's critique. It presupposes that we know who the police are so that we can observe what they do, and it must invoke tacit assumptions about the weighting of different activities. However, a plausible conception of policing must be grounded in knowledge of what the police (as ordinarily understood) do.

Attempts to measure what, in practice, the job of policing amounts to have been made by a number of methods: time budgets compiled by police officers themselves (Banton 1964, chap. 2; Martin and Wilson 1969; Hough 1980; Smith, Gray, and Small 1983, vol. 3; Brown and Iles 1985; Kinsey 1985a and 1985b; Tarling and Burrows 1985; Tarling 1988), analysis of calls made by the public to the police (Punch and Naylor 1973; Ekblom and Heal 1982; Jones 1983; Shapland and Vagg 1987, 1988, chap. 3; Manning 1989; Shapland and Hobbs 1989a), and by direct observation (Cain 1973; Chatterton 1975; Manning 1977; McCabe and Sutcliffe 1978, chap. 4; Holdaway 1983; Smith, Gray, and Small 1983, vol. 4; Southgate and Ekblom 1986; Grimshaw and Jefferson 1987; Hobbs 1988, chap. 8; Shapland and Vagg 1988; Chesshyre 1989; Shapland and Hobbs 1989a). In addition, surveys of public demand for policing in general terms have been the subject of several questionnaire studies and are considered in Section III*E*.

Until fairly recently, a clear consensus reigned in studies of the police role conducted by any of these methods. It confirmed the view of American research that "the vast majority of police man-hours are expended in activity having little to do with law-enforcement, but much to do with social service and peace-keeping" (Sherman 1973, p. 240). As one British researcher expressed it, the police were "a secret social service" (Punch 1979a). This predominance of non-law-enforcement roles arose because the majority of calls for service did not

---

guardians of interest who are entitled to use force to do whatever needs doing" (1982, p. 252). I have suggested a similar line, drawing on both Skolnick and Bittner: " 'The civil police is a social organisation created and sustained by political processes to enforce dominant conceptions of public order' (Skolnick 1972, p. 41). Their specific role in the enforcement of laws and the maintenance of order is as specialists in coercion . . . ultimately the capacity to use legitimate force (Bittner 1970, 1974)" (Reiner 1985, p. 2).

refer to crimes, and because all later research has supported Banton's observation that the police tend to underenforce the law to exercise their discretion to handle matters informally (Banton 1964, p. 127).

At a theoretical level, a number of authors have questioned the conclusion that the police should be regarded primarily as performing a service role. While most calls do not unequivocally refer to a crime, and although the standard police reaction is not to invoke their legal powers, most incidents dealt with do involve an element of, at least, latent conflict and the potential ingredients of a criminal offense. Although usually resolved by means other than the initiation of the legal process, it would be more accurate to describe the bulk of police work as "peacekeeping" or "order maintenance" than as either social service or law enforcement (Wilson 1968; Reiner 1985, pp. 111–16). Furthermore, even when legal powers are not used explicitly, "a benign bobby . . . still brings to the situation a uniform, a truncheon and a battery of resource charges" (Punch 1979a, p. 116).

In recent years, some studies have questioned the orthodox view that police work is primarily not crime related (Jones, Maclean, and Young 1986; Shapland and Vagg 1988; Shapland and Hobbs 1989a). This echoes a changing pattern of results in most other countries, which hitherto had not been thought to apply to Great Britain (Bayley 1985, pp. 120–27). After recognizing that "the attempt to divide calls upon police services into such broad categories as 'crime,' 'service,' etc. . . . is an enterprise doomed to failure and misunderstanding," Shapland and Vagg present an analysis of police message pads in three areas (two urban, one rural), suggesting that, in both urban areas but not the rural area, "potential crime" calls predominated (1988, pp. 36–39).

Although possibly due to different categorizations used by different researchers, it is plausible that shifts in police organization and the experience and reactions of victims (Mayhew, Elliott, and Dowds 1989) have combined to increase the proportion of overtly crime-related police work. In particular, the organization of police work has increased the number of specialists with a law-enforcement function, even though uniform patrol still accounts for the bulk of police manpower (Tarling 1988, p. 5). Policy has also favored the devolution of the investigation of routine crime from specialist criminal investigation departments (CID) to uniform patrol officers. It is thus plausible that police work has, in fact, become more crime oriented in recent years, calling into question one of the orthodoxies of earlier studies of the police.

B. Who Are the Police?

A number of studies have analyzed the demographic characteristics of police officers, usually as a part of a wider research project. There have been two focal points of attention: What sort of people are attracted into the police? How representative are police officers of the population they police? The first question has been of interest because of the assumption that the initial orientations police officers bring to their work due to their social origins and prior experiences may be a factor shaping their subsequent attitudes and behavior during police work. The second question, the social representativeness of the police, has been seen as important in addition because of concerns about equality of opportunity for all groups within the service, as well as the capacity of the police to relate to all social groups. The ethnic, gender, and educational characteristics of police officers have been controversial issues of policy, and official statistics measuring them are regularly published in the annual reports of Her Majesty's Chief Inspector of Constabulary. The social-class composition of recruits is not routinely provided in official reports, but a number of researchers have analyzed it.

There is rough agreement between the major studies on the social background of police officers (Cain 1973, chap. 4; Reiner 1978a, chap. 9; Smith, Gray, and Small 1983, vol. 3, chap. 2). The police do not constitute a complete cross-section of the population. In class terms, they underrepresent the higher and lower ends of the distribution in the population. Most police officers come from skilled manual working-class or lower-middle-class backgrounds (53.5 percent of the sample in Reiner [1978a], e.g.). This is as true of the present police elite as of the rank and file. Just over 60 percent of present-day chief constables come from skilled manual working-class or lower-middle-class backgrounds (Reiner 1988a, 1991). Thus the police at all levels come from social backgrounds that are representative of the majority of the population. "All in all, research findings on the social and economic backgrounds of police officers reveal their typicality rather than their uniqueness" (Bradley, Walker, and Wilkie 1986, p. 163).[13]

Surveys of police officers in the 1970s and very early 1980s suggest that new recruits in that period were drawn to policing primarily because of an intrinsic attraction to the job, rather than the traditional

---

[13] This tradition goes back to Peel's deliberate policy of recruiting men "who had not the rank, habits or station of gentlemen" (Gash 1961, p. 502) in order to make the police mirror the population policed.

instrumental consideration of security as found in studies of recruits in earlier periods (Judge 1972, p. 41). Thus my own study in a provincial force found that 58 percent of post-1960 recruits cited solely intrinsic reasons for joining compared with 36 percent of pre-1949 recruits, with only 11 percent of the younger group giving purely instrumental reasons, as opposed to 43 percent of the older (Reiner 1978a, pp. 159–60). The PSI survey of London police found 18 percent of probationary constables (i.e., with under two years' service) citing job security as a reason for joining, contrasted with 31 percent of officers with over twenty years' service (Smith, Gray, and Small 1983, 3:48–49). These differences in initial orientation to the job suggest that, during the 1960s and 1970s, full employment (and relatively poor police earnings) made policing a career to which people were drawn primarily by aspects of the work itself. It is plausible that in the 1980s this could have changed. Police earnings were raised to a very generous level following the Edmund-Davies report (Committee of Inquiry on the Police 1978), and the Conservative government has maintained its real value by honoring the formula in each annual pay round since. The growth of unemployment in the labor market generally would have contributed further to making the police an occupation which, once again, had the instrumental attraction of security. It might also be hypothesized that the class composition of recruits changed in the 1980s toward an increased middle-class intake. There is no direct evidence on this, although the rise in college graduate recruitment is compatible with the hypothesis.

Debate about the social characteristics and orientation of police recruits has flourished particularly around the vexed question of "police personality." As in the United States and elsewhere, a frequently offered popular and journalistic explanation of the characteristics of police culture and practice has been the claim that the nature of police work and organization—disciplining and being disciplined—attracts a peculiar type of personality with authoritarian tendencies. Until the early 1980s, much of the research suggested that police were not socially or psychologically peculiar to begin with, compared to the population in general, although they came to be socialized into a culture the values of which paralleled those of authoritarianism (Reiner 1985, pp. 101–2; Brogden, Jefferson, and Walklate 1988, pp. 13–20). However, considerable debate was sparked in 1981–82 by a study of police recruits that attracted much publicity and influenced Lord Scarman's report on the Brixton disorders (Colman and Gorman 1982). This research found that "the police force attracts conservative and authoritarian personalities, that basic training has a temporarily liberalising effect, and that continued police service results in increasingly illiberal/intolerant attitudes towards coloured immigration" (Colman and Gorman 1982, p. 1). The study was much debated on methodological issues, especially the adequacy of its control groups (Waddington 1982). However, whatever conclusions are reached about its validity, the majority of studies continue to find that recruits are not initially more prone to authoritarianism than control groups of the general population, although they confirm the ideas of the liberalizing effect of training and the subsequent rise of authoritarianism with police experience (Cochrane and Butler 1980; Brown and Willis 1985). Research on the characteristics of recruits drawn into policing during the 1980s is badly needed, as the picture is likely to have changed due to developments in the labor market. This also means that in a buyer's market the characteristics of police recruits owe more to the decisions of police selectors than to the nature of the job applicants. There is virtually no satisfactory research on police selection (Burbeck and Furnham 1984, 1985) and none on the process by which it is accomplished.

Throughout the last decade, there has been official concern about the unrepresentativeness of the police in terms of ethnic and gender composition (especially at senior levels) and the failure to attract a sufficient proportion of graduates.[14] Research on black police officers has been conducted, and they clearly identify the sources of the problem: perceived racism within the force, both in terms of the "canteen culture" and the difficulties of achieving promotion, and hostility from the black community who regard them as "Uncle Toms" (Holdaway, Spencer, and Wilson 1984; Oakley 1989). The gender imbalance remains marked, despite a considerable change since the Sex Discrimination Act of 1975 that led to the abolition of separate policewomen's divisions and brought about formal integration. (Just over 10 percent of all police officers are women, but there are only thirty-nine who hold the rank of superintendent or above throughout England and Wales, and none above the rank of assistant chief constable.) Research on the effect of the act makes it clear that integration has been formal rather than real. Conceptions of the physical unsuitability of women for physically

---

[14] This latter anxiety goes back to the Royal Commission on the Police Report of 1962, which noted with alarm that there was "no recent instance of a university graduate entering the service" (*Royal Commission on the Police* 1962, para. 308).

tougher aspects of police work, as well as their unreliability for long-term careers due to domestic pressures, combine to affect their deployment and career opportunities (Bryant, Dunkerly, and Kelland 1985; Jones 1986, 1987).

In terms of college graduate recruitment, the 1980s witnessed a considerable expansion as adverse labor-market conditions attracted more recruits with higher educational qualifications (9 percent of recruits in 1988 were college graduates, a slight drop from the mid-1980s high of nearly 12 percent, but a marked increase compared to the 1970s). There is clear evidence that graduates are more likely to reach the top: 25 percent of chief constables and 40 percent of deputy chief constables have college degrees (Reiner 1988a), and indeed the few who enter through the highly selective Graduate Entry Scheme have formal advantages in the promotion system.

Research to date has concentrated on the barriers to recruitment of those groups that are comparatively absent from police ranks. There is as yet no research on the interesting questions of how, if at all, their policing styles vary in practice. The desirability of having representative proportions of blacks, women, and graduates has been assumed, or argued on grounds of equality of opportunity. There is as yet no research assessment of their actual or potential influence on the culture of policing.

C. What Do Police Think?

Much research effort has gone into the delineation and analysis of "police culture." As indicated in the previous section, most researchers have denied that any commonalities of perspective that may be discovered among police officers are due to prior psychological peculiarities of those who join the police. Instead these researchers have followed Skolnick's seminal analysis of the police "working personality": "the police, as a result of combined features of their social situation, tend to develop ways of looking at the world distinctive to themselves, cognitive lenses through which to see situations and events" (1966, chap. 3). The term "police culture" has seemed a more apt label for this notion of a socially structured and generated collective worldview, rather than "working personality," with its individualistic connotations. Police culture has been studied by a number of methods but a rather similar picture emerges from research based on observation (Cain 1973; Chatterton 1975, 1979; Holdaway 1977, 1983; Manning 1977; Punch 1979b; Smith, Gray, and Small 1983, vol. 4; Fielding 1989; Foster 1989; Norris 1989) or interviews (Reiner 1978*a;* Graef 1989). The picture of the central police culture of patrol that has been developed by researchers has amplified,[15] but not substantially altered, the sketch offered by Skolnick's account of the police "working personality."[16]

British accounts of police culture echo Skolnick's themes of suspicion, social isolation coupled with internal solidarity, and conservatism. The perpetual rediscovery of these characteristics is evidently due to their association with certain basic structural features of the police milieu anywhere: the representation and exercise of authority, and the relatively unpredictable danger of encounters—although both the social meaning of authority and the seriousness of danger will vary historically and geographically. A fascinating study of routine policing in Northern Ireland underlines the resilience of police culture even in the most extreme circumstances (Brewer 1990; Magee 1991).

Recent research has more precisely developed the account of police culture. Thus it has been found that the idea of solidarity, while certainly a characteristic of rank-and-file culture, glosses over the structured conflicts according to specialism and rank within the police organization. Many studies have pointed to variants of the division between what American researchers have referred to as "street cops" and "management cops" (Reuss-Ianni 1983). Thus Holdaway has con-

[15] Patrol constitutes the bedrock of police culture for the British police, as for most others. It accounts for 65 percent of manpower (Tarling 1988, p. 5), and only CID accounts for another proportion in double figures (15 percent). All other specialisms—public order, community relations, and training—account for less than 2 percent each, apart from traffic and management/administration, etc. (both 8 percent). There has been no research on the culture of ranks or specialisms other than uniform patrol, apart from recent exploratory studies of detectives (Hobbs 1988, chaps. 4, 8; 1989), fraud investigation (Levi 1987), and of chief constables (Reiner 1991). To all intents and purposes, therefore, studies of police culture have been coterminous with studies of patrol culture.

[16] My claim that Jerome Skolnick's analysis should be seen as the "locus classicus for discussing the police culture" (Reiner 1985, p. 87) has been taken to task for "glossing over the tenuous link between British and American studies" (Holdaway 1989, p. 67). However, Simon Holdaway's own account seems to draw in equal measure on Peter Manning's (1977) semi-American *Police Work* (although he questions its notion of "Anglo-American policing") as well as the thoroughly American *The Narc's Game* (Manning 1980). I am in complete agreement with Holdaway's basic thesis about the need to safeguard "the sociological foundations" of police research and his call for cross-cultural research to pinpoint the "distinctive and shared characteristics" of British and American (and other) occupational cultures (Holdaway 1989, pp. 72–73). However, in his eagerness to establish the strength of a British sociological research tradition on police culture, I believe he underplays the mutual indebtedness of police studies in the United States and the United Kingdom in the 1960s. Jerome Skolnick was a major influence on British work (as were James Q. Wilson, Albert J. Reiss, Jr., Egon Bittner, and others). But they all draw on Michael Banton, and he, in turn, had drawn on Westley's earlier work in the United States.

trasted the gulf between what he calls the "practical professionalism" of the lower ranks and the "managerial professionalism" of the top cops (1977, 1983). A British researcher's study of the Amsterdam police concluded, "Secrecy and solidarity characterise the occupational culture not only in relation to the outside world but also with regard to internal relationships. In particular, there is a deep dichotomy between the values, styles, and vulnerability of lower ranks and senior officers" (Punch 1983, p. 247). My own study of the culture of chief constables shows that there are systematic differences between this and the research findings on rank-and-file culture, as well as many points of overlap. For example, while all studies of police culture emphasize the centrality of the notion of crime as "real" police work, from which the social service aspects of the role are seen as an unwelcome distraction (Reiner 1985, p. 113), chief constables, for the most part, have a broad view of the police role, with crime as only a limited aspect of their work (Reiner 1989c, pp. 184–86).

In addition to qualifying the notions of a solidaristic police culture with reference to interrank conflict, researchers have stressed the variations based on specialism (e.g., mutual rivalry between CID and uniform patrol officers [Smith, Gray, and Small 1983, 3:50–58; Hobbs 1988, chap. 8]). Differences between the personal style of officers have also been identified (Reiner [1985, pp. 103–6] distinguishes four main types on the basis of a review of earlier studies, and these have been confirmed and amplified in later research, e.g., Fielding [1988, chap. 6]; Fielding [1989]). There are also variations in policing styles and culture between different forces that have been noted (e.g., Cain [1973] on rural/urban police differences, which have been amplified by the data in Jones and Levi [1983]). A particularly interesting recent study analyzes the difference in cultures between two adjacent divisions in the London Metropolitan Police, in one of which deliberate management policy seems to have achieved a dilution of the traditional rank-and-file culture that still flourished in the other. The success of these reforms was aided by the characteristics of the area, namely, its highly sensitive reputation as a riot-prone trouble spot (Foster 1989). While all of these studies do reveal the internal variations that exist in culture, qualifying the notion of solidarity, they are variations around a theme rather than yawning chasms.

Research has amplified the ideas of police suspiciousness and social isolation by probing the social perspective of the police and analyzing the structured groupings that officers perceive and distinguish (Reiner

1978*a*, chap. 11; Reiner 1985, pp. 92–97; Holdaway 1983, chap. 6; Smith, Gray, and Small 1983, 4:61–66, and chap. 4). These fundamentally revolve around a division between the rough and the respectable. The former provide the bulk of the police force's clientele, whether as victims, complainants, or suspects. The latter constitute a variety of dangers: antipolice "do-gooders," politicians whose legislation complicates policing problems, and "challengers" such as lawyers, social workers, or doctors who may have professional mandates to penetrate backstage areas of police work. Several writers have stressed how the police officer's map of society is composed of groups distinguished by the potential trouble they pose for the police, "trouble" constituting the mental grid that underpins all police categorizations of people, places, and problems (Norris 1989). However, while the surface of police culture reflects police-relevant categorizations and concerns, these are isomorphic with the place of different groups in the social structure, so that police culture can be seen as a "subterranean process" in the reproduction of power (Shearing 1981; Grimshaw and Jefferson 1987; Brogden, Jefferson, and Walklate 1988, chap. 6; Jefferson 1988). The origin of this structural critique of police culture studies is in the seminal works of McBarnet (1978, 1979), some of the richest theoretical contributions to police research.

This critique links with the conservatism that is implied in all studies of police culture. Researchers have not been allowed to examine directly the political views of the British police (though there has been at least one internal study confirming the plausible hypothesis that police officers are predominantly Conservative supporters [Reiner 1985, pp. 97–99]). Nonetheless, broadly conservative views on moral issues and questions of social policy and "law-and-order" politics have been emphasized at all levels of the force (Brogden, Jefferson, and Walklate 1988, chap. 3; Reiner 1989*d*). These have been translated into police pressure-group activity on a number of occasions (Kettle 1980; Reiner 1980).

Particular facets of conservatism that have attracted special attention are the sexism and racism that numerous researchers have found in police culture in studies ranging over a number of years (Lambert 1970; Cain 1973, pp. 117–19; Southgate 1982; Gordon 1983, chap. 4; Holdaway 1983, pp. 66–71; Smith, Gray, and Small 1983, 4:91–97, chap. 4; Jones 1987; Hanmer, Radford, and Stanko 1989; Reiner 1989*a*, pp. 6–7). Attempts to remedy these problems have been a central concern of recent developments in training, and there has also been extensive discussion of the extent to which these facets of police culture are translated into discriminatory practice. (These issues are considered in later sections.)

Underlying police culture in Skolnick's analysis, there is, in addition to the elements of danger and authority, "a 'constant' pressure to appear efficient" (Skolnick 1966, p. 44), which results in a drive to get results in the form of law enforcement. British studies certainly confirm this, although they also modify the emphasis on the striving for results as a response to external pressure. Rather, the picture that emerges from British work is of a rank-and-file occupational culture built around a value of "real" police work as crime fighting which is seen as both worthwhile and pleasurable (Holdaway 1977, 1983; Smith, Gray, and Small 1983, 4:51–56; Reiner 1985, pp. 88–91; Fielding 1988, chaps. 4, 5; 1989; Hobbs 1988, chap. 8). This normative commitment to police work (at any rate to its crime aspects) is brought in by recruits, who, in recent decades, have been attracted to the job for intrinsic reasons, as the studies cited in the previous section showed (although Fielding [1988, chap. 2] suggests that recruits are initially attracted as much to the service as to the crime aspects of the job). These values have been reinforced by informal socialization processes, but reforms in formal training programs in recent years have been aimed at countering aspects of the rank-and-file culture to make it more congruent with a broader community-oriented conception of the police role and to control its racism and sexism.

D. How Are Police Shaped by Training?

Throughout the 1980s, training has been a major policy issue, and there have been profound changes in organization and philosophy at both probationer and senior officer levels.[17] The changes were stimulated initially by the emphasis given to training questions in Lord Scarman's report on the Brixton disorders (Scarman 1981, pp. 79–84). They were further encouraged by academic criticism of traditional training (Jones and Joss 1985) and by official Home Office research on its deficiencies, especially, but not exclusively, in the areas of community and race relations (Southgate 1982, 1984). In 1982, the Police Training Council established a working party to review probationer

---

[17] There is a succinct yet comprehensive review of these debates and developments in the "Police Foundation Research Noticeboard" compiled by Cathy Bird in *Policing* (1988, pp. 323–29).

training, and it reported in 1983 with a set of recommendations for stage 1 of the training. The program was evaluated over two years by the University of East Anglia's Centre for Applied Research in Education. The center's interim report in 1984 was followed by revisions to the course, and a final report appeared three years later (MacDonald et al. 1987). The results have, in turn, led to the establishment of a Probationer Development Training Team (PDTT), that produced a modular foundation course that has been implemented on a national scale, in a series of stages subject to detailed ongoing evaluation (Elliott 1988). While probationer training has received the most attention, there have also been considerable developments in training for specialists (e.g., community liaison officers [Cochrane and Phillips 1988]), specific tasks (e.g., domestic disputes [Southgate and Marden 1988], interviewing [Shepherd 1986, 1988]), potential senior officers (Adlam 1987), assistant and deputy chief officers, and senior officers (Home Affairs Committee 1989). All of these facets of the 1980s official rethinking of police training are reviewed in a useful collection of essays published by the Home Office Research and Planning Unit (Southgate 1988).

Most of these developments have been subject to in-house evaluative research by police officers, usually in conjunction with academic consultants. Little of this material has been published to date. It appears, however, that most of the in-house evaluations rely on questionnaires as the basis for measuring success. The problem with this approach is evident in the light of the research findings cited in Section IIIB which show that training has, in the past, had a temporary liberalizing effect that is then vitiated by on-the-job informal socialization into rank-and-file culture (Colman and Gorman 1982; Brown and Willis 1985).[18] The one published example of such an evaluation (Bull and Horncastle [1989] on the London Metropolitan Police policing skills training launched in 1982) does incorporate an element of observation of officers at work, as well as an attempt at assessment of their performance by analyzing complaint rates and interviewing members of the public dealt with by the officers studied. On this evidence, the researchers regarded the training package as "a worthwhile achievement of considerable substance and promise" (Bull and Horncastle 1989, p. 98). However, this sanguine conclusion has been "greeted with scepticism" by some critics (McKenzie and Johnston 1988, pp. 221–22) who have pointed out

[18] A point emphasized in American research as far back as Niederhoffer's 1967 account of the growth of police "cynicism" with beat experience.

methodological deficiencies in the research, notably, the absence of an adequate control group. There is, however, evidence in other studies of the potential for sustained attitude change as a result of training, where this is implemented in the context of overall management emphasis in force policy and organization on a "community policing" approach. Thus Brown and Willis (1985) demonstrate that the effects of training to depress police authoritarianism does not survive experience of beat work in a traditionally policed, high-crime-rate police force, but it did continue after probationers began work in a county force with a much publicized "community policing" ethos. Foster (1989) suggests this may even occur in a tough inner-city division in a metropolitan force, provided there is an overall commitment by the managerial hierarchy supporting change.

Almost all the work on training in the 1980s has been of an evaluative kind, focusing on formal training and using primarily quantitative techniques. The one outstanding exception is a five-year study of the informal as well as formal socialization of recruits in a county force and at a training establishment that ran a variety of national and advanced courses as well (Fielding 1988). Fielding combined a variety of methods, but primarily the close qualitative analysis of semistructured interviews and trainee essays at a number of stages during the training period, probation, and first year of service. The results chart a process of informal socialization into an occupational culture that differs both from the values enshrined in formal training and from the recruits' own initial idealism. Fielding's fieldwork (which began in 1979) was completed in the early 1980s before the post-Scarman changes began to bite. For this reason its somewhat pessimistic implications for the likelihood of these reforms succeeding in overcoming the effects of informal socialization may be dismissed by training establishments. This would be unwise in the extreme, for, as Fielding concludes, "the preference of police for experiential learning will not willingly be modified" (Fielding 1988, p. 211). There is a clear need for further research of a more qualitative kind on the experience as well as the longer-term impact of recent training reforms, along the lines of Fielding's study (or its American forebears and counterparts, e.g., Harris [1973]; Van Maanen [1974, 1975]; Bennett [1984]).

E. What Does the Public Think of the Police?

Until the 1980s, large-scale surveys of public attitudes about the police, other than opinion polls commissioned by newspapers, were rare. The main examples are the survey conducted for the 1960 Royal Commission on Police (Morton-Williams 1962) and a survey completed in the early 1970s for the London Metropolitan Police (Belson 1975). Both of these studies, as well as numerous opinion polls, came to very optimistic conclusions about public ratings of the police, although both found that police officers they interviewed were much more pessimistic about how they were viewed by the public. Both studies, in fact, wrote up their results in a way that minimized the extent of disparity revealed by their own data (Whitaker 1964, pp. 15–17; Shaw and Williamson 1972; Brogden 1982, pp. 202–6). These early surveys confined themselves to very broad generalizations about public images of the police, rather than probing respondents' own experiences. It is remarkable, for example, that in Belson's questionnaire, with nearly fifty questions running over eleven pages (in its condensed book form), respondents are never asked directly whether they have had any experience with the police as victims, witnesses, or suspects, even in a section supposedly concerning "contact" with policing (Belson 1975, pp. 82–93).

During the 1980s, however, there has been a considerable growth of survey work probing public views of policing at the national and local levels. (An excellent critical overview is Hough [1989].) This growth of survey work on public attitudes has three main sources: anxieties about apparently declining public acceptance of, and confidence in, the police; the use of surveys to discern public priorities for policing as a kind of surrogate for democratic control over police policy; and as an offshoot of crime surveys primarily concerned with mapping trends and patterns of victimization and offending. All the major surveys have been commissioned by a body with some responsibility for policing, whether it be the Home Office (the three British Crime Surveys: Hough and Mayhew 1983, 1985; Jones 1983; Jones and Levi 1983; Shapland and Vagg 1987, 1988; Mayhew, Elliott, and Dowds 1989); local authorities (the Merseyside Crime Survey: Kinsey 1985a, 1985b; the Islington Crime Survey: Jones, MacLean, and Young 1986; the Nottinghamshire Crime Survey: Farrington and Dowds 1985) or the police themselves (Smith, Gray, and Small 1983).

The information about public attitudes generated by these surveys can be considered under three headings: assessing generalized attitudes toward the police, along the lines of earlier surveys; estimating the public's priorities and preferences in police work; and finding out about respondents' direct personal contacts with the police and their evaluations of these.

1. *Generalized Attitudes toward the Police.*   The meaning of views expressed in response to general questions such as, "Are the police doing a good job?" is hard to interpret. Until very recently, overall ratings of the police remained remarkably robust, at the very high levels indicated by the 1960 Royal Commission and the Belson surveys. This is probably because "unfocused questions about police performance will elicit what one could call a 'sacred cow' response" (Hough 1989, p. 47). If so, however, there are indications that this sacred cow may have become rapidly secularized. A series of opinion polls in 1989, some explicitly comparing their responses to the 1960 Royal Commission, have registered sharp drops in the overall public standing of the police, presumably due to the exceptional number of scandals that hit the headlines over the last few months of 1989 (Reiner 1991).

In terms of generalized questions, the survey of the 1980s had already, however, gone beyond its predecessors in pinpointing pockets of rejection of the police within the overall chorus of approbation. It became clear from the major studies that, even at the level of generalized opinions, views of the police were less favorable among the young, males, Afro-Caribbeans, inner-city dwellers, and the unemployed or economically marginal (Smith, Gray, and Small 1983, vol. 1; Southgate 1984; Jones, MacLean, and Young 1986).

2. *Estimating Public Priorities.*   The results of surveys in which members of the public are asked questions about what problems and offenses should occupy most police time, or which occupy too much time, have been used by both the police themselves and some of their critics as a form of surrogate accountability. Forces (such as the London Metropolitan Police, who have regularly commissioned national opinion polls to ascertain Londoners' policing priorities) use this as a way of demonstrating their responsiveness to public views and portray it as a form of accountability. Critics, for instance, the Islington Crime Survey (Jones, MacLean, and Young 1986, pp. 106–27), emphasize the gap between the public priorities conveyed in their survey and the allocation of public resources in practice. They use this gap to bolster their argument for changing the structure of accountability to put policing policy under the control of democratically elected authorities. In particular, they highlight the contrast between the priority given by the public to crime in survey responses and the predominantly peacekeeping approach of the police in practice.

However, it is arguable on the basis of expressed demand for police interventions (most of which are responsive to calls by the public as the studies cited in Sec. III*A* above show) that the gap lies between generalized public attitudes about police priorities and their effective demand for police services. Actual police practice is a function not only of expressed demand, let alone of generalized attitudes, but is also based on considerations of the likely outcomes and the difficulties and costs involved in various activities. It would seem both undesirable and unattainable to make police policy decisions about resource allocation depend entirely on generalized views of public priorities (Hough 1989, pp. 47–48). However, within the total array of considerations, the results of such surveys must clearly be one factor to take into account. How, and by whom, raises the general issue of accountability, which is considered in Section III*I*.

3. *Evaluations of Contacts with the Police.* Crime surveys have been used as a valuable vehicle for assessing public demands for police service and public evaluations of their contacts with police whether these were police or public initiated. The demands people say they have made of the police are a means of ascertaining the recording practices of the police in response to these reports and of comparing generalized public statements of the priorities of policing with actually expressed calls for service. Public evaluations of their actual encounters with police are an important element in assessing police effectiveness (see Sec. III*H*) and a valuable management indicator. The major surveys of public contacts and assessments of policing (the national British Crime Survey, the local Policy Studies Institute, Merseyside, and Islington Crime Surveys) agree on a number of important major findings:

1. Nearly half the population, 49 percent in the BCS, have some contact with the police during a year, of which about three-quarters are public initiated.

2. The pattern of contact varies greatly between areas. In inner-city areas, the Merseyside and Islington surveys have demonstrated that more demands are made on the police, and these are more often related to crime.

3. Patterns of contact vary for different sections of the population. The police are called on more by nonmanual than manual workers, whites than blacks, young than old, and men than women.

4. Conflictual or adversarial contacts initiated by the police also vary according to the same factors, but in complex directions. Thus young men, inner-city residents, and the more marginal (often unemployed) ranks of the manual working class are more often at the receiving end of such adversarial contacts as being stopped and searched, questioned, or

arrested, as well as figuring disproportionately as callers on police services. However, blacks are more likely to be at the receiving end of adversarial police interventions, but less likely to make calls for service.

5. Reporting patterns by the public to the police and recording practices of the police seem to vary over time (Mayhew, Elliott, and Dowds 1989) and place (Farrington and Dowds 1985).

6. The majority of people who contacted the police to report crimes are at least "fairly satisfied" with the police response. However, the level of consumer satisfaction has clearly declined during the 1980s (Mayhew, Elliott, and Dowds 1989, pp. 26–29). This also varies between groups (ethnic minorities are less satisfied than whites) and places (the inner-city surveys show less satisfaction than surveys from other areas).

7. Those groups that are disproportionately at the receiving end of adversarial police-initiated encounters are clearly more hostile to the police than other groups based on the evidence of all the surveys.

The value of surveys of public experience and evaluation of policing is clear from a policy perspective, and all the bodies with responsibilities for policing are continuing to commission them. However, they also have a potential importance for developing theoretical understanding of the nature of police work and its place in the social structure. This has been relatively untapped as yet because of the policy focus of the surveys, although their results have been incorporated into attempts to develop a theoretical framework for analyzing the police (Reiner 1985, chap. 4; Brogden, Jefferson, and Walklate 1988, chap. 6).

F. Does Policing Deviate from the Rule of Law?

Analyzing the extent and sources of police deviation from the rule of law has been a major concern of American police research from the outset (notably, in Skolnick 1966). Early British research on police culture also emphasized the tenuous relation between formal, organizational, or legal rules and the informal norms of the rank and file that were the immediate determinants of policing practice (Cain 1973; Chatterton 1979; Holdaway 1979, 1983; Manning 1979).

During the 1970s in Britain, the questions of the legal powers of the police and the controls over the exercise of these powers became politicized. On the one hand, a series of causes célèbres, notably the 1972 Confait case (Baxter and Koffman 1983), sparked civil libertarian concern about police violation of the rule of law. On the other hand, the police lobbied effectively on the theme that legal restraints on their powers shackled them in the fight against crime. Civil libertarian anxiety was further fueled by the experience of Northern Ireland, which showed how the rule of law could be eroded by perceived threats to "law and order," even in a United Kingdom which still prided itself on its civility (Boyle, Hadden, and Hillyard 1975, 1980; Hillyard 1981).

Within academic police studies in the late 1970s, a powerful theoretical critique was mounted, questioning the implications of earlier police culture studies (McBarnet 1978, 1979; followed by Brogden 1982, chap. 9; Jefferson and Grimshaw 1982, 1984; Brogden and Brogden 1983; Grimshaw and Jefferson 1987). It was argued in the critique that the vaunted autonomy of rank-and-file police culture was made possible by a "permissive" drafting and application of the rules of law governing police practice. The implication was that police culture was not impervious to the law but could be more rigorously controlled. Whether it was or not depended on the structural pressures on state and police elites who were responsible for the framing and application of the legal rules governing the police.

As a result of these conflicting pressures, the legal powers of the police and the safeguards over the exercise of those powers have been fundamentally reformulated. A Royal Commission on Criminal Procedure was established in 1978 to consider the issues and reported in 1981, having commissioned a substantial body of research on the operation of police powers. Its recommendations eventually resulted in the Police and Criminal Evidence Act of 1984 (PACE) after an exceptionally tortuous parliamentary passage (Reiner 1985, chap. 6; Leigh 1986). The act represents a systematic recasting of the law of police powers and associated questions (Bevan and Lidstone 1985; Freeman 1985; Leigh 1985; Zander 1985). Useful collections of critical essays are Baxter and Koffman (1985), and Benyon and Bourne (1986).

The enactment of PACE has stimulated a substantial body of research to evaluate its effect. (The main sections became operative on January 1, 1986.) In addition to reformulating police powers, it made important changes in the area of accountability, notably, concerning community consultation, and complaints against the police. These issues are considered in Section III*I*. The main source of this research was an initiative launched by ESRC in 1986 under the title "Police Powers and the Prosecution System," with the aim of monitoring and evaluating the effect of PACE. Six studies were commissioned, some of which have begun to publish their results: Gelsthorpe, Giller, and Tutt (1989) on decision making for juvenile offenders; Irving and McKenzie

(1989*a*, 1989*b*) on interrogation (a replication of Irving's 1980 Royal Commission study); Crawford et al. (1990) on the impact of PACE on public opinion; Dixon et al. (1990) on detention in police stations; and McKenzie, Morgan, and Reiner (1990) on custody officers. In addition, a study on search and seizure was commissioned from K. Lidstone of Sheffield University, but findings have not yet been published. Other research has been commissioned by the government departments concerned with PACE, notably, the Home Office: Maguire (1988) on detention and questioning; Willis, Macleod, and Naish (1988) on tape recording interrogations; Brown (1989) on detention; and the Lord Chancellor's Department (Sanders et al. 1989) on access to legal advice in police stations. There have also been a number of small-scale studies by police officers, mostly unpublished. (Examples are Rodie [1988] on custody officers, an unpublished dissertation on the effects of PACE on the charge process done at the Polytechnic of Wales by Sgt. C. Davis of the Avon and Somerset constabulary, and an assessment of the effect of PACE on detective work by Detective Inspector G. Thornton of the Lancashire constabulary, being completed at Manchester University.) Numerous academics have also done work on aspects of the effect of PACE, for example, Thomas (1988) on the implications for social workers; and Stone (1988), Zander (1989), and Feldman (1990) on its interpretation in case law.

All of the studies show that PACE has had profound consequences for police procedures. For example, the process of booking in, supervising, and questioning prisoners is now subject to an elaborate set of routines with a strict timetable and complex recording requirements (Maguire 1988; Brown 1989; Irving and McKenzie 1989*a*, 1989*b;* Dixon et al. 1990; McKenzie, Morgan, and Reiner 1990). Additionally, these studies find that the bureaucratic procedures tend to be followed faithfully. However, it is much more questionable whether the procedures achieve the underlying objectives of adequately protecting suspects while not hampering effective investigation. On the one hand, there has been a chorus of police complaints about the supposedly adverse consequences of PACE on the ability to clear up crime, leading to pressure to erode the suspect's right to silence (McKenzie and Irving 1988). On the other hand, research implies that many of the supposed checks on police powers become mere rubber-stamping routines. For example, the custody officer's duty of ensuring that detention of suspects is necessary in every case has degenerated into a virtually automatic process of authorizing it (McKenzie, Morgan, and Reiner 1990). Similarly, while psychological "tactics" to induce suspects' cooperation in interviews seem to have been inhibited in the early days of PACE, later research suggests they have crept back in, though not to the extent they flourished before the act. (Compare, e.g., Irving 1980; McKenzie and Irving 1987; Irving and McKenzie 1989a, 1989b.)

The right to legal advice has suffered a similar fate. All of the studies show that almost all suspects are informed of their rights, with the consequence that the proportion of suspects consulting solicitors while in custody has gone up considerably compared to the situation before the act (from around 7 percent to around 21 percent; Brown 1989, chap. 3). However, a variety of "ploys" are used by police officers that keep the legal advice rate fairly low (Sanders et al. 1989). For these reasons, it is hardly surprising that a majority of the public remains unaware of the very existence of PACE (Crawford et al. 1990). This is perhaps reassuring in the light of some of the more apocalyptic pre-PACE fears of the advent of a coercive police state (e.g., Christian 1983).

The body of research on the effects of PACE is undoubtedly beginning to yield valuable data on the extent of police deviation from the rule of law, with specific managerial implications about how this can be increased. The pressures of commissioned, policy-oriented research have, however, precluded analysis to date of the implications of the work for theoretical debates about the relation between police culture and practice and the rules of formal organization. All the published work concentrates on managerial and legal issues, and there is a complete absence of sociological variables such as class, race, and gender as possible influences on the impact of PACE, although these have been a key question in most earlier studies of police practice.

G. Are the Police Fair?

The recognition and analysis of police discretion was one of the starting points of police research in the United States as well as the United Kingdom (Goldstein 1960; Banton 1964, chap. 5; La Fave 1965; Wilson 1968; Davis 1969, 1975; Lambert 1970; Reiss 1971). The operation of discretion, however, gives rise to the possibility of differentiation in the treatment of different social groups, and this, in turn, might constitute discrimination, that is, unequal treatment that is not based on legally relevant criteria. The question whether the police do discriminate between different social groups has been an important focus of police research, with the emphasis on race but considerable discussion of class and gender as well.

It has already been noted that different social groups vary in their evaluations of policing. The police on their side see different groups as varying in the problems they cause for policing. What is considered here is research evidence about police practice. Do the police differentially process different social groups? Does this differentiation amount to discrimination?

There is now copious evidence that certain social characteristics are associated with a greater likelihood of being at the receiving end of police powers. Being young, male, Afro-Caribbean, or unemployed or in low paid irregular work are all associated with a greater probability of being stopped and searched, arrested, and charged by the police (Bennett 1979; Brogden 1981; Landau 1981; Stevens and Willis 1981; Tuck and Southgate 1981; Cain and Sadigh 1982; Field and Southgate 1982; Landau and Nathan 1983; Smith, Gray, and Small 1983; Willis 1983; Southgate 1984; Kinsey 1985*a*, 1985*b*; Jones, MacLean, and Young 1986; Brogden, Jefferson, and Walklate 1988, chap. 6; Jefferson 1988; Pearson et al. 1989; Reiner 1989*a*; Crawford et al. 1990). The evidence on policing of women is more fragmentary, but what there is suggests that the police operate with a sharply bifurcated, madonna/whore sexual imagery. Usually women as potential suspects will benefit from "chivalry" if they fit the first image, but if not, they are likely to be treated with a heavier hand (Heidensohn 1985, pp. 51–58; Brogden, Jefferson, and Walklate 1988, pp. 112–23). If they make complaints against the police, those groups who tend to be at the receiving end of police powers are also least likely to have their complaints sustained, being seen as "discreditable" (Box and Russell 1975; Stevens and Willis 1981).

The treatment of different social groups when they appear in the role of victims mirrors the above. In particular, there is lively concern, based on research evidence, about the difficulties women and black people experience with respect to being taken seriously when they report assaults (Edwards 1989; Hanmer, Radford, and Stanko 1989; Crawford et al. 1990).

What has been hotly debated during the 1980s is whether police differentiation is explicable and justifiable by legally relevant differences between racial groups (Waddington 1983, 1984*a*), or whether it is due to police racism (Gordon 1983; Scraton 1985, chap. 5; Gilroy

1987), or to an interaction between the two (Stevens and Willis 1979; Lea and Young 1984, chap. 4; Reiner 1985, pp. 124–35; Benyon 1986; Lea 1986). The problem is that establishing beyond doubt that a "pure" element of discrimination exists, which is not based on legally relevant factors, is methodologically impossible. Observational studies usually conclude that, on the whole, despite expressions of prejudice, the quality of the handling of similar sorts of cases is the same regardless of ethnic group (James 1979; Holdaway 1983; Smith, Gray, and Small 1983, vol. 4, chap. 4). There are certainly many incidents described in observational work that are highly suggestive of discrimination (e.g., Southgate and Ekblom 1986, pp. 65–67), but it is almost impossible to establish racial motivation in particular cases. Statistical analyses of decision making have attempted to isolate a factor of "pure" discrimination in treatment of black suspects, holding constant legally relevant variables. Simcha Landau's (1981) studies of the London Metropolitan Police Juvenile Bureau find, for example, that black youths are less likely to be referred to the bureau rather than charged immediately, and that they are also more likely to be charged than cautioned by the bureau, holding constant all ascertainable legally relevant factors. The problem in taking this finding as unequivocal evidence of discrimination is that the "legally relevant" variables are themselves connected to race. The likelihood of future offending, for instance, is taken as indicated by factors such as single-parent families, unemployed fathers, or being a latchkey child, all of which are themselves correlated with ethnic group.

This points to the artificiality of trying to pursue an element of "pure" discrimination. Differential likelihood of offending and of being subject to police prejudice and discrimination are mutually reinforcing aspects of the structural position of groups at the bottom of the socioeconomic hierarchy. It is this structural location that is the explanation of a vicious cycle of differential pressures leading to offending and differential risk of apprehension, each confirming the other (Reiner 1985, pp. 124–35; Brogden, Jefferson, and Walklate 1988, chap. 6; Jefferson 1988). The police are reproducers rather than creators of social injustice, though their prejudices may amplify it.

Although different social groups have varying experiences and evaluations of policing, both as suspects and victims, survey evidence suggests they have basically similar conceptions of good policing (Smith, Gray, and Small 1983, vol. 1; Gifford 1986, chap. 7; Jones, MacLean, and Young 1986; Crawford et al. 1990). Concern in all groups is as much about police effectiveness as it is about unjust overpolicing. This does not mean that consensus about policing has broken out. There is considerable disagreement about the seriousness of specific problems of crime or disorder in particular places, as small-scale local surveys have pointed out (Shapland and Vagg 1988). One group's fun may be another's disorder, so assessments of what constitutes effective policing are necessarily fraught with ambiguity.

H. How Effective Are the Police?

The Home Office entered the 1980s with a clear awareness of the limited effectiveness of policing as a means of controlling crime (Clarke and Hough 1980, 1984; Morris and Heal 1981). As one Home Office research study put it, "The traditional strategies adopted by the police have but a limited impact on crime" (Morris and Heal 1981, p. 2). One reaction to this was an increasing emphasis on "situational crime prevention" as the favored Home Office tactic in dealing with crime, in which the police play only a relatively marginal role (Clarke 1983). An excellent assessment of the effect of situational and other crime prevention strategies is found in Bottoms (1990).

In following through the implications of this research for policing, however, the government faced considerable problems. Militancy within the police during the late 1970s had resulted in a generous pay recommendation by the 1978 report of the Edmund-Davies Committee, and a formula for linking future police salary increases to the general earnings index. The incoming Conservative government in 1979 pledged itself to honoring this formula. Salaries account for over 70 percent of the police budget, and have been a major factor in making expenditure on policing the fastest growth area of public spending in the 1980s. The costs of policing have increased 55 percent in real terms over the last decade, three times the rate of growth of the defense budget, and six times the growth rate of the education budget.

The police have also been the most special of Mrs. Thatcher's special relationships. Apart from the general ideological affinity she and they share, she has relied on them to control the disorderly fallout from other aspects of government policy, notably the urban disorders of 1981 and 1985, and the mid-1980s militancy of a trade union movement under siege, especially during the 1984–85 miners' strike (Fine and Millar 1985; Geary 1985; Scraton and Thomas 1985; McCabe et al. 1988). Public order policing has become an increasingly significant commitment on the mainland, as in Northern Ireland, and is a source of growing police expenditure on hardware and overtime (Bunyan and Kettle 1980; Manwaring-White 1983; Gregory 1985; Jefferson 1987; Waddington 1987, 1988; Brewer et al. 1988, chaps. 2, 3; Northam 1988).

In consequence, policing becomes almost a blank check, worth, in 1988–89, £1.3 billion. It is hardly surprising that a government not known for its prolix approach to public expenditure should be concerned to pull in the reins. Its intentions were announced in Home Office Circular 114 of 1983 which declared that increases in police resources would depend on a demonstration that existing resources were being used as efficiently, effectively, and economically as possible (the dreaded "3 E's" of the government's Financial Management Initiative in the public sector). The bite did not take effect immediately because of the honeymoon period for police expenditure in the mid-1980s due to urban and industrial disorders. But the message came back in even tougher form in Home Office Circular 106 of 1988, which announced that a case had to be made for each extra constable asked for, showing what his or her specific contribution would be. These circulars, implemented by a beefed-up Her Majesty's Inspectorate of Constabulary, have brought about a reorientation in the management style of police forces.[19] As one Home Office report put it acerbically: "pushed to its limits, the initiative implies a view of the police and other public service as analogous, say, to a shoe factory" (Sinclair and Miller 1984, p. 2). There has been extensive debate in professional circles about the desirability of this new approach (Butler 1984, 1985, 1986; Bradley et al. 1986; Waddington 1986a, 1986b; Chatterton 1987a; Hough 1987). Particular attention has been paid to the thorny question of what sort of performance indicators might be developed for policing (Jones and Silverman 1984; Collins 1985; Reiner 1988b). While researchers and academics have debated the principles, the government's audit commission and Her Majesty's Inspectorate of Constabulary have busied themselves with developing practical measures (Weatheritt 1986, pp. 105–16; Ingram 1987).

Most of the debate about effectiveness and its measurement has either been at the level of first principles or gone by default in the rush

---

[19] They have also provoked a lively debate about incipient "privatization" of policing, stimulated by the growth of the private police sector, by government efforts to encourage citizen volunteers in the Special Constabulary and other guises, and by the North American example (Shearing and Stenning 1987; South 1988; Leon 1989; Johnston 1991; Mawby 1991; Rawlings 1991).

to develop indices in practice. However, one important research project has tried to develop such measures of good practice by action research focused on two key areas of police work (the role of community constables and the handling of domestic disputes). Despite careful methodological planning, the research went awry, due to a combination of technical hitches and lack of wholehearted police cooperation (Horton and Smith 1988; Horton 1989; Smith 1989). The authors come to a final, downbeat conclusion that echoes some earlier critics: "to the extent that the final outcomes of policing are uncertain, decisions about what constitutes good policing practice are a matter of political choice" (Horton and Smith 1988, p. 206).

In addition to generalized debates about police effectiveness, there have been a number of studies attempting to evaluate particular specialties and initiatives. While insider research tends to be the work of partisans for particular schemes and to suffer from a "foregone conclusions" syndrome of predictably happy endings (Weatheritt 1986, pp. 18–19), independent evaluative studies seem to have the opposite tendency: "nothing works." This has been the bottom line of studies of detectives (Burrows and Tarling 1982; Burrows 1986); directed patrol (Burrows and Lewis 1988); crime prevention officers (Harvey, Grimshaw, and Pease 1989); focused patrolling (Chatterton and Rogers 1989); community policing (Fielding, Kemp, and Norris 1989); neighborhood policing (Irving et al. 1989); and neighborhood watch (Bennett 1988, 1989, 1990). In many, if not most, of these cases, the problem lies in "program failure," difficulties in implementing schemes as intended, and it is far from established that the strategies as such could not work. There are, moreover, methodological problems with many of the research designs used in evaluations that minimize the prospects of establishing clear evidence of success (Bennett 1990). However, the quest for improving police effectiveness is more a matter of traveling hopefully than of arriving. A succession of reforms have been met with disappointment after initial enthusiasm. Effectiveness remains a thorny issue in the more general debates about police management and accountability.

I. How Are Police Managed and Controlled?

Underlying all the disparate debates about policing in Britain in the last three decades, there has been a fundamental concern about how the police can be rendered accountable. This has been a peculiarly British concern to a certain extent because of the strength of the doctrine of "constabulary independence" and the traditional suspicion of political control that insulates the police organization from overt subordination to any agency of government. This problem has also been a major concern in Canada (cf. Stenning 1981*a*, 1981*b*; Hann et al. 1985) and has also figured in debates in Australia (cf. Goldsmith 1990) and the United States (cf. Goldstein 1977, chap. 6) but is now lower on the research agenda. However, as many critics have argued, this does not mean policing decisions are not political, only that who makes them and how and why they are made becomes opaque and obscured (Marshall 1965; Jefferson and Grimshaw 1984; Reiner 1985; Lustgarten 1986). In addition to this peculiarly British concern with accountability in the form of the relation between police and government, those problems of police accountability that have been vexing questions in all jurisdictions have also been addressed, notably, the complaints system and the internal accountability of the police rank and file to management.

There is now a voluminous literature considering the constitutional position of the police in the state. The pioneer of this debate in recent times is Marshall (1965), a seminal work demolishing the constabulary independence doctrine. The most comprehensive review of the issues, as well as a cogent statement of the case for local democratic control, is Lustgarten (1986). This is the most prevalent position supported by those at the center or left of the political spectrum (Baldwin and Kinsey 1982; Loveday 1983; Spencer 1985; Downes and Ward 1986; Baldwin 1987; Uglow 1988). Jefferson and Grimshaw (1984) have argued that institutional change alone will not achieve democratic policing. It must be accompanied by an articulation of explicit principles of justice as the basis of decision making (and they argue the case for socialist principles of justice). Reiner (1985, chaps. 6, 7) questioned whether formal constitutional reform would achieve its objectives in the light of the research material on the autonomy of rank-and-file culture and argued it could be counterproductive in particular circumstances (see also Bayley 1983).

Objections in principle to the desirability of local democratic control have come primarily from the police themselves (Mark 1977, 1978; Pike 1985; Oliver 1987). I have analyzed the views on accountability of chief constables as a group (Reiner 1988*a*, 1989*c*, 1991). Some academics have also supported this viewpoint, notably Marshall himself in an influential volte-face from his 1965 position (Marshall 1978; see also Regan 1983; Waddington 1984*b*).

The system for dealing with complaints against the police has also attracted considerable debate, notably about the question of independent investigation and adjudication. The consensus of academic and Center to Left political opinion has long supported a completely independent system (Lustgarten 1986, chap. 9). The police at all levels favored the status quo until 1981, when, in a dramatic change of heart, the Police Federation began to support a fully independent system. However, the majority of chief officers still oppose this (Reiner 1989c). A modicum of independence was introduced in the 1976 Police Act in the form of post hoc review of cases by a police complaints board (which prompted Sir Robert Mark's resignation as metropolitan commissioner). The Police and Criminal Evidence Act (1984) went further in establishing the Police Complaints Authority, which has powers to supervise investigations by the police in serious complaints cases. The Police Federation has bitterly opposed this, raising some cynical doubts about the nature of its commitment to an independent system.

Despite an extensive literature on accountability and control of policing, there has been relatively little empirical research on any aspects of it. Brogden (1977) did some pioneering work on the perspectives of police authority personnel, demonstrating their almost automatic acceptance of police viewpoints. Loveday (1985) made a detailed study of the conflicts between police authority and the chief constable in Merseyside. He has also monitored the development of new forms of police authority in the metropolitan areas since the 1985 Local Government Act abolished the metropolitan authorities, through interviews with key participants (Loveday 1985, 1987, 1990). There have also been recent empirical studies of the views on accountability held by police authority personnel (Day and Klein 1987; Morgan and Swift 1987) and by chief constables (Reiner 1988a, 1989c, 1991).

The Scarman report on the Brixton disorders (Scarman 1981) made a number of recommendations intended to enhance accountability within the existing constitutional framework (Morgan 1987). The most influential of these was the idea of police-community consultative committees, which were further encouraged by Section 106 of the Police and Criminal Evidence Act (1984). Rod Morgan has completed a major evaluative study of these (Morgan and Maggs 1984, 1985; Morgan 1986, 1989). It seems that these committees function more as a means of communicating police perspectives to the public than the reverse, and that their political effect is to legitimate the myth of policing by consent. (Savage [1984] offers a more optimistic interpretation of the potential of consultative committees.)

Another Scarman-inspired attempt to enhance public accountability of police forces was a system of lay visitors to police stations. Following a 1986 Home Office circular, most police forces began to introduce such schemes. These have been evaluated in a study directed by Rod Morgan (Kemp and Morgan 1989). While a valuable initiative in itself, the lay visiting system has been established with fewer powers than Scarman envisaged. The schemes "rely heavily on the establishment of goodwill, trust and cooperation between lay visitors, police and police authority" (Kemp and Morgan 1989, p. 44). However, they do potentially "provide a means of external, impartial scrutiny of formerly hidden areas of police work" (Kemp and Morgan 1989, p. 45).

The other crucial recent reform in the accountability area was the Police Complaints Authority (PCA) and the system of informal resolution that was introduced by the Police and Criminal Evidence Act (1984). Until recently, there has been very little empirical research on the complaints system. The only studies are Box and Russell (1975) and Stevens and Willis (1981), both on the correlates of unsubstantiated complaints (the latter focusing specifically on complaints by ethnic minorities), and Brown (1987) on the views of complainants. However, a major study of the complaints system since the PACE changes has recently been completed (Maguire and Corbett 1989; Maguire 1991). The study reveals considerable lack of satisfaction with the system on the part of complainants and the public at large. Some of these matters, such as the length and secrecy of the process, could be alleviated even without a fundamental change to an independent system. (Indeed, informal resolution of minor complaints goes some way to achieving this.) On the crucial question whether an independent system would achieve more just results, the study is necessarily agnostic. The present investigations (overseen in serious cases by the PCA) do appear to be thorough and conscientious, and it is unclear what the scope for improvement with fully independent investigations would be, other than in terms of public confidence. This seems to be the implication also of British studies of independent systems in North America (Loveday 1988).

The accountability debate has operated largely with a presumed mechanistic model of police organization, in which control of formal policy necessarily carries with it control of policing on the ground. Conversely, the observational tradition of police culture studies has implied that policing practice is largely impervious to formal policy (these models are explored more fully in Grimshaw and Jefferson 1987, pt. 1; Johnston 1987, 1988). What has, until very recently, remained a virtual black box of police research has been study of the culture and practices of the supervisory and managerial ranks of the police organization. In the absence of this, the space has been filled by assumptions about the nature of internal control in police organizations.

In the last few years, there have been some inroads made by empirical studies of police supervision and management. A study of frontline supervision in policing has identified various styles that sergeants adopt, and also analyzed the role of paperwork in supervision by sergeants (Chatterton 1987b, 1989). It paints a picture of sergeants experiencing increasing difficulty in carrying out direct street supervision because of growing workloads and the responsibilities created for them inside stations by the Police and Criminal Evidence Act. In any event, direct supervision created tensions about how to manage the balance between control and taking over, thus undermining subordinates. These tensions generated different supervisory styles for coping with them.

There have been two small-scale studies of policy-making levels in police forces. One studied the demographic characteristics and the workload of the divisional command structure in a Scottish force (Currie 1986). The other was a study of policy conferences and files covering a number of issues in a large city force (Grimshaw and Jefferson 1987, pt. 4). This study found that the character of policy-making varied between issues. Policy issues of a purely administrative kind (e.g., purchase of cars) were discussed in a rational-scientific discourse and resulted in clear decisions and explicit directives. However, issues involving law enforcement (e.g., how to deal with racial attacks) do not result in a policy in the sense of "an authoritative statement signifying a settled practice on any matter relevant to the duties of the Chief Constable" (Grimshaw and Jefferson 1987, p. 204). This is because policy in that sense (as opposed to general statements of intent) would undermine the legal discretion of constables. The analysis of the policy-making process thus suggests that the autonomy of rank-and-file culture ("operational common-sense," as Grimshaw and Jefferson call it) is created by the self-abrogation of police elites, who see explicitly and authoritatively binding policies for handling discretion as contrary to the basic legal conception of the constable's duty of law enforcement.[20]

Another recent study of police policy levels is my own research on

[20] Whether this is true elsewhere may be explored in a study of the making of policing policy on which David Smith of the Policy Studies Institute is embarking. This work will probe the interactions of chief constables, Home Office, police authorities, and other key figures over a range of issues.

chief constables. In it I analyzed the specific characteristics of the careers and culture of chief officers as compared to the rank and file (Reiner 1988a, 1989c, 1989d, 1991). Chief constables come predominantly from the same manual working-class origins as most police, but their families are characterized by strong orientations to social mobility. Their careers set them apart from other police, and they become part of a cohesive national police elite group. They are primarily responsible to central influences, notably, the Home Office, rather than local ones.

A start has evidently been made in the study of policy-making levels and processes in policing. However, the achievement of accountability undoubtedly requires a much more complete understanding of these questions. One source is police history, which researchers have looked to for explanation of the doctrine of constabulary independence that underlies the present accountability structure (Brodgen 1982; Jefferson and Grimshaw 1984), as well as the public trust which generally prevailed until recently (Reiner 1985, chap. 2).

J. How Did Policing Get to Its Current Position?

Arguably, the most distinctive British contributions to police research have derived from historical studies seeking to understand the process by which British police institutions and tradition were formed and developed. Revisionist studies of police history in the late 1960s and 1970s (emanating from the new social history from below of Thompson, Hobsbawm, Rudé, and others) in turn inspired a set of sophisticated Marxist analyses of contemporary British policing (notably Brogden 1982; Jefferson and Grimshaw 1984; Grimshaw and Jefferson 1987).[21]

Revisionist studies of police history were a self-consciously critical reaction to a long tradition of celebratory accounts, which I have previously called "the cop-sided view of history" (Reiner 1985, chap. 1). The orthodox perspective was primarily the work of people with professional police connections. T. A. Critchley, author of the definitive orthodox history, was a Home Office Police Department civil servant (Critchley 1970, 1978). Philip J. Stead was dean of Bramshill Police

---

[21] The other recognizably distinct theoretical traditions in British police studies—the microsociological studies of police culture and the more recent managerial and evaluative police-oriented research—have counterparts in other countries. The studies of policing from a theoretically informed structuralist Marxist perspective seem almost uniquely British.

Staff College and, later, dean of graduate studies at John Jay College (Stead 1977, 1985). Donald Rumbelow was a City of London policeman (Rumbelow 1971), while David Ascoli's study was commissioned by the London Metropolitan Police to commemorate their first 150 years (Ascoli 1979). Charles Reith was a retired tea planter but became a committed police buff (Reith 1938, 1940, 1943, 1956; Robinson 1979).

These "cop-sided" histories presented a picture of the evolution of the British police out of ancient traditions of communal self-policing, becoming "a priceless national heritage that . . . combines the two virtues of all good policing. It sustains our civilisation; and, at the same time, it provides the freedom under the rule of law without which civilisation is worthless" (Critchley 1978, pp. xvii–xviii).

The revisionist histories that appeared in the late 1960s and early 1970s portrayed a very different picture of British policing (detailed accounts of the different approaches are found in Reiner 1985, chaps. 1, 2; Brogden, Jefferson, and Walklate 1988, chaps. 4, 5). The orthodox account had recognized the widespread hostility to the establishment of the police that permeated British society in the eighteenth and early nineteenth centuries but dismissed it as obscurantist or corrupt. The revisionists analyzed these conflicting political currents in terms of their class position and interests, establishing the rationality of antipolice opposition from a variety of perspectives. While upper-class suspicion was rapidly allayed, working-class hostility remained alive much longer, and acceptance of the police in the poorer sections of society continues to be fragile and volatile until today. Police legitimacy was a hard-won, easily lost product of enlightened policies in a favorable context of growing social integration and incorporation. It remains vulnerable to disintegration and deincorporation of marginal strata, as theories of the underclass suggest is happening now (Silver 1967; Storch 1975, 1976; Miller 1977; Philips 1977, 1980, 1983; Cohen 1979; Ignatieff 1979; Brogden 1982, 1987; Reiner 1986).

The history of the police continues to attract a prodigious amount of research attention. More recent work has tended to qualify the pictures presented by either of the above perspectives (although remaining predominantly critical in approach) by identifying the complex variations between places and periods and the ambiguous relations of different classes to the police.[22] There has also been a much greater stress on the

---

[22] These recent more detailed studies hark back to the primarily administrative histories of Hart (1951) and Radzinowicz (1956a, 1956b, 1968) but incorporate a larger social dimension.

continuities between Peel's "new" police and what went before (Brewer and Styles 1980; Bailey 1981; Jones 1982; Emsley 1983, 1987, chap. 8; Steedman 1984; Reiner 1985, chaps. 1, 2; Styles 1987; Palmer 1988; Hay and Snyder 1989).

The history of policing is likely to be substantially revised as a result of ongoing work, in particular on the period from the middle of the nineteenth century (after the much-studied establishment of the "new" police) down to the middle of this century. This period of organizational consolidation has only been researched in terms of specific aspects, although Porter (1987) on the founding of the London Metropolitan Police Special Branch, Jane Morgan (1987) on the policing of labor disputes, 1900–1939, and Hobbs (1988, chaps. 2, 4) on the London CID are excellent histories of these topics. New departures in police history that should prove immensely productive include the collection and analysis of local police archives by Clive Emsley of the Open University (a project which, unlike most historical research, has attracted substantial funding from the ESRC and elsewhere), the gathering of oral histories of the police (Weinberger 1987; Brogden 1991), and studies of police policy-making based on recently released public records (Bottoms and Stevenson 1989). The impact of these new sources that are currently being tapped is likely to deepen profoundly our present understanding of police development.

IV. Police Research in the United Kingdom:
A Concluding Assessment

There are three distinct currents of work that have dominated police research in the United Kingdom. The earliest to develop was the primarily microsociological tradition of studies of the organization, culture, and practices of policing at rank-and-file levels. Partly arising out of a critical reaction to these intraorganizational studies, partly out of political activism, and partly out of a separate tradition of radical social histories of policing, a Marxist analysis of the contemporary police developed in the late 1970s and early 1980s. This attempted to synthesize accounts of the practices and ideology of policing with a macrostructural analysis of the place of the police within the state and society. However, during the 1980s, both traditions have become dwarfed by a proliferation of research within a managerialist, policy-oriented, evaluative paradigm. Motivated and made possible by the movement of policing issues to the center of the political stage, such research has, in fact, flourished at both ends of the political spectrum. It has as its patrons left-wing councils, as well as the controlling institutions of the state apparatus. Many of the producers of this research include the best and the brightest from the earlier research waves. They are not intellectually or politically servile and are often unafraid to bite the hand that feeds them. Their results are often critical of police or government policy.

Nevertheless, there is a danger that the quantitative explosion of police research in the 1980s is not matched by a qualitative expansion of understanding. The first two waves were not without concerns about the policy implications of their work. The police culture studies had clear relevance for understanding and possibly controlling police deviation from the rule of law, discrimination in the exercise of discretion, and lack of accountability to the public. The Marxist work, although owing more to the Marx of the British Museum reading room than the Paris barricades, was evidently fired by a concern for social justice and democracy. Nevertheless, the primary purpose of research in both traditions was understanding the world, even if as a prelude to changing it.

This theoretical intellectual commitment to building up a basic framework for analysis of what is one of the fundamental political and social processes, policing, seems to be absent from even the most meticulous and professional current funded research, despite much greater resource and access opportunities. In their commendable rush to publish, in order to influence policy and practice as much as to keep sponsors off their backs, researchers are more concerned to relate their results to the concerns of practitioners than to relate them to earlier research, to policing in other times, other places, and by other means than formal state police.

There is also a lack of effort to situate particular police research in the wider context of social, political, and economic change at national (let alone international) levels. This must ultimately impoverish even the policy contribution of research, which has to explain broad processes of development that are the basis of specific policy problems. In 1989, I was invited, together with several other researchers, to a consultation with the police staff associations that addressed the problem, as they saw it, of incipient privatization of the policing function, made possible by declining public confidence in the police. This is an example of a real and pressing policy concern that cannot begin to be tackled without a broader understanding of basic economic and social change, not only in the United Kingdom but internationally, as the valuable North American work in this area shows (Shearing and Stenning 1987). British police research is in danger of concentrating on funded, short time-scale projects examining trees while failing to remark on the forest.

The conventional end to an academic article is a plea for more research.[23] It would certainly be unthinkable to argue for less research. However, what is now needed is more synthesis of research, not only in general texts (which has been attempted), but in terms of projects relating themselves to broader theoretical issues as well as other empirical work.[24] It is hoped that this review of research that has been done to date may contribute to this process.

REFERENCES

Ackroyd, C., J. Rosenhead, and T. Shallice. 1980. *The Technology of Political Control*. London: Pluto.
Adlam, Robert. 1987. "The Special Course." *Policing* 3:185–95.
Anderson, Malcolm. 1989. *Policing the World*. Oxford: Oxford University Press.
Antunes, George, and Eric J. Scott. 1981. "Calling the Cops." *Journal of Criminal Justice* 9:165–80.
Ascoli, David. 1979. *The Queen's Peace*. London: Hamish Hamilton.
Bailey, Victor, ed. 1981. *Policing and Punishment in the Nineteenth Century*. London: Croom Helm.
Baldwin, Robert. 1987. "Why Accountability?" *British Journal of Criminology* 27:97–105.

[23] There are, in fact, many important empirical research areas that require more attention. My personal "dream shopping list" would include the observation of police policy-making levels, detective work concerned with serious crime (such as regional crime squads), special branch and political policing, the functioning of the Home Office and Inspectorate of Constabulary, the culture and practice of private security, the inside workings of the selection and promotion processes, and training at higher levels. All of these are unlikely to be serious contenders for access—although, fifteen years ago, few researchers would have predicted the opening up that has occurred in the 1980s of hitherto backstage aspects of policing. Most of these subjects have been studied in the United States, which is clearly still more open to police research. There are two barriers for British police researchers to surmount that are greater than those faced by American researchers. The first is the almost-sacred aura the police in Britain acquired as a symbol of national pride. The second is the greater centralization of the system. Access to police organizations is tightly controlled by the Home Office and the Association of Chief Police Officers; American researchers are more likely to find some sympathetic point of entry in one of the large number of forces in the country.

[24] In essence, I am arguing for a return to the broader eighteenth-century conception of a "science of police" as a branch of political economy (Reiner 1988c), rather than adherence to the more technocratic police science that is dominant at present.

Baldwin, Robert, and Richard Kinsey. 1982. *Police Powers and Politics*. London: Quartet.

Banton, Michael. 1964. *The Policeman in the Community*. London: Tavistock.

———. 1971. "The Sociology of the Police." *Police Journal* 44:227–43.

———. 1973. "The Sociology of the Police II." *Police Journal* 46:341–62.

———. 1975. "The Sociology of the Police III." *Police Journal* 48:299–315.

Baxter, John, and Laurence Koffman. 1983. "The Confait Inheritance—Forgotten Lessons?" *Cambrian Law Review* 14:11–20.

———, eds. 1985. *Police, the Constitution and the Community*. Abingdon: Professional.

Bayley, David H. 1983. "Accountability and Control of Police: Some Lessons for Britain." In *The Future of Policing*, edited by Trevor Bennett. Cambridge: Institute of Criminology.

———. 1985. *Patterns of Policing*. New Brunswick, N.J.: Rutgers University Press.

Belson, William A. 1975. *The Public and the Police*. London: Harper & Row.

Benn, Caroline, and Ken Worpole. 1986. *Death in the City*. London: Canary.

Bennett, Richard. 1984. "Becoming Blue: A Longitudinal Study of Police Recruit Occupational Socialization." *Journal of Police Science and Administration* 12:47–58.

Bennett, Trevor. 1979. "The Social Distribution of Criminal Labels." *British Journal of Criminology* 19:134–45.

———, ed. 1983. *The Future of Policing*. Cambridge: Institute of Criminology.

———. 1988. "An Assessment of the Design, Implementation and Effectiveness of Neighbourhood Watch in London." *Howard Journal of Criminal Justice* 27:241–55.

———. 1989. "The Neighbourhood Watch Experiment." In *Coming to Terms with Policing*, edited by Rod Morgan and David J. Smith. London: Routledge.

———. 1990. *Evaluating Neighbourhood Watch*. Aldershot: Gower.

Benyon, John. 1986. *A Tale of Failure: Race and Policing*. Coventry: University of Warwick, Centre for Research in Ethnic Relations.

Benyon, John, and Colin Bourne, eds. 1986. *The Police: Powers, Procedures and Proprieties*. Oxford: Pergamon.

Bevan, Vaughan, and Ken Lidstone. 1985. *The Police and the Criminal Evidence Act 1984*. London: Butterworth.

Bird, Cathy. 1988. "Police Foundation Research Noticeboard." *Policing* 4:323–29.

———. 1989. *The New Register of Policing Research*. London: Police Foundation.

Bittner, Egon. 1967a. "The Police on Skid Row: A Study of Peacekeeping." *American Sociological Review* 32:699–715.

———. 1967b. "Police Discretion in the Emergency Apprehension of Mentally Ill Persons." *Social Problems* 14:278–92.

———. 1970. *The Functions of the Police in Modern Society*. Chevy Chase, Md.: National Institutes of Mental Health.

———. 1974. "Florence Nightingale in Pursuit of Willie Sutton: A Theory of the Police." In *The Potential for Reform of Criminal Justice*, edited by Herbert Jacob. Beverly Hills, Calif.: Sage.

Black, Donald. 1980. *The Manners and Customs of the Police.* New York: Academic Press.

Blair, Ian. 1985. *Investigating Rape.* London: Croom Helm.

Bottoms, Anthony E. 1987. "Reflections on the Criminological Enterprise." *Cambridge Law Journal* 46:240–63.

———. 1990. "Crime Prevention Facing the 1990s." *Policing and Society* 1:3–22.

Bottoms, Anthony E., and S. Stevenson. 1989. "The Politics of the Police, 1958–1970." Paper presented at the second annual British Criminology Conference, Bristol Polytechnic, Centre for Criminal Justice, July.

Box, Steven, and Ken Russell. 1975. "The Politics of Discreditability." *Sociological Review* 23:315–46.

Boyle, Kevin, Tom Hadden, and Paddy Hillyard. 1975. *Law and State: The Case of Northern Ireland.* Oxford: Martin Robertson.

———. 1980. *Ten Years On in Northern Ireland: The Legal Control of Political Violence.* London: National Council for Civil Liberties.

Bradley, David, Neil Walker, and Roy Wilkie. 1986. *Managing the Police.* Brighton: Harvestor Wheatsheaf.

Brewer, John D. 1990. *Inside the RUC.* Oxford: Oxford University Press.

Brewer, John D., Adrian Guelke, Ian Hume, Edward Moxon-Browne, and Rick Wilford. 1988. *The Police, Public Order and the State.* London: Macmillan.

Brewer, John, and John Styles, eds. 1980. *An Ungovernable People.* London: Hutchinson.

Brogden, Ann. 1981. "Sus Is Dead, but What about Sas?" *New Community* 9:44–52.

Brogden, Michael E. 1977. "A Police Authority: The Denial of Conflict." *Sociological Review* 25:325–49.

———. 1982. *The Police: Autonomy and Consent.* London: Academic Press.

———. 1987. "The Emergence of the Police: The Colonial Dimension." *British Journal of Criminology* 27:4–14.

———. 1991. *On the Mersey Beat: An Oral History of Policing Liverpool between the Wars.* Oxford: Oxford University Press.

Brogden, Michael E., and Ann Brogden. 1983. "From Henry VIII to Liverpool 8: The Complex Unity of Police Street Powers." *International Journal of the Sociology of Law* 12:37–58.

Brogden, Michael E., and David Graham. 1988. "Police Education: The Hidden Curriculum." In *The Political Education of Servants of the State*, edited by R. Fieldhouse. Manchester: Manchester University Press.

Brogden, Michael E., Tony Jefferson, and Sandra Walklate. 1988. *Introducing Policework.* London: Allen & Unwin.

Brown, Andrew. 1988. *Watching the Detectives.* London: Hodder & Stoughton.

Brown, Audrey, ed. 1985. *Models of Police/Public Consultation in Europe.* Cranfield: Cranfield.

Brown, David. 1987. *The Police Complaints Procedure: A Survey of Complainants'*

Views. Home Office Research Study no. 93. London: H.M. Stationery Office.

———. 1989. *Detention at the Police Station under the Police and Criminal Evidence Act, 1984*. Home Office Research Study no. 104. London: H.M. Stationery Office.

Brown, David, and Susan Iles. 1985. *Community Constables: A Study of a Policing Initiative*. Research and Planning Unit Paper no. 30. London: Home Office.

Brown, John, ed. 1984. *Policing and Social Policy*. London: Police Review.

Brown, Louise, and Andrew Willis. 1985. "Authoritarianism in British Police Recruits: Importation, Socialisation or Myth?" *Journal of Occupational Psychology* 58:97–108.

Bryant, Lyn, David Dunkerley, and Gwyneth Kelland. 1985. "One of the Boys." *Policing* 1:236–44.

Bull, Ray, and Peter Horncastle. 1989. "An Evaluation of Human Awareness Training." In *Coming to Terms with Policing*, edited by Rod Morgan and David J. Smith. London: Routledge.

Bunyan, Tony. 1976. *The Political Police in Britain*. London: Quartet.

Bunyan, Tony, and Martin Kettle. 1980. "The Police Force of the Future Is Now Here." *New Society* 53:927–29.

Burbeck, E., and A. Furnham. 1984. "Personality and Police Selection: Trait Differences in Successful and Non-successful Applicants to the Metropolitan Police." *Journal of Personality and Individual Differences* 5:257–63.

———. 1985. "Police Officer Selection: A Critical Review of the Literature." *Journal of Police Science and Administration* 13:58–69.

Burrows, John. 1986. *Burglary: Police Actions and Victims' Views*. Research and Planning Unit Paper no. 37. London: Home Office.

Burrows, John, Paul Ekblom, and Kevin Heal. 1979. *Crime Prevention and the Police*. Home Office Research Study no. 55. London: H.M. Stationery Office.

Burrows, John, and Helen Lewis. 1988. *Directing Patrol Work: A Study of Uniformed Policing*. Home Office Research Study no. 99. London: H.M. Stationery Office.

Burrows, John, and Roger Tarling. 1982. *Clearing Up Crime*. Home Office Research Study no. 73. London: H.M. Stationery Office.

Butler, A. J. P. 1984. *Police Management*. Aldershot: Gower.

———. 1985. "Objectives and Accountability." *Policing* 1:174–86.

———. 1986. "Purpose and Process." *Policing* 2:160–66.

Cain, Maureen E. 1973. *Society and the Policeman's Role*. London: Routledge.

———. 1977. "An Ironical Departure: The Dilemma of Contemporary Policing." In *Yearbook of Social Policy in Britain*, edited by K. Jones. London: Routledge.

———. 1979. "Trends in the Sociology of Police Work." *International Journal of the Sociology of Law* 7:143–67.

Cain, Maureen E., and Susan Sadigh. 1982. "Racism, the Police and Community Policing." *Journal of Law and Society* 9:87–102.

Carrier, John. 1988. *The Campaign for the Employment of Women as Police Officers.* Aldershot: Avebury.

Chapman, Brian. 1970. *Police State.* London: Macmillan.

Chatterton, Michael R. 1975. "Organisational Relationships and Processes in Police Work." Ph.D. dissertation, University of Manchester, Department of Sociology.

———. 1976. "The Police and Social Control." In *Control without Custody*, edited by J. King. Cambridge: Institute of Criminology.

———. 1979. "The Supervision of Police Work under the Fixed Points System." In *The British Police*, edited by Simon Holdaway. London: Edward Arnold.

———. 1983. "Police Work and Assault Charges." In *Control in the Police Organisation*, edited by Maurice Punch. Cambridge, Mass.: MIT Press.

———. 1987a. "Assessing Police Effectiveness: Future Prospects." *British Journal of Criminology* 27:80–86.

———. 1987b. "Front-line Supervision in the British Police Service." In *The Crowd in Contemporary Britain*, edited by George Gaskell and Robert Benewick. London: Sage.

———. 1989. "Managing Paperwork." In *Police Research: Some Future Prospects*, edited by Mollie Weatheritt. Aldershot: Avebury.

Chatterton, Michael R., and Mike Rogers. 1989. "Focussed Policing." In *Coming to Terms with Policing*, edited by Rod Morgan and David J. Smith. London: Routledge.

Chesshyre, Robert. 1989. *The Force.* London: Sidgwick & Jackson.

Chibnall, Steve. 1977. *Law and Order News.* London: Tavistock.

Christian, Louise. 1983. *Policing by Coercion.* London: Pluto.

Christopher, Steve. 1990. "The Who and Why of Police Assaults." *Police Review* 98:20–21.

Clarke, Ronald V. G. 1983. "Situational Crime Prevention." In *Crime and Justice: An Annual Review of Research*, vol. 4, edited by Michael Tonry and Norval Morris. Chicago: University of Chicago Press.

Clarke, Ronald V. G., and Derek Cornish. 1983. *Crime Control in Britain: A Review of Policy Research.* Albany: State University of New York Press.

Clarke, Ronald V. G., and Mike Hough, eds. 1980. *The Effectiveness of Policing.* Farnborough: Gower.

———. 1984. *Crime and Police Effectiveness.* Home Office Research Study no. 79. London: H.M. Stationery Office.

Cochrane, R., and A. J. P. Butler. 1980. "The Values of Police Officers, Recruits and Civilians in England." *Journal of Police Science and Administration* 8:205–11.

Cochrane, R., and S. Phillips. 1988. "The Training of Community Liaison Officers." In *New Directions in Police Training*, edited by P. Southgate. London: H.M. Stationery Office.

Cohen, P. 1979. "Policing the Working Class City." In *Capitalism and the Rule of Law*, edited by B. Fine, R. Kinsey, J. Lea, S. Picciotto, and J. Young. London: Hutchinson.

Cohen, Stan. 1988. *Against Criminology*. New Brunswick, N.J.: Transaction.

Collins, Kate. 1985. "Efficiency Revisited." *Policing* 1:70–76.

Colman, A. M., and P. L. Gorman. 1982. "Conservatism, Dogmatism and Authoritarianism in Police Officers." *Sociology* 16:1–11.

Committee of Inquiry on the Police. 1978. *Reports on Negotiating Machinery and Pay*. Cmnd. 7283. London: H.M. Stationery Office.

Cox, Barry, John Shirley, and Martin Short. 1977. *The Fall of Scotland Yard*. Harmondsworth: Penguin.

Crawford, Adam, Trevor Jones, Tom Woodhouse, and Jock Young. 1990. *The Second Islington Crime Survey*. London: Middlesex Polytechnic Centre for Criminology.

Critchley, T. A. 1970. *The Conquest of Violence*. London: Batsford.

———. 1978. *A History of Police in England and Wales*. 2d ed. London: Constable.

Cumming, E., I. Cumming, and L. Edell. 1965. "Policeman as Philosopher, Guide and Friend." *Social Problems* 12:276–86.

Currie, Cathy. 1986. "Divisional Command." *Policing* 2:318–24.

Davies, John, Lord Gifford, and Tony Richards. 1984. *Political Policing in Wales*. Cardiff: Welsh Campaign for Civil and Political Liberties.

Davis, Kenneth C. 1969. *Discretionary Justice*. Urbana: University of Illinois.

———. 1975. *Police Discretion*. St. Paul: West.

Day, Patricia, and Rudolf Klein. 1987. *Accountabilities*. London: Tavistock.

Ditchfield, J. A. 1976. *Police Cautioning in England and Wales*. Home Office Research Study no. 37. London: H.M. Stationery Office.

Dix, M. C., and A. D. Layzell. 1983. *Road Users and the Police*. London: Croom Helm.

Dixon, David, Keith Bottomley, Clive Coleman, Martin Gill, and David Wall. 1990. "Safeguarding the Rights of Suspects in Police Custody." *Policing and Society* 1:115–40.

Dorn, Nicholas, Karim Murji, and Nigel South. 1991. "Mirroring the Market? Police Reorganisation and Effectiveness against Drug Trafficking." In *Beyond Law and Order: Criminal Justice Policy and Politics into the 1990s*, edited by Robert Reiner and M. Cross. London: Macmillan.

Downes, David. 1983. *Law and Order: Theft of an Issue*. London: Fabian Society.

———, ed. 1991. *Crime and Criminal Justice*. London: Macmillan.

Downes, David, and Tony Ward. 1986. *Democratic Policing*. London: Labour Campaign for Criminal Justice.

Edwards, Sue. 1989. *Policing "Domestic" Violence*. London: Sage.

Ekblom, Paul, and Kevin Heal. 1982. *The Police Response to Calls from the Public*. Research and Planning Unit Paper no. 9. London: Home Office.

Elliott, John. 1988. "Why Put Case Study at the Heart of the Police Training Curriculum?" In *New Directions in Police Training*, edited by Peter Southgate. London: H.M. Stationery Office.

Emsley, Clive. 1983. *Policing and Its Context, 1750–1870*. London: Macmillan.

———. 1987. *Crime and Society in England, 1750–1900*. London: Longman.

Farrington, D. P., and E. Dowds. 1985. "Disentangling Criminal Behaviour and Police Reaction." In *Reactions to Crime: The Public, the Police, Courts and Prisons*, edited by David P. Farrington and J. Gunn. Chichester: Wiley.

Feldman, David. 1990. "Regulating Treatment of Suspects in Police Stations: Judicial Interpretation of the Detention Provisions in the Police and Criminal Evidence Act 1984." *Criminal Law Review*, pp. 452–71.

Field, Simon, and Peter Southgate. 1982. *Public Disorder: A Review of Research and a Study in One Inner City Area*. Home Office Research Study no. 72. London: H.M. Stationery Office.

Fielding, Nigel G. 1988. *Joining Forces*. London: Routledge.

———. 1989. "Police Culture and Police Practice." In *Police Research: Some Future Prospects*, edited by Mollie Weatheritt. Aldershot: Avebury.

Fielding, Nigel G., Charles Kemp, and Clive Norris. 1989. "Constraints on the Practice of Community Policing." In *Coming to Terms with Policing*, edited by Rod Morgan and David J. Smith. London: Routledge.

Fine, Bob, and Robert Millar, eds. 1985. *Policing the Miners' Strike*. London: Lawrence & Wishart.

Foster, Janet. 1989. "Two Stations: An Ethnographic Study of Policing in the Inner City." In *Crime and the City*, edited by David Downes. London: Macmillan.

Franey, Ros. 1983. *Poor Law*. London: Child Poverty Action Group, Claimants' Defence Union, National Association of Probation Officers, and National Council for Civil Liabilities.

Freeman, Michael D. A. 1985. *The Police and Criminal Evidence Act 1984*. London: Sweet & Maxwell.

Gash, Norman. 1961. *Mr. Secretary Peel*. London: Longman.

Gaskell, George, and Robert Benewick, eds. 1987. *The Crowd in Contemporary Britain*. London: Sage.

Geary, Roger. 1985. *Policing Industrial Disputes*. Cambridge: Cambridge University Press.

Gelsthorpe, Loraine, Henri Giller, and Norman Tutt. 1989. *The Impact of the Crown Prosecution Service on Juvenile Justice*. Lancaster: University of Lancaster.

Gifford, Lord. 1986. *The Broadwater Farm Inquiry*. London: Broadwater Farm Inquiry.

Gilroy, Paul. 1987. *There Ain't No Black in the Union Jack*. London: Hutchinson.

Goldsmith, A. 1990. "Taking Police Culture Seriously: Police Discretion and the Limits of Law." *Policing and Society* 1:91–114.

Goldstein, H. 1977. *Policing a Free Society*. Cambridge: Ballinger.

Goldstein, J. 1960. "Police Discretion Not to Invoke the Criminal Process: Low Visibility Decisions in the Administration of Justice." *Yale Law Journal* 69:543–94.

Gordon, Paul. 1980. *Policing Scotland*. Glasgow: Scottish Council for Civil Liberties.

———. 1983. *White Law*. London: Pluto.

Gorer, Geoffrey. 1955. *Exploring English Character*. London: Cresset.

Graef, Roger. 1989. *Talking Blues*. London: Collins.

Greater London Council. 1983. *A New Police Authority for London*. London: Greater London Council.

Greer, Steven C. 1987. "The Rise and Fall of the Northern Ireland Supergrass System." *Criminal Law Review*, pp. 663–71.

Gregory, F. E. C. 1985. "The British Police System." In *Police and Public Order in Europe*, edited by J. Roach and J. Thomaneck. London: Croom Helm.

Grimshaw, Roger, and Tony Jefferson. 1987. *Interpreting Policework*. London: Allen & Unwin.

Hall, Stuart, Chas Critcher, Tony Jefferson, John Clarke, and Brian Robers. 1978. *Policing the Crisis*. London: Macmillan.

Hanmer, Jalna, Jill Radford, and Elizabeth A. Stanko, eds. 1989. *Women, Policing and Male Violence*. London: Routledge.

Hann, Robert G., James H. McGinnis, Philip C. Stenning, and A. Stuart Farson. 1985. "Municipal Police Governance and Accountability in Canada: An Empirical Study." *Canadian Police College Journal* 9:1–85.

Harris, Richard. 1973. *The Police Academy: An Inside View*. New York: Wiley.

Hart, Jennifer. 1951. *The British Police*. London: Allen & Unwin.

Harvey, Linda, Penny Grimshaw, and Ken Pease. 1989. "Crime Prevention Delivery: The Work of Crime Prevention Officers." In *Coming to Terms with Policing*, edited by Rod Morgan and David J. Smith: London: Routledge.

Hay, Douglas, and Francis Snyder, eds. 1989. *Policing and Prosecution in Britain, 1750–1850*. Oxford: Oxford University Press.

Heal, Kevin, Roger Tarling, and John Burrows, eds. 1985. *Policing Today*. London: H.M. Stationery Office.

Heidensohn, Frances. 1985. *Women and Crime*. London: Macmillan.

Hewitt, Patricia. 1982. *A Fair Cop?* London: National Council for Civil Liberties.

Hillyard, Paddy. 1981. "From Belfast to Britain." In *Politics and Power 4: Law, Politics and Justice*. London: Routledge.

Hobbs, Dick. 1988. *Doing the Business*. Oxford: Oxford University Press.

Holdaway, Simon. 1977. "Changes in Urban Policing." *British Journal of Sociology* 28:119–37.

———, ed. 1979. *The British Police*. London: Edward Arnold.

———. 1983. *Inside the British Police*. Oxford: Blackwell.

———. 1989. "Discovering Structure: Studies of the British Police Occupational Culture." In *Police Research: Some Future Prospects*, edited by Mollie Weatheritt. Aldershot: Avebury.

Holdaway, Simon, Christopher Spencer, and David Wilson. 1984. "Black Police in the UK." *Policing* 1:20–30.

Home Affairs Committee. 1989. *Higher Police Training and the Police Staff College*. Vols. 1, 2. London: H.M. Stationery Office.

Hood, Roger. 1987. "Some Reflections on the Role of Criminology in Public Policy." *Criminal Law Review*, pp. 527–38.

Horton, Christine. 1989. "Good Practice and Evaluative Policing." In *Coming to Terms with Policing*, edited by Rod Morgan and David J. Smith. London: Routledge.

Horton, Christine, and David J. Smith. 1988. *Evaluating Police Work*. London: Policy Studies Institute.

Hough, Mike. 1980. *Uniformed Police Work and Management Technology*. Research Unit Paper no. 1. London: Home Office.

———. 1987. "Thinking about Effectiveness." *British Journal of Criminology* 27:70–79.

———. 1989. "Demand for Policing and Police Performance: Progress and Pitfalls in Public Surveys." In *Police Research: Some Future Prospects*, edited by Mollie Weatheritt. Aldershot: Avebury.

Hough, Mike, and Pat Mayhew. 1983. *The British Crime Survey*. Home Office Research Study no. 76. London: H.M. Stationery Office.

———. 1985. *Taking Account of Crime: Key Findings from the 1984 British Crime Survey*. Home Office Research Study no. 85. London: H.M. Stationery Office.

Ignatieff, Michael. 1979. "Police and People: The Birth of Mr. Peel's Blue Locusts." *New Society* 49:443–45.

Ingram, Frank. 1987. "The Audit Commission." *Policing* 3:170–75.

Irving, Barrie L. 1980. *Police Interrogation*. Royal Commission on Criminal Procedure Research Study no. 1. London: H.M. Stationery Office.

Irving, Barrie L., Cathy Bird, Malcolm Hibberd, and Jon Willmore. 1989. *Neighbourhood Policing: The Natural History of a Policing Experiment*. London: Police Foundation.

Irving, Barrie L., and Ian McKenzie. 1989a. *Police Interrogation*. London: Police Foundation.

———. 1989b. "Interrogating in a Legal Framework." In *Coming to Terms with Policing*, edited by Rod Morgan and David J. Smith. London: Routledge.

James, D. 1979. "Police-Black Relations: The Professional Solutions." In *The British Police*, edited by S. Holdaway. London: Edward Arnold.

Jefferson, Tony. 1987. "Beyond Paramilitarism." *British Journal of Criminology* 27:47–53.

———. 1988. "Race, Crime and Policing: Empirical, Theoretical and Methodological Issues." *International Journal of the Sociology of Law* 16:521–39.

Jefferson, T., and R. Grimshaw. 1982. "Law, Democracy and Justice: The Question of Police Accountability." In *Policing the Riots*, edited by D. Cowell, T. Jones, and J. Young. London: Junction.

———. 1984. *Controlling the Constable*. London: Muller.

Jefferson, T., E. McLaughlin, and L. Robertson. 1988. "Monitoring the Monitors: Accountability, Democracy and Police Watching in Britain." *Contemporary Crises* 12:91–107.

Johnston, Les. 1987. "Controlling the Police." *Policing* 3:48–60.

———. 1988. "Controlling Policework: Problems of Organisational Reform in Large Public Bureaucracies." *Work, Employment and Society* 2:51–70.

———. 1991. "Privatisation and the Police Function: From 'New Police' to 'New Policing.' " In *Beyond Law and Order: Criminal Justice Policy and Politics into the 1990s*, edited by Robert Reiner and M. Cross. London: Macmillan.

Jones, David. 1982. *Crime, Protest, Community and Police in Nineteenth Century Britain*. London: Routledge.

Jones, Mervyn. 1980. *Organisational Aspects of Police Behaviour*. Farnborough: Gower.

Jones, Sandra. 1983. "Community Policing in Devon and Cornwall." In *The Future of Policing*, edited by Trevor Bennett. Cambridge: Institute of Criminology.

———. 1986. "Caught in the Act." *Policing* 2:129–40.

———. 1987. *Policewomen and Equality*. London: Macmillan.

Jones, Sandra, and Richard Joss. 1985. "Do Police Officers Survive Their Training?" *Policing* 1:106–25.

Jones, Sandra, and Mike Levi. 1983. "The Police and the Majority: The Neglect of the Obvious?" *Police Journal* 56:351–64.

Jones, Sandra, and Eli Silverman. 1984. "What Price Efficiency?" *Policing* 1:31–48.

Jones, Trevor, Brian MacLean, and Jock Young. 1986. *The Islington Crime Survey*. Aldershot: Gower.

Judge, Tony. 1972. *A Man Apart*. London: Barker.

Kemp, Charles, and Rod Morgan. 1989. *Behind the Front Counter: Lay Visitors to Police Stations*. Bristol: Bristol University, Centre for Criminal Justice.

Kettle, M. 1980. "The Politics of Policing and the Policing of Politics." In *Policing the Police 2*, edited by P. Hain. London: Calder.

Kettle, Martin, and Lucy Hodges. 1982. *Uprising! The Police, the People, and the Riots in Britain's Cities*. London: Pan.

Kinsey, Richard. 1984. *Merseyside Crime Survey: First Report*. Liverpool: Merseyside County Council.

———. 1985a. *Survey of Merseyside Police Officers*. Liverpool: Merseyside County Council.

———. 1985b. *Merseyside Crime and Police Surveys: Final Report*. Liverpool: Merseyside County Council.

Kinsey, Richard, John Lea, and Jock Young. 1986. *Losing the Fight against Crime*. Oxford: Blackwell.

Klockars, Carl. 1985. *The Idea of Police*. Beverly Hills, Calif.: Sage.

La Fave, Wayne R. 1965. *Arrest: The Decision to Take a Suspect into Custody*. Boston: Little, Brown.

Lambert, John. 1970. *Crime, Police and Race Relations*. Oxford: Oxford University Press.

Landau, Simcha. 1981. "Juveniles and the Police." *British Journal of Criminology* 21:27–46.

Landau, Simcha, and George Nathan. 1983. "Selecting Delinquents for Cautioning in the London Metropolitan Area." *British Journal of Criminology* 23:128–49.

Laurie, Peter. 1970. *Scotland Yard*. Harmondsworth: Penguin.

Lea, John. 1986. "Police Racism: Some Theories and Their Policy Implications." In *Confronting Crime*, edited by Roger Matthews and Jock Young. London: Sage.

Lea, John, and Jock Young. 1984. *What Is to Be Done about Law and Order?* Harmondsworth: Penguin.

Leigh, Leonard. 1985. *Police Powers in England and Wales*. 2d ed. London: Butterworth.

———. 1986. "Some Observations on the Parliamentary History of the Police and Criminal Evidence Act 1984." In *Public Law and Politics*, edited by C. Harlow. London: Sweet & Maxwell.

Leon, Claire. 1989. "The Special Constabulary." *Policing* 5:265–86.

Levi, Mike. 1987. *Regulating Fraud*. London: Tavistock.

Lidstone, Ken. 1984. "Magistrates, the Police and Search Warrants." *Criminal Law Review*, pp. 449–58.

Lodge, Tom. 1974. "The Founding of the Home Office Research Unit." In *Crime, Criminology and Public Policy*, edited by Roger Hood. London: Heinemann.

Loveday, Barry. 1983. "The Role of the Police Committee." *Local Government Studies* 9:39–53.

———. 1985. *The Role and Effectiveness of the Merseyside Police Committee*. Liverpool: Merseyside County Council.

———. 1987. "The Joint Boards." *Policing* 3:196–213.

———. 1988. "Police Complaints in the U.S.A." *Policing* 4:172–93.

———. 1991. "The New Police Authorities." *Policing and Society* (forthcoming).

Lustgarten, Laurence. 1986. *The Governance of the Police*. London: Sweet & Maxwell.

McBarnet, D. 1978. "The Police and the State." In *Power and the State*, edited by G. Littlejohn, B. Smart, J. Wakeford, and N. Yuval-Davis. London: Croom Helm.

———. 1979. "Arrest: The Legal Context of Policing." In *The British Police*, edited by S. Holdaway. London: Edward Arnold.

McCabe, Sarah, and Frank Sutcliffe. 1978. *Defining Crime*. Oxford: Blackwell.

McCabe, Sarah, and Peter Wallington, with John Alderson, Larry Gostin, and Christopher Maston. 1988. *The Police, Public Order and Civil Liberties*. London: Routledge.

MacDonald, B., M. J. Argent, J. Elliott, N. H. May, P. J. G. Miller, J. T. Taylor, and N. F. J. Norris. 1987. *Police Probationer Training: Final Report of the Stage II Review*. London: H.M. Stationery Office.

McKenzie, Ian, and Pat Gallagher. 1989. *Behind the Uniform*. Hemel Hempstead: Harvester Wheatsheaf.

McKenzie, Ian, and Barrie Irving. 1987. "Police Interrogation." *Policing* 3:4–22.

———. 1988. "The Right to Silence." *Policing* 4:88–105.

McKenzie, Ian, and Les Johnston. 1988. "Coming to Terms with Policing." *Policing* 4:211–28.

McKenzie, Ian, Rod Morgan, and Robert Reiner. 1990. "Helping the Police with Their Inquiries: The Necessity Principle and Voluntary Attendance at the Police Station." *Criminal Law Review*, pp. 22–33.

Magee, Kathleen. 1991. "The Dual Role of the Royal Ulster Constabulary in Northern Ireland." In *Beyond Law and Order: Criminal Justice Policy and Politics into the 1990s*, edited by Robert Reiner and M. Cross. London: Macmillan.

Maguire, Mike. 1988. "Effects of the 'PACE' Provisions on Detention and Questioning." *British Journal of Criminology* 28:19–43.

———. 1991. "Complaints against the Police: The British Experience." In

Complaints against the Police, edited by A. Goldsmith. Oxford: Oxford University Press.

Maguire, Mike, and Claire Corbett. 1989. "Patterns and Profiles of Complaints against the Police." In *Coming to Terms with Policing*, edited by Rod Morgan and David J. Smith. London: Routledge.

Manning, Peter. 1977. *Police Work*. Cambridge, Mass.: MIT Press.

————. 1979. "The Social Control of Police Work." In *The British Police*, edited by Simon Holdaway. London: Edward Arnold.

————. 1980. *The Narc's Game*. Cambridge, Mass.: MIT Press.

————. 1989. *Symbolic Communication*. Cambridge, Mass.: MIT Press.

Manwaring-White, Sarah. 1983. *The Policing Resolution*. Brighton: Harvester.

Marenin, Otwin. 1982. "Parking Tickets and Class Repression: The Concept of Policing in Critical Theories of Criminal Justice." *Contemporary Crises* 6:241–66.

Mark, Robert. 1977. *Policing a Perplexed Society*. London: Allen & Unwin.

————. 1978. *In the Office of Constable*. London: Collins.

Marshall, G. 1965. *Police and Government*. London: Methuen.

————. 1978. "Police Accountability Revisited." In *Policing and Politics*, edited by D. Butler and A. H. Halsey. London: Macmillan.

Martin, John P. 1988. "The Development of Criminology in Britain, 1948–1960." *British Journal of Criminology* 28:165–74.

Martin, John P., and Gail Wilson. 1969. *The Police: A Study in Manpower*. London: Heinemann.

Matthews, Roger, and Jock Young, eds. 1986. *Confronting Crime*. London: Sage.

Mawby, R. 1979. *Policing the City*. Farnborough: Gower.

————. 1991. "Community Involvement in Criminal Justice." In *Beyond Law and Order: Criminal Justice Policy and Politics into the 1990s*, edited by Robert Reiner and M. Cross. London: Macmillan.

Mayhew, Pat, David Elliott, and Lizanne Dowds. 1989. *The 1988 British Crime Survey*. Home Office Research Study no. 111. London: H.M. Stationery Office.

Miller, Wilbur. 1977. *Cops and Bobbies*. Chicago: University of Chicago Press.

Morgan, Jane. 1987. *Conflict and Order: The Police and Labour Disputes in England and Wales, 1900–1939*. Oxford: Oxford University Press.

Morgan, Rod. 1986. "Police Consultative Groups: The Implications for the Governance of the Police." *Political Quarterly* 57:83–87.

————. 1987. "Police Accountability: Developing the Local Infrastructure." *British Journal of Criminology* 27:87–96.

————. 1989. "'Policing by Consent': Legitimating the Doctrine." In *Coming to Terms with Policing*, edited by Rod Morgan and David J. Smith. London: Routledge.

Morgan, Rod, and Chris Maggs. 1984. *Following Scarman?* Social Policy Papers. Bath: Bath University.

————. 1985. *Setting the PACE*. Social Policy Papers. Bath: Bath University.

Morgan, Rod, and David J. Smith, eds. 1989. *Coming to Terms with Policing*. London: Routledge.

Morgan, Rod, and Paul Swift. 1987. "The Future of Police Authorities: Members' Views." *Public Administration* 65:259–77.

Morris, Pauline, and Kevin Heal. 1981. *Crime Control and the Police*. Home Office Research Study no. 67. London: H.M. Stationery Office.

Morton-Williams, R. 1962. "Relations between the Police and the Public." Appendix 4 of *Minutes of Evidence to Royal Commission on the Police*. London: H.M. Stationery Office.

Niederhoffer, Arthur. 1967. *Behind the Shield*. New York: Doubleday.

Norris, Clive. 1989. "Avoiding Trouble: The Patrol Officer's Perception of Encounters with the Public." In *Police Research: Some Future Prospects*, edited by Mollie Weatheritt. Aldershot: Avebury.

Northam, Gerry. 1988. *Shooting in the Dark*. London: Faber.

Oakley, Robin. 1989. *Employment in Police Forces: A Survey of Police Forces*. London: Commission for Racial Equality.

Okojie, P. 1985. "Chief Constables and Police Interference: The Case of Anderton and Greater Manchester." In *Policing the Miners' Strike*, edited by B. Fine and R. Millar. London: Lawrence & Wishart.

Oliver, Ian. 1987. *Police, Government and Accountability*. London: Macmillan.

Palmer, Stanley H. 1988. *Police and Protest in England and Ireland, 1780–1850*. Cambridge: Cambridge University Press.

Pearson, Geoffrey, Alice Sampson, Harry Blagg, Paul Stubbs, and David Smith. 1989. "Policing Racism." In *Coming to Terms with Policing*, edited by Rod Morgan and David J. Smith. London: Routledge.

Percy-Smith, Janie, and Paddy Hillyard. 1985. "Miners in the Arms of the Law: A Statistical Analysis." *Journal of Law and Society* 12:345–54.

Phillips, David. 1977. *Crime and Authority in Victorian England*. London: Croom Helm.

———. 1980. "A New Engine of Power and Authority: The Institutionalisation of Law Enforcement in England, 1780–1830." In *Crime and the Law*, edited by V. Gatrell, G. Lenman, and B. Parker. London: Europa.

———. 1983. "A Just Measure of Crime, Authority, Hunters and Blue Locusts: The 'Revisionist' Social History of Crime and the Law in Britain, 1780–1850." In *Social Control and the State*, edited by S. Cohen and A. Scull. Oxford: Martin Robertson.

Pike, Michael S. 1985. *The Principles of Policing*. London: Macmillan.

Pope, David Watts, and Norman L. Weiner, eds. 1981. *Modern Policing*. London: Croom Helm.

Porter, Bernard. 1987. *The Origins of the Vigilant State*. London: Weidenfeld & Nicolson.

Punch, Maurice. 1979a. "The Secret Social Service." In *The British Police*, edited by Simon Holdaway. London: Edward Arnold.

———. 1979b. *Policing the Inner City*. London: Macmillan.

———. 1983. "Officers and Men." In *Control in the Police Organisation*, edited by Maurice Punch. Cambridge, Mass.: MIT Press.

———. 1985. *Conduct Unbecoming: The Social Construction of Police Deviance and Control*. London: Tavistock.

Punch, Maurice, and Trevor Naylor. 1973. "The Police: A Social Service." *New Society* 24:358–61.

Radzinowicz, Sir Leon. 1956a. *The Clash between Private Initiative and Public Interest in the Enforcement of the Law*. Vol. 2 of *A History of English Criminal Law*. London: Stevens.

———. 1956b. *Cross-Currents in the Movement for the Reform of the Police*. Vol. 3 of *A History of English Criminal Law*. London: Stevens.

———. 1968. *Grappling for Control*. Vol. 4 of *A History of English Criminal Law*. London: Stevens.

Rawlings, Philip. 1991. "'Creeping Privatisation?' The Police, the Conservative Government, and Policing in the Late 1980s." In *Beyond Law and Order: Criminal Justice Policy and Politics into the 1990s*, edited by Robert Reiner and M. Cross. London: Macmillan.

Regan, David. 1983. *Are the Police under Control?* Research Report no. 1. London: Social Affairs Unit.

Reiner, Robert. 1978a. *The Blue-coated Worker*. Cambridge: Cambridge University Press.

———. 1978b. "The Police in the Class Structure." *British Journal of Law and Society* 5:166–84.

———. 1978c. "The Police, Class and Politics." *Marxism Today* 22:69–80.

———. 1980. "Fuzzy Thoughts: The Police and Law and Order Politics." *Sociological Review* 28:377–413.

———. 1985. *The Politics of the Police*. Brighton: Wheatsheaf.

———. 1986. "Policing, Order and Legitimacy in Britain." In *Research in Law, Deviance and Social Control*, vol. 8, edited by S. Spitzer and A. Scull. Greenwich, Conn.: JAI.

———. 1988a. "In the Office of Chief Constable." In *Current Legal Problems 1988*, vol. 41, edited by R. Rideout and J. Jowell. London: Stevens.

———. 1988b. "Keeping the Home Office Happy." *Policing* 4:28–36.

———. 1988c. "British Criminology and the State." *British Journal of Criminology* 28:138–58.

———. 1989a. "Dixon's Decline: Why Policing Has Become So Controversial." *Contemporary Record* 3:2–6.

———. 1989b. "The Politics of Police Research." In *Police Research: Some Future Prospects*, edited by Mollie Weatheritt. Aldershot: Avebury.

———. 1989c. "Where the Buck Stops: Chief Constables' Views on Police Accountability." In *Coming to Terms with Policing*, edited by Rod Morgan and David J. Smith. London: Routledge.

———. 1989d. "Thinking at the Top." *Policing* 5:181–89.

———. 1990. "Police and Public Order in 1989." In *Contemporary Britain: An Annual Review*, edited by P. Catterall. Oxford: Blackwell.

———. 1991. *Chief Constables*. Oxford: Oxford University Press.

Reiner, Robert, and Joanna Shapland, eds. 1987. "Why Police? Special Issue on Policing in Britain." *British Journal of Criminology*, vol. 27, no. 1.

Reiss, Albert J., Jr. 1971. *The Police and the Public*. New Haven, Conn.: Yale University Press.

Reith, Charles. 1938. *The Police Idea*. Oxford: Oxford University Press.

———. 1940. *Police Principles and the Problem of War*. Oxford: Oxford University Press.

————. 1943. *British Police and the Democratic Ideal*. Oxford: Oxford University Press.

————. 1956. *A New Study of Police History*. London: Oliver & Boyd.

Report of Her Majesty's Chief Inspector of Constabulary, 1988. 1989. London: H.M. Stationery Office.

Reuss-Ianni, Elizabeth. 1983. *The Two Cultures of Policing*. New Brunswick, N.J.: Transaction.

Robinson, Cyril D. 1979. "Ideology as History." *Police Studies* 2:35–49.

Rock, Paul. 1988. "The Present State of Criminology in Britain." *British Journal of Criminology* 28:188–99.

Rodie, John. 1988. "The Undervalued Custody Officer." *Policing* 4:4–27.

Rolph, C. H., ed. 1962. *The Police and the Public*. London: Heinemann.

Royal Commission on the Police. 1962. *Final Report*. Cmnd. 1728. London: H.M. Stationery Office.

Rumbelow, Donald. 1971. *I Spy Blue: The Police and Crime in the City of London from Elizabeth I to Victoria*. London: Macmillan.

Sanders, Andrew, Lee Bridges, Adele Mulvaney, and Gary Crozier. 1989. *Advice and Assistance at Police Stations and the 24 Hour Duty Solicitor Scheme*. London: Lord Chancellor's Department.

Savage, Stephen. 1984. "Political Control or Community Liaison?" *Political Quarterly* 55:48–59.

Scarman, Lord. 1981. *The Scarman Report: The Brixton Disorders*. Cmnd. 8427. London: H.M. Stationery Office.

Scraton, Phil. 1985. *The State of the Police*. London: Pluto.

————, ed. 1987. *Law, Order and the Authoritarian State*. Milton Keynes: Open University Press.

Scraton, Phil, and Kathryn Chadwick, eds. 1987. *In the Arms of the Law*. London: Pluto.

Scraton, Phil, and Paul Gordon, eds. 1984. *Causes for Concern*. Harmondsworth: Penguin.

Scraton, Phil, and Phil Thomas, eds. 1985. "The State vs. the People: Lessons from the Coal Dispute." Special issue. *Journal of Law and Society*, vol. 12, no. 3.

Shapland, Joanna, and Dick Hobbs. 1989a. "Policing Priorities on the Ground." In *Coming to Terms with Policing*, edited by Rod Morgan and David J. Smith. London: Routledge.

————. 1989b. "Looking at Policing." In *Crime and Criminal Policy in Europe*, edited by Roger Hood. Oxford: Centre for Criminological Research.

Shapland, Joanna, and Jon Vagg. 1987. "Using the Police." *British Journal of Criminology* 27:54–63.

————. 1988. *Policing by the Public*. London: Routledge.

Shaw, M., and W. Williamson. 1972. "Public Attitudes to the Police." *Criminologist* 7:18–33.

Shearing, Clifford D. 1981. "Subterranean Processes in the Maintenance of Power." *Canadian Review of Sociology and Anthropology* 18:283–98.

————. 1984. *Dial-A-Cop*. Toronto: University of Toronto, Centre of Criminology.

Shearing, Clifford D., and J. S. Leon. 1976. "Reconsidering the Police Role." In *Final Report: International Seminar on Police Research*, edited by L. Van Outrive and S. Rizkalla. Montreal: University of Montreal, Centre for Comparative Criminology.

Shearing, Clifford D., and Philip C. Stenning, eds. 1987. *Private Policing*. Beverly Hills, Calif.: Sage.

Shepherd, Eric. 1986. "The Conversational Core of Policing." *Policing* 2:294–303.

———. 1988. "Developing Interview Skills: A Lifetime Perspective." In *New Directions in Police Training*, edited by Peter Southgate. London: H.M. Stationery Office.

Sherman, Lawrence W. 1973. "The Sociology and the Social Reform of the American Police: 1950–1973." In *The Ambivalent Force*, edited by A. Neiderhoffer and A. S. Blumberg. 2d ed. Hinsdale, Ill.: Dryden.

———. 1983. "After the Riots: Police and Minorities in the U.S. 1970–1980." In *Ethnic Pluralism and Public Policy*, edited by N. Glazer and K. Young. London: Heinemann.

Silver, Allan. 1967. "The Demand for Order in Civil Society." In *The Police*, edited by David Bordua. New York: Wiley.

Sinclair, Ian, and Clive Miller. 1984. *Measures of Police Effectiveness and Efficiency*. Research and Planning Unit Paper no. 25. London: Home Office.

Skolnick, Jerome H. 1966. *Justice without Trial*. New York: Wiley.

———. 1969. *The Politics of Protest*. New York: Bantam.

———. 1972. "Changing Conceptions of the Police." In *Great Ideas Today*. Chicago: Encyclopaedia Britannica.

Skolnick, Jerome H., and David H. Bayley. 1986. *The New Blue Line*. New York: Free Press.

———. 1988. *Community Policing: Issues and Practices around the World*. Washington, D.C.: U.S. Department of Justice, National Institute of Justice.

Smith, D. A., and J. R. Klein. 1984. "Police Control of Interpersonal Disputes." *Social Problems* 31:468–81.

Smith, David J. 1989. "Evaluating Police Work." *Policing* 5:254–64.

Smith, David J., Jeremy Gray, and Stephen Small. 1983. *Police and People in London*. 4 vols. London: Policy Studies Institute.

Smith, Philip Thurmond. 1985. *Policing Victorian London*. Westport, Conn.: Greenwood.

South, Nigel. 1988. *Policing for Profit*. London: Sage.

Southgate, Peter. 1982. *Police Probationer Training in Race Relations*. Research and Planning Unit Paper no. 8. London: Home Office.

———. 1984. *Racism Awareness Training for the Police*. Research and Planning Unit Paper no. 29. London: Home Office.

———, ed. 1988. *New Directions in Police Training*. London: H.M. Stationery Office.

Southgate, Peter, and Paul Ekblom. 1986. *Police-Public Encounters*. Home Office Research Study no. 90. London: H.M. Stationery Office.

Southgate, Peter, and Florence Marden. 1988. "Police Training for Handling Domestic Disputes." In *New Directions in Police Training*, edited by Peter Southgate. London: H.M. Stationery Office.

Spencer, Sarah. 1985. *Called to Account*. London: National Council for Civil Liberties.

Stead, Philip J., ed. 1977. *Pioneers in Policing*. New Jersey: Patterson Smith.

———. 1985. *The Police of Britain*. New York: Macmillan.

Steedman, Carolyn. 1984. *Policing the Victorian Community*. London: Routledge.

Stenning, Philip C. 1981*a*. *Police Commissions and Boards in Canada*. Toronto: University of Toronto, Centre of Criminology.

———. 1981*b*. "The Role of Police Boards and Commissions as Institutions of Municipal Police Governance." In *Organisational Police Deviance*, edited by Clifford D. Shearing. Toronto: Butterworth.

Stephens, Mike. 1988. *Policing: The Critical Issues*. Hemel Hempstead: Harvester Wheatsheaf.

Stevens, Philip, and Carole F. Willis. 1979. *Race, Crime and Arrest*. Home Office Research Study no. 58. London: H.M. Stationery Office.

———. 1981. *Ethnic Minorities and Complaints against the Police*. Research and Planning Unit Paper no. 5. London: Home Office.

Stone, Richard. 1988. "PACE: Special Procedures and Legal Privilege." *Criminal Law Review*, pp. 498–507.

Storch, Robert. 1975. "The Plague of the Blue Locusts: Police Reform and Popular Resistance in Northern England, 1840–57." *International Review of Social History* 20:61–90.

———. 1976. "The Policeman as Domestic Missionary." *Journal of Social History* 9:481–509.

Styles, John. 1987. "The Emergence of the Police: Explaining Police Reform in Eighteenth and Nineteenth Century England." *British Journal of Criminology* 27:15–22.

Tarling, Roger. 1988. *Police Work and Manpower Allocation*. Research and Planning Unit Paper no. 47. London: Home Office.

Tarling, R., and J. Burrows. 1985. "The Work of Detectives." In *Policing Today*, edited by K. Heal, R. Tarling, and J. Burrows. London: H.M. Stationery Office.

Taylor, Ian, Paul Walton, and Jock Young. 1973. *The New Criminology*. London: Routledge.

Thackrah, J. R., ed. 1985. *Contemporary Policing*. London: Sphere.

Thomas, Terry. 1988. "The Police and Criminal Evidence Act 1984: The Social Work Role." *Howard Journal of Criminal Justice* 27:256–65.

Thornton, Peter. 1985. *We Protest*. London: National Council for Civil Liberties.

Tierney, John. 1989. "Graduating in Criminal Justice." *Policing* 5:208–23.

Tomasic, Roman. 1985. *The Sociology of Law*. London: Sage.

Tuck, Mary, and Peter Southgate. 1981. *Ethnic Minorities, Crime and Policing*. Home Office Research Study no. 70. London: H.M. Stationery Office.

Uglow, Steve. 1988. *Policing Liberal Society*. Oxford: Oxford University Press.

Van Maanen, J. 1974. "Working the Street." In *The Potential for Reform of Criminal Justice*, edited by H. Jacob. Beverly Hills, Calif.: Sage.

———. 1975. "Police Socialisation." *Administration Science Quarterly* 20:207–28.

Waddington, P. A. J. 1982. "Conservatism, Dogmatism and Authoritarianism in the Police: A Comment." *Sociology* 16:592–94.

———. 1983. *Are the Police Fair?* Research Paper no. 2. London: Social Affairs Unit.

———. 1984*a*. "Black Crime, the 'Racist' Police and Fashionable Compassion." In *The Kindness That Kills*, edited by D. Anderson. London: SPCK.

———. 1984*b*. "The Role of the Police Committee: Constitutional Arrangements and Social Realities." *Local Government Studies* 10:27–49.

———. 1986*a*. "Defining Objectives." *Policing* 2:17–25.

———. 1986*b*. "The 'Objectives' Debate." *Policing* 2:225–34.

———. 1987. "Towards Paramilitarism? Dilemmas in Policing Civil Disorder." *British Journal of Criminology* 27:37–46.

———. 1988. *Arming an Unarmed Police*. London: Police Foundation.

———. 1989. "Review of G. Northam: Shooting in the Dark." *British Journal of Criminology* 29:296–98.

Ward, Tony. 1986. *Death and Disorder*. London: Inquest.

Weatheritt, Mollie. 1986. *Innovations in Policing*. London: Croom Helm.

———, ed. 1989. *Police Research: Some Future Prospects*. Aldershot: Avebury.

Weinberger, Barbara. 1987. "Towards an Oral History of the Police." *Journal of the Police History Society* 2:36–38.

Weinberger, Barbara, and Herbert Reinke. 1989. "Law and Order in the Industrial City: An Anglo-German Comparison." Paper presented at the annual meeting of the Social Science History Association, Washington, D.C., November.

Westley, W. 1970. *Violence and the Police*. Cambridge, Mass.: MIT Press.

Whitaker, Ben. 1964. *The Police*. Harmondsworth: Penguin.

Willis, Carole F. 1983. *The Use, Effectiveness and Impact of Police Stop and Search Powers*. Research and Planning Unit Paper no. 15. London: Home Office.

Willis, Carole F., John Macleod, and Peter Naish. 1988. *The Tape-recording of Police Interviews with Suspects: A Second Interim Report*. Home Office Research Study no. 97. London: H.M. Stationery Office.

Willmott, Peter, ed. 1987. *Policing and the Community*. London: Policy Studies Institute.

Wilson, James Q. 1968. *Varieties of Police Behavior*. Cambridge, Mass.: Harvard University Press.

Young, Jock. 1988. "Radical Criminology in Britain." *British Journal of Criminology* 28:289–313.

Zander, Michael. 1985. *The Police and Criminal Evidence Act 1984*. London: Sweet & Maxwell.

———. 1989. "PACE Four Years On: An Overview." *Northern Ireland Legal Quarterly* 40:319–32.

David H. Bayley

Comparative Organization of the Police in English-speaking Countries

ABSTRACT

In order to describe adequately the national organization of police,
it is necessary to distinguish the number of autonomous forces,
the coordination of jurisdictions among them, and the territorial
and functional distribution of commands within them. Among the five
English-speaking countries of Australia, Canada, Great Britain, India, and
the United States, the number as well as the coordination of forces varies
sharply. As a result, differences in scale are so great as to call into
question the value of using either forces or police stations as units of
managerial analysis. Surprisingly, the scale of jurisdictions does not affect
the number of command levels within forces. One implication of this is
that the concept of centralization/decentralization must be grounded
in considerations of scale. Differences in national structures of policing
depend on political settlements achieved at the time countries were
formed. Differences in functional organization are smaller among
countries than structural ones, and they depend on professional outlooks
shared internationally. Finally, very little is known about the effects of
police organization on goals and objectives. The entire subject is shrouded
in unexamined assumptions often unintelligently applied.

The organization of the police is a curious subject. To begin with, it is
boring. Everyone in policing has sat through endless briefings about
command structures, internal organization, and the ranks of personnel.
Police departments hand out charts about these matters as hostesses
distribute party favors. Such information is essential in order to find
one's way around a police department, but no one pretends it is fun to

David H. Bayley is professor in the School of Criminal Justice, State University of
New York at Albany.

learn. Nor is it often studied as if it were intrinsically important. Knowledge about police organization is used like a road map—once you get where you are going, you stuff it in the glove compartment. At the same time, police fight their most bitter battles over changes in organization. And politicians think abolishing or amalgamating police forces is tantamount to changing the constitution. Efforts at the reform of policing inevitably, and too often exclusively, focus on questions of location, scope, and chain of command. Proposals to assign detectives, for example, to patrol commands or to base traffic units in police stations can be as controversial as selling condoms in a convent. So what is one to do with a subject that is variously perceived to be boring, basic, inconsequential, fateful, and diversionary?

I explore this topic, first, by describing the variations in police organization among countries, focusing on the five largest English-speaking democracies—Australia, Canada, Great Britain, India, and the United States. The comparative net could be thrown more widely to include, for example, authoritarian countries, but the differences would be less informative to an American audience. These five countries, with India as the outlier for cultural reasons, presumably have something to learn from one another. In this comparative exercise I ignore private policing and concentrate on policing conducted by governments.

Second, I explore theoretical propositions that explain national differences in police organization. Specifically, I try to account for variations in two aspects of organization that have been described: the spatial organization of command, including both the number of autonomous forces in a country and the dispersion of command responsibility within forces, and the functional organization of police forces, meaning the way in which work of different types is coordinated. Although I describe differences in rank structures, too, I do not try to explain them. Together these three chartable aspects of police organization constitute the steel frame of policing, constraining and preoccupying all who work as police officers or study police operations.

Third, I address the nagging question of whether organization makes a difference. Are the police right in thinking organizational matters are worth fighting about or are the rest of us right in thinking they are distracting and inconsequential?

In order to carry out this agenda, this essay is organized into six sections: Section I, forces; Section II, commands; Section III, functions; Section IV, personnel—which compares aspects of police organization among the sample countries—Section V, explanation—which explores factors that might account for variations in organization—and Section VI, significance—which discusses whether organization is important to the conduct of policing.

I. Forces

Among the five English-speaking democracies of Australia, Canada, Great Britain, India, and the United States, there is enormous variation in the number of autonomous general-purpose police forces (autonomous in the sense that they are created, supported, and directed by units of government that cannot be directed with respect to policing by other units of government).[1] The United States has by far the largest number of autonomous forces; Australia the least. In descending order, Australia has seven state police forces and a federal force that does general-purpose policing only in the capital territory. India has twenty-two state forces, plus national units stationed in nine Union Territories. Great Britain has forty-three forces, consisting of forty-one provincial forces and one each in the City of London and the surrounding London metropolis.[2] The City of London is the financial sector of London, in effect, its Wall Street.

Canada, with 461 police forces, represents a sizable jump in multiplicity. They consist of ten provincial and 450 municipal forces plus the Royal Canadian Mounted Police (RCMP). Counting forces in Canada is tricky. Municipalities and provinces are allowed by the British North America Act (1867) to organize their own police. All Canadian provinces have done so, but many municipalities have not. But several of the provinces and many of the municipalities that have created police forces have not wanted to go to the bother and expense of doing it on their own. Instead they have asked the RCMP to do it for them on contract. Thus, eight of the ten provinces and 191 of the 450 municipal forces are actually composed of units of the RCMP paid and directed by local authorities. Only the provinces of Ontario and Quebec have their own non-RCMP police. The RCMP conducts general-purpose

[1] I am grateful for help in this research given me by students in my graduate class in comparative policing, specifically, Lisa Bellamy, Mike Karecki, Craig Masterson, Craig Penet, and Jill Wallace.
[2] Great Britain should be understood to refer here to England and Wales. Technically the name for the country is the United Kingdom of Great Britain and Northern Ireland. It consists of England, Wales, Scotland, and Northern Ireland. Statistical information about police and crime in the United Kingdom usually covers only England and Wales.

policing in its own right only in the vast Northwest and Yukon Territories. So how many forces does Canada have? Four hundred and sixty-one by one count; 363 if all the contracted forces are lumped into the RCMP.

If counting forces in Canada is tricky, in the United States it is impossible. At least it has not been done. Forty thousand was the figure that was cited for many years (President's Commission on Law Enforcement and Administration of Justice 1967). It was credited to the redoubtable Bruce Smith (1940). In the late 1960s the U.S. Department of Justice undertook a survey to find out how many forces there were. It concluded that there were approximately 14,901 "enforcement agencies," 14,000 of them maintained by local governments (Law Enforcement Assistance Administration 1970). However, because this survey excluded governments covering less than 1,000 persons, which according to estimates ranged from as few as 10,000 to as many as 25,000, many people thought there could be at least 25,000 separate police agencies in the United States. This chaotic situation has now been stabilized by the U.S. Department of Justice, which annually provides a figure on the number of American police forces, carefully noting that it is "based on weighted sample results, not an enumeration" (Jamieson and Flanagan 1989, p. 78). The estimated figure for 1987 was 15,118, consisting of 11,989 local forces, 3,080 county sheriffs' departments, and forty-nine state forces. Assuming these estimates to be reasonably accurate, slightly over one-third of governments in the United States have raised their own police.[3]

Police forces, even when they can be counted, are lousy units of analysis because they vary so enormously in scale. The largest jurisdictions by a long shot are in Australia and Canada, then India, Britain, and last the United States. Police forces in Australia cover 337,400 square miles on the average.[4] Australia's seven state forces cover an area that is almost as large as the United States minus Alaska and Hawaii.[5]

---

[3] The International Municipal Management Association (1989) gives 39,798 as the number of governments in the United States in 1987, excluding school districts and special districts, some of which may have their own police.

[4] Throughout this essay data on police strength come from local sources unless otherwise noted, and information about area and population comes from *The World Almanac and Book of Facts, 1989* (World Alamanc 1989); and the *Statistical Abstract of the United States* (U.S. Bureau of the Census 1989).

[5] The Australian Federal Police is the eighth force, but it has general police responsibility only for the Australian Capital Territory, which is similar in status to Washington, D.C.

The police force of Western Australia alone covers an area that is about the size of the United States east of the Mississippi River (975,000 square miles).

In order to appreciate the relative size of these countries, and hence the extent of territory that is parcelled out among constituent police forces, refer to figure 1, which shows each of the countries drawn to the same scale. Information on average number of officers, population, and territorial coverage for constituent police forces in the five English-speaking countries is provided in table 1.

Although there are 450 municipal police forces in Canada, most of its territory is covered by ten provincial forces and the RCMP in the two far northern territories. Assuming that the area of the municipal forces is small relative to the whole, then the provincial forces would cover 362,500 square miles on the average.

India too has vast police jurisdictions. Its twenty-two state forces cover an area that is 40 percent of the size of the mainland United States.[6] The average state police jurisdiction is about 58,000 square miles.

Police jurisdictions in Great Britain and the United States are on an altogether different scale from Australia, Canada, and India. Police jurisdictions in England and Wales, which together are slightly smaller than Oregon, average about 1,357 square miles. This makes them smaller than India's police jurisdictions by a factor of forty-three. British police forces cover territories the size of American counties. Most police forces in the United States cover even less territory. Computing an average would be meaningless because American forces often overlap in their jurisdictions and are attached to levels of government formed on very different scales. State police jurisdictions are larger on the average than others but are confined to unincorporated areas or highways. County police usually share authority with state and municipal forces. If counties did all of the policing in the United States, police jurisdictions would average 983 square miles—appreciably smaller than Britain's. Most of the American population, however, is covered by police forces that operate within even smaller boundaries. If local police forces divided up all the territory among them, in effect abolishing state and county jurisdictions, the average would be smaller again,

---

[6] The land area of the United States minus Hawaii and Alaska is 2,962,031 square miles. Of the twenty-two Indian states, it is 1,267,105 square miles. Indian territories, which are separately policed, encompass 3.6 percent of total land area.

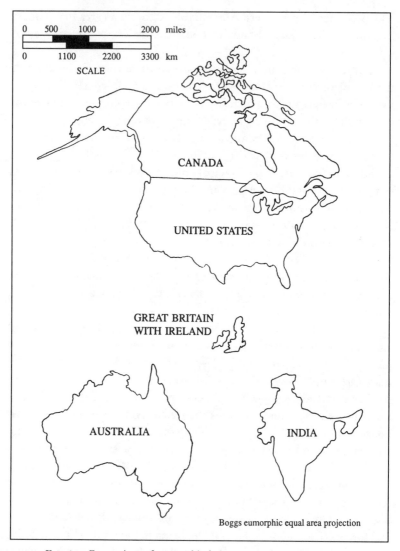

FIG. 1.—Comparison of geographical size among the study countries

about 252 square miles each. So the United States has a few police jurisdictions of substantial size, but the vast majority are minuscule compared to the other four English-speaking democracies.

Huge disparities also exist among the police forces of these countries in terms of the number of officers employed and the size of the populations covered. Proving again that the number of police officers is deter-

TABLE 1

Parameter Averages for Constituent Police Forces in
English-speaking Countries, 1988–89

Countries	Officers	Population	Territory (Square Miles)
Australia	4,978	2,296,000	337,400
Canada	114*	56,089	8,651
Great Britain	2,247†	1,162,000	1,357
India	40,506	36,362,000	58,000
United States	36.7*	16,139	N.A.

SOURCES.—U.S. Bureau of the Census (1989); World Almanac (1989).
NOTE.—Data for India are from 1982. N.A. = not applicable.
* These figures are approximate.
† This figure does not include London.

mined largely by population, the rank order of the countries by officers per force and populations per force are identical.[7] India has gigantic forces that are responsible for enormous populations. The average size of an Indian force is almost half again as large as New York City's, approximately 40,506.[8] The largest force, with 136,403 officers, is in the state of Uttar Pradesh. The smallest is in Sikkim, with 1,700. Indian forces are responsible for populations averaging 36,362,000—almost five times larger than the population of New York City.

The next largest forces are in Australia, although far behind India's. Australian police forces average 4,978 police officers and cover populations of 2,296,000 (Bayley 1990).

In Great Britain, London has an enormous force—approximately 28,000 officers—while the forty provincial police forces are much smaller, averaging 2,247 officers. The London police are responsible for 7,202,000 people (Reiner 1988); the remaining forty-two forces for about 1,189,000 each.

Canada, like the United States, is difficult to generalize about because its police forces vary so widely in scale. Lumping all the provincial and municipal forces together, whether contracted to the RCMP or not, the average force has 114 officers and covers 56,089 people. The

[7] For a discussion of the relation between the numbers of police personnel and population, see Bayley (1985), chap. 4.
[8] Due to the slowness of reporting official figures in India, these data are not up-to-date (Ministry of Home Affairs 1982). Since the size of forces has grown since then, the general point about the relative size of Indian forces is not affected.

average is distorted, however, by a few large forces, such as the Provinces of Ontario and Quebec, which have 5,500 and 5,000 officers, respectively. Seventy-two percent of Canadian forces have fewer than twenty officers (Murphy 1990). Among the 259 noncontract municipalities, only twenty-four have more than 250 officers. Relative, then, to India, Australia, and Great Britain, Canada has small forces for the most part.

The United States has the smallest forces of these five countries, covering small populations. If its police officers were distributed evenly among the 15,118 state, county, and local forces, there would be 36.7 in each and they would cover populations of 16,139 each.[9] This calculation is misleading, however, because one-fifth of all police officers are employed in twenty-five large departments (U.S. Bureau of Justice Statistics 1987).[10] Subtracting the largest forces and their personnel from all police agencies, the average per force is about thirty sworn officers covering 15,093 people. So the United States has mostly small departments responsible for few people, but it has more large departments, averaging 3,800 officers, than Australia or Canada.

In all of these countries the national government plays a very limited role in general-purpose policing. The dominance of local policing might have been expected in Australia, Canada, India, and the United States, which have federal systems, but it is true of Britain as well. It should also be noted that while the constituent federal units all maintain police forces—states in Australia, India, United States, and provinces in Canada—they do not necessarily monopolize policing. Monopolization at the state level occurs only in Australia and India. In Canada and the United States, the constituent federal units allow subordinate governments to create police forces if they choose.

General-purpose policing by the central government is done straightforwardly in three of these five countries. The Australian Federal Police (AFP) does it in the Australian Capital Territory (ACT), which is in effect Australia's District of Columbia. The RCMP does it in the Yukon and the Northwest Territories. And India does it in nine Union Territories.[11]

---

[9] There were 555,364 police officers in the United States, excluding federal personnel, in 1987 (Jamieson and Flanagan 1989).

[10] These twenty-five cities employ 95,911 police officers.

[11] Washington, D.C., is policed by a local force as is Ottawa, Canada's capital. In fact, in Ottawa there are a municipal force and three independent suburban ones. The RCMP is responsible only for the grounds of Parliament House.

At the same time, all five central governments have personnel with powers of investigation and arrest who can be used in connection with national responsibilities. In Australia and the United States, where each state has its own criminal code, the Australian Federal Police and the Federal Bureau of Investigation (FBI) have preeminent authority to enforce federal statutes. The same is true for the RCMP in Canada and the Central Bureau of Investigation in India, even though both countries have unified criminal codes. Britain's position is equivocal. The London Metropolitan Police—Scotland Yard—is responsible to Parliament, not to local government, and can be directed by the Home Secretary to undertake national investigations and law enforcement. It can, therefore, be regarded as both a local and a central government force. MI5, Britain's domestic security service, has authority to investigate subversion throughout the island as well as to make arrests, although arresting is usually left to local forces as a matter of courtesy.

The numerical strength of central government personnel with police powers is difficult to compare for two reasons: the category "police" is ambiguous, and information about all personnel who might qualify is not readily available. Indeed, these problems complicate descriptions of national police systems more generally. But a reasonably good description can be made if one distinguishes three kinds of police. First, there are police with full powers of access, arrest, and investigation for any criminal offense throughout the territory of the authorizing government unit. These are what I have called general-purpose police forces. "Cops," in other words, usually uniformed. Second, there are special-purpose police who may have powers of enforcement throughout the country but exercise them only in connection with a narrow range of offenses, such as tax evasion, securities fraud, illegal immigration, black-marketing, and environmental pollution. These "police" officers specialize in investigation and work mostly out of uniform. Third, there are general-purpose police whose jurisdiction is limited to particular territories within the wider boundaries of the authorizing government unit. For example, on military bases, railroad yards and rights-of-way, public-housing estates, airports and bus depots, atomic energy facilities, and docks and shipyards. Such special-area police may be created by any unit of government but seem most common under national authority. I call these ancillary police forces, and "police" need not be put in parentheses.

General-purpose police are the heart of policing in any country, making up the bulk of police personnel. Special-purpose police are usually authorized by national governments. Examples include Australia's National Crime Authority, created in 1984 to combat organized crime; America's Secret Service for the protection of the president and other VIPs; India's Border Security Force; and Britain's MI5. Ancillary police forces—the third category—include the New York City Transit Police, which is the seventh largest police force in the United States,[12] the U.S. Army's Military Police, the British Transit Police, the Indian Railway Protection Force, the British Atomic Energy Constabulary, and the Canadian National Railway Police. My impression is that these forces are increasingly being amalgamated into surrounding general-purpose police forces. This happened recently to the railway police in the Australian states of Victoria and South Australia. There is considerable discussion at the moment about consolidating the New York City Transit Police with the New York Police Department.

Therefore, in order to determine the role of the central government in policing these five countries, it would be necessary to enumerate all three categories of forces and then count the personnel in them. This would be a difficult job. Even for the United States, I have been unable to find a comprehensive list of national government agencies with general-purpose, special-purpose, and ancillary police units, let alone data about personnel or budgets. What I can say is that while only the national governments of Australia and Canada have created general-purpose police forces—namely, the AFP and the RCMP—all five national governments have established special-purpose as well as ancillary police agencies. At the same time, I suspect that the presence of the national government in policing is most apparent to the general public in Canada and the United States due to the prominence respectively of the RCMP and the FBI. I doubt if the public is very aware of national government police agencies in Australia, Britain, or India.

One final comment needs to be made about the structure of police—from now on referring only to general-purpose police—in these English-speaking countries. National structures vary not only with respect to the number and size of autonomous forces but also in the existence of "system." In all these countries except the United States, citizens are subject to the authority of only one general-purpose police force at a time. The jurisdictions are coordinated. In Australia and India, separate state forces have exclusivity; in Canada, either munic-

---

[12] It had 3,900 personnel in 1987, slightly more than Washington, D.C., and slightly less than Houston, Texas (U.S. Bureau of Justice Statistics 1987, p. 8).

ipal or provincial/territorial forces; and in Great Britain, provincial forces or the London Metropolitan Police. Only the United States allows overlapping police jurisdictions, where citizens may be subject simultaneously to enforcement by city, county, and state police. As Bruce Smith said over fifty years ago, "there is . . . no such thing in the United States as a police system, not even a set of police systems within any reasonably accurate sense of the term" (1940, p. 22). America is not, however, unique in this respect in the world more largely. Lack of jurisdictional coordination also occurs in Italy, the former Soviet Union, Spain, Belgium, and Switzerland.

The police systems of the five largest English-speaking democracies are characterized by multiple independent police forces. All of them except the United States coordinate coverage of their multiple forces. If one level of government chooses to create a general-purpose police force, the others do not. America's system, unique in this sample, is what I call "multiple uncoordinated" (Bayley 1985, chap. 3). America's curious nonsystem cannot be attributed to federalism since Australia, Canada, and India are federal, too. Neither can it be attributed to the absence of a national criminal code since Australia does not have one either. Canada, Britain, and India, however, do. The United States is stranger than it knows.

II. Commands

In order to describe the organization of police in a country, it is not enough to determine how many autonomous forces there are. That tells where legal/political responsibility for creating and maintaining police forces lies. It does not show where command is actually exercised. This is especially obvious for very large police forces. Can one believe, for example, that command of Australian police operations is actually lodged at seven state police headquarters in a combined area that is as large as the mainland United States? But the same question should be asked about command in Saskatchewan, Uttar Pradesh, London, and New York City.

Despite the enormous variation in the scale of police forces among these countries, the formal structure of command is surprisingly invariant. There are usually only four levels of command, encompassing force headquarters at the top and ending at police stations, no matter whether the force is municipal, state, or provincial. For example, provincial forces in Britain have four levels of command—headquarters, divisions, subdivisions, and stations. So too does London—headquarters, areas, districts, and stations. Australian cities, like Adelaide and Sydney, have the same command levels as the far-flung hinterlands. The New York State Police and Canada's provincial police have one less—headquarters, troops/districts, and stations/detachments. New York City has three command levels, although a fourth has been inserted in the borough of Manhattan.[13] As city size declines in North America, the number of command levels declines. Medium-size cities such as Edmonton, Alberta, and Denver, Colorado, have only two—headquarters and stations. In America's mostly small police forces, all operations are directed from a single police facility. There is a hierarchy of ranks but no spatial decentralization of command. The most elaborate command hierarchy occurs in India, where there are commonly six levels—headquarters, range, district, subdivision, circle, and station.

Since command structures are fairly invariant despite differences in the scale of forces, it follows that police stations vary enormously in area and population. Like police forces, they should not be treated as a homogeneous class of units. The general pattern is that rural police station areas are extensive with small populations while those of urban stations are small with large populations. Among the five countries, police stations range in size from 24,751 square miles covering 7,448 people in the Northern Territory, Australia, to 3.2 square miles covering 76,453 people in New York City. Between these two extremes, Indian stations average 114 square miles covering 10,766 people in Uttar Pradesh, the most populous state, and Canadian provincial stations average 3,710 square miles covering 13,342 people.[14]

The point is that, although police stations are the basic unit of operation, they are very dissimilar. They are not even commanded by the same rank of officer. In the United States most stations are commanded by chiefs. In Australia they are commanded by sergeants. And it is not true that only very small stations are turned over to comparatively junior ranks. Indian stations are commanded by subinspectors but are units of enormous scale by American or British standards. Royal Canadian Mounted Police stations, too, are commanded by sergeants but are the equivalent of entire American police forces. Subordinate officers,

---

[13] Headquarters, borough, and precinct. In the borough of Manhattan, Manhattan North and South.
[14] The calculation for Canada is for the eight provinces policed by the RCMP on contract. Ontario and Quebec are excluded. Canada's station areas are actually slightly smaller in extent because one should exclude the 450 municipal jurisdictions.

often relatively young in terms of service, are given command responsibilities in Australia, Canada, and India that would be unthinkable in
the United States and Britain. It also follows that either the United
States is paying chief's wages for sergeant's work or sergeants are
dreadfully underpaid elsewhere.

While command in most forces appears decentralized in terms of
territorial organization, it is not clear that this is true in fact. Although
the issue can only be judged by close observation of operations in
several forces at police station level, the need for devolution of command responsibilities is perceived in all these countries. Senior commanders complain that subordinate supervisors do not want to manage,
while station-house commanders complain that they are not given an
opportunity. Both are probably right. Certainly most station commanders seem to be preoccupied with filling out duty rosters, accounting
for the use of equipment, and managing overtime. Few of them seem to
build budgets, allocate resources according to local needs, or develop
strategic plans. They are supervisors, not managers. This appears to be
true, once again, regardless of the scale of police forces.

This leads to an important observation. Talk about centralization
and decentralization is generally meaningless. Recommendations about
them are made ritualistically, without recognizing that costs and
benefits will not be the same among forces if the scales of operation are
very different. Although spatial decentralization of command is generally seen as a good idea, especially in order to enhance responsiveness
and strategic discrimination, equal amounts of it across similar command hierarchies in forces of substantially different scale is unlikely to
produce the same effects. Can generic decentralization be the solution
to fundamental command problems in New York City, for example, as
well as Western Australia, Suffolk as well as Uttar Pradesh, and the
New York State Police as well as Edmonton? Conversely, should centralization be expected to produce greater disciplinary control in forces
as different as Toronto and the Northern Territory? The jurisdictions
of some forces are smaller than those of stations in others. People
conjure with the concept of centralization/decentralization in a vacuum,
failing to study its effects in practice in organizations of different sizes.
This is another consequence of uncritically using police forces as units
of analysis.

The concept of centralization/decentralization is even more misleading in descriptions of the organization of national police systems. The
United States is usually described as having a decentralized police

system. So too is Australia. Yet the one has over 15,000 police forces, the other only eight. Moreover, some countries, such as France, have centralized systems which are smaller than forces in decentralized countries, such as Australia. The problem is that centralization/decentralization is applied both to *countries* referring to the number of forces and to *forces* referring to the number of territorial commands. The solution is to recognize that the concept of centralization/decentralization can be predicated on both countries and forces. Command may be organized nationally in terms of the number of autonomous forces as well as in terms of areas within forces. To capture fully the variety that occurs with respect to the organization of policing within countries, one needs to distinguish the number of autonomous forces and also the distribution of command responsibilities within forces, the latter described behaviorally rather than formally insofar as possible.

To put this point another way, if centralization/decentralization is applied to countries, then multiplicity creates decentralization; if it is applied to forces, then multiplicity does not. This has an important implication for policy. Americans are wrong in thinking that the only way to create the benefits of decentralization is to establish multiple forces. And the British are wrong in thinking that the creation of a national police force inevitably eliminates the possibility of developing community-responsive local commands.

If both dimensions of police centralization/decentralization were taken into account in descriptions of national police systems, a neat fourfold matrix would be generated (Bayley 1985, chap. 3). See table 2. All cells of the box are alive because any force can be either centralized or decentralized, just as any country can have one or several general-purpose police forces.[15]

By adding the feature of coordination with respect to the territorial coverage among multiple forces, a typology of police structure can be constructed that is both discriminating and reliable. The major judgmental element involves characterizing degrees of centralization within forces. Using this scheme, one is now in a position to make useful

---

[15] An important complication to note is that command is not the only function that may be subject to centralization/decentralization. A single police force may have decentralized command but centralized procurement. Similarly, several forces may share training facilities, in effect centralizing them, but recruit separately. To make accurate generalizations about centralization/decentralization either within forces or within countries, it is necessary to generalize across functional areas of police activity.

TABLE 2
The Structure of National Police Systems

	Dispersal of Command	
Number of Forces	Centralized	Decentralized
Single	Sri Lanka	Japan
	Singapore	
	Poland	
	Ireland	
	Israel	
Multiple:		
Coordinated	France	Canada
	Finland	Australia
	Great Britain	India
		West Germany
Uncoordinated	Italy	United States
	USSR	Mexico
	Belgium	
	Switzerland	

SOURCE.—Adapted from Bayley (1985).

comparative statements. The United States has more forces than other countries of the sample but not the most decentralized. Australia has the fewest forces of the sample, but each force is quite decentralized, at least formally. Among the five countries, the United States is unique in an unexpected way. It has achieved decentralization through the creation of a larger number of autonomous forces, while most of its forces are relatively centralized. It is also the only country among the large English-speaking democracies where territorial coverage is not coordinated.

III. Functions
Police forces are organized in terms of function—the nature of work performed—as well as the command of territory. And frequently they do not coincide. Indeed, the only functional speciality within policing that conforms to the organization of spatial commands is patrol, known outside the United States variously as "operations," "general duties," or "uniforms." "General duties" is probably the most descriptive designation since it indicates that these personnel are prepared to do anything—patrol, emergency response, criminal investigation, order maintenance, traffic enforcement, or crime prevention. Two other

functional commands are standard, except in very small departments, namely, criminal investigation and traffic control. Unlike "general duties," these commands do not appear in every geographical unit of organization. Their representation tails off in the smaller command jurisdictions, such as police stations. In jurisdictions of very large scale, they cluster at intermediate command levels—below headquarters but above police stations—where they are available for local assignment but are not wasted by permanent posting to very small areas.

The lack of coincidence between spatial and functional commands creates enduring problems for all police forces. Criminal investigators (detectives) and traffic specialists are very jealous of their specialized status; they want to be distinguished from generalist officers. Consequently, there is often a tug-of-war between commanders who are responsible for territory, usually "general-duties" personnel, and functional commanders who are responsible for tasks. Who controls police officers on the ground—the spatial chain of command or the functional chain of command? Arguments about authority between spatial and functional commanders often hamper operations, generating disputes that must be referred to headquarters for resolution. Although in most forces territorial commanders are designated as paramount, most of them know from bitter experience that if they intrude too often into specialist matters complaints will be lodged at headquarters and they will be discreetly told to lay off.

Specialization also produces problems of coordination for rank-and-file personnel in the field. General-duties officers often resent having to hand over interesting criminal cases to plainclothes detectives from remote headquarters. They are made to feel like ignorant menials. So their response to crimes sometimes becomes perfunctory, even though research shows that they may be in the best position to collect information that will be critical for solution (Greenwood and Petersilia 1975; Eck 1983). Sometimes formal policies are laid down to guide the relationship among front-line investigators and generalists—concerning the type of cases each group should handle, the time generalists are allowed to spend on any investigation, or the assistance generalists may ask from investigators. With respect to traffic enforcement, generalists usually share the responsibility with specialists, but they are not nearly as keen. Most generalists either do the minimum enforcement required by their supervisors or pay attention only to egregious violations of traffic rules, such as drunk or reckless driving. Traffic officers suffer from the perception that they are doing "Mickey Mouse" work, not integrally related to the crime-fighting mission of the police.

Data on the proportion of personnel doing different sorts of work is difficult to obtain. Not only is it rarely collected at national levels, but even individual police forces cannot quickly produce it. Rarely, for example, do breakdowns on the strength of different functional commands appear in annual reports. As a result, one cannot readily chart longitudinal trends with respect to the growth or decline of different functions. A critical aspect of the evolution of policing is invisible. At the same time, officers in every large force are absolutely sure which units have "won" or "lost" in the bureaucratic wars for personnel. Invidious rumors feed on ignorance.

Here are some gleanings about the relative strength of different functional specialties from the five countries. General duties is the largest specialty in policing, accounting for about 60 percent of personnel worldwide. Sixty percent of personnel are general-duties officers in Australia, 56 percent in the United States, and 43 percent in Great Britain (Jones 1980; Police Executive Research Forum 1981, pp. 581 ff.; Bayley 1990). For criminal investigation, the numbers are 15 percent in Australia, 9.8 percent in the United States, and 13.9 percent in Great Britain.[16] For traffic, the figures are 10 percent in Australia, 9 percent in the United States, and 10 percent in Great Britain.

Because criminal investigation represents the essence of modern policing, it has enormous prestige within every force. Ambitious officers aspire to be selected for it. In many American departments, detective is a rank to which officers are promoted. India also limits criminal investigation by rank but in another way: officers below noncommissioned rank (constables and head constables) may not investigate crimes or even make arrests unless a serious crime occurs in their presence. Such crimes are nicely called "seizable offences."[17] In the other countries, it is a prized assignment, but all ranks are represented in it. Except in very small police departments, criminal investigation branches are organized into squads dealing with particular kinds of offenses—

---

[16] The American data are based on returns from 122 police agencies serving populations of 50,000 or more. A figure for the proportion of specialist officers averaged over all American forces would be misleading because of the presence of many very small agencies, which would have few specialists, and a few very large ones, which would have many.

[17] In law they are known as "cognizable offences."

homicide, burglary, arson, "major crimes," commercial fraud, sex offenses, auto theft, dacoity (rural banditry—India), and "gold stealing" (Western Australia).

Detectives are also generally responsible for investigating and monitoring people who may foment public disorder, organize subversive political movements, or attack government personnel or facilities. Australian, Canadian, British, and Indian forces are more forthright about this than American forces. They designate such units as the Special Branch, a contraction of "Special Irish Branch" created by the London Metropolitan police in 1884. Even where the name is not used, officers will matter-of-factly say "this is our special branch." American forces, especially large ones, certainly do special branch work, but they do not readily admit it and disguise the existence of such units (Bouza 1976; International Association of Chiefs of Police 1976; American Friends Service Committee 1979; Marx 1988).

Security surveillance is the area of policing where central governments play an important role—the RCMP in Canada, MI5 and the Special Branch of Scotland Yard in Great Britain, the Central Bureau of Investigation in India, and the Federal Bureau of Investigation in the United States. Covert penetration and surveillance of dissident political groups became so notorious in Canada and the United States during the 1960s and 1970s that those governments investigated and implicitly censured the RCMP and the FBI, respectively. The FBI was forced substantially to deemphasize surveillance aspects of counterespionage, while the RCMP's security/intelligence branch was abolished and its functions transferred to a newly created, independent Canadian Security Intelligence Service (Halperin et al. 1976; Wilson 1980; Mac-Donald Commission 1981).

Traffic regulation and enforcement is not a highly regarded specialty. Many senior officers consider it a burdensome nuisance that embitters their relations with the public without contributing to the prevention of crime. Talk about turning it over to nonpolice agencies, as has been done with the regulation of motor-vehicle parking, is common but has been done, to my knowledge, in only two English-speaking jurisdictions—New Zealand and Western Australia. The practice continues in New Zealand but was discontinued in Western Australia after an experiment lasting from 1975 to 1982.

Most police forces also maintain heavily armed units trained in handling violent confrontations with individuals or groups—such as hostage takings, sieges, terrorist attacks, and mob violence. In Australia,

Canada, Great Britain, and the United States, these units are small. Perhaps due to the worldwide influence of American television, they are generically referred to as SWAT units even when the local name may be different.[18] India, however, is another matter. Almost a quarter of police personnel were maintained in armed formations in 1981 (Ministry of Home Affairs 1982, p. 140). According to informants, the proportion is even higher in 1990. The armed police are separately recruited, trained, and commanded from the unarmed, more numerous civil police. Although armed units spend most of their time guarding government installations, their primary purpose is to serve as ready reserves in case of large-scale rioting between caste or religious groups, violence connected with strikes and boycotts, or the tumult of mammoth political demonstrations (Bayley 1969, 1983a).

Until recently, police in all these countries except the United States handled the prosecution of cases that could be tried before courts of first instance—magistrates rather than trial courts. India gave up the practice in 1974, creating separate directorates of prosecution in the states. Great Britain, where the practice originated, gave up police prosecutions in 1985, transferring the function to the Crown Prosecution Service. Only Australia and Canada continue to use police as prosecutors, but many senior officials would like to give them up.

Although aggregate data are lacking, new functional specialties are beginning to emerge in all these countries. They are crime prevention, often attached to enlarged community/public affairs units; centralized criminal intelligence collection and analysis, sometimes with field personnel (collators) in every police station; and research and development. These appear to be the "growth" areas of contemporary policing.

IV. Personnel

Although all these countries except India recruit to the police at the bottom rank only—constable or police/patrol officer—their rank structures vary considerably. Ranks are most compressed in the United States, where six are standard; they are most elongated in Australia, where there are thirteen in three states. See table 3. In between are the RCMP, India, and provincial Great Britain. There is a marked similarity in rank titles among commonwealth countries, reflecting the histor-

[18] There is no agreement about what "SWAT" stands for. Some say it is "Special Weapons and Tactics," others "Special Weapons Attack Team," and a few "Several Weirdos Armed to the Teeth."

TABLE 3
Ranks and Commands

Australia	Canada		Great Britain	
	RCMP	Edmonton	Provinces	London
Commissioner	Commissioner	Chief	Chief Constable	Commissioner
Deputy Commissioner	Deputy Commissioner	Deputy Chief	Deputy Chief Constable	Deputy Commissioner
Assistant Commissioner	Assistant Commissioner	Superintendent (station)	Assistant Chief Constable	Assistant Commissioner
Commander or Chief Super-intendent*	Chief Superintendent	Inspector	Chief Superintendent	Deputy Assistant Commissioner
Chief Superintendent	Superintendent	Staff Sergeant	Superintendent	Commander
Superintendent	Inspector	Sergeant	Inspector (station)	Chief Superintendent
Chief Inspector	Staff Sergeant (detach-ment)	Constable	Sergeant	Superintendent
Inspector	Sergeant		Constable	Inspector (station)
Sergeant 1st Class	Corporal			Sergeant
Sergeant 2nd Class	Constable			Constable
Sergeant 3rd Class (station)				
Senior Constable				
Constable				

528

India	United States	
	General	New York City
Inspector-General	Chief	Commissioner
Deputy Inspector-General	Assistant/Deputy Chief	Deputy Commissioner
Superintendent	Captain	Chief of Department
Deputy/Assistant Superintendent	Lieutenant	Chief
Inspector	Sergeant (detective)	Assistant Chief
Subinspector (station)	Police Officer	Deputy Chief
Head Constable		Inspector
Constable		Deputy Inspector
		Captain (station)
		Lieutenant
		Sergeant
		Police Officer

SOURCE.— Adapted from Bayley (1985).

* In three states.

ical influence of Britain. The rank structures in the giant cities of London and New York are also very long, very similar to Australia. Curiously, although India uniquely allows stratified recruitment—to constable, assistant subinspector, and deputy/assistant superintendent—it has a more egalitarian rank structure than the Aussies. Lateral or outside recruitment to very senior positions in most forces is possible but rare.

Unfortunately again, information about the proportion of personnel in different ranks is not readily available. It appears that operational nonsupervisory personnel—constables and police/patrol officers—constitute from 75 to 90 percent of force strength (Government of India 1985; Swanton and Hannigan 1985, p. 516; Carter et al. 1989, p. xi; *Economist* 1990, pp. 55–56). See table 4. India has significantly more personnel at the lowest rank than the other countries. First-line supervisors are proportionately most numerous in Australia, fewest in India and the United States. The prospects for promotion to this rank—usually sergeant—are therefore best in Australia, worst in India and the United States, and middling in Great Britain. Recognizing that judging the equivalence of ranks is inexact, it appears that a larger proportion of personnel are in senior ranks—above the rank of first-line supervisor—in the United States than in Australia, Britain, or India. The Indian rank structure especially is a more squat wide-based pyramid than the others.

In all countries the command of police stations, the lowest level of operation control, is in the hands of second-line supervisors—lieutenants and captains in the United States, inspectors in Australia and Britain, staff sergeants in the RCMP, and subinspectors in India.

There is a general appreciation among police in all countries that communication is being frustrated by elaborate rank differentiations. The problem is particularly intense in India where there are three rank strata—rank-and-file, noncommissioned officers, commissioned officers—with little promotion between them. In all countries, ranks do not seem to coincide with well-defined command tasks. They establish hierarchy but not functional responsibilities. There is a good deal of discussion in professional circles about compressing ranks in order to encourage participant management and the devolution of operational decision making from central headquarters.

V. Explanation

The problematic elements of police organization that I will try to explain are the following: multiplicity of autonomous forces within coun-

TABLE 4

Proportion of Police at Different Ranks

	Australia	Great Britain	India (Civil Police)	United States
Senior	4.5	5.8	.8	13.3
Middle management	20.0	15.9	8.5	11.7
Rank and file	75.0	78.0	90.7	75.0

NOTE.—Percentages do not add to 100 due to rounding.

tries, command decentralization within forces, and development of functional specializations. As a general proposition, I submit that variation across countries is greatest with respect to the multiplicity of autonomous forces and least with respect to matters of internal organization. This is because the autonomy of police agencies is closely connected to politics, while internal organization responds to the promptings of the police profession, which has always been highly international. The implication of this proposition is that, as nations develop, convergence in the organization of police will occur more within forces than in the relations among forces (Bayley 1977).

National structures of policing reflect decisions about the geographical distribution of political power. They emerge early in national histories, and they change very little subsequently. The rank order of Australia, Canada, Great Britain, India, and the United States in terms of the number of autonomous forces would be the same in 1860 and 1990, that is, from about the time organized police forces emerged in respective national histories to the present. The gaining of independence in Australia, Canada, and India made no difference. In ascending order of multiplicity, there would be, then and now, Australia, India, Great Britain, Canada, and the United States.

In Australia, for example, which began European settlement in 1788, a state force was established in South Australia in 1838, Victoria in 1853, Western Australia in 1861, Queensland in 1864, and New South Wales in 1862. All of this occurred well before independence in 1901. Although Tasmania became a state in 1857, it did not consolidate its police forces until 1899. A force was established in the Northern Territory by the national government in 1911. From the very beginning, then, police power was monopolized by the governments of colonies, subsequently states. There was hardly any tradition of policing by local government. This situation continues today, with little public pressure for the disaggregation of the enormous state police jurisdictions.

Canadian policing began in Ontario and Quebec, the early settled eastern provinces, and was based on municipalities, very much like the United States. As Canada expanded westward, however, a unique police system developed. In order to ensure "peace, order, and good government," as the British North America Act of 1867 said, the provinces were given responsibility for the administration of justice. In 1873 the national government created the Northwest Mounted Police with responsibility for policing west of Ontario. As provinces were created out of the western wilderness, they developed their own police, replacing the "mounties." In 1928, however, provinces, and later municipalities, began to ask the Royal Canadian Mounted Police, as it was renamed in 1920, to undertake policing on their behalf "on contract." Consequently, most municipal police departments today, although operating under provincial authorization and supervision, are to be found in Ontario and Quebec, while the Royal Canadian Mounted Police serves as a general-purpose police force mostly in the prairies, the far west, and the maritimes. It operates exclusively under national direction only in the Yukon and the Northwest Territories.

Consolidation of small municipal forces into larger ones stopped with the creation of several regional police forces in the early 1970s. In the future, the number of forces will undoubtedly rise marginally as some municipalities with rising populations decide to command their own forces. A more important change would occur if the western provinces decide, as some have threatened, to raise their own forces rather than contract with the RCMP. This would not, however, change the number of autonomous forces since these provinces direct the police now, even if the personnel wear RCMP uniforms.

British policing has been based on local authorities at least since the Statute of Winchester, 1285. Because Justices of the Peace could appoint and direct constables, as set forth in the Justice of the Peace Act of 1361, their law-enforcement power gradually supplanted that of the king's sheriffs (Pringle n.d.; Parker 1937; Reith 1948; Royal Commission on the Police 1962; Critchley 1967). After the establishment of the London Metropolitan Police in 1829, local governments successively copied Peel's model, but the national government did not require organized police forces throughout the country until the County and Borough Police Act, 1856. Jurisdictions were not rationalized, leading to the elimination of many small ones, until the Local Government Act, 1888 (Critchley 1967, chap. 4). After 1856, the number of autonomous forces declined steadily—from 239 to forty-three (Martin and Wilson

1969). By 1960, on the eve of the creation of the Royal Commission on the Police, the number had fallen to 123. A further substantial decrease occurred in the early 1970s with the consolidation of local governments generally, producing the present number of forty-three.

Although Britain seems firmly attached to the principle of local accountability of police, the structure of policing has always been determined by central initiative through Parliamentary statutes. Britain does not have a federal system, with powers reserved to constituent units. The central government developed the London Metropolitan Police in 1829, required its emulation by local communities after 1856, and determined the number and scale of local police jurisdictions thereafter. Although public opinion remains dead set against the creation of a national police force, Britain may be moving in that direction in fact. Since 1886 the central government has paid an increasing share of the cost of local policing—currently 51 percent. The Home Office plays a substantial role in the selection and training of chief constables, and its policy directives are increasingly accepted by chief constables as authoritative (Reiner 1988). Moreover, during public order crises, often growing out of labor disputes, mechanisms have developed for coordinating police action throughout the country. The appearance of decentralized local control continues to be important in British politics, but in reality the central government has created the structure of policing and powerfully influenced its operating policies.

Indian policing was a provincial responsibility under the British and continued as a state responsibility after independence. The number of state forces has increased slightly since then as linguistic and ethnic communities have successfully gained statehood. This will undoubtedly continue, especially in the few remaining "territories" that are governed directly by New Delhi. Barring major splits in existing states, the number of police forces is unlikely to go beyond thirty, which is just over double the number in 1947.

American traditions of policing have always been local, and there is no sign of change. The only flutter of structural departure from tradition occurred around the time of the Civil War when several states experimented briefly with taking over policing in major cities—for example, in Baltimore, Detroit, New Orleans, Cleveland, San Francisco, New York, and Boston (Richardson 1974). During the early twentieth century state forces arose, but instead of supplanting existing forces, they filled in the unpoliced space between them. Faced with the country's uncountable proliferation of forces, the President's Commission on Law Enforcement and Administration of Justice (1967) urged consolidation. Although there was some interest initially, the movement, which was never strong, now seems stalled (Mastrofski 1985). For example, only four of 3,096 county sheriffs' departments have amalgamated with large surrounding cities in the last few years.[19] In fact, the effectiveness of local forces may be improving as they learn to share resources cooperatively with one another (Henderson 1985). This occurs most commonly with respect to communications facilities, hardly ever for patrolling. At the same time, the balance of police authority, as opposed to its territorial structure, is being affected slowly by the nationalization of certain crimes, empowering federal agencies, usually the FBI, to expand the ambit of operations. Such a trend may be occurring in other countries as well. It is an important development to keep track of.

On a larger world scale of comparison these five English-speaking countries are more similar than different. None has a centralized police system, although the number of constituent forces varies considerably—from eight to over 15,000. This conforms to my general finding that, in the modern world, democratic political regimes are highly associated with decentralized police systems and authoritarian regimes with centralized ones (Bayley 1985, chap. 3). Moreover, they conform to the general proposition that structural centralization occurs when the formation of new political communities—in this case nation states—is met with violent resistance (Bayley 1985, pp. 69–70). Australia, Canada, India, and the United States are all federal systems formed largely through consent. Great Britain's unity, too, was not imposed by the sword, although there may be some Scots who would argue with that.

Australia, Canada, Great Britain, India, and the United States have decentralized police systems because they were formed largely without violence from preexisting political entities. And they will remain decentralized if threats to national authority are nonviolent or short-lived. India faces just such a crisis today in Punjab state and is governing there under emergency powers that, in effect, federalize law enforcement. The federal government of the United States, too, used its army to police the South immediately following the Civil War. In contrast, the Canadian government conceded cultural and linguistic rights to

---

[19] They were Miami, Jacksonville, Las Vegas, and Carson City. Private communication from the National Sheriffs' Association, February 1990.

Quebec in the early 1970s in order to preserve its federal integrity without resort to force.

In sum, the decentralized police structures of these five countries can be explained by the relative absence of violence accompanying state building. The differences among them with respect to the number of autonomous police forces is explained by differences in patterns of political settlement. Prolonged resistance to central authority by constituent units can produce either a weakening of federalism (centralization) or a strengthening of federalism (decentralization). In times of turmoil, given the political traditions of these countries, one would predict the latter. If, however, resistance to central authority was undertaken by the populace generally and the constituent units could not contain it, then centralization of policing might occur. This happened in small ways during both World Wars in all these countries, illustrating the principle that "police systems are more likely to be centralized if mobilization demands by the state are high and popular resistance of a violent sort is encountered" (Bayley 1985, pp. 70–71). It may be happening today in India and, more arguably, in Britain.

There has been a sharp debate among historians about the importance of collective violence in developing modern police forces in the nineteenth century. I would like to separate my argument from it. Many historians have argued that serious and persistent rioting, especially in large cities, and the fear of its continuation, precipitated the political decision to create forces organized and paid by government (Reith 1948; Lane 1967, 1980; Silver 1967; Bopp and Schultz 1972; Tobias 1972; Brown and Brown 1973; Richardson 1974; Storch 1975; Grabosky 1977; Gurr, Grabosky, and Hula 1977; Miller 1977; Walker 1980; Harring 1983). Others have argued that the influence of rioting has been exaggerated, that the bankruptcy of previous ordering mechanisms was widely recognized at the time, and that police were reformed because of less dramatic macrosocial changes (Radzinowicz 1957; Critchley 1967; Levett 1975; Field 1981; Monkkonen 1981; Emsley 1983; Reiner 1985). The point that should be noted is that however important rioting was in creating organized policing by government in the nineteenth century, it did not produce centralized police forces in any of these countries, apart from India under a colonial administration. Localism triumphed, based on whatever dispersed political centers were valued in each country.

It is a mistake to talk about police reform in the nineteenth century as being a case of "centralization." Compared to France, Italy, and Spain, the Anglo-Saxon countries reformed their forces within distinct preexisting subnational structures. The significant change in the policing of Australia, Canada, Britain, and the United States was not primarily in the scale of police organization but in the creation of substantial regulated bodies of police preventively deployed in public places. Collective tumult may have contributed to these changes, but it did not affect national structures. The reason rioting did not was that it was not perceived as a threat to the political distribution of authority existing at the time. It may have threatened the class basis of political power but not its geographical organization. The Civil War in the United States did threaten its geographical organization, as did separatism in Quebec, and as does terrorism in Punjab today. Chartism in Great Britain, however, and the turmoil surrounding passage of the Reform Bill in 1832 did not threaten the structure of state power, nor did labor unrest later in the century in the United States.

Turning to the dispersal of command responsibilities within police forces, any connection between it and external circumstances is hard to discern. One problem is vagueness in operationalizing "centralization." Centralization of command within forces is generally associated, especially in the United States, with the professional model of policing developed during the early decades of the twentieth century (Walker 1976; Monkkonen 1981; Kelling and Moore 1987). But in what sense was command centralized—discipline, hiring, promotion, patrol, criminal investigation, community contact, or finance and audit? "Centralization/decentralization" are too vague to wrap around changes encompassing the development of features as diverse as specialized criminal investigation capability, redefinition of the police role, reform of personnel management, attenuation of political control, and the introduction of technological aids. Much was going on; only some of it might be called centralization/decentralization. The concept needs to be grounded so that one can pinpoint its permutations historically, thus beginning to establish a sense of what might have been impelling it.

Furthermore, the so-called professional model gained ground not only in the United States during the early twentieth century but in the other countries as well. Even India was seized by the necessity of reforming the police: the only major systematic examination of policing in India between the Police Act of 1861 and independence came under the auspices of the national Police Commission in 1902–3. This coincidence of organizational reforms among all these countries suggests either that sociopolitical circumstances were remarkably similar or professionalism had a life of its own in police circles internationally. The latter would seem to be the case and is happening again today. "Community-oriented" and "problem-oriented" policing are the hottest ideas in Australia, Britain, Canada, and the United States. The Indian police, too, though preoccupied with communal and separatist violence, are talking about the need to engender community trust, enhance command responsibilities at the grass roots, and enlist the public in crime prevention.

Unable to untangle the historical causation of events that are so similar in so many different milieus, I would suggest three points. First, "centralization/decentralization" are code words for reform used by practitioners and scholars regardless of what is actually going on. Second, changes in the location of command both functionally and geographically are often undertaken as part of reform even though they have no vital, or even clearly perceived, connection with new organizational objectives. And, third, reform is always justified in terms of external conditions. That is the way it is made to seem rational and necessary. But this does not mean that such circumstances are causal in an empirical sense.

The functional organization of police, too, relates more to a professional, and international, zeitgeist than to changes in local circumstances. Note again three facts: with the exception of India's large armed reserves, all five of these countries have the same major specializations—patrol, criminal investigation, and traffic; each specialization has relatively the same strength in terms of personnel across the countries; and the specializations appear to have developed more or less at the same time historically despite variations in the occurrence of macrosocioeconomic events, such as urbanization and industrialization. These three points would continue to apply, I think, if the examination were expanded to almost any number of countries.

Criminal investigation, the most important specialization to emerge in the last two centuries, first appeared in London in 1842. It did not become a sizeable command, however, until 1878 (Critchley 1967, pp. 160–62). Bombay, Calcutta, and Madras developed criminal investigation divisions (CIDs) in the 1880s, undoubtedly influenced by Britain's example. Criminal investigation departments were added in the provincial forces after the 1902–3 Police Commission (Bayley 1969, chap. 2). Criminal investigation became a major specialization in the United States around the turn of the century, although small numbers of detectives were to be found in large cities fifty years before (Richardson

1974; Monkkonen 1981; Marx 1988). The very first unit may have been a three-man group created by the Boston police in 1846 (Lane 1967).

The hypotheses developed by historians to explain the change in American police during the opening decades of the twentieth century would not account for the development of criminal investigation as a specialization across so diverse a group of countries. These hypotheses include the rise of a capitalist class (Harring 1983), relatively affluent nativists concerned with unruly immigrants (Fogelson 1977), and revenue pressure (Peterson 1981). Applying a very broad historical brush, we find that criminal investigation emerged well after the onslaught of industrialization in Britain, during its heyday in the United States and Canada, and well before it in Australia and India.

In the absence of more detailed comparative analysis, the best explanation for functional developments within police seems to be the evolution of professional perspectives that are shared among police and informed members of the public about the appropriate role for the police and the most useful strategies for carrying it out. These perspectives are transnational, certainly among English-speaking countries, and once institutionalized have a life of their own (Bayley 1975).

VI. Significance

Does the organizational framework of policing make a difference to the quality of police operations? Almost everyone thinks so. Politicians, supposedly mirroring public opinion, are reluctant to tamper with traditions of multiple autonomous forces. National police forces, even substantial amalgamations, are anathema. Structural decentralization is considered essential to the protection of the "ancient liberties of Englishmen," while centralization is associated with authoritarian repression. Police officials respond to any crisis—corruption, crime, race relations—with organizational reforms, usually the creation of a new unit, task force, or command. Scholars, too, have associated organizational changes, especially within forces, with key developments in policing during the last century. In the United States, for example, decentralization of command was integral, we are told, to the "political model" of nineteenth-century policing; centralization to the science-based crime fighting of the "professional model"; and decentralization to the "community-oriented" model of the 1980s (Kelling and Moore 1987).

But are the changes in police organization really instrumental? Officers charged with reexamining the command structure of the Victorian police in Australia in the late 1980s wryly named their task force "Project Arbiter," after Petronius Arbiter of Rome, circa A.D. 50, who said: "We trained very hard—but it seemed that every time we were beginning to form up into teams we would be reorganized. I was to learn later in life that we tend to meet any new situation by reorganizing: and a wonderful method it can be for creating the illusion of progress while producing confusion, inefficiency, and demoralisation." It often seems that the impulse to improve is expended in battles over form. Police officers know the cynical truth of the expression "plus ça change, plus c'est la même chose." Changing organizational boxes is to policing what curriculum reform is to universities—a fractious exercise periodically repeated whenever the institution is challenged.

What is needed, then, is a serious examination of the assumptions about the importance of organizational variables. In order to do this, one must stipulate areas of likely impact and then study the differences that changes in organization make. As a beginning to this much-needed enterprise, I shall summarize what little I know about the difference police organization makes.

Neither the number of autonomous forces nor the extent of command centralization/decentralization within forces has any effect on human rights and political freedom. Australia, Britain, Canada, India, and the United States are all vibrant democracies, but they vary considerably in the multiplicity of forces as well as the command organization within them. If there is a threshold effect, so that below a certain number of forces freedom is more at risk, it would have to be less than Australia's eight. And the scale of centralization would need to be larger than Western Australia—hardly likely considering that it is already larger than Great Britain, Japan, and Texas combined. Furthermore, authoritarian polities sometimes have decentralized police systems—for example, Prussia, the Soviet Union, and the American South before the civil rights movements, while notable democratic countries have centralized ones—such as Denmark, Ireland, Sweden, New Zealand, and France. Persuaded by such comparisons as well as the logic of politics, the British Royal Commission on the Police (1962) said: "We therefore summarize our opinion on this matter by observing that to place the police under the control of a well-disposed government would be neither constitutionally objectionable nor politically dangerous; and if an ill-disposed government were to come into office it would without doubt seize control of the police however they might be organized. If reasons are to be found for continuing a system of local police forces, therefore, they must be found elsewhere" (p. 46).

With respect to community responsiveness of the police, the experience of Australia and Japan shows that a large number of autonomous forces belonging to local governments is not essential. American public opinion is wrong about this. American faith in local forces confuses structural autonomy with command decentralization within forces. Japan has achieved remarkable community responsiveness through its koban system, despite having a substantially unified police system. The Australian states of New South Wales and South Australia are developing consultative committees for their police stations, even though the jurisdiction of each force is enormous. Conversely, New York City has a local police force, but it is questionable whether communities within the city feel the police are accountable to them. In order for the multiplication of forces to ensure community responsiveness, I suspect that the scale of the police force must be very small—like an American township. For the most part, therefore, if communities want to make police responsive, they must learn to insist on command decentralization.

Although considerable attention has been given to the effect of police strength on crime rates and victimization, there are hardly any studies of the effect of variations in police organization (Morris and Heal 1981; Bennett 1983). The best evidence comes from the Police Services Study of sixty-one police departments in the United States. Contrary to what the President's Commission on Law Enforcement and Administration of Justice had thought, large police forces were not more effective than small ones (Ostrom et al. 1973, 1977). In fact, residents in communities with small police forces reported fewer criminal victimizations and faster response times, and had more favorable opinions about police service.

Reanalyzing that rich data set, Robert Worden has recently found that citizens' satisfaction is only weakly related to the size of police departments when one controls for the socioeconomic character of neighborhoods, background of respondents, experiences with the police, styles of local government, and other perceptions of police performance. Moreover, the smaller departments had the better evaluations (Worden 1989).

With respect to the costs of policing, Steve Mastrofski, surveying

American studies, found that consolidating small departments rarely produced economies of scale; cooperative sharing of resources through contracting showed mixed results; duplication of services among small departments was rare and sharing common; and patrol coverage on the street was more intense in small departments (Mastrofski 1985). Apparently not wanting to disappoint the proponents of consolidation too much, Mastrofski concluded that research to date did not show that consolidation was a bad idea.

Finally, centralization of command was once thought essential to the elimination of improper police behavior, particularly corruption and the misuse of force. It was the hallmark of reform during the Progressive Era, carrying with it tighter disciplinary controls and closer supervision. Today this conventional wisdom is being challenged. Centralized control cannot be effective, some contend, in the instrumental sense. It is too cumbersome, perhaps even counterproductive (Maas 1973; Daley 1978; Sherman 1978; Walker 1988). Centralization gives the impression of control but not the reality. Instead, police departments are being encouraged to develop a sense of mission in all officers, stressing the general values that should infuse all activities (Brown 1989). Discipline would come through socialization and peer reinforcement rather than through the stipulation of rules, covert investigation, and condign punishment (Bayley 1983*b*). Such an approach is compatible with the decentralization of operational commands. Indeed, if command decentralization leads to more collegial management, it might assist in "imprinting" the morality of the organization throughout its ranks more successfully.

If what I know about the effects of organization on police performance is at all reflective of what is in fact known, then this science is still in its infancy. It has barely proceeded as far as producing good case descriptions, still less comparative ones. The organization of the police is a boring topic because it has not been examined to discover if it truly makes a difference. It is viewed so equivocally because it has not been taken seriously intellectually. This is ironic considering the resources, effort, and emotion vested in it by the police themselves. The neglect of organization as a subject for analysis is our fault—police managers, policy analysts, and academic scholars who care about the police. The solution is to use organizational charts for more than getting around in a police organization; they must be treated as independent variables in empirical research. The slender results already obtained indicate that we will probably be surprised.

REFERENCES

American Friends Service Committee. 1979. *The Political Threat to Political Liberty*. Philadelphia: American Friends Service Committee.

Bayley, David H. 1969. *The Police and Political Development in India*. Princeton, N.J.: Princeton University Press.

————. 1975. "The Police and Political Development in Europe." In *The Formation of National States in Western Europe*, edited by Charles Tilly. Princeton, N.J.: Princeton University Press.

————. 1977. "The Limits of Police Reform." In *Police and Society*, edited by David H. Bayley. Beverly Hills, Calif.: Sage.

————. 1983a. "The Police and Political Order in India." *Asian Survey* 23:484–96.

————. 1983b. "Accountability and Control of Police: Lessons for Britain." In *The Future of Policing*, edited by Trevor Bennett. Cropwood Conference Series no. 15. Cambridge: Institute of Criminology.

————. 1985. *Patterns of Policing*. New Brunswick, N.J.: Rutgers University Press.

————. 1990. *Toward Policing 2000*. Adelaide: National Police Research Unit.

Bennett, Richard R. 1983. "Police Personnel Levels and the Incidence of Crime: A Cross-sectional Investigation." *Criminal Justice Review* 8(2):32–39.

Bopp, William J., and Donald D. Schultz. 1972. *A Short History of American Law Enforcement*. Springfield, Ill.: Charles C. Thomas.

Bouza, Anthony V. 1976. *Police Intelligence: The Operations of an Investigative Unit*. New York: AMS Press.

Brown, Lee P. 1989. "Community Policing: A Practical Guide for Police Officials." *Police Chief* (August), pp. 72–82.

Brown, Lorne, and Caroline Brown. 1973. *An Unauthorized History of the RCMP*. Toronto: James Lewis & Samuel.

Carter, David, et al. 1989. *The State of Police Education*. Washington, D.C.: Police Executive Research Forum.

Critchley, T. A. 1967. *A History of the Police in England and Wales, 1900–1966*. London: Constable & Company.

Daley, Robert. 1978. *Prince of the City*. New York: Panther, Granada.

Eck, John E. 1983. *Solving Crimes: The Investigation of Burglary and Robbery*. Washington, D.C.: Police Executive Research Forum.

Economist. 1990. "An Old Force on a New Beat." (February 10), pp. 53–59.

Emsley, Clive. 1983. *Policing and Its Context, 1750–1870*. London: Macmillan.

Field, John. 1981. "Police Power and Community in a Provincial English Town: Portsmouth, 1815–1875." In *Policing and Punishment in Nineteenth Century Britain*, edited by Victor Bailey. New Brunswick, N.J.: Rutgers University Press.

Fogelson, Robert M. 1977. *Big-City Police*. Cambridge, Mass.: Harvard University Press.

Government of India. 1985. *Statistical Abstract of India*. New Delhi: Government of India.

Grabosky, Peter N. 1977. *Sydney in Ferment: Crime, Dissent, and Official Reaction, 1788–1973*. Canberra: Australian National University Press.

Greenwood, P. W., and J. Petersilia. 1975. "The Criminal Investigation Process." In *Summary and Policy Implications*, vol. 1. Santa Monica, Calif.: RAND.

Gurr, Ted R., Peter N. Grabosky, and Richard C. Hula. 1977. *The Politics of Crime and Conflict: A Comparative History of Four Cities*. Beverly Hills, Calif.: Sage.

Halperin, Morton H., et al. 1976. *The Lawless State: The Crimes of the U.S. Intelligence Agencies*. New York: Penguin.

Harring, Sidney L. 1983. *Policing a Class Society*. New Brunswick, N.J.: Rutgers University Press.

Henderson, Lori M. 1985. "Intergovernmental Service Arrangements and the Transfer of Functions." *Municipal Yearbook*. Washington, D.C.: International City Management Association.

International Association of Chiefs of Police. 1976. *History of Police Intelligence Operations, 1880–1975*. Gaithersburg, Md.: International Association of Chiefs of Police.

International Municipal Management Association. 1989. *Municipal Yearbook, 1989*. Washington, D.C.: International Municipal Management Association.

Jamieson, Katherine M., and Timothy J. Flanagan. 1989. *Sourcebook of Criminal Justice Statistics—1988*. U.S. Department of Justice, Bureau of Justice Statistics. Washington, D.C.: U.S. Government Printing Office.

Jones, J. Mervyn. 1980. *Organisational Aspects of Police Behavior*. Westmead, United Kingdom: Gower.

Kelling, George L., and Mark H. Moore. 1987. "From Political Reform to Community: The Evolving Strategy of Police." Unpublished manuscript. Cambridge, Mass.: Harvard University, Kennedy School of Government.

Lane, Roger. 1967. *Policing the City: Boston, 1822–1885*. Cambridge, Mass.: Harvard University Press.

———. 1980. "Urban Police and Crime in Nineteenth-Century America." In *Crime and Justice: An Annual Review of Research*, vol. 2, edited by Norval Morris and Michael Tonry. Chicago: University of Chicago Press.

Law Enforcement Assistance Administration. 1970. *Criminal Justice Agencies in Pennsylvania*. Washington, D.C.: U.S. Government Printing Office.

Levett, A. E. 1975. "Centralization of City Police in Nineteenth Century United States." Ph.D. dissertation, University of Michigan, Ann Arbor.

Maas, Peter. 1973. *Serpico*. New York: Viking.

MacDonald Commission. 1981. "Commission of Inquiry concerning Certain Activities of the RCMP." *Freedom and Security under Law*. Ottawa: MacDonald Commission.

Martin, J. P., and G. Wilson. 1969. *The Police: A Study in Manpower*. London: Heinemann.

Marx, Gary. 1988. *Undercover: Police Surveillance in America*. Berkeley and Los Angeles: University of California Press.

Mastrofski, Stephen D. 1985. "Police Agency Consolidation: Lessons from a Case Study." In *Police Practices in the 90s: Key Management Issues*, edited by James J. Fyfe. Washington, D.C.: International City Management Association.

Miller, Wilbur R. 1977. *Cops and Bobbies: Police Authority in New York and London, 1830–1870*. Chicago: University of Chicago Press.

Ministry of Home Affairs. 1982. *Crime in India*. New Delhi: Government of India.

Monkkonen, Eric. 1981. *Police in Urban America, 1860 to 1920*. Cambridge: Cambridge University Press.

Morris, Pauline, and Kevin Heal. 1981. *Crime Control and the Police: A Review of Research*. Home Office Research Study no. 67. London: H.M. Stationery Office.

Murphy, Chris. 1990. Outline of remarks for the Conference on the Future of Canadian Policing, Winnipeg, March.

National Sheriffs' Association. 1990. Personal communication with author, February.

Ostrom, Eleanor, et al. 1973. *Community Organization and the Provision of Police Service*. Beverly Hills, Calif.: Sage.

———. 1977. *Policing Metropolitan America*. Washington, D.C.: U.S. Government Printing Office.

Parker, J. L. 1937. "Law and Police." In *European Civilisation: Its Origins and Development—Economic History of Europe since the Reformation*, edited by Edward Eyre. London: Oxford University Press.

Peterson, Paul. 1981. *City Limits*. Chicago: University of Chicago Press.

Police Executive Research Forum. 1981. *Survey of Police Operational and Administrative Practices—1981*. Washington, D.C.: Police Executive Research Forum.

President's Commission on Law Enforcement and Administration of Justice. 1967. *The Challenge of Crime in a Free Society*. Washington, D.C.: U.S. Government Printing Office.

Pringle, Patrick. n.d. *Hue and Cry: The Story of Henry and John Fielding and Their Bow Street Runners*. London: William Morrow.

Radzinowicz, Leon. 1957. *A History of English Criminal Law and Its Administration since 1750*. New York: Macmillan.

Reiner, Robert. 1985. *The Politics of the Police*. New York: St. Martin's.

———. 1988. "In the Office of Chief Constable." In *Current Legal Problems, 1988*, vol. 41, edited by R. Rideout and J. Jowell. London: Stevens.

Reith, Charles. 1948. *A Short History of the British Police*. London: Oxford University Press.

Richardson, James F. 1974. *Urban Police in the United States*. Port Washington, N.Y.: Kennikat.

Royal Commission on the Police. 1962. *Final Report*. Cmnd. 1728. London: H.M. Stationery Office.

Sherman, Lawrence W. 1978. *Controlling Police Corruption: The Effects of Reform Policies—Summary Report*. Washington, D.C.: Law Enforcement Assistance Administration.

Silver, Allan. 1967. "The Demand for Order in Civil Society: A Review of Some Themes in the History of Urban Crime, Police, and Riot." In *The Police: Six Sociological Essays*, edited by David J. Bordua. New York: Wiley.

Smith, Bruce. 1940. *Police Systems of the United States*. 2d ed. New York: Harper & Row.

Storch, Robert D. 1975. "A Plague of Blue Locusts: Police Reform and Popular Resistance in Northern England, 1840–1857." *International Review of Social History* 20:62–90.

Swanton, Bruce, and Garry Hannigan. 1985. *Police Source Book 2*. Canberra: Australian Institute of Criminology.

Tobias, J. J. 1972. "Police and Public in the United Kingdom." *Journal of Contemporary History* 7:201–20.

U.S. Bureau of the Census. 1989. *Statistical Abstract of the United States*. Washington, D.C.: U.S. Government Printing Office.

U.S. Bureau of Justice Statistics. 1987. *Special Report: Police Departments in Large Cities, 1987*. Washington, D.C.: U.S. Department of Justice, Bureau of Justice Statistics.

Walker, Samuel. 1976. "The Urban Police and Crime: A Review of the Literature." *Journal of Police Science and Administration* 4:252–60.

———. 1980. *Popular Justice: A History of American Criminal Justice*. New York: Oxford University Press.

———. 1988. *The Rule Revolution: Reflections on the Transformation of American Criminal Justice, 1950–1988*. Madison, Wis.: Institute for Legal Studies.

Wilson, James Q. 1980. "The Changing FBI—the Road to Abscam." *Public Interest* 59:3–14.

Worden, Robert. 1989. "Police Department Size and Police Performance: An Exploration into Alternative Explanations." Paper presented at the annual meeting of the Academy of Criminal Justice Sciences, Washington, D.C.

World Almanac. 1989. *World Almanac and Book of Facts, 1989*. New York: World Almanac.

Eric H. Monkkonen

History of Urban Police

ABSTRACT

American police grew in per capita strength from the mid-nineteenth
century until the first decade of the twentieth when they reached their
present strength. Their hierarchical organization, communication
capacity, and uniformed visibility made them civil servants of general
resort, called on to run soup kitchens, inspect boilers, standardize
weights and measures, and recover lost children. Not until the end of
the nineteenth century did they begin to focus more narrowly on crime
control; in so doing they diminished their varied range of social services,
which included the overnight housing of thousands of homeless people.
The broad range of police activities and their complex relationship to
cities in their formative era has made them the subject of increasing
historical research.

Historians working in the field of American crime and justice have
produced a massive body of scholarship, a recent, selected collection
of articles alone consuming over 7,000 pages in sixteen bound volumes
(Monkkonen 1990). A significant portion of this work deals with the
police as opposed to a more holistic view of the criminal justice system
or, alternatively, of the whole city government. The police have attracted the historian's attention for many reasons, ranging from simple
curiosity to questions about urbanization, crime control, and the history of society. Although no one concept or paradigm has guided this

Eric H. Monkkonen is professor of history, University of California, Los Angeles.
He wishes to thank the participants at the conference on Modern Policing, Washington,
D.C., 1990, for their extensive and useful comments. In addition, Mark Haller has
helped him rethink many issues posed here, and he thanks him.

research, the result has been a rich and valuable set of empirical studies.

A decade ago Roger Lane (1980) published in *Crime and Justice* a synthetic article on urban policing that newer work expands in several different directions. This essay follows the directions of the new research, emphasizing areas where substantive gains have been made. The intention here is to examine the areas where there is new knowledge rather than to write a completely new history of policing. That task grows ever more complex, especially for the years after World War I. Historians have, for the most part, concentrated on the earlier years for several reasons. First, the history of the nineteenth-century United States has captured intense research excitement in many fields, and the police have given historians an avenue of investigation with a unique perspective (Monkkonen 1982). Second, in most characterizations of periods in U.S. history, the Progressive Era, closed by World War I, culminates in many of the principles and issues that undergird the major intellectual, social, and political developments of the remainder of the twentieth century. Finally, modern social science has much better documented the post–World War II era, so that the challenge of historical recovery and analysis has not been as great for more recent historical events.

The new studies have deepened our understanding of the origins of the police, their functional roles, their relationship to criminal behavior and public order, police organizations as employers and controllers of labor, the police professionalization movement, the complex and unique situating of police in the larger political order, and the growth and change of nonurban police—private and federal, in particular. In addition, we now have a fuller picture of police as they became regular components of the urban service sector and essential participants in the criminal justice system.

Sections I and II of this essay summarize my book on the police (Monkkonen 1981a), supplementing its research and analysis with other new and relevant work. Section I stresses the social and political innovation represented in policing, while Section II emphasizes that the fundamental aspect of U.S. policing as a component of local government has made police a part of urban services. The essay then turns in Section III to new research publications focusing on police as employers. Section IV examines police relations with organized labor. Section V turns to those issues in police reform that have attracted historical research, while Section VI focuses on policy issues in the

context of a federal political system. The conclusion delineates future
research needs and directions.

I. Police as an Innovation

Police are relative newcomers to the Anglo-American criminal justice
system. The Constitution does not mention them. Early city charters
do not mention them, either, for the simple reason that, as we know
them, police had not been invented. Instead, cities had loosely organized night watches and constables who worked for the courts, supplemented by the private prosecution of offenders through lower-level
courts (Steinberg 1989). The night watch and day constable, dating
from the Middle Ages, were familiar comic figures in Shakespeare's
plays and were not replaced until the 1820s, when London police were
reorganized by Robert Peel. The police precedent for the United
States, as is well known, came from the establishment of the Metropolitan Police of London in 1829. Peel used his military experience in
Ireland to create a social control organization midway between a military and a civil force (Palmer 1988). The new police solved both tactical
and political problems: they were cheaper than a military force; they
created less resentment; and they were more responsive to civil authorities (Miller 1976).

Constables were responsible to civil and criminal courts. They supported themselves by fees, which came from serving warrants and civil
papers and arresting offenders. The victim of an offense had to seek a
constable, paying for his actions. Ferdinand's (1980) study of Boston
showed that a few constables often took the initiative in making drunk
arrests, apparently to make a continuous income. The fees for catching
an offender or for restitution could often be higher than the value of a
stolen object, but Steinberg's new work (1989) suggests that these fees
were no deterrent to many poor people using the criminal justice system. His work also shows that the constables could be sidestepped,
victims going directly to local aldermen's courts.

Night watch did just that: they were to raise the hue and cry in case
of an offense or to sound an alarm for a fire. The usual criticism of
them was that they slept, used their noisy rattles to warn off potential
offenders, and ran from real danger. The *New York Gazette* asserted
that the watch were a "Parcel of idle, drunken, vigilant Snorers, who
never quelled any nocturnal Tumult in their lives; but would, perhaps,
be as ready to join in a Burglary as any Thief in Christendom" (quoted
in Peterson and Edwards [1967], p. 324). These criticisms are difficult

to evaluate, but they do suggest that the night watch, who were either citizens doing required volunteer service or, more likely, their paid substitutes, were not in any way a serious crime-fighting organization.

There are four important innovative features of the new police as created in the United States in the nineteenth century. First, the new police had a hierarchical organization, with a command and communications structure resembling the military. This gave them an ordered and centralized hierarchy with an immediate communication superiority to all other urban organizations as well as the preceding constable watch system. Even without an electronic communications system (call boxes or police telegraphs first, then the telephone, which came a little later in the nineteenth century), the simple chain of command meant that a citizen could report an offense to an officer who would in turn relay the information to headquarters, which could then distribute the information back down the line. While no doubt the system operated with less than perfect precision, in the traditional constable watch system, this was even less likely to happen. Haller's (1970, 1976) work on Chicago shows that, after 1930, centralization increased further, especially with the introduction of radio cars and the decreased importance of the local station house. Since under the prepolice constable watch system the constables had gained their incomes from fees, the structural incentive encouraged them to follow up promising (i.e., high-fee-generating) leads themselves.

Second, increasing functional differentiation in revised city governments located the police under the executive rather than the judicial branch—previously, constables and watches had been part of the lower courts.[1] As a part of the mayor's executive office, the police were no longer general factotums for courts, which freed them from civil court activities. This shift had to accompany the abandonment of fees for service, for civil fees had been a part of the constabulary incomes (Steinberg 1989). This shift also sent the American police down a different developmental path from the English police, who long remained much more active and involved in preparing and prosecuting criminal cases than did their American counterparts. Until very recently, most English prosecutions were carried out by police officers and police solicitors. The shift also ensured a structural antagonism between the courts, prosecuting attorneys, and the police as the divide

---

[1] It is necessary to caution that this distinction overdraws the notion of executive, legislative, and judicial branches, for aldermen held courts (Surrency 1974).

in responsibilities took on greater ideological content in the twentieth century. This antagonism, usually characterized as an aspect of adversarial justice, was not at all intended and distinguishes the United States from other nations.

Third, the uniforms made the police visible, hence accessible, to all, whether neighbors or strangers, and this essentially made them the first and, for a long time, the only officials easily seen by the public. Uniforming, an integral part of their new organizational model, generated consternation and some amusing anecdotes for police historians. At first the uniforms were mocked by commentators and shunned by police officers. Called "popinjays" in Boston, ridiculed as "expensive and fantastical" in New York, derided as "livery" in Chicago, and refused by an officer in Philadelphia as "derogatory to my feelings as an American," uniforms were a difficult part of the transformation (Lane 1967, p. 105; Richardson 1970, p. 65; Johnson 1976, pp. 172–76, respectively). Americans valued greatly their freedom to wear what they pleased. Previously, only soldiers and servants of the wealthy had been seen on the streets in such outfits. But the uniforms instantly increased citizen access to patrol officers, now visible for the first time. This visibility, for instance, combined with a centralized communication system, accounted for the sudden turn to the police by parents of lost children; prior to police availability, parents had had to conduct frantic, random community searches (Monkkonen 1981a, pp. 109–28). In addition, uniformed officers were easier for their superiors to find and control.

Fourth, the police were conceived to be active: that entailed patrol (they were expected to discover and prevent crime), regular salaries and lines in the city budget, and free prosecution of criminal offenders. Conceptualized as bringing regular and more effective crime prevention to the city, this new activity contrasted with the constables' responsive, fee-based work. City officials hoped that regular patrol would prevent crime by scaring would-be offenders. If successful, of course, then fees for catching offenders would no longer be a fair way of paying for police services. So the new police had to have regular salaries that were to be a part of the city budget. An unexpected consequence of this was free prosecution of offenders: no longer did a victim have to calculate the value of a stolen pair of boots before calling a constable. Steinberg's research (1989) in the Philadelphia aldermanic court records suggests that people may have been quite willing to pay a fee to prosecute neighbors. He argues that one reason for creating the

Philadelphia police was to stop frivolous private prosecutions.[2] The regularity of the salaries made the police jobs more attractive, hence their almost immediate seizure as political plums to be handed out by the political party gaining the mayor's position. From this then developed the use of police in political control, police officers sometimes deterring voters and generally working for a partisan control of the ballot boxes (Jordan 1980). And this development, in turn, meant that as immigrant voting machines grew, immigrants had access to these city jobs early on. The image of the Irish cop had a genuine basis in reality, even in cities like New Orleans.

Steinberg's (1989) important work on Philadelphia shows that, prior to the police, a vigorous system of private prosecution had kept the aldermen and mayor busy adjudicating minor criminal offenses. He argues that this system, though corrupt, kept the citizenry in easy and constant contact with the law and that the police for their first two decades mainly pursued arrests for public-order offenses, the petty larcenies and assaults being handled by these lower and more neighborhood-based courts. Steinberg's book adds an additional dimension to what local criminal justice systems looked like prior to the police, revising the work on the constable watch by Ferdinand (1980), who emphasized their inefficiency and unsystematic entrepreneurialism. Steinberg raises new sets of complex questions for further analysis in the history of crime control and policing in his argument that the police deliberately, albeit slowly, eroded the vigorous involvement of the urban poor and laboring classes in the justice system. That is, regular patrol by salaried officers in theory reduced corruption, increased the availability of the police for consistent service, and removed the opportunity for frivolous complaints and prosecution by those with the money to pay fees. Did the modern police in fact decrease crime control and make the justice system less easily accessible?

Steinberg's work depends in part on a scholarly find, the fragmentary logs of three aldermen. Few of the numerous aldermen apparently kept written records, which means that a more systematic comparison than he attempted will depend on historians discovering new records. Nevertheless, until Steinberg's book, no historian even had the idea of looking for such materials, and his work opens an exciting new set of questions. In addition to such logs, police historians have already

---

[2] To be sure, the reporting of offenses had liabilities because witnesses were on occasion still locked up.

uncovered a rich lode of systematic sources (Monkkonen 1979, 1980). These include detailed annual reports, internal records, less regularly preserved blotters (the daily log of station activities), and, for the nineteenth century, detailed newspaper accounts. Most police departments have written histories that vary widely in quality and coverage (see Monkkonen [1981a], pp. 164–68, for a bibliography). In addition to these specifically police-oriented sources, there are records produced by courts, coroners, and carceral institutions. Most of these are manuscripts, but state governments produced annual summaries of court, prison, and jail activities. In addition, the federal censuses have interesting data, rendered difficult to use by their inconsistency from decade to decade.

II. Policing as an Urban Service

The new kinds of police work came as costly service innovations to American cities, stingy city governments often resisting the transition specifically because of the new claims on city budgets (Schneider 1980). Uniformed police spread across the United States to most cities in the three decades between 1850 and 1880. It sometimes seemed that local incidents, most typically riots, "caused" a city to change its police force to the modern form. But in general, a city's rank size among American cities determined the order in which police were adopted, the spread of police innovation following a diffusion curve typical for all sorts of innovations (Monkkonen 1981a, pp. 49–64). Some historians (Blackburn 1979; Rippy 1985) have argued that police were created in response to rising crime, but there is little empirical evidence to support this because most social scientists now assume that the long-run trends in crime rates have been downward (Gurr 1989). More to the point, those creating police forces would have had little way of detecting rising crime. Riots had long been a part of American urban life, and historians have been able to describe in considerable detail the political ends of riots as conscious social forms (Schneider 1980; Gilje 1987). New York City, for instance, had major nineteenth-century riots in 1806, 1826, 1834, 1837, 1849, 1855, 1857, 1863, 1870, 1874, 1900 (Monkkonen 1981a, p. 196). At best, one could say that the creation of the police force reflected a growing intolerance for riots and disorder, rather than a response to an increase in crime. Gallman (1988) has shown that this was the case for Philadelphia, a city with a long tradition of rioting, where he argues that citizens no longer accepted public outbursts.

The police grew in per capita strength from around 1.3 per thousand in the 1860s, stabilizing at two per thousand in 1908, which is around the current ratio. Examined more carefully, the growth data suggest two eras of expansion, the first up to about 1890, when the police forces became permanent fixtures of city government, and the second in the decade of the 1890s when the police force again and finally expanded in strength. As a reciprocal to the increasing number of police per capita, the proportion of patrol officers fell from around 95 to about 75 percent by 1920. Toward the end of the nineteenth century, the actual number of patrol hours per officer may also have declined, for not only did the proportion of patrol officers decrease, but the two-shift system (twelve hours on, twelve hours off) yielded to the more humane three-shift system in this era (Monkkonen 1981a, pp. 144–45). Certainly, the twentieth century saw declining patrol hours per officer. Watts (1981a), using more precise data for the St. Louis police department, has estimated police hours available for patrol since 1900, accounting for vacation and workweek changes. He concludes that, since the nineteenth century, hours per officer on the street have consistently declined, as one might expect given the general decrease in the length of the working day. Using officer hours worked for the period 1958–62 as a base, police worked about 80 percent more at the end of the nineteenth century, about 20 percent more between 1907 and World War II, about 10 percent less after 1962 (Watts 1981a, p. 671, n. 15). At least for time allotted to patrol, police presence began declining within four decades after their introduction to cities.

Once in place, city police almost immediately began doing things unexpected by their original creators, whose expectations were more along the lines of crime prevention. Along with arresting offenders, the police took in tramps, returned lost children by the thousands, shot stray dogs, enforced sanitation laws, inspected boilers, took annual censuses, and performed myriad other small tasks. Their unique communications organization and street presence virtually forced them to become city servants as well as crime-control officers. Simultaneously, with a pull toward urban service came a surprising inability to fulfill other crime-related functions, most notably riot control and catching of offenders whose crimes crossed many local government districts (e.g., thieves on railroads). Unpredictable in their ability to control strikes, police sometimes sided with strikers (e.g., as happened in Homestead, Pennsylvania, in 1892). Fogelson (1989) shows that urban elites created armories in response to strikes and riots beginning in the post–Civil War era, signaling their clear recognition that police skills did not include antiriot mobilization. As the contributor to the *Cyclopedia of American Government* stated: "Labor riots, particularly against strike breakers, sometimes [had] the sympathy of the police" (McLaughlin and Hart 1914, 3:584).

From very early on police did something for which they had not been created: they dispensed forms of welfare in response to the pressing demands of citizens. It is important to be clear about this particular transformation: in the mid-nineteenth century, all welfare was a local responsibility. The federal government took no such responsibility until the early twentieth century. State governments accepted limited responsibility for the blind and mentally ill and juveniles in need of reform (Schlossman 1977; Brenzel 1983; Dwyer 1987). County governments accepted responsibility for paupers, a group confined to the severely disabled, the old and infirm, and pregnant destitute women (Hannon 1984*a*, 1984*b*; Katz 1986). City governments took on all others, from orphans to the homeless. Police departments were the front line of encounter for a good many of such needy people. Station houses contained separate dorm-type rooms to house overnight "lodgers." Each city varied in what it provided, but the accommodations were primitive and limited to a few nights. A police officer recorded each person's name and sometimes rather detailed information (age, place of birth, occupation, "whither from," and destination). Such police service did not go unnoticed, either by the poor or by city officials.

Toward the end of the nineteenth century and into the 1920s, many reformers worked to dismantle station house lodging. Jacob Riis, in his autobiography, complained bitterly about his and his dog's maltreatment by the police when he stayed in stations in New York City and Camden, New Jersey, after his arrival in the United States in the 1870s (Monkkonen 1981*a*, p.92). Later his bitterness fused with the critiques of police commissioners like Theodore Roosevelt, who argued that the presence of tramps was degrading and threatened police officers with contagious diseases.[3] At the same time, other reformers in major eastern cities worried about the consequences of the indiscriminate giving of overnight lodging. They argued that this accommodation did nothing to reform the bad habits of the poor; scientific charity

---

[3] Berman (1987), in telling the story of Roosevelt's career as New York City police commissioner, captures nicely this transition and its linkage to the larger program of the progressive movement, rationalization, efficiency, and an end to corruption.

should not be indiscriminate. Instead, some reformers encouraged cities to substitute municipal lodging houses for police lodging, requiring delousing and work from the overnight lodgers. Such reforms carried through at least in Boston and New York, much to the unhappiness of the lodgers who preferred dirty but no-strings-attached shelter. By the 1920s, police were out of the lodging business; only rarely have social welfare histories shown an awareness of this important role taken on by the police (Katz 1986).

It seems almost natural to ask today why this simple police activity should have been allowed to disappear, especially since there is no evidence suggesting that the police themselves complained. But in the context of the original crime control impetus behind their creation, and the changing focus of their range of activities, the disappearance of lodging makes more sense. Social welfare reformers, and some police chiefs, began to differentiate the components of the "dangerous class," and tramps became, to them, the unemployed rather than dangerous. After the 1890s, police really did focus more and more on crime control. So did the other loose components of the criminal justice system. For example, Friedman and Percival, in their study of Alameda County, California, show that in this period "criminal justice shifted away from amateurs and part-timers toward full-time crime handlers" (1981, p. 194).

Other tests confirm the change in police focus from both broad welfare and crime control to more concentration on crime control. For instance, the correlation in most major cities between arrests for criminal offenses (as opposed to public-order offenses) and numbers of police per capita increased after 1890. A recent analysis of arrests for murder and other felonies, lodgers, and police strength in the twenty largest American cities more precisely confirms 1894 as the turning point, the moment when police began to respond more directly to crimes of violence as measured by murder arrests (Bijleveld and Monkkonen 1991). At the same time, police focused their attention on other felony crimes, while continuing to slough off their burden of temporarily housing the homeless and even reducing the numbers of people arrested for public-order misdemeanors.

The narrowing focus of police on crime in turn came with a new set of external pressures, including demands for efficiency, honesty, and crime control. Coordination of departments began at the modest scale of sharing information. The Police Chiefs Union, founded in 1893 (to become the International Association of Chiefs of Police), started a modest bureau of identification at some point in the 1890s.

Their efforts did not meet with success because of the nature of the federal system. Voluntary contributions from city police departments could not provide adequate or consistent funding for this national activity. Not until Theodore Roosevelt became president were police leaders to see the creation of the Federal Bureau of Investigation (FBI), some twenty years later (Dilworth 1977; Uchida 1983). A range of local changes paralleled these fledgling national coordinating efforts.

In this context, the question of the police role in maintaining public order gains new significance. Compared to their British predecessors, Miller (1976) argued, the new police in the United States envisioned their role as keepers of public order, dispensing summary justice immediately on the street (see also Friedman and Percival 1981, pp. 80–81). Police jobs had high rates of turnover, in part because of their nature as political plums in cities with rapid regime transitions and in part because high residential mobility characterized all of urban America. Turnover ensured that police professionalization issues never mattered for the nineteenth-century officer. And for the whole police organization, the keeping of lodgers had no logical role conflict with arresting drunks and felons: all of these activities involved control of what was then called the "dangerous class." The cessation of control of the "dangerous class" came with the first reforms of police corruption in the 1890s, followed by new emphases on investigative techniques like fingerprinting (around 1905) and with the slow change of the job from political plum to career occupation. By the end of World War I, police were in the business of crime control. Other city- or state-run agencies had taken over their former noncrime control activities.

It should be noted here that the dating of the turn to crime control is based on police behavior. Additional evidence suggests that, over the decades of the early twentieth century, the crime-control model became more explicitly drawn. Douthit (1975), for instance, presents evidence that, in the 1920s and 1930s, an effort to create a professional police brought with it an even more refined focus on crime control that excluded all other forms of social conflict. In the mid-1920s the concept of a "war against crime" was popularized by businessman Mark Prentiss (who wrote in the popular magazine *Current Opinion*) at the same time that somewhat more serious work was being conducted by crime commissions or crime surveys in twenty-four states (Douthit 1975, pp. 318–19). President Coolidge's National Crime Commission (1925) brought national attention to the movement, and President Hoover created a better-known National Commission on Law Observance and Enforcement, usually referred to as the Wickersham Commission, that published fourteen reports and had research conducted by such experts as August Vollmer, Zechariah Chafee, Jr., Newton Baker, Edith Abbott, Mary Van Kleeck, Sam B. Warner, Miriam Van Watters, Clifford Shaw, and Henry Mckay (Walker 1981, pp. 173–75). These national commissions and the high publicity earned by J. Edgar Hoover marked an image-setting finale to the much longer swing of the police mission to crime control.

Not all scholars agree that the 1890s mark the transition to a crime-control model for the police. In a debate over policing practice and public-order arrests, Watts has argued that crime-control-oriented policing was not finalized until the 1940s, an argument based on internal documents as well as quantitative evidence from the St. Louis police. In contrast, Wertsch, in a close documentary analysis of the Des Moines police department, argues for a change in the 1920s: a "methodological change in policing that drew its attention away from public disorder offenses toward the more urgent task of protecting lives and property" (1987, p. 448). Therefore, while there is agreement that a shift from public-order control to crime control did occur, the precise timing remains in dispute (see also Watts 1981a, p. 658). Several factors probably affected this transition and its city-to-city variability, just as several factors affected the initial adoption of uniformed police. More precise examination may well establish a parallel: an early but longer-lasting transition, say from 1890 to 1920, in those large cities with both progressive reform movements on many fronts and with innovative police departments, with a later but quicker transition in smaller cities.

A declining per capita rate of arrests for drunk offenses may also have resulted solely from this shift in emphasis, although there is strong, if contested, evidence suggesting that drinking itself has been in a long decline since the mid-nineteenth century (Rorabaugh 1979; Monkkonen 1981c, 1983; Watts 1983a; Wertsch 1987; Blocker 1989). The complexity of the topic and the question of policy is most dramatically illustrated by the articulated policy change in the Cleveland police in 1908. Under Chief Fred Kohler, the police adopted the "golden rule" in 1908, assisting drunks home or ignoring them. As the seventh largest American city, Cleveland was often looked to as a model for reform.[4] Arrests for drunk offenses plummeted from 18,743 in 1906 to a low of 909 in 1912, the most visible impact being between 1907 and

---

[4] Note that, although Cleveland's arrest trends are not typical of most cities, it is included here for its observed policy shift and to exemplify how Progressive Era reforms moved the police toward the goal of crime control.

1908 when the arrests fell by 80 percent. Patrol officers each arrested an average of about 37 drunks per year in 1906 and less than two per year in 1912. But this dramatic policy change simply followed on a more complex trend in Cleveland where arrest rates for drunkenness had fallen from as early as 1873 until the mid-1890s, and the peak in 1906 was the result of a decade of increased aggressiveness in arrests for drunkenness. Kohler's policy could actually be interpreted as a return to an earlier pattern. Thus a probable scenario that links policy to public behavior is that more decorous behavior had begun to prevail on the city streets as the long nineteenth-century campaign against excessive drinking slowly spread its influence. In the larger context of growing urban order and political progressivism, the police themselves shifted toward a crime-control orientation and simultaneously reconsidered the effectiveness of arresting drunks.

Whether or not public behavior became less disorderly, it is very clear that the policing of drunkenness had been in a long downswing prior to the movement in the 1970s to decriminalize public drunkenness. And when the question of drunkenness is considered in the context of public order, more broadly defined, the notion of a shift in police action from order maintenance to crime control remains a major argument from the past decade's research. It should still be considered as a hypothesis worth more systematic exploration. At least one pair of scholars is doing this. A project by Weinberger and Reinke (1989) compares two industrial locations, Manchester, England, and Wuppertal, Germany, for the period 1890–1930. Based on the American work and on work for England that argues that urban policing had aggressively reduced criminal offenses until the 1890s (Gatrell 1980), they seek to expand further and make more precise the relationship between police and public order and issues of social welfare. They have already found important differences from the American experience and evidence that suggests that the shift away from welfare concerns may not have occurred until after World War I. In Britain a police orientation toward class control was "self-evident" (Weinberger and Reinke 1989, pt. 1, p. 14). In Germany, the police explicitly focused on controlling worker politics and unions, and at the same time separate health and sanitary police were created to implement growing expertise in these fields (Weinberger and Reinke 1989, pt. 2, pp. 8–9).

III. Police Departments as Employers
In the United States, through their organizational tie to the mayor's office and to local partisan politics, police departments have been im-

portant as employers of some immigrant groups, most notably the Irish. This held true even for southern cities; in 1850, over one-third of the New Orleans' police force had been born in Ireland (as opposed to the Irish population, which was about one-fourth of the city population) (Rousey 1983, p. 62). Rousey quotes northern visitor Frederick Law Olmstead's encounter with a police officer in New Orleans in 1854: when he asked for directions, "a policeman, with the richest Irish brogue, directed me back to the St. Charles" (p. 61). Nativist politicians purged the police of most of their immigrant officers in the late 1850s, but by 1870 the Irish were back in the department. Summarizing the experience of seventeen southern cities, Rousey discovered that Vicksburg and Memphis both had fifty percent of their officers born in Ireland as late as 1880 (if children of immigrants were included, this proportion would probably have been much higher). He concludes that "a large Irish role in southern urban policing was the rule" for most of the nineteenth century (p. 80).

Several recent studies by Watts (1981*b*, 1982) analyze police hiring practices in St. Louis in great detail using personnel data that include persons not hired. The results of his work provide a unique source of information on twentieth-century police departments. Between 1917 and 1969, one-third of St. Louis's recruits had had a previous local arrest record (Watts 1981*b*, p. 82). The median age of recruits, around thirty at the beginning of the twentieth century, dropped slowly as policing changed from a job, typically one of several in a man's life, to a career (p. 84).

As the twentieth century began, even a heavily German city like St. Louis had an Irish police force; only 3 percent of its population had been born in Ireland, compared to one-third of its police force (Watts 1981*b*, p. 100). Of more importance was that, at the turn of the century, the total ethnic composition of police, fire, and watch organizations reflected the immigrant heritage of the city, three-fourths of whom were immigrants or children of immigrants, a figure somewhat less than that for Milwaukee, New York, or Chicago (Fogelson 1977; Watts 1981*b*, p. 99).

At the turn of the century 6 percent of St. Louis's population was black; its police department appointed its first two black police officers in 1901. Watts points out that Democrats controlled the police department and that virtually all of the city's black voters were Republicans, which suggests that politics combined with racial exclusion to account for the small number of black officers (1981*b*, pp. 105–6; 1981*c*). A

Republican governor in 1920 admitted fifteen black officers to the department, and in the immediate post–World War II era, when black voters shifted to the Democratic party, 10 percent of all new recruits were black (Watts 1981*b*, p. 107). Watts argues (1981*b*, p. 109) that many changes in the racial and ethnic composition of the St. Louis police in the twentieth century were actually the result not of reform but of larger "societal changes," such as the black shift to Democratic politics.[5]

Probably the most significant result to come from Watts's intense analysis of the individual career patterns of police officers is his discovery that over the course of the twentieth century, "no truly 'typical' pattern ever emerged" (1983*b*, p. 224). The average tenure of police officers varied highly at the beginning of the century and continued to vary through the 1970s. Moreover, actual individual careers belied the seemingly clear structural reforms and the appearance of a transformation of the police from a relatively simple and unpredictable internal structure to a highly structured and rationalized bureaucracy. Watts's conclusion that the "police in St. Louis failed to establish a uniform, coherent career pattern for its members" (1983*b*, p. 224) provides a cautionary note to the strong impression most scholars carry of the police as a Weberian bureaucracy in the process of professionalization.

IV. Police and Labor

Police control of labor in the United States has been much less direct and open than in Germany, and the recent historiography reflects a surprisingly ambiguous though still incomplete picture that is tied in large part to issues in private policing. In spite of notorious incidents, like the Memorial Day Massacre in Chicago in 1937, when police killed demonstrating workers, most recent labor history does not paint a completely antilabor picture of American police and organized labor. In fact, until the defeat of striking police officers in Boston in 1919 ended police unionization efforts for almost a half century, police themselves were often a part of the American labor movement (Walker 1980, pp. 166–69). One of the best-known labor historians, Herbert Guttman, pointed out that police sometimes sided with striking workers (Guttman 1977; see also Johnson 1976). This usually occurred in smaller cities where police budgets depended on taxes paid by workers.

[5] Watts (1982) also demonstrates in an analysis of promotion practices that the only meaningful variable for promotion is seniority.

In small cities, police officers were often related directly to strikers or were from the same labor pool. And finally, in small cities, labor parties often gained considerable political power: Terrence V. Powderly, the founder of the Knights of Labor, also gained the mayor's seat in Scranton, a town racked with antilabor violence (not by the police). According to Walker, as far as the police were concerned, "Powderly resembled his predecessors" (1978, p. 85), making the police a part of his political machine and trying to get the city council to enlarge the force. In larger cities, police officers did not know or were not related to strikers, so at least the personal element of police/labor amicability was missing.

By far the most systematic and wide-ranging examination of police labor relations has not come from labor historians, however, but from a police historian, Sidney Harring (1983). In a study of Great Lakes cities, he has identified a strong antiunion bias of the police in Buffalo, Chicago, and Milwaukee (under a socialist government). He argues vigorously that the police in these and other cities acted as shock troops for local capitalists, pacifying and controlling local labor under the dictate of local businessmen. In Chicago, for instance, Harring (1983, pp. 121–27), has identified extensive strikebreaking activities by the city police, especially after 1910. Though his evidence for Chicago is very persuasive, it is less so for other cities where his arguments remain widely disputed and highly controversial. For instance, in Chicago in 1905, in Oshkosh in 1898, and in Akron in 1913, police "weakness" failed to curb strikes, and either private guards or the militia intervened (Harring 1983, pp. 125–31). But until further systematic research is completed, Harring's work stands as the best study of police and labor to date (Lane 1984; Terrill 1986; for a new look at police and labor, see Clark [1991]).

In one of the most famous labor disputes in the United States, the lockout in Homestead, Pennsylvania, in 1892, local police sided with the locked-out workers; Carnegie's plant officials had to hire nearly 400 Pinkerton agents to support them. The agents attacked the strikers from barges in the river, resulting in three agents and ten strikers being killed (Morn 1982, p. 103). This incident highlights two long traditions: that the police have local political ties by virtue of their local funding, and that their responsiveness to local circumstances created an opportunity for private enterprise, the private police.

In a careful institutional history of the Pinkerton National Detective Agency, Frank Morn (1982) has provided a badly needed narrative history of the most visible and oldest form of private policing, the detective. He shows how this famous agency quickly moved from "detection to protection," becoming a "private army of capitalism." He argues that "railroad expansion [in the 1850s] quickly exposed the weaknesses of police work in a country enamored of federalism" (Morn 1982, p.24). Once a train left a city, it had no police protection: in a long-distance trip it passed through many small police regions. Pinkerton capitalized on this gap in governance in the railroad industry by providing private contractual services where no public services were available. Among other things, Pinkerton's agents "tested" employee honesty (e.g., theft by conductors) as trains rolled across the countryside. Later his business expanded to capture similar opportunities in other industries and began to include strikebreaking in instances where neither local police nor militia could or would provide assistance. In all situations, the private sector either filled in governmental interstices or took on possibly illegal activities, for instance, employee testing that involved "sting"-like operations, where Pinkerton agents tried to bribe conductors to let them ride without tickets. Agents then filed reports to the companies, who fired corruptible conductors. The question remains whether Pinkerton operatives in fact blackmailed or extorted money on occasion.

Reviewing Morn's book, Jeffreys-Jones observes that it is "the first serious monograph on private detective agencies" (1983, p. 266). He clarifies how Allen Pinkerton's prolabor radicalism was also antistrike and anticommunitarian and how in the United States Pinkerton could be a reformer yet also work against all labor violence. Moreover, Jeffreys-Jones sets a research agenda for more work to be done on the history of private detective agencies as part of the history of private policing, including divorce work and family law, with a suggestion of new primary sources. His brief but important essay provides the starting point for the next round of historical research.

Yet the role of such private armies did not pass unscrutinized. The Homestead incident shocked the nation and prompted a federal investigation that resulted in no federal legislation but in antidetective legislation in many states (Morn 1982, pp. 91–109). The irony of the Pinkerton agency's antilabor reputation came from Allan Pinkerton's widely publicized prolabor radicalism that had forced him to leave Scotland in the 1840s. The company was embarrassed by the Homestead fiasco and actually did little strike work for ten years after it. However, antilabor activity could include more than strikebreaking, and by the

1930s the company was a leader in the industrial espionage field, with over 1,000 operatives in all major unions (Morn 1982, p. 187). Again the focus of an embarrassing federal investigation and exposé, the Pinkerton agency left these activities by 1940, slowly moving into the private security business (Morn 1982, p. 192).

Private police like the Pinkerton and Burns agencies gained their economic advantage by moving across political regions, using means of dubious legality, and working only for the moneyed. But they were not the only private police, for another form of nonmunicipally controlled police has been present in American cities since the 1890s, consisting of privately employed off-duty police officers and, more important, public officers appointed and employed solely by private organizations. Rebecca Reed's (1986) work on Detroit has shown how these officers, their commissions issued by the police department, grew in numbers as crime (indicated by the homicide rate) and population increased while the per capita police budget decreased (p. 5). About one-fourth of these officers were employed by other municipal agencies, and about two-thirds were employed by businesses (p. 10). In essence, businesses hiring these officers simply eliminated the services of detective agencies. She also has evidence that the police department was "reluctant" to let the police be used in strikes and that these privately employed police may have been business's response to the official aversion to strikebreaking (pp. 11–13).

Recent work on a famous teamsters strike in Minneapolis in 1934 supports Reed's insights. The so-called Citizens' Alliance was in fact a group of businessmen vigilantes who supplemented the police in the strike. Formed in 1917 to keep Minneapolis an "open shop" city, it successfully "eliminated the political threat of the WPNPL [Working People's Nonpartisan League of the Minneapolis trade unions] and the NPL [Nonpartisan League], deunionized the Minneapolis police, maintained an effective intelligence service, and helped establish a Highway Patrol and a Bureau of Criminal Apprehension headed by men it could trust" (Millikan 1989, p. 233). Its political clout and credibility ended when its members tried to drive and guard trucks to keep goods flowing in the strike. Armed with clubs and guns, the vigilantes actually got into armed conflict with the strikers, where their amateurish aggression resulted in deaths. After this misadventure, one in which the governor intervened on the side of the strikers, the Citizens' Alliance did not disband but instead hired parapolice to do investigative and patrol work (Millikan 1989). In essence, this private group used force of dubious legality to supplement the legitimate police when they were unwilling to step over the bounds of legitimate action.

V. Reforming Police

Often police have stepped over bounds of legitimate action, and corruption has been a persistent problem in U.S. policing. The Lexow Commission (created by the New York State Legislature in 1894), gained national prominence during its investigation of the New York City police and a subsequent exposé of corruption (Berman 1987, pp. 23–29). Similar reforms occurred in other large cities for the next three decades (Fogelson 1977). Sherman (1978) has observed that waves of scandal and reform have run in twenty-year cycles since the Lexow Commission investigation of New York City police corruption. He argues that "virtually every urban police department in the United States has experienced both organized corruption and a major scandal over that corruption" (Sherman 1978, p. xxiii). Reforms following scandal, he contends, have often been successful, but control of scandal, like control of crime itself, is hampered by fundamental freedoms. As opposed to most crime, however, scandal arises under fairly predictable conditions, usually surrounding vice operations. Historians have shown the long connection of police corruption with prostitution, drugs (including alcohol when illegal), and gambling (see Haller [1990], pp. 212–13, for a good brief summary; Best 1981; McKanna 1984). The potential for scandal is made most clear in those episodes when cities tried, for health reasons, to regulate prostitution without legalizing it. By the turn of the century, local political machines depended on these semilegitimate vice districts, the bribes from vice entrepreneurs funding the machines. (In some cases, elected nonmachine governments depended on the revenues from such fines, e.g., the small city of East Grand Forks, Minnesota, in the pre–World War I era [Sylvester 1989].) Since the 1960s, federal investigations of police corruption have reduced the ability of local vice entrepreneurs to control police (Haller 1990).

Earlier police historians had envisioned the first decades of the twentieth century as the dawn of scientific policing, a notion associated with Berkeley's famous chief August Vollmer, Richard Sylvester of Washington, D.C., the International Association of Chiefs of Police, and the serious communication among scholars and various segments of the crime control community through the pages of the *Journal of Criminal Law and Criminology*, which began publication in 1909 (Johnson 1981, p. 70). Yet recent work has made this clean, Progressive Era picture more complex. For instance, as Watts's work (1983*b*) has shown, the emergence of a more professional police force did not result in more orderly career paths for St. Louis police officers, implying that the bureaucracy did not have the organizational rationality earlier observers had envisioned.

Nor did shedding by police of service activities and focusing on crime-related arrests conform to the professional picture being painted by prominent police officers like August Vollmer. Vollmer, elected town marshall of Berkeley in 1905, where he supervised a force of three nonuniformed officers, soon became famous and influential. He achieved publicity in local and national newspapers, wrote extensively in the professional journals, and published several well-respected books. His innovations included a counseling clinic with a psychiatric social worker, Elisabeth Lossing, and an aggressive policing policy that emphasized intervention in personal affairs and prevention through methods prescribed by the latest ideas of the mental hygiene movement (Liss and Schlossman 1984). The most recent scholarship on Vollmer denies his widely acclaimed genius without denigrating his considerable achievements: "Rather than an original thinker, Vollmer's strengths lay in finding ingenious practical applications of ideas he borrowed from others, in carefully supervising the implementation of a wide variety of technical and procedural innovations, and, perhaps, most importantly, in maintaining high personal involvement and exercising decisive leadership in community affairs that impinged on police functions" (Liss and Schlossman 1984, p. 81).

It is important to see the shift Vollmer represented and advocated as not directly countering the narrowing police function or as returning to the multiservice police of the nineteenth century. His intervention and social work orientation and his genuine sympathy for and stern guidance of troubled people were directed toward the end of crime prevention. Earlier, police had taken in the homeless as a sort of municipal housekeeping. This function was in fact technically implied by the legal notion of "police power" that meant the power of a state or its local governments literally to do housekeeping, from cleaning streets to creating an orderly public arena. Vollmer's new and generous vision of policing was oriented toward the prevention of individual criminal actions.

This same vision enabled police to respond in new ways to old problems. During World War II, vicious race riots in several cities took the lives of African Americans and Mexican Americans. More to the point, the police not only failed to control the riots but were in many cases part of the problem. Thurgood Marshall compared the Detroit police to the Gestapo; some police officers saw the riots as providing fuel for Nazi anti-American propaganda (Walker 1980, p. 231). From these experiences, Milwaukee police chief Joseph Kluchesky earned a national reputation for his race relations training program in Milwaukee in 1944. In the same year, the International City Manager Association published a manual on police relations with minority groups that became widely used throughout the United States. Walker found twenty-two cities adopting some race relations training between 1943 and 1950 (to be sure, in some cities this involved little more than a two-hour lecture) (Walker 1980, pp. 236–38). However, the lack of urban riots after World War II until the 1960s never really tested the effectiveness of these programs or their companion antiriot strategies, leaving the police with untested and feebly implemented programs when the urban riots of the 1960s began (Walker 1980, p. 242).

While much has been written about the urban riots and the civil rights movement, no historian has yet tackled these episodes and the police roles in them in a systematic way. For instance, the Little Rock police attained considerable notoriety in 1957 and 1958 for their morally repugnant refusal to protect black children in the school integration crisis. Did such outrages as these, exposed on the national television, prompt public support for stronger federal standards in all areas of law enforcement? Did the question of racial fairness make an impact in other cities that did not gain media attention? Atlanta marketed itself as the "city too busy to hate" at the very same time. Did other urban boosters strive to make their cities and police fairer for latent economic incentives? And in the 1960s, did the impact of seeing riots on national television have an equal if different impact (Williams and Murphy 1990)?

VI. Federal-Local Policy Issues

As these visible urban problems in which the police were inextricably involved gained public attention, scholars turned to researching local police departments. The work of the 1960s and 1970s focused intensely on local aspects of policing, on detailed studies of individual police departments, and on questions of the social side of policing (see Kelling and Stewart [1991] for the best survey of this recent history). Implicit in all of the work was the recognition that policing in the United States was an activity done by local governments. Historians ignored issues of larger political entities in order to assess the details of the actual local systems. But now some historians whose earlier work began in the arena of the local police have turned toward these other issues relating to the nature of the federal system and policing. In so doing they bring their sensitivity to the all-too-often ignored importance of the local system and its relations to the federal system. The significance of their work is in its clear comprehension of the high visibility of federal levels of policing and of federal policing's relatively small scope compared to local policy. This work represents only a beginning. The working out of the appropriate theoretical context has only begun (Miller 1986). The work of Athan Theoharis (1978, 1981) has focused on the issues of "intelligence and legality" and the long conflict they represent within the mission of the FBI. Ernest Alix (1978) has published a unique study on a single criminal offense, kidnapping, which includes an examination of the federalization of this crime and its incorporation into the purview of the FBI. But most work on the FBI has not considered the context of policing or the nature of criminal law in the United States, and as a result, it is too often journalistic, attending to particular aspects without relating them to any larger context, or deals with abuses, in particular, FBI abuses of power.

Wilbur Miller's work (1989) represents a pioneering approach to federal law enforcement. Examining the issue of collecting federal revenue on alcohol production in the South, he highlights both the scope and limits of this early form of federal policing. While he draws no explicit comparison with current drug enforcement today, the contemporary comparison with the too-often romanticized illegal production of the nineteenth-century drug of choice, liquor, is obvious. The revenue collectors were sometimes corrupt; moonshiners often resisted violently, killing ten revenue collectors between July 1877 and June 1878 (Miller 1989, p. 201); there was also internal violence in the moonshine business. After 1879, federal troops accompanied revenue collectors (Miller 1989, pp. 206–8). People in rural communities, often women, did not all approve of the illegal liquor and secretly informed to the revenue collectors. The question of moonshine, Miller makes clear, is the question of state penetration into illegal business, just as it is today with nonalcoholic drugs. Successful federal efforts were characterized by consistent and fair prosecution, a system of fines and suspended sentences that could be revoked if the defendant resumed illegal alcohol production. By the end of the nineteenth century, popular support for moonshine had dramatically eroded because of the consistent and judicious federal effort, so that moonshiners were often denounced as "gangs of lazy, bad men . . . of general worthlessness" (Miller 1989, p. 212). While for Miller the important contrast in the research is with federal failure to enforce civil rights, he might well have made the contrast with current efforts on drug enforcement.

One hopes that further work on federal policing will supplement Miller's work so that we may begin to understand the nature of policing across the American social and political landscape. His central argument is perhaps of more interest to historians and political scientists than to those in the criminal justice fields: the historiography that emphasizes the failure of Reconstruction to protect black citizens in the South "overlooks the internal revenue system, a product of the Civil War that became a permanent element of expanded national authority" (Miller 1989, p. 196). This insight suggests that "expanded national authority" and policing do have an important connecting link: federal laws are enforced through a wide variety of organizations, and too often writers attend only to the FBI as a unique institution. One hopes that Miller's recentering of thinking about national law enforcement by highlighting a forgotten aspect of national policing will provoke other historians into looking at other federal policing systems—the park police, for instance, as examined by Mackintosh (1985) in an internal history that does not link this agency to the broader context of police history or the police of Washington, D.C., which in spite of their federal mandate have a past quite like that of other cities (*Statutory History* 1985).

David R. Johnson's (1991) work on federal policing combines two approaches, one emphasizing federal crime—counterfeiting—and the other focusing on large bureaucracies and state building. He argues that the "fitful" and "obscure" process behind the creation of a federal police followed from the creation of federal authority over currency during the Civil War (Johnson 1991, pp. 1, 7). Subtly using currency and counterfeiting as his topic, Johnson directly relates the question of state building to the chasing of counterfeiters, showing how the creation of a nation-state required a strong currency, which in turn boosted the creation of a small national police. He details how both criminals and federal agents operated in a local and highly irregular manner. Stuart Traub (1988), writing on the use of rewards in the American West, has evidence that both local governments and U.S.

marshalls, reporting directly to the attorney general, used rewards as an attempt to compensate people for catching, and often killing, known offenders. He argues that rewards were a rational way to communicate and provide crime control in lieu of an efficiently organized state, although he notes that the system encouraged murder rather than trials (Traub 1988, p. 299). Unlike Johnson, he links his analysis neither to theoretical questions surrounding local and federal policing nor to state building, clearly the essential missing element in the U.S. West.[6]

Craig Uchida's work on the early FBI clarifies its origins in the Bureau of Investigation, begun by President Roosevelt in 1908. He provides a clear bridge to local policing by showing how this federal organization was begun by a politician expert in the ways and limitations of city police from his term as New York City police commissioner. Roosevelt mandated that the Bureau of Investigation initiate criminal investigations for crimes spreading beyond local felonies—beginning with political land frauds. While not explicitly understood as a structural problem related to the federal system, Roosevelt's agency indeed focused on those felonies that were simply beyond the scope of local police. Rather than seeing Roosevelt's actions as purely politically motivated, one might instead draw a comparison with Progressive reformers in the late nineteenth and early twentieth centuries, who, Jeffreys-Jones contends (1978), exaggerated the amount and fear of labor violence in order to accomplish their electoral and legislative goals. In other words, reformers exaggerated fears to accomplish somewhat different ends.

Some of this recent police history has raised policy issues that cut across other features of local governments and services. Police, like schools, provide labor-intensive services that do not seem to be easily replaced by technology. Greater bureaucratic complexity has not broken down tasks to simple elements easily performed by machines, and such does not seem to be a realistic expectation. Local governments have the potential of doing some things much better than they now do (e.g., traffic control), but policing and schooling do not have such rosy futures. Perhaps this is one reason why they both remain at the center of controversy: the jobs get no easier, and the bureaucracies no more efficient with the passage of time and the growth of expertise. Equally important, the efficiency of these labor-intensive services seems to have

---

[6] For the best description of local violence in the West, see McGrath's (1984) study of mining towns.

an inverse relationship to city size: at some size, the bigger the city, the more costly and perhaps less efficient the service, whether school or police (Monkkonen 1983).

The history of police raises some difficult theoretical questions about urban government and has unclear implications for policing. Paul Peterson (1981), in *City Limits*, argues that policing is an "allocational" function of city government, meaning that it is neutral in relation to the city's long-run expectations for increased or decreased revenue. As the history of the police makes clear, their functional change over time renders Peterson's analysis problematic, while at the same time making his overall model even more useful. In the nineteenth century, police clearly performed part of the city's welfare or distributional function. As the police shifted to a crime-control emphasis, they became essential to the city's promotional functions in that they helped provide a safer environment for urban economic activities.

Following Peterson's larger argument, that distributional activities migrate to the highest, most geographically capacious, level of government, while promotional activities stay at the smallest geographical units of government, then his theory could help describe and explain why policing changed from broad class control to more narrow crime control. Given the historic limitations of American policing to small locales and the strong tradition prohibiting the creation of a state or national police system as in Europe, the police came under steady pressure to change what they did. As distributional actors, cities were under competitive constraints to spend less on welfare services, including those accomplished by the police, while at the same time they were under pressure to attract revenue-enhancing activities by providing crime-free environments. The fixed location of American police would then account for their turn to crime control and away from welfare in contrast to the continued welfare and broader service orientation (class control) of European police (Weinberger and Reinke 1989). This constraint would also help account for the relatively low amount of development of crime-control-oriented policing at the state and federal levels despite tremendous political and social pressure for more effective crime control. Crime control, then, would not migrate to the national level until local revenue enhancing disappeared, an unlikely scenario given the long history of local government. If one imagines an international scenario in which the United States will have to make itself crime-free to attract investment, then might crime control move to broader levels of government?

VII. Conclusion

The research of the past decade gives scholars a much deeper context and much greater empirical knowledge in which to understand current policing. As Lane's essay of 1980 synthesizes the pioneering generation of police historians, this essay builds on the maturing field. This generation has had the advantage of a growing body of research and a broad spectrum of theoretical perspectives, from the Marxism of Sidney Harring to the interdisciplinary approach of John Schneider. It has been much more synthetic than the work of the pioneering generation of the 1960s and 1970s. My overview and history (Monkkonen 1981*b*) pulled information from dozens of late nineteenth- and early twentieth-century local police histories. In addition, it and the articles of Watts introduced new levels of statistical analyses to the field. Friedman and Percival's (1981) study of Alameda County looked at the whole criminal justice system—police, the courts, law, lawyers, offenders, jails, the media. Schneider's (1980) work on Detroit mapped arrests and police distribution, and tied the social and economic geography of the city to the nineteenth-century development of its police and crime. And Emsley (1983) published the first scholarly history of policing in Europe and England, enabling American scholars to begin to appreciate more deeply the complex differences between North America and Europe.

This new stage of sophistication was matched on another level, too. On the international scene, a loose affiliation of scholars known as the Dutch Group put together international scholarly conferences on crime history. Organizing a larger meeting in conjunction with the seventh International Economic History Congress in Edinburgh in 1978, this group created a new, more formal, organization and publication, the *International Association for the History of Crime and Criminal Justice Newsletter* in 1979. Published by the Fondation de la Maison des Sciences de l'Homme in Paris, the newsletter began the complex task of coordinating and informing researchers about the varied and rich research being conducted around the world in criminal justice history (Monkkonen 1984). The work of this group introduced Americans to the historical sociology of Norbert Elias, whose generous theoretical approach underwrites much contemporary European scholarship. One year later in the United States, the journal *Criminal Justice History* appeared. An annual serial, it publishes international scholarship and with its first issue established itself as a serious scholarly journal.

The research developments discussed in this essay suggest a diverse research agenda. For instance, Steinberg (1989) raises a two-pronged challenge, the first to find sources that will permit the documentation of prepolice modes of criminal justice. He has found fragmentary evidence on alderman's courts. We need similar sources on church courts; Kasserman (1986) has documented the Methodists' exclusion of a young woman for prostitution, while Waldrep (1990) has systematic evidence on church trials and county court trials for a rural county in late nineteenth-century Kentucky. He argues that a decline in church trials preceded a rise in felony court prosecutions. Similar work also must be done in labor union court records. Garlock (1982), for instance, has documented the Knights of Labor courts in the late nineteenth century, showing that the expulsions mainly were for offenses having to do with union affairs but that the court structure of the union was specifically designed as a fairer alternative to the existing police and judicial machinery. He quotes Terrence Powderly: "They [working men] have long perceived that at the hands of advocates, justices and police, they get an immense amount of *law*, but no *justice*" (p. 29). Finally, excellent recent studies of vigilantism and crime show the need for further systematic work on the power of the state and crime control (Ball 1980; Little and Sheffield 1983; McGrath 1984; Ethington 1987). We also need comparable, systematic research on the constable watch system. This is essential if we are to understand the transition to the police and a formal, state-run, justice system.

Steinberg's (1989) second challenge is his argument that in many ways the quantity as well as quality of local crime control decreased after the introduction of the police. This is a stimulating assertion and should attract the research efforts of historians.

Work by McDowell and Loftin (1984) provides a model for research design in historical studies. Constructing a long fifty-year data series of police behavior and expenditures, and paying careful attention to the population denominator, they reexamine the role of expenditures on policing in Detroit. While they find a weak relationship between expenditures and apprehension rates, their article is of more importance for its demonstration of the feasibility of doing long time-series research. Its research design is clearly generalizable to other sites, and it should provide a beginning orientation for future studies.

How do police relate to issues of public order, from misdemeanors to riots? In spite of all the research, there has yet to be a research design capable of convincingly testing counterfactuals, that is, asking what cities would have been (or be) like without the police. Schneider

(1980) has systematically examined the relationship of police to riots in the mid-nineteenth century, looking also at cities where there were no riots. (He argues that Detroit Germans and Irish had residential and journey-to-work patterns that minimized the friction that caused riots in other cities.) No historian has examined twentieth-century riots and police in such a systematic way. If urban rioting declined with the introduction of policing, did this reflect effective riot control, the consequence of a visible control mechanism, or an independent increase in urban order? The late nineteenth-century decline in violent crimes and in accidental deaths suggests the latter, but a project specifically designed to test these alternatives has yet to be conducted (Lane 1979; Gurr 1989).

We still need to know far more about the police themselves. Were nonurban police and private police so active in labor control that the local police could remain relatively absent? What has been the impact of police training and civil service rules (Johnson 1981)? Did the slow change in police technology indicate a resistance to innovation detrimental to crime control? Did the transition from more generalized class surveillance and control to crime control wipe out an important urban welfare service? The question of productivity in a labor-intensive service like policing (and also school teaching) implicitly plagues most analyses: little has been done to estimate the contributions of technological change to productivity and then to estimate the total changes in policing.

The question of police and order has special significance for southern cities, where the work of Rousey on New Orleans suggests a very different development path from the North's. Rousey (1984) has also shown how New Orleans in the second half of the nineteenth century was far more violent than northern cities. This extended to the police, often with disastrous results. In the period 1863–90, police officers more often shot bystanders than did civilian shooters. In addition, police officers were more likely to be killed by fellow officers than by civilians (p. 57).

Rousey shows how the police of New Orleans were essentially a military force, patrolling the city primarily to control slaves (Rousey, n.d.). It is not yet clear whether we should even call the "city guard" police, for with their swords, armory, and uniforms, they much more represented a European style urban military: they were at first called, in 1805, the Gendarmerie. The New Orleans police were demilitarized later in the century, and the post–Civil War police represented the city's first modern police system. The contrast between the South and the North in the pre–Civil War era suggests that an unfree society cannot support a modern police system. Systematic comparison both of organization and behavior can make clearer these regional differences and in the process show how the issues of liberty, partisan politics, and the legitimacy of the state directly affect policing. Thus further opportunities for police history research go in several directions, from policy to urban political theory to fundamental issues of democracy and liberty.

REFERENCES

Alix, Ernest K. 1978. *Ransom Kidnapping in America, 1874–1974: The Creation of a Capital Crime*. Carbondale: Southern Illinois University Press.

Ball, Larry D. 1980. "Militiary Posses: The Territorial Militia in Civil Law Enforcement in New Mexico Territory, 1877–1883." *New Mexico History Review* 55:47–69.

Berman, Jay S. 1987. *Police Administration and Progressive Reform: Theodore Roosevelt as Police Commissioner of New York*. New York: Greenwood Press.

Best, Joel. 1981. "Keeping the Peace in St. Paul: Crime, Vice, and Police Work, 1869–1874." *Minnesota History* 47:240–48.

Bijleveld, Catrien C. J. H., and Eric H. Monkkonen. 1991. "Cross-sectional and Dynamic Analyses of the Concomitants of Police Behavior." *Historical Methods* 24:16–24.

Blackburn, Bobby L. 1979. "Oklahoma Law Enforcement since 1803." Ph.D. dissertation, Oklahoma State University, Department of History.

Blocker, Jack S., Jr. 1989. *American Temperance Movements: Cycles of Reform*. Boston: Twayne.

Brenzel, Barbara M. 1983. *Daughters of the State: A Social Portrait of the First Reform School for Girls in North America, 1856–1905*. Cambridge, Mass.: MIT Press.

Clark, Thomas. 1991. "The Limits of Liberty: Courts, Police and the Rights of Labor in California, 1890–1927." Ph.D. dissertation, University of California, Los Angeles, Department of History.

Dilworth, Donald C. 1977. *Identification Wanted: Development of the American Criminal Identification System, 1893–1943*. Gaithersburg, Md.: International Association of Chiefs of Police.

Douthit, Nathan. 1975. "Police Professionalism and the War against Crime in the United States, 1920s–1930s." In *Police Forces in History*, edited by George L. Mosse. Beverly Hills, Calif.: Sage.

Dwyer, Ellen. 1987. *Homes for the Mad: Life inside Two Nineteenth-Century Asylums*. New Brunswick, N.J.: Rutgers University Press.

Emsley, Clive. 1983. *Policing and Its Context, 1750–1870*. London: Macmillan.

Ethington, Phillip J. 1987. "Vigilantes and the Police: The Creation of a Professional Police Bureaucracy, 1847–1900." *Journal of Social History* 21:197–227.

Ferdinand, Theodore N. 1980. "Criminality, the Courts, and the Constabulary in Boston, 1702–1967." *Journal of Research in Crime and Delinquency* 17:190–208.

Fogelson, Robert. 1977. *Big City Police*. Cambridge, Mass.: Harvard University Press.

———. 1989. *America's Armories: Architecture, Society, and Public Order*. Cambridge, Mass.: Harvard University Press.

Friedman, Lawrence M., and Robert V. Percival. 1981. *Roots of Justice: Crime and Punishment in Alameda County, California, 1870–1910*. Chapel Hill: University of North Carolina Press.

Gallman, James M. 1988. "Preserving the Peace: Order and Disorder in Civil War Pennsylvania." *Pennsylvania History* 55:201–15.

Garlock, Jonathan. 1982. "The Knights of Labor Courts: A Case Study of Popular Justice." In *The Politics of Informal Justice*, edited by Richard Abel. New York: Academic Press.

Gatrell, V. A. C. 1980. "The Decline of Theft and Violence in Victorian and Edwardian England." In *Crime and the Law: The Social History of Crime in Western Europe since 1500*, edited by V. A. C. Gatrell, Geoffrey Parker, and Bruce Lenman. London: Europa.

Gilje, Paul A. 1987. *The Road to Mobocracy: Popular Disorder in New York City, 1763–1834*. Chapel Hill: University of North Carolina Press.

Gurr, Ted Robert. 1989. "Historical Trends in Violent Crime: Europe and the United States." In *Violence in America*, vol. 1, *The History of Crime*, edited by Ted Robert Gurr. Beverly Hills, Calif.: Sage.

Guttman, Herbert G. 1977. *Work, Culture, and Society in Industrializing America*, pt. 4, "Local Behavior and Patterns of Labor Discontent in Gilded Age America." New York: New Viewpoints.

Haller, Mark H. 1970. "Civic Reformers and Police Leadership: Chicago, 1905–1935." In *Police in Urban Society*, edited by Harlan Hahn. Beverly Hills, Calif.: Sage.

———. 1976. "Historical Roots of Police Behavior: Chicago, 1890–1925." *Law and Society Review* 10:303–23.

———. 1990. "Illegal Enterprise: A Theoretical and Historical Interpretation." *Criminology* 28:207–35.

Hannon, Joan Underhill. 1984a. "The Generosity of Antebellum Poor Relief." *Journal of Economic History* 44:810–21.

———. 1984b. "Poverty in the Antebellum Northeast: The View from New York State's Poor Relief Rolls." *Journal of Economic History* 44:1007–32.

Harring, Sidney. 1983. *Policing a Class Society: The Experience of American Cities, 1865–1915*. New Brunswick, N.J.: Rutgers University Press.

Jeffreys-Jones, Rhodri. 1978. *Violence and Reform in American History*. New York: New Viewpoints.

———. 1983. "The Defictionalization of the American Private Detective." *Journal of American Studies* 17:265–74.

Johnson, Bruce C. 1976. "Taking Care of Labor: The Police in American Politics." *Theory and Society* 3:89–117.

Johnson, David R. 1979. *Policing the Urban Underworld: The Impact of Crime on the Development of the American Police, 1800–1885*. Philadelphia: Temple University Press.

———. 1981. *American Law Enforcement: A History*. St. Louis: Forum Press.

———. 1991. *Crime and Power: Counterfeiters, the Secret Service, and the Nation State, 1865–1900*. Unpublished manuscript. San Antonio: University of Texas at San Antonio, Department of History.

Jordan, Laylon W. 1980. "Police and Politics: Charleston in the Gilded Age, 1880–1900." *South Carolina Historical Magazine* 81:35–50.

Kasserman, David R. 1986. *Fall River Outrage: Life, Murder, and Justice in Early Industrial New England*. Philadelphia: University of Pennsylvania Press.

Katz, Michael B. 1986. *In the Shadow of the Poorhouse: A Social History of Welfare in America*. New York: Basic.

Kelling, George L., and James K. Stewart. 1991. "The Evolution of Contemporary Policing." In *Local Government Police Management*, edited by William A. Geller. Washington, D.C.: International City Management Association.

Lane, Roger. 1967. *Policing the City: Boston, 1822–1905*. Cambridge, Mass.: Harvard University Press.

———. 1979. *Violent Death in the City: Suicide, Homicide, and Accidental Death in Philadelphia*. Cambridge, Mass.: Harvard University Press.

———. 1980. "Urban Police and Crime in Nineteenth-Century America." In *Crime and Justice: An Annual Review of Research*, vol. 2, edited by Norval Morris and Michael Tonry. Chicago: University of Chicago Press.

———. 1984. Review of *Policing a Class Society: The Experience of American Cities, 1865–1915* by Sidney Harring. *Journal of American History* 71:650–51.

Liss, Julia, and Steven Schlossman. 1984. "The Contours of Crime Control in August Vollmer's Berkeley." *Research in Law, Deviance and Social Control* 6:79–107.

Little, Craig B., and Christopher Sheffield. 1983. "Frontiers and Criminal Justice: English Prosecution Societies and American Vigilantism in the Eighteenth and Nineteenth Centuries." *American Sociological Review* 48:796–808.

McDowell, David, and Colin Loftin. 1984. "Conflict, Crime and Budgetary Constraint: Police Strength in Detroit, 1927–1976." In *The Politics of Urban Fiscal Policy*, edited by Terrence McDonald and Sally Ward. Beverly Hills, Calif.: Sage.

McGrath, Roger. 1984. *Gunfighters, Highwaymen, and Vigilantes: Violence on the California Frontier*. Berkeley and Los Angeles: University of California Press.

McKanna, Clare. 1984. "Hold Back the Tide: Vice Control in San Diego." *Pacific History* 28:54–64.

Mackintosh, Barry. 1985. *United States Park Police: A History*. Washington, D.C.: U.S. Government Printing Office.

McLaughlin, Andrew C., and Albert B. Hart, eds. 1914. *Cyclopedia of American Government*. New York: Appleton.

Miller, Wilbur R. 1976. *Cops and Bobbies: Police Authority in New York and London, 1830–1870*. Chicago: University of Chicago Press.

———. 1986. "Police and the State: A Comparative Perspective." *American Bar Foundation Research Journal*, no. 2 (Spring), pp. 339–48.

———. 1989. "The Revenue: Federal Law Enforcement in the Mountain South, 1870–1900." *Journal of Southern History* 55:195–216.

Millikan, William. 1989. "Maintaining 'Law and Order': The Minneapolis Citizens' Alliance in the 1920s." *Minnesota History* 51:219–33.

Monkkonen, Eric H. 1979. "Municipal Reports as an Indicator Source: The Nineteenth Century Police." *Historical Methods* 12:57–65.

———. 1980. "The Quantitative Historical Study of Crime and Criminal Justice in the United States." In *History and Crime: Implications for Contemporary Criminal Justice Policy*, edited by James Inciardi and Charles Faupel. Beverly Hills, Calif.: Sage.

———. 1981a. *Police in Urban America, 1860–1920*. New York: Cambridge University Press.

———. 1981b. "A Disorderly People? Urban Order in Nineteenth and Twentieth Century America." *Journal of American History* 68:539–59.

———. 1981c. "Toward an Understanding of Urbanization: Drunk Arrests in Los Angeles." *Pacific Historical Review* 50:234–44.

———. 1982. "From Cop History to Social History: The Significance of the Police in American History." *Journal of Social History* 15:575–91.

———. 1983. "The Organized Response to Crime in the Nineteenth and Early Twentieth Centuries." *Journal of Interdisciplinary History* 14:113–28.

———. 1984. "The History of Crime and Criminal Justice after Twenty-five Years." *Criminal Justice History* 5:161–65.

———. 1990. *Crime and Justice in American History*. Westport, Conn.: Meckler.

Morn, Frank. 1982. *"The Eye That Never Sleeps": A History of the Pinkerton National Detective Agency*. Bloomington: Indiana University Press.

Palmer, Stanley H. 1988. *Police and Protest in England and Ireland, 1780–1850*. New York: Cambridge University Press.

Peterson, Arthur E., and George W. Edwards. 1967. *New York as an Eighteenth Century Municipality*. Port Washington, N.Y.: Friedman.

Peterson, Paul. 1981. *City Limits*. Chicago: University of Chicago Press.

Reed, Rebecca. 1986. "Private Employees/Public Badges: 'Additional Patrolmen' in the Policing of Detroit." Paper presented at the annual meeting of the Social Science History Association, St. Louis, October.

Richardson, James F. 1970. *The New York Police: Colonial Times to 1901*. New York: Oxford University Press.

Rippy, Felix. 1985. "Crime and the Beginnings of the Muncie Police Force." *Indiana Social Studies Quarterly* 38:5–18.

Rorabaugh, William J. 1979. *The Alcoholic Republic: An American Tradition*. New York: Oxford University Press.

Rousey, Dennis C. 1983. "Hibernian Leatherheads: Irish Cops in New Orleans, 1830–1860." *Journal of Urban History* 10:61–84.

————. 1984. "Cops and Guns: Police Use of Deadly Force in Nineteenth-Century New Orleans." *American Journal of Legal History* 28:41–66.

————. n.d. "Out of the Orbit of Mars: Demilitarizing the New Orleans Police, 1805–1836." Unpublished manuscript. State University: Arkansas State University, Department of History.

Schlossman, Steven. 1977. *Love and the American Delinquent: The Theory and Practice of "Progressive" Juvenile Justice*. Chicago: University of Chicago Press.

Schneider, John C. 1980. *Detroit and the Problem of Order, 1830–1880: A Geography of Crime, Riot, and Policing*. Lincoln: University of Nebraska Press.

Sherman, Lawrence W. 1978. *Scandal and Reform: Controlling Police Corruption*. Berkeley: University of California Press.

A Statutory History of the United States Capital Police Force, Ninety-ninth Congress, First Session. 1985. Washington, D.C.: U.S. Government Printing Office.

Steinberg, Allen. 1989. *The Transformation of Criminal Justice: Philadelphia, 1800–1880*. Chapel Hill: University of North Carolina Press.

Surrency, Edwin C. 1974. "The Evolution of an Urban Judicial System: The Philadelphia Story, 1683 to 1968." *American Journal of Legal History* 17:95–123.

Sylvester, Stephen G. 1989. "Avenues for Ladies Only: The Soiled Doves of East Grand Forks, 1887–1915." *Minnesota History* 51:291–312.

Terrill, Richard J. 1986. Review of *Policing a Class Society: The Experience of American Cities, 1865–1915*, by Sidney Harring. In *Criminal Justice History: An International Annual* 7:206–7.

Theoharis, Athan G. 1978. *Spying on Americans: Political Surveillance from Hoover to the Huston Plan*. Philadelphia: Temple University Press.

————. 1981. "The Presidency and the Federal Bureau of Investigation: The Conflict of Intelligence and Legality." *Criminal Justice History* 2:131–60.

Traub, Stuart H. 1988. "Rewards, Bounty Hunting and Criminal Justice in the West: 1865–1900." *Western Historical Quarterly* 19:287–301.

Uchida, Craig D. 1983. "Policing the Politicians: Theodore Roosevelt and the Origins of the F.B.I." Paper presented at the annual meeting of the Academy of Criminal Justice Sciences, San Antonio, March.

Waldrep, Christopher. 1990. "'So Much Sin': The Decline of Religious Discipline and the 'Tidal Wave of Crime.'" *Journal of Social History* 23:535–52.

Walker, Samuel. 1978. "The Police and the Community: Scranton, Pennsylvania, 1884–1886, a Test Case." *American Studies* 19:79–90.

————. 1980. "The Origins of the American Police-Community Relations Movement: The 1940s." *Criminal Justice History: An International Annual* 1:225–46.

————. 1981. *Popular Justice*. New York: Oxford University Press.

Watts, Eugene J. 1981*a*. "Police Priorities in Twentieth Century St. Louis." *Journal of Social History* 14:649–74.

————. 1981*b*. "St. Louis Police Recruits in the Twentieth Century." *Criminology* 19:77–113.

————. 1981*c*. "Blue and Black: Afro-American Police Officers in Twentieth Century St. Louis." *Journal of Urban History* 7:131–68.

———. 1982. "Patterns of Promotion: The St. Louis Police Department, 1899–1975." *Social Science History* 6:233–58.

———. 1983*a*. "Police Response to Crime and Disorder in Twentieth Century St. Louis." *Journal of American History* 70:340–58.

———. 1983*b*. "Continuity and Change in Police Careers: A Case Study of the St. Louis Police Department." *Journal of Police Science and Administration* 2:217–24.

Weinberger, Barbara, and Herbert Reinke. 1989. "Law and Order in the Industrial City: An Anglo-German Comparison." Paper presented at the annual meeting of the Social Science History Association, Washington, D.C., November.

Wertsch, Douglas. 1987. "The Evolution of the Des Moines Police Department." *Annals of Iowa* 48:435–49.

Williams, Hubert, and Patrick V. Murphy. 1990. "The Evolving Strategy of Police: A Minority View." *Perspectives on Policing*, no. 13.

Author Index

Subject Index